FRONTIER OF DREAMS

Nigel Brown, *Potted History*

FRONTIER OF DREAMS

The Story of New Zealand

TVnz

our nation. our voice.

Edited by Bronwyn Dalley & Gavin McLean

Hodder Moa

National Library of New Zealand Cataloguing-in-Publication Data
Frontier of dreams : the story of New Zealand / edited by
Bronwyn Dalley and Gavin McLean. 1st ed.
Includes bibliographical references and index.
ISBN 1-86971-006-1
1. New Zealand—History. I. Dalley, Bronwyn, 1963- II. McLean, Gavin.
993—dc 22

A Hodder Moa Book
Published in 2005 by Hachette Livre NZ Ltd
4 Whetu Place, Mairangi Bay
Auckland, New Zealand

Published under licence from Television New Zealand Limited
Text © Crown copyright 2005
The moral rights of the authors have been asserted.
Design and format © Hachette Livre NZ Ltd 2005

Designed and produced by Hachette Livre NZ Ltd
Printed by Everbest Printing Co. Ltd, China

Front cover: Patrick J Hogan, *View of Auckland*, 1852, Auckland Art Gallery, Toi o Tamaki
Back cover: Chart of New Zealand used by Captain James Cook, 1770, Museum of New Zealand, Te Papa Tongarewa

Contents

The Authors

Neill Atkinson, Historian at the Ministry for Culture and Heritage, specialises in politics and government, transport, the labour movement and the social history of working people. He has published *Crew Culture* (2001), *Rewarding Service* (2002) and *Adventures in Democracy* (2003). *Hell or High Water: New Zealand Merchant Seafarers Remember the War*, his latest book, appears in 2005.

Bronwyn Dalley is Chief Historian at the Ministry for Culture and Heritage. She has published in social and cultural history, particularly in relation to welfare, sexuality, crime, daily life and public history. Her books include *Family Matters* (1998), *Living in the 20th Century* (2000), and *Past Judgement: Social Policy and New Zealand History*, co-edited with Margaret Tennant (2004). Bronwyn is completing a study of sexuality, gender and culture in urban centres between the 1860s and 1920s.

David Green has spent two decades editing and writing history, mostly for the Ministry for Culture and Heritage. With Kai Tahu as well as English whakapapa, he has always been fascinated by this country's race relations. He has investigated coercive aspects of this subject in entries in the *Dictionary of New Zealand Biography* and the *Oxford Companion to New Zealand Military History*. David is also researching the significance of European sports for Maori in the 19th century. He is currently co-writing histories of the artillery and of government auditing.

Ian McGibbon, General Editor (War History) at the Ministry for Culture and Heritage, has published widely on foreign policy and military history. His works include the two-volume official history of New Zealand's involvement in the Korean War and two guidebooks on First World War battlefields, the Western Front (2001) and Gallipoli (2005), as well as editing the *Oxford Companion to New Zealand Military History* (2000). In 2004 Hodder Moa Beckett published his *New Zealand and the Second World War*. He was made an Officer of the New Zealand Order of Merit for services to historical research in 1997.

Gavin McLean, Senior Historian at the Ministry for Culture and Heritage, specialises in business, local and imperial history, and has also written extensively on transport, exhibition and heritage history. His recent books include guides to Oamaru, Dunedin and Wellington, *Captain's Log: New Zealand's Maritime History* (2001), *100 Historic Places in New Zealand* (2002), *Rocking the Boat? A History of Scales Corporation* (2002) and *We Were Different: The Tasman Express Line Story* (2004). Gavin is completing a history of New Zealand's governors and governors-general, and is writing histories of publisher Reed and of Helicopters (NZ) Ltd. He is also co-editing, with Kynan Gentry, *Heartlands*, a collection of essays by historians on historic places.

Claudia Orange, Director of History and Pacific Cultures at the Museum of New Zealand Te Papa Tongarewa, is responsible for leading the museum's research, curatorial and collection management functions in those areas. She was General Editor of four of the five volumes of the *Dictionary of New Zealand Biography* (1990–2003), and saw it online in 2002, also serving as Acting Chief Historian (1997–2000). She was awarded the OBE in 1993 and received the University of Auckland's Distinguished Alumni Award in 1997. Her research interests are race relations and the Treaty of Waitangi, her most recent publication being *An Illustrated History of the Treaty of Waitangi* (2004).

Jock Phillips is General Editor of *Te Ara: The Encyclopedia of New Zealand* in the Ministry for Culture and Heritage. He took up this position after serving for 13 years as Chief Historian. Jock has taught American and New Zealand history at Victoria University, where he founded and was the first director of the Stout Research Centre for New Zealand Studies. He has written or edited 10 books, of which the best known is *A Man's Country: The Image of the Pakeha Male — A History*.

David Young, a former journalist, specialises in history and conservation, people and the land. His *Our Islands, Our Selves: A History of Conservation in New Zealand*, appeared in 2004. His other books are *Woven by Water: Histories From the Whanganui River, Faces of the River, Matahina: A Power in the Land*, and *Values as Law*, a history of the Resource Management Act. He worked on the staff of the *NZ Listener* before editing *Terra Nova*. David has worked on several television productions, including the award-winning *One Land, Two People*. He has also been engaged with iwi and Treaty claims, museum work, and is currently writing a book on the endangered blue duck. In addition to contributing to this volume, David wrote scripts for *Frontier of Dreams*.

Acknowledgements

In 2000 Ray Waru and Vincent Burke from Whakapapa Productions Ltd commissioned the History Group of the Ministry for Culture and Heritage to develop a conceptual framework for a 13-part television history of New Zealand. New Zealand On Air funded Whakapapa to contract the Group to supply general background essays for the scriptwriters and the researchers for the television series. Guided by Jock Phillips (who led the concept development), Claudia Orange, Manuka Henare and Ranginui Walker, the Group assembled a project team drawn from the Ministry and from academia.

The writers for the background essays were:

episode 1	Geoffrey Irwin and Matt McGlone
episode 2	Janet Davidson and Dame Anne Salmond
episode 3	Dame Anne Salmond and Manuka Henare
episode 4	Claudia Orange
episode 5	Danny Keenan and Judith Binney
episode 6	Gavin McLean
episode 7	Erik Olssen
episode 8	Ian McGibbon
episode 9	Miles Fairburn
episode 10	Malcolm McKinnon
episode 11	Bronwyn Dalley
episode 12	Jock Phillips
episode 13	Charlotte Macdonald

Ranginui Walker contributed to episodes 7 and 9–13. Although Whakapapa scriptwriters and the authors of this book have in some cases adapted the foundation essays considerably to meet the requirements of the television series and of this book, we would like to acknowledge our debt to those pathfinders.

We also thank Jock Phillips and Claudia Orange for staying with the project and adapting their earlier material to book form, despite moving to positions of responsibility elsewhere, as General Editor of the Ministry's *Te Ara: The Encyclopedia of New Zealand*, and as Director of History and Pacific Cultures, Museum of New Zealand Te Papa Tongarewa, respectively. For this book we welcomed to the writing team Neill Atkinson and David Green from the History Group and David Young, who recently completed a history of conservation for us under contract.

At Hachette Livre NZ Ltd we thank Managing Director Kevin Chapman and Editorial Director Warren Adler for taking on a project of such size, complexity and urgency and for trusting us to deliver on time. Managing Editor Jane Hingston scheduled everything, liaised between the general editors, Hachette Livre editorial and production staff and Whakapapa Productions (especially Ray Waru, Vincent Burke, David Filer and Louise Callan); she always pleaded and prodded diplomatically and also helped us by hunting down illustrations and other resources. Craig Violich put everything together with care and flair and freelance editor Jeanette Cook skilfully edited the text.

The archives, libraries and photographers who gave permission to use illustrations are acknowledged in the captions (and further information on artworks is given in the List of Artworks on page 400). We would, however, like to offer special thanks to the Alexander Turnbull Library, especially Joan McCracken, Heather Mathie and Marian Minson, who quickly got used to us ransacking their filing cabinets and who also offered many helpful suggestions for alternatives to elusive shots. For additional help with photographs we would like to thank the Department of Conservation, and from the Ministry for Culture and Heritage, Jane Hutchings, Fran McGowan, Simon Nathan and Redmer Yska.

Bronwyn Dalley & Gavin McLean
April 2005

Foreword

I am writing this on the evening of 25 April 2005, ANZAC Day. Since early morning I have been listening to radio coverage of the commemoration events that have been held up and down the country. The television programmes that have been broadcast today have added to my knowledge of the events that occurred at Gallipoli and have made it easier to understand and empathize with those who fought and died in the battle.

The aim of the television series, *Frontier of Dreams*, is similar to, but wider than most of the history programmes seen on screen. Most programmes pick a moment in history; we have to tell a national history — and we are doing it all.

The challenge of the series that was the impetus for this book is to use television's unique attributes to help us understand and empathize with the people who laid the foundation of the nation. We hope the television series and this book will give New Zealanders a real understanding of the context and complexities of the story of New Zealand. Inevitably we have simplified some of that story but we hope that we have also suggested there is a depth and intelligence in our history. We also want to trumpet loudly that we have a history that is rich in character and incident and worth knowing about.

The series name was suggested by Jock Phillips who argued that every shipload of migrants and every generation of New Zealanders has a special vision for the country. Every group of immigrants from the Polynesians a thousand years ago to the Wakefield settlers of the 1840s and the new Asian arrivals today see the country as a blank page on which to write their own stories. In some ways New Zealand preserved its idea of frontier well into the 20th century.

As we prepared for the series I experienced two revelations. The first was that New Zealand was the last major landmass in the world to be discovered by modern humans. We really were the last frontier.

The second revelation was about demographics. I learned that between 1860 and the 1880s our population doubled to about half a million and by the time the Vogel immigrants had settled in we were a fully formed country. In the course of a couple of generations we were created whole as a functioning political economy with a mix of mostly British people and Maori and we would not change much until a new wave of Pacific Island migrants arrived in the 1950s. I had thought our basic cultural makeup had taken years to form but in fact it had happened very quickly.

There are, of course, at least two histories in New Zealand. The other main one is Maori. Once colonial settlement became a reality the displacement of Maori became inevitable. Maori lands were confiscated and the establishment of the Native Land Court made it easier to take land from Maori. We hope the series helps to put Maori history into a context with Pakeha history and that the past will help inform the present and make it easier to understand some of the things that motivate Maori actions today.

Many people helped make the series and we (Vincent Burke and I) would like to thank all of them. Specifically we would like to thank the people who shared their personal stories with us.

Even a long series and a big book can only scratch the surface of our history. We hope viewers and readers will explore their own frontiers and embrace the story of New Zealand for themselves.

Ray Waru & Vincent Burke
Co-producers Frontier of Dreams
April 2005

In 2005 history fascinated New Zealanders. They were studying it in schools and universities, reading it (making *The Penguin History of New Zealand* a bestseller) and engaging with it, lodging Treaty claims, salvaging artefacts from the path of the Wellington bypass or wondering if Oamaru might join the pyramids on the World Heritage List. Thousands saw Hollywood's take on Alexander the Great, partied at Napier's Art Deco Weekend or, like these folk at Hood Aerodrome in Masterton, watched the old warbirds go through their paces.

Jane Hutchings

Introduction

History is the new black. Interest in New Zealand's past has never been greater. This may be a nation that prides itself on its relative youth — these islands were among the last habitable places on the planet where humans settled — but we are rapidly accumulating history per capita. History is everywhere — museums, family histories, historic places, historical novels, memorials and books. It is in carvings and waiata, in advertisements, in the court-rooms, on the screen and over the airwaves. Every Kiwi knows or thinks they know something about our past, and a good number like to share their opinions on talkback radio and in letters to the editor. New Zealand, it seems, cannot get enough of itself.

Frontier of Dreams: The Story of New Zealand grows from and adds to the lively interest in our past. It is a general history of major events, personalities, themes and issues. Here is a highlights package of New Zealand's past; for like other general histories, *Frontier of Dreams* 'accepts a responsibility to generalise' rather than exploring topics and individuals in full.[1] All books about history involve choices of what to include and this book is no different, so readers should look to the references and bibliography for more detailed treatments of particular issues. Drawing on recent scholarship, and using a range of written and visual sources, this book presents our history in an accessible and lively way. It tells familiar stories, and less familiar tales as well, in new ways, offering insights into the diverse forces that have helped shape the nation and its peoples.

The book partners a television series of the same name. The Frontier of Dreams project — the series and the book — was developed by Whakapapa Productions and the Ministry for Culture and Heritage. The project was planned at the turn of the millennium when many New Zealanders were reflecting on this country, where it had come from and where it was heading. Other nations' stories — Ken Burns's *Civil War* and Simon Schama's *A History of Britain* — played on our screens, so it seemed timely to re-examine New Zealand's general history on screen and in print, taking advantage of the latest developments in historical scholarship and television documentary making.

A team of archaeologists, historians, scientists, and specialists in matauranga Maori (Maori knowledge), who are listed in the acknowledgements, produced a 'storyline' or road map for each of the television episodes. The storylines suggested arguments, issues, themes and interpretations that could be used in developing scripts suitable for presenting history on television where the emphasis is on the visual rather than the written word. In turn, the scripts guided but did not constrain the writers of this book, which stands alone as a history of New Zealand and complements the television episodes.

Our authors all have some association with the Ministry for Culture and Heritage, and a number also prepared the original storylines for the television series. Some write about their specialist areas — Ian McGibbon on the context of the First and Second World Wars, Claudia Orange on the Treaty and its times, David Young on the natural world — while others — Neill Atkinson, David Green, Jock Phillips, and the two general editors, Bronwyn Dalley and Gavin McLean — have elsewhere written on aspects of New Zealand's cultural, heritage, labour or social history.

New Zealand's national story has been told many times. Individual iwi tell their particular accounts of this land and its peoples. Each generation of historians and writers produces another history of New Zealand. 'General' histories published in the last two decades fill a modest bookshelf; this millennium alone has seen the publication of a half-dozen or so. Sales of Michael King's *The Penguin History of New Zealand*, published in 2003 and promoted as 'a new book for a new century', topped the 100,000 mark within a year of its release.[2] That book remained at the top of the book charts more than a year after its publication, far outpacing sales of biographies of All Blacks, traditional best-sellers here.

New Zealand television has been slower to portray our general history, or indeed much local history at all. The most recent attempt at a national history, *Our People, Our Century* (2000), presented the past primarily through family histories, and a multi-part documentary exploring women's experiences appeared in 1993. We have to go back to 1981 and *Landmarks* for the last general treatment of New Zealand on the small screen. Bite-sized chunks of the past have been preferred by producers, funding agencies and the programmers. Over several seasons the series *Epitaph* traced famous and infamous characters through their headstones, and slices of New Zealand culture aired in *The Game of Our Lives* (1996) and *Give it a Whirl* (2003), examining rugby and popular music respectively. War has been a favourite, with *New Zealand at War* (1995), *The New Zealand Wars* (1998), and *Colour of War — The Anzacs* (2003). Nostalgia, rather than more serious attempts to explore the past, has featured too, particularly in series such as *The Way We Were* (1995 and 1997).[3]

Whatever the medium, each telling of New Zealand's story reflects the life and times of those relating it. The storytellers generally agree on a clutch of core issues and — most of the time — that rather unfashionable concept of 'the facts': Abel Tasman cruising the coastline in 1642, the signing of the Treaty of Waitangi in 1840, Labour's triumph in 1935, and so on. But there are usually important differences in how these events are interpreted: the weight given them, their consequences, and what the turning points and major themes in our history may be. We have national stories rather than a single national story, and the act of telling our history, like history itself, is a work in progress.

Historian James Belich noted that we once thought New Zealand's story mundane and tame; the excitement and the big drama of the past occurred elsewhere.[4] *Frontier of Dreams* starts from the assumption that New Zealand has been and continues to be a vibrant place. Each writer brings a commitment to presenting its past to readers in entertaining and informative ways. Our history shows action and pathos. There are heroes, ratbags and ordinary souls; there is rebellion, bloodshed and peace-making; and there is innovation and creativity, adoption and adaptation. New Zealand has followed international trends, and sometimes led them; the nation has stood alone and played a part in global events. New Zealand history is anything but boring.

SCREENING HISTORY

Frontier of Dreams is the biggest history documentary series made in New Zealand in 20 years, drawing on the talents of a multidisciplinary team of historians, archaeologists and scientists and a television production team of over 40 people, including directors, researchers, writers, editors, graphics designers, film crews and many others who provided specialist skills in prop making and costume design. The producers — Whakapapa Productions — used historical and news film footage, stills, ephemera, sound recordings and historic places, and used actors to re-enact some of the key stories. In 2004 Whakapapa reconstructed a section of trenches in a quarry in South Auckland (below). In the top photograph make-up artist Wendy Nowell-Usticke works with the actors.

Some themes in this book emerge from the *Frontier of Dreams* television series. Two themes follow the title. This land, and sometimes the ideas and efforts of its peoples, have been on the frontier. New Zealand was on the edge of the world, for Polynesian navigators, for British and European settlers in the 19th century, and for more recent migrants from the Pacific and Asia. There have been events here that have been cutting-edge, for New Zealand has long liked to see itself as leading the world — the first to see the sun, the first nation where women got the vote, the first to provide state pensions to the aged, and so on. The frontier, physical or psychological, has been intimately connected with aspirations — dreams — of making a

different life. Migrants made a choice to come here; few travelled across the Pacific or halfway round the world by accident. At times hopes and dreams drove the country forward and had a significant effect on its development, as in the aspirations of rangatira and iwi in the 1820s, gold-seekers' visions of riches in the 1860s, and the reforming zeal of governments in the 1890s, the 1930s and the 1980s.

Other important themes are developed. One is New Zealand's relationship with the rest of the world. *Frontier of Dreams* firmly sets our national story in an international context, not necessarily to draw comparisons with the rest of the world — this is not a comparative history — but to indicate the connection between us and the outside world. New Zealand history has been played out in and with the wider world, whether in geological processes, migration stories, cultural exchange, trade, or the sharp or blunt ends of diplomatic relations.

Within the national story are regional and local variations, however, and these form another theme. There have been linked and separate issues for North and South, town and country, and province and centre, which have changed over time as fortunes ebbed and flowed. Sometimes those regional variations have been intimately connected with relations between Maori and Pakeha; life before the 1960s for the largely rural Maori population followed a very different trajectory from that for the predominantly urban Pakeha. Socio-economic status, population structure, public services and more besides have differed from one region to the next. Once upon a time Maori communities in the Bay of Islands were on an economic high supplying goods to the dispersed Pakeha settlements, Dunedin was bigger and richer than Auckland, Hamilton was a one-cow town, and Hokitika had a pub on just about every corner. Ethnicity or different cultural backgrounds have marked regions, areas within regions and locales: a Scottish south, an Irish west, a Polynesian Auckland, an Asian Howick.

How peoples have adapted to this land, and how cultures have developed either in isolation or in response to others, are also strands that run through the chapters. Most of this land's human history has been a story of development within these islands but apart from the wider world. The rich and complex Maori world — te ao Maori — emerged over the course of half a millennium. Its resilience has been tested ever since first contact, and while much was lost, much still remains. Relations between the two main cultures, Maori and European or Pakeha, embody much of the process of cultural adaptation and development and are

Waves of migrants have washed over New Zealand in the last 800–900 years and each has its own culture, as this 1930s Shaw Savill & Albion poster suggests. Alexander Turnbull Library, Eph-A-SHIP-1931-01

a core issue in this book. The Treaty of Waitangi was signed in 1840 between representatives of various iwi and the British Crown, and this country still grapples with trying to come to some agreement about its interpretation and the way ahead.

New Zealand culture and ways of life are also explored. Attention is paid to the texture of the past, and the illustrations have been chosen to evoke a sense of people, place and daily life. Alongside major political developments and economic changes are discussions of New Zealanders' material lives — their food, their dress, their houses. People work, play, make families, sing songs, go to the movies, shop, grow old; here is a history that conveys some of the rhythms of life in the past. Yet *Frontier of Dreams* does not overtly search for a distinct New Zealand identity and there is no attempt to point to any particular time or event and claim, 'Here, now, is New Zealand'. Rather, our authors trace New Zealand as a work in progress, a shifting amalgam of lifestyles, beliefs and practices that emerge from the process of living in this land.

Issues of change and continuity are important in history, and *Frontier of Dreams* is no exception. Some of the turning points suggest the coming of big changes: the brief encounter between Dutch sailors and Maori in 1642 or the ones between Englishman James Cook's crews and Maori from 1769; the signing of the Treaty of Waitangi in 1840; the first shipment of frozen meat in 1882; the emergence of the Liberals in the 1890s; the economic depression of the 1930s; the effects of the marriage and baby booms from the late 1940s; Maori urbanisation from the 1960s. Such events are reasonably well known but there are other major events or changes discussed here that may be less known, or at least are not considered much in general accounts of our past. The Musket Wars of the early 19th century, discussed in chapter 3, are a case in point. Casualties were at least 20,000, more than New Zealand's in either of the world wars of the 20th century. The effects on Maori society were devastating, and combined with the full impact of colonialism from the 1850s, long-lasting.

Frontier of Dreams also reassesses whether some events were as momentous as once thought. The Orwellian date of 1984 has been a beacon in our recent history, denoting enormous change and, in the view of many, an end to the world as it was. Yet commentators, including the authors in this book, are reconsidering the period: did New Zealand have a revolution, a counter-revolution, or an attitudinal shift in the 1980s and 1990s, or did some of the big economic changes begin much earlier? And what about the period since reform with a capital R ran out of steam in 1993?

The period from the end of the First World War until the election of the first Labour government in 1935, and that from the end of the Second World War until the mid 1960s come under reconsideration too. These years have often received a bad press, from historians and from those who lived through them. Because they were bookended by wars or by major cultural shifts, they are often viewed as in-between times, historic doldrums; economic downs and ups, a massive breeding binge,

and general social conservatism reigned. But these were periods of energy and innovation in high and popular culture, and of flourishing consumerism as all manner of goods flooded the market. The continuities between the years after the First World War and those after the Second are explored here; war punctuated, rather than created a boundary.

The structure of 13 chronological chapters and the turning points in this book take their cue from the television series. New Zealand's long and still unfolding story begins in geological time — 130 million years back when the supercontinent Gondwanaland began to break apart; the first chapter traces the emergence of these new islands from the sea. The epic Polynesian navigation throughout the Pacific brought the world into first contact with these islands when New Zealand's 'human' time began less than 1000 years ago. The explorers made landfall about 1200 AD and colonisers — maybe only 200 in 10 waka over the course of a century — followed to this strange land of giant birds and ancient forests. Making it to these islands was one thing, but making the land home was a different matter entirely. The second chapter traces this process and looks at the development of Maori culture and knowledge. The story of cultural adaptation to this land begins with the morphing

Agricultural and Pastoral shows were part of the rhythm of life. Almost every town seemed to have one. On 'show day' shops might shut and everyone would deck themselves out in their finery. Farmers competed to show the best cow, the best merino, the biggest cabbage. Local manufacturers filled tents with their finest products and commercial agents displayed new machinery. Mums bottled. And everyone gawped.

of Polynesian into Maori; there would be many more cultural transformations as migrants realised or adapted their dreams of making it in a new country.

Splendid isolation at the bottom of the world would never last. Chapters 3, 4 and 5 examine the meeting of Aotearoa and the world, and look at the varied relationships that Maori and European forged to live alongside each other in the same land. Early encounters often went badly, but there was co-operation and exchange, trade and intermarriage, sharing and adaptation, especially when Aotearoa remained distinctly Maori. The wider world arrived with a vengeance once Maori and the British signed the Treaty of Waitangi in 1840; the meaning and implications of that document have been to the fore in relations between the two peoples ever since. Cultures collided within Maoridom and between Maori and settlers as open warfare punctuated the 1840s and the 1860s.

Regional differences surged to the forefront from the mid 19th century, and chapter 6 examines these. While war raged in the North and a government was established, the South Island got on with the job of laying the foundations for some of the building blocks of modern New Zealand: gold, pastoralism, and the building of port cities from which wool and meat flowed to foreign shores. Boom times for the growing Pakeha population, although not for the Maori, saw the rise of cities and a modern economy with all the excitement and changes they entailed.

The boom unleashed a rollercoaster, and the country hurtled along as the later 19th century segued into the first decades of the 20th. Four chapters look at different aspects of this long rollercoaster ride. Chapter 7 charts the shift from economic depression to comfort, with New Zealand leading the world in social reforms and giving itself the epithet of 'God's Own Country'. The turnaround hit Maori too, and new leaders emerged who tried new ways of bringing Maori out from under the debilitating effects of colonialism. New Zealand followed and led. Where Britain went, we went — to war in South Africa, and then to the killing fields of Gallipoli and the Western Front, examined in chapter 8, where the price of Empire was crippling. For New Zealanders intent on making happy homes, the subject of chapter 9, the rollercoaster was roughest through the 'jazz age' of the 1920s and '30s as economic depression hit, then hit again. Always understated in their actions, New Zealanders responded with a quiet revolution when they tossed out an old political order and brought in a new. Once more, government charged ahead with economic and social reform. New Zealand's welfare state blossomed and everything seemed so good that in 1940 the country put itself on show for months in a triumphant celebration of progress over the 100 years since the signing of the Treaty of Waitangi. Another world war was a shocking reminder of the world outside our social laboratory.

The final three chapters cover the enormous social, cultural and economic changes of the last 60 years. Many of the roots of contemporary New Zealand lay in the 1950s and early 1960s, discussed in chapter 11: a breeding binge; the

Chunuk Bair, painted some 80 years after the battle. Gallipoli occupies centre stage in our national mythology and some argue that we forged our national identity here. The First World War ended the so-called long 19th century, but the 1920s and 1930s share themes with the 1950s and 1960s. Wars may not necessarily be major turning points in our history.

relocation of Maori from country to city; the vast expansion of suburbs and urban centres, notably Auckland; the shifting economic and political relationship with the United States and the United Kingdom. Interaction of national and global, and national and regional, loomed large during the later 1960s and through the 1970s. New Zealand's culture, social outlook and mores all felt the effects of the wider world. Economic shifts on the other side of the world rocked the country and the cost of being friends with the superpowers was felt as Kiwis headed off to fight wars in Vietnam. Blokes drank beer and cruised the streets in Mark II Zephyrs, but this was also a time of rebellion, of women's lib and black power, and a generation gap, as chapter 12 suggests.

The last chapter looks at the period since 1984. The baby-boomers who crowded the schools in the 1950s, then donned walk shorts, jeans or tie-dyed skirts in the early 1970s, grabbed power in the 1980s. Kiwis led the global pack again in dismantling and restructuring almost everything, but the world was always there — and here — whether in shocks like the *Rainbow Warrior* bombing and the share-market crash, or the cultural diversity gained through migration from Asia and elsewhere. Biculturalism and the role of the Treaty were to the fore like never before. The past unfolds continuously, so the historian's usual safety valve of avoiding recent events is dispensed with. *Frontier of Dreams* comes to 'the present' at the beginning of 2005 and moves into the mid 21st century by way of demographic and cultural predictions of New Zealand as it could be.

Fotopress

A tryst with Destiny? Historians have been accused of marginalising religion's role in the national story. In 2004, however, Brian Tamaki's Destiny Church, a new-style evangelical church that appealed to many Maori and Pacific people, made history as it marched down Wellington's Lambton Quay to oppose the Civil Unions Bill. The legislation was passed.

Evening Post Collection, Alexander Turnbull Library, F-21844-¼

Most people got on with life despite the ups and downs of the political and economic cycles. These rowers, woolly-headed in the fashion of the 1970s, fine-tune their strokes on unusually calm Wellington waters while in the background the harbour board's earth-movers tear up the waterfront to create Frank Kitts Park for the office workers from the tower blocks.

Chapter 1

We love to argue over who got here first, and when. Kennett Watkins painted *Departure of the six canoes from Rarotonga for New Zealand* in 1906 at the height of S Percy Smith's 1350 AD Great Fleet myth. Now Smith is myth, too, but his date was close and he appreciated Polynesian navigational abilities better than some later scholars.

K Watkins, Auckland Art Gallery, Toi o Tamaki

The Last Place on Earth

Prehistory–c. 1300

People reached Australia, New Zealand's nearest neighbour, about 50,000 years ago, after crossing Ice Age seas that were less extensive than they are now — 130 m below today's levels. The English Channel did not even exist when the earliest of our human ancestors reached Britain, our other ancestral launching pad. But unlike the routes to Britain and Australia, there were no land bridges or short raft hops to New Zealand. Getting here took the greatest maritime migration in pre-industrial history, which accelerated about 3500 years ago as a new wave of seafarers fanned out into the vast reaches of the Pacific Ocean. During that epic journey they adapted to become Polynesians.

Journey's end, at the southernmost limit of their reach, was New Zealand, where they arrived less than 1000 years ago. And a strange place it was. The islands of New Zealand were cloaked in ancient podocarp forests that would have looked familiar to diplodocus dinosaurs. But they were, geologically speaking, and as their Dutch name suggests, the new land from the sea. Caught at the crunch point between the Pacific and the Indo-Australian tectonic plates, 'Moa's Ark' had been on the geological equivalent of a bucking bronco ride since breaking loose from Gondwana and rafting eastwards on the Pacific Plate. With their cargo of ancient plants, flightless birds, mouse-sized crickets and heaving, spouting volcanoes and geysers, these islands — the last large ones to be settled by human beings — were a work in progress.

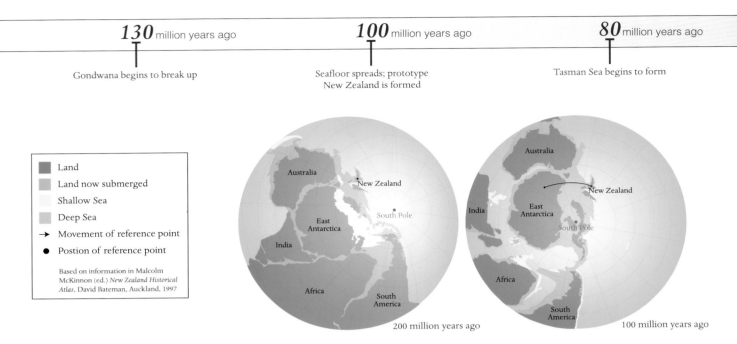

130 million years ago — Gondwana begins to break up

100 million years ago — Seafloor spreads; prototype New Zealand is formed

80 million years ago — Tasman Sea begins to form

Land
Land now submerged
Shallow Sea
Deep Sea
→ Movement of reference point
● Postion of reference point

Based on information in Malcolm McKinnon (ed.) *New Zealand Historical Atlas*, David Bateman, Auckland, 1997

200 million years ago

100 million years ago

Land moving as fast as fingernails grow

About 130 million years ago part of the land we call New Zealand began to shear away from its parental landmass, the supercontinent Gondwana. It was a time when dinosaurs trampled the earth and birds as we know them had barely begun to evolve. Three threads run through the story of this ever-changing landmass: the continuous destruction and re-creation of its landforms, its daunting isolation, and the distinctive paths its ancient life-forms took. The effects of a prolonged exile from their species in Gondwana brought forth some unusual animals; many retained the characteristics of ancient Gondwana, but their exile also led to adaptations that made them distinctive, if not bizarre. Significantly, for all that time New Zealand remained essentially mammal-free. And humanity did not put its foot into it until 1000 years ago, by which time life on this archipelago had become like that on another planet.

New Zealand's formation took place around the time that Gondwana began to rupture into the jigsaw of pieces which, riding on tectonic plates, spread out to become continents. Africa made an early separation, pulling away from its old bedfellow, South America. Then, about 100 million years ago, a rupture formed along the seam of the Australian piece of the Gondwana jigsaw. As the seafloor spread, a slither of old Gondwana fused with sediments that had eroded and washed off its northern shore and accumulated in the rift, then headed east. These extensive sediments formed the New Zealand mini-continent, extending from New Caledonia in the north to south of Campbell Island. They included today's Lord Howe Rise, the Norfolk Ridge, the Chatham Rise and the Campbell Plateau. The total mass, much of it submerged, came to about half of the area of modern Australia.

Eighty million years ago the Tasman Sea began to form. A new ocean floor continued to spread for the next 20 million years. Then late in the day — 15 to five million years back — as ice sheets closed across the previously temperate, palm-decked Antarctic, Tasmania and Antarctica went their separate ways. Into this opening flowed the waters and wonders of the Antarctic Convergence, providing everything from starfish to krill. This pattern of warmer water meeting colder still sets the currents, winds and weather for the Southern Ocean, maritime New Zealand's number one talking point.[1]

Carried out into the ocean on the convulsive seam between the Indo-Australian and Pacific tectonic plates, New Zealand became more distinctive the further it travelled. Eventually it acquired that state that still defines it in every way, extreme isolation, standing about equidistant from Australia and Australia's old geological Siamese twin, Antarctica.[2] Today it is about 2000 km from each of them. Its old links to New Caledonia in the north became less distinct, with connections only evident along sea ridges. New Zealand's distinctiveness became defined in terms of both its geological characteristics and its cargo of plants and animals.

During the period 40 to 20 million years ago a new plate boundary — a new rupture — spread along the Macquarie Ridge. Emergent New Zealand straddled this. Its size was such that it stretched to New Caledonia. Then, in the traction set up

The Last Place on Earth

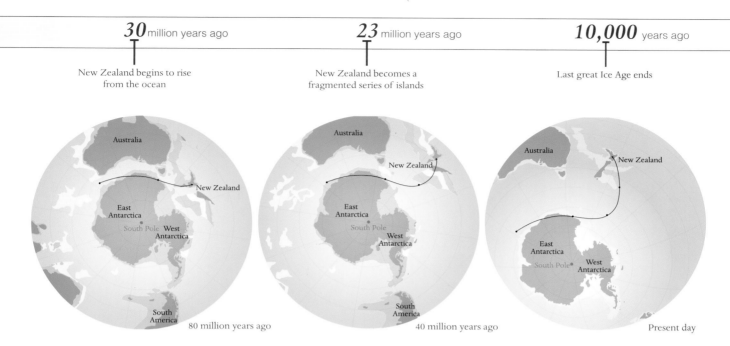

30 million years ago

New Zealand begins to rise
from the ocean

23 million years ago

New Zealand becomes a
fragmented series of islands

10,000 years ago

Last great Ice Age ends

80 million years ago

40 million years ago

Present day

between the two tectonic plates, its spine was put under such pressure that the great divide of its emerging two main islands rose up, eventually stretching terrestrial New Zealand into the mountainous country we have today. At the same time, these forces carried New Zealand further away from its nearest geological cousins, Australia and New Caledonia, with whom it shares more flora than the other, now scattered, pieces of the Gondwana jigsaw.

Over time New Zealand was pushed and pulled up, down and sideways, killing off many species from what eventually became an archipelago. As the underlying rocks cooled, much of the land sank under its own weight. This leached its future soils while extensive rain, down-cutting rivers and coastal erosion also sapped the land's nutrients. Seas continued to rise.

Thirty million years ago, its uplands leached and weathered, New Zealand again pushed up out of the ocean. The tectonic plate boundary activated the landmass and uplift outstripped erosion, exposing more and more land. At the beginning of this New Zealand had been a low flat plain, with probably as little as 18 per cent of it remaining above water.[3]

Activity at the new plate boundary formed the New Zealand we recognise today. In the period between 12 and five million years ago, the Alpine Fault movement lifted more and more land out of the sea. At the same time, the lava of fiery volcanism formed such places as the Coromandel, Banks and Otago peninsulas.

Rugged and proud though our mountain chains are, they are just babies in their geological cradles. They were formed only between five and three million years ago. This explains how, for

example, the Manawatu River can be older than the mountains it cuts through; it was there before they existed and it cut down as they continued to rise.[4] The main axial mountains of the Southern Alps continue to rise at 17 mm a year but a matching amount of annual erosion keeps them from reaching higher. The Southern Alps are so new that the rocks sitting atop Mount Cook/Aoraki, our highest peak, were a million years ago below today's sea level.

Periodically, ice ages blanketed much of the South Island and as far north as the Tararuas with snow and ice. This profoundly affected the ability of most life-forms to survive here and

Life took on some bizarre forms in islands that lacked mammalian predators. Here weta, kissing cousins to crickets and grasshoppers, grew huge and flightless, filling ecological niches occupied by mice elsewhere. Maori called them 'gods of ugly things', and none is bigger or uglier than this wetapunga, which when pregnant can reach a thumping 70 g — as heavy as a small bird.

21

CONVEYORS OF CONTINENTS

Based on Jeffry Aitken, *Rocked and Ruptured*, Reed, 1999

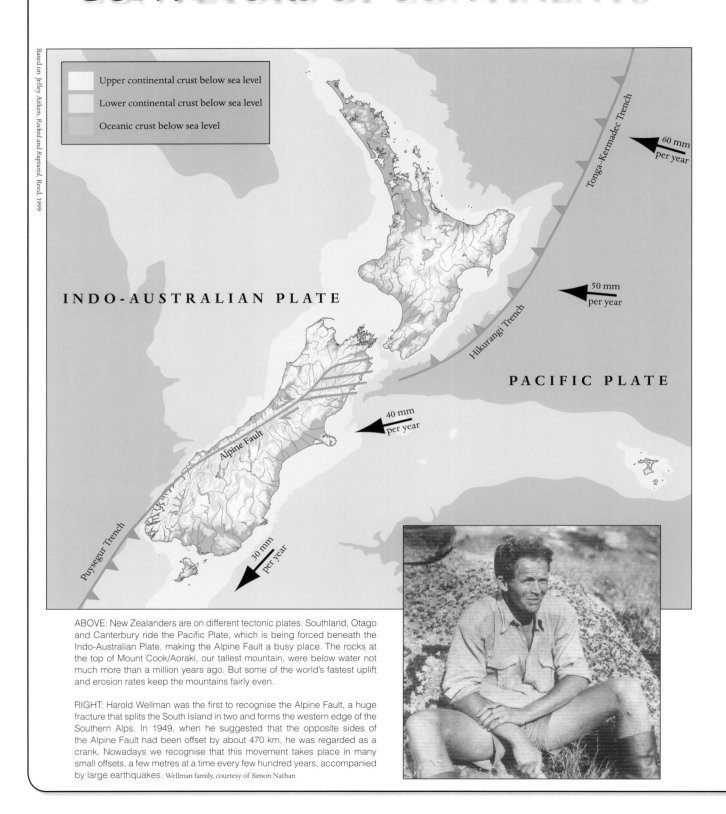

Upper continental crust below sea level

Lower continental crust below sea level

Oceanic crust below sea level

INDO-AUSTRALIAN PLATE

PACIFIC PLATE

Tonga-Kermadec Trench

60 mm per year

50 mm per year

Hikurangi Trench

40 mm per year

Alpine Fault

30 mm per year

Puysegur Trench

ABOVE: New Zealanders are on different tectonic plates. Southland, Otago and Canterbury ride the Pacific Plate, which is being forced beneath the Indo-Australian Plate, making the Alpine Fault a busy place. The rocks at the top of Mount Cook/Aoraki, our tallest mountain, were below water not much more than a million years ago. But some of the world's fastest uplift and erosion rates keep the mountains fairly even.

RIGHT: Harold Wellman was the first to recognise the Alpine Fault, a huge fracture that splits the South Island in two and forms the western edge of the Southern Alps. In 1949, when he suggested that the opposite sides of the Alpine Fault had been offset by about 470 km, he was regarded as a crank. Nowadays we recognise that this movement takes place in many small offsets, a few metres at a time every few hundred years, accompanied by large earthquakes. Wellman family, courtesy of Simon Nathan

Until the development of plate tectonics about 30 years ago, it was difficult to understand how the earth worked. Our planet is unique in the solar system, with continents moving like conveyor belts on great plates driven by convection heat generated at the planet's fiery core. Continental drift helps explain many hitherto imponderable questions, in particular why some continents, thousands of miles apart, share plants and animals that have common species origins.

One of the pioneers of modern geology, Harold Wellman from Victoria University College, demonstrated near Murchison that earthquakes and fault movements changed New Zealand's land surface in even the short time that elapsed between his geological surveys. Our Alpine Fault is one of earth's most spectacular geological boundaries. Scientists estimate that the section running between Milford Sound and Blenheim has been shunted laterally 470 km by movement along the fault.

The North Island sits on the Indo-Australian Plate as does the South Island west of the Alpine Fault. East of the fault is the Pacific Plate. As scientists Trevor Worthy and Richard Holdaway say, the plates 'are converging at about 42 mm per year or about the speed our fingernails grow. This is 42 kilometres in a million years.' They collide through the Cook Strait region. As a result, in the zone between Marlborough and East Cape, the Pacific Plate dives beneath the Indo-Australian Plate in a process called subduction — the driving down of cold, dense organic crust into the hot mantle of the earth. When this occurs pressure zones are formed, and these are where earthquakes are most frequent. The energy released in an earthquake can take hundreds of years to accumulate. As most New Zealanders know, it is usually discharged in a few seconds. As the Pacific Plate sinks it depresses the surface of the earth, creating a vast submarine trench, the Hikurangi Trench, which becomes the Tonga–Kermadec Trench that reaches as far as Tonga.[5]

also created some of our most formidably sheer landscapes, particularly around Fiordland. Some plants found pockets where conditions were not so harsh, so there were remnant populations at the extremities of the South Island, Fiordland and Nelson, for example. Ice killed off many plants. About 30 million years ago the eucalypt (gum tree) and the acacia (wattle) became extinct here. In other places, plants made their escape by climbing to colonise higher, sheltered places.[6] Just 15,000 years ago, during the great Ice Age, glaciers scraped out a path down to the coast with their slow, scouring pot-mitts of moraine and ice until they overhung the very edge of the ocean, then more than 100 m below today's levels. When warmer weather returned and sea levels rose, they brought many changes to islands that were blessed with a considerable coastline.[7]

Fire made its contribution in the form of extensive volcanism. New Zealand sits uneasily atop part of the Pacific rim of fire. Every now and then across New Zealand explosive magma from the earth's inner core spews out igneous materials — ignimbrite, andesite, basalt, obsidian and rhyolite. At times this volcanism

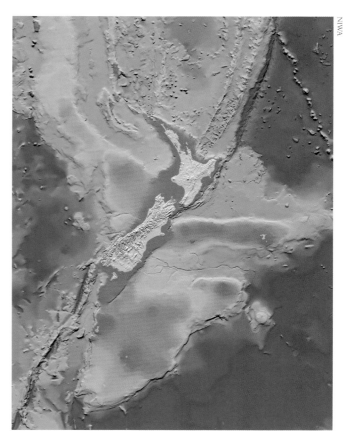

NIWA

Most of the New Zealand 'mini-continent' is underwater, as this striking image of the islands, continental shelves, trenches and submarine valleys shows. Ironically, those tectonic forces that rattle our teacups and break our sleep are largely responsible for keeping our islands above water, rather than a kilometre below the sea where they would otherwise be.

has been extreme. Just 1800 years ago a volcano blew its head off to become Lake Taupo. It is estimated that in the space of a few minutes 30 cubic kilometres of volcanic material exploded out of the earth. The resulting pyroclastic flow travelled almost at the speed of sound, destroying forest across a diameter of 160 km in a few seconds.[8] Ash showered the country as far south as Banks Peninsula. But this was not unusual; such activities have occurred on average once every 1000 to 2000 years for the past 100,000 years. In such ways does the earth renew its surface. Seed-carrying birds do the rest.[9]

A mere 600 years ago, with mesmeric suddenness, Rangitoto appeared above the waters of the Waitemata Harbour. Most promontories around Auckland — Mounts Eden, Wellington and Hobson, for example — are volcanoes. This region's volcanic forces are far from extinct. The Pacific rim of fire runs out through the Taupo volcanic zone, heading east to the Bay of Plenty's White Island, still a regular performer; even on quiet days its fumaroles produce geysers of steam and its surface is covered in sulphur and igneous rock. White Island is one of a string of such volcanoes. The rest are still submarine.

These powerful and diverse forces make New Zealand about as varied geologically as it is possible to be, deservedly earning its nickname 'the Shaky Isles'.

Ancient species and ingenious adaptors

Over millions of years, New Zealand has shifted considerably northwards. Its three main islands lie across degrees of latitude from 33 to 47. Add the associated islands to the north, the Kermadecs, and to the south the Auckland Islands, and the range, for a relatively small landmass, is enormous.

Described as temperate, New Zealand has a mean Celsius temperature range of about 16 degrees in the north to 10 degrees in the south. While the country is subject to the prevailing westerlies, the latitude range means that it can support an extraordinary diversity of life. The vegetation varies according to which side of the main divide it grows on, as these mountains also divide our weather. Our seas host corals and subtropical fish in the north and krill, squid, whales, and penguins and other sea birds in the south. Within the larger system are smaller patterns. Warm currents, for example, bear down on the west coast of the South Island, ensuring a richness of marine life, including fish and birds.

Generally, climate determines what grows where; and the resulting habitats, again generally, determine what animals live where. But soils usually become sparser the higher you climb. At higher altitudes plants have to adapt more ingeniously in order to survive, whereas on the lowlands, which are often river-fed if not river-formed, the rich silts and loams sustain the largest trees and the richest vegetation. On the Canterbury and Otago sides of the main divide tile-like deposits of flat, broken greywacke are common, and among this scree,

Mount Ruapehu blows its top in June 1996. New Zealand is one of the world's major volcanic centres.
JR Keys, Department of Conservation, Te Papa Atawhai

which is home to 25 alpine plants from a variety of families, a lizard and a number of insects, including spiders, are found. On both sides of the tops, tall snow-grass tussocks efficiently hold and release rainfall into the high country, allowing for a more even balance in the catchments below.[10]

Mammals and flowering plants evolved shortly before New Zealand struck out from Gondwana. The fossil record shows evidence of abundant life. Until 25 years ago it was believed that land-based dinosaurs had never reached here, but amateur fossicker Joan Wiffen turned that belief on its head with her extraordinary find of the toe bone of a megalosaur — a 3-m, meat-eating theropod — in the remote Te Hoe Valley near Napier in 1979.[11] Scientists now believe that several different groups of dinosaur once dwelt here. As well, there were primitive birds, a host of insects, lizards and reptiles, and primitive mammals. Recently in Central Otago, a crocodile fossil was uncovered, dating back to an era when waters were warmer here.

Although ancient New Zealand lay within reach of Antarctica, tropical sea currents warmed this country. Paradoxically, once it shifted further north, the currents from the now much colder Antarctic cooled its climate. The New Zealand archipelago's extensive latitude has enabled plants inherited from Gondwana to range themselves across different climate zones. Foremost are the podocarps — big, long-lived conifers that have changed little in 190 million years. Podocarps include rimu, which grows for up to 1000 years, with trunks 60 m tall. Another podocarp, kahikatea, perhaps the most ancient tree of our forests, often grows to 60 m and thrives in the moist dark soils edging rivers and wetlands. As ecologist Geoff Park says:

> *Kahikatea is the supreme survivor. The basket fruit of the forest . . . connects us to a birdless, flowerless world in which huge ammonites stalked the sea-floor and pterodactyls the air. The most remarkable thing about a kahikatea landscape . . . is that the trees are the oldest things your eye encounters, not the mountains. Kahikatea persists from an old, swampy, worn-down tropical archipelago, utterly different from the cool, young, mountainous New Zealand of today.*[12]

The other stately podocarp, the totara, prefers well-drained soils, grows to 30 m and sometimes lives for 1800 years. Matai and miro also prefer drier areas.

In the north and down to Whakatane stand the staunch kauri forests, trees of such immensity that they were prime targets for early foresters. The largest measured had a girth of over 20 m.

All these trees are accompanied by lower-storeyed forest trees, often broadleafs, with clinging vines and epiphytes, worts, fungi and mosses.

The higher country is the realm of the beech (tawhai), another direct descendant of the Gondwana inheritance. Beech, which are communal trees, cover much of the South Island. Small-leafed, hardy and growing up to 30 m, the beech is the most predominant species of the higher ground and montane (lower ranges) country. Most varieties can survive in poor, rocky harsh conditions. Above them are the tussocks.

New Zealand changes so fast and so often that almost no assertion about conditions for life can be made without immediately qualifying it. For example, some of the creatures that live here are amazingly old, but at the same time, are in the midst of newness. This has never been more so than over the past five million years when both plate tectonics and volcanism have been especially active and climate changes, particularly those brought on by periods of glaciation, have also tested the animal and plant life of the region. As volcanoes erupted the land was scoured and scorched as well as enriched with minerals. Yet entire great podocarp forests bounced back in the Taupo region within 1500 years of the Taupo eruption.

Some of our big estuarine and coastal wetlands, such as Ellesmere, Pauatahanui and Ohiwa Harbour, evolved after the last Ice Age (about 12,000 years ago).[13] They include a mixture of fresh and briny water, mudflats, salt marshes and sandy shores where tidal movements stimulate cycles of abounding life. Wetlands are the most productive ecosystems on the planet, rich in special plant life and teeming with insects and worms for the birds and fish that breed or sojourn here. The development of these places led to an explosion in these forms of life. Many of the birds they attract are migratory, as are most of the fish. Some of our most distinctive native birds are found in these places, including the Australian-originating white-faced and white herons and the spoonbills, as

New Zealand has more than 600 species of alpine plants, which makes them rather prolific considering that present-day mountains did not exist until a few million years ago. At high altitudes these plants have to work hard to survive. The spaniard plant in the foreground of this view of the Matukituki Valley is a handsome member of the carrot family, but as mountain climbers will have learned, it has evolved needle-sharp spines to ward off browsers.

Neville Peat, Department of Conservation, Te Papa Atawhai

Claire McMeekin

well as some of the long-distance migrants such as terns, godwits, sandpipers and oystercatchers.

Everything that happens here, life-evolving and life-dissolving, takes place against a backdrop of continuous change. There never has been a steady state in which it could be said, 'this is the original, native New Zealand'. But if the place was isolated for 80 million years it was not completely airtight. One of the more interesting plants to drift here was the mangrove, that guardian and filter of the waters of the northern coast, which probably arrived just 10,000 years ago. New Zealand was a giver as well as a receiver. It also cast its seed across the ocean, with the result that the hebes, for example, took up residence in South America and the Pacific Islands, and the kowhai blooms on coastal islands in the South Atlantic.[14]

Over millions of years, in the absence of mammalian predators, a number of birds became ground-dwelling and flightless. Some also became large, gigantic even. Of these, those that come first to mind are the moa, some standing well above the height of a person, and the kiwi. The world's largest parrot, the tree-climbing kakapo, is another big bird. Yet another is the extinct giant eagle.

A much larger array of birds that retained the power of flight were also able to breed on the ground, if not in it. Many were seabirds, like the titi that nested in burrows on land. (Titi is a Maori word for a range of migratory petrels, prions and shearwaters whose fatty chicks produce the still sought-after 'mutton birds'.) We can only speculate as to the numbers of seabirds, but two points are worth making in this regard. One is that throughout the Pacific — and New Zealand is no exception — the birds of the sea rose above the islands and atolls in such

WJ Cooper, Department of Conservation, Te Papa Atawhai

The kauri is New Zealand's largest, grandest tree, hosting a wide range of plant and animal life. Kauri once grew as far south as Southland, but two million years ago a change in climate limited them to north of a line between Kawhia and Te Puke in the North Island. Waipoua Forest's old-timers Tane Mahuta (girth 13.77 m, height 51.5 m) and Te Matua Ngahere (girth 16.21 m, height 29.9 m) have been living here since before the arrival of humans and even before Rangitoto Island appeared.

Wetlands, such as these tarns and peat land between the lagoon and the sea at the Waituna Wetlands Scientific Reserve, are often termed 'the quiet places' but they are also immensely valuable breeding and feeding grounds for birds, fish and plants. Waituna Wetlands, in Southland, is no exception. It is home to a number of birds, including the threatened giant kokopu and banded kokopu, the New Zealand shoveler, variable oystercatcher, the South Island oystercatcher, the South Island fernbird, the New Zealand dotterel and the banded dotterel.

clouds that they were navigational aids to seaborne Polynesians. And such were the numbers in New Zealand that one species alone, petrels, over the previous five million years very likely would have significantly enriched at least some New Zealand forest with their guano.[15] Many other seabirds — gulls, prions, fulmars, gannets and shags — became part of our ecological way of life. The largest, the albatross, has a wingspan of 3.3 m.

But the birds that have attracted the greatest attention of the scientific world were the ground birds. Eleven species of moa and five species of kiwi are part of a group of birds that, together with the emu and the cassowary, are called ratites — from the Latin name for a breastplate that once supported wings. Recent DNA work on ratite bones suggests that the kiwi is more closely related to the emu–cassowary group than to the moa. It seems that the kiwi, famed for its flightlessness, quit the fragmenting hunting grounds of Gondwana about 15 million years after New Zealand broke away from it. The kiwi had to make its way across water — and perhaps did so by flying, a power that it may then still have possessed.[16]

Canoes to dare the clouds of heaven

Earth could not be a more misleading name for this planet, 70 per cent of whose surface is covered by oceans and seas. The Pacific Ocean is just one of Earth's oceans, but it is the largest and the deepest, covering more than a third of the planet's surface and containing over half of its free water. It has an area of approximately 180 million square kilometres. More than 30,000 islands pockmark the Pacific, ranging in size from Australia to minuscule coral islands, but they make up only a tiny percentage of its surface area. In fact, you could merge all the continents back into a single landmass, plonk it in the Pacific and still leave room for some water. Not surprisingly, many early European navigators likened crossing the Pacific to travelling through a desert. Five hundred years ago one of Ferdinand Magellan's chroniclers spoke of 'a sea so vast the human mind can scarcely grasp it'.[17]

The Pacific's name — given by a Juan-come-lately, Portugal's Magellan, just 500 years ago — is as misleading as the name Earth. The Pacific is anything but pacific. Along its ring of fire, nearly 300 active volcanoes vent steam and smoke. Typhoons sweep through the equatorial regions, and earthquakes unleash tsunami (tidal waves).

But to people accustomed to sea voyaging, seas are highways, not barriers. Even today, no other form of transport can move large amounts of cargo long distances so effectively. While life at sea had its perils, it was tame compared to those of the land: swollen rivers, parched deserts, impenetrable jungles,

Claire McMeekin

Before people reached these islands New Zealand was one of the great seabird centres of the world. Seabirds by the hundreds of millions fed in this country's waters, like these gannets at Muriwai.

Canterbury Museum

The bird that arouses the most enduring curiosity is the moa. When the great anatomist Richard Owen (pictured above), working from a bone delivered to England, pronounced that this was part of a flightless bird heavier than an ostrich, Victorian science was transfixed. More than a century later we remain no less entranced by a bird whose stature matched its antiquity, frustrated perhaps by the idea we missed seeing it by a narrow, but often debated, period of time. The largest of the moa — which recent studies have proved to be female — stood more than two metres tall and weighed 200 kg. Moa lived in a variety of habitats; during the last few million years smaller species tended to occupy the humid forests, the larger the scrub or open ground. They filled a niche elsewhere occupied by herbivores, mainly mammals. Or at least they did until a particularly dangerous mammal species appeared on the beaches in canoes 800 years ago.

precipitous peaks and passes, dangerous animals and, worst of all, robbers, brigands and tribal warlords who regarded squeezing travellers and traders as a legitimate business activity. Even so, such journeys cannot have been undertaken lightly. So why did the people who became Polynesian launch themselves into the unknown?

Although middens or DNA samples are least useful in uncovering motives, scholars have not been shy in offering suggestions. Some point to universal human traits — a sense of adventure, the desire to explore, the quest for riches, the wish to trade, or the desire for greener pastures. Others suggest that warfare, disease or population pressure drove people out. Or were they fleeing enemies or being exiled? We do not know. There was probably no single reason, but it is likely that 'pull' factors outweighed 'push'. Since population densities on most islands were probably lighter when voyagers were setting out, we may assume that people were not driven out by starvation. Archaeologist Patrick Kirch suggests that part of the explanation may be found in the recurring stories throughout Polynesia of the trickster Maui, who as the younger brother in a patriarchy of rigid succession lines may have had a raw deal. In such a society there were, for younger brothers, issues of what is called mana. 'Usually in these sagas, it is the younger brother that leaves the home island to sail over the horizon in search of a new land where his line can be established as foremost.'[18]

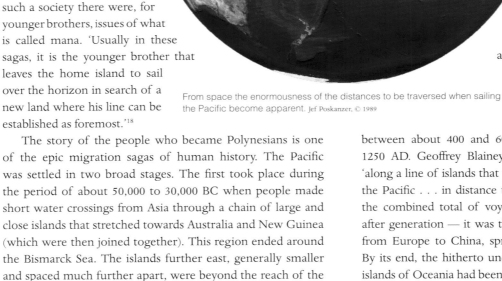

From space the enormousness of the distances to be traversed when sailing the Pacific become apparent. Jef Poskanzer, © 1989

The story of the people who became Polynesians is one of the epic migration sagas of human history. The Pacific was settled in two broad stages. The first took place during the period of about 50,000 to 30,000 BC when people made short water crossings from Asia through a chain of large and close islands that stretched towards Australia and New Guinea (which were then joined together). This region ended around the Bismarck Sea. The islands further east, generally smaller and spaced much further apart, were beyond the reach of the simple voyaging technology of the time. Nevertheless, the area covered in this first stage was impressive, what anthropologist

Geoffrey Irwin calls a 'voyaging corridor'. Here islands are seldom more than 100 sea miles (185 km) apart. They can be reached with simple craft and may be detected comparatively easily by reading changes to swells, cloud formations, or by observing the movements of birds. The weather, too, is helpful. The seasonal reversals of the north-west monsoon and the south-east trade winds enabled these most ancient of navigators to move around, fairly sheltered between the northern and the southern cyclone belts. This zone is a big navigational incubator.

Then about 6000 years ago a new wave of people moved down from the region of south China–Taiwan. Those who settled the northern coastal fringe of New Guinea and the Bismarck Archipelago moved out into the wider Pacific Ocean between 1500 and 1000 BC. There were several stages. The first stage was from the Bismarcks to Fiji, Tonga and Samoa (with the exception of Fiji, what is known as West Polynesia), where ancestral Polynesian society was readily identifiable by 500 BC. Academics are still debating whether the flow was continuous or whether there was a pause in East Polynesia, but what is certain is that the flow was eastwards and then south-west, finally dissipating in the next stage in Hawai'i, Easter Island (Rapa Nui) and New Zealand. Radiocarbon dating is hazy with such recent dates, but East Polynesians are likely to have arrived at Hawai'i and Easter Island between about 400 and 600 AD and New Zealand around 1250 AD. Geoffrey Blainey wrote about a gradual diffusion 'along a line of islands that formed a kind of Milky Way across the Pacific . . . in distance travelled along an east-west line — the combined total of voyage after voyage made generation after generation — it was the equivalent of a journey on land from Europe to China, spread over more than 4000 years'.[19] By its end, the hitherto unclaimed atolls, reefs, volcanoes and islands of Oceania had been occupied by an estimated 1,230,000 Polynesians, now composed of about 450 distinct cultures speaking as many languages.[20]

LAPITA PEOPLE

The languages are described as Austronesian, but these people shared many other things in common. They were coastal dwellers, highly proficient seafarers in their ocean-going outriggers and they also knew how to hunt and fish, to farm chickens and pigs and to practise forms of horticulture, such as the cultivation of tubers. Living either on beach terraces close to reef passages or on small offshore islands, the 'Lapita peoples transformed Oceanic rainforests into a landscape of high productivity'.[21] But they were also highly adept ocean navigators and makers of tools, fish hooks and decorative items, integrating the economies of land, shore and sea to harvest all of the riches their Pacific abodes offered. On the shoreline, for example, they gathered seaweed and molluscs; they pulled the bulk of their protein from the inshore fishery but they also trawled the deep-sea fishery and, apart from its fish, harvested turtles and porpoises. Their most remarkable material legacy is their pottery, which has been located from New Guinea to such places as Tonga, Samoa, Fiji and New Caledonia — across 4300 km of the Pacific. And carbon dating reveals that the Lapita diaspora, moving at the rate of 20 km per generation, was one of the most rapid such events in the world.[22] In fact, they went much further. Linguistic analysis suggests that one branch of these Austronesians went on to travel as far west as Madagascar. In the eastern direction they touched the coast of South America.

The pottery that came to be known as Lapita took its name from the place where it was found in New Caledonia in 1917, although it was first identified by a Jesuit priest on the island of Watom, in the Bismarck Archipelago early last century. Distinctive in design and execution, Lapita pottery has been characterised by four evolving styles, ranging from 'Polynesian plainware' to carved paddle styles. Some styles display humanoid heads, many involve zigzags, triangles and repeating curved designs. For reasons not entirely clear, the throwing of Lapita pots came to an end in Polynesia early in the first millennia AD, but the passing of Lapita work heralded the emergence of a new, Pacific culture. [23]

This Lapita pottery fragment, dated approximately 1000 BC, depicts a human face incorporated into the intricate geometric designs. It was unearthed in the Santa Cruz group of islands, south-east of the Solomon Islands. Department of Anthropology Photographic Archive, University of Auckland

We can also scuttle two ideas, briefly fashionable 50 years ago, of accidental drift and of South American origins for the Polynesians.[24] While storms and navigational errors may have played a minor part in the process on occasion, the Pacific could not have been settled so thoroughly and so quickly by a bunch of incompetents. We know that the Polynesian craft were large and seaworthy enough to transport people, plants and goods in the quantities needed to sustain new settlements. They were colonisers, not castaways.

Despite the efforts of the media-savvy Thor Heyerdahl, we can also sink the suggestion that South Americans settled Polynesia.[25] Though modern raft voyages have proved little more than that modern people can sail traditionally-made craft to places that they already know to exist, archaeological, linguistic and DNA evidence shows that the ancient Polynesians reached South America, where they picked up the sweet potato. But they did not put down roots there themselves for the simple reason that the continent was already settled.

The sea change in our view of ancient Polynesian voyaging has been considerable. Anthropologists, linguists, medical researchers, mariners and the descendants of the ancient voyagers themselves have all had a hand in reconstructing this remarkable tale. In laboratories, computer simulations have created pictures of winds and currents, producing new insights into ancient voyaging. At sea, David Lewis, 40 years ago, sailed a catamaran from Tahiti to New Zealand without instruments to prove the viability of sailing by star observations; and a decade later Ben Finney built *Hokule'a*, a Hawai'ian double-hulled canoe (albeit in modern materials), which he sailed without instruments from Hawai'i to Tahiti. Following in the pioneering wakes of these two men, other mariners and adventurers have tested theories — and themselves — by sailing long distances, recreating ancient voyage pathways.

Those ancient craft were truly 'canoes to dare the clouds of heaven'.[26] The European explorers who first encountered these vessels were impressed by them, more so than some later armchair admirals.[27] In calm conditions, those explorers watched Polynesian craft literally sail rings around their own arthritic ships. Polynesians were the greatest navigators of their age, although as historian James Belich notes, 'they are in danger of being deified rather than merely superhuman'.[28] Many of their navigational techniques would have been familiar to mariners elsewhere around the globe. European sailors, too, felt the swells, observed clouds, water colour and bird flight patterns, sniffed the breeze and looked for drift objects in the sea. As the *Endeavour* approached New Zealand in late September and early October 1769, Cook's log was full of references to observations of this sort.[29]

David Lewis quibbled at the use of the word 'canoe', asserting that they were really ships before slipping back into the c— word. They were big — throughout Oceania they averaged 16–25 m in length (some exceeded 30 m, about the same length as Cook's *Endeavour*, although smaller in overall size). And they

Ben Finney's double-hulled voyaging canoe *Hokule'a* approaching Waikiki, Hawai'i.

were mostly planked vessels, not dugouts like the New Zealand, Hawai'ian and Marquesan inshore paddling craft familiar to modern readers. True, they were lashed together, not nailed, but that gave a flexibility in a seaway that brought safety and strength. The lashings needed renewal, but not within the timeframe of a single Pacific voyage. In Polynesia the three main varieties became the Tahitian and the Tuamotuan pahi, which were twin-hulled, two-masted sailing vessels 16–22 m long; the Tongan tongiaki, with a sizeable platform; and the Fijian ndrua. More manoeuvrable than the tongiaki, the ndrua has one hull shorter than the other, the shorter hull acting more like an outrigger.[30]

Unlike some Micronesian vessels, the double-hulled canoes in Polynesia generally tacked in the European manner. They were less effective, as they could comfortably sail no closer to the wind than about 75 degrees. In practice this meant that a shallow draft, double canoe had to tack for 7.2 km, compared to the 2.6 km of a modern keeler yacht, to make good one sea mile (1.85 km) against the wind.[31] But mariners could select seasonal wind patterns suitable for their otherwise efficient crab-claw shaped sails. Cook trailed a patent log behind a tongiaki and was impressed by its average of seven knots close-hauled. He also noted that pahi could outsail the *Endeavour*, although almost anything could do that — his bluff-bowed Whitby collier was no ocean greyhound. Nevertheless, twin-hulled Polynesian voyaging canoes could cover a very creditable distance in a day, point to point, under reasonable sailing conditions, enabling them to cover long distances safely and reliably.

While double canoes could carry nothing like the amount a deep-draft European ship of the same length could, they were obviously capable of sustaining prolonged voyaging.

David Lewis (1917–2002), born in Britain, but brought up in New Zealand, always called himself a New Zealander even if he was also a Polynesian under his skin. In the 1960s he gave up doctoring and took his family to sea in the cruising catamaran *Rehu Moana*. Pragmatic, earthy and colourful, Lewis sank the desk wallahs' theories by sailing the *Rehu Moana* 2960 km from Tahiti to New Zealand. This showed that it was possible to sail long distances without the aid of Western navigation tools.

An observer with Cook, who reported tongiaki carrying between 80 and 100 people, considered them capable of 'keeping the sea' for long periods. Joseph Banks said that Tahitian vessels 'carry a tolerable stock in hollow Bamboes'.[32] Carrying fresh and fermented food supplies, they could remain at sea for months, which at the 100 to 150 miles (185–277 km) a day they could cover under reasonable wind conditions, equated to 3000 to 4500 miles (5550–8325 km) — the distances that had to be crossed for the settlement of several island groups to take place. Their twin hulls, held together by a broad platform, had room for a sizeable shelter.

Early navigational skills

'All navigators must be able,' Ben Finney notes, to '(1) orient themselves and set an accurate course toward their destination; (2) keep track of position en route and make any necessary course corrections; (3) make landfall on the island or place along a coastline to which they are heading.' The rotation of the earth causes stars to appear to rise in the east and set in the west, following recognisable paths that Polynesian navigators used to orient themselves. Canoes often left from known landmarks, lining up against a horizon star. Since stars change their bearings, and are generally only useful as markers for about an hour after rising, 10 or 12 may be needed in the course of a night to maintain a correct course.[33] This is called the 'star path' and is just one of the important elements in the mental map the navigator creates in his head. Other contributions can come from the stars — like Polaris in the north — that appear fixed over the North or South Pole, or from major constellations such as the Southern Cross. In daylight the navigator's attention switches to the rising and setting of the sun, drawing in secondary information from the ocean swells and the direction of the wind. Here, feel is as important as sight. If that sounds complicated, it is; it requires constant vigilance and the use of all the senses, as you literally feel, see and sniff your way across the sea.

Once at sea, a navigator must keep track of his vessel's progress in order to keep it on its proper track, guarding against errors caused by current set, leeway (sideways wind-drift under sail) and gale-drift. Before the days of modern navigational instruments, Western sailors talked about 'dead reckoning', calculating their position from their estimates of the course their ships had sailed and how far they had travelled from their last known position — in other words, keeping a running estimate of position as a voyage proceeds. Polynesian sailors did the same but used a completely different conceptual system, carrying a mental reference point (an island) in their heads. Obviously new waters brought unfamiliar currents, but a wary navigator would have a fair idea of the relationship between currents and

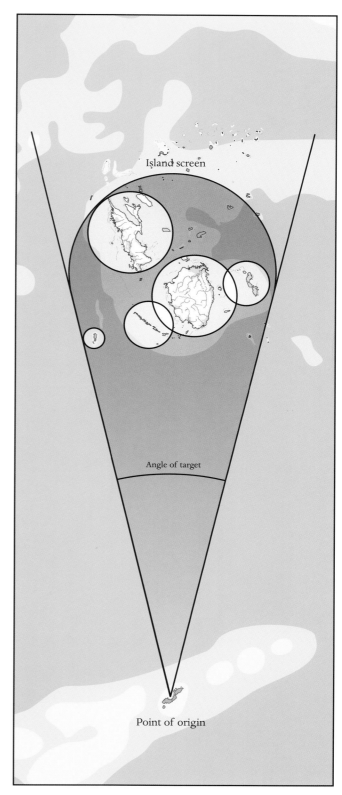

An 'island screen' is the area within which the existence of an island can be detected from out at sea. The evidence may include the presence of offshore feeding birds, cloud formations and the effect of land on ocean swells.

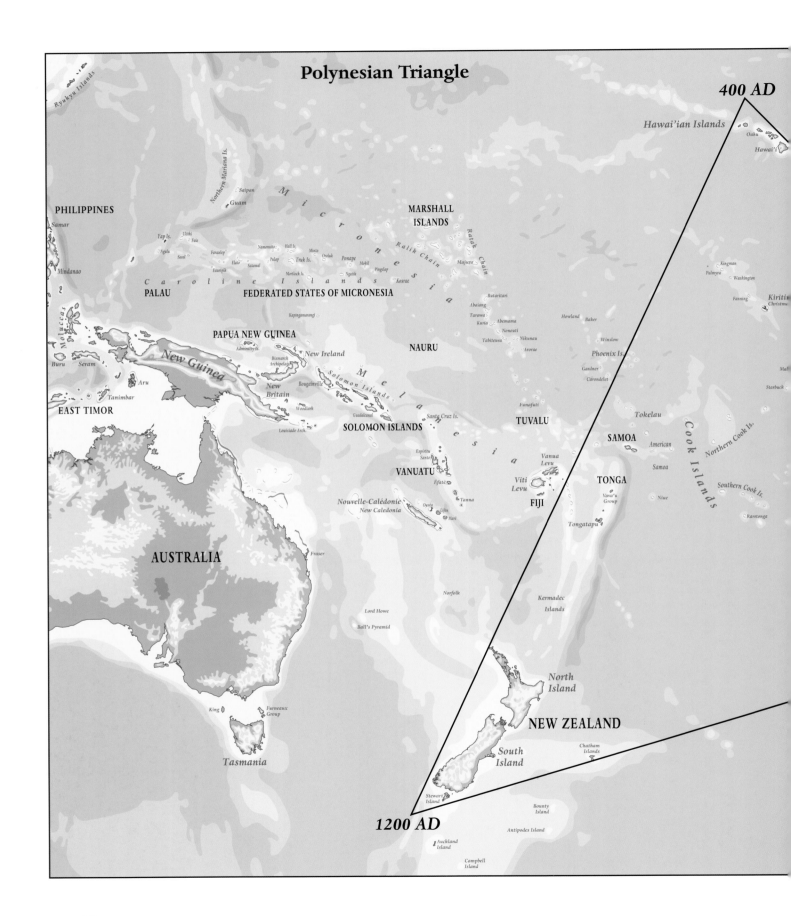

Polynesian Triangle

400 AD

Hawai'ian Islands

Oahu

Hawai'i

Ryukyu Islands

PHILIPPINES

Samar

Mindanao

Northern Mariana Is.

Saipan

Guam

Micronesia

MARSHALL
ISLANDS

Yap Is. *Ulithi*
Faia

Ngulu *Sorol*

Namonuito *Hall Is.* *Minto*

Faraulep *Orolak*

Elato *Satawal* *Palap* *Truk Is.*

Eauripik *Mortlock Is.* *Ngtik*

PALAU

CAROLINE ISLANDS

FEDERATED STATES OF MICRONESIA

Kapingamarangi

Moluccas

Buru *Seram*

EAST TIMOR

Aru

Tanimbar

New Guinea

NEW GUINEA

PAPUA NEW GUINEA

Admiralty Is.

Bismarck Archipelago

New Ireland

New
Britain

Bougainville

Woodlark

Solomon Islands

Guadalcanal

Louisiade Arch.

SOLOMON ISLANDS

Santa Cruz Is.

Melanesia

Ponape *Mobil*

Pingelap

Kosrae

Butaritari

Abaiang

Tarawa

Kuria *Abemama*

Nonouti

Tabiteuea *Nikunau*

Arorae

NAURU

Howland *Baker*

Winslow

Phoenix Is.

Gardner

Carondelet

Ralik Chain

Ratak Chain

Majuro

Kingman

Palmyra *Washington*

Fanning

Kiritim
Christm

Mal

Starbuck

Funafuti

TUVALU

Espiritu
Santo

VANUATU

Efate

Vanua
Levu

Viti
Levu

Tanna

FIJI

Nouvelle-Calédonie
New Caledonia

Ouvea

Lifou

Maré

Tokelau

SAMOA

American
Samoa

TONGA

Vava'u
Group

Niue

Cook Islands

Northern Cook Is.

Southern Cook Is.

Rarotonga

Tongatapu

AUSTRALIA

Fraser

Norfolk

Lord Howe

Ball's Pyramid

Kermadec
Islands

North
Island

NEW ZEALAND

Chatham
Islands

South
Island

King

Furneaux
Group

Tasmania

Stewart
Island

1200 AD

Bounty
Island

Antipodes Island

Auckland
Island

Campbell
Island

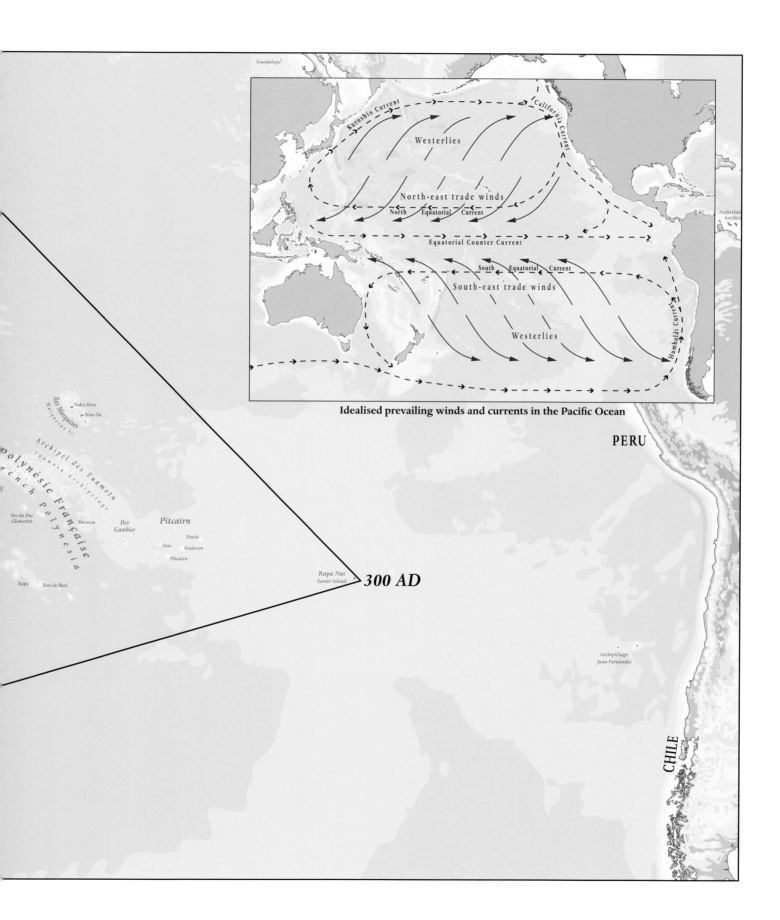

Idealised prevailing winds and currents in the Pacific Ocean

Kuroshio Current

California Current

Westerlies

North-east trade winds

North Equatorial Current

Equatorial Counter Current

South Equatorial Current

South-east trade winds

Westerlies

Humboldt Current

Guadalupe

Netherlands Antilles

PERU

Nuku Hiva
Hiva Oa
Îles Marquises
Marquesas Iss.

Archipel des Tuamotu
Tuamotu Archipelago

Polynésie Française
French Polynesia

Îles du Duc
Gloucester
Mururoa
Îles Gambier

Pitcairn

Ducie
Oeno Henderson
Pitcairn

Rapa Nui
Easter Island

Rapa Îlots de Bass

300 AD

Archipiélago
Juan Fernández

CHILE

KUPE

Did the Polynesian explorer Kupe carry out the first advertising campaign for New Zealand? Legends differ, but in one popular version he is said to have discovered Te-Ika-a-Maui (the 'Great Fish of Maui' or the North Island), while pursuing the octopus Te Wheke-o-Muturangi. After fighting Muturangi at Rangi-whakaoma, Kupe sailed down the island — which still bears many names associated with him and his crew — and returned to the Pacific to brag about this strange place.

The Kupe story as told by Rangi Hetet (carving) and Erenora Puketapu Hetet (tukutuku). Maui and the Wellington taniwha Ngake and Whataitai are on the left-hand column. On the right Kupe (top), holding his adze Rakatuwhenua, is grappling with the octopus Te Wheke-o-Muturangi (centre); his daughters Matiu and Makoro are at the bottom. The Southern Cross features prominently at the top of the tukutuku. Museum of Wellington City and Sea

the prevailing winds; as Lewis noted, there was a tendency for 'errors due to short-term fluctuations to neutralise each other'.[34] Leeway can be calculated by sighting back along the centreline of the canoe and observing the angle between the wake and this projection of the course being steered. Speed and time, both essential for measuring distance covered, could also be estimated with experience.

The third of Finney's points, making a landfall, is less difficult than some may think. On the page of an atlas the islands of the Pacific may look like needles in a haystack, but they are numerous and they tend to cluster together in chains. Wayfinders, therefore, learned to aim for 'island blocks' or 'screens' of islands. The Hawai'ian Islands, for example, stretch more than 1600 km from east to west across the ocean; the Tuamotus stretch 880 km north to south and 800 km east to west. 'You do not aim towards an individual puko tree but towards a grove of puko trees,' Tongan navigator the Hon. Ve'ehala told Lewis, 'only then do you look for your particular tree.'[35] In other words, aim for the largest possible target. But it was still important to be able to 'read' the sea itself, since the distortions created by islands expanded the target size far beyond that of the atolls and the islands themselves. When a navigator detects a change to the regular oceanic swell, it is usually because an island or an atoll has bent it, either around an island coming towards him or reflected back at him if he is sailing with the current. With experience a navigator can detect the distortion created by even the tiniest atoll from 30 km or more away, far better than the distance of 10–15 km from which he can see a low atoll with trees.

Other signs include drift objects such as wood or seaweed. When David Lewis approached New Zealand in the *Rehu Moana* in the 1960s, he detected floating vegetation up to 370 km

This bronze casting of Kupe Raiatea, his wife Hine Te Aparangi and the tohunga Pekahourangi, originally sculpted in plaster by William Trethewey for the 1940 Centennial Exhibition, stands on the Wellington waterfront. Gavin McLean

offshore. Clouds, too, are important. At sea they pile up over islands, often forming distinctive 'eyebrow' or inverted 'v' shapes before dissipating; constant vigilance is needed to detect these characteristic breaks in the drifting cloudscape. Then there is the loom above an island created by sunlight or moonlight reflecting up from either white sand or a smooth lagoon. Phosphorescence — flashes and streaks of light emanating from land — can also be seen across long distances.

Birds, too, are excellent indicators of unseen landmasses. Seabirds such as the noddy tern return to land daily, flying out from islands in the morning and back to them in the late afternoon, so their flight paths offer clues to the direction of land and its possible distance away. The noddy tern ranges up to about 65 km in total daily but other birds can cover much longer distances. As a general rule, the more birds feeding at sea, the closer you are to land. Even the smell of the land may be detected before it is seen.

Once one island is located, seafarers can move within the screen checking known landmarks (if the island is familiar), getting directions from the inhabitants (if it is peopled) or settling there if it is uninhabited.

To minimise the risks of exploring unknown seas, the early mariners sailed eastwards against the prevailing easterly trade winds using brief periods of westerlies, knowing that the easterlies would always return to get them home again if necessary. 'Practically every radiocarbon date in the remote Pacific supports the view that colonisation went first against the prevailing winds and only then across and down them.'[36] 'Without a doubt it is safest to sail first in the direction which is normally upwind because one can expect the fastest trip back,' Geoffrey Irwin argues. He should know, having modelled the winds of the Pacific on computer and also battled them aboard yachts:

JOURNEY'S END

The final phase of Polynesian colonisation of the Pacific was to settle the extremities of what was referred to as 'the Polynesian Triangle' — Easter Island, Hawai'i, and New Zealand. This occurred about 300, 400 and 1200 AD respectively. Why people reached as far south as this is a mystery. The Kupe story puts the blame on a bait-stealing octopus and it is likely that nature beckoned in the form of migrating birds. Long-tailed cuckoos migrate from tropical Polynesia to New Zealand in September and shearwaters fly south a month later. Their annual departures would tell that land lay south, though not, of course, how far away it was.

By this stage the distances to be covered were truly immense. New Zealand and the Chathams were the extreme test of Polynesian navigation, lying far south of the tropics in seas and weather patterns quite different to those of the likely homelands of East Polynesia (the Society Islands and the Marquesas in particular). Fortunately, after leaving the Cook Islands, Norfolk Island and the Kermadecs could act as stepping stones. The evidence suggests that both were first settled just under 1000 years ago.

Nevertheless, crossing the trade routes was a demanding voyage, even if they did break the journey at Rarotonga, 2560 km to the north. Although the map of generalised westerlies on page 33 may suggest that the winds would have been against a voyage to New Zealand, there are short seasonal breaks when winds are more favourable. An old Maori memory of a sailing direction was to point the prows of the canoe towards the setting sun, or just to one or the other side of it, during the months of October or November; this suggests that the first explorers may have set out in early summer before the start of the cyclone season, sailing with easterly tailwinds across the top of summer high pressure

New Zealand marked the end of Polynesian colonisation. Not long after it was settled the frequency of voyaging began to fall. The three isolated points of the Polynesian Triangle — New Zealand, Hawai'i and Easter Island — became effectively marooned. Although voyaging survived in the more closely settled Micronesia, the Societies and western Tuamotus, and the Samoa, Tonga and Fiji region, about 20 small and isolated 'mystery islands', including Norfolk, the Kermadecs (Macauley Island is shown below) and Pitcairn, appear to have been abandoned. These were stepping-stone islands no longer needed after voyaging declined. Department of Conservation, Te Papa Atawhai

The hard way is really the easy or safe way and this simple paradox is one of the keys to explaining the trajectory of human settlement . . . sailing upwind also provides the means to find the way home by latitude sailing. This was evidently developed during the settlement of Polynesia and simply involves using the altitude of known stars to return to the latitude of one's origin island, while still upwind of it, and then running with the wind along the latitude.[39]

systems. Or they may have headed south on the northerlies at the leading edge of an advancing front. 'Sooner or later, a canoe crossed the trades into the variables and arrived at the right time to pick up freshening northerlies perhaps 200 miles ahead of a typical front and then flew south before them, initially from choice and then perhaps driven in a near-gale for a day or a night as the front closed in.'[37] Afterwards the canoe would be well placed to make a landfall in clearing weather on the Northland coast.

David Lewis concluded that the return voyage, against the trade-wind belt and aiming for the comparatively small screen of the Cooks, would have been 'difficult navigationally, and would be subject to the mischance of unseasonably prolonged headwinds'. But as the *Hokule'a*'s 1986 New Zealand–Tonga–Tahiti voyage showed, 'it would be difficult, but far from impracticable'.[38]

Being able to return home was crucial. The first colonisers followed the first explorers, and New Zealand was hit time and again by new arrivals. But it seems this influx did not last long. For reasons still not completely understood, voyaging declined soon after the first settlement, isolating the islands' Eastern Polynesian colonists. Not that it mattered much. There were worlds aplenty to explore in this vast new homeland and plenty to get used to. That much had been apparent even before toes trod sand. According to an old Maori story, the voyagers saw trees ablaze with red as they approached the shore. Thinking them full of red-feathered birds, the joyous sailors flung their treasured head-dresses of red feathers into the sea. 'The chiefly colour of Hawaiki is cast aside for the chiefly red of the new land that welcomes us,' one sailor said in anticipation, only to discover that they had seen not birds, but the bright red blossoms of the pohutukawa tree which blooms on the north-eastern side of the North Island between late November and January. One dream, at least, had already fizzled out on the frontier.

Te 'Au o Tonga, a double-hulled pahi, closes on Auckland after a voyage from Apia in 1996, throughout which it averaged 16.7 kph.

Chapter 2

Landfall in southern seas. The Polynesian colonists found a strange new land, larger, colder and more varied than anything they had previously encountered. A scene from *Frontier of Dreams*.

Whakapapa Productions Ltd

Treasure Islands
c.1300–1642

Making it to these islands was one thing, but for the Polynesians who settled here, making them their own was something else. In short order, these voyagers explored the coastline and the interior, camping wherever possible at those fertile interchanges between salt and freshwater where fowl, fish and shellfish abounded, and where they could hunt marine mammals and the huge flightless moa that seemed there for the taking. So plentiful was all this food that they could live as semi-nomads, as hunter-gatherers, although they held on to the foods they had brought with them, keeping their precious kumara tubers dry for that rainy day.

During their first 200 years they used up most of the easily available food and burnt off about half of the extensive forest cover of the main islands. As the easy meat diminished and as their numbers grew, horticulture became increasingly important north of Banks Peninsula. Out of this came a growth in tribalism, accompanied by the rise of the fortified pa and a gradual increase in warfare. There was also a growth in artistry: carving, waiata, oratory, the weaving of cloaks for the ariki (chiefs). The making of haka and pounamu finery are all expressions of tribal mana and of a distinctive Polynesian adaptation to this unique archipelago.

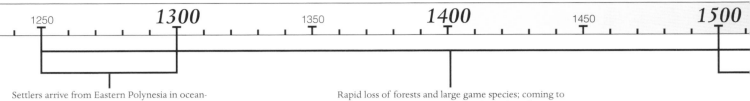

1250   **1300**   1350   **1400**   1450   **1500**

Settlers arrive from Eastern Polynesia in ocean-going canoes; exploration, identification of resources and suitable locations

Rapid loss of forests and large game species; coming to terms with a less varied diet, limited conflict

Arrival and exploration

At first sight the main islands of New Zealand must have seemed astonishing. To those Polynesian voyagers who reached here about 800 years ago this country was large, bigger in every way: tall mountains, big rivers, broad plains, huge trees, vast forests, huge animals. And uninhabited. Nothing in the stories that had led them here could have conveyed how big the new territory was, far larger than anything they had seen before. The island of Rarotonga — a point of departure for some of the voyaging waka — would fit inside Wellington Harbour, or Whanganui-a-Tara as they came to call it.

The second immediate impression was that the archipelago was rich in food, fresh water and forest. Protein was everywhere. Beneath their outriggers, estuarine fish shoaled and broached in numbers unimaginable today. The tidal zone was decked in shellfish. On the rocky shore fresh food lounged about for the taking, for the fur seals and sea elephants had known no terrestrial predators. Many shorelines heaved and wheeled and teemed with birds, their raucous choruses especially deafening at sunrise and sundown.[1]

As they pushed into estuaries and nosed up rivers, the Polynesians soon noticed that the vegetation produced neither the rich fruits, the coconuts nor (except very rarely) the stone-fruit they had known in the islands they had left behind. That was not a problem at first, for this new land was full of big birds, many of which, astonishingly, simply scuttled away across the ground, for they were flightless. In more open areas huge birds, some taller than a person and carrying on their haunches alone more than enough meat to satisfy an extended family group, browsed the trees and grasses as if in some eternal dream.

The new settlers' first landfall was almost certainly on the east coast of the North Island. Two landing spots favoured by both archaeology and tribal accounts are North Cape and the Coromandel Peninsula. The traditions of at least four major founding waka — Tainui, Matatua, Horouta and Nukutere — tell us that they landed first in the eastern

Bay of Plenty — some state explicitly that the place was Whangaparaoa, out on the East Cape. Voyaging re-enactments in the late 20th century suggest that winds and currents will still fetch up a canoe headed south from the region of the Society Islands to this part of New Zealand. A black-lipped pearl shell lure found at a coastal site at Tairua, eastern Coromandel, is one of the very few archaeological items scientists are certain came from the ancestral land Maori call Hawaiiki, one of several places

Maori forts and moa-hunting sites

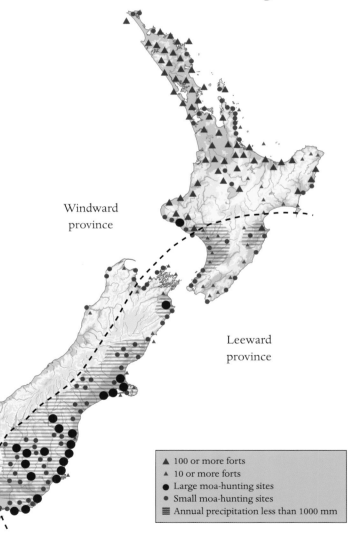

Windward province

Leeward province

- ▲ 100 or more forts
- ▲ 10 or more forts
- ● Large moa-hunting sites
- • Small moa-hunting sites
- ≡ Annual precipitation less than 1000 mm

Archaeologist Atholl Anderson has suggested dividing early New Zealand into a 'windward province' and a 'leeward province'. Pa (forts) predominate on the 'windward province' and moa-hunting sites on the drier 'leeward province'.

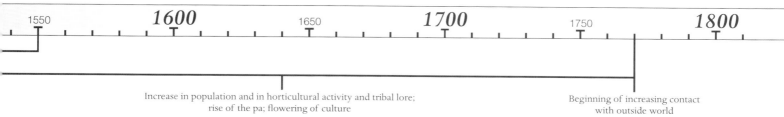

Increase in population and in horticultural activity and tribal lore;
rise of the pa; flowering of culture

Beginning of increasing contact
with outside world

in Eastern Polynesia. From this single tenuous link a landfall following an ocean voyage is confirmed. And sometimes there are matches between what modern science can demonstrate and the persistent accounts from Maori oral traditions that are still shared on marae.

Modern genetics research confirms that a number of canoes arrived in groups, in series over perhaps a century and not necessarily from the same Polynesian islands. Mitochondrial DNA research in 1998 suggests strongly that there were at least 50 women, probably about 70, from a group of between 100 and 200 arrivals. There were not, as ethnologists asserted in the late 19th century, just seven canoes — but there may have been as few as ten.

Their tohunga-navigators are well known in Maori lore. The earliest remembered are those who had located and circumnavigated these islands before the settlers, giving their names to features of the coastline that — while smudged by more recent arrivals' naming — still endure. The journeying of Kupe, for example, has been remembered in Matakitaki-a-Kupe (Kupe's lookout place) alongside Cape Palliser. Similarly, Mana, the island south of Kapiti off the Wellington coast, is more completely known as Te Mana o Kupe ki to Moana Nui a Kiwa, while Matiu, one of Kupe's daughters, gives her name to the larger island in Wellington Harbour.

Long before the establishment of those traditions, the new arrivals energetically shaped up to the task of discovering precisely what these islands contained, not just in the way of food, but also suitable locations for living and materials for tools. For serial voyagers like the Polynesians, this was standard practice, their equivalent of a geological survey. 'Match-fit' and confident from their recent oceanic voyage, within a short time they had mind-mapped every bit of coast and offshore island. They were thorough. Signs of firing in pollen samples from swamps indicate that, within a few years of arrival, they had spread themselves, however thinly, across both main islands on the big estuaries and lagoons, the inviting river mouths that gave easy access to both ocean and hinterland. Here food was most varied and plentiful. And from here the entire coastline of New Zealand was accessible to their waka. Trade flourished quickly, and telltale argillites from Rangitoto (D'Urville Island) and obsidian from Tuhua (Mayor Island) in

the Bay of Plenty were soon scattered widely across New Zealand. The early knives and scrapers, made only in the Murihiku, the south of the South Island, were large 'blades' wrought mainly from Central Otago silcrete. They were probably the preferred tool for butchering moa. Unlike the casual construction of the smaller tools made from obsidian and chert, they were struck with skill from carefully prepared cores by artisans. There is evidence too that greenstone was

Whakapapa Productions Ltd

A typical Maori coastal unfortified village (kainga) reconstructed for *Frontier of Dreams*.

BONES VERSUS SEEDS

Did Maori forebears make it to New Zealand about the time of Jesus Christ? Recent possible evidence of arrivals earlier than those who came here in about 1250–1300 AD has been indicated in rat bones. Polynesians, and before them their Lapita ancestors, have eaten rats for millennia, carrying them out into the Pacific on their voyages. There are many Polynesian stories and whakatauaki (proverbs) tied up with them.[2] Work by Richard Holdaway in the late 1990s tested the bones of kiore (Polynesian rats) by radiocarbon dating. On the strength of this controversial work, he con-cluded that since rats could not have got here unassisted, people must have visited New Zealand about 2000 years ago. But apart from the bones, there was no evidence that they had remained here. Only in the last year or so Janet Wilmshurst, a

Janet Wilmshurst, Landcare Research, Manaaki Whenua

Landcare palaeo-ecologist, has put these theories to the test. Knowing that forest tree seeds are a favourite food of kiore, she core sampled peat soils in both Taranaki and Coromandel. She also excavated some buried seeds. These were radiocarbon dated in order to detect just when rats first appeared in New Zealand. The answer has provided a challenge to the Holdaway camp. The first signs of rats appeared at both sites very close to the now widely accepted — in both Maori tradition and modern research — arrival time of c.1250–1300 AD.[3]

Since Pacific rats (kiore) cannot cross large distances over sea by themselves, they must have accompanied people. Know how long these rats have been here and you have a fair idea of how long people have been here. So far Janet Wilmshurst's testing of seed cases has not found any with evidence of rat teeth marks older than 1250–1300 AD.

Dick Veitch, Department of Conservation, Te Papa Atawhai

located early on, but its exploitation and the challenging trails for humping it out of the steep valleys of Westland would not be developed for some time.

As a people whose culture is steeped in whakapapa (genealogy), Maori traditional accounts of the early movements of waka around the coast hold riches of detail to this day. These waka provided the foundations for what later became tribes. The people descended from the Tainui canoe that set forth from Rangiatea in the Society Islands, for example, still tell how, having reached Whangaparaoa on the east coast, their forebears explored Hauraki, Waitemata, then portaged to Manukau and eventually on to Kawhia Harbour and south to the Mokau, the traditional border between Tainui peoples and Taranaki. The massive anchor stone of the Tainui canoe remains a hallowed tribal taonga at Maniaroa, Mokau.[4]

The very words used by the new arrivals indicate, as people from a warmer, different climate and environment, how they found their new land. For example, huka-rere, the seafarer's word for flying foam, became the word for snow while ua-whata, or stone rain, became the word for hail. Plants sometimes were familiar to them from other islands and, where there were similarities, old names got attached to new plants. The rimu with its drooping leaves, for example, was named for the Polynesian limu, a word for seaweed. The milo, a tree renowned in Polynesia for its good grain, gave its name to the New Zealand miro.[5] The word in the islands for a tiger shark became, in New Zealand water environments, the word for a guardian spirit, a taniwha. The Polynesian word for a mound of earth or tuber

planting, puke, became a hill. The original term moa referred to a chicken, and the Maori word uru retains its essential old meaning as a grove of trees.[6]

The arrival date of 1250–1300 AD, widely accepted by tradition, science and modern history, also coincides with the pollen sampling work by Matt McGlone. This shows that firing of forest on a large scale began very close to this time. The Polynesians who came here were not only highly skilled sailors, they were hunters and gardeners who brought with them their own ideas about how to manage forested landscapes. From early days they burnt areas for cultivation and clearing. They packed into their canoes domesticated animals, the kiore and the native dog (kuri), for new lands. They also carried seeds and tubers. Among these were the gourd plant, yam, taro, kumara, Pacific cabbage tree and the much-travelled Asian mulberry, source of tapa cloth. The kumara tuber, already a token of Polynesian contact with South American people many years before, was to become a distinctive part of cultural life in the upper half of the North Island.

By contrast, at the southern end of the South Island, where cool mean temperatures and shorter summers made cultivations far more difficult, the Polynesians retained their more mobile hunter-gatherer lifestyle, moving between the high country and the sea according to seasonal rhythms and natural food cycles. They, too, fired about half of the forest. Archaeology has revealed how Polynesians lived in those early days, some 700 years ago. There are examples from Aotearoa, as the North Island was known, and Te Wai Pounamu (the South Island) that cast light on intimate details of early settlement.

A LINK TO THE PACIFIC PAST

Archaeological evidence of early Maori ancestors is scarce. This shank of a fishing lure, found at Tairua in the Coromandel, is one of a very few items from New Zealand archaeological sites that were actually brought from Polynesia. It was excavated from an archaeological site in 1964 and is made from the shell of a black-lipped pearl oyster found only in the tropics. Early Polynesians would have brought it with them when they voyaged to New Zealand, and its design could suggest that it came from the Marquesas. The layer in the midden where it was found has been carbon-dated to between 1267 and 1392 AD.

Auckland Museum

The walled gardens that would have been familiar to Palliser Woman, abandoned over 600 years ago, can still be traced through the topsoil on the windy southern Wairarapa coast.

BELOW: An example of the kind of wharepuni the Palliser Woman would have slept in is available to the modern world through the efforts of archaeologists and by Ngati Hinewaka and Te Papa Tongarewa to create Makotukutuku Whare. Although it is a 16th-century house, it remains quite Polynesian and not dissimilar to what she would have known. Her house was simply ornamented, but built in traditional style, rectangular, slightly asymmetrical, with a porch, door and a stone-lined fire, vented through the roof, burning in the centre. There are four upright posts down the middle line to hold the ridgepole. Beneath the largest pole the jawbone of a dog had been placed, probably a ritual involved with the construction of the house. It was probably covered in raupo, bark, moss and reeds. Museum of New Zealand, Te Papa Tongarewa

Palliser Woman and Makotukutuku House

In addition to what Maori tradition tells us, archaeology reveals details of how they lived. Our equivalent of England's Lindow (Peat Bog) Man is the more recently extant Palliser Woman, a skeleton named for the place she came from. She was buried in a shallow shingle grave late in the 14th century near the mouth of the Makotukutuku River, close to her hamlet in eastern Palliser Bay, Wairarapa. From her remains archaeologists can tell that she was 162.6 cm tall, had given birth to between two and four children and suffered from arthritis and severe wear and abscessing of her teeth. The arthritis can be put down to a life of physical hardship, the dental problems to a diet that involved ingestion of excessive amounts of sand — probably from the fern root she chewed on. She was no older than 40 but died from what would have been considered old age in that culture.

Hers was one of several small villages from which the people made seasonal trips to the nearby Aorangi Mountains to catch such birds as parakeets and tui. But most of their food came from the sea. Walled gardens were located on old raised beach ridges and swales nearby where, in prepared soils, kumara and gourds were grown from the 14th to the 16th century. When not gardening, she gathered shoreline seafood — especially paua, topshells, limpets and crayfish.

Some of the fish eaten at the village were caught inshore using circular hooks of bone and shell, but when sea conditions were suitable the men caught fish such as barracouta and kahawai by trolling lures behind canoes. Rats and eels were trapped close to the village and domestic dogs were killed to supplement the meat of sea mammals such as dolphins and seals. During the summer months, food gathering included items for preservation. The long hours of daylight were fully occupied with the splitting of eels and other oily fish for drying, and the weaving of kete for storage.[7]

Even within a few years of arrival the early settlers had adapted to their new environment, discovering ways of applying their imported culture and technologies to the demands of a new and different land. By the late 15th century the people of Palliser Bay, their beaches destabilised by inundation and erosion possibly triggered by tsunami, had moved inland.[8] But all over New Zealand, the Polynesians had either bent to what they could not change in their new home, or they had bent it to their needs. In this process of survival, they moved gradually from being Polynesian to becoming tangata whenua, the people of this land. Maori, a word meaning 'ordinary', was not how these increasingly tribal people would have described themselves.

But the sheer availability of flesh meant that the new settlers still had much to learn about survival. The fur seals were not only common throughout much of the New Zealand coastline,

they weighed up to 200 kg and had a greater percentage of edible meat than the moa. Within 150 years of their arrival the hunters had butchered their way through the seal rookeries of most of the North Island. The sea lions and sea elephants suffered a similar fate. The demise of the moa in most places took little longer. 'Although small groups of moa must have survived in more remote locations, the main populations were extinct by AD 1400,' wrote Worthy and Holdaway.[9]

Using harpoons they also occasionally hunted dolphins and other marine mammals, including smaller whales. Lacking the technology to take larger whales, they were not averse, however, to making use of beached whales. Indeed, one of the earliest stories of Polynesian landfall on these islands is from Tainui and is also told by Te Arawa. It speaks of Tainui coming in to Whangaparaoa and laying claim to a beached whale by way of a long mooring rope. However, Tainui were elaborately tricked by the slightly later arrivals in the Te Arawa canoe, captained by the trickster Tamatekapua. By burning a new rope to age it and passing it beneath the Tainui rope Te Arawa led Tainui into believing that the whale was in fact subject to an earlier claim by those of his canoe. This also meant believing that Te Arawa had beaten Tainui to making first landfall on these islands.[10]

In the South Island, where moa were more widely distributed, probably because the bigger river plains made for the more open, scrubby domains that they preferred, these great birds, like the

Rod Morris, Department of Conservation, Te Papa Atawhai

Tucker time. Despite popular mythology, marine mammals such as this breeding colony of Hooker's sea lions were a more important part of Polynesian/Maori diet than moa. By the time of European arrival, fur seals, sea lions and sea elephants had been wiped out from many places and were still numerous only in the south and on the offshore islands.

Artist's reconstruction of cooking kauru (cabbage tree roots) in umu ti.
B Fankhauser

easily available fur seals and sea lions, immediately became a prime target. Again, archaeology, notably at sites at the mouth of the Shag and Wairau rivers, has uncovered evidence that in places where they were plentiful they were killed and butchered. They were also hunted on navigable river flats, and from the interior the meat was carried out on the Maori mule: the reed raft or mokihi.

At Shag River mouth, North Otago, 6000 moa were killed and dismembered, probably within a relatively short period, in the 14th century by parties of mobile hunters. At Papatowai, on the South Otago coast, some 7000 moa were taken in just 50 years. Only the best cuts were taken. If these were sites of considerable waste, possibly this was at a time when Maori were still labouring under the illusion that food horizons were boundless. Later practices of preserving and storing food had yet to take hold. Wairau Bar, Marlborough, is somewhat different because here, where some 9000 moa were killed, a hunting station became a permanent village — presumably because there were adequate alternative food supplies. Such slaughter was also accompanied by extensive raiding of the huge moa eggs, each one equivalent to 100 hens' eggs — a square meal in oval form by any whanau's standards. This attack on both ends of the moa life cycle doomed them to extinction.[11]

If Shag River is one indication of how the newcomers lived in the South Island, the transient hunting shelter on Lee Island is another, and one of a number of island camps in the southern lakes area that were used for hundreds of years until well into the 19th century. Again archaeology has drawn back a veil from the site and, through painstaking analysis, created something of the now lost world of the more nomadic peoples of the south. This was a place from which systematic, seasonal hunting of fowl in the forest was conducted. Prey included kakapo, which were usually hunted in late summer with the help of torches and dogs. Native pigeons were also taken in large numbers, using traps and spears; kaka were enticed with decoys and snared, and parakeet were taken. Anderson and McGovern-Wilson wrote that it is possible later occupants of the shelter 'were on the routeway from Foveaux Strait to the bowenite sources in Milford Sound and to settlements at Martins Bay and elsewhere on the southern West Coast', as well as to greenstone sources in the Lake Wakatipu watershed.[12]

Yet another feature of life in the south were the umu ti, widely distributed in South Canterbury, Otago and Southland. These were circular pits, often two metres deep, usually with raised rims. In large umu or hangi pits the stems and roots of ti (cabbage trees) were baked, their sugars caramelised. Some pits reach back to the earliest period of settlement and — like many Maori activities — display evidence of the creation of an elaborate, communal process:

Ten to twenty people took one to two days to make one pit, collect and arrange the firewood in layers and collect and pile stones up to the top of the pit. Thousands of kilograms of stone could be used in a single umu. Early in the morning the fire was lit, and as morning drew on the stones became hot. The pits were raked to spread out the stones. At midday earth was raked over the stones, spread over with leaves and the baskets were piled up to the top of the pit. When it was full, the baskets were covered over with mats (tapora) woven from ti leaves trimmed from the stems, and were splashed with water and buried with earth so that no steam could escape.[13]

Motutapu

In the North Island, on Motutapu Island at the Sunde site the remains of a dwelling not only provides evidence of how early Maori lived in the north, but also the most positive proof that they were involved in an event that, in any people's cosmology, was truly astonishing. Although these still active volcanoes have been quiet in the Auckland area for several hundred years, in the 14th century the placid waters of the Waitemata Harbour erupted and were unutterably altered by the sudden birth of a new volcano, Rangitoto. Periodically the new arrival erupted, showering Motutapu in ash. In New Zealand's echo of Pompeii, the evidence is still there that the tangata whenua 'hot-footed it' through the ash:

The occupants of the Sunde site made gardens on the banks of a small stream soon after each ash shower. Subsequent showers preserved the marks of their digging sticks and, even more spectacularly, their footprints . . . the clear tracks were left by gardeners carrying baskets of sand from the edge of the stream for adding to the fertile ash.[14]

A new event such as this taxed the range of gods of the wider Polynesian world. According to some traditions it required the discovery of a new one, Ruaumoko. He was the youngest son of the foundational ancestors, Rangi and Papa, still at the breast of his mother, Papatuanuku, when brother Tane forced his parents from their prolonged clinch, bringing forth Te Ao Marama, the world of light.

Graham Harris, The Open Polytechnic of New Zealand

Although kumara could not be grown in most of the South Island, it was a vital food source to the Polynesian settlers and their Maori descendants elsewhere. Here are three pre-European varieties, (from left) 'Rekamaroa', 'Hutihiti' and 'Taputini', somewhat different to the kumara commonly seen in New Zealand today, which was introduced by Europeans during the 19th century.

THE MYTH OF THE MOA HUNTERS

As late as the 1960s archaeologists fed a popular belief that before the Maori there had been an earlier Polynesian race who spread themselves across New Zealand. It tied in with still persistent Maori beliefs that there had been people living here before they arrived. Moa hunters, stated the 1966 official New Zealand encyclopaedia, settled here between 500 and 1000 AD, possibly earlier than 500 AD. They lived off the abundance of moa in many sites, from Coromandel to Taranaki to Wairau Bar and sites in Otago and Southland. When the moa died off, this apparently peaceful people did too, to be replaced by the Classic Maori.[15] It was nonsense.

Kevin Jones, Department of Conservation, Te Papa Atawhai

BELOW: The so-called moa hunter camps and moa butcheries were seasonal hunting bases. Most were on the coast at the mouths of rivers (the largest, at the Waitaki River mouth, contains the remains of anything from 29,000 to 90,000 moa), but the big birds were hunted inland, too. Chris Gaskin's reconstruction of a hunting camp is at Cairnmuir Mountains behind the Cromwell Gorge on the banks of the Hawks Burn. C Gaskin, Department of Conservation, Te Papa Atawhai

ABOVE: The killing fields. This aerial photograph shows the Wairau Bar, one of New Zealand's most-studied archaeological sites. Although the amount of shells (1600 tonnes) far outweighed the moa bones (25 tonnes), moa have lodged themselves more firmly in the popular imagination. Most such hunting sites were seasonal, and people took fish and marine mammals, as well as other birds in addition to moa.

Further north, at Pouerua, near Kaikohe in the Muriwhenua, evidence of continuous living for perhaps 800 years fits with traditional accounts. The site is the heavily terraced and long-abandoned Nga Puhi pa and gardens in the cone of an old volcano. In a number of ways, particularly the use over time of the site for living and for defence layered over many hundreds of years, it resembles that of Otatara, another great pa site, of Ngati Kahungunu in Hawke's Bay. Even today, in pasture, it is possible to see below the sward at Pouerua the hundreds of stone mounds every few metres where it seems Maori grew bottle and fruit gourds. On one of the many terraces are numerous kainga, as well as a central citadel at its heart. Some house sites have been investigated. One proves to be a long-used place where once a pataka (raised food house) stood. The prehistoric house, built later than the pataka, was larger than those found typically on the heavily human-stippled surface of this cone. Archaeologists have concluded that this was a winter home:

This is indicated by evidence of food storage at locations which were well removed from the kumara gardens which surround the cone . . . It is also probably true that some of Pouerua's prehistoric inhabitants moved seasonally. They are likely to have spent summers fishing on the coast. Some time in autumn was presumably spent eeling on the inland waterways. Gardening would take precedence over other activities in late winter–spring and autumn. Pigeons would be taken when the miro were ready.[16]

Effects of Maori settlement

One of the most profound effects of the Maori upon the New Zealand landscape was deforestation. Upon arrival, about 90 per cent of the main islands were covered in forest. By 1840 about half of the North and South Island had been deforested by fire. Based on his analysis of pollen sampling in peats and bogs, Matt McGlone estimates that much of the clearing took place in the first 300 years

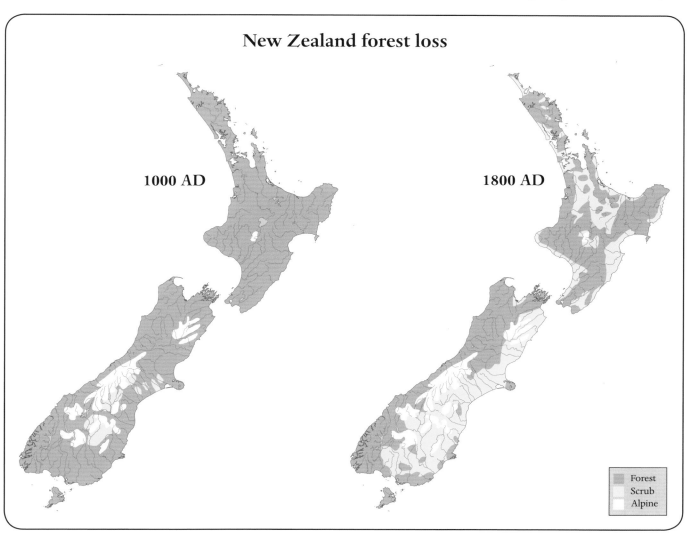

New Zealand forest loss

1000 AD

1800 AD

Forest
Scrub
Alpine

of settlement and 'on a grand scale'. Within 200 years the great lowland podocarp forests of the eastern South Island were gone, destroyed by fire. In the 200 years before 1500 AD the beech forests of the same region went the same way, the deforestation accelerating natural erosion. Much of the west and south of the South Island was spared because of higher rainfall that kept the forest wet. Similarly, in the North Island in the first 200 years of settlement deforestation was rapid, but it was less widespread because the climate was wetter. 'Destruction of forest and aggradation apparently continued until about 400 [years ago].'[17]

Some of the firing was for gardening. Some was simply to clear otherwise almost impenetrable forest where bracken, whose root became an important source of protein for Maori, soon established itself. Since it is evident that Maori also retained some valued trees, especially the tallest in the forest — the kahikatea — for their fleshy stone-fruit which were attractive to humans as well as pigeons, the extensiveness of firing has puzzled some commentators. 'Forest lacked a food resource of the same magnitude and reliability of bracken root,' palaeontologist McGlone explains. 'Many forest vegetable foods are scattered, slowly replaced, or of low nutritive value; birds were easily obtained only at certain seasons and time consuming to hunt, the more vulnerable species having been exterminated, or nearly so, early in prehistory. Lack of food in the forests is indicated by the low numbers of Maoris in heavily forested areas.'[18]

Forty varities of local plants were exploited for their food. Maori needed only follow the birds for much of it — the berries of the miro, hinau and tawa, for example — and the trails of the kiore to the sweet bracts of the kiekie.[19] The karaka's highly

toxic berries, once carefully processed by boiling and decanting, also made a desirable food, hence the presence of such trees at old camp sites. But it was the replacement of forest with scrub, grasses, bracken and swamp that unlocked the productivity of the land for the new arrivals, building a platform for what would later become a more sustainable way of life.

The deliberate firing, hunting and the random predations of rats quickly reduced the populations, if not the entire species, of many animals. It was not just the seals and their kin whose dwindling numbers were pushed to remote corners of the country. Apart from the moa a host of ground birds was extinguished. In the end, of all the large browsing birds only the takahe survived — and then only by the skin of its beak — in remote Fiordland. Apart from the 11 or 12 species of moa, the Maori killed off 20 other species of birds, including the giant Haast's eagle, the native goose, great goshawk, and the adzebill, and pushed a number of others close to extinction, including the native quail. Until it disappeared from view the Haast's eagle was the world's biggest such bird, its raptor beak capable of ripping into the vital organs of a great moa. Maori also drove out the tuatara and some birds from many mainland areas, leaving them to survive almost entirely on offshore islands.[20] Many other birds went the way of the moa during the pre-European era. The smaller flightless birds lost to the kiore's single-handed endeavours included wrens, snipe and the smaller petrels.[21] Though not usually straying far from camp, the kuri added to the destruction. The moa's problem was the same as that of the other birds that were lost: a combination of factors resulting from the new incursions. Effects included loss of habitat,

A ripper of a raptor. Haast's eagle, the largest eagle known to have lived, was top predator until Maori killed off many of its main prey species. Its huge claws killed by crushing and by causing severe bleeding. The eagle could kill a 200-kg moa and would also have posed a serious threat to unwary humans. This computer-generated reconstruction was produced for the *Frontier of Dreams* television series.

MAORI LIFE IN THE 1600s

Kohika, a recently excavated Ngati Awa lake village in the wetlands of the lower Rangitaiki River system, displays many of the characteristics of life in the late 17th century.

Central to village life was its location, not far from the sea but at the junction of the Rangitaiki and Tarawera rivers and also affording access to the interior. From here the inhabitants commanded a diversity of food and other resources of the coastal and inland dunes, swamps, river levees and flood plains. During their occupation they repeatedly burnt off the dense forests, changing the landscape to one of scrub and fernland with forest remnants. This enabled the spread of valued carbohydrate foods, including bracken fern, ti and tutu. They also cultivated these fertile lowland soils. Wetland resources, such as flax, raupo, puha, fish and water birds, and harvesting from the nearby marine environment were also vital to their survival.

Archaeologists have uncovered bird spears, digging and weeding tools, and Mayor Island obsidian used for tools. Evidence of a rich tradition of woodcarving, including that on a paddle and possibly a waka, have been found. One elaborately carved and several lightly carved pole and thatch houses have been identified.

There was, somewhat surprisingly, an almost complete absence of weapons and little evidence of fighting. However, many dogs, a whale, a seal and possibly humans were eaten and their bones were made into tools.

It appears that a major flood eventually drove the Ngati Awa away.[22]

LEFT: A tiki pendant made of human bone which was unearthed at Kohika. Geoffrey Irwin, Department of Anthropology, University of Auckland

BELOW: A recreation of the Kohika village, looking northwards across the lake to the dunes and sea, based on artefacts uncovered during the excavation. The lakeshore vegetation of raupo, flax and cabbage trees with stands of kahikatea and kanuka shown in this sketch is based on the pollen record. Geoffrey Irwin, Department of Anthropology, University of Auckland

MORIORI OF THE CHATHAM ISLANDS

Moriori is the common name given to the people who colonised the Chatham (Rekohu) and Pitt (Rangiauria) Islands around the fourteenth century from the New Zealand mainland. The tiny islands' wet, windswept and often cool conditions were off-set by abundant fish and bird life. Since horticulture here was unthinkable, their food was almost entirely marine-sourced — protein and fat from fish, fur seals and the fatty young of seabirds. Moriori lived sustainably by keeping their birth rate low (they castrated some boys), by regulating sea mammal stocks and by honouring ancestor Nunuku-whenua's ban on warfare and cannibalism. They remained pacificists even after mainland tribes invaded in 1835, devastating Moriori culture, language and popu-lation. Popular myths held that Moriori were inferior, or even extinct, but recently they have revived their identity and culture, culminating in January 2005 with the renewal of the covenant of peace at the new Kopinga marae on the Chatham Islands. Moriori culture is characterised by a dependence on bird and sea life, by dendroglyphs (tree carvings or rakau momori) and by a distinctive dialect.

This is one of the few remaining examples of Moriori carved figures, and is known as 'Hatitimatangi'
Museum of New Zealand, Te Papa Tongarewa

intolerance of predation and inability to cope with the pressure imposed by humans and the company they kept.

At the time of Polynesian arrival, there were 245 species of which 176 were endemic to the archipelago. 'The 32 terrestrial and freshwater species [of birds from 129 taxa] that became extinct in the prehistoric period did so as the result of at least 600 years of adjustment to the presence of Polynesians, kiore . . . and dogs,' wrote Worthy, Holdaway and Tennyson.[24]

The rise of the tribes

The population expanded rapidly on the easy pickings, then had to learn how to cope with leaner fare. With the big game gone, food was harder-won and, overall, diet became more bland — a mixture of fern root, ground birds, shellfish, fish and, when available, kumara. Horticulture grew in importance, changing not just the physical but also the cultural landscape. Since kumara was grown at the outer limits of its climatic tolerance, Maori painstakingly built up specially draining, north-facing soils to improve cultivation. As the need for gardening became more significant, so the need for organisation, initially based on small whanau groups, increased. Over several centuries gardening became more important, and never more so than on the greater Tamaki Isthmus where kumara fields spread over some 2000 ha — a vast horticultural enterprise by anyone's standards.[25] On the warm Waimea Plains in Nelson, carefully imported gravels and sands were used for the same purpose by Ngati Tumatakokiri and are still extensive. When James Cook sailed into Anaura Bay on his first and second voyages his men saw 40–80 ha in cultivation, enclosed by a paling fence of reed stalks, with pre-emptive rat traps set nearby.[26] Once grown, the precious tubers then had to be stored in special pits, dry, rodent-free and well-insulated. Sometimes cave-like structures were made, sealed with a suitable door. Many were like cellars under pitched roofs.

Evolution to this stage of tribalism had two main pressures: an increasing tendency to more localised lifestyles based on a kainga or village and the demands of horticultural rhythms in the working year. This meant a subsequent reduction of the nomadic, hunter-gatherer lifestyle (except south of Banks Peninsula, where the climate was cooler and the population smaller).[27] The considerable planning and industry involved in horticulture demanded greater tribal loyalty and tribal hierarchies. To secure the authority of this emerging tribal identity, people looked to their canoe origins, to their chiefly lines and their mythology. The very word for tribe, 'iwi', means the bones of the ancestors.

Accompanying this was the development of a change in consciousness, based on a greater emphasis on lore rooted in the tribe. Over hundreds of years of storytelling beneath the stars and of oratory on the paepae (where elders spoke), the explanations of where people came from, the human and superhuman ancestors, were woven together in rich tribal traditions of narrative, song and art. At base was whakapapa, ancestral lineage, the alpha and omega of Maori being. 'Deification of ancestors' was the beginning of Polynesian religion. Inevitably, belonging to a tribal or sub-tribal group and to the land would also involve defending the values embodied in these groups — and what they came to regard as their property, their gardens. In these ways began the rise of the pa.

Pa were not unknown in some of the ancestral Polynesian homelands. But nowhere else in Polynesia has a readiness for war been so widespread. They did not become a feature of the landscape for about 250 years — only appearing once a more settled way of life was established. And they were essentially (98 per cent) in the North Island only and always 'in horticultural zones or areas where large-scale fern root gathering was possible', as Hirini Mead puts it. 'The extent to which northern communities in regions suitable for kumara growing depended on garden crops was probably primarily determined by the state of political relationships, with gardening predominating in times of peace.'[28]

Disputes within hapu would have been common in competitive Maori society. The ability to defend oneself against near relatives would at times have been important. Sometimes these differences spilled into larger, tribal-based conflicts. But as rules became more important, so too came the need to settle disputes. The whakatauaki (proverb), 'He kai koura nui te rere' — 'war is a devouring flame kindled by a spark' — is based on a recognition of how easily a slight could turn into conflict. Although tribal lore is replete with accounts of war and of killing and cannibalism, archaeological findings have not been able to verify such stories on the same scale. Cannibalism was practised,

there is no question, and within the period of early European contact some particularly gruesome eyewitness accounts have been recorded. But archaeological work thus far suggests that tribal renditions have often been exaggerated for rhetorical effect. However, more than 7000 sites of former pa are known to exist.

Pa were not normally places of habitation, but of refuge. Characteristically they were defensive in character, built wherever possible on the most unassailable headlands of shore, river and ravine that the locale allowed, but close to the kainga and to habitations. In some places, such as at the Muaupoko defences at Papaitonga, they were erected on artificial islands in lakes. Often they were surrounded by wooden palisades, but they were usually made more impregnable by a series of scarps, ditches, embankments and palisades, each of which had to be breached by an enemy before the population and its food stores could be reached. An adequate water supply was an obvious advantage. Over several centuries before European contact the pa became the centrepiece of mana Maori, not simply a practical device, but also an expression of the power of the tribe and its chief.

With the development of tribes and agriculture came other, more intensive communal food gathering, from the sea and to a lesser extent rivers and lakes. In broad terms, barracouta was the preferred species in the south, taken with rods from canoes at the rate of four a minute; snapper was the choice of the north. Seabirds overflew and sometimes landed on many craggy parts of the archipelago, but it was in the islands of Foveaux Strait where the practice of mutton-birding has remained a distinctive activity among some of the hapu of Ngai Tahu. Cooked in their fat and then sealed in the hollow bowls of sea kelp, mutton birds or titi were (and remain) a tribal delicacy. Early in the European contact period, shark-hunting was undertaken and there were still massive efforts to fish with large nets off the Muriwhenua coast. Descriptions of these activities

The patu was a highly effective weapon at close quarters and those owned by distinguished warriors were well known. 'Te Whiu', an argillite patu, was once owned by Tuhoe chief Maru-Wahia. Alexander Turnbull Library, Curios-019-018

MAUNGAKIEKIE (ONE TREE HILL)

Perhaps there is nothing new in Auckland's congestion and sprawl. Studies have shown that the iconic extinct volcano Maungakiekie, or One Tree Hill, was first occupied at least 500 years ago. It had location, location, location. From its peak people could watch out over the adjacent rich horticultural lands — the huge undulating volcanic stone fields and small clumps of houses, now buried beneath the streets and buildings of the modern city. It was also close to the fisheries of the Waitemata and the Manukau.

The soft scoria made it easier to construct the defensive works that are so visible from the air. Almost unimaginable amounts of earth were moved on Maungakiekie and the nearby cones, all by hand tools, a massive undertaking by Pacific standards. Maungakiekie's earthworks are the mightiest of the lot, a major system of linear defences across the southern approach and six strongpoints. The cone was extensively terraced (to provide living areas and food storage pits) and scarped (to provide artificially steep banks that would slow down or exhaust attackers). Ditches, wooden palisades and fighting platforms would have completed the defences. In times of war as many as 1000 people may have gathered here, though there would have been long periods of peace and we should not over-emphasise the fighting. Maungakiekie was no longer occupied by the 18th century. Whakapapa Productions Ltd

indicated a number of aspects that, together, again amount to considerable tribal organisation: careful preparation, including the making of nets and the readying of canoes and manpower and their deployment; knowledge of the availability of the fish at certain times; and a take that, while substantial, appears to have been sustainable.[29]

From the estuaries, wetlands, streams, rivers and lakes beside which they usually lived or camped, Maori harvested cress, gathered freshwater mussels and caught crayfish, patiki (flounder) and juvenile fish, not least of which was the fry of the native *galaxiids* that in late winter and early spring swarmed in their tidal tonnes heading upriver. There were also ducks to lure and eels to trap. It was a life based on close observation of nature, with the year cast into four great agricultural seasons: of preparation, planting, cessation and harvest. As the botanising early missionary William Colenso noted: 'Their year commenced with spring; to which, and to the proper planting season, they were guided by the rising of certain constellations, particularly of Pleiades and of Orion; by the flowering of certain trees . . . by the mating, moulting and change of note of bird.'[30]

Once the catches had been made, ahead still lay the even more daunting task of preparation, preservation and storage of the food. The one exception to this may have been the eel, which could be taken in, say, early autumn and held live and writhing in big baskets suspended in water for eating during the leaner months of winter. Eels were also dried. If there was a price for coming to this land, it was undoubtedly hard work. Food varieties may have been limited, but Maori generally did not want for sustenance. But it took work, much of it by women, to turn it into food. While Maori women had been paddlers of canoes in the early days, that practice did not continue. Instead, in tribes that were for the most part seeded by horticulture and blooded by militarism, men dominated, and women took up much of the slack on the domestic front.[31] Maori survival and comfort was founded on a seasonal round of gathering and planting, harvesting and trap-laying, hunting and preserving, fishing and drying. In addition, there was also the usual round of cooking, mending, minding children and — in keeping up with tribal life, hapu gossip — running the tribe. Colenso got the measure of this in an article published in 1880:

The ancient New Zealander had great plenty of good and wholesome food, both animal and vegetable, but all such with them was only to be obtained by labour, in one shape or the other, almost unremitting. To them, Nature has not been over-indulgent as she has been to their relatives in the more Eastern and tropical Isles of the South Pacific . . . But all such constant labour and industry was doubtless in their favour, helping to 'the survival of the fittest' and causing the development of a finer race, both physically and intellectually.[32]

F Wright, Auckland Art Gallery, Toi o Tamaki

Capable of carrying a hundred or more paddlers, waka taua were built of kauri or totara and represented a huge investment of time and tribal resources. Guided by tohunga tarai waka (canoe-making experts), experienced carvers worked under strict conditions. Tane Mahuta, the forest god, was propitiated before a tree was felled. Women and children were kept clear of the work site, as was food, and the men wore special garments — or sometimes nothing — while working on the hull. The entire process, from selecting the tree to completing the canoe, could take up to two years.

As a race the Maori thrived, their numbers growing from a few canoes to what may have been around 100,000 people within 500 years — about the time James Cook arrived.[33] But their lifespans, generally, were not enhanced. It may be because few Maori made old bones that practices emerged such as whangai — adopting out children to other relatives.

Flowering of culture and trade

Although Maori society was based on hard work, it was also organised in such a way that a tribe could produce specialists, supported by other workers. So from about 250 years after arrival until the first 50 years of European contact, Maori — for that is what these people had now become — produced extraordinary artisans in considerable numbers. In a society in which whakapapa was pre-eminent, foremost were the carvers — the keepers of tribal knowledge, who depicted it in whakairo (carving). In one East Coast tradition, carving was an art discovered by Ruatepupuke, in a visit to the underworld beneath the ocean, the realm of Tangaroa, to find his son. The carved house was the focal point for the tribe and its gatherings. At the heart of this was the pou manawa or central carved ancestral figure holding up the meeting house, often supported by other notable ancestors. Carving was also a commanding feature in other decoration of the house, including the tekoteko figure on

Gavin McLean

Gavin McLean

In the limestone country of North Otago and South Canterbury (above), caves hold the fading traces of rock art (top right), ranging from ancient times to the European era.

the outside apex of the front of the house and the amo (barge boards). In some tribes pataka (food storehouses) were decorated too with carving, as were wahora (gateways) and commemorative prows, the latter raised to a vertical position. The tokotoko stick, an aid for an orator speaking on whakapapa matters, would also be an object of knowledge rendered by carvers with great care. High carving was also worked on wakahuia, or treasure boxes, and sometimes on funeral caskets of chiefs.[34]

If these expressions of tribal history and mana were for peaceful purposes, not surprisingly, carving was also often extraordinary in the way it was put to use for war. Decorative talismans and assertions of mana on war canoe prows and raised sternposts and gunwales, and even hoe or paddle handles, could be elaborate and imposing. So too were the taiaha, or fighting sticks, deftly wielded by the samurai of Maoridom in close fighting. Sometimes boundary posts and even bird perches were carved. All these were rendered in wood, but Maori also worked in bone and in stone, their greatest treasures conferred upon the chiefly ranks being in greenstone, as objects such as hei tiki, and as the ceremonial short fighting club or patu, and adzes.

The craft and art of the women was in fabric, enormous effort being made in the dressing of flax and the woven panels of the meeting house, the tukutuku panels, their rectilinear designs in contrast to the curvilinear carvings. But intricate dog hair and kiwi feather cloaks also became an emblem of Maori high culture. In the colder climate the tropical standby of aute (mulberry) for tapa cloth failed to produce sufficient material for their clothing needs. So the abundant harakeke (New Zealand flax) became the thread for weaving that, with great skill, formed the basis of nearly all clothing. This was not without considerable experimentation and the development of a new weaving technique (aho rua) to

Much skill went into carving taurapa (canoe sternposts) such as this one. It is clearly very old but little is known about it. It has been attributed to Nga Puhi.
Museum of New Zealand, Te Papa Tongarewa

make the kind of clothing — aprons, kilts, capes and cloaks — that modesty required and climatic conditions demanded.[35] Harakeke also provided the cord for rope and the twine for binding. The skills of weaving were applied to other objects of great beauty and utility, such as the kete or kit bag, the hingaki nets that caught the eels and the corfs in which they were stored live over winter months.

Another legacy of Maori culture is the rock art of the limestone country, 95 per cent of it in South Island caves and shelters, mostly in North Otago and South Canterbury. Almost all South Island rock art describes birds, fish, dogs and humans. At Craigmore, South Canterbury, what seems to be a depiction of the now extinct eagle is outlined on the roof of a shelter.

It was not simply a north–south divide that determined how Maori lived. New Zealand's variable, distinctive regions, with their differing climates and resources, set up the patterns that would eventually characterise the people who lived there and what it was they had to trade. If fishing and particular fish were a speciality of certain coastal tribes, equally the piharau (lamprey) was the prize of certain villages among the eel-harvesting culture that was essential to life on the Whanganui River.[36]

Birds and birding were what differentiated the prowess of the people who hunted the rich forests north of Taupo from, say, the Kahungunu people who lived beside the Ruamahanga River in the Waka a paua area of Kahutara. Apart from its abundant eels, a speciality of the Wairarapa river plains was its totara. This had the double advantage of being highly suitable for dugouts and of standing close to a river down which these dugouts could be taken in batches to the sea, for trade across Cook Strait in Nelson argillites, if not Nelson greenstone.

As the culture consolidated and as pounamu became to Maori what diamonds are to modern society, the trade in greenstone, which had different names for its different colorations, became an essential part of tribal life. To meet this demand a network of trails was established into and out of the remote and inaccessible country in which it is located. The best known of these trails today followed the valleys and passes, such as the Greenstone and Browning, that penetrate the Southern Alps. But all of the major river systems of the South Island, from the Kawatiri (Buller) to the Haast Pass and even the very rugged country of Fiordland, are known routes for the conveyance of pounamu.

One of those publicised by early European travellers is along the often wild, unnavigable Poutini (West) Coast. A daunting feature is its bluffs, framing the bays and river mouths from the mouth of the Grey River northward. Some of these could be traversed only by way of Maori rope ladders; some, like an infamous specimen at Te Miko (Perpendicular Point), near Punakaiki, dangerously frayed in 1846 when Charles Heaphy hauled his dog up it like a sack of potatoes. Terrifying vertigo was reported on the same ladder in a member of a party led by Julius von Haast.

In 1983 the 400-year-old remains of one 'sherpa's' endeavours on another of these challenging trails was found in a Southland rock shelter. This was a nifty backpack made from plaited flax strips — the only known one of its kind left to us. A fitting accompaniment were the sandals, paraerae, made from either flax or the leaves of the ti (cabbage) tree; the latter material, preferred for its toughness, was used for paraerae worn in the snows and rough terrain of the mountain passes. Thomas Brunner wrote that a pair of these sandals, which took a couple of hours to make, would last several days in these tough conditions.[37]

Belief and culture

The idea of the indivisibility of all things is central to Maori culture. It is there from the outset on any marae visit, in a mihi (greeting) that will usually contain explicit linkages between the chief, as an embodiment of the tribe, the mountain and the river. Tuhoe/Tuwharetoa writer Chris Winitana sums it up:

> Because our life is holistic in nature, we see ourselves in our mountains, our rivers and lakes, and even in the trees and birds. They are all inextricably part of our own physical lineage . . . One part of me comes from the Tuhoe tribe of the Urewera bush. In our traditions, Hine-pukohurangi, the mist, married Te Maunga, the mountain, and had Potiki, the ancestor from whom our tribe descends . . . In the story relating to the voyage of Te Arawa canoe at the time of the migration from Hawaiiki, mention is made of Ngatoroirangi, the high priest. He is my blood ancestor, 25 generations removed. We still chant and intone the prayers he offered to the gods almost a thousand years ago.
>
> In my mother's tribal lands of Tuwharetoa from the Lake Taupo district, there is a saying which runs, Tongariro is the mountain, Taupo is the sea, Tuwharetoa is the tribe, Te Heuheu is the chief.[38]

POUNAMU: TAONGA WITH MANY FACES

E rere taku wairua, ki te wai pounamu
Mau, ka huraina te ara pounamu
I sleep and my spirit journeys to the waters of greenstone
My dreams reveal their resting place

Pounamu, or greenstone, takes several forms, each of which has an explanation in Maori stories.

Inanga (whitebait) is pearly-whitish and grey-green. It may be transparent and finely textured.

Kawakawa, so named because it resembles the leaf of the kawakawa tree, has strong dark greens and lighter shades.

Kahurangi is translucent, lightish green with darker streaks and, being flawless, is quite rare.

Kakotea is streaky dark and spotted black.

Tangiwai, highly translucent and olive to blue-green in colour, is found near the entrance to Milford Sound and is from bowenite stone, whereas the others are nephrite.

New Zealand nephrite jade, greenstone, pounamu, call it what you like, has been prized for centuries. It was valued for its beauty and for its quality of keeping sharp edges, and Maori fashioned it into personal ornaments such as hei tiki (neck pendants), kuru and kapeu (ear pendants), mere pounamu (greenstone weapons), and toki (adzes). This adze blade, found at the remote Wairaurahiri River mouth, is thought to be 500 years old, explaining its similarity to adzes found elsewhere in the Pacific. Museum of New Zealand, Te Papa Tongarewa

A complex set of rituals governed the gathering, preparation and consumption of food. Some chiefs and tohunga were so sacred that they could not profane their hands with food and had to be fed by others.

For Maori, there is no separation between the past and the present — the past is all and it informs all action, even all art. Key words to this understanding are mua, meaning 'front', but which also means 'before' and 'first', and muri, meaning, 'behind', 'the rear, the sequel', 'the time to come' and also 'the future'. As Hirini Mead explains:

> Thus the past is constantly in view of ego and the present is changing into the past, as each event occurs. Logically, the known world is the past, out of which Maori art emerged. The unknown is the future, which cannot be seen. What has happened to us is history and it is this that defines our present position.[39]

This is a view of the world that is entirely consistent with one in which ancestors are the source of all being and whose presence in spiritual form continues to guide and inform the living, the tangata whenua or people of the land.

'The tangata whenua idea is about human potential and is predicated on mana, tapu and mauri,' says Raukawa scholar and teacher Charles Royal.[40] Mana of chieftainship is explained by Te Rangi Hiroa: 'The mana of chief carries the meaning of power and prestige,' a quality inherited on his death by his son. 'The greater the prestige acquired by the family and the tribe, the greater the mana that was inherited.' A wise and just chief at home or a successful leader on the battlefield added to his mana. Credit for tribal success, no matter who did it, was focused on

the chief: 'the mana of a chief was integrated with the strength of the tribe.'

The power of a chief is sharply demonstrated in the control he exercised in the midst of battle, as exemplified by North Taranaki Ngati Tama chief, Uereta, who successfully led his taua (war party) through a succession of tiered defences to the heart of the enemy:

> The chief of the defenders knew that one of his ancestors had come from a leading family of the Ngati Tama, and in this knowledge there was an inkling of hope that he and his surviving tribesmen might be saved from annihilation. He stood on the topmost parapet and called down for the leader of the war-party. Uerata rose with spear in hand and gazed upwards. The desperate chief voiced his petition, 'O Uerata, what token from the past do you have for me?' Uerata recognised the claim, raised his spear horizontally above his head with both hands, and then deliberately broke it across his knee. Without a word, he turned his back and walked down the slope on his homeward way with his warriors following quietly behind him. It was a grandstand play, but only a chief of great mana could have accomplished it.[41]

In such ways, the mana of a chief is only heightened — more so than had he simply advanced to finish off his enemies.

The terms mana and tapu, with noa (the reciprocal of tapu) are concepts that journeyed out of Polynesia with the waka that came to New Zealand. Widely and consistently used in Polynesia for 2500 years, they went hand in hand with each other and were inseparable. Mana means 'power, supernatural force'; tapu 'prohibited, sacred or under ritual restriction', explain Patrick Kirch and Roger Green.[42] Their power is well illustrated through ariki or chiefly authority, inherited from a chiefly line, but added to or diminished by an individual's actions. The respect and awe with which a chief is sometimes greeted is stated in the greeting to an ariki: 'Haere mai te mana, mai te tapu, haere mai te wehi' — welcome to power, welcome to sanctity, welcome to dread.

Such was the power of tapu concentrated in a head, a chief's hair cuttings had to be disposed of so that no harm would befall anyone who might come in contact with them. Similarly, no one else could drink from the container used by him. But its application was far wider. Tapu was the means by which laws could be upheld without a police force — especially when it came to protecting property and food sources in the sea, on the shore, in forests and in horticulture. The sanction meant that there would be unpleasant results for those who refused to acknowledge a tapu and breached its power. Tapu was also applied to certain work, such as house and waka building, to ensure that diligence and focus were applied to it until its completion.[43]

The power of tapu is dramatically demonstrated in the case of Ngatokorua, who was in a party that, having been defeated, knew that he would not only die, but that he would be eaten. Worse than both of these outcomes was the Maori belief that being reduced to the status of common food was a stigma to be endured by succeeding generations; it was the most vicious assault on a family's mana and enemies would have no hesitation in reminding victims' families of it. So, as Te Rangi Hiroa explains, Ngatokorua broke off the head of his spear, hiding it in his hand when his arms were bound behind him. Then freeing himself with this 'knife' he made out that he was still bound until, as a final request, he was to hongi the conquering chief as a last gesture. Pulling the chief down towards him, he repeatedly stabbed him. 'The blood gushed down and Ngatokorua daubed it over his face and body before the startled warriors could shower blows upon him. Ngatokorua died happy. His body had been rendered tapu to the war party by the blood of their chief and they could not eat him.'[44]

The other framework within which all of Maori society went about its business was that of utu, a law of reciprocity that ensured that hospitality and gifting and other such gestures of kindness were never forgotten and always amply repaid. Just as the sacred, tapu, had its opposite, expressed in the idea of noa, or the profane, so too under the law of utu negative, unfriendly, hostile acts were to be acknowledged and paid back with interest. Not to do so was to experience a loss of mana. Cook may have ensured such a loss in the eyes of both Maori and crew on his second voyage to New Zealand when he decided against punitive action after some of his crew were killed and eaten in the Marlborough Sounds.

Yet there were exceptions to the law of utu. A notable case concerns the avenging Nga Puhi warrior of the Musket Wars, Hongi Hika. His life had been spared in a close encounter along a western beach in the Far North with neighbouring Ngati Whatua from Kaipara. The Ngati Whatua chief decided to invoke protection ritually by drawing a line in the sand at the very back of the flying heels of Hongi, who was retreating as fast as he was able from a lost battle. How the Ngati Whatua must have regretted that edict. Notoriously, when Hongi became armed with muskets, it was Ngati Whatua who felt his

wrath as much as anyone. In this case, the usual healing binds of intertribal marriage had not been entered into afterwards, thus failing to secure this gesture in lasting peace.

Underlying all forms, all life, is the life force itself, mauri — 'a spiritual essence, a non-material core, a life principle' without which there is nothing. 'The fruiting of the trees, the abundance of birds and rats, the vigorous growth of the forest as a whole, all hinged upon the preservation of the mauri intact and unharmed. Fisheries, too, had their mauri representing their productivity, as had all other types of natural resources, and man himself.' Mauri was an intangible, but essential, unseen force, as electrical power is today; but everything in nature 'had its physical basis and its psychic counterpart; material form, and vital essence,' writes Raymond Firth. Thus mauri, he says, was capable of being affected by humans — of being contaminated or of being destroyed by human beings. For this reason there were powerful prohibitions against carrying cooked food through a forest, for instance.[45] It was the role of the tohunga to mediate and, through his powers, restore a mauri of his people's resources, or perhaps destroy that of an enemy's.

But soon mauri, together with all other Maori beliefs and even the very gods of this world, would find themselves in contest with another. The new people who breached the 500 years of isolation and experience that had created the Maori world would not destroy these beliefs. But they brought with them new technology, new animals and plants and, more challenging than all of these, new ideas that would shake Maori being to its foundations.

Warriors brandish a mixture of Western weapons such as muskets and axes along with more traditional items, but HG Robley's 1864 painting of a Maketu taua captures the vigour and ferocity of a war party under the disciplined leadership of a great chief. HG Robley, Alexander Turnbull Library, A-080-051

Chapter 3

In the first two centuries of contact, Europe knew New Zealand's coasts better than its hills and valleys as waves of entrepreneurs, explorers and desperadoes worked their way through its natural resources. This painting shows whalers preparing to process their catch at a shore whaling station, probably Te Awaiti.

When Worlds Collide
1642–1839

In 1642 Europe and te ao Maori discovered each other. It was a fleeting, stinging encounter, leaving four Dutchmen dead and an enigmatic squiggle on Europe's charts to show for it.

From the late 18th century, however, Europe's reach lengthened and it mapped New Zealand's shores, if not the minds of its inhabitants. Although other nations participated, Britain predominated, neatly positioned from 1788 in New South Wales, its open-air prison-cum-trading post. From the 1790s on, a polyglot mixture of sealers, whalers, woodcutters and flax merchants mined the New Zealand quarry, often abetted by Maori, who traded these raw materials, along with labour and sex, for the products of the West. Some venturesome Maori in turn travelled overseas to learn what they could of the wider world. There were many misunderstandings, and firearms intensified intertribal warfare; but the races co-operated surprisingly well and some Europeans even settled here as 'Pakeha Maori'.

This was not yet colonisation, and for a while the Colonial Office shared the Protestant missionaries' hopes that the islands might evolve into an independent, God-fearing country. Western notions of nation were alien to Maori though, and plans by powerful joint stock companies to create neo-Europes, modern capitalist colonies, finally forced Britain's hand. As 1839 drew to a close a Royal Navy officer was preparing to cross the Tasman to plant the flag.

Europe discovers New Zealand: 1642 and all that

Commander Abel Janszoon Tasman is off most New Zealanders' radar, even though his name graces a sea, mountain, glacier, national park, local authority, barcode reader and scores of other enterprises. We prefer to remember James Cook rather than the Dutch, French, Russian, American, Austrian and other European or neo-European explorers who poked their prows into our waters between the mid 17th and the mid 19th centuries.

That era, 'The Age of Discovery' of the old textbooks, saw Europe lay the foundations of a new global civilisation based on maritime commerce and naval supremacy. Until then Europeans had been mainly coastal voyagers who seldom strayed far from the sight of shore. But they had been honing their shipbuilding and navigational skills progressively over the centuries and several advances came together fortuitously in the Middle Ages. One, the Mediterranean carvel system (plank on frame), used less wood than the northern clinker system (overlapping planking), making ships lighter, larger, faster and cheaper. Then, by combining square rig and fore-and-aft sails in one ship, shipwrights enabled it to sail better under more wind directions. Soon Portuguese caravels and Spanish galleons were crossing vast distances.

In the late 16th century the Dutch developed the *fluyt*. Cheap and simple to operate and able to stow plenty of cargo for its size, the *fluyt* and its foreign imitators could stay at sea for months or years.[1] Ships like this made the Dutch Republic a major maritime power by the 17th century, spearheaded by the gargantuan Dutch East India Company, which operated trading 'factories' throughout South-East Asia. In 1642 Anthony van Diemen, Governor-General of the Dutch East Indies, sent Tasman off in the *Heemskerck* and *Zeehaen* to hunt *Terra Australis Incognita*, the fabled 'Great South Land' that geographers thought counterbalanced Northern Hemisphere landmasses. After skirting 'New Holland' (Australia), the Dutch sighted a 'land, uplifted high', just off Punakaiki, on 13 December 1642. Assuming we ignore the believers in pre-European 'discoverers' — with their claims of lost Chinese cities, Tamil bells, Spanish helmets or space gods — this sighting made Tasman and his crew the first non-Polynesians to see the place.[2] Five days later they anchored in Golden Bay.

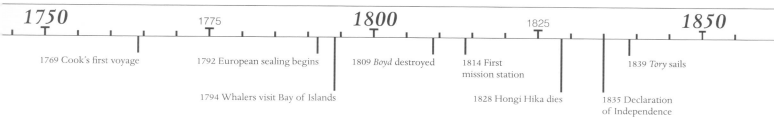

1750   1775   *1800*   1825   *1850*

1769 Cook's first voyage   1792 European sealing begins   1809 *Boyd* destroyed   1814 First mission station   1839 *Tory* sails

1794 Whalers visit Bay of Islands   1828 Hongi Hika dies   1835 Declaration of Independence

Their timing was bad. Local politics were tense and pickings were poor. Two canoes of suspicious Ngati Tumatakokiri paddled out to inspect the newcomers and issued a ritual challenge with incantations and shell trumpets. 'It is possible they had decided these were spirits of some sort,' Anne Salmond speculates, 'since in early times when people were afraid of ghosts at night, they commonly blew trumpets and shouted to frighten them away.'[3] The Dutch, unaware that 'the Maori convention was to take the offensive in an uncertain situation', ordered their trumpeters to respond and unwittingly accepted the invitation to fight.[4] Next morning, to their shock and dismay, a waka rammed a cockboat crossing between the *Heemskerck* and the *Zeehaen*, killing four Dutchmen.[5] After fending off a larger attack with gunfire, Tasman's ships fled what Tasman called Murderers' Bay. For just over a fortnight the ships worked their way up the west coast of the North Island and then swung off into the Pacific. No one had set foot ashore and their draughtsmen would leave the sketchy outline of parts of this unfriendly land hanging off the map like a big question mark. Even the name they gave it, Staten Landt, left no imprint. In Europe an unknown cartographer rechristened it Nieuw Zeeland, 'New Land From the Sea', geologically sounder than the later, equally European application of Aotearoa, 'Land of the Long White Cloud' to islands that then had no single name.[6]

Tasman's enigmatic squiggle kept hopes of a southern continent alive for another hundred years or more, by which time Britain had overhauled the Dutch as a sea power. So it fell to the Royal Navy to fit out a ship for a voyage that redrew the map of the world and established James Cook as the greatest navigator in history.

Cook was born in 1728 at Marton-in-Cleveland, in Yorkshire, the second son of a Scottish day labourer. After learning the ropes in merchantmen, Cook dropped rank to join the navy, where he rose through sheer professionalism in a service notoriously slow to reward merit. Cook made a name for himself in North American waters for his draughting ability and his cool-headedness and was a natural choice for a voyage of exploration. The navy got it right. To quote the *Dictionary of New Zealand Biography*, he was 'a genius of the matter of fact: a systematic, professional and thorough explorer, who knew just how far to take his ships and his men ... In his relations with indigenous, peoples he was essentially a creature of his time, carrying to the Pacific a compassionate version of British concepts of justice, which he endeavoured to adapt to new circumstances.'[7] His official instructions were to observe the Transit of Venus from Tahiti, but the hidden agenda of the Lords of the Admiralty was to find and claim the great southern continent.

LEFT: After fleeing Murderers' Bay, Tasman sailed north up the western coast of the North Island. This drawing by Isaac Gilsemans shows the *Zeehaen* and the *Heemskerck* close to Three Kings Islands. The two Maori men outlined against the skyline appear as giants, possibly the result of the distorting effect of imperfect telescopes. I Gilsemans, Alexander Turnbull Library, PUBL-0105-004

ABOVE: Haunted? Driven? James Cook famously wrote that his ambition led him 'not only farther than any other man has been before me, but as far as I think it possible for a man to go'. William Hodges's dark portrait of him in captain's undress uniform comes closest to capturing the complexity of the man. W Hodges, National Maritime Museum, Greenwich

Joseph Banks collected most of the adulation back in London. Benjamin West's portrait depicts him as the trophy-laden conquering hero of science, wearing a Maori flax cloak with a fine taniko border. A taiaha, a canoe paddle and an adze are on his right and at his feet is a book containing plant specimens, and other Pacific artefacts.

Typically, Cook chose not a dashing frigate, but a humble coastal collier, the Whitby 'cat' *Endeavour*. HM bark *Endeavour* was 33.2 m long and just 8.8 m across — smaller than the ferries that today run between Auckland and Devonport.[8] Into this small wooden world that normally accommodated 20 crew, Cook crammed a bewildering quantity of spares, weapons, scientific materials, 'trifles' for natives and supplies for 18 months at sea. Those supplies included bread in bags and butts, flour, beef and pork in casks, 5500 litres of beer and some of Cook's pet cures for scurvy. Last but not least were 85 sailors, marines and scientists, a cast of characters whose names now litter the hills, capes and seas of the globe. Two stand out. During the voyage the wealthy young naturalist Joseph Banks eased Cook

out of his rightful place in the Great Cabin and on his return would take centre stage, overshadowing the great navigator himself. With his servants, dogs and 'coat with silver frogs', the dandyish Banks was the English Enlightenment personified, rational when not being foolish, curious about everything, fond of wine, women and song, and not averse to slumming it when occasion demanded. The second tall poppy has had a leg-up from anthropologists. Tupaia was a Tahitian chief/priest who befriended the British and asked to accompany the ship. Banks welcomed Tupaia, believing he might 'keep him as a curiosity, as well as some of my neighbours do lions and tygers'.[9] Tupaia would not live long enough to play pet for Banks in London, but he impressed Britons and Maori alike. Cook admired Tupaia's knowledge of Polynesia, his navigational skills and his ability to converse with Maori. If, as Salmond suggests, Tupaia made a more lasting impression on Maori than Cook, that would be ironic. Tupaia, as aristocratic and egotistical as Banks, looked down on Maori as country cousins, cannibals who did not even keep pigs, the Polynesian staple.

Two worlds touched briefly again in 1769 when surgeon boy Nicholas Young ('a son of a Bitch', one shipmate thought) sighted some peaks through the haze inland of Turanganui, modern Poverty Bay, so named by Cook because it afforded him little but grief.[10] Cook playfully reversed the order of his names and renamed a Tai Tokerau headland Young Nicks Head. Next day the *Endeavour* anchored about a mile offshore. The curious Britons could see fortifications, canoes on the water and smoke rising from the beach. For Maori the encounter must have been even more electrifying. Was the *Endeavour*, with her tall masts and billowing sails, a floating island? Or a great bird? Were her crew, who did that very un-Maori thing, row facing backwards (Maori paddled facing forward), goblins from the sea?

Once again a misinterpretation of a Maori challenge led to bloodshed, Maori blood this time, when three young *Endeavour* crewmen, frightened by a warrior party's challenge, fired warning shots and later real shots when a chief raised his lance and appeared about to throw. Next day Tupaia and Cook made

some progress, Tupaia communicating easily with the twitchy locals, and Cook pressed noses with one man, but shooting broke out again after another man stole a sword. Then Cook made things worse by kidnapping some fishermen from their canoe. 'The local people must have been profoundly relieved when on the morning of 11 October the *Endeavour* raised its anchor and sailed south out of the bay.'[11]

But not out of New Zealand or out of history. Cook proved that New Zealand was a set of islands, but there remained a hope that the southern continent lurked hereabouts. Cook made two more voyages, basing himself at Dusky Sound and Queen Charlotte Sound. The second voyage (1772–75) in HMS *Resolution* and HMS *Adventure* was the greatest voyage in history. During his four years away from home he crossed the Antarctic Circle, extinguished any faint hopes of a southern continent and successfully tested a copy of H-4, Harrison's chronometer, the mechanical clock that enabled mariners to estimate longitude accurately for the first time. Cook's charts threw new light on the Pacific and on New Zealand in particular. The last one was not replaced by the Royal New Zealand Navy until late last century. Cook's third and last voyage (1776–80) with HMS *Resolution* and HMS *Discovery* took him in search of the north-west passage. By now he was tired and his patience was fraying. He paid the price at Kealakekua Bay in February 1779 when Hawai'ians attacked and killed him.

Cook still overshadows the other European explorers. The French, Britain's great continental rivals, were also pushing the geographical boundaries of the Enlightenment and in December 1769 Jean-François de Surville and Cook actually passed within 48 km of each other as they each rounded Northland. De Surville knew New Zealand's bad reputation but had too many crew sick to be fussy. On 17 December he anchored in Doubtless Bay (which he named Lauriston Bay) and had a relatively peaceful stay, marred only by the theft of a dinghy and bloodless French retaliation. Three years later another Frenchman, Marc-Joseph Marion du Fresne, entered the Bay of Islands where he and 26 other officers and men were

Contrasting views of Cook's controversial landfall at Gisborne. ABOVE: John Elder Moultray called his earlier work 'It is a God!' Cook and his men were as mortal as the people whose isolated world they disturbed, but for each side this encounter was both exciting and traumatic. BELOW: FFC Huddleston's more modern reconstruction, also from the shore, looks out across the mouth of the Turanganui River to the *Endeavour*, looming less large. It also hints at the richness of life in 'Poverty Bay'.

killed for violating a fishing tapu; French utu left 250 Maori dead. Later French visitors included Bruni d'Entrecasteaux (1793), Louis Duperry (1824), Dumont d'Urville (1827 and 1840), Laplace (1831) and Lavaud (1840–43), supplemented by Spaniard Alejandro Malaspina's 1793 expedition, later British ones by George Vancouver (1791), Robert FitzRoy (1835) and Ross (1840) and a visit by the Russian, Bellingshausen (1820). Later even Austria sent a scientific expedition.

The latecomers found a world far different to that encountered by Tasman. Maori society was changing — 'the world in a whirl', as one chief put it — and whalers, traders, missionaries and farmers now lived among Maori, many having married into the local real estate. Maori still called the shots but their society was going through a period of rapid change as it adapted to the abrupt end of its long isolation.

French artist Louis Auguste de Sainson visited New Zealand in 1827 aboard Dumont d'Urville's *Astrolabe*. This lithograph of his artwork shows Maori buildings from Tolaga Bay and the Bay of Islands just a generation before colonisation. LA de Sainson, Alexander Turnbull Library, C-010-024

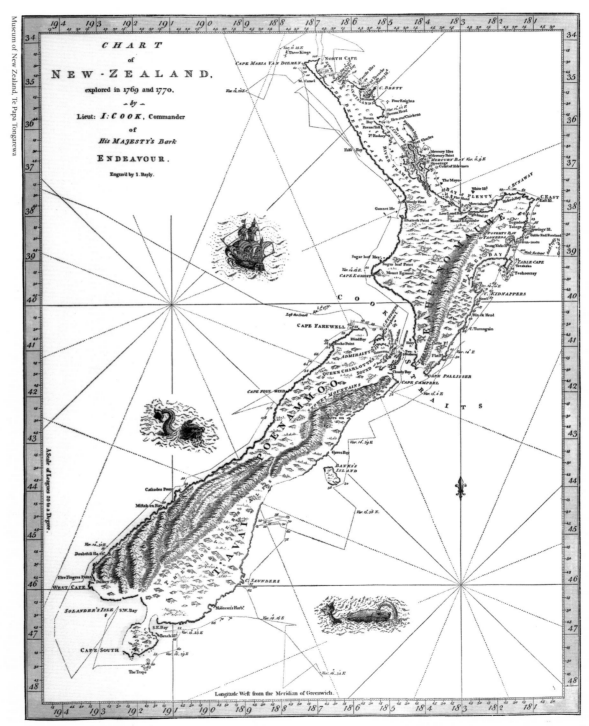

The chart of New Zealand drawn by Captain James Cook.

Until the 17th century mariners had no reliable way of fixing longitude, the position on an east–west line. Latitude (the distance north or south of the equator) could be established by using a compass and by sighting the sun, but for longitude they had only the unreliable 'dead reckoning' until English clockmaker John Harrison perfected a small, reliable watch that kept time at sea. H-4, a large pocket watch, would change navigation. James Cook took K-1, a copy of H-4, on his second voyage and described it as 'our faithful guide through all the vicissitudes of climates'. Now mariners could find their way anywhere in the world by cross-referencing against grids of co-ordinates. With this revolution came the perfection of maps and charts, and in this James Cook was a master. His beautiful map of New Zealand connected Stewart Island to the mainland and had Banks Peninsula as an island but is otherwise a remarkable achievement. Chronometers and accurate maps gave European seafarers an enormous advantage over those of other cultures, but we should not forget that they also used many of the same techniques that the Polynesians used, studying swells, sea colour and depth, clouds, birds, and drifting wood and plant life. Cook's journal was full of such references as he approached New Zealand for the first time in October 1769.

Harrison's number 4 chronometer, c.1760.
Mary Evans Picture Library

Mining the quarry:
sealers, whalers and merchants

European commerce began in the deep south, Murihiku as local Maori called it. In November 1791 George Vancouver's ships called at Dusky Sound where at Cook's old anchorage in Pickersgill Cove they 'drank a cheerful glass to the memory of Capt Cook'.[12] Their reports of rich fur-seal rookeries delighted entrepreneurs from New South Wales, who had almost exterminated Bass Strait's seals and were looking for fresh killing fields. Next year the *Britannia* left a sealing party in Fiordland, the first of Murihiku's tally of European New Zealand's firsts: first shipwreck, first shipyard, first house and the largest European 'settlement' until the 1830s. But that settlement was not planned. It was an accident. In 1795 the unseaworthy *Endeavour* (not Cook's ship) limped into Facile Harbour with the *Fancy*. They were there to refit and to complete a schooner left behind by the *Britannia* sealers, but their stay became longer than planned when the *Endeavour* fell apart, stranding 244 sailors, sealers and convict stowaways, who were left to cope with the rain and the sandflies.

Murihiku became New South Wales's bloody frontier. For months at a time gangs of 30 to 40 men lived ashore, sometimes sheltering under canvas or overturned boats. It was cold, wet, unpleasant work. John Boultbee, a gent slumming with sealers in Murihiku, fended off Maori, but he knew that the heavy surf and surges around the rookeries were a greater danger. Most visitors described sealers as rough, violent and drunken; but despite that, and their contempt for 'scholards', 'swells' and gentlemen, the sealers fancied themselves as middle class. That might have

Sealing vessels at anchor in Halfmoon Bay, Stewart Island. Sealers were the first Europeans to spend much time in New Zealand. It was brutal, dangerous work. Once the men got in among the seals they 'set up a yell to confuse them . . . then begins the slaughter, the men hitting right & left as fast as they can with their clubs, until there is not a seal left; after which they then commence skinning'.

been stretching the point for the gargantuan Thomas Chaseland. Genial, 'at least when sober', and feared and respected by everyone because he spoke the language of utu, on one occasion Chaseland avenged an attack on a sealing party by storming into a kainga and slaughtering everyone he found. But by 1810 the big operators were moving on from Murihiku's depleted rookeries. The seals were not safe yet, but over-culling and changing fashions had cut the industry down to size just in time.

The forestry industry began about the same time at the other end of New Zealand. In 1794 Edgar Dell took the brig *Fancy* to Doubtless Bay before sailing down to 'the River Thames', the Firth of Thames, seeking the stands of timber mentioned by Cook and Banks. Dell's men spent several months cutting and dressing timber for spars and planks for East India Company ships. After 1798 ships visited the Coromandel Peninsula and Northland for spars. The Royal Navy sent the *Dromedary* and *Coromandel* to New Zealand in 1820 to collect timber, even though kahikatea made poor spars and kauri cost more than Virginia spars.[13] Almost a hundred timber ports sprang up in the late 1820s and the 1830s, clustered in Northland, Hauraki, Bay of Plenty, the Wellington region, Cloudy Bay, Banks Peninsula and on the Otago and Southland coasts. Most had just a single European resident or two, but in the Bay of Islands, the Hokianga and at the bigger southern whaling stations, larger groups could be found. Ngati Hao chief Patuone visited Sydney in 1826 to promote Hokianga as a trading base and returned with the agent of a Sydney firm to complete arrangements for

the sale of land at Horeke.[14] Soon there was a mill and shipyard at 'Deptford', as Horeke was called, and by the 1840s 'the kauri forests had been cleared well back of the coasts of the Bay of Islands, Whangaroa and Hokianga'.[15]

The whaling industry was the 18th-century equivalent of today's petroleum industry. Whale oil was used for lighting, cooking, tanning and as a lubricant. Europeans seldom ate whale meat, but baleen (whalebone) strengthened chair-seats and corsets and made fine buggy whips. There were two types of whaling: pelagic (ocean) whaling from ships and shore whaling.[16] They overlapped, but pelagic whaling began here in the mid 1790s, concentrating on the lucrative sperm whales and humpbacks. Shore whaling began in the late 1820s to exploit the southern right whales that swam seasonally through Cook and Foveaux straits and calved in bays along New Zealand's east coast. Southern rights — large, docile and slow — were the 'right' ones to hunt because they floated when dead.

Some of the first convict transports had been whale ships, so it was hardly surprising that they started whaling in the Tasman Sea in 1791. Whale ships could be smelled a mile away but 'the smell of whales, alive or dead, was the smell of money'.[17] Between November and April they put into anchorages throughout Northland, around Cook Strait, Banks Peninsula and Murihiku. At times the waters of the Bay of Islands were thick with them. They were mainly British at first, American later on, but also included ships from New South Wales, France (the French ships favoured Banks Peninsula), the Netherlands,

The timber industry flourished in pre-colonial New Zealand. A boat was towing spars to be loaded aboard the barques *Francis Spaight* (foreground) and *Bolina* (rear) off GF Russell's timber yard at Kohukohu in December 1839 when artist Charles Heaphy visited in the New Zealand Company vessel *Tory*. Note the cannon by the flagstaff. C Heaphy, Alexander Turnbull Library, C-025-020

Whaling stations and grounds

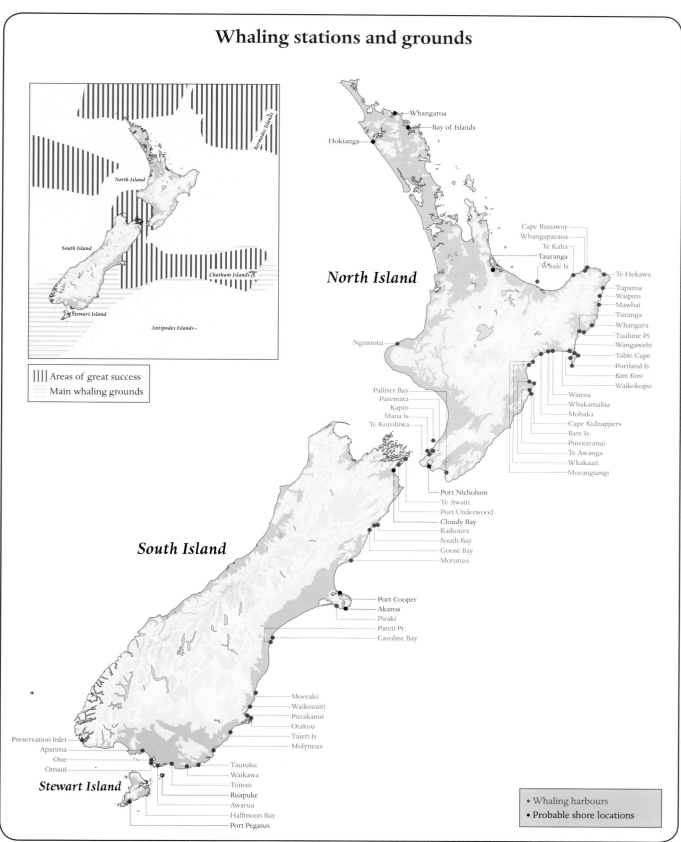

North Island

South Island

Stewart Island

Kermadec Islands

North Island

South Island

Chatham Islands

Stewart Island

Antipodes Islands

||| Areas of great success

Main whaling grounds

Whangaroa
Bay of Islands
Hokianga

Cape Runaway
Whangaparaoa
Te Kaha
Tauranga
Whale Is

Te Hekawa
Tuparoa
Waipiro
Mawhai
Turanga
Whangara
Tuahine Pt
Wangawehi
Table Cape
Portland Is
Kini Kini
Waikokopu

Ngamotu

Palliser Bay
Paremata
Kapiti
Mana Is
Te Korohiwa

Wairoa
Whakamahia
Mohaka
Cape Kidnappers
Bare Is
Putotaranui
Te Awanga
Whakaari
Moeangiangi

Port Nicholson
Te Awaiti
Port Underwood
Cloudy Bay
Kaikoura
South Bay
Goose Bay
Motunau

Port Cooper
Akaroa
Piraki
Pateti Pt
Caroline Bay

Moeraki
Waikouaiti
Purakanui
Otakou
Taieri Is
Molyneux

Preservation Inlet
Aparima
Oue
Omaui

Tautuku
Waikawa
Toitois
Ruapuke
Awarua
Halfmoon Bay
Port Pegasus

• Whaling harbours
• Probable shore locations

Based on information in Harry Morton, *The Whale's Wake*, UOP, Dunedin, 1982

and feathered a Sydney debt-collector. Later commentators may have found themselves agreeing with the American trader John Knight, who preferred the 'barefaced villains' to the 'respectable' merchants and the missionary traders whom he considered 'the greatest sharpers and [who] descend into the meanest and lowest subterfuges of any men I ever before fell in with'.[19]

The hell-hole of the Pacific? When Edward Markham visited the Bay of Islands in 1834 he observed that 'thirty to five and thirty sail of Whalers come in for three weeks to the bay and 400 to 500 Sailors require as many Women', but thought that 'the sailors have done as much towards Civilising the Natives as the Missionaries have'. While ships' masters stocked up on food, water and timber, their crews sought alcohol and women. Alcohol was seldom short. In those days the foul-quality rum went by the name of fighting rum, so much belligerence did it brew. Women were equally abundant. According to Belich, the sex industry was the precursor of New Zealand's more familiar export earners, wool, gold, meat and dairy products. Prostitutes were generally low status women, pimped by the chiefs. This oldest trade sometimes involved coercion and sometimes brought disease, but the sex industry was not all bad. At a gun for the tribe and a frock for the woman, each coupling 'represented a tenfold improvement on the yield for women's work and it was far more than any man could make'; 'sex was one industry where Maori men at least could snigger back'.[20]

They could do with some laughs. The Maori discovery of the wider world had begun badly. In 1793 Lieutenant-Governor King had two Northland Maori, Tuki Tahua and Ngahuruhuru, kidnapped and taken to Norfolk Island to teach convicts how to work flax, a mistake since flax preparation was women's work and beneath the dignity and knowledge of the two men, who were later returned home. Soon, though, Maori were shipping out aboard whalers voluntarily, eager to see the sights and to earn money. Whale ship captains valued their boatmanship, strength and discipline so highly that hundreds were serving at sea between the 1820s and the 1840s. 'The natives of New Zealand are a robust and enterprising yet docile race, and . . . prove orderly and powerful seamen,' London ship owners reported.[21] Maori often sailed together on the same ships and worked their way up the ranks, becoming harpooners or even officers. One was chief mate aboard the *Francis*; only nationality (or race?) kept another from the master's job on the *Earl Stanhope*. Maori quickly became a familiar sight in Sydney, where the governors put up chiefs such as Te Pahi, Ruatara and Matara. Already the New Zealand propensity to seek greener pastures in Australia was establishing itself. At a gala day at Hobart in 1838 Maori made up a third of the 90 oarsmen.[22]

'Give her line give her line
Down she goes through the foaming brine
Sponge the side where the flying coil
Marks the monster's speed and toil'

For boat crews the danger increased when the harpoon struck. Frightened, enraged and in pain, the whale usually dived, dragging boat and crew off on a 'Nantucket sleigh ride'. A powerful whale could tow a boat for miles.

the German states, Portugal, Denmark and Canada. These were the roistering visitors who earned the Bay of Islands' main town, Kororareka, its reputation as 'the Hell-hole of the Pacific'. Mission printer William Colenso muttered that it was 'notorious for containing a greater number of rogues than any other spot of equal size in the universe', and Charles Darwin called Kororareka residents 'the veriest refuse of society'.[18] But the prudish and the pious said that of many early 19th-century seaports. By 1836 Kororareka had a temperance society, but grog shops probably still outnumbered wowsers and the town's inhabitants knew how to treat authority's lackeys; they tarred

*'But lo her giant strength is broke
Now she turns a mass of lead
The mighty mountain whale is dead'*

So went 'A Whaler's Song', which concluded with the hope that a fair lass would remember 'The hardy tar who on seas afar / Risked his life for her lamp to fill'.

Whalers are cutting blubber from a whale in John Hewside Clark's near-idyllic rendering. In reality it was a dangerous and dirty job (circling sharks added to the hazards) and the seas were seldom as placid as this.

In any society sex, gunpowder and money make an explosive mix, so it is remarkable how well Maori and Europeans got on here. Thankfully they often wanted different things — Maori and Europeans competed for seals, but not for whales, timber, or flax — but it also helped that each usually preferred to trade rather than fight. Frederick Maning recalled that flax traders put out boarding nettings, armed their crews and never allowed more than five Maori aboard at a time but most traders were realists. Here the early 19th-century phase of imperialism when British military superiority was less pronounced, so different from the later era of Gatling gun and steam frigates, typified the 'collusions that imperial appetite necessarily imposed on the British, a small people who could therefore be caught and caught out'.[23] Europeans trod warily.

Even so, there were clashes. One of the more significant took place in Taranaki in 1834. Te Awaiti whaler John 'Jacky' Guard and his family were returning from a visit to Sydney when their barque *Harriett* blew ashore near Cape Egmont.[24] Everyone made it ashore safely, but the Taranaki tribe plundered the wreck; then Ngati Ruanui attacked the castaways, killing 12 sailors and capturing the rest. John Guard and several companions escaped and went to Sydney to obtain a ransom for Betty Guard, her children and the others. There he changed his mind. Maori had been getting on his wick lately. They had pillaged his ship *Waterloo* after it went ashore on Waikanae Beach a year earlier, and a Ngai Tahu taua (war party) had killed and eaten three Maori workers at his Kakapo Bay station. So Guard persuaded New South Wales Governor Richard Bourke to teach his wife's kidnappers a lesson. He returned to Taranaki with HMS *Alligator*, the government schooner *Isabella* and part of the Sydney garrison. Using what some condemned as excessive force, they recovered the prisoners after shelling and burning a pa. Betty Guard's experiences raised more questions than answers. A lurid account in the *Sydney Herald* had her stripped naked, dragged off, tomahawked (but saved by a large comb in her hair) and forced to watch displays of cannibalism. Other accounts had her treated well by Chief Oaoiti. That second story may also have been the origins of rumours of her bearing twins fathered by the chief.

Jacky Guard was one of the new shore whalers. Like pelagic whaling, shore whaling was seasonal, taking place between autumn and early winter from stations that clustered thickest around the Kapiti Coast, Cook Strait and eastern and southern New Zealand. The stations were crude wooden or thatched huts. They reeked of whale oil, and rats and fleas abounded. But

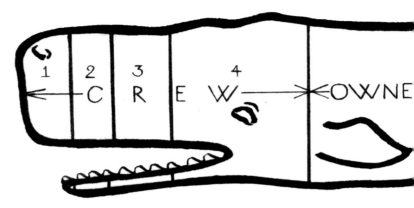

'They will rob you they will use you
Worse than any slaves
Before you go a-whaling boys
You best be in your graves'

Alexander McLintock's diagram of where the profits went supports the gloomy lines of 'The Whalemen's Lament'. AH McLintock, Alexander Turnbull Library, A-191-009

Kororareka in 1840 as Louis Le Breton, surgeon on the corvette *L'Astrolabe*, saw it, crowded with whale ships. L Le Breton, Hocken Library, University of Otago

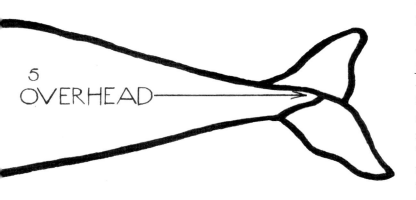

5 OVERHEAD		
1	CAPTAIN'S SHARE	16/240
2	THREE OFFICERS DIVIDE	14/240
3	SIX BOAT-STEERERS DIVIDE	18/240
4	TWENTY CREW DIVIDE	40/240
5	OWNERS AND OVERHEAD	152/240

Sydney merchants could set up five or six shore stations for the price of a single ship. Guard established the first at Te Awaiti in 1827 (although it was not fully operational until 1830–31). Other well-known shore whalers were Dicky Barrett from Te Awaiti, Joseph Thoms from Marlborough and Porirua, the Wellers — George and Edward — at Otago, Purakanui and Taieri Island, Johnny Jones at Waikouaiti, John Hughes at Moeraki and Thomas Howell from Riverton. Here men with colourful nicknames like 'Geordie Bolts', 'Flash Bill', 'Fat Jackson' and 'Black Peter' worked hard and played hard. 'Casks of rum, usually of such foul quality that it was said to smell worse than the decaying whale scraps, assumed equal importance to casks of meat in the station supplies', but most were well run and the men generally kept the working and the drinking seasons separate.[25]

In the early 1800s several attacks on ships earned New Zealand the reputation as the cannibal coast. In 1808 the crew of the schooner *Parramatta* paid dearly for wounding three Maori and for trying to sail without paying for a cargo. An evil wind blew the *Parramatta* back ashore near Cape Brett, where all were killed. Even more notorious was the burning of the *Boyd*.[26]

Guards Bay in Port Underwood typified the small shore whaling stations that dotted New Zealand's coast. The grave in the foreground belongs to Rangiawa (Kuita), the wife of Mr Wynen. W Fox, Alexander Turnbull Library, B-113-015

INSET: As early as 1804 an American whale ship found a 'New Zealand prince . . . Vary [sic] happy & well contented' on another whaler. Ruatara, the missionaries' first protector, travelled widely on several whaling, sealing and convict ships, as did other adventurous Maori. Here a Maori man and woman relax on board a ship with the crew. British Library

Walter Wright's famous 1908 oil is now described as 'documentary racism', erroneous in many details. But the burning of the *Boyd* at Whangaroa in 1809 fuelled the European depiction of New Zealand as a 'cannibal coast'.
W Wright, Auckland Art Gallery, Toi o Tamaki

Much has been written about this 'Saga of Cultural Clash', which cast a pall over European-Maori trading relationships. These relationships had been developing promisingly thanks to those early boundary-crossers and cross-cultural travellers, Governor Philip King of New South Wales and Hikutu chief Te Pahi. Te Pahi visited Norfolk Island and Port Jackson in 1805, staying with his sons at Government House for three months. King gave them iron tools, fruit tree seedlings, livestock and other gifts. A keen but critical observer of Europeans and Aborigines, Te Pahi even considered sending some of his people to New South Wales to learn to become shepherds.

This promising start came unstuck thanks to rival Whangaroa Maori, who in 1808 believed that Captain James Ceroni from the *City of Edinburgh* had placed a curse on their little-used harbour after disease struck. They would not be so welcoming when the next ship, the spar trader *Boyd,* called in 1809. Unfortunately her master had abused a Ngati Uru chief, Te Ara, who took utu by luring the captain and some of the men ashore and murdering them. Te Ara's party returned after dark, clad in the dead sailors' clothes. They boarded the brig and killed most of the passengers and crew before someone accidentally blew up a powder keg, setting the ship on fire. Te Pahi tried to rescue some of the survivors but was wrongly identified as guilty by the crews of the whalers. They raided Te Puna in revenge, wounding Te Pahi, who died in 1810 in an intertribal skirmish. The *Boyd* 'Massacree' set back trade for several years, a broadsheet printed in London warning would-be merchants, 'touch not that cursed shore lest you/These Cannibals pursue'.[27]

The Musket Wars

For most of the first four decades of the 19th century ferocious intertribal wars raged throughout this green and unpleasant land. Unlike the later 'New Zealand Wars' (in which only some thousands of adult Maori participated), the shooting, clubbing and cannibalism of these wars crimsoned both main islands and even bloodied some of their outliers, making them truly national in scope. But few general histories give them much space. The duration, the impact and even the name of these wars is debateable. One historian suggests calling them Potato Wars, another downplays the importance of muskets (believing they had more impact in the later wars), while a website euphemises them away as 'Maori on the Move'. But what is beyond doubt is that they were unequalled for their ferocity and their extent. The butcher's bill for these wars is as hazy as many of the events, but even if scholars now discount an earlier estimate of 80,000 deaths from fighting or disease, the lowest recent guesstimate, 20,000 plus, exceeds the New Zealand casualties in either of the two world wars; and if measured in terms of casualties per head of population, they were even worse. One battle alone, Matakitaki in the Waikato in 1822, may have cost 2000 lives, almost the body count for the entire New Zealand Wars.

The fog of these wars obscures all but the names of a few protagonists who did their fighting under the noses of journal-keeping Europeans or who lived long enough to make themselves useful or meddlesome to later colonisers. Men like Hongi Hika in the Bay of Islands or Te Rauparaha around Cook Strait have entered common folklore, generally demonised or romanticised in settler storytelling as the hooliganish 'before' that had to make way for the desirable 'after' of a God-fearing,

home-owning democracy. There is much more to it than that, although as Angela Ballara, the Musket Wars' latest historian cautions, 'if the main impression of these events is of a confusing plethora of names of chiefs, hapu, people killed, the names of their killers, words spoken, by whom and other innumerable details, then the right effect has been produced. These words were about people: individuals who killed or were killed, and the reasons for these killings.'[28] There were plenty of them 'taken by the hand of death / on the pathway of Kapa — the sign of manliness', as a female relative of chief Tiwaewae grieved in her waiata in 1824.[29]

Mana and utu drove Maori warfare, Ballara reminds us. In te ao Maori, people were born with mana, the psychic power and authority inherited from the powers of the gods among their ancestors. The higher a person's status, the more mana he or she had, but everyone except for slaves had some. Although mana knitted the fabric of society together and ordered relationships, it was also fragile. Just as it could be enhanced, so could it be lost or diminished, putting reputations or even lives at risk. Damage the mana of a senior person and you harmed the group's mana. The words repayment and reciprocity come closer to the meaning of utu in English than revenge. That helps to explain why 'utu was not a moral choice: in Maori cultural terms it was an absolute necessity'.[30] Mana would be lost if utu was not taken. There were, of course, other reasons for going to war. Men also fought for land, for resources and for the sheer hell of it, just as men have done in every society.

A complex system of tikanga (customary rules and rights) or rikanga (customary practices) organised society, with warfare being the ultimate sanction for breaching these codes. Warfare was endemic in late 18th- and early 19th-century New Zealand,

Warriors perform a haka in front of the pa at Ohinemutu.

The enormous, elaborately decorated war canoes, waka taua, could carry more than 150 men.

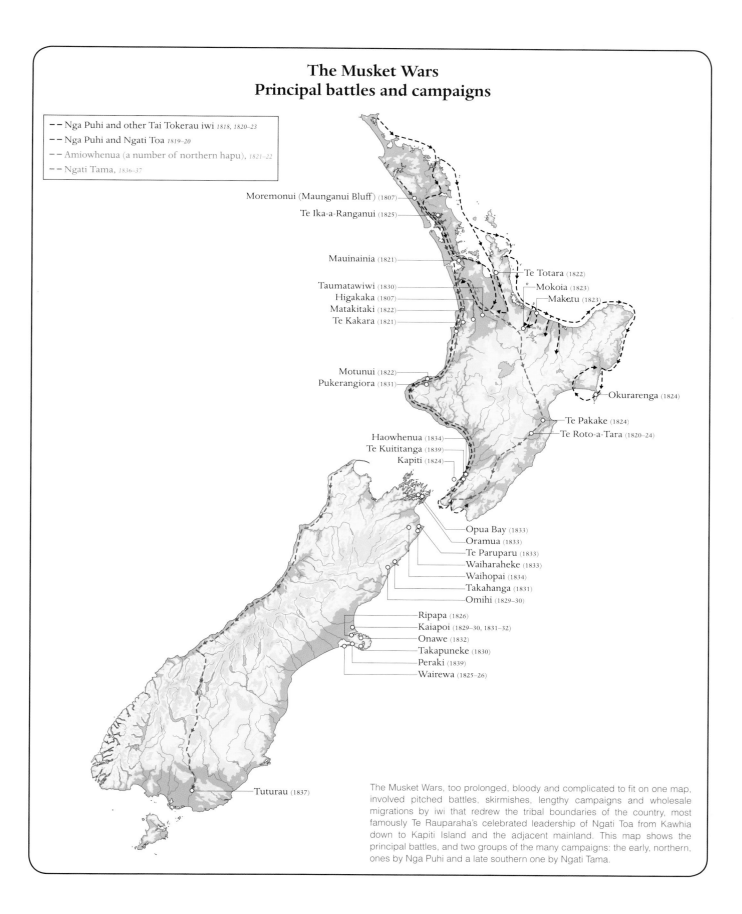

The Musket Wars
Principal battles and campaigns

- – – Nga Puhi and other Tai Tokerau iwi *1818, 1820–23*
- – – Nga Puhi and Ngati Toa *1819–20*
- – – Amiowhenua (a number of northern hapu), *1821–22*
- – – Ngati Tama, *1836–37*

Moremonui (Maunganui Bluff) (1807)
Te Ika-a-Ranganui (1825)

Mauinainia (1821)
Te Totara (1822)
Taumatawiwi (1830)
Mokoia (1823)
Higakaka (1807)
Maketu (1823)
Matakitaki (1822)
Te Kakara (1821)

Motunui (1822)
Pukerangiora (1831)

Okurarenga (1824)

Te Pakake (1824)
Te Roto-a-Tara (1820–24)

Haowhenua (1834)
Te Kuititanga (1839)
Kapiti (1824)

Opua Bay (1833)
Oramua (1833)
Te Paruparu (1833)
Waiharaheke (1833)
Waihopai (1834)
Takahanga (1831)
Omihi (1829–30)

Ripapa (1826)
Kaiapoi (1829–30, 1831–32)
Onawe (1832)
Takapuneke (1830)
Peraki (1839)
Wairewa (1825–26)

Tuturau (1837)

The Musket Wars, too prolonged, bloody and complicated to fit on one map, involved pitched battles, skirmishes, lengthy campaigns and wholesale migrations by iwi that redrew the tribal boundaries of the country, most famously Te Rauparaha's celebrated leadership of Ngati Toa from Kawhia down to Kapiti Island and the adjacent mainland. This map shows the principal battles, and two groups of the many campaigns: the early, northern, ones by Nga Puhi and a late southern one by Ngati Tama.

in part because Maori society was a patchwork of small independent communities — some argue that it was made up of hapu in these times, rather than iwi — without any larger political or legal institutions to appeal to. Marriage alliances often kept the peace, as did diplomacy, the use of peacemakers, or simply skedaddling out of harm's way. Since the death of high-status people required more utu, protagonists could minimise bloodletting by killing slaves or people of lower station. Taua muru, raiding parties that stripped offenders of their goods, also kept violence to containable levels. In general, Maori tried hard not to draw the blood of close relations, but in such a fragmented, highly personalised society, and particularly during the heat of battle, matters could quickly spin out of control. Killing someone by mistake, killing too many high-ranking people or inadvertently breaching someone's mana or property rights could all be grounds for war.

When did the wars start? Since chiefly mana had a long pedigree and intertribal warfare was endemic, any starting point must be entirely arbitrary. Nevertheless, it is worth remembering that although muskets intensified the carnage over time (as did cannon, iron weapons and implements such as swords and axes), the motivation for this warfare was entirely traditional. Furthermore, until the mid to late 1820s the impact of European

Strategically close to Cook Strait, Kapiti Island watched over trade routes in addition to providing a place of refuge. Te Rauparaha let several whalers and traders use the island. Whaling was already declining when John Gilfillan sketched the original watercolour from which Walter Bowring did this copy, Jillett's (sometimes spelled Gillett's or Gillet's) whaling station spread out along the Waiorua beach. W Bowring, Alexander Turnbull Library, D-018-012

weaponry on the battlefield was probably less important than we commonly suppose. Many of the early muskets flogged off by traders were the wretched 'trade muskets', short-ranged (20 to 30 m at best) flintlocks, slow to reload and prone to misfire or clog.[31] They usually lacked bayonets, making them useless in the hand-to-hand phase of fighting. But like any new technology, muskets emboldened their owners and had shock value when used against people unfamiliar with them. Warriors got more proficient with them over time and altered their fighting tactics to accommodate the new weapons.

The trigger for the wars is often taken to have occurred in 1807, the year that Ngati Whatua ambushed a 500-strong Nga Puhi taua (war party) near modern-day Dargaville, killing 150. Among the survivors of the battle of Te Kai-a-te-Karoro (the 'Seagulls' Feast') was a minor Nga Puhi chief, Hongi Hika, who lost two brothers there. This would have been cause enough for utu, even if he took his time to exercise it against Ngati Whatua. The various hapu and groups of hapu that made up Nga Puhi were disparate and at first inclined to fight among themselves. What made them important collectively was their early monopoly on European technology and resources, although, ironically, some of the longest-legged taua were launched by hapu with the smallest number of muskets: for example, Ngati Whatua and western Nga Puhi's Te Amiowhenua ('Encircling of the Land') expeditions to the Cook Strait region.

But Hongi, leader of the northern Nga Puhi faction, did add a new edge to the fighting in 1821 when he returned home from England where he had met King George and helped Cambridge academic Professor Samuel Lee and missionary Thomas Kendall prepare a Maori language grammar. At Sydney on the way back, Hongi bought several hundred muskets, which he used between 1821 and 1823 on several extraordinarily successful and bloody campaigns against Ngati Paoa of Tamaki, Ngati Maru of Thames, Te Arawa of the Bay of Plenty and the Waikato tribes. By now muskets were numerous and important. And so were potatoes, as James Belich reminds us. While it would be going too far to rename the wars the Potato Wars, the humble spud did give Maori a reliable surplus with which to sustain war parties for longer than traditional crops could. Potatoes joined pigs, flax and smoked heads as the commodities traded for guns; 150 baskets of spuds and eight pigs would buy one gun in the Bay of Islands in 1814. Flax was important south of the Bay.

As the first to have guns in quantity, Hongi made the most of them. Between 1821 and 1827, when he received the wound that would kill him a year later, Hongi and his shifting alliances within Nga Puhi slaughtered thousands, enslaved just as many and looted canoe-loads of treasures and heirlooms. European observers were as horrified as Maori. Frederick Maning, the 'Pakeha Maori' memorialist and champion yarn spinner, felt that a friend who in 1822 had paid a cartridge-box of shells for a Maori woman 'who was just going to be baked' had paid 'a great deal more than she was worth' but conceded that 'humanity does not stick at such trifles'.[32] More typical were the pained diary entries of the missionaries, traders and others, who when able to escape being drawn into the conflicts, watched victorious war parties troop past their doors, bearing human flesh by the basket-load. 'Ten slaves have passed this settlement laden with human flesh; and considerable quantities have been sent to other districts,' Paihia missionary Henry Williams wrote in his diary on 13 February 1828.[33]

Even more famous than Hongi was Te Rauparaha, composer of the 'ka mate, ka mate' haka. European observers tended to call him the 'Napoleon of New Zealand' on good days and 'the old Sarpent' on others. Like Hongi, Te Rauparaha also trickled down. In 1822, with his small, vulnerable Ngati Toa iwi, he began his epic trek down to the Cook Strait region, fighting and accumulating alliances as he went. After a spectacular victory there in 1824, Te Rauparaha turned Kapiti Island into a combination bolthole and trading base. From here he victualled and loaded whalers and flax-trading vessels and made war on his adversaries. It was New Zealand's nearest thing to an African-style conquest state.[34] Te Rauparaha ravaged the mainland off Kapiti but is best remembered for his campaigns against the

Te Rauparaha took his defeated, outnumbered Ngati Toa tribe from Kawhia to the new territories at the other end of the North Island. A military genius, he quickly saw the advantage of muskets. Ngati Toa's great migration changed the tribal structure of New Zealand forever. E Abbot, Hocken Library, University of Otago

KAIAPOI

The Ngati Tuahuriri chiefs defending Kaiapoi were not caught napping during the campaigning season of 1829. They knew about Te Rauparaha's bloody rampage through the Marlborough Sounds and Omihi. After the Kai Huanga feud they had adapted the pa for musket warfare. It was surrounded by deep swamps on three sides (which also supplied fresh water to the defenders) and the fourth, southern side had been reinforced by massive, bulletproof wooden defences, fitted with flanking projections and openings for muskets. They had plenty of guns. Ngati Toa and allies were encamped nearby, claiming to have come peacefully to trade. Some did, indeed, enter the pa and trade guns, which turned out to be defective, for pounamu. In revenge for an insult, and under circumstances that were disputed, Ngai Tahu ariki Te Maiharanui wiped out Te Pehi Kupe, Te Pokaitara, Te Aratangata and his companions. Te Rauparaha and Te Rangihaeata, who had remained outside, launched an attack, but failed to break through the defences and retired after killing all the prisoners taken at Omihi and cooking and eating them in full view of the occupants of the pa. The message was plain. He would be back and Kaiapoi Ngai Tahu would be on the menu next time.

Te Rauparaha returned in the summer of 1831–32, having taken Kaikoura on the way down. The southern chief Taiaroa came up and launched spirited attacks on Ngati Toa, but lacked the numbers to break the siege, which drew on as Te Rauparaha's men sapped their zigzaggy way slowly towards the palisades, bundling manuka at the front and roofing over the saps to protect the workers. After three months the huge brushwood piles rested ominously against the palisading on the southern side of the pa, accumulating faster than the defenders could remove them. Te Rauparaha, reinforced by a Ngati Rarua taua led by Niho, was just waiting for the right wind to set them alight. Seeing the inevitable, Taiaroa and his men retired one night. The defenders lit the manuka themselves in the hope of driving the flames back on the attackers but at a crucial moment the wind swung to the south, throwing it back onto the dry palisades, which burst into flames. 'In the wild confusion caused by the raging gale carrying a blast of choking smoke and dust into the pa, with flames and flying debris, Te Rauparaha's men were soon inside the defences.'[35] Three or four hundred died that day, hundreds more were captured 'and at least one group was massacred'.[36] Many defenders fled through the swamps in the confusion, but for days takahi taua (raiding groups) scoured the countryside, killing or raping any they came across.

mainland's Ngai Tahu. In the late 1820s the southerners had been more interested in killing each other, fighting the aptly named Kai Huanga 'Eat Relations', a bloody civil war between the tribe's northern and southern sections. Victory went to the better-armed southerners in 1828, two years before Te Rauparaha fell on the weakened northerners. For three years he rampaged through northern Ngai Tahu lands, with devastating effect. The battles and sieges still resonate: Kaikoura, Kaiapoi and Takapuneke and Onawe pa at Akaroa, among others.

In the Takapuneke attack Te Rauparaha used the trading brig *Elizabeth* as a Trojan horse, tricking Ngai Tahu into thinking that it was just another innocent trading vessel. They captured Ngai Tahu visitors to the ship, then launched a dawn attack on the pa's unsuspecting inhabitants. Three hundred were killed, cooked and eaten and others enslaved. Imprisoned aboard the charnel ship, Te Maiharanui and his wife strangled their 12-year-old daughter to spare her sufferings. Near Otaki, Te Maiharanui was hung upside down and had his throat pierced so that the widows of Te Pehi Kupe, Te Pokaitara and Te Aratanga (whose husbands had died at Kaiapoi) could drink his blood. The *Elizabeth*'s master, Captain John Stewart, was reviled for his part in Te Rauparaha's subterfuge, but escaped prosecution at Sydney on a technicality.

The killing peaked in the early 1830s and then fell away sharply. There were still some prodigious feats, most notably Te Puoho, who in 1836 and '37 led a small Ngati Tama taua 1500 km from Golden Bay down the length of the West Coast, over the Southern Alps and across Central Otago and inland Southland to Tuturau, where Tuhawaiki defeated him.

The Maori economy changed dramatically in the first half of the 19th century, as Cyprian Bridge's 1845 watercolour of a pa (probably Tamati Waka Nene's pa at Okaihau) shows. European crops such as potatoes (right) could be sold for cash or weapons and trade goods. The pa itself features strengthened palisade walls and musket-holes around the base.

Some limited fighting also took place in parts of the North Island as late as 1843 and '44, but most of the heat had gone from the intertribal wars by the end of the 1830s. Why? Just as in determining the causes of the wars, there is no single, simple answer. War-weariness certainly played a part. A great deal of blood and treasure had been lost by a population that was also coming under pressure from new infectious diseases and from pushy colonists. In strictly military terms, the proliferation of muskets had evened up the balance of terror, reducing the likelihood of winning easy one-sided victories.[37] So, too, had changes to pa construction and to battlefield tactics, by evening up the balance between attack and defence. 'The wars diminished in lethality as differentials declined in each region . . . They began when and because some Maori had muskets and potatoes, and stopped when and because everyone had them.'[38]

Another factor was the growing impact of European culture. The Christian message of peace, largely ignored for a decade and a half, grew more attractive as an alternative means of breaking the cycle of violence by 'going mihinare [missionary]' and embracing a new value system. This was especially attractive to people enslaved by conquest. Young Maori seafarers and whalers returning materially rich also probably felt constrained by traditional lines of chiefly authority and subverted or ignored them. Finally, too, the impact of land purchases by Europeans was making itself felt. These were early days yet, but as large tracts of land changed hands and as shiploads of settlers fanned out from their coastal beachheads, tribal boundaries were becoming frozen and increasingly irrelevant to the newcomers. Maori still called the shots, but by the mid 1840s traditional wars of conquest and immigration were becoming impossible.

Settlers, not sojourners: mihinare, Pakeha Maori and shagroon colonists

The Devil may have the best tunes but, in New Zealand, missionaries, more habitual writers than most of their contemporaries, have cast a deceptively long shadow over our early 19th-century past. Their most enduring monument, Kerikeri, the 'cradle of New Zealand', glosses up the iconic mission station of the Church Missionary Society (CMS); there the country's oldest buildings, the 1822 Mission House and the fortress-like 1835 Stone Store, both elegantly preserved, overlook the yachts in the inlet. But for the site of the first station, you must drive north-east a few kilometres and then walk down a steep farm road to deserted Rangihoua Bay, where it takes sharp eyes to detect beneath the grass the faint archaeological impressions of houses, paths and a sawpit. It was here between 1814 and 1832 at Oihi Mission Station, overshadowed in every sense by towering Rangihoua pa, that

Marsden preached his famous first sermon; here that he privately flattered himself the 'English flag' would wave until Maori 'enjoyed all the happiness of British subjects'; here that his dependent missionaries, having failed to convince the 'barbarian savages' of the superiority of other than martial civilisation, traded in civilised arms; here that brotherly love waxed so hot that teacher Kendall stabbed blacksmith Hall with a chisel, only to be repelled by horse-pistol fire. And here that nary a convert to Christianity was made.[39]

Christianity, like whaling, sealing, gun-running and the other blessings of Western civilisation, launched itself at New Zealand from convict-ridden Sydney. Here the Reverend Samuel Marsden concocted his crusade to Anglicise Polynesians, more malleable he hoped than convicts or Aboriginals. As beamy as the tankers that call at the refinery named after him, Marsden gets mixed reviews from god-bothered historians: the evangelicals 'dressed like crows; seemed joyless, humourless and sometimes hypocritical; they embalmed the evidence poor historians need to read in tedious preaching'.[40] Marsden was that and more. Australians know him as the 'Flogging Parson' and he could be scratchy when crossed. But he was also energetic, determined and generous, ever ready to dip into the fortune some criticised him for accumulating, to proselytise Polynesians.

Even so, it took long enough. Although he had been thinking about a New Zealand mission for several years, Marsden had had to wait until 1807 to return to London. There he set about enlisting the support of the CMS and recruiting lay settlers to prepare the way for ordained ministers, for Marsden believed that indigenous people had to be 'civilised' by learning to read, write and farm like good British yeomen before they were ready for the Christian message: God followed goods. It was another two years before he could return to Sydney, accompanied by William Hall, a joiner, and John King, a rope maker, the first lay missionaries or 'mechanics' (as artisans or skilled workers were then called), who would soften up Maori. Also aboard the ship was a godsend, Ruatara, the Nga Puhi chief he had befriended in Britain.

At Sydney delay followed frustrating delay. After the *Boyd* incident the Colonial Office vetoed further settlement. Then the CMS rejected Marsden's grand proposal to link the Sydney, Tahiti and New Zealand missions. As a result, the first missionary mechanics, Hall and Thomas Kendall, did not reach

J Backler, Alexander Turnbull Library, G-620

ABOVE: 'Commerce and the arts have a natural tendency to inculcate industrious and moral habits,' Samuel Marsden believed. 'The attention of the heathen can be gained, and their vagrant habits corrected.' Convict artist Joseph Backler painted Marsden in Sydney, where he was known as 'the Flogging Parson'.

BELOW: Ruatara offered Marsden protection for his first mission station at Rangihoua in the Bay of Islands. The pa occupied a prominent site, while the missionaries built their Oihi station to the right on a steep slope. M Clayton, Auckland Museum

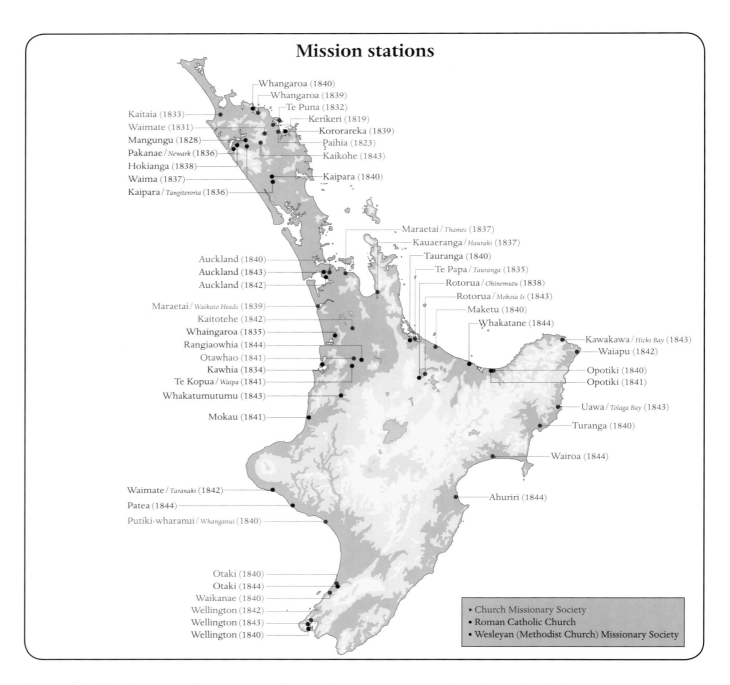

Mission stations

Whangaroa (1840)
Whangaroa (1839)
Te Puna (1832)
Kerikeri (1819)
Kororareka (1839)
Paihia (1823)
Kaikohe (1843)

Kaitaia (1833)
Waimate (1831)
Mangungu (1828)
Pakanae / *Newark* (1836)
Hokianga (1838)
Waima (1837)
Kaipara / *Tangiteroria* (1836)

Kaipara (1840)

Maraetai / *Thames* (1837)
Kauaeranga / *Hauraki* (1837)
Tauranga (1840)
Te Papa / *Tauranga* (1835)
Rotorua / *Ohinemutu* (1838)
Rotorua / *Mokoia Is* (1843)
Maketu (1840)
Whakatane (1844)

Auckland (1840)
Auckland (1843)
Auckland (1842)

Maraetai / *Waikato Heads* (1839)
Kaitotehe (1842)
Whaingaroa (1835)
Rangiaowhia (1844)
Otawhao (1841)
Kawhia (1834)
Te Kopua / *Waipa* (1841)
Whakatumutumu (1843)
Mokau (1841)

Kawakawa / *Hicks Bay* (1843)
Waiapu (1842)
Opotiki (1840)
Opotiki (1841)
Uawa / *Tolaga Bay* (1843)
Turanga (1840)
Wairoa (1844)

Waimate / *Taranaki* (1842)
Patea (1844)
Putiki-wharanui / *Whanganui* (1840)

Ahuriri (1844)

Otaki (1840)
Otaki (1844)
Waikanae (1840)
Wellington (1842)
Wellington (1843)
Wellington (1840)

• Church Missionary Society
• Roman Catholic Church
• Wesleyan (Methodist Church) Missionary Society

the Bay of Islands until June 1814. There on 22 December Marsden landed at Rangihoua Bay, Ruatara's patch, where on Christmas Day he preached that famous first sermon. Quoting from Luke 2:10, he told a big congregation to 'behold, I bring you good tidings of great joy', with Ruatara translating for him.

The seed fell on barren land, literally and metaphorically. Marsden and his CMS crew energetically planted mission stations — Kerikeri in 1819, Paihia in 1823, Waimate in 1831, Te Puna in 1832, and so on — but his obsession with wheat growing made few converts. Bay of Islands Maori had been growing potatoes (more

nutritious and productive than the finger-sized kumara), Indian corn and other vegetables and raising pigs to victual shipping since the 1790s, but why labour to produce wheat when imported flour was plentiful and cheap? Nor did they like the Christian gospel. The missionaries' protectors, Ruatara at Rangihoua, or Hongi Hika at Kerikeri, listened politely and let children attend the stations' schools, but they rejected the low-church mechanic missionaries' gloomy emphasis on 'an angry God always on the alert to damn their souls to eternal fires'. As Waikato, the young chief from Rangihoua who accompanied Hongi to Britain in

1820 and '21, put it: 'The People at the Warree Karakeah (Missionary House) and the *Karaheah itself* (Preaching) was no good for the NZd man.'[41] In any case, no chief was yet ready to sacrifice the mana that conversion would entail.

In fact, Maori and missionary drew the conversion game in the turbulent 1820s. The brighter, broader-minded missionaries were particularly susceptible to Maori ideas, and to Maori bodies. Thomas Kendall, an enduring figure in New Zealand literature and 'an emotional, idealistic and self-torturing man, driven by evangelical zeal and seeking perfection, although believing at the same time in his own deep imperfection', went native. Marsden sacked him for trading in guns and for adultery with a Maori woman.[42] A decade later William Yate, another of the more linguistically gifted CMS toilers, was 'given the bum's rush by Marsden and his horse . . . shot in his stead' for dallying with Maori youths.[43] Marsden had also dismissed his first ordained minister, the Reverend John Butler, in 1823 and the CMS mission only got its house in any semblance of order after the arrival of the Reverend Henry Williams, 'as much a match for the domineering, absentee Marsden as he was for the chiefs, who recognised the battle-proven naval veteran as a fellow warrior'.[44]

Williams put the bickering brethren back on their feet. He built a schooner to reduce their dependence on Maori and traders. He dropped Marsden's 'civilisation first' policy and made them master the Maori language and preach the gospel. It took time to work (Williams himself was only really fluent from 1828) but in 1829 and '30 the CMS finally broke the 14-year drought by baptising several Maori at Paihia. In the next decade about 3000 would 'go missionary'. 'Te Atua, the God of the Bible, was on the move.'[45] Why? The missionaries were more numerous, more confident and more fluent. They also had better tracts and grammars, appealing to the Maori interest in literacy. Scholars disagree about the extent and sophistication of Maori literacy.[46]

In 1820 James Barry painted chiefs Waikato (left) and Hongi Hika (centre) in London, where they were visiting with the Reverend Thomas Kendall (seated, right). Hongi was the CMS's chief protector and a leading protagonist during the Musket Wars. Kendall was drawn into Maori language and custom, to Marsden's horror. 'By prying into the obscene customs and notions of the natives with a vitiated curiosity, his own mind has become so polluted that it will be very difficult for him to purify his ideas.'

But if the literacy–Christianity link sometimes underestimates the Maori interest in spirituality, it must also be admitted that Maori interest in reading and writing was profound and similar to that expressed elsewhere in Polynesia. Perhaps more importantly, Hongi's death also freed the missionaries from the taint of being his creatures and 'began the process that released it [Christianity] from Northland to the rest of the country'.[47]

For their part Maori, who had happily embraced European trade and schooling while holding true to their own cosmology, began to explore Christianity. 'Karakia Maori were increasingly replaced by karakia mihinare, although the point should be made that this often occurred *without* Maori relinquishing a belief in their own gods. In this sense, perhaps, Maori did not so much convert *to* Christianity as convert Christianity . . . to their own purposes.'[48] To the delight of the tribally inclined, several versions clamoured for their custom. The Wesleyans had arrived in 1822 and to the horror of the British Protestants, French Catholics would land at the Northern Hokianga in 1838.

The Protestant missionaries have been accorded a high place in the settler pantheon. In 1939 Lord Bledisloe even wrote to the CMS to 'exculpate the great Archdeacon Henry Williams — after the lapse of 100 years — explicitly and definitely' as a centenary gift to the dominion.[49] (Williams had been expelled from the Society in 1849 for what Bledisloe wordily termed his 'alleged deviation from the path of strict integrity in connection with purchases of land in the North Auckland Province of New Zealand'.) These missionaries played their part, of course, but equally if not more important were those less obsessive scribblers, journal keepers

Missionary propaganda. 'The Power of God's Word' is a plate from an 1856 book and purports to show the Williams brothers, Henry and William, calming hostile Maori with words from the Bible. In reality missionary peacemaking was limited.

and public commentators, the shagroon (early) settlers and the whaler/traders of Old New Zealand who had lived more or less on terms with Maori New Zealand.

Maori had spoken of 'our Pakeha' and had competed to obtain trophy Europeans who would attract ships, muskets and other trade goods. 'Traders, ship-captains, labourers, employers of labour, these were to be honoured, cherished, caressed, protected and plucked,' Frederick Manning wrote, 'plucked judiciously . . . so that the feathers might grow again.'[50] At the whaling stations, owners and managers married women of high status, while workers married women of lesser rank. In doing so, they were marrying into the local real estate, offering technical and business advice to the iwi or hapu and sometimes even military assistance. Edward Markham, a Pakeha Maori of Old New Zealand said, 'it is not safe to live in the country without a chief's daughter as protection'.[51] John Howell, who ran the Jacobs River (Aparima River) station with nearly 60 Europeans and 200 Maori, learned the hard way. Ngati Mamoe treated his refusal to take a wife as an insult. 'After an altercation he married Kohikohi, daughter of Horomona Patu, of Centre Island; she brought him a dowry of a large area of land between the Waimatuku Stream and Jacobs River.'[52]

Pakeha Maori were the first Europeans to settle permanently among Maori and to adopt most if not all of their customs. Frederick Maning painted himself centre stage in Old New Zealand in the much-reprinted book of that name. They were a diverse crew. Some set down deep roots, founding enduring dynasties (though not without the odd glitch). In 1823 Danish mariner and whaler Phillip Tapsell was married by missionary Thomas Kendall to Maria Ringa, who decamped the same day. The knot tied by Marsden seven years later to Karuhi, sister of Nga Puhi chief Wharepoaka, proved more enduring. At the invitation of Te Arawa chiefs of Rotorua, Tapsell settled at Maketu later that year. After the death of Karuhi, he took as his wife Hine-i-turama (Hineaturama) Ngatiki, a high-ranking woman of Ngati Whakaue of Te Arawa.

Villains made better copy. Take Charlotte Badger, the corpulent convict who crashed heavily onto the stage of history in 1806 when she and fellow lag Catherine Hagerty helped pull off a successful mutiny on the *Venus* off Tasmania. If the raciest account is believed, this pistol-packing mama dressed in male clothing, flogged the captain and raided another ship to seize supplies and weapons. Months later the other mutineers set down the women, their partners and Charlotte's child at Rangihoua Bay. There Charlotte lived with a Nga Puhi chief as the first wahine Pakeha Maori, disappearing from the record only after twice turning down offers of rescue. The good ship *Venus* went on down the coast, trailing trouble in its wake, kidnapping two Nga Puhi women and selling them to southern chiefs who subsequently ate them. Later the ship came to grief and its crew also ended up in the pot.

Early 20th-century historian James Cowan immortalised the liar and deserter, Kimble Bent, who fought with Maori during the 1860s. A shadier, shadowier figure was John 'Jacky' Marmon. The *Dictionary of New Zealand Biography* lists him under the categories 'sailor, convict, Pakeha-Maori, interpreter, shopkeeper, sawyer, carpenter, soldier' only, one suspects, because the editors lacked categories for 'braggart, liar and knave', characteristics he played up in disreputable old age as he peddled his Old New Zealand tales to northern papers. Fact and fiction collide messily in Marmon's life. As the son of Sydney Irish, he already had two strikes against him in the eyes of the Hokianga Wesleyan missionaries who described him as 'the terror of the river'.[53] Convicted of theft, he deserted and settled there in 1823, where he married Ihipera (Isabella), daughter of Hone Kingi Raumati, though that did not stop him from having affairs with other Maori women. He became fluent in Maori and made himself into a kind of Pakeha tohunga. 'Very little art is required to dupe a Maori in matters connected with his religion,'

ABOVE: Danish Pakeha Maori Phillip Tapsell crossed several cultural boundaries. Born as Hans Homman Jensen Falk, he changed his name to Phillip Tapsell and posed as a Manxman to get to sea. He was a sailor, whaler and trader. Like many he sold guns but he also acted as a local peacemaker. He is photographed with his daughter Kataraina. Steffano Webb Collection, Alexander Turnbull Library, G-8956-1/1

RIGHT: Maori adopted European-style boats and houses. These early photos may have been taken at The Neck, Stewart Island in the 1860s. The cottages are early-style European houses, and like their settler counterparts are firetraps with their weatherboards, wooden chimneys and thatched roofs. Richard Taylor Album, Alexander Turnbull Library, E-296-q-154-2

the old villain later crowed.[54] He also sold grog, sheltered runaways and opposed the Treaty of Waitangi. Many accounts mention his involvement in Maori warfare and his delight in cannibalism. *Dictionary* writer Roger Wigglesworth paints a far less lurid picture but concedes that his 'criminal record, his close association with the Maori, his bellicose temperament and the widespread belief that he had been a cannibal' meant that this short, ruddy-faced man with a penchant for top hats 'was the bogeyman with whom errant Hokianga children were threatened'.[55]

But most Pakeha Maori were not bogeymen and some clerics even got on well with them. Bishop Selwyn, a champion swimmer and oarsman in his youth, was so at home in New Zealand seas that one sailor rashly admitted that 'to see the Bishop handle a boat was almost enough to make a man a Christian'.[56] Selwyn, the physical embodiment of muscular Christianity, felt that 'the whalefishers impart a considerable amount of civilisation to the natives', and 'praised the men's love for their children, the half-caste, bilingual youngsters who daily bridged the cultural divide'.[57] It is doubtful that many of those stations ever paid their way for long, so when whaling declined, their Maori wives followed the retired whalers to small 'shagroon' colonies scattered about the coast, where the men took up boatbuilding, fishing, and subsistence farming. These were settlements such as James Spencer's Bluff, Southland, bought from Maori in 1824, where he established a fishery and trading store, grew wheat, ran cattle and pigs and employed 21 Maori and Europeans who lived in six cottages. 'Since that date there has been a population living on the site in European fashion.'[58] Long before the British Colonial Office relaxed its opposition to formal colonisation, and before Wakefield's hordes swept in, (predominantly European) men and (mainly Maori) women such as these were first-footing in the nation-building business.

Mr Nobody's flag and declaration

As the 1830s unfolded, a string of unpleasant events encouraged even those Britons philosophically opposed to colonisation to reconsider. The endemic warfare was disturbing enough; but foreigners' participation in the shrunken heads trade, or — like Captain Stewart of the brig *Elizabeth* — taking sides in intertribal warfare, shook policymakers just as badly. Never mind that many 'outrages' were exaggerated or that they were remarkably rare; considering the frequency of contact between Maori and foreigners, they made bad news, and that coloured thinking.

The CMS still opposed colonisation. But lawlessness and — as anti-papist Francophobes almost to a man — the fear of French Catholicism may have encouraged them to extend a tentative feeler towards Mother Britain. In September 1831 rumours of French annexation plans had 13 northern chiefs 'under an unknown degree of missionary influence' petition King William IV to be their friend and to guard their land against 'the tribe of Marion', as Maori had called the French since encountering Marion du Fresne.[59]

The Colonial Office was still dominated by the humanitarians, led by Under-Secretary James Stephen, who believed that full-scale colonisation would harm Maori.[60] So in 1831 when New South Wales Governor Sir Ralph Darling recommended appointing an official British Resident to prevent further *Elizabeth*-style incidents, Lord Goderich, Secretary of State for the Colonies, watered down even this modest proposal. Darling suggested an army officer supported by a small detachment of soldiers, but Goderich specified a civilian and scotched the troops. He also made New South Wales pay his salary and enact laws enabling it to punish crimes committed 'in Islands situated in the Southern or Pacific Ocean not being within His Majesty's dominions'.[61] Legal opinion quashed the idea

of legislating for a foreign country, so young James Busby landed at Waitangi in May 1833 as British Resident armed only with his wits.

Busby has had a poor deal from historians, who rate his viticultural expertise above his diplomatic skills. He was capable enough; but he made few close friends and he grew more argumentative and egotistical over time. Regardless of his personal qualities, he faced an impossible task. As Resident — a lowly post — he was a glorified race relations conciliator, mediator and gatherer of trade statistics. He had no authority, no budget and no clout beyond the support of a passing Royal Navy warship. Nor did he have friends in court. New South Wales' new Governor Sir Richard Bourke, a Whig, liked this young Tory about as much as he liked the drain on his treasury. Setting what would become a recurring theme in New Zealand public architecture, Bourke halved the size of the prefabricated house that Busby had had designed for him. So Busby went down in history as the 'man-of-war with-out guns'. As the Austrian Baron Karl von Hugel (an observer of events, and someone who, while critical of them, liked Busby) put it, 'he has no power over a ship's crew whose captain complains of their conduct, and so they regard him as Mr Nobody'.[62] That is how he looked to Bourke, who read Busby's increasingly whingeing reports with disdain.

But Busby did solve some disputes and he did his best to encourage the 'settled form of government' Bourke wanted. On 20 March 1834 he held a meeting of northern chiefs on his lawn at Waitangi. Like so many events then it had something to do with ships. Thomas Raine had been building them

Sydney newspapers lampooned 'Mr Borer Busby Junior' and the *Dictionary of New Zealand Biography* notes that an English visitor 'with shrewd insight, observed that Busby was simply not "Devil enough" to deal with a situation that called for a man of some "Nouse"'. He could be prickly, but a Resident's powers were strictly limited. R Read, Private Collection, Alexander Turnbull Library, Non-ATL-P-0065

at Hokianga for several years, so it came as a rude shock when Sydney Customs officers seized the *Sir George Murray* in 1830 for breaching British navigation laws by sailing without a flag or register. They gave her a temporary trading licence but Busby decided that a local flag and shipping register would reassure settlers and Maori that trade was safe, and might foster greater Maori political collaboration.

Sydney agreed and sent the flag. But it was insufficiently red (the colour of mana), so missionary and ex-naval officer Henry Williams sketched three designs, which Bourke had made up. In March 1834 Busby invited northern chiefs to choose one. Busby's dispatches spin-doctored this gathering with a veneer of dignity and importance that would have surprised von Hugel.[63] Busby allowed no debate. When asked to choose, the puzzled chiefs who 'had no notion what their war canoes or other craft had to do with that flag, or who was going to give them the flag which they needed, the cost of which they estimated at a dozen or more of their fattest pigs', fumbled the vote; the first three chose different flags, then most 'said they did not care which flag was chosen'.[64] After some prodding by one of Williams's Maori Christians, they selected (in a close vote) the St George Cross (thicker, accentuating the red) on a white background 'with a canton of dark blue, which contained a red cross fimbriated black, each quadrant of this smaller cross featuring a white eight-pointed star'.[65]

Scholars, who have recently assigned the incident more importance than did von Hugel, speculate that it owed something to the missionary flag. Certainly their St George cross would have been familiar. The stars may have represented the Southern Cross and the blue background may have represented the sea.[66] But any old seadog could just as well have suggested the White Ensign of Henry Williams's old service, to which the new flag bore a superficial resemblance. HMS *Alligator* fired a 21-gun salute to the 'Flag of the Independent Tribes of New Zealand' (which was then hauled down and packed away for shipment to Sydney for formal approval). Then the Europeans sat down to a fine lunch while the chiefs got a cauldron of 'children's porridge or flummery', stirred with a broom handle. The flag was gazetted in New South Wales on 19 August 1835, but a muddle gave it a white fimbriation instead of black and the stars became six-pointers. There was no pre-colonial New Zealand register (Busby issued certificates) but for the next few years Williams's flag fluttered in front of Busby's residency and elsewhere. It flew in the Bay of Islands for several years and at the tribal elections for King Potatau Te Wherowhero in the late 1850s, although we should note that Maori flew many flags; Binney records that 'Christian pa often adopted the blue or white ensign and added their own words, crosses and stars'.[67]

Ironically, the 'Maori flag', used sometimes as a symbol of protest in the 19th century, had its moment in the limelight in 1840 when William Wakefield gave Lieutenant-Governor Hobson the constitutional collywobbles by flying a slightly modified version at Port Nicholson. Even more ironically, that version of the 'flag of independence' (with six-pointed stars, and without a white edge to the cross) became familiar to generations of New Zealanders as the house flag of Shaw Savill & Co (later Shaw Savill & Albion), the shipping line that carried more colonisers here than any other.[68]

colonists rioted and departed, and the man who would be king found himself lord of a mere 325 ha of rural backwater. He later tuned pianos in Auckland. But simple jealousy may have had as much to do with the Declaration as de Thierry. In 1835 Thomas McDonnell had been appointed Honorary Additional British Resident. At the Hokianga he had done what Busby had failed to do in the Bay of Islands — ban liquor sales. In Governor Bourke's mind at least the Declaration 'appears to have been intended to subvert the local law [prohibition] passed at Hokianga' and to give the impression of dynamism.[70]

Thirty-four northern chiefs signed Busby's Wakaputanga o te Rangatiratanga o Nu Tirene, the Declaration of Independence of the United Tribes of New Zealand. The short handwritten document, later run off by the mission printery, asserted the independence of Nu Tirene (New Zealand) under the rule of

Sydney merchants Raine, Browne and Ramsey established a shipyard at 'Deptford Dock Yard' at Horeke on the Hokianga, where they built several ships and traded in timber and flax. Augustus Earle's 1827 watercolour captures the brig *New Zealander* in frame.

On 28 October 1835, a day and a half after getting a letter from an eccentric Frenchman, Busby called northern chiefs together again to sign a Declaration of Independence 'into which Maori had had no input'.[69] The Frenchman was the former gaolbird 'Baron' Charles Philippe de Thierry. As colourful as his name and about as genuine as his self-given title, de Thierry declared that he would make himself sovereign in chief of a colony in New Zealand. That was par for de Thierry's wobbly course. Ten years earlier he had tried to persuade the Dutch to make him viceroy of New Zealand, and he had gone on to appoint himself king of Nuka Hiva in the Marquesas. The bogus baron later fetched up in the Hokianga in mid 1837 with 60 settlers recruited in Sydney, but the land purchased for him by Thomas Kendall was disputed, his

the 'United Tribes of New Zealand'. Its second article — there were just four — put 'all sovereign power and authority within the territories of the united tribes of New Zealand . . . entirely and exclusively in the hereditary chiefs and heads of tribes in their collective capacity', power only being delegated by them to people 'appointed by them in Congress assembled'. The hereditary chiefs and heads of tribes agreed to meet 'in Congress' at Waitangi each autumn to frame laws. They thanked the King of England [sic] for acknowledging their flag, promised to treat Britons fairly and sought protection from any attempts upon their independence. Bourke, put out by Busby's precipitate action, saw some merit in the Declaration, although he would have preferred not to read the second clause.

THE FLAG OF THE UNITED TRIBES

The 'Flag of the United Tribes of New Zealand', chosen in 1834 as a flag of convenience for the protection of European-owned New Zealand trading vessels, has acquired more complex symbolism over time, often being flown as a flag of protest or of cultural assertiveness. Edward Markham's watercolour (below) summarises the reason for its existence, with two musket-toting Maori looking out over a schooner. The sketch (top right) was sent by New South Wales Governor Bourke to King William IV for formal approval. The colour plate (lower right) was published in an Admiralty book of flags in 1845.

National Flag

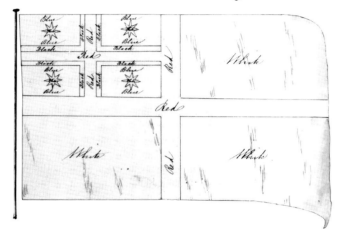

Selected by the assembled Chiefs of New Zealand in the presence of George R Lambert Esqre Captain of His Majesty's Ship Alligator and James Busby Esqre British Res Wyatanga, Bay of Islands, 20th of March 1835.

Busby to Governor, 20 March 1834 CO 209/1, Australian Joint Copying Project, Public Record Office, London, courtesy of Archives New Zealand. The date, 1835 in the original, should have read 1834.

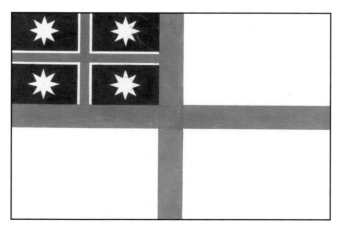

James Laurenson Collection, Alexander Turnbull Library, MS-Papers-0009-09/01

The Secretary of State for the Colonies, Lord Glenelg, more positive than his officials, advised the King to recognise the new polity as far — note the reservation — 'as may be consistent with a due regard to the just rights of others and to the interests of His Majesty's subjects'.[71] The reply was given apparently without much thought for the legal consequences, creating the problem that 'if Britain chose to intervene formally, the independent status of the country would have to be either qualified or nullified'.[72] But, as the *Alligator*'s punitive expedition showed, out here the Royal Navy effectively called the shots, not scraps of paper, for 'Europe could now plant itself anywhere on the surface of the globe within reach of naval cannon'.[73]

Busby went on collecting signatures. He had 52, almost exclusively northern chiefs, by 1839 on what he pompously called his 'Magna Charta of New Zealand'. But to what effect?[74] As historian Claudia Orange observed, 'no one knew better than Busby that the Declaration was no substitute for effective government'. In a fragmented, war-weary land where tiny hapu, as often as iwi, claimed most peoples' loyalties, 'there was no indigenous political structure upon which to base a united congress'.[75] The weakness of the Maori polity was acknowledged in the Declaration's third clause, which 'cordially invite[d] the Southern tribes to lay aside their private animosities and to consult the safety and welfare of our common country, by joining the Confederation of the United Tribes'. In other words, 'the Declaration represented something more like a regional goodwill agreement rather than a national document of truly constitutional significance'.[76] No congress ever sat beside Busby's white house, even though he ordered timber for its assembly building.

By then British politicians had given up on an independent New Zealand. An earlier New Zealand Company had sent out two ships in 1826, but like de Thierry's expedition, it added little to the slow build-up of foreigners in New Zealand. Probably only about 2000 were living here by the end of the decade, most more or less integrated into the Maori world and living more peacefully and lawfully than later yarn spinners would have us believe. But that was about to change. As the 1830s drew to a close joint stock companies in Britain and France were chartering ships to plant substantial colonies, mini neo-Europes, in New Zealand where Sydney speculators claimed to have bought mind-boggling amounts of land from Maori. So far hapu and iwi had been able to assimilate trophy Europeans into te ao Maori, but could they cope with the long white crowd headed for the land of the long white cloud? Even the most hands-off missionaries and Colonial Office bureaucrats now feared they could not. Reluctantly, in late 1837 British parliamentarians came around to the idea that only annexation could prevent chaos and bloodshed. The flag would follow trade.

Chapter 4

The landing of Lieutenant-Governor Hobson at Waitangi on 5 February 1840, a brilliant fine day. Outside Busby's grounds, stalls sold refreshments: pork, cold roast meat, pies and baskets of bread, and stout, ale, brandy and rum. Provisions were ready for Maori too — a half tonne of flour, five tonnes of potatoes, 30 pigs and other goods. Ships had all their flags flying. It was a gala occasion for the Bay of Islands.

M Clayton, Auckland Art Gallery, Toi o Tamaki

Flags and Nations
1839–1852

Strong strands of idealism were embedded in the treaty-making and events of 1840. Most of the groups involved in New Zealand's annexation and settlement had dreams that the new colony would exhibit relationships of a new kind between settlers and indigenous peoples. The Treaty of Waitangi embraced this dream, but the Treaty parties had different expectations of what the partnership and sharing of power on the ground would be. Immigrants to New Zealand also had aims and dreams — of economic security through land and trade — and these soon gave rise to competition with Maori.

The Wakefield settlements were based on 'systematic colonisation' principles. But when applied to the realities of the colonial frontier, these proved faulty. Maori in the Cook Strait settlements were forced to adjust. Their hopes of securing the benefits of a settlement that they could control were rapidly overwhelmed by the influx of large numbers of settlers, whose interests soon dominated. Wakefield settlers were at the forefront of the push for independence through self-governing institutions, and these were granted in the 1852 constitution.

Auckland, meanwhile, was demonstrating the inter-dependence of Maori and Pakeha – something of the 1840 partnership ideal. It also showed that unplanned settlement could grow as well as or better than planned settlement. A frontier capital and garrison town, Auckland was never at risk during the Northern War of 1845 to 1846. But its Maori character and its capital status would be lost in the 1860s wars.

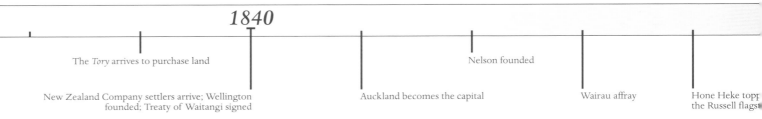

1840

The *Tory* arrives to purchase land

Nelson founded

New Zealand Company settlers arrive; Wellington founded; Treaty of Waitangi signed

Auckland becomes the capital

Wairau affray

Hone Heke topp the Russell flags

Conflicting ideas on colonisation

Complex issues of empire were being debated in Britain in the 1830s. How should new areas be colonised? And how could colonisers ensure that indigenous peoples were treated justly? Could the needs of the two ever be reconciled? In 1838 the frontiers of the British Empire were about to expand to absorb New Zealand. Some saw it as a test case that might supply possible answers, although opinions on the likely outcome were not universally optimistic that it would benefit Maori. Much depended on the goals of those involved in New Zealand's future, and among the key players in the colonisation process those goals varied.

Two of London's influential actors were colonising entrepreneur Edward Gibbon Wakefield and James Stephen, permanent head of the Colonial Office. On the New Zealand frontier two key groups were involved — British missionaries, supported by their London metropolitan headquarters, and Maori.

Wakefield began to develop his theories on colonisation in the 1820s. He offered a solution to what he argued was an excess of labour and capital in Britain. His scheme would make emigration an attractive investment, especially to cultured classes. He planned 'civilised' colonisation — close-settled farming communities able to afford the infrastructure of schools, churches and halls. A privileged, land-owning class would be served by an ample supply of carefully selected labourers, who might eventually own land too. Profit for the scheme's organisers would come from land bought cheaply from the Maori and sold at a 'sufficient' price to the first purchasers. The profits would also cover the fares of the

A youthful Edward Gibbon Wakefield, known as EGW, in 1823. He conceived his colonisation theories in America and nurtured them during a three-year gaol sentence for abducting a 15-year-old schoolgirl heiress, Ellen Turner, in 1826. His theories were applied unsuccessfully to a South Australian experiment in 1834. New Zealand provided the perfect place to trial his scheme again. A Wivell, Alexander Turnbull Library, A-042-023

labourers. And so the outcome would be a settlement along the lines of an idyllic English farming community, and at the same time a tidy return for investors.[1] A New Zealand Association formed in 1836 was converted into the New Zealand Company in 1838. Wakefield now courted the British authorities to win support for his colonisation scheme. He promoted the notion of incorporating Maori chiefs into his plan. They would be encouraged to become brown, landed gentlemen and ultimately play their part in the government of a mixed, class-structured community. Reserves put aside from purchased land would cover the needs of chiefs and their people and would increase in value beside European-owned sections. Since they were scattered among Pakeha, such reserves were not likely to appeal to Maori; but the intention was to influence government attitudes, not please Maori.

Wakefield borrowed his ideas on Maori from theories then being circulated by humanitarian lobbyists in Britain. The record of dealings with native peoples in British colonies was given publicity in an 1837 parliamentary report, which revealed that ill-treatment and disease were often the norm and led to extermination of native races. The Aborigines Protection Society had documented the grisly tale of British imperial expansion and its impact on indigenous peoples. Founded in 1836, the society was active in raising public consciousness. In its aim to secure for all men 'an equality of natural rights', the society theorised that colonisation would help civilise the Maori through 'political amalgamation'. Maori and British would live together peacefully in

Northern War	Otago founded	Canterbury founded	New Zealand Constitution Act

a single political community, shaped to a class structure similar to that of Britain. In New Zealand it would not evolve in quite that way; but the ideal of amalgamation of Maori and Pakeha, faulty as it was, was nonetheless embedded in the country's early colonisation theories, and its currents would continue to run strongly throughout New Zealand's history after 1840.[2]

Theories, debates and plans on colonisation were the order of the day at the Colonial Office. Its cautious permanent head, James Stephen, strongly evangelical and influenced by humanitarian ideals, hoped that settlement in New Zealand — and he thought it ultimately inevitable — might be different from elsewhere in the Empire. The indigenous race would receive fair and just consideration. British relations with the Maori would establish a new pattern.

Stephen was associated with the London-based leaders of the Church Missionary Society (CMS) who, like the Wesleyan Missionary Society (WMS), opposed colonisation and endeavoured to influence official policy in the 1830s. Maori acceptance of Christianity was gaining momentum in the mid 1830s after several decades of barren missionary labour. Colonisation could jeopardise this and greatly weaken missionary influence. The missionaries also feared the violence that often erupted when uncontrolled settlers engaged with indigenous races. And they knew that Maori would not countenance extensive or forceful intrusion. By the end of the 1830s, however, the CMS and WMS and their New Zealand missionaries reluctantly accepted that British annexation had to come. The rule of British law was preferable to a likely chaotic situation with Wakefield settlers arriving.

Annexation by Britain was also desirable in order to shut out the French. Fears of French intrusion had earlier been stirred by visiting French warships and by the adventurer de Thierry. By the mid 1830s increasing numbers of French whalers were using New Zealand harbours. A French settlement scheme, being planned in 1839, would follow at Akaroa in 1840. French interest in New Zealand was one of several factors assessed by the Colonial Office in 1839, but historians differ in the weight they give it in British decision-making.

By the late 1830s Maori felt the changes in their society brought about by the growing intrusion of European and mission influence. Since 1769 there had been 70 years of Maori–

The Colonial Office, at 14 Downing Street, close to the present British Prime Minister's residence. The Colonial Office was the hub of the Empire, where decisions were taken that determined the lives of millions on British colonial frontiers. The building was demolished in 1876.

James Stephen, Permanent Under-Secretary at the Colonial Office from 1836 to 1847. His antagonism to Edward Gibbon Wakefield and his associates coloured Colonial Office thinking in the years before 1840 as the Office struggled with the Wakefield clique's settlement schemes. Wakefield's supporters reciprocated that dislike, calling Stephen 'Mr Mother Country' or 'Mr Over Secretary'.

Alexander Turnbull Library, F-104159-½

Alexander Turnbull Library, F-9032-¼

EMIGRATION
TO
NEW ZEALAND

Important to Farmers and small Capitalists.

The Court of Directors of the *New Zealand Company* having received numerous applications for passages from persons of the above description, and being desirous of facilitating the emigration to *New Zealand* of persons of the industrious classes, who do not fall within the regulations entitling them to a *Free Passage*, and also small Capitalists to whom the costly Accommodation usually provided for Cabin passages would be unsuitable, *Notice is hereby given*, that Cabin Passages to ... and NELSON may be obtained in the splendid new Ship,

PHŒBE,
Burthen 500 Tons, lying in the West India Docks,

Chartered by the Company to Sail from the PORT OF LONDON positively on the 15th of November next, on the following terms:—

The price of a Chief-Cabin Passage, with a liberal dietary, will be 50 guineas for a married couple, & 30 Guineas for a single adult person: and that of a Fore-Cabin Passage will be £20 per adult. The prices for children will be in the proportions fixed by the Passengers' Act, or as the Directors may fix in the case of large families.

Families who may desire it, may have extra space for their Accommodation upon payment of a proportionate additional Sum. One Ton Freight will be allowed to Chief Cabin and Half a Ton to Fore-cabin Passengers, FREE OF CHARGE; EXTRA FREIGHT will be allowed by the Directors in their discretion, at the rate of 45s. per Ton measurement, and 25s. per Ton dead weight.

The Company will appoint an experienced Surgeon, and will provide Medicines and Medical Comforts.

Applications for Passage or Freight, to be addressed to the Secretary of the New Zealand Company, *Broad Street Buildings;* or to J. STAYNER, SHIP & INSURANCE BROKER, 110, *Fenchurch Street, London*, on or before SATURDAY, 15th OCTOBER next.

A Deposit of £10 will be required for every Chief-Cabin Passage, and of £5 for every Fore-Cabin Passage, which must be paid to the Company, or to J. STAYNER, on or before the 15th October, and the remainder of the Passage-Monies previous to Embarkation.

By Order of the Court,

New Zealand House, Broad Street Buildings,
September 14th, 1842.

JOHN WARD, Sec.

A. ECCLES, Printer, 101, Fenchurch Street

Emigration to New Zealand was popularised by New Zealand Company propaganda produced by well-organised spin doctors. Their base was at the grandiosely named New Zealand House in London, and their agents were located in key provincial towns. By 1842 they were well organised, their advertisements appealing to farmers and small capitalists, offering 'a liberal dietary', plenty of baggage space and medical comforts. This type of advertising, aimed at a better class of emigrant, was typical of their operations. Pictorial Collection, Hocken Library, University of Otago

European contact. Maori had travelled out of the country as crew on whaling ships. Pakeha had been adopted into tribes. New knowledge, skills and trade had been adapted and widely adopted by Maori communities, though with great variation from one area to another. In the 1830s literacy (in Maori) was eagerly sought after and there was wide experimentation with new mannerisms and in lifestyle, most notably in clothing, in housing, and in a move towards a money economy. Adoption of new crops and of boats to replace waka were among the indicators of change.

But change came at a price. In the 1820s tribal warfare had spun almost out of control, until a balance of armaments and a degree of exhaustion had blown the whistle in the 1830s. These factors, coupled with violence caused by lawless frontier riffraff, laid some basis for Maori acceptance of a British intervention that might bring peace and a new order. But Maori and European alike soon summed up the appointment of James Busby as British Resident in 1833 as nothing more than a stopgap measure that relied on the influence of respectable settlers and the missionaries. And they, too, became increasingly fed up with the Busby appointment. By the late 1830s, this holding operation seemed less viable to the Colonial Office. Officials held a clutch of appeals from missionaries and traders, and disturbing reports of intertribal fighting. A half-year journey lay between dispatch of a report from New Zealand and its arrival at the Colonial Office, so there was no way to check such information. Officials reluctantly accepted that their worst fears of inevitable frontier deterioration were true. Yet like all appeals, some had substance, others were exaggerated.

Officials were also pondering over the New Zealand Company plans for sending out settlers. Having failed to secure government support and desperate to secure land before further British intervention, it decided to act. In May 1839 its ship *Tory* left England with agents on board, charged with buying land for settlement at Port Nicholson (Wellington) and elsewhere.

The first of several shiploads of emigrants left in September, with no assurance that land had actually been purchased, but with high hopes of forming the ideal settler colony on Wakefield's systematic principles.

The British government, too, had come to a decision on New Zealand but it was slow to act. Early in 1839 Captain William Hobson RN accepted the appointment of consul to an independent New Zealand. He faced a challenge he had probably not expected, nor was well prepared for. In 1837 he had carried out an inspection visit to New Zealand, calling at only a few coastal spots. He had reported to his superiors in terms he knew would meet their inclination to defer action — he advised that a few locations be acquired and developed as enclaves of British settlement in a Maori New Zealand. In India such colonies were called 'factories'. His own opinion was that Britain should acquire sovereignty over the whole country. Busby felt the same and was not slow to suggest this to the Colonial Office.[3]

Through 1839 Hobson had discussions with officials. Colonial Office debates on what should be done in New Zealand swung back and forth for about eight months. A number of factors had to be considered. Officials sought legal opinions about the international status of New Zealand. The country did not shape up in official estimation as a fully fledged nation state because it had no central government. Britain had nonetheless recognised New Zealand as independent in several parliamentary acts in the 1820s. Busby's initiatives had also given status to the country's independence — in the selection of a flag chosen by chiefs in 1834 at Waitangi, and the Declaration of Independence first signed there in 1835 by the 'United Tribes' of New Zealand and accepted by Britain. It was obviously desirable to have this sovereign independence transferred formally to Britain by treaty.

Officials were aware that other nations would be interested in the outcome of events. Large French and American whaling fleets were working New Zealand waters and using its harbours.

William Hobson had served in the Royal Navy for many years, operating in pirate-infested and disease-ridden Caribbean waters. Conscientious and cautious, in an 1837 report on New Zealand he had suggested only limited intervention, which was all he believed acceptable to the Colonial Office at that time. But to his wife Liz he confided his convictions that Britain should acquire sovereignty to protect investment, control settlers and keep other nations out. He believed Maori to be in decline through diseases. MA Musgrove, Rex Nan Kivell Collection, National Library of Australia, NK5277

They could be resentful and perhaps protest if Britain seized the country without Maori consent. An American consul, James Clendon, was appointed in 1839.

Officials were also keenly aware that peaceful settlement depended on securing Maori agreement to British administration. But how to get that agreement was the issue. They were unsure of Maori understanding of events. Would Maori leaders think that by selling land they had lost the sovereignty over it? Would they understand what was meant if they were asked to 'cede sovereignty' over the whole country by signing a 'treaty'? There were no easy answers. For a while officials talked about securing a localised surrender of power and authority, with Maori rights to the rest of the country guaranteed and the national flag respected. But after his 1837 visit, Hobson was convinced that this would not be adequate; Britain should try to get sovereignty over the whole country.

When Hobson sailed for New Zealand in August 1839, with his wife Eliza and their children, he held authority to make a treaty for sovereignty over either all or part of the country. His instructions from Lord Normanby, the Secretary of State for Colonies, told him to get the 'free and intelligent consent' of chiefs to the treaty and to deal with them 'openly'.[4] They also explained why Britain had decided to make a move in New Zealand — not because of the small settler group of only 2000 people, but to control the thousands of expected emigrants and to protect the rights of Maori. The instructions then briefly outlined the business of setting up a colony. Frugality was to be the byword; the expenses of the new administration would be covered from revenue raised in the colony. Buying land cheaply from Maori and selling it at a profit would be the major source of revenue.

Normanby's instructions revealed an important shift in the government's attitude to New Zealand during 1839. When Colonial Office officials had first thought about plans for a British colony in New Zealand, it was for a Maori New Zealand in which settlers would somehow be accommodated. But, by the time Hobson got his instructions, the plan was for a settler New Zealand in which Maori would have a special 'protected' position.

The shift occurred as settlement outside of British control became a certainty and the Colonial Office determined on action to protect Maori. But historian Peter Adams discerned the weakness of the Maori position and its implications for the future: 'Underlying the humanitarian idealism and the promise of impartial and equal protection lay fundamental attitudes of cultural and racial superiority.'[5] Equal treatment would ultimately depend on the Maori becoming brown Englishmen and women, and participation would mean amalgamation and the submergence of Maori in a European world.

The making of the Treaty of Waitangi

Hobson's ship, HMS *Herald*, dropped anchor off Kororareka on Wednesday 29 January 1840. A spell in Sydney had prepared him for the tasks ahead. He was the sworn-in lieutenant-governor of any territory gained, brought with him a motley assortment of officials (the dregs of Governor Gipps's table, quipped a critic), and was ready with a proclamation that title to land would be valid only if bought from or approved by the Crown. A treaty had no doubt been on the Gipps–Hobson meeting agenda, but Hobson sailed into the Bay of Islands without one.[6]

The anxious-to-please Busby hurried on board. His offer to organise a meeting of chiefs at Waitangi the following Wednesday was accepted and he scurried away to send out invitations. Meanwhile, Hobson began to write out a treaty with the help of his staff and with missionary advice. Busby declared the notes inadequate and on 3 February provided a draft treaty that included three articles. It incorporated the points that Britain wanted: that the chiefs would give up

Henry Williams (1792–1867), senior missionary and key translator and negotiator of the Treaty, told the chiefs at Waitangi to listen carefully. He said the missionaries fully approved of the Treaty and that it was 'an act of love' towards Maori on the part of the Queen. The Treaty would be like a fortress against any foreign power (the French) that might have designs on the country.
JI McDonald, Alexander Turnbull Library, NON-ATL-P-0020

'sovereignty'; and that Britain would take complete control over all transactions in land, both buying it from the Maori people and selling it to settlers. It offered the Maori 'protection' and 'all the rights and privileges of British subjects'. It also confirmed and guaranteed Maori possession (individually and collectively) of their lands, forests, fisheries and other properties as long as they wanted to retain them. In Busby's opinion this promise was essential to get Maori agreement.

Hobson then asked Henry Williams to translate the treaty into Maori which the missionary did, with his 21-year-old son Edward, on the evening of 4 February. It had to be a rushed job; chiefs were already arriving for the great meeting next day.

But one certainty is that by 1840 Williams had decided to do his best to get Maori agreement and the translation could be key to that. The result was not an exact mirror of the English, and it was ambiguous on crucial points. But it was ready for the meeting on 5 February.

That day dawned fine and warm and cicadas shrilled noisily. From early morning the Bay of Islands came alive with waka heading for Waitangi. Settlers' boats joined the stream; traders, missionaries and their wives turned out in Sunday best dress. Dominating the Waitangi lawn was an enormous marquee made of sails and decorated with flags. New South Wales mounted police paraded in their scarlet uniforms. Maori, some

These three chiefs were lively speakers at the Waitangi meeting of 5 February 1840. They are (from left), Hakiro, Waka Nene and Rewa. Nene chided other chiefs at the meeting for telling Hobson to go away and pressed him to stay.

The missionary realised he held a key role, essential to the success of Hobson's mission. Like Busby, he knew that if the treaty took away too much power from chiefs there was little chance of getting their agreement. Did he set out to mask the treaty's real intention — the establishment of British sovereignty and a Crown colony? Or did he believe that in the humanitarian climate of 1840 there was a fair chance of striking a balance between government authority (kawanatanga), and Maori authority (te tino rangatiratanga)? And did Hobson confide in Williams honestly about his official instructions, which were usually kept private? There are no sure answers.

with guns, sat smoking and talking while Europeans strolled up and down. There was a buzz of excitement among the crowd when Hobson arrived about 9 a.m. Formalities finished, Hobson moved to the marquee with the French Catholic bishop JBF Pompallier hot on his heels. Purple-robed and sporting his glittering crucifix and ruby ring, the bishop upstaged the drab, black-clad English missionaries and seized a prime seat in the marquee. On a raised platform at one end Hobson sat down at a table covered with the Union Jack. Others took up positions wherever they could. Over 200 Maori rapidly filled up the sitting room in the main space, with several hundred more outside,

SIGNING THE TREATY

Hobson was surprised when summoned ashore late in the morning of 6 February. He arrived alone and in plain clothes, but for his plumed hat. Several hundred Maori were waiting, but only Busby, a few missionaries and a dozen Europeans had turned up, including Pompallier. Nervous and uneasy, Hobson kept repeating that it was not a 'regular public meeting', he would take only signatures and allow no discussion. But before anyone could sign, Pompallier gained Hobson's agreement to a public guarantee that there would be freedom of religion. Infuriated by this Catholic triumph and failing to dissuade Hobson, Williams had to translate the promise. He linked his favoured Anglican and Wesleyan churches, and then the two he held in contempt, Maori custom (ritenga) and the Catholics. The guarantee was not written into the Treaty but is sometimes referred to as the fourth article.

As a satisfied Pompallier left, Colenso seized the opportunity to put a question no one else dared to ask: Did Hobson think the chiefs really understood the Treaty? It had not been explained adequately, and if Maori later felt cheated, they would hold the missionaries respons-ible. An exasperated Hobson impatiently pointed out that the chiefs had heard Williams read the Treaty in Maori. It was the missionaries' job to keep their converts 'peaceable enough'; for the rest 'we must do the best we can with them'.[7] And so the signing began, on a clean copy produced overnight by missionary Richard Taylor.

Busby called up the chiefs by name, starting with Hone Heke. Each signing was followed by a handshake and greeting from Hobson: 'He iwi tahi tatou.' ('We are [now] one people.') The words had weight, especially for Christian chiefs; peace would unite tribes, and under the Treaty Maori and British would be linked, as subjects of the Queen and under the one God.

LEFT: This is all that remains of the Treaty copy signed at first at Waitangi and then elsewhere in the north and at Auckland. Chewed by rats and stained by water, it was finally rescued and preserved.

Department of Internal Affairs/Archives New Zealand

RIGHT: Catholic Bishop Pompallier stood out with his purple robes and his elaborate crucifix. Like most such imaginative reconstructions, this illustration incorrectly depicts Hobson in his full uniform.

Over 40 Maori leaders put their name or moko on the Maori Treaty that day.[8] Three thundering cheers closed this second meeting, and Colenso was left to distribute gifts: two blankets and some tobacco to each person signing. In Hobson's report he noted that 26 of the chiefs who signed had also signed the 1835 Declaration of Independence. That, he wrote, 'must be deemed a full and clear recognition of the sovereign rights of Her Majesty over the northern parts of this island'.[9] If he knew that the English and Maori Treaties were different, he was not going to admit it. Two days later the *Herald* ran up all her flags and fired a 21-gun salute in honour of the new British colony of New Zealand.

More Treaty meetings were soon set up, at Waimate, and at Mangungu on the Hokianga Harbour, where a thousand Maori gathered. Experienced traders and seasoned travellers to Australia, Hokianga Maori were deeply suspicious of British motives, sceptical about any sharing of power and critical of the British treating Aborigines 'like dogs'. But after

a day's debate, and reassured that they were a 'special' people, signing began around six in the evening. Hobson now had 200 copies of the Maori Treaty printed before heading south to the Hauraki Gulf. Then a combination of exhaustion, disagreements with the *Herald*'s captain, the peppery Joseph Nias, and a howling north-easterly gale brought on a stroke. Hobson retreated north to recuperate and responsibility for the Treaty work was delegated.

Over the next six months, at least nine copies of the Treaty were taken around New Zealand for signing.[10] The negotiators were missionaries, an army captain, Hobson's officials, and a trader. Some areas missed out; many gave the Treaty a mixed reception and some chiefs refused to sign. When Hobson finally held the nine copies that came back to him, he was able to report that over 500 chiefs, including around a dozen women, had given their agreement. For Hobson this represented a mission achieved. For Maori, it was the beginning of the end of their power, though this was not at all apparent at first.

Pompallier Diocesan Centre, Auckland

The Treaty trail

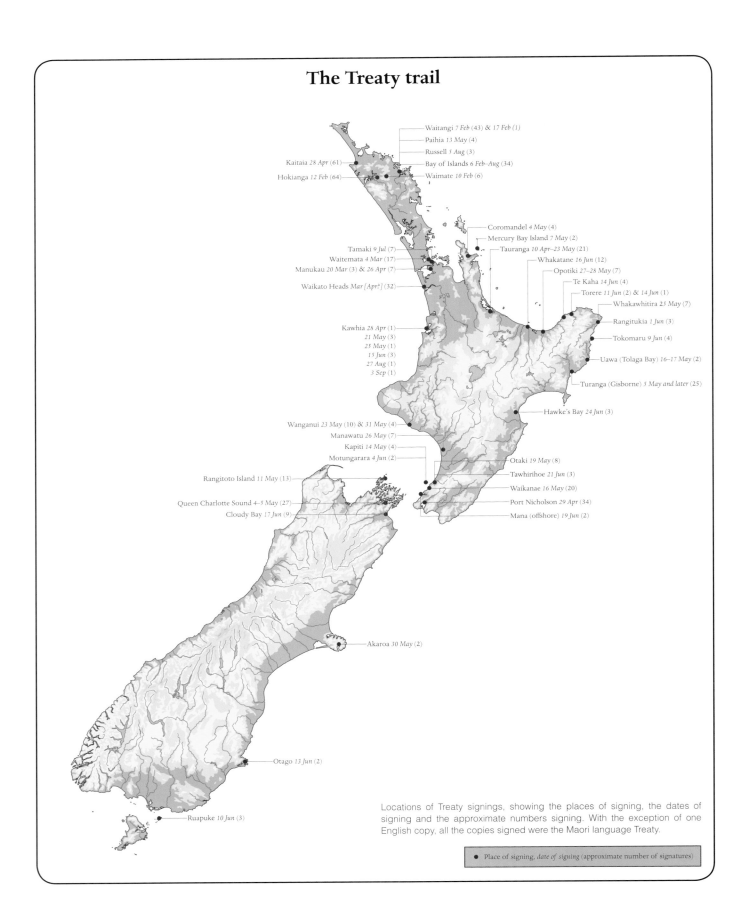

Waitangi *7 Feb* (43) & *17 Feb* (1)
Paihia *13 May* (4)
Russell *5 Aug* (3)
Bay of Islands *6 Feb–Aug* (34)
Kaitaia *28 Apr* (61)
Hokianga *12 Feb* (64)
Waimate *10 Feb* (6)

Coromandel *4 May* (4)
Mercury Bay Island *7 May* (2)
Tamaki *9 Jul* (7)
Tauranga *10 Apr–23 May* (21)
Waitemata *4 Mar* (17)
Whakatane *16 Jun* (12)
Manukau *20 Mar* (3) & *26 Apr* (7)
Opotiki *27–28 May* (7)
Te Kaha *14 Jun* (4)
Waikato Heads *Mar [Apr?]* (32)
Torere *11 Jun* (2) & *14 Jun* (1)
Whakawhitira *25 May* (7)
Kawhia *28 Apr* (1)
Rangitukia *1 Jun* (3)
21 May (3)
Tokomaru *9 Jun* (4)
25 May (1)
15 Jun (3)
Uawa (Tolaga Bay) *16–17 May* (2)
27 Aug (1)
3 Sep (1)
Turanga (Gisborne) *5 May and later* (25)

Hawke's Bay *24 Jun* (3)

Wanganui *23 May* (10) & *31 May* (4)
Manawatu *26 May* (7)
Kapiti *14 May* (4)
Motungarara *4 Jun* (2)
Otaki *19 May* (8)
Rangitoto Island *11 May* (13)
Tawhirihoe *21 Jun* (3)
Waikanae *16 May* (20)
Queen Charlotte Sound *4–5 May* (27)
Port Nicholson *29 Apr* (34)
Cloudy Bay *17 Jun* (9)
Mana (offshore) *19 Jun* (2)

Akaroa *30 May* (2)

Otago *13 Jun* (2)

Ruapuke *10 Jun* (3)

Locations of Treaty signings, showing the places of signing, the dates of signing and the approximate numbers signing. With the exception of one English copy, all the copies signed were the Maori language Treaty.

● Place of signing, *date of signing* (approximate number of signatures)

while Europeans hung back against the tent walls. Bright sunlight picked out the vivid colours of the flags. It was going to be a long, hot day.

Hobson held English and Maori copies of the Treaty. He first explained his intentions to the few dozen Europeans and then spoke to the Maori, with Williams translating. British people were free to go wherever they chose, he explained, and the Queen was always ready to protect them or restrain them but outside British territory she had no authority. 'Her Majesty the Queen asks you to sign this Treaty,' he said, to give her that power. The Treaty was also an offer of British protection, which Maori had often asked for.[11] Then he read out the Treaty in English. Williams followed, reading the Maori Treaty.[12]

This rather sober opening to the hui now gave way to an animated debate, punctuated with theatrical flourishes. A space was cleared for speakers. One by one, each chief rose, strode back and forth, and fired verbal shots at missionary, trader and British government alike. William Colenso, mission printer, furiously scribbled some notes, which he later published.[13]

Ngati Kawa leader, Te Kemara let go the first salvo. He had no intention of ending up 'a worm, a crawler' under the British. 'We are not whites, nor foreigners,' added Rewa, a Kororareka chief. 'This country is ours . . . we are the governor — we, the chiefs of this our fathers' land.' Te Ruki Kawiti, Ngati Hine leader, echoed these sentiments, as did others. Hakiro was brutally frank. 'We are free. We will not have a governor . . . go back, return, walk away.' Tall and massively built, with a 'deep sepulchral voice', Tareha of Ngati Rehia took the floor. 'We only are the chiefs . . . We will not be ruled over.' Dressed in a 'filthy piece of coarse old floor matting loosely tied around him', Tareha flourished a bunch of dried fern-root, at one time a basic vegetable for Maori. If intended to disclaim the need for European clothing and food items, his performance possibly had the reverse effect. Perhaps it was intended to.

And there were grumbles. Middlemen were buying up produce and pigs from Maori and selling at three times the amount to Pakeha. Whai of Ngai Tawake asked: 'Will you remedy the selling, dealings, and the cheating, lying, and stealing of the whites?' He doubted that Hobson would act or deal with the man who had cursed him the previous day, a grievous offence to Maori.

For five or six hours the chiefs had spoken for and against the Treaty. Few had welcomed Hobson. The CMS's first convert, Rawiri Taiwhanga of Ngati Tautahi and Ngati Rahurahu chief Hone Heke were exceptions. So, too, was the Hokianga chief, Tamati Waka Nene of Ngati Hao, who urged him to stay and to be 'a father, a judge, a peacemaker'. Patuone, his brother, agreed.

This was too much for Te Kemara who cried out, 'No! Go away.' Kemara said that if chiefs and Hobson were going to be equal in rank and power, it would be right, but if not, then he would say no. Eyes flashing and hands crossed as if handcuffed, he shouted, 'Shall I be . . . like this?' Then suddenly he seized Hobson's hand, shaking it over and over and roaring out in English, 'How d'ye do, eh, Governor? How d'ye do, eh, Mister Governor?' Everyone was convulsed with laughter, and the meeting closed with three cheers for the governor.

That night, groups of Maori debated the Treaty as they camped at Te Tii marae near the Waitangi river mouth. Europeans were bragging 'insultingly' that the country was gone and Maori were now only slaves (taurekareka). Williams told them that they would be 'one people with the English, in the suppression of wars, and of every lawless act; under one Sovereign, and one Law, human and divine'.[14] This reassurance, or tiredness and a shortage of food, must have turned the tide of opposition, because by the morning of 6 February most were keen to sign and get home. Some had already left. The missionaries raced to organise a meeting. Strike the iron while it is hot, they no doubt thought.[15] A meeting was called immediately and by the end of the day more than 40 Maori leaders had signed the Treaty.

Maori had accepted the Treaty for reasons that varied from one region to another. Most saw it as a useful move to advance tribal power. Chiefs expected a special relationship with Britain in which authority would be shared and Maori interests protected. The confirmation and guarantee of rangatiratanga — Maori sovereignty of a corporate kind — conveyed a sense of security. Chiefs would manage their own people, while the new administration — the kawanatanga — would control troublesome settlers and land sharks. But acceptance of change and of the need for experimentation were also critical factors for some who signed. Given the extent of change in the previous 70 years, especially in areas of regular and extensive contact, they knew the clock could not be turned back. All anticipated the benefits of settlement, and thought to control it.

In the end, however, the Treaty relationship was a personal one with the great British chief, Queen Victoria, whose navy dominated the world. Maori had covenanted with her as head of the English church and state. This understanding had a Maori parallel, for a chief might also hold the rank of a tohunga, a religious leader. And missionary influence was crucial in the kind of understanding Maori had of the Treaty and in getting Maori agreement.

Some would later hold Nga Puhi responsible for taking the first step in signing the 'tiriti parakete' (blanket treaty); the tribe most experienced in dealings with foreigners must have known what they were doing.

In the final event, then, the treaty-making was a very muddled business. Three months after Waitangi, Hobson heard that New Zealand Company settlers at Wellington had formed a government, enacted laws and appointed magistrates. Furious over such uppityness, he proclaimed British sovereignty over the whole country on 21 May — over the North Island by cession (most Treaty copies were still to come in) and the South Island on the grounds of Cook's discovery (of dubious international legality).

This move also forestalled any claims by a French colonising venture about to settle at Akaroa. In the 1830s paranoia over possible French designs on the country's sovereignty had spooked Busby, missionaries and Maori, but in the period 1839–40 the French bogey seemed about to materialise. The Nanto-Bordelaise Company was gathering up prospective settlers. The French government agreed to provide limited support by sending a 'royal commissioner' ahead of colonists. It was not out to assert sovereignty but to get the 'core of a French possession' in place by a 'semi-official and symbolic occupation'.[16] When Commissioner Charles-Francois Lavaud sailed into the Bay of Islands in July 1840, it was enough for Hobson. He took no chances and post haste dispatched Captain Stanley in the *Britomart*, with two magistrates who would hold a court session at Akaroa. By this farcical manoeuvre, Hobson reckoned to give evidence of British sovereignty.

In October 1840 the Treaty and Hobson's proclamation were gazetted in London. Tact, flattery, guile, bluff and a degree of subterfuge had all been part of the diplomatic baggage in creating the new colony. The British government would do its best for Maori, but the balance between Crown colony authority and chiefly authority had not been defined. Disillusion amongst Maori set in when a weak, fledgling administration started to flex its muscles. Maori were also shocked by the speed with which settler numbers began to increase, especially in the Wellington region.

Contemporary press comments bit hard. The *Bay of Islands Observer*, 7 July 1842, grumbled that:

For the good people at home, the affair [the Treaty] was made to assume the appearance of one of the purest pieces of philanthropy on the part of England in favour of the Natives to protect them against European aggression; but the simple truth is, disguise it as we may, that under this cloak of benevolence, has been practised the greatest hypocrisy, to obtain possession of the country honestly, if possible, but, nevertheless to obtain it.

This watercolour by Charles Heaphy, painted in 1841, looks across Wellington towards the south-east. Te Aro flat in the centre is flanked by Brooklyn and Mt Cook to the right and Mt Victoria to the left.
C Heaphy, Alexander Turnbull Library, C-025-009

The Wellington and Nelson settlements

Two weeks before the signing of the Treaty at Waitangi, the first of six ships, carrying some of the 1300 New Zealand Company migrants, arrived at Wellington. Most of the migrants were from London or England's south-east and south-west.

For the cabin passengers the many months at sea were often boring. For steerage passengers they were sometimes unbearable. Hit by fearful storms, each roll of the ship plunged passengers about, tossed them onto filthy mattresses, with water washing from side to side, bedding soaked, crockery smashed and boxes banging around. Babies were born, children died; foetid air, screams and no privacy were all part of the scene.

Before setting out on the voyage, the settlers were told that one-acre [0.4-ha] town sections and 100-acre [40-ha] farms on fertile, easy country would be surveyed ready for their arrival. In the months of hardship at sea, settlers' hopes were buoyed by such expectations. But as the ships sailed through a dangerous entrance into a bleak Wellington harbour, faith in company promises sank. It was not the new Britannia settlers had expected.

Lieutenant John Wood described first impressions. 'The passengers were all on deck straining their eyes to catch a glimpse of civilization. Little was said, though disappointment was visible on the countenance of everyone.'[17] Even optimists were silenced by the rugged hills and dense forest to the water's edge. Surveys had hardly begun. There was no real wharf at the edge of Petone's sandy foreshore where the first settlers huddled.

As ships unloaded, the beach soon became 'a scene of concentrated chaos' with 'casks and bales, beds and pianos, clocks, cruet-stands, warming-pans, family portraits and packages', some washed up high by the incoming tide.[18] Te Atiawa chiefs Te Wharepouri and Te Puni were welcoming and provided fresh vegetables and fruit. But within weeks, storms, floods and other problems raised settler anger and protest to fever pitch. Disappointment and bitterness ran deep. For their part, Maori were astonished by settler numbers; they asked if the whole English tribe were migrating, and showed signs of panic.

William Wakefield, the company's agent and brother to Edward Gibbon Wakefield, was neither decisive nor helpful. Carrying cash and trade goods to the value of £6000, he had headed the *Tory* advance party that arrived the previous September. His brief was to purchase 445,000 ha of flat, fertile land near a harbour, and as much other land as possible. He was absent to the north when the surveyors arrived. Despairing of terrain in the inner Wellington harbour, the surveyors struggled to make a grandiose company town plan work in the Hutt Valley. Then Wakefield agreed to surveys starting at the western end of the harbour — an area occupied by Maori, who had settlements at Nga Uranga, Kaiwharawhara, Pipitea and Te Aro. As sections were marked out, Maori disputed sales and resisted settlers who muscled in.

The town plan, slapped upon a largely broken terrain elsewhere, created a clutch of hopelessly steep streets and useless sections. Out at the Hutt, some settlers began to develop small properties, although communication with the Thorndon/ Te Aro area (which was named 'Wellington' late in 1840) was not good until earthquakes (in 1848 and 1855) raised the narrow shoreline and created a passable track.

Problems over surveys, land titles and land claims soon produced insecurity among would-be settler owners. Wakefield's claim that he had bought over eight million hectares from the Maori in the Cook Strait region was outrageous. This became clear when land claims were investigated by the impartial William Spain, appointed by the British government. Wakefield did all he could to embarrass and impugn Spain's acts, and to deny the jurisdiction of his claims commission. But the testimony of Dicky Barrett (translator in the original land sale), Te Puni and George Clarke Jnr (government agent) revealed how imperfect or non-existent many purchases were. Explanations had left

William Spain, Land Claims Commissioner.
Special Collections, Auckland City Libraries

C Heaphy, Alexander Turnbull Library, A-145-010

Meeting of the New Zealand Company's ships *Tory* and *Cuba* in Cook Strait 1840.

Maori believing they would retain their settled areas, whereas the company's aim was to redistribute the Maori occupation sites, cultivations and burial places among settler sections. Barrett swore that Maori had not sold either Te Aro or Pipitea, a revelation that caused the company's claim to collapse. This might have deterred settlers in those areas but they pressed on regardless.

Wakefield knew he faced the likelihood of ferocious Maori opposition. Several iwi occupied the Wellington town and nearby region, which had both been contested in the previous 20 years. By 1840 Ngati Toa chiefs Te Rauparaha and Te Rangihaeata were dominant on the Kapiti Coast, while Te Atiawa were powerful around the harbour areas. Wakefield offered to pay compensation to the Maori but refused to let them retain their settlements, cultivations and burial grounds. He went ahead with allocating reserves nonetheless, but provided only 40 ha scattered around the town for Maori,

plus another hundred 40-ha sections of rural land, much of it on hillsides that Maori could not cultivate.

In mid 1842, when surveyors attempted to lay out sections on Porirua land, Te Rangihaeata and his people resisted. Settlers clamoured for the chief's arrest but Police Magistrate Murphy refused and bloodshed was avoided. Yet over time it was a combination of bullying and force that secured settler might and rights.

But Wakefieldian strength did not carry the day with Hobson. The company's moves early in 1840 to establish some form of local authority had prompted his hasty proclamation of sovereignty over the whole country. The company was bitterly disappointed that Hobson refused to make Wellington the capital. Thereafter relations were frosty and there were tensions between Wellington and

A youthful Arthur Wakefield in the early 1820s. Leader of the Nelson settlement, he joined the party that set out to capture Te Rauparaha, a decision that ended in his death in the Wairau Valley.
Alexander Turnbull Library, F-18885-½

Te Aro pa, c.1842. Pencil drawing attributed to Edmund Norman.

E. Norman, Alexander Turnbull Library, A-049-001

Auckland over the policy and practice of the colonial administration. Stringent press attacks were levelled at the much-hated government in Auckland. Local resentment was always at simmering point over some matter or other and was particularly bitter about the Treaty. It held back development by restraining settler desire to dominate the Maori. In the local forums for debate — newspapers, pubs and gaming houses — the demand grew for settler self-government.

Meanwhile, the fortunes of the New Zealand Company were boosted in November 1840 when it received a charter from the British government. This encouraged plans for two new settlements: New Plymouth and Nelson.[19] (A small settlement had already been set up at Wanganui because of the land shortage in Wellington.)

Leadership of the larger Nelson project was given to William Wakefield's brother, young Arthur, who sailed for New Zealand in May 1841. He selected a site for Nelson on Blind Bay, estimating he had the 121,406 ha needed; but there was a shortfall of 66,773 ha, and the site's disadvantages soon became obvious. The land was of very mixed quality, often stony or swampy. Sections were frequently inaccessible, and even company agents admitted that much of it was useless. Since four-fifths of the purchasers were absentee owners, ideals of concentrated and co-operative settlement evaporated. Even 'suburban' sections might be 30 km from town, and rural sections were even further.

The company was unwilling to exchange worthless land for unsold sections, and settler legal action only tardily led to additional compensatory land. In 1856 unsatisfied land claims arising from company transactions still amounted to 39,659 ha. Nelson settlers also had to fight for a decade to recover funds set aside for education, religion and steam navigation — company directors had appropriated these for their own use.

The early years were miserable for settlers. The proportion of capitalists to labourers was greater in Nelson than in Wellington. Only one-twelfth of land sold was owned by resident capitalists, and these owners were of very modest means; yet around 300 labourers migrated to Nelson. Labourers 'revolted' during 1843 over rates of pay and terms of work. The crisis passed, adjustments pacified the men and some had become small farmers by the end of the decade. But it was pastoralism that pulled Nelson out of depression.

The great gathering of pioneer ships in Wellington Harbour on 8 March 1840. William Wakefield aimed to intimidate Maori. He ordered shows of cannon fire from the parading company ships to show who was in charge. Matthew Thomas Clayton painted the scene, basing it on a description by EJ Wakefield.
M Clayton, Alexander Turnbull Library, C-033-005

ABOVE: Te Rangihaeata had a reputation for being a firebrand. He was at the forefront of resistance to settler claims to disputed land in the Porirua district and in Marlborough, and he avoided Grey's attempt to capture him.

BELOW: Nelson was a better site than Wellington, but there was simply not enough farmland to support the Wakefield dream of a thriving market town and port, serving a close-knit agricultural community. And as in Wellington the result was dispersal of settlement, and costly road and bridge construction. Settler land blocks were often some way apart, which added to the discomfort and isolation.

Arthur sought a solution in expanding into the Wairau Valley, some 70 km to the east of Nelson.[20] In April 1843 when surveyors began work there, Ngati Toa leaders Te Rauparaha and Te Rangihaeata angrily denied they had sold Wairau and wanted Spain to hear the case. They interfered with surveyors' work and burnt their raupo hut. Sufficient cause for an armed expedition to arrest the two chiefs on a charge of arson, said Nelson leaders. Forty-nine armed special constables were led by Police Magistrate Henry Thompson, an eccentric, excitable 28-year-old with little nous or self-control. His aim to arrest Te Rauparaha, one of the most feared war chiefs in the country, was ill conceived and the expedition ill executed.

At the Tuamarina Stream the Nelson group exchanged words with the chiefs. Te Rauparaha kept his cool and held fiery Te Rangihaeata in check, while friendly Puaha appealed on the Bible for peace. But the Europeans were spoiling for a fight. Thompson waved handcuffs about in his excitement. No one knows who fired the first shot. In the fracas that erupted there were a number of casualties. Between two and six Maori were killed, including Te Rangihaeata's wife and Te Rauparaha's half-brother. Te Rauparaha reluctantly consented to Te Rangihaeata exacting utu by dispatching the Europeans with blows to the head, and 22 were killed, including 13 who surrendered.

It was a disaster for the Nelson settlement and sent shock waves through the whole country. The first blood had been spilled, and peaceful settlement and co-operation between settler and Maori was shattered. Feeling ran high in the company settlements, and men armed themselves and drilled.

When troops from Auckland arrived in Wellington some of the heightened tension began to ebb, and wise counsel moderated more extreme settler attitudes. Many thought the Nelson settler group had acted most unwisely at Wairau. And so the goal of resuming peaceful settlement still seemed achievable.

Less likely to succeed were the ideals of the Wakefield

scheme. Settler confidence was fading fast. The Wakefield dream had turned sour. The scheme is a 'most vicious game of chance, instead of a sound system of colonisation . . . Strength consists in union and combination of capital and exertion; this is Wakefield's own theory — but Wakefield's Practice is very different, he is the scatterer of settlements, the enemy of cheap government, and the curse of all colonies.'[21]

Realities of the new land forced the abandonment of Wakefield's ideal, compact and gentlemanly farming community. Rural 100-acre [40-ha] lots were more often than not many kilometres out of town. Further dispersal of settlement — against the Wakefield ideal — finally created Wellington's long-term economic development through pastoralism. In the early 1840s Charles Clifford, Frederick Weld and Charles Bidwill pushed their way round the Palliser Bay coast and into the Wairarapa where their sheep flocks flourished under hired management. Their leasehold arrangements with local Maori were advantageous to both Maori and settler. Families established themselves in town and country, with settler wives and sometimes Maori partners too.

The balance needed between capital, labour and land ownership in an ideal colony was a much-vaunted key aspect of the scheme. In practice it did not work. The system of land purchase — shares that were balloted for in England — undermined the balance from the outset by encouraging speculation. Three-fifths of Wellington's purchasers were absentees, and among the migrants with capital there were too many bent on using their land merely for speculative purposes. The ballot system also meant that land was not allocated on the basis of need; merchants who needed waterfront sections had to purchase the property in New Zealand.

There was also an initial overabundance of labour and a lack of local capital. Employers were in short supply and a good deal of land remained non-productive. The company had guaranteed

AH & AW Reed Collection, Alexander Turnbull Library, F-38720-½

Samuel Revans about 1860. He was one of Wellington's few entrepreneurs, producing its first newspaper only a month after landing on Petone Beach, then turning his hand to farming in Evans Bay and later in the Wairarapa. A bitter opponent of the Wakefields, he did not spare them in his scathing attacks in the press.

SAMUEL PARNELL
AND THE LABOURING CLASS

As a skilled labourer, Samuel Parnell's services were in demand. From the moment he touched shore he insisted on setting his own terms of employment — an eight-hour day — and encouraged others to follow. Labour associations were quickly set up and terms of employment laid down. Working-class families did most breaking-in of the land, leasing between half a hectare and about four at low rents, growing crops and vegetables, and keeping a few dozen cows. The marked independence of labouring men challenged Wakefield class-structure theorising and his 'ideal balance' from the outset. The successful ones were grudgingly admitted into Wellington's more genteel social life. The frontier had its own way of levelling relationships.

Samuel Duncan Parnell, photographed in 1890, 50 years after he landed on Petone Beach.

employment for labourers at £1 a day plus rations, but within two years Wellington slid into recession, as cash expended on surveys had run out and private capital was short. In January 1843 London directors ordered William Wakefield not to employ any labour whatsoever. He reduced those on relief and, with winter approaching, sent 50 families into the bush to survive as best they could. Some disenchanted settlers voted early with their feet and moved to Auckland and elsewhere. By 1848, only an estimated 85 of Wellington's 436 original capitalists remained.

Few aspects of the Wakefield scheme had survived the frontier challenge. Plans made in London had simply proved impractical in New Zealand. And in the final winding-up of the company's affairs, its debt of £200,000 was transferred to the young colony. Yet the scheme had been successful in one undeniable result — settlement. Despite the alternative open to British migrants, the short and cheap journey to North America, the Wakefield scheme had successfully persuaded thousands of settlers to choose the longest immigrant route in the world and to migrate to distant New Zealand. With the passage of time, the scheme's shortcomings were overlooked, the public viewed the results more kindly, and Edward Gibbon Wakefield's star rose in the historical firmament.

Hobson's choice — Auckland

The settlement of Auckland was an altogether different matter. Early in 1840 Ngati Whatua chiefs visited Hobson in the Bay of Islands, and invited him to build a new capital on their land to the south, Tamaki-makau-rau ('Tamaki desired by a hundred lovers').

This isthmus between the Waitemata and Manukau harbours was a bridge between north and south, and gave access to waterways on the east and west coasts of the North Island. But in the 1820s it was ravaged by warring Nga Puhi, and became a highway for various tribes as they passed to and fro on war expeditions. A weakened Ngati Whatua withdrew to the protection of Waikato allies. Ngati Paoa on the Tamaki River, their tribe decimated in Nga Puhi attacks, had retreated to the Hauraki Gulf.

The exodus had left the isthmus deserted until the mid 1830s, when Ngati Whatua began cautiously to return to their lands on the Manukau — at Karangahape, Mangere and Onehunga — and to Orakei, where they planted gardens. Their invitation to Hobson had more than one purpose. They wanted protection as well as the advantages of settlement.

During his March 1840 visit with the Treaty, Hobson

Sales of Tamaki land 1840–44

1 Mataharehare, Opou and [Maunga] Whau Block, September 1840, 1214 ha.

2 Kohimarama Block, 28 May 1841, c. 2400 ha, southern boundary ill defined.

3 Waitemata to Manukau Block, 29 June 1841, c. 4800 ha.

4 Manukau Road Purchase, 14 September 1842, 81 ha.

5 Corridor of Land — between Blocks 2 and 3 and south of Remuera Road, bought by Europeans during 1844 when Govenor FitzRoy waived Crown Pre-emption.

6 Remuera–Orakei lands which Ngati Whatua wished to preserve.

This map does not indicate small purchases and Old Land Claims eg. of Fairburn, Hamlin and Dalziel.

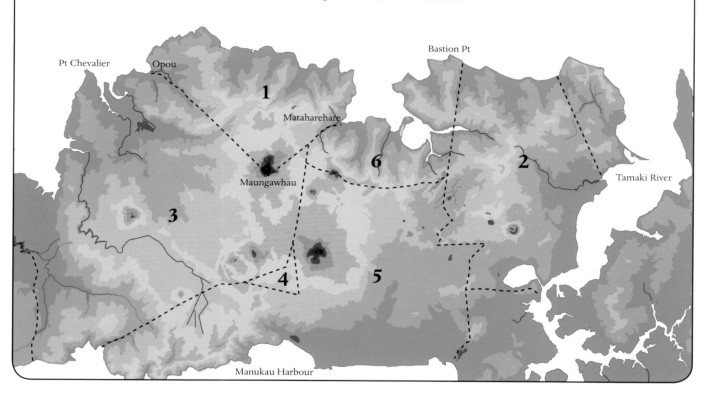

reconnoitred the isthmus. The site had the great advantage of ample fertile land, as well as numerous bays on both harbours. He took little time to decide to move from the Bay of Islands to this new capital, Auckland (named after his patron the First Lord of the Admiralty, Lord Auckland). With the aid of troops, staff and money, coupled with good organisation, the shift was accomplished without difficulty. On 15 September 1840 the *Anna Watson* arrived from the Bay of Islands carrying seven officials and 32 skilled workers with their wives and children.

Three days later the first purchase of 1214 ha from Ngati Whatua gave the government little trouble. It was marked by the erection of a flagstaff near present-day Queen Street, the raising of the British flag, and a 21-gun salute. The advance party busied itself setting up temporary dwellings. More permanent government buildings were soon erected, including a prefabricated Government House. Hobson and his staff arrived in March 1841.

The little settlement quickly took shape. Guided by the contours of the land, acting surveyor-general Felton Mathew laid out what critics called the town's 'spider-web' plan. 'Cobweb' Mathew was chastised by his contemporaries and the plan modified. A giant Trafalgar Circus, roughly the present site of Auckland University and Albert Park, did not eventuate. But Mathew's foresight in allowing for reclamation of Commercial Bay's tidal foreshore paid off; within 50 years it was transformed into the commercial area of seafront Auckland and gave the local authorities a source of leasehold income and security for loans. On the Waitemata Harbour bays soon became defined by names that suggested either their use or their occupants: Official Bay, Mechanics Bay, Judges Bay. Freemans Bay was named after

The British flag first hoisted on the Waitemata, 18 September 1840.

A young John Logan Campbell in the uniform of the Albion Archers, 1839.

Hobson's secretary, but was soon known as Waipiro (grog) Bay for the carousers who frequented it.

With land for the town surveyed and divided by the end of 1840, the first government sale of town sections by auction was held the following April, with a second sale in September. The first set the pace and tone of Auckland as a place for speculation and enterprise. Suburban and country lots sold were within the vicinity of the town, and prices were exceptionally high.

Ngati Whatua were keen to sell more land and in June 1841 the Waitemata to Manukau Block went to the Crown. Tribal leaders were careful to release only land they clearly marked out. Settlements, cultivations and the precious area of Remuera down to the harbour they reserved for their own use. In May 1841, however, Ngati Paoa sold the Kohimarama Block — roughly the area of Auckland's present eastern suburbs — a sale that infringed on Ngati Whatua's eastern land boundary. And then in 1844 Waikato tribes began selling land that threatened Ngati Whatua's Remuera 'nest-egg'.[22]

At government land sales sections initially sold at such a gross profit that Maori were stunned and evaluated the government's profits as unfair. Even more astonishing to Maori was the fact that much of the land sold was soon subdivided by purchasers and sold again. Yet while entrepreneurial settlers made a killing, the high prices were not a deterrent to settlement. During Auckland's first two years the population steadily grew.

Settlers came from all corners. Already on the scene were the Scotsmen William Brown and John Logan Campbell. Campbell left his home on Motukorea (now known as Browns Island) in the Waitemata Harbour in 1840 and set up his small tent and a trading store on shore. His business acumen would bring riches and a reputation as the 'father of Auckland'.[23]

A trickle of settlers now started to flow faster, though there was no organised immigration. Towards the end of 1840, 40 settlers arrived from Australia, the first of a steady migration, while others were attracted to the town from various spots in the Hauraki Gulf and Coromandel. Some — like the lawyer and later premier, Frederick Whitaker — followed the capital from the north. On the Manukau Harbour, a small English settler group began to settle at Cornwallis in 1841, but some soon shifted to Auckland.

In October 1842 the first emigrant ships arrived in the Waitemata, the *Duchess of Argyle* and the *Jane Gifford*, bearing 552 settlers, including impoverished labourers and their families from Paisley, in the Scottish lowlands. Soon after, two ships brought 72 boys between 12 and 20 years of age from the Parkhurst reformatory on the Isle of Wight. Auckland citizens thought them socially unacceptable and objected. The experiment was not repeated.

New settlers were provided with temporary shelter and contract work on roading, if they wanted it. But wage rates were low and newcomers were reluctant to take up the offer. According to David Rough, harbourmaster-cum-public works supervisor, he had more success by letting contracts to parties of new arrivals. Shortland Street was the most developed thoroughfare by 1844, with Queen and Princes Streets also formed and metalled. Roads were pushed out to Newmarket, Tamaki and Onehunga, sometimes using Maori labour under contract.

With skilled labour in short supply, most new arrivals found some employment, often on the land. By May 1843, 162 ha were under cultivation; by September 1844 this had increased threefold. New settlers, not wanting to go too far from town, bought land mainly to the south. The Great South Road was started about 1843; by 1851 it had been metalled as far as Otahuhu, and in good weather was passable as far as Drury.[24]

Political and public life in the little settlement could be lively. Business Auckland tended to be suspicious and critical of government, and in the early years local newspapers waged merciless attacks on Hobson. Life was also full of uncertainties. Investigations into pre-1840 land claims caused uneasiness among both Maori and Pakeha, and continued to do so for years. Even more disturbing was the brutal Bay of Islands murder of the Roberton family and a chief's granddaughter. Maketu, a Nga Puhi man, was brought to trial in Auckland and hanged in 1842. It was the first real test of Maori acceptance of British justice. Northern Maori co-operated — Maketu's guilt was not in dispute and British law coincided with utu — but the case might have closed differently had they not wanted to avoid intertribal bloodshed.[25]

Hobson's choice of Auckland as the colony's capital enraged the Cook Strait company settlers, and his actions ensured their continuing chagrin. He requested that the Colonial Office direct immigration to Auckland where the climate was more congenial and the soil more productive; and he successfully advertised for carpenters, bricklayers and other skilled labourers from Wellington, to where they had been brought at company expense. Persistent attacks from Wellington included a petition for Hobson's recall, one of many ingredients in the provincial rivalry between Auckland and Wellington that persisted through

E. Ashworth, Alexander Turnbull Library, A-275-007

Maori watch in the foreground as Auckland takes shape in the distance c. 1843. Government House occupies the fenced area in the centre right, and the late afternoon sun silhouettes the spire of St Paul's Church against Mount Victoria across the harbour.

JL Campbell, Campbell Papers, Auckland Museum

Campbell sketched this scene of Commercial Bay in December 1840, showing tents and the government store (from which the bay, long reclaimed, took its first European name).

E Ashworth, Auckland Art Gallery, Toi o Tamaki

By 1843 Commercial Bay showed all the signs of a rapidly growing settlement.

a greater part of the 19th century. But then dissatisfied Auckland settlers petitioned London for Hobson's recall too. Hobson saved everyone the trouble. Unwell from the moment he arrived in New Zealand, he died from another stroke in September 1842.

In its first years Auckland's gradual economic development was based on the timber and gum trade, and on general commerce. There was no major staple export that would have attracted more settlers and capital, and farmland took time to break in. Settlers initially depended on local Maori for supplies. Gentle and charming Mary Martin, wife of the colony's chief justice, admitted how much they relied on Maori for firewood, pork, fish and vegetables.

The town was soon in part also supplied by market gardens, orchards and small farms close by. But Maori remained essential to Auckland, providing services such as raupo shelters for incoming settlers. From as far away as the Bay of Plenty came produce for sale, and a substantial Maori market operated at the foot of Queen Street. By the early 1850s up to 2000 canoes a year arrived in the port, and a growing number of Maori-owned coastal vessels carried goods from greater distances. The town's traders were dependent on the Maori trade, and shops stocked goods to satisfy Maori tastes.[26]

Then gold discoveries in California in 1848 and Australia in the 1850s opened up markets for Auckland's produce and building materials. Between 1851 and 1853 this stimulated a doubling of the area under cultivation within 24 km of Auckland. By then

PJ Hogan, Auckland Art Gallery, Toi o Tamaki

Auckland in the early 1850s seems to be a well-established township. On closer acquaintance the raw nature of its planning and roadways was evident. The Horotiu Stream running down Queen Street became an open sewer until the 1860s, when it was filled in. The street was a quagmire in winter and butchers fouled the air with the cast-out entrails of slaughtered animals rotting in warm weather. For years Auckland was a dirty town, ravaged at times by fevers.

the settlement had a third of the colony's white population and provided 43 per cent of its public revenue.[27] Some of its settlers were wealthy men. Yet there was no stability in the export of produce, and Auckland's local commerce continued to be its most certain source of income. For years, too, Auckland's economic wellbeing depended heavily on government funds.

The high prices of the first government land sales were not repeated for some time and, as land sales throughout the colony declined, government income shrank. Together with customs duties, income from land sales was the main source of revenue. A recession through 1843 and 1844 hit Auckland commerce hard. Then a new governor, Robert FitzRoy, arrived at Christmas 1843. FitzRoy tried to solve the colony's financial problems by increasing revenue through an unauthorised issue of debentures, and by stimulating land sales. He waived the Crown's right of pre-emption and allowed direct settler purchase of land from Maori with payment of fees to the Crown. The moves complicated the land alienation system and simply added to the government's problems. A year later pre-emption was restored and the debentures redeemed. FitzRoy would pay for his administrative failures, but not before he had faced the first major challenge to British authority.

Hone Heke's July 1844 attack on the Russell flagstaff led eventually to war in the north. Panicky Auckland settlers, numbering fewer than 3000, trembled for their safety, though at no stage was the town at risk. Nga Puhi chief Patuone was situated

on the northern flank of the town and on the southern side was the Waikato chief Te Wherowhero, who also had a cottage in Auckland Domain; both pledged to protect the town. And when the war was over in 1847 and rumours still circulated that Heke might attack the settlement, Te Wherowhero promised that it would be over his dead body. Nonetheless, between 1847 and 1852 Auckland accepted 721 imperial army pensioners, known as Fencibles. By 1851 almost 30 per cent of Auckland's population comprised the regular army and the Fencibles group.

With government based in Auckland, the town always held a number of officials, and army officers of rank. These formed the upper crust of 'society' along with capitalists and gentleman farmers. But the business community dominated. Some of the merchants took up manufacturing, experimenting with exports, and investing in farms and mines. Their public role was as considerable as their social position was unchallenged, and from their ranks came legislators and town councillors. They could expect to go to the Government House ball on the sovereign's birthday.[28]

Social life for most settlers, though, revolved around home visits, picnics, church, school and the odd party or entertainment. But whether ball, picnic or regatta, Maori were part of the scene. Auckland's distinctive Maori character would last for a decade and more. And then the mixing and interdependence of Maori and Pakeha interests would be overwhelmed by settler interests and by war. The cost for Auckland would be loss of its status as the colony's capital.

J Williams, Rex Nan Kivell Collection, National Library of Australia

Auckland was a garrison town, dominated by the Albert Barracks. The Fencibles, retired soldiers, brought wives and families from England and established four outposts on the town's outskirts — at Otahuhu, Panmure, Howick and Onehunga — where they developed the land while being available to fight if required. This never proved necessary and these settlers were absorbed into the communities that developed around them.

This view of British troops attacking Kawiti's pa at Ohaeawai in July 1845 was painted by Cyprian Bridge, one of the senior officers.

Robert FitzRoy was 38 when he became governor in 1843. Eight years earlier, when an unknown artist produced this lithograph, he had commanded the *Beagle's* round-the-world voyage and with Charles Darwin aboard had visited the Bay of Islands. In 1854 he headed Britain's first weather office, but the strain led to suicide in 1865.

The Northern War

Only a month after his arrival late in 1843, FitzRoy headed south to settle Wellington's land issues and to deal with the Wairau disaster. Six months had passed and tensions were still high. But FitzRoy showed little sympathy for the families of men killed at Wairau and upbraided Nelson settlers for causing the fiasco. This earned him such enmity that Nelsonians began a campaign for his recall.

Although Te Rauparaha and Te Rangihaeata expected firm government moves, FitzRoy gauged that the colony could ill afford a major confrontation. He simply chastised the chiefs for their actions. Company settlers were outraged. Feelings between the races remained fragile and were not helped as settler and Maori jostled for land in the Hutt.[29] And then, five months later, Heke's attack on the Russell flagstaff led to the Northern War.[30]

Times had changed with the arrival of the first governors. Certain measures affecting the colony rankled with northern Maori: in particular customs duties, government regulations such as prohibitions on cutting kauri, and the removal of the capital from Russell to Auckland. Goods were more expensive and land sales had diminished. Maori income had dropped. And settlers, more confident with a British administration to back them and less dependent on Maori goodwill, were not so inclined to recognise Maori cultural sensitivities. Sometimes the Europeans could be downright rude or aggressive. In these changing times chiefs recognised a loss of the power they had exerted over Europeans before the signing of the Treaty.

FitzRoy considered Heke's attack on the flagpole as of very great importance. After some hesitation he tried unsuccessfully to parley at a September meeting of chiefs, held at the Waimate mission station.

On 11 March, after two further attacks on the flagpole, Heke cut down the flag for the fourth time, while Kawiti's men moved on the town. In the confusion both Maori and European were killed. And then a powder magazine blew up, the town was looted by Maori and by some Europeans, and its citizens fled to Auckland.

The loss of the fifth-largest town in the colony and £50,000 of property was a serious blow to British prestige. The attention of the whole colony was now bent upon the struggle that was bound to follow. FitzRoy knew he had to take punitive measures. But while he waited for reinforcements from Australia, a secondary war began in April between Waka Nene and Heke. The conflict was over settling old tribal scores. Heke ended up badly wounded; Kawiti did not take part. This utu was a sideshow to the main war between anti-government Maori and British forces, and overlapped it.

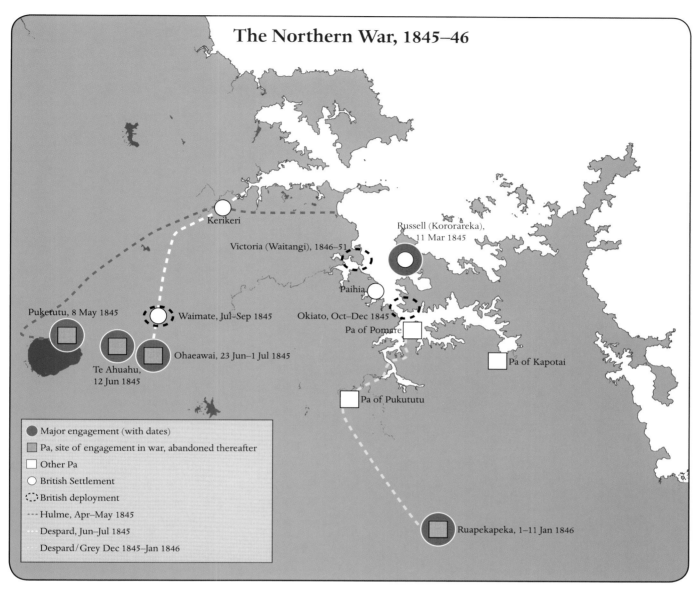

The Northern War, 1845–46

Kerikeri

Russell (Kororareka),
11 Mar 1845

Victoria (Waitangi), 1846–51

Paihia

Puketutu, 8 May 1845

Waimate, Jul–Sep 1845

Okiato, Oct–Dec 1845

Pa of Pomare

Ohaeawai, 23 Jun–1 Jul 1845

Te Ahuahu,
12 Jun 1845

Pa of Kapotai

Pa of Pukututu

Ruapekapeka, 1–11 Jan 1846

Major engagement (with dates)

Pa, site of engagement in war, abandoned thereafter

Other Pa

British Settlement

British deployment

--- Hulme, Apr–May 1845

Despard, Jun–Jul 1845

Despard / Grey Dec 1845–Jan 1846

One cause of northern discontent was the investigation of pre-1840 land sales. The investigations and the retaining by government of 'surplus' lands (if there were any) was hotly debated by Maori and seen as a breach of the Treaty. Promises had been made that lands unjustly taken would be returned to Maori.

Apart from minor actions there were three engagements in the Northern War — assaults on Heke's Puketutu pa and on two pa built by Kawiti, at Ohaeawai and at Ruapekapeka. The British did not come off well. Heke had expected British retaliation and constructed Puketutu pa close to Lake Omapere. It was not entirely finished when British forces attacked on 8 May. Fifty-two troops were killed and wounded, and around the same number of Maori. Kawiti's forces contributed to repelling the British attack. It had been a close thing though. As historian James Belich observes, in combat on open ground it was clear that British forces had the edge on a similar number of Maori. The lesson was learnt and Maori struck open combat off their list of battle tactics.[31]

In June, Colonel Henry Despard arrived from Sydney with 200 men and artillery. With Nene and his warriors, he attacked Ohaeawai. Despard gravely underestimated Kawiti's military skills. In a suicidal assault over 40 were killed and 70 or more wounded. Kawiti had few losses and moved on to prepare Ruapekapeka pa.

After this disaster FitzRoy tried unsuccessfully to negotiate, but his time was up. The British government disapproved of his financial management. His term ended with the arrival of his successor, George Grey, in mid November.

Grey came with more money, more troops and more resources. Determined to end hostilities, he issued an ultimatum to Heke and Kawiti: negotiate or face attack. Neutral Maori were

HEKE'S ATTACKS ON THE FLAGPOLE

The mission-educated Hone Heke was a volatile character. Intelligent and sharp, he could also be truculent, surly and sulky.[32] Before and after 1840 he was troublesome to the settlers, making several sorties on Kororareka in the early 1840s to 'stir'.

In mid 1844 Heke reckoned that the Union Jack flying on a large flagstaff above the settlement could be taken as the symbol of British sovereignty. He created a fuss around town, and on 8 July 1844 he cut down the flagstaff.

In January 1845 Heke was joined by Te Ruki Kawiti who had also signed the Treaty, very reluctantly, in May 1840. Both were convinced that the British flag had deprived chiefs of their mana and stood for the loss of their country to the British. Bringing down the flag would strike at British sovereignty, without inflicting a blow at settlers or valuable economic benefits. And so down came the flagstaff again, twice in that month.

A blockhouse and guard were placed nearby and FitzRoy asked for more troops. But during the night of 10 March Heke's forces surrounded the blockhouse and severed the flagstaff for the fourth time, an action that led to the outbreak of the Northern War.

LEFT: Hone Heke, at left, and Eruera Maihi Patuone.
GF Angas, Alexander Turnbull Library, PUBL-0014-01

AD McCormick, Alexander Turnbull Library, A-004-037

Heke fells the flagstaff at Kororareka.

Alexander Turnbull Library, F-37353-½

Te Ruki Kawiti — Ngati Hine leader and warrior.

warned they would be treated as rebels unless they honoured the Treaty. The inveterate letter-writer Heke challenged the governor's right to the land. 'Do you return to your own country, which was made by God for you. God made this land for us, and not for any stranger or foreign nation to touch.'[33]

Grey's answer was to move over a thousand troops inland. Armed with cannons, mortars and rockets they bombarded Kawiti's hilltop pa, Ruapekapeka, on 10 January 1846. When troops entered the pa on the following day they found it all but deserted. Heke brought his forces in at the rear of the pa; he and Kawiti lost men but then slipped away. There were 40-odd British casualties (about a dozen killed). Neither war leader wanted to continue the fight and they quickly settled their differences with Nene.

The consummate spin doctor Grey claimed victory and Maori submission, which pleased settlers and his masters in London. But as Henry Williams noted, Heke's cause had not been settled and the chief was still at large. Grey had no time for Williams, however (and would conspire to have him dismissed from the Church Missionary Society). He preferred to let the north settle down. He decided not to confiscate any land, the flagstaff was not re-erected, and in time the battle leaders were pardoned. The war cost northern Maori lives and resources. It was a lesson they would not forget.

In the country as a whole Grey then demonstrated that the government was in control. With a large force he arrived in Wellington to resolve the tussles between Maori and settlers over land in the Hutt. He declared martial law in March 1846 and embarked on a mission to reduce the mana of Te Rauparaha and Te Rangihaeata. Te Rangihaeata gave him the slip, retreating from Porirua Harbour into the Manawatu, not to be caught. But Te Rauparaha was captured as he slept and held prisoner. When the old war leader returned 18 months later, he was a spent force. The signals to Maori were clear. A challenge to British sovereignty would be met with force. And power would also gradually be established by other means, largely authorised by the pen.

Grey soon asserted authority over law and land matters. He disestablished the Protectorate of Aborigines, largely staffed by young offspring of missionaries and so disliked by company settlers, and set up the Resident Magistrate system. In his Land Ordinance of 1846 he aimed to have only the Crown deal in land; there was supposed to be no leasing from Maori.[34] Yet the Wairarapa continued to open up, leases did not cease, and settler demands now drove Grey into buying more land. Almost all of the South Island was purchased and large areas of the North Island.

By the end of 1853 over 700,000 Wairarapa hectares were acquired for just over £9000 (the sale included the Tararua range, so the usable total was a little less than 400,000 ha). There were promises of churches, schools and mills for the Maori. In 1853 and '54 the Wairarapa Small Farms settlements were developed, Greytown and Masterton under the aegis of their own association, and Carterton and Featherston as Wellington provincial government settlements. The four settlements slowly expanded, with settlers pushing further north into bush. The small farms survived, carried largely by enterprises on larger holdings — sawmilling and pastoralism — that took the district into more certain economic prosperity in the 1860s.

From the mid 1850s the colony had had a settler legislature and the new provinces had their own governing councils. Grey had bought time over battles for the land, but he found it impossible to silence the cry for self-government. The Colonial Office had recognised the need when the colony was established; and in face of Wakefieldian pressure the 1846 New Zealand Constitution Act was passed by the British Parliament.[35] The Act split the country into two provinces, New Ulster (to the north of a line drawn east from the mouth of the Patea River) and New Munster (to the south). Heavy with governing structures, the constitution gave limited self-government and limited franchise: only male property owners who met an English literacy test could vote, and this effectively excluded most Maori.

Grey argued that if the constitution were introduced it would provoke an armed Maori uprising. He managed to have the constitution suspended for five years but he was playing for time. Settlers were infuriated, especially in the New Zealand Company settlements, and clamoured for the right to govern themselves.

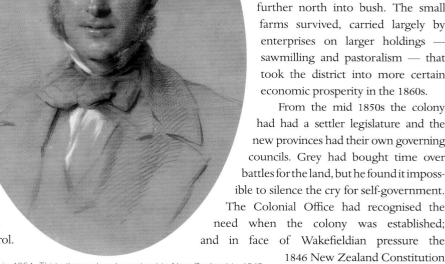

George Grey in 1854. Thirty-three when he arrived in New Zealand in 1845, Grey became the most important government figure in New Zealand's early colonial history. Governor for two terms (almost 15 years) and premier for two years, he was sympathetic to Maori and intensely interested in their culture, but nonetheless bent on assimilating them into a British state.
G Richmond, Auckland Art Gallery, Toi o Tamaki

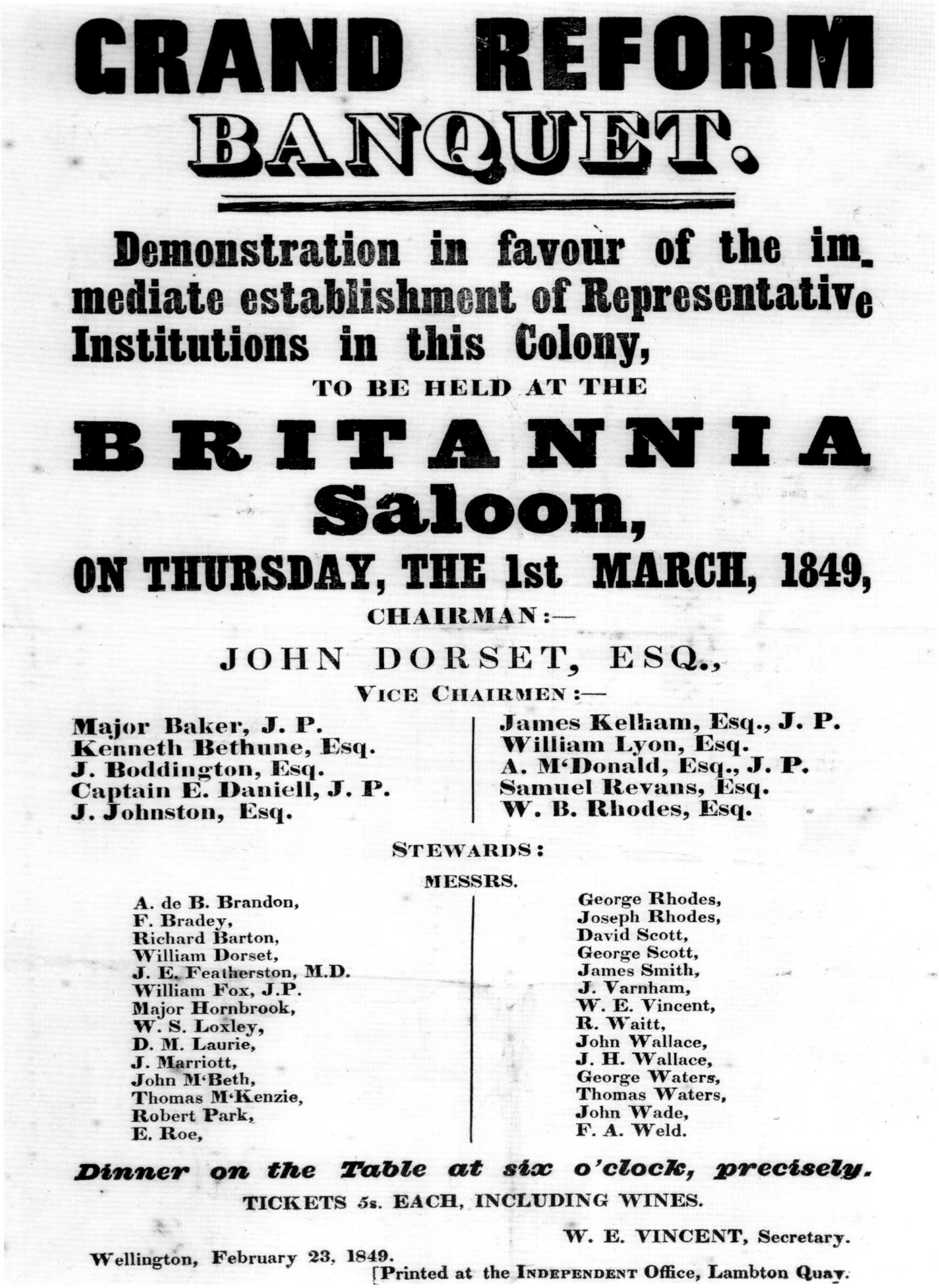

GRAND REFORM BANQUET.

Demonstration in favour of the immediate establishment of Representative Institutions in this Colony,

TO BE HELD AT THE

BRITANNIA Saloon,

ON THURSDAY, THE 1st MARCH, 1849,

CHAIRMAN:—

JOHN DORSET, ESQ.,

VICE CHAIRMEN:—

Major Baker, J. P.	James Kelham, Esq., J. P.
Kenneth Bethune, Esq.	William Lyon, Esq.
J. Boddington, Esq.	A. M'Donald, Esq., J. P.
Captain E. Daniell, J. P.	Samuel Revans, Esq.
J. Johnston, Esq.	W. B. Rhodes, Esq.

STEWARDS:

MESSRS.

A. de B. Brandon,	George Rhodes,
F. Bradey,	Joseph Rhodes,
Richard Barton,	David Scott,
William Dorset,	George Scott,
J. E. Featherston, M.D.	James Smith,
William Fox, J.P.	J. Varnham,
Major Hornbrook,	W. E. Vincent,
W. S. Loxley,	R. Waitt,
D. M. Laurie,	John Wallace,
J. Marriott,	J. H. Wallace,
John M'Beth,	George Waters,
Thomas M'Kenzie,	Thomas Waters,
Robert Park,	John Wade,
E. Roe,	F. A. Weld.

Dinner on the Table at six o'clock, precisely.

TICKETS 5s. EACH, INCLUDING WINES.

W. E. VINCENT, Secretary.

Wellington, February 23, 1849.

[Printed at the INDEPENDENT Office, Lambton Quay.

The Grand Reform Banquet at Wellington in March 1849. To promote the cause of self-government, constitutional associations in Wellington and Nelson organised such reform dinners and meetings, which were memorialised in the local newspapers, and obtained support from the Colonial Reform Society in London.
Alexander Turnbull Library, Eph-D-POLITICS-1849-01

Suspension of the Act gave them a focus for agitation. A few returned to England to put the case in person. When the Otago and Canterbury settlements were established in 1848 and 1850 respectively, articulate and able men like John Robert Godley added their support to the call for a constitution. Though there were differences of opinion on the type of constitution, all wanted change.

With the constitution suspended and no local government, Grey divided the colony into the two provinces proposed under the 1846 Act. Provincial legislative councils — comprising officials and nominees — were established. New Ulster's never met. New Munster's did not work well. Settler resentment simmered over this stopgap situation.

At Colonial Office bidding, Grey drew up a proposal for a constitution, which the home government passed as the New Zealand Constitution Act 1852.[36] The following year the Act came into affect. It allowed for a General Assembly of two chambers: an elected House of Representatives, which still exists, and above it a nominated Legislative Council, disestablished in 1950. The country was divided into six (eventually ten) provinces, each governed by an elected superintendent and elected provincial council. The provincial councils were subordinate to the central government and initially were largely dependent on it for funding. New Zealand would not be a federation but a united colony.

The House of Representatives, with between 24 and 42 members, was to be elected every five years; the provincial councils every four. Every male over 21 with a certain amount of property was entitled to vote and could do so in each electorate in which he held property. This largely excluded Maori males, who in the main had communal land-holdings. The expectation expressed in the 1850s — wishful thinking of course — was that Maori were a long way along the path of amalgamation; they would soon have individual land ownership to entitle them to the franchise.

The Act allowed for 'native districts', but these were never introduced nor taken seriously by the New Zealand government. The Act gave settler government wide powers over legislation and finances, although the governor retained responsibility for Maori policy. He could also veto provincial legislation; and Acts passed by the central government he could approve, veto or refer to the British government (which held responsibility for foreign affairs).

With electoral districts set up, the first polls were held between June and October 1853. The seats were not hotly contested. Travel and time taken in attending assembly sittings in Auckland deterred many from standing. The provincial councils became the most lively political scene, their concerns focusing on local affairs — education, land, immigration, development of an infrastructure, and above all, finance. For two decades there would be a struggle over the powers and rights of the provincial

governments and their relationships with central government.

Grey went on his way in 1853, leaving a rather confused political situation. Constitutional associations had argued for responsible government, for elected assemblies had little power unless the governor was obliged to take the advice of ministers, backed by a majority of members of the House and responsible to it. After a muddled assembly in 1854, the Colonial Office settled matters by instructing the governor (Acting Governor Wynyard) to introduce responsibility.

Fourteen years after the signing of the Treaty, it seemed that the settlers were close to taking absolute control. Their leaders were largely drawn from the Wakefield settlements. By 1858 the fast-growing Pakeha population had drawn even with the declining Maori one, and would rapidly overtake it. And by 1858 Heke, Kawiti, Te Rauparaha and Te Rangihaeata were all dead, and Maori leadership was passing to a younger generation. That year Kawiti's son Maihi Paraone, together with 400 other Maori, re-erected the flagstaff on Russell's Maiki Hill.[37] It was a gesture of commitment to the government, to the dream of a Maori–Pakeha partnership and a mutually beneficial relationship. The north would stay a zone of peace. But further south other tribes were planning action that would challenge settler power.

JE Collins, Canterbury Museum, CM 321A

Edward Gibbon Wakefield in 1850 looks every bit the colonial patriarch. But when the great theoriser and publicist finally migrated to Wellington in 1852, he was soon disillusioned with colonial life. Grey left and so avoided the battle with Wakefield that might have occurred in early parliaments.

Chapter 5

Pai Marire karakia, held by the Te Hau fanatics at Tataroa, New Zealand, to determine the fate of their prisoners, by Lieutenant Herbert Meade, shows Pai Marire believers in procession around a niu pole near Taupo in 1865. Through the religion and the wars it sparked, Maori tried to come to terms with a world turned upside down. The painter, one of the two bound figures seated at right, was lucky to survive to tell his tale.

The Explosive Frontier
1852–1884

In the early 1850s, Maori owned most of Te Ika a Maui — the North Island. The majority of the island's 60,000 Maori lived in Te Tai Tokerau (Northland) and Waikato. In the north, Europeans were confined to the Bay of Islands and the vicinity of Auckland — the colony's capital, and its commercial and military centre. The rest of the 20,000 Pakeha, three-fifths of them male, were concentrated in the Wakefield settlements. Co-operation and communication between these settlements was limited. Most Europeans in the North Island were camped on the edge of Polynesia. Maori had the upper hand in economic potential, cultural vitality and military strength.

Three decades later, the North Island was home to 180,000 Pakeha and only 40,000 Maori, who were still declining in numbers while white immigrants were pouring in by the shipload. Most of the good land was now in the hands of the settlers, and much of the rest of it would soon be for sale. Power had passed decisively from Maori to Pakeha within a generation. This revolution had been accomplished by economic, political, judicial and cultural, as well as military, means. But the changes were not black and white. More Maori allied themselves with Pakeha than fought against them. Unable to beat the world's strongest colonial power, they found new ways to live with it.

New Zealand Constitution Act
gives settlers self-government

Pakeha population exceeds Maori;
Te Wherowhero becomes Maori king

Taranaki War;
Kohimarama conference

Waikato War

Native Land Court establ

A Maori golden age?

Many settlers arrived from Britain without farming skills, and in the early 1850s Europeans owned little arable land in the North Island. Maori had both land and skills, an advantage they were encouraged to make the most of by missionaries and by the autocratic governor, Sir George Grey. These men believed they knew what was best for Maori — advice that also served their own interests. Successfully growing crops for a market economy required English virtues like thrift and self-discipline. Missionaries hoped that as they learned such values, their congregations would also start to give Christianity more than lip service. Model communities, like the one set up by the devout Ngati Haua chief Wiremu Tamihana at Peria, near Matamata, pointed the way. Grey wanted to turn young Maori men into brown-skinned Pakeha who supported their families by farming. If the land could somehow be prised from Maori hands, they would become wage labourers. Some already were, some of the time. Ngati Maniapoto men built roads in Auckland in 1846; European forestry entrepreneurs relied on Maori to fell and drag trees.

Missionaries and government officials gave Maori ploughs, seeds and agricultural education. Thanks to a thirst for innovation and a desire for status, collectively worked farms flourished. Production was often more important than appearances. The fences protecting crops from foraging pigs were rough manuka affairs. Water-powered flour mills were the pride of many hapu — even those with little land suitable for growing wheat. Nearly 60 large mills were begun in the North Island between 1846 and 1860, half in Waikato.[1] Costing up to £500 to build, some were never completed and others fell into disrepair despite help from the government's Inspector of Native Mills.

Always great sailors, Maori now owned ships. Chiefs competed with each other to acquire them. Cutters and schooners — small vessels of 10 to 20 tons — were ideal for carrying produce, consumer goods and people. Owning a ship was a visible marker of wealth and a reminder that in the mid 19th century, Maori power and status remained high. By 1858 there were 53 Maori-owned vessels in Auckland province. Each had cost several hundred pounds and needed constant maintenance. Whaleboats, which were cheaper and more practical, did not come into vogue until the late 1860s, 20 years after schooners.

Maori played a key role in the European economy, and they did so on their own terms. The bustling Auckland market was the hub. Waka laden with produce — fish, fruit, and the ever-popular spud — ringed the wharf. Maori hawked their wares in muddy downtown streets. Cutting a hard bargain seemed to come naturally; they were notorious for 'chaffing with the most persevering assiduity for a copper more for a head of cabbage, or . . . an additional [ha'penny] for a kit of corn'.[2]

North Island iwi

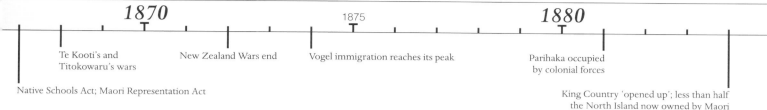

1870   1875   *1880*

Te Kooti's and   New Zealand Wars end   Vogel immigration reaches its peak   Parihaka occupied
Titokowaru's wars   by colonial forces

Native Schools Act; Maori Representation Act   King Country 'opened up'; less than half
the North Island now owned by Maori

The Waikato and Hauraki tribes supplied nearly all Auckland's vegetables and flour. The gold-rush in Victoria from 1851 stimulated food production still further. The government's Maori-language newspaper exhorted its readers to grow wheat and potatoes for the Australian market. So they did. In 1854 nearly 2000 canoes brought more than £16,000 worth of produce to Auckland and Onehunga. Much more came in small sailing ships. Chatham Islands Maori made their Moriori slaves grow potatoes for the Californian goldfields.

Maori were slowly increasing their immunity to European diseases. If they could keep their land, it seemed, they would be able to support themselves in a modern economy. But in 1856 flour and potato prices collapsed as Australian production increased. The slump was compounded by the over-investment in mills and schooners, which encouraged sales of land or timber to clear debt; soil exhaustion from overcropping; and an increasing preoccupation with politics. Many Maori now learned the hard way that in a market economy, wasteful investment would be punished.

While Maori prospered and competed among themselves, many northern settlers lacked land. By the mid 1850s, only about 10 per cent of Auckland province had been bought by Pakeha.[3] Much of this land was owned by speculators willing to hold onto it until they could make big profits — only one per cent of the province was in European-owned cultivations or pasture.[4] The sharp lawyers Thomas Russell (soon to found both the New Zealand Insurance Company and the Bank of New Zealand) and Frederick Whitaker (a key political figure until 1890) were the most prominent members of an Auckland elite whose political, commercial and personal interests were often entwined.

To the south, Grey's land purchase agent, the canny Scot Donald McLean, bought much of Wairarapa, southern Hawke's Bay and Rangitikei from its Maori owners in the early 1850s. Pastoralists with dubious leases from local hapu could now get legitimate titles, and their sheep could more safely graze. With small farm schemes also being established in Wairarapa, the success of Wellington province was finally assured after the uncertainties of its first decade.

The kainga of Te Arakanihi, at Mohaka in northern Hawke's Bay, embraced the farming boom of the 1850s. More than 30 people would die here at the hands of Te Kooti in April 1869. AJ Cooper, Alexander Turnbull Library, A-235-004

Trouble in Taranaki

The fact that New Plymouth province was not renamed Taranaki until 1859 summed up its problem — the 25,000 ha available for occupation by its 3000 Europeans stretched little beyond the outskirts of the town that had been established by the Plymouth Company in 1841. Elsewhere along the west coast of the North Island from Wanganui to Port Waikato, Maori still held land that immigrants had hoped to deforest and plant in pasture and crops. In Taranaki, uncertainty over the actual extent of early land purchases was compounded in 1848 by the return of 600 Maori, mainly Te Atiawa, from Waikanae, where they had moved during the Musket Wars. Led by the dignified Wiremu Kingi Te Rangitake, the migrants reoccupied and began farming commercially 'a splendid tract of land covered with luxuriant fern' at Waitara that Donald McLean was anxious to purchase.[5]

Subsequent intertribal violence alarmed Taranaki's Europeans. Many shared James Richmond's sentiments: 'I imagine that a day will come not long hence, when the preposterous Waitangi treaty will be overruled . . . and the ridiculous claims of the natives to thousands upon thousands of acres of untrodden bush & fern will be no longer able to damp the ardour & cramp the energies of the industrious white man.'[6] Some settlers appreciated the beauty of the new land they were 'breaking in'. The more sensitive among them, like James's sister Jane Maria, occasionally admitted to doubts about what they were doing: '[One] afternoon when [I was] walking from Aunt's home to ours, the scene was . . . quite ghastly in ugliness . . . the wide road was full of deep ruts . . . with here and there an old giant stump sticking up in it, the clumsy looking fences on each side of the road, and beyond, the fields full of stumps of all sizes and shapes . . . were the only things I could see . . . nothing more dreary looking could be imagined.'[7]

Burning the Taranaki bush for farming was an ugly business. Both the men and the dog in William Strutt's 1856 painting seem to be taken aback by the forces they have unleashed.

At a large meeting in 1854 Taranaki iwi resolved to stop selling land. From 1855 British troops garrisoned New Plymouth. The settlers were formed into a militia in 1858. The following year, the high-minded — and stiff-necked — Governor Thomas Gore Browne bought part of the Waitara Block from a minor Te Atiawa chief, despite Kingi's protests. Two views of ownership clashed: a senior chief asserted his mana over land to which the government had determined — at least to its own satisfaction — others were the 'lawful proprietors'. When a survey of the contested land was obstructed by Kingi's people in February 1860, martial law was declared and war seemed inevitable. Kingi had told Gore Browne in 1859: 'These lands will not be given up by us into the Governor's . . . hands, lest we resemble the sea-birds which perch upon a rock: when the tide flows the rock is covered by the sea, and the birds take flight, for they have no resting-place.'[8]

Maori traders *On the Beach, New Plymouth* in another William Strutt painting.

WHAT'S IN A NAME?

The interracial warfare that erupted in Taranaki in 1860 flared up time and again across the North Island for a dozen years. People still argue not just about the details of what happened, but which side won battles and even campaigns. As history has been rewritten, the names of the 20-odd separate conflicts between 1845 and 1872 have also changed. At the time colonists generally referred to them by region, key incident or presumed chief evildoer. For instance, the War in the North was also the Flagstaff War and Heke's War; it was followed by a pair of Taranaki Wars and the Waikato War. As campaigns multiplied and previous battlegrounds were fought over again, settlers found it easier to speak collectively of the Maori Wars. The Kingites called the Waikato War Te Riri Pakeha — 'the white man's anger'.

From the 1960s academic historians began to write of the Land Wars (usually meaning just the 1860–72 conflicts) or the Anglo-Maori Wars. But the fighting was not only about land; and it was not a straightforward contest between British and Maori either, for these were also civil wars. The 'New Zealand Wars' originally meant those fought among New Zealanders — meaning Maori — in the decades before 1840 (what we now call the Musket Wars). But the 1860–61 Taranaki War was sometimes called the New Zealand War, especially overseas and by its Pakeha opponents. James Cowan's determination to be fair to both sides led him to title his pathbreaking 1920s oral history *The New Zealand Wars*. James Belich's adoption of the same title for his magisterial 1986 history of the wars cemented its use. None of the iconoclasts who have chipped away at Belich's work have yet done him much damage — or come up with a better name for this bitter period, even though the wars barely touched the mainland.

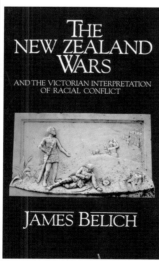
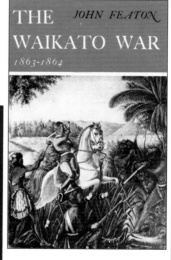
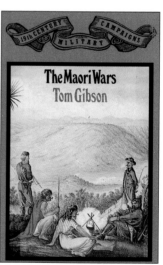

FROM LEFT TO RIGHT: James Cowan (*The New Zealand Wars and the Pioneering Period, vol II*); James Belich (*The New Zealand Wars and the Victorian Interpretation of Racial Conflict*); John Featon (*The Waikato War, 1863–1864*); and Tom Gibson (*The Maori Wars: The British Army in New Zealand, 1840–1872*).

The first shots in the main phase of the New Zealand Wars rang out in Taranaki early in 1860. A decade of bloodshed and suffering began with simple aims on both sides. Pakeha wanted to enforce 'the Queen's law', Maori wanted to keep their land. The year-long Taranaki War was something of a war by proxy. British regular soldiers fought to safeguard current and future settlers, and to discourage 'rebellion' in Waikato — the heartland of Maori independence — as much as to defeat it in Taranaki. In the short term, they achieved none of these goals.

With the might of the British Empire behind them, the soldiers and settlers were cocky. Time and again — in this conflict and later — they underestimated Maori skills and strategic nous. In March 1860, Kingi's men quickly built a modern artillery-resistant pa on the disputed land. After this had withstood a day's bombardment, they happily abandoned it. Successful Maori war leaders understood that pa were expendable but warriors precious.

When an expedition to rescue outlying settlers was attacked, all hell broke loose in New Plymouth. After the alarm guns were fired, 'a stream of women were to be seen hurrying up the steep path into the barracks . . . some . . . with a child under each arm, without either hat, bonnet or shawl — some with a bundle hastily thrown together, and many seemed utterly bewildered amidst the confusion and noise of women crying, children screaming, and the eager, anxious questions to know what it was all about'.[9] The volunteers returned safely after midnight to the 'deafening cheers and mad excitement' of their relieved families.

While settlers huddled in town in increasingly unsanitary living conditions, their opponents took over the countryside, harvesting crops, slaughtering livestock, and looting homes and farm buildings. Colonel Emilius Gold's thousand soldiers concentrated on protecting New Plymouth and could not catch either Te Atiawa or their southern allies, Ngati Ruanui and Taranaki, in the open. Bolstered in June by taua (war parties) on tours of duty from Waikato — 1500 warriors in all during the

New Plymouth was an armed camp in 1860. Military and settlers alike suffered from disease, and more than 100 died. Eight hundred civilians, mostly women and children, were shipped off to Nelson as refugees. E Harris, Alexander Turnbull Library, C-030-010

war — the Maori won a crushing victory at Puketakauere, a deceptively strong pa complex near Waitara. Here they were led by the Atiawa chief Hapurona, 'a little, fiery man with a jealous temper and great military talent'.[10] Twenty-nine of the 350-strong British strike force were killed; many were tomahawked and left to rot in a swamp renamed Te Wai Kotero ('the putrid pool'). This was a shattering blow to colonial morale; the Auckland newspaper *Southern Cross* described it as 'the worst reverse we have ever suffered in all our engagements with the natives'.[11]

The bewhiskered and jowly General Thomas Pratt then took charge of a force that eventually numbered 3500.[12] Superior firepower helped him win some skirmishes in the second half of 1860, but his opponents were still elusive. In December he tried a new approach, attacking Kingi's pa at Te Arei by digging a covered trench towards it. The settlers despaired. 'The General . . . will . . . get to where the Natives

are in from ten to fourteen days. And . . . when he gets there the Natives will be as far off.'[13] Kingi's men mockingly offered to dig the trench themselves for 1s 6d an hour. Though new-generation artillery came into action in March 1861, informed local colonists felt 'more depressed and hopeless than ever. General Pratt's conduct looks more and more idiotic.'[14]

With both sides weary of the struggle and no end in sight, a ceasefire took effect on 18 March. Gore Browne agreed to look again at the Waitara purchase. Before James Belich's *The New Zealand Wars*, most historians accepted the government's claim of victory. But the majority of the 'rebel' leaders never signed the peace agreement, and the Taranaki settlement was left with less land than before the war. Its farms were crippled by pillaging for which no compensation was ever paid. Many would not be reoccupied for years. About 400 fighters lay dead — roughly equal numbers of Europeans and Maori. Distrust and discontent would smoulder for decades.

The Taranaki ceasefire was brokered by Wiremu Tamihana, one of the leaders of a Maori nationalist movement that had developed during the 1850s. Grey had noted shrewdly in 1847 that peace and improved communications were making co-operation among tribes much easier — and growing Pakeha pressure for land was making it necessary. The catalysts for kotahitanga (unity) were not traditional leaders, but young, literate, Christian chiefs like Matene Te Whiwhi and Tamihana Te Rauparaha of Otaki, the mission station famed for producing the most 'advanced' Maori in the country.[15] From 1853 this pair made several trips around the North Island advocating a confederation headed by a king. Only by creating their own institutions could Maori preserve their identity and protect their land.

After a huge hui at Lake Taupo in November 1856, the elderly Waikato chief Potatau Te Wherowhero — Auckland's former protector — eventually agreed to accept the kingship if this would rally support for Maori sovereignty. 'New Zealand is ours — I love it!,' enthused another aged chief.[16]

Firth Family Papers, Alexander Turnbull Library, F-93198-½

Wiremu Tamihana was a churchman militant. His Christianity was as important to his actions as his belief in Maori sovereignty.

Te Wherowhero was installed as king by Wiremu Tamihana at hui held at Ngaruawahia and Rangiaowhia in June 1858. Hapu who declared allegiance to him placed their lands under his mana — they could not be sold. As well as an embargo on the advance of Pakeha settlement — new roads were opposed with growing vehemence — the Kingitanga, as it became known, sought self-government for Maori-held areas. 'Soon they had their own flag, newspaper, records, councillors, magistrates, constables, and a surveyor.'[17] Tamihana was busy drafting a legal code based on models developed at Peria.

Gore Browne responded by calling a Maori conference at Kohimarama, Auckland, in July 1860. About 200 chiefs turned up, including representatives of iwi like Te Arawa, who had not signed the Treaty of Waitangi; but chiefs from Taranaki and Waikato who were 'in rebellion' were not invited. This assembly reaffirmed the Treaty and pledged unanimously 'to do nothing inconsistent with their declared recognition of the Queen's sovereignty, and of the union of the two races'.[18] But it neither endorsed the government's policy in Taranaki nor condemned the Kingitanga — many thought it possible to serve both monarchs. Gore Browne was humiliated by the standoff reached in Taranaki in April 1861 and demanded that the Kingitanga submit 'without reserve, to the Queen's sovereignty and the authority of the law', or face the consequences.[19] This was an offer that could only be refused, and he began planning to invade Waikato in the spring. By then, however, he was governor of tranquil Tasmania. Fearing an expensive war, the Colonial Office had pinned its hopes on its 'native' expert, Sir George Grey.

The Kingites, as the settlers dubbed them, were also preparing for war. This 'Kingite War-song' was still being chanted 50 years later:

Ka ngapu te whenua
Ka haere nga tangata ki whea?
E Ruaimoko
Purutia!
Tawhia!
Kia ita!
A . . . a . . . a ita!
Kia mau, kia mau!

The earthquake shakes the land;
Where shall man find an abiding-place?
O Ruaimoko (god of the lower depths)
Hold fast our land!
Bind, tightly bind!
Be firm, be firm!
Nor let it from our grasp be torn![20]

The Waikato War

The Waikato War was the heavyweight contest that decided the North Island's future. It opened up a vast area to settlers, and blunted Maori ability to resist further inroads. The Waikato iwi and their allies fought desperately for their lands, livelihoods and families. Thanks to their skill and bravery, most survived to fight other kinds of battles. But once the imperial superpower applied itself, there was little chance they could hold on to their homes or resources. Except when fighting flared briefly on both coasts in the summer of 1868/69, European dominance in the North Island would never again be threatened.

While serving as Britain's man in South Africa, Grey had gained more experience in race relations. Back in Auckland's Government House in late 1861, he moved to reduce the appeal of the Kingitanga through an imperial strategy as old as the Romans: indirect rule. His 'new institutions' promised Maori limited self-government. Local runanga (assemblies) in which only men could take part would be grafted onto the customary informal gatherings. They would administer laws, hold courts and settle disputes. The pay offered for clerks, legal assistants, police and mailmen tempted uncommitted hapu like those living along the lower Waikato River to use the new institutions. But Grey's determination to 'dig around the King until he falls' struck many as a prelude to war. An uneasy peace lasted for a year or so. Grey used it to extend the Great South Road from Drury towards the Waikato River, protecting it with forts such as Queen's Redoubt at Pokeno. Its military function was clear.

Grey also persuaded the Colonial Office to send reinforcements, claiming that the Kingites were poised to attack Auckland. This is doubtful. But by mid 1863 about 4000 imperial troops were available in the province, enough to invade Waikato. Some arrived battle-hardened after helping to put down the British Empire's earlier 'native difficulty', the 'Indian Mutiny'. In April 1863 Grey ordered the reoccupation of the Tataraimaka Block in Taranaki, which had been held by Maori as compensation for Kingi's Waitara Block. By the time the Waitara Purchase was formally abandoned in May, fighting had broken out again in Taranaki. As war fever grew in Auckland, newspapers echoed the view of most settlers: the Maori must be shown that they were subjects of the Queen. For most Pakeha, a desire to occupy the fertile land of the Waikato basin stemmed less from personal greed than from a belief that it was wrong for Maori to hold on to so much 'waste' land. Many welcomed the imminent clash between 'civilisation' and 'barbarism'.

An engraving from *The Illustrated London News*, 'The Devil's Nest', showing the military road over the Bombay Hills. This road was vulnerable to guerrilla attacks until the bush alongside it was cleared. Alexander Turnbull Library, PUBL-0033-1863-476

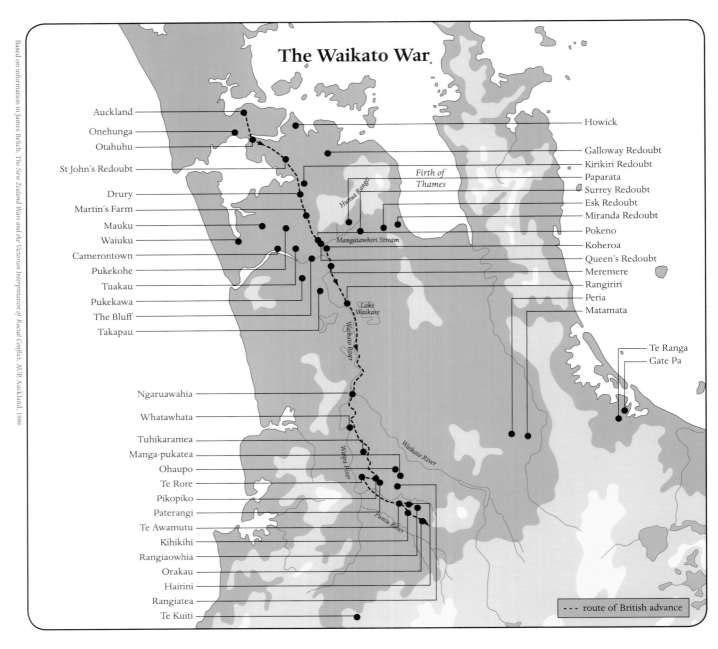

Based on information in James Belich, *The New Zealand Wars and the Victorian Interpretation of Racial Conflict*, AUP, Auckland, 1986

The Waikato War

Auckland
Onehunga
Otahuhu
St John's Redoubt
Drury
Martin's Farm
Mauku
Waiuku
Camerontown
Pukekohe
Tuakau
Pukekawa
The Bluff
Takapau
Ngaruawahia
Whatawhata
Tuhikaramea
Manga-pukatea
Ohaupo
Te Rore
Pikopiko
Paterangi
Te Awamutu
Kihikihi
Rangiaowhia
Orakau
Hairini
Rangiatea
Te Kuiti

Howick
Galloway Redoubt
Kirikiri Redoubt
Paparata
Surrey Redoubt
Esk Redoubt
Miranda Redoubt
Pokeno
Koheroa
Queen's Redoubt
Meremere
Rangiriri
Peria
Matamata

Te Ranga
Gate Pa

Firth of Thames

Hunua Range

Mangatawhiri Stream

Lake Waikare

Waikato River

Waipa River

Waikato River

Puniu River

--- route of British advance

On 9 July 1863, Grey ordered all Maori living between Auckland and the Waikato River to swear allegiance to the Queen and give up their arms, or face expulsion. Most left with whatever they could carry. They were never compensated for their losses. Three days later, General Duncan Cameron's troops crossed the Mangatawhiri Stream into Kingite territory. This tall Scotsman with 'a large hookey nose and small grey eyes' had warfare in his blood and had made his name in the Crimean War. New Zealand in 1861 was every officer's dream mission — a wartime command — and Cameron arrived as 'one of the most accomplished officers in the British army'. He left four years later with his reputation here much diminished.[21]

The core Waikato iwi — Ngati Haua, Ngati Maniapoto, and Waikato proper — were united against the British. Other tribes had difficult choices to make. Which side would they choose? Would blood ties override expediency? Ngati Paoa, for example, tended to support the Crown despite being linked to Waikato by both kinship and traditional alliances; their territory around the Hauraki Gulf lay between the settlers' capital and the Waikato heartland. Europeans missed such shades of grey. And while hapu took different sides, most North Island iwi sent contingents to support the Kingitanga, and others provided logistical support. As Grey's agent in Waikato put it: 'All the tribes of New Zealand either support or sympathize with the

Waikatos. That all have not actually risen in arms against us is no proof to the contrary: for one Maori tribe can carry on the war better, if other tribes remain neutral, and furnish supplies.'[22]

The Kingites had stockpiled ammunition and supplies south of Auckland. Their vigorous guerrilla campaign against Cameron's supply lines stalled his advance for three months. Meanwhile, outlying settlers scuttled to safety in Auckland. As convoys and pickets along the Great South Road came under attack from the nearby forest, soldiers were diverted to fell trees and build and man new redoubts. On 7 September, a British depot at Camerontown on the lower Waikato River was destroyed by Ngati Maniapoto raiders, cutting the alternative supply route via the Waikato Heads. Guerrillas based in the Hunua ranges were pursued — largely ineffectively — by an improvised 'Moveable Column' (mobile force) of picked regulars and a new 'bush fighting' unit of colonists, the Forest Rangers. By the end of October, 6000 men were protecting Cameron's supply lines. Able at last to advance safely, he bypassed the Maori defences at Meremere by ferrying his 2000-strong strike force upriver. The defenders had thought the steamers' draught was too deep. They withdrew rather than face attack from both front and rear.

The odds were stacked against the Kingites. The British had superior weapons and logistics. Their opponents had no effective artillery, and most of their weapons were obsolete trade muskets. These were, however, easy to maintain and effective at close range. Cameron's men had the latest rifles and artillery, steamers and gunboats, and an efficient supply system. His goal was to bring about a major battle in which enough warriors were killed or captured to persuade the Kingites that fighting on would be futile. Their aim was to stop the British moving upriver past Taupiri mountain to Ngaruawahia, the King's capital. Here the Waipa River joins the Waikato, and both rivers are navigable by small craft for a long way upstream. To forestall an advance into their heartland, the Kingites built a new defensive line at Rangiriri, 20 km south of Meremere, across the kilometre-wide isthmus between the Waikato River and Lake Waikare.

Defending their homes and heritage imposed enormous stresses on Maori. Unlike Britain, they had no full-time army and produced little or no economic surplus. They could not keep fighters permanently in the field. Men had to go home periodically for rest and recreation, and to plant and harvest crops and tend livestock. On any given day up to a third of the force might be in transit, available neither to fight nor to produce food. The Kingites generally managed to co-ordinate warriors from diverse sources, and developed efficient systems for supplying them. Women literally carried much of the burden. However, hapu and iwi continued to grow food independently — there was no co-ordinated Maori war economy. This was

Charles Heaphy's sketch *Earthworks of Rangiriri Pa* evokes the scale of the central redoubt at Rangiriri. It must have seemed insurmountable to the men of the 'forlorn hopes' who stormed it.

a fatal weakness against a well-organised enemy. The effort that had gone into constructing and defending the Meremere line had temporarily depleted the Maori capacity to wage war. Although Rangiriri's defences were nearly finished when the British attacked on 20 November, they were occupied by only about 500 warriors, mostly local Waikato men — not enough to man them properly.

The Rangiriri line could not be completely encircled. So long as it was held, the defenders would be able to escape by waka across Lake Waikare. Therefore the best chance for a decisive British victory was a frontal attack followed by close pursuit. Troops were ferried upriver to cut off retreat to the south. This backstop force had trouble landing, and Cameron's main body did not attack from the north until late afternoon. The under-manned trenches towards the river were soon occupied, and Cameron then ordered a series of assaults on the central redoubt by infantry, naval and artillery units. After the battle, he was criticised for this apparently reckless decision, so at odds with his usual caution. But the real strength of the redoubt could not be seen by reconnaissance from the river. Cameron's quartermaster-general dismissed it as 'just a common embankment with a fence cut in front of it'.[23] But as night fell it was still held by the Kingites, as were the trenches to the east. About 40 men lay dead on each side.

During the night some of the defenders slipped quietly away through the trenches and were paddled across the lake. Among them were Te Wherowhero's son, Matutaera, who had succeeded him as King, and Wiremu Tamihana. Maori wounded were also evacuated. Meanwhile the British 'bivouacked on the wet ground, disgusted and disheartened'.[24] Next day tragedy became farce. At dawn the defenders raised a white flag in response to one flying on a steamer. They meant to negotiate, but were soon trying to wave away soldiers who thought they had surrendered and swarmed inside the defences. Cameron was happy to take advantage of the situation and demand the arms of the 180 men (and a few women) who were still in the redoubt. Taken to Auckland as prisoners, they eventually had some revenge. Concerned about conditions on the prison hulk *Marion*, Grey invited them to stay at his Kawau Island property in August 1864. They soon escaped to the mainland, where many holed up in a hilltop pa while others terrified new settlers over on the Kaipara. Persuaded to come down to the coast, they drilled regularly — and enjoyed a hearty Christmas dinner — before accepting safe conduct back to Waikato at New Year.[25]

The loss of more than 200 fighting men at Rangiriri was soon followed by the evacuation of the King's capital, and Tamihana sought peace. In early December, Grey crowed to the Colonial Secretary in London that 'the neck of this unhappy rebellion is now broken'.[26] He knew this was not true. The King would never surrender unconditionally, as the British demanded. His forces were already digging in on the 'Paterangi line', about 40 km south of Ngaruawahia. The scale of these defences reflected the importance of the agricultural heartland around Rangiaowhia, compared to which 'the country from which

they had been expelled was of slight value'.[27] Four large pa and several smaller ones were linked in the largest and most complex system of modern pa ever built. The British crawled towards them through the Waikato summer. Cameron's strike force, now 3000 strong, had to be supplied and his lengthening line of communications had to be protected; and one of his two steamers had sunk in the Waipa.

Once again, the Maori Achilles' heel was lack of numbers. Fifteen hundred men dispersed along this line could not guard every path, and Cameron with 1200 men successfully negotiated a rough track past Paterangi on the night of 20 February. He pushed on to Rangiaowhia, where civilians were killed by Colonial Defence Force cavalry and Forest Rangers in house-to-house fighting with the kainga's few surprised defenders. This incident became a cause célèbre — partly because some were killed trying to surrender, and also because Cameron had supposedly promised that Rangiaowhia would not be attacked. As the area was a key base for the Kingite war effort, it is unlikely he had made such a promise.

Hoping to lure the main Kingite force into a decisive pitched battle, Cameron pulled back to Te Awamutu. But the Maori fought only a delaying action at Hairini that bought time to withdraw.

This photograph shows the size of the Paterangi defences. Cameron's men were lucky that a local Maori was willing to guide them around Paterangi.

The Kingites' 'Maginot line' had fallen. They had saved their army but lost some of their richest land and economic resources. The colonial soldier Gustavus von Tempsky witnessed their reaction: 'Never . . . shall I forget the expression of dismal wonder in the faces of the Mission-Maoris when my rangers marched into the courtyard . . . [of St John's Church at Te Awamutu] . . . Could they see our arrival calmly, when the very fact of this arrival indubitably announced that this great bulwark of Maoridom, Paterangi, had either fallen, or had proved useless.'[28]

After another battle at Orakau (see page 140), Ngati Maniapoto's heartland was still protected by three strong pa south of the Puniu River, which the Kingites began calling the aukati (boundary). They would oppose any advance across it. Ngati Haua and Ngati Raukawa manned other pa to the east. Unable to destroy the King's army, Cameron took 1700 men to Tauranga to cut off a source of reinforcements and supplies. Rawiri te Puhirake, the feisty Ngaiterangi chief, fortified Pukehinahina (the Gate Pa). On April 29, this was bombarded by the greatest concentration of artillery used in the wars. Once its parapet had been breached, soldiers and sailors poured in. But much of the bombardment had missed the small pa, which was so strong that most of its 200 defenders had survived in underground bunkers.

Unexpected fire from below demoralised the attackers; 31 were killed and those who could soon fled. The distraught Cameron 'dashed his field-glass on the ground, turned his back on the fugitives, and retired to his tent to conceal his emotion'.[29] The Maori withdrew after dark, leaving 19 dead behind them.

Two months later, the British avenged Gate Pa when they surprised about 500 Maori in the act of digging rifle pits at Te Ranga, killing about 70. But the earlier disaster had convinced Cameron that he could not capture a completed modern pa manned by disciplined defenders. He admitted this laconically to Grey: 'Experience has shown me that it is not generally desirable to attack such positions.'[30] Beginning during the Northern War, Maori engineers had solved the apparently insoluble — how to win defensive battles despite vastly inferior numbers, and with only muskets against rifles and modern artillery. They had developed trench and bunker systems that could stand up to bombardment, incorporated deceptively weak or strong features that confused the gunners, and included firing positions and salients from which volleys of musket fire could be suddenly unleashed onto attacking troops. But even these unsung geniuses were ultimately no match for the resources that were brought to bear against them.

General Duncan Cameron — fifth from right in the second row, in front of the wheel of the gun carriage — poses with members of his staff and Royal Artillerymen on the morning of the battle at Gate Pa.

ORAKAU

"If men are to die the women and children can die also."

FRONTIER FILMS LTD. PRESENT
THE N.Z. CENTENNIAL EPIC

REWI'S LAST STAND

STARRING
RAMAI TE MIHA
LEO PILCHER
STANLEY KNIGHT

A RUDALL HAYWARD PRODUCTION

Rudall Hayward remade his 1925 feature film, *Rewi's Last Stand*, which he had based on James Cowan's *The New Zealand Wars*, for the 1940 New Zealand centennial. Hayward's decision to emphasise a fictional interracial love affair was no help at the box office. New Zealand Film Archive

The three-day battle at Orakau dominates the imagery of the New Zealand Wars. It has been portrayed in fiction, song and film. Yet it was an almost accidental act of defiance that was doomed before it began. The Ngati Maniapoto war leader Rewi Maniapoto was travelling east to talk strategy with Tamihana when he came across a party of Tuhoe and Ngati Raukawa who were spoiling for a fight after fleeing Paterangi without having one. Unable to change their minds, he predicted disaster:

> Tokotokona na te hau tawaho koi toko atu
> I kite ai au i Remu-taka ra,
> I kite ai au ma taku kui ki Wai-mata-e
> Tohungia mai e te kokoreke ra
> Katahi nei hoki ka kitea te karoro tu-a-wai
> I tu awaawa ra
> Ma te kahore anake e noho toku whenua
> Kai tua te ra e whiti ana,
> E noho ana ko te koko koroki
> I ata kiki tau.

This was the gist of it:

> Listen to me, Tuhoe. Waikato is destroyed. I alone survive. If we fight, as you propose, I alone will survive. I have seen the evil omen, the lone gull on the waters. If I fight again, no one will live in my lands. Only by not fighting may I retain them. If we fight, the sun will shine on a land without people. I will be the only songbird left, but I shall be mute. Do not fight at Orakau. If you must fight, fight at Te Tiki-o-Te Ihingarangi, at Maungatautari.[31]

Yet Rewi — out of kinship and loyalty — decided to join the hotheads, and about 250 warriors, accompanied by 50 women and children, fortified Orakau in late March 1864. The site was chosen to provoke the British; it was only 5 km from their base at Kihikihi.

The true strength of the hastily constructed pa was disguised by its low walls and the peach trees that surrounded it. But it could easily be encircled. It also lacked an internal water supply, and was incomplete when 1100 soldiers arrived on 30 March. Tuhoe, who had met few Europeans, were awed: 'What a numberless people are the Pakeha. They covered the land.'[32] After several frontal assaults failed, Brigadier-General Carey resorted to artillery bombardment and sapping. By noon on 2 April Cameron had arrived with reinforcements, the sap had reached the pa, and the defenders, without food or water, had almost run out of ammunition. The destruction of the garrison (including Rewi) seemed only a matter of time. But in mid-afternoon the defenders broke through the British lines. About 80 were killed, but the rest fought off cavalry and Forest Rangers, hid in a swamp till nightfall, and then escaped across the Puniu River.

Civil war and self-reliance

By mid 1864, Grey and Cameron — with 18,000 troops — had conquered a good deal of the northern North Island. The area covered on a map by the King's tapu bowler hat marked out the 'Rohe Potae' — his remaining territory. The government decided to pay for the war by confiscating land, including the half-million hectares it had occupied in Waikato, where military settlers built blockhouses and took up sections along the de facto border. But real peace was nearly a decade away.

The first challenge came from the Pai Marire ('Goodness and Peace') movement of the visionary south Taranaki prophet Te Ua Haumene, who promised to regain Maori their birthright. Te Ua named his church Hauhau — the spirit of God in the wind ('Te Hau') would carry his prophecies to the faithful. In autumn 1864 his followers launched attacks in Taranaki and Wanganui; in August he rebaptised King Matutaera and renamed him Tawhiao ('Bind the People'); from December messengers travelled across the island to Turanga (Gisborne) preaching resistance as they went. The missionaries seemed to have failed Maori, and Te Ua was just one of many prophets springing up in this time of troubles whose teachings combined Christianity with traditional beliefs.

In early 1865 Cameron mounted a tentative campaign from Wanganui into south Taranaki. A year later his successor, Major-General Trevor Chute — 'the Kerry Bull'[33] — completed the journey to New Plymouth, crushing unco-ordinated resistance before getting lost in the forest behind Mount Egmont. On his return along the coast Chute accepted the surrender of Te Ua, who had lost his radical fervour. British regulars were now being steadily withdrawn, amid arguments about how much the colony still owed for their services. In 1867 their place was taken

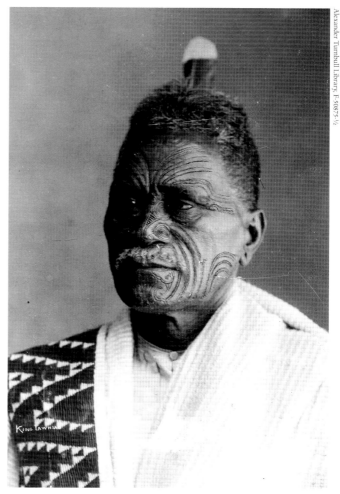

Tawhiao Matutaera Potatau Te Wherowhero, tall and elaborately tattooed, led the Kingitanga through 34 years of war and peace.

Te Kooti's War was increasingly fought by Maori against Maori. This Te Arawa detachment of the Armed Constabulary has captured Te Kooti's war flag at Lake Rotokakahi, just south of Rotorua, in February 1870.

by the Armed Constabulary, a small but increasingly efficient army. Its commandant was a career soldier turned Hawke's Bay runholder, George Whitmore, 'a small man, trimly bearded, with a steely gaze'.[34] Whitmore was competent and energetic, but also 'hypocritical, elitist, arrogant, and tactless', and 'a contemptible little brute'.[35] In the same year Grey was sacked as governor and replaced by Sir George Bowen, who was more pompous than Grey but also more in tune with the limitations of the governorship in a democracy. In future, 'native policy' would be both paid for and determined by the settler government. This was now based in Wellington, which had clamoured to become the capital for some time.

Things had hotted up when Te Ua's emissaries ignored his instructions to behave peaceably and incited the killing of the government spies Carl Volkner (a missionary) and James Fulloon in eastern Bay of Plenty in 1865. To settlers used to the comparative chivalry of previous campaigns, this was a new kind of barbarism. Punitive expeditions by colonial units, Te Arawa and Wanganui kupapa (pro-government Maori) were followed by the confiscation of much of this area. The East Coast and Poverty Bay were also ablaze. After a Ngati Porou civil war along the Waiapu River, Pai Marire adherents were defeated near Turanga in November 1865 by a mostly Ngati Porou force keen to settle some old scores with local iwi. These small campaigns set the pattern for the rest of the New Zealand Wars by being fought mainly between Maori. During the battle at Waerenga-a-hika in November a Rongowhakaata man, Te Kooti Te Turuki, who was fighting on the government side, was arrested for allegedly helping the enemy. In 1866 this former 'terror to the district',[36] who had become a successful trader, was among nearly 200 men exiled to the Chatham Islands.

Te Ua Haumene, the founder of Pai Marire.

Pukohu tairi ki Poneke ra,
Ki te kainga ra i noho ai te Minita.
Ki taku whakaaro ka tae mai te Poari
Hai noho i te whenua o Kotitia nei,
Pa rawa te mamae ki te tau o taku ate.
E te iwi nui, tu ake ki runga ra,
Tirohia mai ra te he o aku mahi!
Maku e ki atu, 'Nohia, nohia!'
No mua iho ano, no nga kaumatua!
Na taku ngakau i kimi ai ki te Ture,
No konei hoki au i kino ai ki te hoko!
Hi! Hai aha te hoko!

Yonder the mist hangs over Wellington,
The home of the Minister.
I fear that the Board will come
To live in this land of Kootitia,
And I am sick at heart.
All my people, be watchful,
See the evil of these things!
I say to you, 'Remain, remain on the land!'
It is from former ages, from your ancestors!
Because my heart has searched out the Law,
For this reason I abhor selling!
Hi! Why sell![37]

There are no known photographs and few sketches of Te Kooti. This drawing of him addressing a meeting in Rotorua is dated 1887, but he is not known to have visited the town in that year. It may have been made in 1883.

TE KOOTI'S WAR

Poverty Bay settlers used him as a bogeyman to frighten naughty children. To them he was an 'arch-rebel' who created a blood-bath for incomprehensible religious reasons. Many Maori who crossed his path also feared him — with good reason. Some saw him as unjustly accused, a Moses-like figure who had delivered his people from exile. His biographer, Judith Binney, observes that 'almost all the Maori stories that are still told of Te Kooti place him as the guardian of the land, and of the people's autonomy'.[38] He was also a prolific composer of waiata. However he is remembered, he was a central figure in the turbulent late 1860s.

Te Kooti became leader of the whakarau (the prisoners on the Chathams) by developing a religious movement — Ringatu ('The Upraised Hand') — which resembled Pai Marire. His first service promised the exiles divine deliverance: 'Thy children shall come again to their own border.'[39] In July 1868 he gave the Almighty a hand by masterminding their escape in a captured schooner. After landing south of Gisborne, he and his followers (including their families, who had been allowed to join them on the Chathams) took a month to reach safety near Waikaremoana. They won three engagements against local volunteers and kupapa on the way. In November Te Kooti returned to Poverty Bay with a vengeance, killing about 50 people in a night-time raid on Matawhero, where his family's land had been occupied by Europeans after his exile. He took many prisoners and holed up on top of Ngatapa mountain. Like Orakau, this had neither a water supply nor any apparent way out. Yet when the position became untenable at New Year 1869 after five days of siege, Te Kooti and his followers managed to escape down a cliff. Many of the 140 men who were caught in the subsequent chase were executed by Ngati Porou kupapa or Te Arawa regular soldiers. Some were prisoners from Matawhero.

After Ngatapa, Te Kooti could raid, run and hide, but he was no longer much of a military threat. With a price on his head, he was offered sanctuary in the Urewera, and from there he descended on Mohaka and Whakatane to exact bloody utu. But his attempts to impress the Kingitanga ended in October 1869 at Te Porere, south of Lake Taupo, where he lost a battle in another poorly chosen position at the cost of 37 lives. From then on, Te Kooti and his dwindling band of followers were hunted mercilessly by Ngati Porou, Arawa and Wanganui kupapa until they escaped to the King Country early in 1872.

To thank Tawhiao for sheltering him, Te Kooti transformed Tokanganui-a-noho at Te Kuiti into one of the best carved and painted meeting houses of the post-war era. He composed many more waiata in this new exile. One, 'He waiata tohutohu' ('A song of instruction'), urged Tuhoe not to sell their land to the government (see far left).

Museum of New Zealand, Te Papa Tongarewa

Te Kooti's flag was captured at Te Porere. According to Binney, the moon symbolised the new world, which would be won with the aid of the fighting cross. The letters WI are thought to evoke the Holy Spirit.

TITOKOWARU'S WAR

At New Year 1869, 605 of Wanganui's 'Wives, Mothers and Daughters' begged Queen Victoria 'to avert the extinction of ourselves, and those dearest to us, under circumstances equal to if not exceeding the barbarities perpetrated in . . . Poverty Bay'.[40] Belich has called the man they were afraid of, Riwha Titokowaru of Ngati Ruanui, 'the best general New Zealand has ever produced' because of his skill at building deceptively strong pa.[41] Unlike Te Kooti, Titokowaru posed Whitmore the question that Cameron had been unable to answer: how to kill or capture the defenders of a well-designed modern pa. Whitmore had far fewer resources than Cameron, and he, too, never solved this riddle.

Titokowaru was grim, deep-voiced, and commanding, but 'by no means good-looking', particularly after he lost an eye in a botched Pai Marire attack on New Plymouth in 1864.[42] In mid 1868 he took up arms against the land confiscation that was accompanying the construction of a road from Wanganui towards New Plymouth. After turning to ritual cannibalism and invoking the traditional war-god Uenuku, he began to be credited with supernatural powers. His small but growing army won victory after victory and seemed unstoppable.

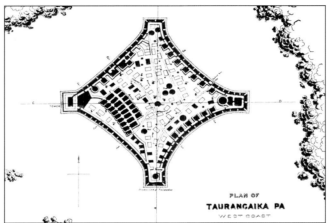

PLAN OF
TAURANGAIKA PA
WEST COAST

Tauranga-a-ika was Titokowaru's masterpiece. Even the cocky Whitmore confessed later that 'no troops in the world' could have stormed this 'really strong pah'.
From a survey by J. Buchanan, 1869, in James Cowan, *The New Zealand Wars*, volume II

More than 50 Wanganui kupapa and Armed Constabulary (including von Tempsky) were killed, and farms near Wanganui were plundered. Land values in town plummeted by 75 per cent, and the demoralised citizens felt even more threatened when Whitmore and most of his trained troops went east in pursuit of Te Kooti.

While they were away, Titokowaru built a formidable modern pa at Tauranga-a-ika, 30 km north-west of Wanganui. When Whitmore came back to attack it on 2 February 1869, he risked losing the core of his army. If he had, the few British troops still in the colony could not have sustained the war effort, and the Kingitanga might have reoccupied its lost land. Belich asserts that this would have meant not 'European extermination or expulsion, but . . . a return to the race-relations situation of 1859: a British periphery co-operating economically with a much larger Maori hinterland'.[43] This last chance for a biracial New Zealand was lost when Tauranga-a-ika was abruptly abandoned by its defenders. Titokowaru's army melted away — supposedly after he was found with another man's wife. Never in New Zealand's history has the personal been more political.

Taking the land

As the settlers flexed their newly self-reliant muscles, conquest was backed up by law. In 1863 the Whitaker–Russell government — Auckland's business elite in thin disguise — passed a Suppression of Rebellion Act, which suspended the normal legal rights of anyone suspected of being 'in rebellion'. They could be detained indefinitely and tried by military courts martial. The New Zealand Settlements Act authorised the confiscation of the land within proclaimed districts. Some would be allotted to military settlers; the rest could be sold by the government to cover the cost of the war. Compensation would be paid or land returned only to Maori who could prove they had owned land within the district, and had not rebelled. However it was spun, this was all about punishment and teaching Maori a lesson the effects of which would be felt for decades.

In December 1864, more than one million hectares in Waikato, Bay of Plenty and Taranaki was confiscated. Later in the decade, more was taken in Taranaki and eastern Bay of Plenty. Other strong-arm tactics were used to acquire land on the east coast. Although about half the confiscated land was eventually returned or paid for, this process took decades and was riddled with

Artist Kennett Watkins's view of the death of the Prussian adventurer turned Armed Constabulary officer, Major Gustavus von Tempsky, at Te Ngutu o te Manu in September 1868. It shows his men's confusion but trivialises Titokowaru's defences. Most of his warriors did not stand nonchalantly in trees or crouch behind logs, but concealed themselves in purpose-built firing positions.

anomalies. In Waikato, all the occupied territory was confiscated. So the Waikato iwi lost almost all their land, Ngati Haua about a third of theirs, Ngati Maniapoto virtually none. The 'loyal' Maori of the lower Waikato eventually had land returned to them — but little good land. On the other hand, much of the land proclaimed as 'confiscated' outside Waikato was for years taken only on paper. Maori naturally assumed that the confiscation had been abandoned, and were resentful — some to the point of armed resistance — when it finally happened.

As fighting died down in Waikato, several regiments of military settlers, including the Forest Rangers and many men recruited from the declining goldfields of Victoria and Otago, took up properties between Ngaruawahia and the aukati. The future Hamilton, Cambridge, and Alexandra (Pirongia) were laid out in town sections. Country allotments ranged upwards according to rank from the 50 acres allocated to privates. Rations were provided for only one year, and many walked away before their three years of service ended. Others sold up as soon as they got title, daunted by the task of building houses and reclaiming swamps. Many of those in for the long haul, who picked up additional sections cheaply, were officers. The Maori they had displaced were now refugees, reluctant long-term guests of Ngati Maniapoto or Ngati Tuwharetoa.

Military settlers and their families did it tough as they carved farms out of the Waikato bush. Many gave up and went back to town.

Claimants in their Sunday best flocked to Land Court hearings like this one at Ahipara in the far north around 1880. Often they had to stay on for weeks before being heard.

Maori owned some flax mills, but not this one at Clevedon, south of Auckland. As they lost land and capital, many became wage labourers for Pakeha owners.

Maori land that was not confiscated was opened to purchase by Europeans by a legal revolution. The Native Lands Act 1865 set up a system for converting customary title into individual title. At first, there could be no more than 10 names on each deed. When large blocks were awarded, most of those with an interest missed out if chiefs chose to pocket the sale proceeds. Although the 10-owner limit was removed in 1873, there was still no provision for collective title. Native Land Courts sitting around the country issued titles that could be sold, leased or mortgaged in the usual way. The Crown also kept buying Maori land to onsell to the immigrants who were flooding into the country.

The Land Court has gone down in history as 'te kooti tango whenua' — 'the land-taking court'. Ironically, this term was first recorded in 1867 by Major Reginald Biggs, the self-serving Poverty Bay magistrate who confirmed Te Kooti's exile, occupied his land and pursued him relentlessly when he came back in 1868. Te Kooti had a terrible revenge, killing Biggs and his family at Matawhero.[44] The court has also been called 'a veritable engine of destruction' of Maori customary rights,[45] part of a system which provided 'a show of justice' but not its substance.[46] Unlike Grey's, this 'new institution' definitely had teeth. Yet some historians argue that Maori litigants effectively ran the Land Court themselves for their own purposes.[47] This is a living court: its files are still consulted extensively during the Treaty claims process.

The process by which titles were granted certainly made it likely the land would be sold. It began when a customary owner applied to have his or her interest individualised. Often an owner was encouraged to do so by an intending buyer. Rival claimants had to appear in court to plead their cases — absence could be fatal to their chances. All paid a daily fee to attend the court, and most had to hire interpreters and lawyers. Whole communities became temporary migrants, often staying in hotels. (Maori were by now as fond of alcohol as Pakeha, and the price of a bottle of whisky could be several acres of marginal land.) The court eventually split up blocks into many portions, which were surveyed at the owners' expense. If they decided to sell — often by now the only way they could clear their debts — 10 per cent duty was payable on the proceeds. Those who could afford to keep their land often lost access to it when their neighbours sold up, forcing them to follow suit. When part of a block was reserved from sale, this was typically only for 21 years, after which this land too could be partitioned and sold.

Court hearings often dragged on, because evidence for customary title was always complex and frequently contradictory. This was not a simple matter of Pakeha dispossessing Maori; Maori were also pitted against each other. The Musket Wars were relitigated for decades. Some hapu wanted to sell land mainly because this would prove they owned it. Customary give-and-take within hapu tended to give way to self-interest, with the claimants who were eventually granted title behaving as private owners rather than the trustees of collective property. The kind of authority over substantial areas of tribal land that was claimed by rangatira like Wiremu Kingi withered away as the law ground on.

Some chiefly families who held onto substantial landholdings or other assets built mansions and sought mana in the Pakeha world. Others spent the proceeds of land sales on status symbols. Innumerable hui and a spate of church and meeting-house building also depleted resources while solving few problems. As immigrants and investment flooded in from Britain, it was increasingly difficult for Maori to compete. Maori did not lose their talent for doing business, but the relatively level pre-1860 playing field had disappeared. They were 'not so much shut out of, as left behind by, the colonial economy'.[48] With mechanised wheat farming booming on the South Island plains, for example, only about 10 Maori-owned flour mills operated in Auckland province after the wars.[49] In the Hauraki district, expensive tramways and steam-powered mills were needed to work the inaccessible timber still in Maori hands. Quartz gold mining was risky and cost a fortune to get into. Only flax milling offered Maori any entrepreneurial scope. Where decent farmland remained in Maori ownership, such as the 850-ha Te Huruhi Block on Waiheke Island, crops were grown and flocks reared on a commercial basis. Other hapu sold their forests or dug kauri gum — under economic pressure, kaitiakitanga (guardianship) was giving way to exploitation. Those dispossessed through the Native Land Court process often had no choice but to move. By the 1870s most North Island shearing gangs were Maori, and many shearers joined the seasonal trans-Tasman circuit. Wage labourers often worked and travelled in whanau groups, but broader hapu and iwi ties were loosened.

During the 1870s, the South Island provinces were linked by railways. Better communications made regional governments a luxury, and the provinces were abolished in 1876. Things were less straightforward in the north, although telegraph and road communication between Wellington and Auckland was established in the early 1870s. The route was pragmatic and strategic, but far from direct; it went via Napier, Taupo, Rotorua and Tauranga. The fact that the two Rohe Potae — the territory of the Kingitanga and the Urewera — had been prised apart was symbolised by Governor Bowen's lightly escorted ride along the new coach road in April 1872, while Te Kooti was still being hunted. Bowen even spent a night at Opepe, the scene of a 'massacre' of volunteer cavalry by the guerrilla leader's men less than three years before. The road was built by two main groups: troops with time on their hands, and Maori. Land for public works could be confiscated from 'rebels' without

Museum of New Zealand, Te Papa Tongarewa

In the decades to come Maori culture would continue to adapt itself to the new world. Painted rafter ends at Ruaihona (Te Teko) depict faces on playing cards.

compensation, and many of the road-building contracts were awarded to local chiefs. Bowen observed that 'the policy pursued for the pacification of the Highlands of New Zealand is . . . the same [as] that adopted in the last century for the pacification of the Highlands of Scotland. The true weapons of conquest have been in both cases the spade and the pickaxe.'[50]

As well as British flags (to replace Hauhau ones) and paid employment, many of Bowen's hosts asked for schools that would teach Pakeha knowledge in the English language. The emphasis on commercial enterprise in the 1850s, followed by political ferment and war, had blunted the earlier enthusiasm for literacy among Maori. Most mission schools had closed in the 1860s. To replace them, the Native Schools Act 1867 set up a system of primary schools supervised by the Native Department. Charles Heaphy's argument in Parliament has a familiar ring: 'Any expenditure in this direction would be true economy, as the more the Natives were educated the less would be the future expenditure in police and gaols.'[51]

Local communities provided the land and helped fund buildings and salaries. By 1880 about 1400 pupils were attending 57 native schools, most north of Auckland, in Te Arawa and Ngati Porou country, and in the South Island. Only a few had Maori teachers. The churches now concentrated on teaching slightly older pupils at boarding schools. In areas where the races were intermingled, Maori attended general schools alongside Pakeha; some Pakeha children were taught at native schools.

Also in 1867, Maori were given four seats in the 76-member House of Representatives. Maori were then about one-fifth of the population, so this was far from equal representation (although about 2000 Maori men who met the property qualification were also on the general roll). Pragmatism, not principle, lay behind this gesture. Special goldfields seats were being created in the South Island, and the Maori seats would preserve the interisland balance of power. A term or two in the House could also reward a kupapa chief for his loyalty. Among the first Maori members in 1868 were Wanganui's self-styled 'General' Mete Kingi Paetahi, who had saved the town from the invading 'Hauhau' in 1865, and the Ngati Kahungunu warrior Tareha Te Moananui. Participation was low to begin with; Mete Kingi was not opposed, and Tareha won by 34 votes to 33. Most Maori MPs until the 1890s knew little English and could take little part in debate.

Although to the settlers they appeared to be entering Parliament as tokens, the Maori MPs were also new actors in the ongoing adaptation of European forms to Maori ends. Another facet of this process was the formation in the 1870s of many komiti (committees) to spread information, promote local issues, and administer justice outside the Pakeha system. Ngati Kahungunu's komiti was especially active, co-operating with others to organise intertribal hui in Hawke's Bay that attracted growing numbers of delegates.

As long ago as the early 1850s, when the New Zealand Constitution Act was implemented, Wiremu Tamihana had suggested a Maori parliament paralleling that of the settlers. Now Henare Matua of Porangahau revived the idea of kotahitanga (unity) that was to flower in the Maori parliaments that met from the late 1880s, and were countered from 1894 by the Kingitanga's rival Kauhanganui (great council). Meanwhile, another self-styled parliament met annually at Orakei in Auckland from 1879 to 1881. This mostly kupapa assembly was heavily subsidised by the government, which hoped to replicate the Kohimarama conference of 1860. Like their predecessors, however, those attending spent much time protesting against breaches of the Treaty of Waitangi.

WG Baker, Museum of New Zealand, Te Papa Tongarewa

Isolation inside the King Country did little for Maori living conditions.

Henare Matua was also the driving force behind the Repudiation movement of the mid-1870s. This kupapa-inspired pressure group denounced the land sales that had allowed a few runholders, including McLean and the Reverend Samuel Williams, to amass large estates in Hawke's Bay. They had Pakeha allies, and a novel mixed-race commission of inquiry was set up. Though this found — implausibly — no evidence of fraud, its litany of procedural irregularities and unfairness did encourage the abandonment of the 10-owner rule.

Endings and beginnings

Disillusioned kupapa were bad enough. But Pakeha found it 'intolerable that large centres of population should be cut off from each other by vast spaces of country which Europeans were not even allowed to traverse'.[52] The main trunk railway from Auckland reached Te Awamutu in 1880. It could go no further south until the standoff with the Kingitanga was resolved. Life along the aukati resembled the popular image of the American West at this time. All male settlers and most Maori men carried guns. The roads between blockhouses were patrolled regularly by Armed Constabulary and Waikato Cavalry. Alexandra (Pirongia) was a frontier town of 200 whose few sober citizens were regularly alarmed by armed men on horseback. Whatiwhatihoe, just across the Puniu, was quieter, especially after Tawhiao imposed an alcohol ban — but it did hold regular race meetings. Pakeha who strayed across the aukati were sometimes killed, and Maori fleeing British justice found sanctuary in the King's Country. On the other hand, Kingites often passed through Alexandra to sell produce, buy consumer goods, and attend hui and horse races. And some Pakeha men lived across the border with Maori kin — seven at Te Kuiti (the King's capital) alone in 1875. Holes were appearing in the aukati.

By the early 1870s the Kingitanga was also crumbling from within. Ngati Haua had started selling land even before their chief Wiremu Tamihana died in 1866. Two-thirds of the King Country's 7000 inhabitants had fled there from outside the

Rewi Maniapoto, the hero of Orakau in 1864, came to terms with the settler state from 1879. He is shown here with Te Rohu Maniapoto and two children.
Parihaka Album, Alexander Turnbull Library, F-113715-½

Rohe Potae. As the irreversibility of the loss of land sank in, there were tensions with Ngati Maniapoto. Loyalty to Tawhiao — who had founded a new non-violent religion, Tariao, with similarities to Pai Marire — became virtually confined to the Waikato tribes. Living conditions were poor — probably worse than those of pro-government iwi, although theirs was partly a temporary prosperity financed by selling land. The Kingitanga was no threat to anyone beyond its borders. On the other hand, the government — all too aware of the costliness of war — hesitated to force open those borders.

The politicians were soon back in touch. In early 1869, an emissary from Tawhiao was received by Bowen at Government House. Later in the year, Native Minister Donald McLean met Rewi Maniapoto and a representative of the King inside the Rohe Potae. From then on, northern kupapa leaders and the government agent WG Mair shuttled across the aukati with the frequency and self-importance of UN representatives. At first they had little success. After Grey came to power yet again, this time as premier, in 1877, he attended several large hui in the King Country. These foundered on Tawhiao's insistence that all the confiscated land be returned. Not all the 'conversations' involved policy. The activities of Grey's Native Minister, John Sheehan, an alcoholic and 'a regular ram among the native women', gave rise to bilingual humour:

Solo: 'Ma wai taatou e hauti?'	Who do we shout [buy a drink]?'
Chorus: 'Ma Te Hiana.'	'Sheehan.'
Solo: 'Ma wai tatou e ai?'	Who do we f***?'
Chorus: 'Ma Titiana.'	'Titiane.'[53]

The official entertainment during the negotiations included multi-faith church services (Christian, Tariao, Hauhau and Ringatu) and dances — not with poi, but polkas, waltzes, quadrilles and the schottische. Those lucky enough to attend a rival hui called by Rewi Maniapoto at Waitara had even more to occupy them: an art exhibition and reserved seats at the Star pantomime and the Imperial theatre; luxury tinned

SHOWDOWN AT PARIHAKA

The main phase of the New Zealand Wars was bookended in Taranaki. In 1872 the elderly Wiremu Kingi joined the growing community at Parihaka that was led by Te Ua's successors, Te Whiti-o-Rongomai and his brother-in-law Tohu Kakahi. This pair looked like Old Testament prophets, and often sounded like them. Te Whiti in particular had a poetic turn of phrase: 'Look for the fog the Darkness the smoke. Look. It shall shoot forth from these. It shall not come when the sea is smooth, but when its waters are troubled then it shall strike the Shore. The sign of the Son of God.'[54]

As elsewhere, land was the issue at Parihaka. Anomaly had piled on injustice since Titokowaru's War fizzled out in 1869. All the coastal strip had been confiscated — at least in theory — in the mid 1860s, but British writ did not yet run between the Waingongoro and Stony (Hangatahua) rivers. Land was awarded here to kupapa, but they couldn't take it up. Much 'confiscated' land was later also 'bought' by government agents who openly 'greased the palms' of Titokowaru and others. The former scourge of the settlers was now in business supplying them with grass-seed. He remained a threat as the muscle behind Te Whiti and Tohu. Their growing mana as symbols of resistance to colonisation made Parihaka the largest Maori settlement in the country by the late 1870s.

The government could tolerate preaching, but not an unyielding determination to hold onto the land. Grey's ministry began surveying the fertile Waimate plains, north of the Waingongoro, in 1878. Obstruction of the surveys intensified after Titokowaru's valuable cocksfoot crop was

In 1881 Parihaka was the largest Maori community in New Zealand. Its residents — seen here gathered on the central marae — supported themselves by farming.

damaged. Through the winter of 1879, Te Whiti sent teams of ploughmen onto settlers' land. The soldiers of this 'holy army of martyrs' were arrested and shipped off to build roads in Dunedin. John Hall's conservative government, which replaced Grey's later in the year, ordered an inquiry into the whole West Coast lands issue — and passed legislation to hold the prisoners without trial until the inquiry had reported. Potential warriors had to be kept far away from Parihaka.

Surveying continued, and 600 soldiers resumed work on the coast road. Once this was completed, resistance to the confiscation would be difficult because troops could be rushed wherever they were needed. When the roadmakers neared Parihaka in mid 1880, fences they cut down were repeatedly replaced. Like the ploughmen, the fencers were arrested. Both groups were released after the commission of inquiry recommended that large reserves be set aside from the confiscated land — more than 50 ha for every Maori in Taranaki. The Waimate plains was sold off at high prices — £6 an acre — and small farmers began to move in. Te Whiti still refused to negotiate.

In October 1881 the government took advantage of the absence in Fiji of the 'nigger-loving' governor, Sir Arthur Gordon, and gave Te Whiti an ultimatum. When this was ignored, a 1600-strong force of Armed Constabulary and volunteers descended on Parihaka. Their advance on 5 November was opposed only by 'skipping-parties of girls'. Bryce read the Riot Act to an entirely peaceful gathering. Te Whiti then came forward . . .

towards a man who called him with a voice now more powerful than his own and turned his back upon the scene of many a rhapsody, unfulfilled prophesy and fervent address; and yet not without dignity did he move through the lane of grey shirted and stalwart constabulary; for even in that hour of trial he was every inch a chief and his grizzled hair and beard and smiling handsome face created anything but an unpleasing impression.[55]

Te Whiti and Tohu were held without trial in gentlemanly exile in the South Island. Titokowaru was bound over to keep the peace after a brief hunger strike. Hundreds of ancient fowling pieces and assorted hunting weapons were confiscated from Maori all over Taranaki. Fifteen hundred Parihaka residents from other iwi were sent home, many

of them identified by an informer. Women were raped during night raids by drunken troopers, and the homes of those evicted were demolished. Parihaka would be rebuilt — with piped water and electricity — after Te Whiti and Tohu returned from exile in 1883, but they would never regain wide influence. Their legacies were their philosophy of non-violence, the size of the Maori reserves in Taranaki — and ongoing bitterness. In 1996, for example, a Waitangi Tribunal report controversially described the experience of Taranaki Maori as a 'holocaust', and ranked the dispersal of the Parihaka community alongside 'the most heinous action of any government in any country in the last century'.[56] A 2004 Treaty settlement proposal to return ownership of the Waitara Block to Te Atiawa was strongly opposed by many lessees.

Erueti Te Whiti-o-Rongomai III.

Alienation of Maori land to 1884

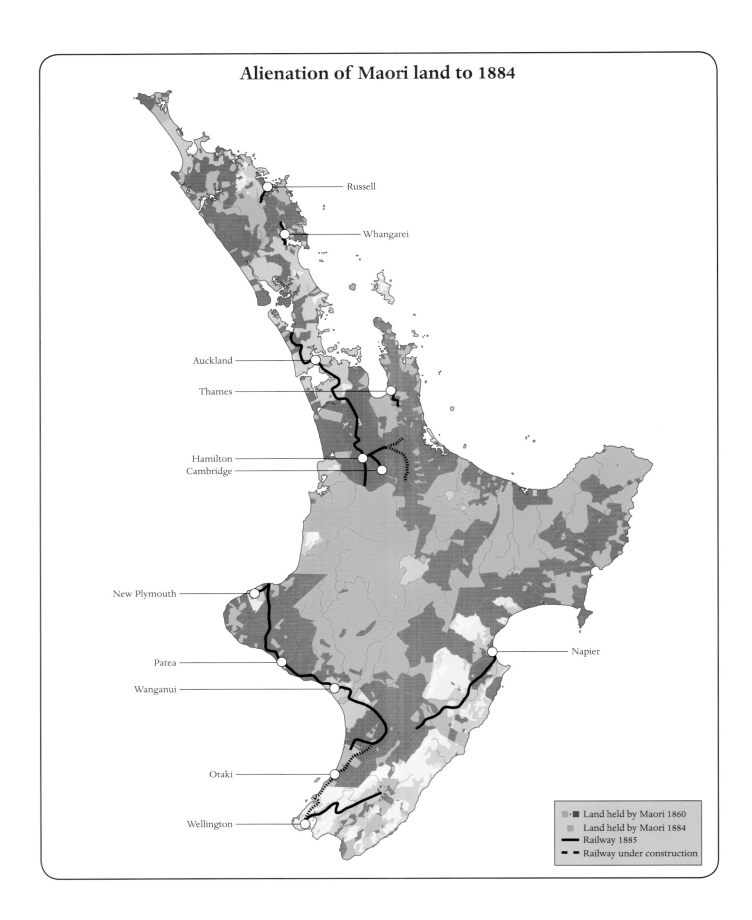

Russell

Whangarei

Auckland

Thames

Hamilton
Cambridge

New Plymouth

Napier

Patea

Wanganui

Otaki

Wellington

Land held by Maori 1860
Land held by Maori 1884
Railway 1885
Railway under construction

food, 'good ale and wines, and "three-star brandy". Nor did the women lack of anything they longed for, in costumes, chemises, skirts, silk handkerchiefs and ties'.[57] Everything was paid for by the government.

Any chance that a Maori 'state-within-a-state' might endure in the central North Island ended in 1879, when Rewi was received like royalty in Auckland. The government built him a house on its side of the border, and he bought a gun shop. Tawhiao rode into Alexandra with 500 followers in 1881 — to lay down his guns, not to fire them. Although he still rejected the government's terms, the 'shadow of an authority claimed by a person of the native race' was 'fleeting away', as the new Native Minister, John Bryce, put it.[58] Tawhiao travelled on by train to enjoy a fortnight of 'more congratulations and honours than ever fell to the lot of any man in Auckland',[59] then returned to symbolically open a bridge over the Waipa.

Now certain that the wars were over, the government agreed to pardon all former 'rebels', including Te Kooti, in 1883. (The prophet was to provoke one last war scare by planning to visit Poverty Bay in 1889. Four years later he died the accidental death he had long ago foreseen for himself.) Ngati Maniapoto came to terms with the government, agreed to the railway crossing their territory, and put their land through the Land Court. Tawhiao appealed to both Queen Victoria and Bryce for self-government. The Constitution Act allowed for local Maori autonomy, but the game was up. The Kingitanga had run out of bargaining chips.

By the mid 1880s, Maori had lost control of the North Island. But were they doomed to die out entirely? Some used the evolutionary theories of Charles Darwin and Herbert Spencer to argue that Europeans would supplant Maori because they were not just physically stronger, but superior in every way. The decline since the 1850s in Maori numbers and economic clout seemed to bear this out. By 1891 the 42,000 Maori — including nearly 5000 'half-castes' — were only six per cent of New Zealand's population.[60] Infant mortality was so high that Maori life expectancy at birth was in the mid 20s, less than half that for non-Maori.[61] Maori still owned 40 per cent of the North Island, but much of this was poor land and some of it was leased to settlers on very generous terms. About 2000 Maori had been killed during the wars, and many more had since died in the epidemics to which they remained vulnerable. Even in the 1918/19 influenza epidemic, the Maori death rate would be seven times that for Europeans.

But though Lindauer and Goldie were soon painting pictures with titles like *The Memory of What Has Been and Never More Will Be*, there were other straws in the wind. The number of 'half-castes living as Europeans' was growing fast. And if infant mortality could be cut, overall Maori numbers would soon revive. Star pupils at Hawke's Bay's Te Aute College, which was now turning out young Maori scholars and gentlemen, would soon be leading lights in a new public health system. Te Aute boys were also playing British games with passion and skill. New forms of competition with each other, and with Pakeha, were evolving. From this perspective, Maori did not look at all like a dying race.

Athol Williams Collection, Alexander Turnbull Library, F-61582-½

Many young Maori embraced the new world. These prefects at Te Aute College were photographed a few years after John Thornton began reinventing it as an English public school in 1878. Thornton felt that playing English sports helped 'build character'. It certainly helped improve relations across the racial divide.

Chapter 6

Dunedin, 'New Zealand's First Great City', bathes in sunshine and prosperity about 1870, a world apart from the bush, redoubts and military camps of the North Island wars. The 1865 Exhibition building is prominent in the left foreground and First Church sits atop the reduced stump of Bell Hill, centre rear. The business heart of the city — and of the colony — is in the Exchange in the distance, just past the church. Harbour reclamation continues apace.

J Irvine, Lady Sidey Collection, Hocken Library, University of Otago

The Rush To Be Rich

1848–1882

Just as Maori had been thin on the ground in Te Wai Pounamu, so too had Europeans before the 1860s. The 'Middle Island', as many still called the South Island, bobbed behind the North, which had the capital, the major towns, most of the people and almost all of the armed conflict. But from 1861 all but the last distinction was turned on its head. The discovery of gold in Otago and Westland brought the one brief period in our history when more people lived south of Cook Strait than north of it. But it was more than a temporary blip in demographics. The 1860s and the 1870s were also the decades of increased population (largely through migration), port cities and pastoralism, in other words of building a modern, export-dominated capitalist economy recognisably similar to the one we have now. In the two decades from 1861 to 1882 large cities emerged, linked by central government, telegraphs, steamships, a modern railway, and roads of varying quality. Companies that still survive planted their roots in this period, along with others whose old premises have left their imprint on our townscapes. Welcome to the building blocks of modern New Zealand.

1845   *1850*   1855   *1860*

Otago settlers arrive   Canterbury settlers arrive   Otago gold-rush

Settling (and unsettling) the southern frontier

On 8 June 1861 the *Otago Witness* reported that Gabriel Read had found gold 'shining like the stars in Orion on a dark frosty night' just outside Lawrence. By Christmas 14,000 people — several times Dunedin's pre-rush population — were under canvas on the Tuapeka and Waipori fields. The first of New Zealand's big rushes — Otago 1861, Westland 1864 and Thames 1868 — was on. Dunedin almost emptied out. 'We cannot resume our Arcadian simplicity: greatness is forced upon us,' the *Witness* complained. The rush to be rich swelled Otago's population by 400 per cent between 1861 and 1864, when Dunedin began its 17-year reign as our largest city. The 'Edinburgh of the South', or 'Mud-edin' as the wags had called it, surged from 2000 in 1860 to 20,000 in 1864.[1] In 1879, long after the rushes had ebbed, 288,537 of the colony's 463,729 non-Maori people still lived south of

Once the easy stuff had been panned, miners found themselves resorting to more capital-intensive (and environmentally destructive) methods such as sluicing, seen here at the Blue Spur site, Gabriel's Gully.

Cook Strait, Otago (131,999) and Canterbury (104,293) far outweighing Auckland (90,132) and Wellington (57,926).[2] Read's fossicking had transformed New Zealand. Settler numbers had taken 20 years to crawl from 2000 to 60,000; in the next 20 they soared to 470,000, explaining why in 1865, with the help of the new southern politicians, Wellingtonians snatched the capital status they had craved since 1840.

Some of the earliest contact between Europeans and Maori had taken place along the southern fringes of Te Wai Pounamu. But large settlements of the type planned by Wakefield and his protégés required more land than that. Kai Tahu (Ngai Tahu in northern dialect) chief Tuhawaiki and companions had airily 'sold' enormous tracts of land while visiting Sydney in 1838, but colony-building only became possible after FitzRoy terminated Crown pre-emption in 1844. That year Frederick Tuckett, the New Zealand Company's chief surveyor, bought the Otago Block (216,102 ha) for £2400 for the projected Scottish settlement. Governor Grey stepped up land purchasing. In 1847 missionary's son Henry Kemp negotiated the Wairau Purchase from Ngati Toa for £3000. Then came the biggest of them all, the Canterbury Block, or 'Kemp's Purchase' in June 1848. A century and a half later the Waitangi Tribunal would complain that the purchase:

Gold made modern New Zealand. Tents and tailings stretch as far as the eye can see in this 1862 photograph of Gabriel's Gully, which is already looking like an ecological disaster as miners clear the topsoil from their claims. Already Otago, a disputatious provincial backwater, is poised to pole-vault over the war-wracked northern provinces to become New Zealand's most populous and prosperous province.

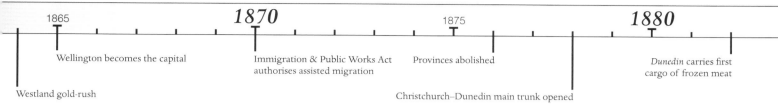

1865   *1870*   1875   *1880*

Wellington becomes the capital   Immigration & Public Works Act   Provinces abolished   *Dunedin* carries first
authorises assisted migration   cargo of frozen meat

Westland gold-rush   Christchurch–Dunedin main trunk opened

. . . of 20 million acres [8.1 million ha], almost one-third of the country, was conducted carelessly, especially with regard to boundaries and the size and location of reserves, yet Grey and Lieutenant-Governor Eyre both approved the meagre 6359 acres [2573 ha] of reserves allotted to Ngai Tahu owners from this block. It does seem, though, that most of the leading chiefs of the hapu whose lands were purchased either signed the deed themselves or gave their consent to it.[3]

Further purchases followed at Banks Peninsula, Murihiku and elsewhere, culminating in the Arahura Purchase in 1860. The prolonged history of selling by southern chiefs, hazy boundary setting, the low prices paid and the failure to create many of the promised reserves would sow a minefield of confusion and grievances.

Otago and Canterbury began in 1848 and 1850 respectively, founded by New Zealand Company affiliates, the Otago and Canterbury Associations. This second Wakefield wave aimed to create godlier, more socially homogenous societies and drew on the Free Church of Scotland and the Anglican Church respectively. There was many a slip between lip and chalice, of course, for neither province was a *tabula rasa*. For a start, a small Maori population — Ngati Tama, Ngati Kuia, Te Atiawa, Ngati Koata, Ngati Rarua and Rangitane around Nelson and Marlborough, and Kai Tahu and Katimamoe over the rest of the island — occupied a sparse string of mainly coastal sites. Their numbers had been falling. The Musket Wars were the principal cause, but imported European diseases and the loss of women to European partners also contributed.[4] By the 1840s and 1850s the population that was once perhaps 5000 had dropped to 1500–2000. But southern Maori were no passive victims. Kai Tahu leaders had coped well with the pre-1848–50 settlers and would go on doing so until the influxes of the 1860s and the 1870s completely swamped and marginalised Maori and early settlers alike.

For several decades sealers and whalers had also been operating mainly along Murihiku's southern fringe, where they had intermarried with Maori and formed shagroon colonies. According to Atholl Anderson, by 1864 people of mixed race were 24 per cent of

the Otago/Southland Maori population (68 per cent of which was around Foveaux Strait). From around 1840 this Old New Zealand stew had been flavoured by a small contingent of French colonists at Akaroa and here and there by wealthier colonisers getting in ahead of systematic colonisation — the Rhodes and Deans families in Canterbury or Johnny Jones at Otago. Their produce helped feed infant Dunedin and Christchurch, but here, as in the north, their sheep also undermined the Otago and Canterbury Associations' Wakefieldian plans for concentrated, socially ordered settlements. So, too, would passenger lists of settlers who were neither as godly nor as select as the elect would have liked, despite the use of terms such as 'Canterbury Pilgrims' or attempts to maintain the Wakefieldian distinction between 'colonists' and 'emigrants'.

Southern purchases of Maori land

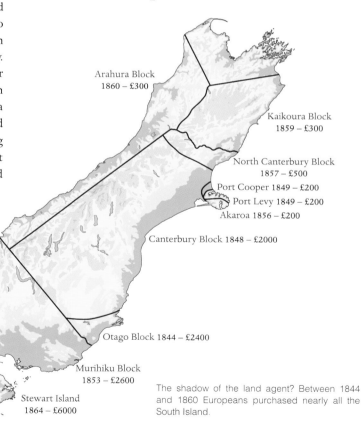

Arahura Block
1860 – £300

Kaikoura Block
1859 – £300

North Canterbury Block
1857 – £500
Port Cooper 1849 – £200
Port Levy 1849 – £200
Akaroa 1856 – £200

Canterbury Block 1848 – £2000

Otago Block 1844 – £2400

Murihiku Block
1853 – £2600

Stewart Island
1864 – £6000

The shadow of the land agent? Between 1844 and 1860 Europeans purchased nearly all the South Island.

Each settlement would struggle in the 1850s, confounding believers in God's City on Earth and systematic colonisers alike. Canterbury came closest to the Wakefield model, thanks to deep Anglican pockets capitalising it adequately and the opportunity to learn from the mistakes of others. The land had been surveyed and immigration barracks built before the *Charlotte Jane, Cressy, Sir George Seymour* and the *Randolph* dropped their picks in Lyttelton Harbour in December 1850. The Canterbury leaders, John Godley and James Fitzgerald, were bright and flexible and quickly appreciated that pastoralism was the key to success. After Godley dropped the 'sufficient price' in 1851, Australian pastoralists and others rushed to set up viable units. Otago's leaders took longer to learn the lesson, but after William Cargill reduced land prices by 75 per cent, the province's population increased from 3796 in 1856 to 12,691 in 1860, a satisfying rise, but still leaving Otago lagging behind its northern rivals.

That is why so many Otago settlers welcomed news of Read's discovery. The New Zealand rushes were smaller than those in California and Victoria, but the diggings still drew in people as fast as ships and their legs could carry them. Dreams rose and fell whenever the Gold Escort came into town. 'Geologically the whole Province appears to be one extensive gold field!' the *Witness* exulted.[5] Prices rose steeply, but so did land values, and population growth increased the range of goods and services available to settlers. Reflecting on the marvellous improvements going on, the *Witness* thought only a poulterer was lacking. A new spiderweb of shipping services reinforced already strong ties to the Australian colonies, Victoria especially. Businessmen, hawkers and entertainers followed the diggers across the ditch and people and commodities flowed back, explaining, for example, why some Australian buildings are constructed of Oamaru

stone. Australia left its mark in language — Erik Olssen blames the miners for enhancing New Zealanders' skill at swearing — and in place names. Dunedin's hotels included the Adelaide, Aldinga, Australasian, Ballarat, Bendigo, Geelong, Melbourne, Melbourne Club, and the Rose of Australia, and goldfields dancing girls rejoiced in names like 'Ballarat Sal', 'Melbourne Liz' or 'Sydney Kate'.

Those pubs remade Dunedin. Hotels and taverns never lacked patrons in the days when public halls were rare, the streets were bogs, and alcohol was prescribed as a health restorer. Here people could read the newspapers, gossip, seek work, form clubs and even conduct public business. For added diversions there were rat-pits (where dogs competed to kill the largest number of rodents), billiards tables, and the Victorian precursor to karaoke, 'free-and-easies' (songs, poems or instrumental offerings). Naturally the law was sometimes bent or broken. Landlords licensed to sell beer often 'sly-grogged' the heavier stuff, as did stores with 'bottle licences', and there were many unlicensed dives. It was claimed that 200 full-time prostitutes plied their trade in Dunedin in 1864. By 1872, when Canterbury enforced the discriminatory Contagious Diseases Act, Christchurch had 80 on the game.[6]

King of gold-rush Dunedin's livelier side was physician turned publican, Shadrack Jones. When the Provincial opened in 1859 as Sibbald's Hotel, Dunedin was a quiet, muddy town, but by the time Jones and Charles Bird bought it, as many as 200 miners at a time were flocking off each ship, all seeking food and lodgings. By charging snoring drunks three shillings a night for a shakedown on the floor, Jones struck pay dirt without leaving the comforts of town. New Zealand's first real theatrical entrepreneur, he had, like his customers, come via Victoria.

TOP: Governor in all but name. John Godley stayed only two years in Canterbury, but his pragmatism and dogged leadership set the province on the right course. Wakefield paid him the compliment of saying that 'the affair lost its soul and body when it lost Godley, who both thought and acted for everybody'. Alexander Turnbull Library, F-5079-½

BOTTOM: Saloon running was so much more fun than doctoring, Shadrack Jones decided. For four glorious years the florid, dandyish Jones ruled the gold-rush entertainment scene in Dunedin. Alexander Turnbull Library, F-4362-½

Restless and mercurial, with his 'chequerboard waistcoat, fat cigar, lavish jewellery and bulldog at heel', he made himself Dunedin's leading impresario and was a keen follower of the racetrack. He turned his saleyards behind the Provincial into a unique theatre, screening out the animals at night and setting up a hinged stage. 'The theatre, christened the Royal Princess, had only boxes and pits for humans; the stalls were for the four-legged patrons who at times were not loath to add their comments on the endeavours of the actors.'[7] Jones added a better theatre to the Commercial Hotel for star turns such as the Christy Minstrels and The 'Inimitable' Charles Thatcher. The Provincial prospered. 'When Jones took over the Provincial . . . business merely hummed. Jones soon had it throbbing.'[8] Jones turned it into the depot and booking office for the Cobb & Co coaches running between Dunedin and Gabriel's Gully. Clubs, societies and sporting bodies met here. The Provincial expanded with its owner's girth and he stuck his pudgy fingers in all sorts of commercial pies until he outreached himself. In 1864 he brought out the All-England cricket eleven, hoping to make a pile; but they arrived late, the roof blew off the main stand and the first match coincided with Dunedin's worst fire.

Most settlers welcomed the changes brought by gold — a consumer-led recovery as modern economists would put it. The main naysayers were the Free Church founders, who had been losing ground even before then. But it fell to Cargill's son, Edward Bowes ('EB') Cargill, to fire the most famous shot for the dwindling dream by urging 'that, notwithstanding the great influx of rogues and vagabonds, settlers should preserve their "Old Identity".' This was a bit rich, for EB had squeaked into Otago in 1858, barely a stiff upper lip ahead of the Victorian flood. Smug Scots Presbyterian jibes at the 'New Iniquity' — the mainly Australian newcomers — inspired Shadrack Jones's top entertainer, Thatcher, to lampoon them in one of our first pop hits, 'The Old Identity':

> *Go on in the old fashion*
> *And ne'er improve the town*
> *And still on all new comers,*
> *Keep up a fearful 'down'*
> *Don't alter your Post Office —*
> *Let that old Jetty be —*
> *And thus you'll be preserving*
> *The Old Identity*[9]

Swamped and ridiculed, the theocratic hardliners retreated. The more introspective fought the introduction of hymns and music to kirk services, the more pragmatic went with the cash flow, tut-tutting occasionally from institutions such as the Dunedin Club or later the Otago Early Settlers' Association. EB quickly made his peace (and his money) with the 'New Iniquity'.

F Weld, Alexander Turnbull Library B-139-004

Last and luckiest, Canterbury's leaders benefited from observing the earlier settlements' mistakes and so had the immigration barracks ready, a jetty in place and the town sections surveyed before the first settlers arrived in 1850. Lyttelton presented a tidy enough appearance, but those hills virtually cut off port from plains.

Alexander Turnbull Library, F-4505-½

These two photographs of Princes Street, taken just nine years apart, show how gold transformed Dunedin. In the top photograph, taken in 1861, the footpaths are rough and unpaved, the fence rail is collapsing and most of the buildings are single-storey wooden structures. The road lived up to 'Mud-edin's' nickname whenever it rained. By 1870, however, Princes Street had been transformed. The road still lacks something, but the pavements are sealed, there are streetlamps and the buildings are imposing masonry structures.

Alexander Turnbull Library, G-1662-10X8

THE OTAGO ASSOCIATION

The Otago settlement had its origins in a schism that rocked the Presbyterian Church in Scotland in 1843. 'The Great Disruption' saw a third of church members, angered by attempts to remove a congregation's right to appoint its minister, break away to form the Free Church of Scotland. Historians have tended to paint the grizzled Captain William Cargill and the stern, puritanical Reverend Thomas Burns as Free Church fanatics who dreamed of making Otago a new Geneva, a Free Church, a small-farmer society in which the morals were as straight as the fence lines and hedgerows. Both were more complex than that. Burns's rough reign aboard the *Phillip Laing* on the way out in 1848 was as close to a Free Church theocracy as they got. They persecuted their Anglican rivals ('the Little Enemy'), Burns shamefully at times, and Burns was also a harsh disciplinarian, but he also supported workingmen's rights and education for women. The English, who never really understood either man, loved to ridicule Cargill, whose insensitivity and nepotism irked many, and whose speaking skills were poor, but the old soldier was a pragmatist whose sheer determination carried the settlement through trying times. The magnificent, soaring spire of Dunedin's First Church (1873) symbolises the utopian dream of the 'city on the hill' but it also symbolises the influence of Clementina Burns. For all their carping about 'the Little Enemy', both Burns and Cargill had married Anglicans.

The Reverend Thomas Burns was a nephew of the Scots poet Robert Burns and a symbol of Free Church beliefs. In Otago he travelled widely to minister to his congregation, warred with the Anglican 'Little Enemy', but had less daily influence than Cargill.

James Brown caricatured Cargill, who always 'wore a blue bonnet, with a flaming red toorie in the centre, sucked on a stunted black pipe, and carried a shepherd's tartan laid across his left shoulder'. Yes, he was a dour, inflexible Scot, and a poor organiser, but despite that he held the small, disputatious community together.

'The people are Scotch. They stopped here on their way home to heaven — thinking they had arrived,' Mark Twain said sarcastically. First Church, Free Church Dunedin's surprisingly Anglican-looking symbol, suggests that they were more adaptable than we sometimes think. Gavin McLean

Dunedin was the chief beneficiary of gold fever; but it was remade, not made, by gold. In Central Otago and on the West Coast, on the other hand, towns literally sprang into existence overnight. Stories of lucky strikes fired the imagination, none more so than Americans Christopher Reilly and Horatio Hartley's 39.5-kg haul from the Dunstan field in August 1862. They 'did not wash anything unless we thought it would pay a poundweight a day'.[10] Within a week thousands had descended on the field. The same wintry conditions that had dropped river levels to expose the gold for Reilly and Hartley proved nightmarish for the ill prepared, killing some miners and driving many more back to Victoria. Seven thousand fled the fields, but the opening of the Dunstan brought a renewed surge in 1863. The gross migration of 45,730 people to New Zealand that year was unprecedented. By that summer there were 24,000 miners on the Otago fields, over a third of all non-Maori New Zealanders.

peaceful most of the time, a good thing in view of the near-absence of police, courts and lockups. 'On the rare occasions when arrests were made the prisoner, for want of a gaol, was usually chained to a rock or heavy log'.[12] Certainly the goldfields were more orderly than those of California or Victoria. There were several reasons for this. Otago already had a basic infrastructure in place and many of the 'Old Identity' had beaten the 'New Iniquity' to the fields. The province was racially fairly homogenous and its government pragmatic; the provincial authorities quickly gave miners voting rights, did not impose too many onerous direct taxes and fees, and the police took a moderate but firm line. The miners formed what Hearn called 'structured mobs' and towns such as Lawrence or Waitahuna soon took on the trappings of permanence.[13] Waitahuna had a temperance society by 1861.

Drink tents and hotels provided popular meeting places on the goldfields. Here the licensee, his wife and their patrons pose in front of the Derby Inn at Waitahuna Valley. Alexander Turnbull Library, F-21439-½

Miners lived a distinctive lifestyle, sporting the goldfields uniform of moleskin pants, blue shirt, wide-awake hat and boots. Overwhelmingly young and male, they lived on mutton, drank, swore and worked hard. At first they made do with tents and calico shanties. The fields had plenty of 'dirty shanties' — disreputable sly-grog houses or tents — and early hotels were often mere 'refreshment tents', but they were sociable places; miners played cards, two-up and billiards, danced together ('stag dancing' it was called), went pig hunting, and as early as 1861 staged Caledonian games at Weatherstons. Certainly they had an irreverent attitude to toffs and to authority, but that has been exaggerated by romantic nostalgia — 'there were no lynchings, no vigilantes, no Eureka and very few murders'.[11] The orderliness of the diggings varied — Tuapeka was relatively law-abiding, the Wakatipu fields less so — but most were

But that did not mean there was no friction. Miners with memories of struggles with Victorian squatters hated pastoralists, whose sheep were sometimes fair game and their outbuildings a handy source of firewood. One miner caught despatching a sheep red-handed pleaded self-defence, declaring that he killed any sheep that bit him! But the runholders gained more than they lost, for the miners created a vast new market. Many runholders charged royally for meat and transport. City financiers, importers and manufacturers also coined it, especially after sluicing and stamping became the norm. Indeed, as much money was made from extracting cash from diggers as the diggers ever made from extracting colour from the ground. Servicing industries mushroomed, including everything from ship chandlers and provedores in the ports to the touring players who entertained on the fields.

HOKITIKA

Hokitika's rise was remarkable, springing from nowhere, 'one of the wonders of the age'.[14] Within months it became a port-of-entry and the commercial capital of the West Coast. But it was 'a boom-town in the classical Wild Western style, in both function and architecture'.[15] The *Lyttelton Times* described a place where:

> The Commissioner lives in a tent, the wardens are accommodated ditto; prisoners are locked into a couple of twelve feet square wooden boxes; the court-house is a flimsy weather-boarded affair, about the size of a small cottage; hotels are cabbage trees, calico, unseasoned boards and corrugated iron, tricked out with desperately big signs and load bars; houses, tents, hovels and V-huts of so unsubstantial a character as to baffle description. Many of them seem to be nothing but masses of rags and old iron, the sort of rubbish that is usually found in a marine store.[16]

Revell Street, the main street, was so narrow 'that two men may almost shake hands across it', and some idea of its inhabitants' priorities may be gauged from the fact that 67 of its 246 buildings in September 1865 were hotels. Revell Street later got the ultimate clean-up when breakers rolled in and swept many shanties off their foundations and out to sea. By 1867 Hokitika, 'besides being the fastest growing port in the Empire' was, with 4866 inhabitants, New Zealand's sixth-largest town.

ABOVE: Hokitika was a goldfield 'mushroom capital'. Here we look over the wooden facades of its business heart out to the river where, typically, several ships lie stranded in the distance.
West Coast Historical Museum

LEFT: Hotels, shops and livery stables. Revell Street displays a typical gold-town commercial heart in 1867.
Alexander Turnbull Library, F-2702-¼

BELOW: Ships line Hokitika's Gibson Quay at the height of the gold boom. They were the lucky ones; many never made it across the treacherous bar.
Museum of Wellington City and Sea

Westland, sometimes called Australia's easternmost gold-rush, mushroomed even faster and was more strongly Victorian in flavour. Within months of Maori finding gold in the main branch of the Hohonu (Greenstone) Creek early in 1864, shopkeepers were chartering steamers to bring diggers to the Coast. After a short lapse of time and more exploration, attention shifted to the port from Hell, Hokitika, with its lethal entrance and snag-infested river. The first steamer entered the river on 20 December, cutting the costs of provisions by £25 a tonne, and soon hundreds were camped on and around the sandy isthmus, 'one vast pile of driftwood'. The prevailing winds, which dictated sailing patterns, gave Melbourne merchants the jump on their Christchurch counterparts. Westland's population peaked at 29,000 in 1867 and Hokitika was briefly the colony's leading export port.

On both fields men predominated, but women found jobs in the goldfields and the surrounding towns. Recent research by women historians has emphasised the inadequacy of the old 'damned whores' or 'God's police' stereotypes.[17] Although few in number — there were still only 30 women for every 100 men in Otago in 1867 — women often worked with their husbands or kin hotelkeeping or storekeeping. Isabella Graham, a Melbourne nurse, was at the respectable end of the spectrum. She went from Victoria to Hokitika, Ross and Okarito where she married and nursed the sick while bearing her children.[18] Another woman, 'Little Biddy of the Buller', prospected with two male companions, sporting the moleskin trousers of her calling, every bit as partial to tobacco and a drop of the hard stuff as the men. But the Devil often has the better tunes even when croaked drunkenly by the likes of Barbara Weldon. She found her way to Dunedin in 1863 from Melbourne and quickly became known as 'the most drunken and disorderly woman in Dunedin', no mean

feat then. Weldon may have had a face like the back end of a Cobb & Co coach, but she scratched a miserable living on the game here until 1869 when the authorities literally ran her out of town by putting her on the coach to Hokitika. She spent the rest of her life as 'a perfect pest outside the Gaol, and a continual source of trouble when in Gaol'.[19] She had plenty of company. That year Maria Clark, 'Porpoise Maria', was sent down for two months in gaol for brawling with another prostitute in the middle of Revell Street.[20]

The Chinese were a special case. The first one landed in Dunedin in 1863, to be chased through the streets.[21] But by 1865 Otago businessmen were rethinking things as people upped stakes for the West Coast diggings. Otago's population dropped from 67,000 in early 1864 to 47,000 in 1865, enough to jolt the Dunedin Chamber of Commerce into inviting Chinese miners from Victoria, although the statement that 'an increase of population, even were it in the shape of chimpanzees, would be preferable to no population at all' suggested that it was not going to offer red-carpet treatment.[22] Otago provided a solitary Chinese constable to help them find their feet, but more than covered the cost of his wages by increasing customs duties on rice and opium. By 1871 there were 2641 Chinese, or 'Celestials', in Otago, 100 to 300 each in Arrowtown, Naseby, Macraes, Lawrence, Waipori, Nevis, Bannockburn and Lawrence. By 1876, 4000 were mainly picking over ground abandoned by European miners (who, nevertheless, howled about race contagion). Almost entirely male (only nine of the 5004 Chinese here in 1881 were women), these hardy, mainly Cantonese migrants built their own isolated little communities. Entrepreneurs such as the Sew Hoys prospered after the rushes in Dunedin commerce and manufacturing, and even put down dynastic roots, and the second generation branched into market gardening and

BELOW: In 1878 Oamaru artist Edward Augustus Gifford immortalised settler capitalism; a steam train, herald of progress, races along the new main trunk line, tall buildings and chimneys catch the afternoon sun, and ships stand off the bay. EA Gifford, North Otago Museum

retailing; but most were sojourners, as James Ng puts it, working here to earn enough to buy a house back home. Many failed, returning home in coffins, and those who stayed did so in the face of hardening official opinion, poll taxes, language tests and the view that 'there is about as much distinction between a European and a Chinaman as that between a Chinaman and a monkey', as Premier Richard John Seddon later said.

Gold-mining would later revive in both Otago and on the West Coast from the 1890s with gold dredging, but by then it was as capital intensive as that other big extractive industry, coal. Steamships, trains and power plants all needed coal, supplied from mines in Otago and Southland and the West Coast: 162,000 tonnes in 1878, 227,350 tonnes in 1879 and 295,260 tonnes in 1880.[23] On the Coast, where coal was king, the Westport Coal Company ruled. Its main mine was at damp, dangerous and dreary Denniston, a miserable gimcrack clutter of corrugated iron and weatherboard buildings clinging precariously to a bleak plateau, shrouded in fog for weeks on end and bathed with steady drizzle.

It may have bucketed down but little grew there apart from rust, emphysema and the politics of dissent. The soil was so thin they had to send bodies down for burial elsewhere. But between 1879 and 1967 these mines, with their 'Eighth Wonder of the World', the self-acting or counterweighted incline, would transport 13 million tonnes of coal from the plateau to Westport. It was a technical triumph. The incline plunged precipitously, 548 m over just 1670 m, some grades as steep as 1 in 1.25 (or 80 per cent)! Two water-operated brakes slowed the counterbalancing wagons (descending full wagons pulled up empty ones) down the inclines to the railhead at Conns Creek. But because few of the Coast's independent-minded gold-miners wanted to work in the company's highly disciplined mines, it had to advertise in England for miners in 1879. It offered British miners free passages but the new recruits got a cool reception from some colonial workers. The rise of the big company and the big pastoralist was setting the stage for the industrial and political unrest of the decades to come.

ABOVE: Jane Deans arrived in Canterbury in 1853, more than 10 years after John, to whom she had become attached. They had barely two years together before he died. Undaunted, Jane stayed on to bring up her children and to consolidate a Canterbury dynasty. When she died in 1911, Cantabrians mourned a pioneering icon. Canterbury Museum, 12504

Pastoral frontiers

In 1875, like an Old Testament god, the Reverend Alexander Todd looked out over North Otago's fields, homesteads, the ships in the bay, 'a line of railway stretching northward near the shore, and many other indications of civilisation', and saw that it was good. What a pleasant contrast the smoke, steam and dust made to the 'long dreary period when the aboriginal race spent a miserable and monotonous existence on the land, incapable of extracting from it the rich treasures which it enclosed . . . It was well that the dismal Maori period came to an end, to usher in a second, brief but important, in its place, when flocks of sheep began to browse on the hills and valleys around.'[24] Jane Deans felt the same up north. 'All [the Canterbury Plains] was waiting the advent of a white race of people to reclaim them and make them useful or beautiful as a garden.' No shrinking violet, Jane survived early widowhood to impose her will on the Canterbury landscape she loved. Deans Cottage, an 1843 cottage at the edge of suburban Riccarton Bush, leadenly interpreted as a shrine to pioneer, plough and progress, is New Zealand's closest shot at a log cabin legend.

Although the Canterbury and Otago Associations initially tried to control the price of land, they had neither the markets nor the labour force to sustain intensive agriculture; 'by 1849 every competent judge knew that the colony's future lay in pastoralism'.[25] Sheep numbers had been climbing since the mid 1840s when Frederick Weld, CR Bidwill and Charles Clifford drove their flock into the Wairarapa, where they spread out onto land leased from Maori. From there sheep nibbled their way across Hawke's Bay, Marlborough and then down into Canterbury, Otago and Southland,

taking advantage of the eastern tussock lands created by early Polynesian burning. Adopting the proven Australian pattern of sheep ranching and 'protected and encouraged by quickly hatched land laws', pastoralism took off. Since land could support 10 sheep for every cow and wool was an exportable commodity, whereas meat was not then, sheep numbers climbed. There were 223,000 in 1851, 1,530,000 in 1858, and 2,761,000 by 1861.[26] By the 1870s there were 13 million, 10 million in the South Island.[27] Wool exports rose from about 405,000 kg in 1851 to 3,562,800 kg by 1861, mostly merino. From the 1860s the south would also have many small and semi-subsistence holdings, especially around the coastal and urban fringes, where men and women sold their labour during harvest season or worked on road or railway construction and maintenance, but the dominant figures were the big runholders.

One small but interesting community sidelined by the pastoralists were the mixed-race communities that had emerged in the wake of southern sealing and whaling. Research on Murihiku's mixed-race communities has shown that Maori–European hybridisation here followed a very different path to that of the north. Southern families were 'mainly patrilocal, that is, the Maori women partners left their communities and went to live in European or mixed race settlements where they brought up their children in predominantly European ways . . . Post-European southern Maori history was, as a result, one of largely unremarked racial and cultural assimilation.'[28] 'That's why I'm four generations from Maoridom now,' Syd Cormack wrote recently, 'because they married European all the time. It seems that higher

The pastoralists got most of the land, but here and there small Maori and Maori–Pakeha communities persisted, combining small farming with traditional fishing and seasonal gathering. Richard Taylor took this photograph of 'The Kaiki at The Neck of Stewart's Isle' around the 1860s. Alexander Turnbull Library, E-296-q-158-1

ranking ones married Europeans — or a lot of them did.'[29] This self-chosen assimilation was the closest New Zealand came to developing a bi-culture like the Metis of Canada, and a warning against applying the Pakeha–Maori typology too rigidly. Small Kai Tahu communities — kaika (kainga in the northern dialect) — clung to traditional coastal sites, such as Foveaux Strait, Otago Peninsula, Moeraki, Temuka, Banks Peninsula, Kaiapoi and Kaikoura, often blending farming with fishing, residual whaling and farm labouring. Inadequate reserves gave the Maori of Waihao 'little choice but to enter the farm economy of the surrounding districts as seasonal workers while engaging in subsistence agriculture or gardening on their meagre reserves'.[30] But even so, some patterns of life persisted, notably mutton-birding, leaving one historian with 'the impression of Ngai Tahu riding both European and Maori horses, shifting balance from one to the other as circumstances required.'[31] A Maori scholar saw 'a tiny, almost invisible minority of the people . . . whose choice was between self-destruction and clinging to the edges of Pakeha power. Most Kai Tahu chose survival.'[32]

Runholders bought and leased swathes of tussock and native grasslands, keeping bracken and manuka in check by burning. At first they did without fencing, relying on natural boundaries and outriders before turning to the cheap new wire fencing. They controlled scab, the biggest threat, by separating flocks and by dipping sheep in a mixture of tobacco water and spirits of tar.[33] In 1874 there were 616 freeholds of over 2000 ha each and 1124 Crown pastoral leaseholds, averaging 5040 ha each.[34] Grain — wheat and oats mainly — was also a substantial product, providing 10–20 per cent of exports during the 1870s. The south's tiny population had held back cropping, but the population booms of the 1860s created a market for flour for breadmaking and for oats to fuel horses. 'By 1867, some 55,000 acres [22,258 ha] north and south of Christchurch were planted with wheat, oats and barley. North of the Waimakariri River there were 572 small farms (perhaps

William 'Ready Money' Robinson was one of Canterbury's great 'sheep lords'. He built up the vast Cheviot Estate in North Canterbury and did not let even the lack of a port stop him. By 1886 he had over 100,000 sheep and was coining it. C Johnson Collection, Alexander Turnbull Library, PAColl-5564-002

40 per cent of the provincial total) with an average of 33 acres [13.4 ha] in crop.'[35] Grain, which paid more stable prices than wool, also benefited from the new metal ploughs and the railways, which cut the cost of transport to the ports. But wool was king.

Forget quaint notions of colonial gentry, for few runholders were gentry, despite their occasional pretensions. Like their city counterparts, most had lower-middle-class roots. To the latest historian of the south's wealthy, they 'were largely people who had done very much better for themselves in the colony than they could ever have done at home', but they were only middle class by imperial standards. They worked for a living.[36] Although they lived and breathed the gospel of self-improvement, most had helped their chances of getting on by getting in early, and by having access to capital, as two of the more colourful examples will show.

William Robinson — 'Ready Money Robinson' to his friends and foes — hailed from England but had made his money selling stock in South Australia before buying land on the Cheviot Hills. Since North Canterbury was so sparsely populated, he built his own slipway at Port Robinson and a bridge over the Hurunui. In 1888 he completed a large homestead and 'Cheviot Hills became a self-sufficient pastoral kingdom and a symbol of runholder wealth'.[37] In 1882 Robinson's 37,171 ha were valued at £279,392, second only to GH Moore's Glenmark.

Cheviot Homestead burned down a long time ago but other grand homesteads survive. Few are more distinctive than Robert Campbell's three-storeyed Elizabethan Gothic mansion (1879), which stands alongside equally impressive stone stables at Otekaieke near Duntroon. Its spiky limestone silhouette still hints at the prickliness of its first owner, Eton-educated Campbell.[38] His family had made its money with New South Wales wool, and he came to Otago in 1860 to look for land, suitably early and cash-rich. Campbell did so well, on his own or in partnership with his father, that he eventually held almost 400,000 ha. In good years he made profits of £30,000. Before dissipating himself in drink,

Campbell sat in both houses of Parliament when it suited him (he resigned in 1869 to honeymoon in London and he later took long absences from the Legislative Council for British jaunts), dominated the Waitaki County Council, sat on the Oamaru Harbour Board and invested in the local railway.

Campbell achieved his dream of endless acres at the cost of others' humbler dreams of a pound for shearing a hundred sheep. Cheap labour was almost as important to pastoralists as cheap land and they fought out New Zealand's first big industrial stoushes with shearers in the south. Shearing was seasonal and trans-Tasman: New Zealand shearers crossed to the Australian colonies to shear between June and November and returned with their Australian colleagues to shear the New Zealand clip. At first, labour shortages kept wages up, but from the 1860s runholders tried to force them down. In 1867 'Ready Money' Robinson tried to enforce a shed agreement. The main battle, however, was fought out on both sides of the Waitaki. Oamaru, where a shearers' union was formed in 1873, was the shearers' union stronghold. 'From this time on North Otago became the centre of an organised campaign by shearers involving strikes in most pastoral areas of New Zealand.'[39] The core demand was the rate of £1 per 100 sheep. Strikes at Kurow and Elephant Hill forced up North Otago and South Canterbury rates; but runholders also combined, 28 owners of 34 stations coming together in 1873. By 1875 there were strong unions at Oamaru and Dunedin; but next year runholders, led by Robert Campbell, held out for 17s 6d.[40] The union urged arriving shearers to report in at Oamaru, where it offered them board, but Morven Hills owners set a rate of 16s 8d and held out, thanks to cheaper Australian labour.[41] As the restored bunkroom at Totara Estate shows, the rewards from those broad acres were shared very unequally.

Building beachheads: ports

'By Ships We Live' was the Otago Harbour Board's motto, a sentiment they would have shared at Port Chalmers's rival, Oamaru. Oamaru grew from an open roadstead with an unenviable reputation for wrecks and strandings that existed even before the great storm of 3 February 1868. That storm burst rivers from the Waimakariri to the Clutha, battering buildings, ships and crops. When the gale struck at about 11 a.m. the beach master ordered ships out of the anchorage, where four lay moored to cables. Two coasters scudded out but the big wool ships took longer to comply, and in mid afternoon the *Star of Tasmania* parted her cable. The crew dropped the anchor, but its cable snapped, sending the *Star* into the breakers, where waves broke clean over her. Passengers and crew huddled miserably on the forecastle fearing death in the dark until, after many attempts, a rescuer put a line aboard, enabling all but four to scramble ashore, many badly bruised. By then the *Water Nymph* had also gone ashore, fortunately without loss of life, as had the coaster *Otago* after wild seas carried away her rudder. The storm had also wrecked the jetty. A week later the victims were buried in the midst of a torrential thunderstorm that so flooded the graves that they had to be bailed out before the coffins could be lowered.[42] No wonder they called drowning 'the New Zealand death'.

The events of the 3rd and 4th of February knocked confidence in Oamaru (and also in Timaru, where the storm also wrecked ships). In 1872 the Oamaru dock trust (later the harbour board) started constructing a breakwater. It was 12 m wide, 11 m high, built from 20–25-tonne blocks and capped by masses of concrete, all positioned by 'one of the largest travelling steam cranes ever constructed'.[43] For 12 years contractors struggled against increasingly deep and rough water before sinking the last monolith early in 1884, at a total distance from the shore of about 560 m. The breakwater and the wharves it protected were an engineering triumph but a financial albatross, costing about £280,000. When the Oamaru Harbour Board defaulted on payments on its London loan, the *Financial Times* muttered about 'the recklessness or worse of colonial borrowers'.[44]

Why did Oamaru, just 4000 people in 1870, borrow so much to build this artificial harbour? Quite simply, it had no choice. Settlement depended on shipping, as the statistics showed. In 1880 the main southern centres were Dunedin (40,880) and Christchurch (22,946), followed by Nelson (6804), Invercargill (6683), Oamaru (5098)

and Timaru (3791) — all seaports or adjacent to one. The largest inland centre, Ashburton, had just 1200 inhabitants.[45] 'Port or perish!' was the booster's cry. Nelson, with a poor port, had tumbled from the ranks of the Big Five centres of the 1840s and 1850s.[46] Oamaru never broke into the Big Five, but it gave it a good try, exemplifying the New World model that demonstrated that 'port cities, at the expense of smaller towns . . . capture and control the wealth generated by their hinterlands'; they could 'easily construct railways fanning out into these narrow hinterlands and offer freight concession to draw trade and commerce away from smaller, competing towns'.[47]

'PORTS OR PERISH!'

In early colonial New Zealand everyone and everything moved by water. William Strutt's sketch of the beach at New Plymouth (opposite page, left) in 1855 shows the problems that settlers faced. Cargo had to be double-handled in and out of surfboats and canoes, it had to be surfed ashore at great risk and ships could anchor only under favourable conditions. Oamaru shared the same problems, and in 1872 began building a breakwater (opposite page, right) to enclose part of the bay. The harbour works are shown as they appeared around 1879 (below), far from complete but already providing a safe haven for shipping.

New Plymouth's open beach typified the dangerous landing places that settlers struggled to turn into safe ports.

ABOVE: By the late 1870s Oamaru's harbour was still incomplete, but already the breakwater had made it a safe export port.

BELOW: In 1872 Oamaru began building the breakwater on which its survival depended. EA Gifford, North Otago Museum

The story had been similar at Christchurch, which hankered after a viable outlet to Lyttelton Harbour, isolated by the Port Hills, the western edge of a submerged volcano. While the 'Canterbury Pilgrims' sweated their way up over the steep, narrow Bridle Path to get to Christchurch, heavy goods had to be unloaded at Lyttelton, put aboard small craft, bounced across the perilous Sumner bar and taken up to Ferrymead. There they were unpacked again and put into wagons, pulled from late 1863 by New Zealand's first locomotive, the *Pilgrim*, for the last leg of the journey to Christchurch. Ferrymead was a miserable stop-gap. Lyttelton was — and remains — the only logical deepwater port.[48]

People had been dreaming about driving a tunnel through the hills almost as soon as the 'Summer Ships' arrived in 1850. After William Sefton Moorhouse — 'Railway Billy' — won the provincial superintendency in 1857, he took just a year to convince his council to think very big by approving one of the longest tunnels yet contemplated and the first in the world to go through the walls of an ancient volcano, all to link two towns with a combined population of just 3000. But the provincial council spent heavily to link port and town, despite the opposition of some politicians.[49] GR Stephenson, nephew of railway pioneer George Stephenson, prepared the estimates; but when British contractors let him down, Moorhouse sailed to Melbourne to get a better deal. On 17 July 1861, in appalling weather, he turned the first sod of the 'Canterbury railway tunnel'. Being Christchurch, the event was hierarchical. While the elite banqueted in a large marquee, 1500 sodden folk rioted over the quality of the beer. The work was arduous. Miners prepared the tunnel faces with picks and long chisels, then fired gunpowder charges and returned to load the spoil into wagons. It was stuffy, wet work, and in one very bad stretch an iron shield had

ABOVE: Christchurch commemorates William Sefton Moorhouse with a wide avenue, a fitting gesture for the man who railroaded citizens to connect the town and its port. On his return from arranging the finance and the contractor, Moorhouse was met at the Heathcote ferry by a cavalcade of 100 horsemen and a band playing 'Oh Willie, we have missed you' and 'Hail the conquering hero comes'. W Bowring, Alexander Turnbull Library, G-505

BELOW: Until the coming of the railway, even the smallest places took pride in their ports. This is one casualty of the main trunk line, Karitane, Waikouaiti Bay, as George O'Brien saw it in 1867. G O'Brien, Otago Settlers' Museum

to be built over the miners so that they could keep working. At the rate of about 3 m a week the two faces shuffled towards each other. Breakthrough came in 1867. Plenty of nightshift work lay ahead, but by December passenger trains were running.

Once the ports were secure, railways spread across the plains to feed the products of the pastoral economy down to them. Otago and Canterbury began their own systems in the early 1870s, but it took Colonial Treasurer Julius Vogel's 1870 budget to put them all on the same track. Vogel gave the railway network a high priority and his technical advisors settled on a narrow gauge (1.07 m) to expedite construction. The South Island main trunk dominated railroad building during this time and it snaked its way across the Canterbury Plains, handicapped principally by the challenge of bridging the broad, braided riverbeds. In all, 12 km of bridges would be required to complete the task. Like the Lyttelton tunnellers and Oamaru's breakwater builders, the men working on the main trunk often laboured under arduous conditions. On the hilly approach to Dunedin men were roped together as they hacked a path across a rock face high above Blueskin Bay.[50] The South Island main trunk opened three decades ahead of the North Island one, the Christchurch to Dunedin section on 7 September 1878 and Dunedin to Invercargill on 22 January 1879. It revolutionised transport. By the late 1870s, for those who could afford the price of a ticket, rutted roads, fords and slow river punts were a thing of the past. Now they could travel from Dunedin to Christchurch in 10 hours 55 minutes.

DL Mundy, Canterbury Museum, 9200

It might not have been the eighth wonder of the world, but to the men who built Christchurch's economic lifeline to the world under primitive, difficult conditions, it must have seemed like that. This is the rail tunnel's Lyttelton portal in February 1867. Provincial Engineer Edward Dobson sports the white top hat.

Canterbury Museum, CM 2130

The spoil from the tunnel formed the reclamation for the new Lyttelton wharves.

ABOVE: The restored migrants' quarters on the *Star of India* (ex *Euterpe*) give an indication of how crowded conditions would have been.

BELOW: The *Star of India* in full sail. Thad Koza, Maritime Museum of San Diego

John Wright, Maritime Museum of San Diego

Building up the numbers: Vogel's immigrants

Several times a year the only seaworthy survivor of our greatest immigrant boom bends its canvas and leaves its pier at the San Diego Maritime Museum to take a turn around the bay. These days she is the barque *Star of India*, a name bestowed by salmon packers, but we knew her as the *Euterpe*.[51] In all but speed, the *Euterpe* typified the migrant ships of the Vogel era. The *Euterpe* is 62 m long, 10.7 m broad and her mainmast towers 38 m above deck, making her smaller than a modern factory trawler. Yet between 1873 and 1898 she made 18 voyages to New Zealand, bringing out nearly 2000 immigrants.[52] For their descendants, perhaps for all British New Zealanders, the *Euterpe* is *the* ancestral waka.

Shaw Savill bought the *Euterpe* to cash in on the boom created by Julius Vogel's Immigration and Public Works Act 1870. Vogel was our most colourful 19th-century politician after Sir George Grey. Born into a London Jewish family in 1835, he reached Dunedin in 1861, via Victoria. There he settled into his old love, journalism, helping to launch the *Otago Daily Times*, our first daily. Vogel happily mixed print, politics and business with a love of good food and wine. In Dunedin he dramatised a novel, gave indifferent attention to provincial council and central government business and edited the *ODT* until 1868 when he parted company with it. Next year he moved to Auckland and into government. Between 1869 and 1876 Vogel held several posts before returning to Britain as Agent-General.

Although Vogel had followed gold, he knew that 'a steady influx of settlers was needed, not the tidal rush and ebb of the diggers'.[53] His remedy was to spend £10 million on development, £1.5 million of that on immigration. New Zealand was simply uncompetitive otherwise. In 1874 it cost a migrant £15 (five months' earnings for an Oxfordshire agricultural labourer) and the voyage took 75 to 115 uncomfortable days. The United States, on the other hand, cost Britons just £4 and took only 5 to 10 days, and Canada offered free passages and free land. That is why emigration to New Zealand 'was but a small leak in the Atlantic pipeline'.[54] Of the 4.5 million Britons who emigrated between 1861 and 1885, only 17 per cent went to Australasia. Even in the peak years of 1874 and 1875, New Zealand grabbed just five per cent of the British exodus. About 100,000 assisted migrants, 93 per cent from the United Kingdom, came here during the 1870s — just over half the net inflow in that decade.

Labour leaders worried about assisted migrants driving down wages, but with gold production falling, wool prices tumbling, capital works virtually on hold, immigration at its lowest level since 1857 and with the war debt to pay, most colonists hoped that carefully selected immigrants would reinvigorate the economy. In introducing the legislation, Vogel made it clear that he did not intend to import the Old World problem of the pauperised 'submerged one-tenth': 'the refuse populations of large towns and cities, composed of beings hopelessly diseased in mind and body, deficient in all capacity for useful labour, vagrant and idle alike by habit and inclination, paupers by profession, and glorifying in being so'.[55] Could Wakefield have put it any better?

The migrants came from different places. Australians, many of them short-term migrants, were more numerous than Britons in the 195,000 who came here during the 1860s but Britons would predominate in the 197,000 of the 1870s. Scots were significantly overrepresented (20.9 per cent of migrants in 1871–80, about double their representation in the United Kingdom), as were Irish (22.4 per cent, higher than their 16.7 per cent share of the United Kingdom population in 1871, with the Protestant north of Ireland being overrepresented).[56] The English were not only underrepresented but came from certain clusters, the West Counties (Devon, Cornwall and Somerset), South Midlands (Oxford and Gloucester) and the London hinterland counties of Surrey, Essex and Kent. Whatever their origins, the newcomers helped to even up the sex ratio. In 1871 the ratios for people over 20 had been 66 per cent men to 34 per cent women. By 1891 it was 56 per cent to 44 per cent. And, of course, many Vogel migrants went to the North Island.

Organising immigration on this scale required something better than the systems used by the old New Zealand Company or by the provincial authorities. In 1872 and 1873, John Brogden & Sons tendered to recruit 2172 English immigrants, the so-called 'Brogdenites'. They were overwhelmingly farm labourers — the favoured occupational group — although 450 had navvying, mining, building or general labouring backgrounds, and some would find work constructing southern railways.[57]

But central government did most of the recruiting, led by the country's Agent-General in London, Isaac Featherston, who framed new regulations to replace the provincial ones. 'These offered assisted passages to agricultural labourers, navvies, shepherds, country mechanics and domestic servants who were "sober, industrious, of good moral character, of sound mind, good health" and intended to go to New Zealand to work for wages. Single women between the ages of 15 and 35 could

An unknown artist captures the emotional moment in 1848 when migrants from Wakefield's 'anxious classes' board a boat for the steamer that will carry them down the Clyde to the ship that will take them out to the Free Church colony in Otago.

Sir Julius Vogel was one of colonial New Zealand's most important politicians, deeply committed to 'progress' and 'development'. He later returned to Britain where, among other things, he wrote a futuristic novel, *Anno Domini 2000* or *Woman's Destiny*, in which women held the highest government posts; so he might not have been surprised to return to find Governor-General Dame Silvia Cartwright chatting to Prime Minister Helen Clark and Speaker Margaret Wilson.

sign a note promising to repay their entire fare after arrival but single men and married couples had to pre-pay part in cash.'[58] Featherston's staff conducted lecture tours, approved emigrants and oversaw ship departures. More than 100 immigration agents (paid 10 shillings commission per adult migrant) supported the peripatetic lecturers and recruiters. These local agents were typically teachers, booksellers, lawyers and estate agents, and although of varying quality and effectiveness, they publicised New Zealand, helped by the National Agricultural Labourers' Union (which was battling employers). Further up the social ladder, the Female Middle Class Emigration Society recruited young women to go out as governesses.[59]

A slow start inspired Otago and Canterbury to re-establish their own immigration agencies.[60] By 1873 Vogel had bowed to pressure and offered free, rather than assisted passages, and land grants for relatives nominated by colonists. That, a recession in North America, and a rural lockout in southern and eastern

Fire was the great fear in wooden ships. In November an Auckland-bound ship, the *Cospatrick*, caught fire west of the Cape of Good Hope. All but three of the 473 aboard died, many of them perishing days later in the boats. S Calvert in *Illustrated New Zealand Herald*, Alexander Turnbull Library, PUBL-0047-1875-09

England, pushed up numbers. Thirty-two thousand assisted migrants flooded in in 1874, the peak year.

Finding ships was important. The Albion Line and Shaw Savill dominated the New Zealand trade until 1873, when the Christchurch-based New Zealand Shipping Company, led by merchant Charles Wesley Turner, won the main government contracts. The ships of the 1870s were larger and better than earlier ones. Graceful, sharply raked bows and finer hull lines produced the 'clipper' look, and iron hulls, iron shrouds and stays gave more stability and speed. Speed was the only characteristic the *Euterpe*, 'one of the slowest boats afloat', lacked. The ship took 143 days to make one passage from Britain to Lyttelton, and draughtsman Joshua Charlesworth, who endured a 134-day voyage in 1879, gnashed his teeth and wrote that 'the ship can't go close enough to the wind for she is considered very poor at tacking'.[61] His fellow passenger, stonemason George Lister, wrote 'it takes a gale to drive her along, and then they are obliged to take sail in'.[62]

Charlesworth and (second-class passenger) Lister, have left accounts of that voyage in 1879. Like most immigrant ships, the *Euterpe* left London, where Lister's experience typified the 'confusion, distress and bewilderment [that] prevailed at every embarkation', which Charlotte Macdonald recorded, with its 'great jumble of strange faces, voices, bags and boxes in the unfamiliar surroundings of the main deck where emigrants gathered to watch the constant passing of members of the crew, dock workers, friends, relatives and officials'.[63] The *Euterpe* left the massive East India Docks, a community of its own, with 400 clerks, 4000 watersiders and the crews and passengers of up to 250 ships. Dock entrances were locked at night and staff went around at nine each evening extinguishing lights.

Once the jostle and noise subsided, migrants discovered that 'ships continued to be a microcosm of the class structures those in steerage hoped they had left behind'.[64] Passengers were segregated by class, marital status and gender. First-class and second-class passengers had the space beneath the poop (the upper aft deck). Forward were the more numerous assisted immigrants, closer to the waterline and therefore more likely to spend days battened down in stormy seas. Their berths or 'horse stalls' were partitioned by cheap, thin timber, knocked up for the outward voyage and knocked down for the return, when wool, grain and kauri gum replaced people. They occupied each side of the 'tween deck, four people shoehorned into compartments approximately 2 m by 2 m. The 'tween decks were so cramped that the mess tables had to be hoisted up to the deckhead when not in use. In well-regulated ships a 'mess captain' maintained discipline in his little section, drawing stores, supervising food preparation, and ensuring that things were tidy for the master's daily inspection.

The assisted migrants' bill of fare looked adequate, but spoilage, vermin or skimping by unscrupulous shipowners or masters could reduce that. The food was fair until the fresh meat and vegetables ran out. 'It is not often we can eat the Meat as it stinks so, we just throw it over in the sea,' Lister complained.[65] Saloon passengers ate well while the livestock lasted but when they were gone it was salt beef, barrelled pork, tinned mutton, highly smoked bacon, preserved potatoes, carrots and hard biscuits. The *Euterpe Times*, the shipboard paper, talked about 'Rats à la Paris' and Charlesworth called for fresh potatoes, less salt junk and pork, two galleys, a ship's baker and a rat catcher. 'The rats ate part of my boots last night, we are swarmed with them,' he grumbled as the ship lay off Canterbury.[66]

The rats may have been the happiest denizens of this cramped, dark world, where headroom was just 1.8 m to 2.4 m. What 21st-century visitors to the pristine *Euterpe* miss is the smell. Spew, sweat and shit mingled with the stench of cargoes past and present. 'Vermin, including lice, were commonly present,

ABOVE: Voyage's end. The *Euterpe* lies alongside the Shaw Savill & Albion shed at Port Chalmers, one of the principal destinations for the Vogel immigrants. DA de Maus Collection, Alexander Turnbull Library, G-2136-¹/₁

BELOW: This *Illustrated Australian News* engraving of immigrants landing at Lyttelton captures some of the sense of bustle at the wharfside whenever passengers disembarked. Along with the port and government officials there would be relatives and friends searching for loved ones, boarding room touts waiting to pounce on 'New Chums' and employers seeking workers. Alexander Turnbull Library, F-81746-½

and rats were endemic to all ships at all periods.'[67] Disease also flourished. Passengers were inspected before embarking, but illness (and pregnancies) could slip through. Some ships' doctors were drunken quacks — the *Euterpe*'s passengers petitioned for a new doctor even before they left the docks.[68] Since a family with six children could expect to lose one on the voyage, migrating was, as historian James Belich says, playing 'New Zealand roulette with their children'.[69]

At sea, conditions alternated between lengthy stretches of boredom and episodes of life-threatening drama. Boredom predominated, especially in a slow ship. Passengers looked forward to little diversions such as Sunday services, the ship's newspaper, concerts, dancing on deck and crossing-the-line ceremonies. 'There were lots of songs but tune had left many of the singers,' Lister wrote, but his diary showed how eagerly he anticipated such events. *Euterpe* passengers fished, caught albatross, recorded when their ship 'spoke' to passing vessels and watched the sea and weather. Male passengers and crew also fought. The third mate loved bullying and one night 'a saloon passenger got drunk and offered to fight any man in the ship'.[70] On 2 December the master stopped the sale of beer.

They survived several dramas. In the Thames a steamer hit the *Euterpe*, forcing it back. Books love to stress the perils of racing through freezing iceberg-infested southern seas; but that was tame compared to the crowded English Channel, where the *Euterpe* spent three miserably seasick weeks battling contrary winds, unable to break out. Passengers discovered that this was no place to linger on 20 September when they were called on deck and ordered into their cork vests as the New Zealand-bound *Hurunui* bore down on them. Only a last-second wind shift averted disaster, but even so, the ships' sails touched briefly as they slid past each other. You can still sense the sigh of relief in Charlesworth's diary for 31 September: 'Out of the Channel, a day of rejoicing to all on board.'[71] There were later scares: the sound of a heavy biscuit barrel rolling along the deck convinced jumpy passengers that the masts were falling and there was little sleep the night the ships' yards flicked the waves as it powered through the southern ocean in a shrill gale. But the *Euterpe* avoided the greatest threats, disease and fire.[72]

The *Euterpe* made port safe and sound a couple of days before Christmas. Port officials pronounced the immigrants healthy, sparing them detention on Quail Island. 'It seems rather queer to have Xmas in the middle of summer when fruit is ripe,' Lister wrote, but he liked the look of the little town with its wooden houses 'a little distance apart and not built close together like they are at Home'.[73] For Charlesworth, too, the promise of a dream's fulfilment was there. 'The new land is all around us, also new scenes and faces, and boats are busily bringing us fresh provisions on board and friends of the passengers coming to see them is quite pleasant to see.'[74]

An almost-instant urban society

The solid air and studiedly anachronistic Greek and Venetian facades of Oamaru's limestone buildings are deceptively ancient, for no place better exemplifies how remarkable the speed of establishment and the growth of New Zealand's towns and cities was in world terms.[75] Oamaru, just a hut or two in 1857, was a town of 2000 by 1864 and 4000 six years later. By 1891, 37.8 per cent of New Zealanders lived in towns or cities of 2500 people or more,[76] behind Australia (48.7 per cent), but ahead of the United States (36.1 per cent).[77] More and more New Zealanders lived in these coastal beachheads of a maritime Empire.

But Oamaru's elaborate facades offer a chocolate-box view of the 'Architecture of Prosperity'. In the days when it was the best-built town in the colony, its streets also harboured wooden shacks, tents, dives and potholes. They were paved not with gold but mud, dust and dung. It was the same elsewhere. 'Godley, who is only aristocratic to us,' John Cookson observes, 'was often in the blue shirt and dungarees of the colonial man.'[78] Like

Oamaru's building facades, the starched, stuffy studio portraits of Victorian settlers mask the fact that clothing had to cope with the mud and excrement, that covered the streets. Dunedin's privies, 5-m-deep holes topped by a rough wooden closet, disgorged their contents when it rained hard and long. Still, that was better than the stretch of town where the *Otago Daily Times* sniffed out flax bushes surrounded by 'extensive middens of stinking, obnoxious, decomposing vegetable and animal matter'.[79] 'Boots! Boots! Boots', colonial newspapers advertised and you can bet that women as well as men wore them.

Mud and muck bred disease. KC McDonald examined Oamaru in 1878. Its youthful citizen's youth and vigour were no protection against infectious diseases. Oamaru had a death rate of 12 per 1000. With one baby in 12 failing to survive its first year, it paid to have wealthy, healthy parents. The colony's overall birth and death rates compared favourably with industrial Britain's, but 'death rates from "filth" diseases in the 1870s and 1880s were worse: 4.4 per 1000 in 1879 compared with 3.4 in Britain'.[80] Swampy, smoky and smelly, low-lying Christchurch was 'notoriously New Zealand's unhealthiest city in the 1870s',

ABOVE: As this 1862 photograph of the slopes between Dunedin's High Street and Maclaggan Street shows, many citizens had to put up in tents and wooden shacks. This part of town was alongside the notorious 'Devil's Half-Acre' slum area. Alexander Turnbull Library, F-4367-½

BELOW: Settler capitalism put on its best face in servicing towns such as Oamaru, which they called the best-built and most mortgaged town in New Zealand. Here is a typical mix of buildings: a bank (left) and an insurance company (right) and at the end of Itchen Street a grain elevator, a reminder of the 1870s grain boom. Gavin McLean

a dubious honour virtually guaranteed in 1866 when politicians sold off the pipes imported for a drainage scheme. Shit, slops and the hospital's untreated waste flowed through the streets into the Avon, feeding 'Christchurch Fever'. Christchurch's general death rate of 30.4 per 1000 was double that of the rest of the colony in 1875.[81] In 1875 and '76 a typhoid epidemic killed 152 Christchurch citizens.[82]

Canterbury made partial amends with the most extensive public relief scheme in the colony. The Canterbury Hospital and Charitable Aid Act 1864 authorised a special property rate and by 1875 the province was spending over £4000 annually on institutions such as the hospital, asylum and industrial school and £600 on a 'charitable aid gang', which worked under supervision.[83] Supporting this were the private charities such as the Christchurch Home for Servants of Respectable Character

that Harriet Simpson had run in Worcester Street in the 1860s. Otago, in keeping with the Scottish system, relied more heavily on private philanthropy. The haunting symbol of this was 'The Benny' in Caversham, founded in the early 1860s and housed from the 1880s in the massive brick bulk of the Otago Benevolent Institution. Supported entirely by donations, garden parties, fetes and the like, in 1874 it supported 55 children, 17 men and four women, 'the adults being mainly helpless cripples'.[84] In 1867 the Neglected and Criminal Children Act was passed to protect children abandoned in the wake of the gold-rushes.

The best way of keeping out of places such as 'The Benny' was by owning a house. This could generate income, and a garden and chooks put food on the table. In later life Harriet Simpson, for example, worked as a dressmaker and took in boarders. The little wooden houses clustering Lyttelton's slopes

PROVINCIAL AND LOCAL GOVERNMENT

The end came for the provincial governments in 1876. There had been six of them, plus four breakaways, one of which, Southland, had its furniture seized by creditors. Today Southland's tiny premises are leased as a shop by the Historic Places Trust, but the Canterbury buildings still exude the sense of pride and permanence of a system that at its peak mattered more to settlers than distant Wellington. By the 1870s, however, they were being squeezed between central government — Vogel's development plans — and new tiers of local administration, city and borough councils and specialist bodies such as harbour boards. In 1868, for example, Timaru's 1000 residents got a mayor, six councillors and a town clerk to preside over the affairs of 'the 150 homes and the couple of dozen clay and shingle streets that made up the municipality of Timaru'. Typically, they met in the Club Hotel.[85]

Canterbury Provincial Council Chambers. Gavin McLean

that so enchanted George Lister represented security for their owners. Historian Trevor Burnard reminds us just how much investment was absorbed by the building and servicing of low-density cities, possibly 50 per cent of private capital formation. Christchurch and Oamaru were essentially suburban from the beginning, 'riding or driving cities' quite different from earlier 'walking cities' such as Sydney. Expensive to build and costly to service with roads, sewerage and lighting, their spacious suburbs grew nevertheless, their residents providing the principal motor of growth. 'Occupational fluidity encouraged some self-sufficiency but, more importantly, emphasised mutuality; there was a constant exchange of goods and people', with house construction and the provision of services creating work for many.[86] Wooden houses of modest size predominated, but every place had its wealthy enclaves like Dunedin's High Street and Royal Terrace.

Gaols, courthouses and police stations were important features in towns such as Oamaru, which was anything but quiet, with larrikins even disrupting church services by banging on windows, shouting or throwing stones. 'Almost all of the hotels remained open until midnight and, despite the law, most of them permitted gambling, dancing and singing,' Olssen noted. 'In each year convictions for drunkenness in Oamaru trebled the national figure. Men fought, swore and pissed in public.' Dunedin's *Age* called Oamaru 'that drunken metropolis'. Wild orgies spilled out into the streets from scores of unlicensed grog shops, which masqueraded as boarding houses. In 1881 the *Oamaru Mail* growled about the existence of 32 sly-grog shops and 12 brothels in addition to the legal premises.

Pubs were important parts of the infrastructure that towns and cities created during this period. By the end of the 1870s even the smallest towns were adding or upgrading bridges, roads, telegraphs and, in many cases, railway stations. Rail killed the flyspeck settlements that it bypassed, but larger settlements along the iron route quickly accumulated many of the accoutrements of civilisation: hotels, stockyards, churches, public halls and schools. Thornbury, inland from Riverton in Southland, 'was one of the townships whose growth dates and coincides with the coming of the railway', which went through in 1879. That year the *Western Star* carried an advertisement. 'Notice!' it exclaimed, 'Will shortly be offered by auction the township of Thornbury. Particulars later.' The subdivider offered sites on terms of 50 per cent down, the balance over two years at eight per cent. Like most railroad settlements, Thornbury had a minor boom, the private and public sectors each making their contribution. That year the landowner-developer opened the Thornbury Junction Hotel. Next year he added refreshment rooms, by which time the stationmaster was doubling as the postmaster. A general store opened in 1880 and a second hotel in

1885. Soon other settlers added a hall, store, bakery, granary, smithy, saddlery, butchery, bookmakers, and in 1883 a school. Religion was not overlooked. The Presbyterians had been worshipping nearby since 1867. In 1882 the Anglicans opened St Leonards, saving a journey to Riverton on the railway surfaceman's trolley.[87]

Education was important. Otago founded the first university in 1869, not surprising given the province's wealth and the Scottish respect for education. Scottish primary schools were better than English ones, and Scots abroad continued the tradition of ensuring that their daughters were almost as well educated as their sons. When the new university opened in the Exchange on 5 July 1871, offices and shops shut to let people watch the ceremonies. The first four professors were male, as were the first students, but in 1878 Caroline Freeman — not a Scot, but perhaps the next best thing, a Yorkie — became the first matriculated woman to enrol at the University of Otago. Teaching while studying, the redoubtable Freeman walked the 11 km home to Green Island after lectures until failing health forced her to take rooms in Dunedin. She endured the sexism of GS Sale, Professor of Classics, and passed the first section of her BA in 1881. In 1885 she became Otago's first female graduate.

Most colonial youngsters were lucky just to get to secondary school, which would not be free until the 1930s. Schools varied in size and quality. 'Big School' and other early buildings attest to Christ's College's (1851) ambitions, but other institutions also aimed high. In 1861 Nelson College opened its new building, 'of the best heart of totara procurable, and with the blessing of God and five coats of paint, it will be a credit and ornament to Nelson for many years to come.'[88] Such elitism sometimes got up the noses of other colonists. In Oamaru the gifted and scholarly vicar of Columba Church led a strident campaign against public education reserves being monopolised by Waitaki Boys' High, which set up outside the town boundary and was seen as an elitist institution with Etonian pretensions. These were, notice, *boys'* highs. Visitors to Oamaru may contrast the fine sweep of the Boys' High buildings with the cramped former county council building lent to the girls' institution.

In fact, of course, many colonial children would have loved to go to either school. Most received more elementary education in more rudimentary places. The Education Act of 1877 provided 'free, secular and compulsory' primary education for everyone and created a triple-tier administrative system comprised of a Wellington-based Department of Education, district education boards and an imperfect plethora of community-based school committees. Maori children had the option of attending the primary schools set up under the 1867 Native Schools Act, where they spoke English as much at the insistence of their Maori parents as the authorities.

SOUTHERN CAPITAL

In the 1870s were launched Shacklocks, Mosgiel Woollens, the Westport Coal Company, the big pastoral firm NMA, Standard Insurance, National Insurance and the Colonial Bank. Biggest of all was the Union Steam Ship Company, formed by Dunedin and Scottish capitalists in 1875 and directed by colonial-born James Mills. Mills was the son of a customs officer, but profited from getting to Otago early (1849) and by impressing the whaler turned businessman, Johnny Jones. In its first three years, the Union Company took over its main coastal rival and the main trans-Tasman line. By the mid 1880s it had tied up the coal industry. Ten years before it issued this colourful montage of its home city, architect David Ross designed one of the city's most palatial office blocks for Mills, its roofline a riot of minarets, ironwork and flagpoles, complete with an observatory dome, from which he could watch ships come up the harbour. Maybe the centre of the facade, surmounted by 'a pyrament with an emblematic design (globe, anchor, cable etc) enclosing a clock', symbolised Mills's ambition and reach? Or the Dunedin business community's? Unlike the UK-born 'Father of Auckland', John Logan Campbell, Mills, the first colonial-born New Zealander to be knighted, achieved the colonial dream by retiring to London with his fortune.

James Mills was colonial New Zealand's most powerful entrepreneur. In just two decades he made the Union Steam Ship Company the country's largest business. Gavin McLean

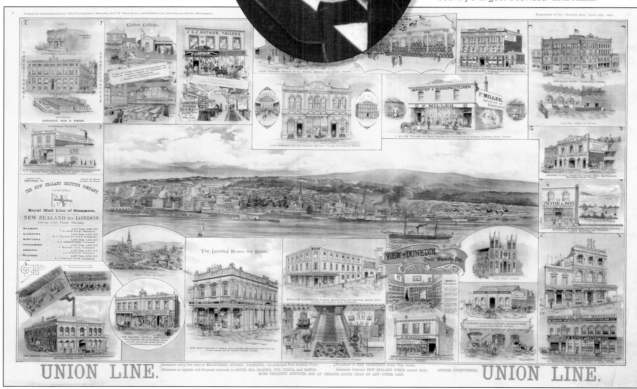

Dunedin's biggest company celebrates. In 1893 the Union Steam Ship Company issued this colour supplement showing the city and featuring its finest buildings. Alexander Turnbull Library, Eph-E-BUILDINGS-Dunedin-1893-1

Most businesses were male-dominated but women ran small schools, boarding houses and stores. Maria Sophia Pope was a well-known southern shopkeeper. This remarkable widow immigrated to Canterbury in the late 1850s. In 1862 she and daughter Sarah opened a shop in Market (now Victoria) Square, Christchurch, selling goods that became more varied as she prospered. Pope was a shrewd trader and survived the burning of her shop in 1868 after a neighbour lit a fire to disguise a murder. By 1882 she no longer lived on the premises and the business, dominated by female Popes until the 1920s, spawned several branches, trading until comparatively recently. Further south, widow Hannah Ward Barron bought a Bluff boarding house and went on to buy the Club Hotel in 1880, the first step in assembling a major portfolio of Bluff premises.[89]

But the period was also important for the founding of enterprises that took the colony and the world as their market. Dunedin, in particular, spawned many companies that became household names throughout New Zealand. Start-ups in the 1860s included stock and station agents Wright Stephenson & Co, music dealers Charles Begg & Co, coffee merchants W Gregg & Co, cordial manufacturers Lane's Ltd, engineers A & T Burt, drapers and woollen millers Ross & Glendinning, ironmongers A Briscoe & Co and John Edmond Ltd, merchants Neill & Co, publisher H Wise & Co, carriers NZ Express Co, and soap manufacturers McLeod Bros among others. Little wonder, then, that in 1865 the colonial and provincial governments built an Indian Raj-style building in Great King Street to house the New Zealand Exhibition, New Zealand's first. An impressive

31,250 visitors viewed it just 17 years after the *John Wickliffe* and *Philip Laing* had dropped anchor off Port Chalmers.

The period closed with the historic sailing of a ship. This was the *Dunedin* with New Zealand's first cargo of frozen meat for London. Until 1882 most of the sheep meat raised here had to be boiled down or wasted. There simply was too much even for people as meat-addicted as colonial New Zealanders to consume, a disappointment to farmers who would have liked their pound of flesh as well as their wool. The Australia–New Zealand Land Company's general manager, William Saltau Davidson, who had been following Argentinian and Australian experiments closely, persuaded the Albion Line to put a Bell-Coleman cold-air coal-powered refrigerating plant aboard a sailing ship. No one had ever tried to export across such distances without steamships and without freezing works on shore, but Davidson had Thomas Brydone, manager of the company's Totara Estate (outside Oamaru), erect a killing shed for the carcasses, which were railed to Port Chalmers. On 15 February the *Dunedin* sailed carrying 4311 carcasses of mutton, 598 of lamb, 22 pigs, 2226 sheep tongues, 246 kegs of butter and two passengers. She landed the cargo in perfect condition, delighting the shippers, who got good prices for their meat.[90] It was a red-letter day. True, the benefits of refrigeration would take years to spread throughout New Zealand, which was by then preoccupied by a spreading depression, but that key technical breakthrough, coming on top of membership of the British Empire and sustained by the rising incomes of British consumers, would make New Zealand that fortunate rarity, a primary producer with first-world living standards.

The ship that changed our destiny. The success of the *Dunedin*'s 1882 voyage with frozen meat gave New Zealand a new source of wealth. She is seen here in dry dock at Port Chalmers early in her career. DA de Maus Collection, Alexander Turnbull Library, G-12669-½

The Historic Places Trust has preserved Totara Estate, where the first export sheep were slaughtered. This is the men's quarters. Gavin McLean

Chapter 7

At the start of this period Auckland lagged behind Dunedin. By the end of it, it had pulled away from the other main centres, establishing a lead it never relinquished. Depression still stalked Queen Street in 1889 when Belgian artist Jacques Carabain finished this painting, but the handsome new buildings made at least the second part of balladeer Charles Thatcher's crack about 'Auckland town of shams and swells/ Drains and mud and horrid smells' obsolete.

J Carabain, Auckland Art Gallery, Toi o Tamaki

God's Own Country

1878–1913

In the three and a half decades between 1878 and 1913 New Zealanders rode a wild rollercoaster. They went from colony to dominion, declined to become Australians and acquired a Lilliputian empire of their own. They went steam-mad, emigrated, drifted north, and flocked to the cities. The Maori race got off its deathbed and produced new leaders who tried new responses to the challenge of colonisation. New Zealanders began the period in the severest depression in our history and ended it some of the wealthiest people on Earth, grown fat on feeding Britons. That depression and a determination to banish Old World ills from New World dreams radicalised many and sparked a search for solutions. Paradoxically, although they lived in a 'country without strikes', two of our three great national strikes occurred, the second of which, fought out in city streets, brought them closer to revolution than before or since. But there was stability, too. Party politics replaced factionalism and our longest-serving government presided over God's own country, as 'King Dick' Seddon liked to call it. New Zealanders gave women the vote, built the social laboratory of the world and almost banned booze. By the end of all these ups and downs they had fashioned an enduring consensus, pragmatic, egalitarian and fair-minded.

LEFT: God's own's King Dick stealing the show. His hold on people was such that when an opponent asked an old miner in his electorate to vote for him the old chap looked startled. 'Is Dick dead, then?' Alexander Turnbull Library, F-58363-½

185

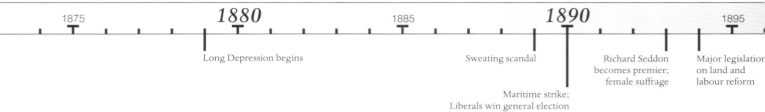

1875   *1880*   1885   *1890*   1895

Long Depression begins   Sweating scandal   Richard Seddon becomes premier; female suffrage   Major legislation on land and labour reform

Maritime strike;
Liberals win general election

'God's own country, but the devil's own mess': progress runs out of steam

The end of the 1870s rang down the curtain on two decades of exceptional economic growth. New Zealanders had become accustomed to seeing 'progress' stamp its mark on their land with wooden wharves, iron rails, steel bridges and brick buildings. The new woollen mills and clothing factories, thickest along the Otago and Canterbury coasts, were creating jobs for thousands of men and women, and work for builders, engineers, transport firms and coal merchants. Government trains and Union Company steamers cut travel time and costs, and knitted the country together, enabling canny manufacturers like Speight's to capture national or even overseas markets for the first time. Taranaki parliamentarian EM 'Ironsand' Smith, who saw gold in 'the hiron hores lying on the beach', thought the 'Britain of the South' would become an industrial giant.[1] And who, admiring the towering chimney and the serried, saw-toothed roofs of Ross & Glendinning's hulking Kaikorai Valley mill or the wagons shuttling endlessly up and down Westport Coal's incline, could doubt that?

But a serpent lurked in this New World Eden. Rabbits had been nibbling farmers' yields even before grain and wool prices plateaued and fell around 1878. Then the City of Glasgow Bank failed, its woes mistakenly blamed on Australasian pastoral investments. Nervous City of London bankers put colonists addicted to borrowing for capital gain on starvation rations. The 'Long Depression' settled over the colony, lingering like a heavy fog from 1879 until 1895. Historians debate its severity but not that it strangled growth in a colony until then sheltered from global recession by state borrowing; nor that it radicalised the migrants of the 1860s and the 1870s. The south felt the chill first. In a reversal of the gold-rushes, thousands fled Otago and Canterbury for prosperous Victoria; many who stayed put preferred to invest their money there.[2] The 1881 census had bad news for Dunedin; Auckland had edged ahead of it again. Some towns actually lost people. Oamaru's population, 5791 in 1881, fell below this level for the next 40 years. The drift north was here to stay. Between 1886 and 1891, 100,000 New Zealanders, including many skilled workers, emigrated.

For a while Auckland, always more in step with the still-healthier Australian economy, rolled along on a speculative boom. The Queen City had prospered, its merchants' pockets jingling with Thames gold. They invested in brewing, timber and publishing. Industries grew fat, but land speculation, 'the colonial vice', seduced even a bishop who purred that land bought on Karangahape Road had appreciated by 300 per cent

Alexander Turnbull Library, Eph-F-Meat-Gear-006

Rabbits, first recorded in 1838, were the nibbling edge of the 'ecological imperialism' of the 19th century, the peskiest of the pests plaguing one of Earth's most fragile landscapes. In 1887 in Otago alone, the state lost £32,803 in rents as tenants abandoned rabbit-degraded Crown land.[3] Runholders built rabbit-proof fences, fumigated or stopped up burrows, sowed poisoned carrots, shot millions of rabbits and released dogs, stoats, weasels and ferrets, largely in vain, for rabbits reached plague proportions throughout the high country in the 1890s. The problem ebbs and flows, but has not gone away. Not even the best efforts of the Marlborough Rabbit Trapping and Meat Export Company, could make much of a dent in their numbers.

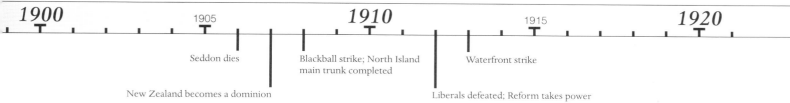

1900   1905   **1910**   1915   **1920**

Seddon dies

Blackball strike; North Island main trunk completed

Waterfront strike

New Zealand becomes a dominion

Liberals defeated; Reform takes power

in little more than a decade.[4] After a large fire in 1873 tightened up the rules, ornate warehouses and public buildings such as the customs office and art gallery sprang up. Suburbs — inner suburbs to us but dauntingly distant then — started to snake out along the main roads, and steam ferries served the thinly populated North Shore. In 1880's bubble economy skilled labour was scarce. They said that there 'was not a man without work, unless he be infirm, dissolute, or lazy'.[5] Then came the reckoning. In 1885 and '86 Auckland's economy crashed fast and hard. The Northern Steamship Company reported a loss and the National Bank wrote off £100,000 of capital, beginning 'a 10-year banking crisis which affected the whole colony'.[6] In 1887 the Bank of New Zealand stunned everyone by failing to pay a dividend for the first time. Many leading businessmen went under, and even John Logan Campbell and Thomas Russell lost much of their fortunes as they struggled to meet their interest bills. The collapse of the huge, inelegantly named Union Steam-Saw Moulding Sash and Door Company made the timber industry 'stink in the nostrils of ye publick'.[7] The capitalists' credibility crashed along with their fortunes. Credit tightened, loans were called in and businesses once thought solid closed their doors. 'Whole streets had not a soul in them,' one settler recalled, and cottages in 'distant' Ponsonby were let for free.[8] More than 11,000 people were declared bankrupt in the 1880s

and Auckland's Wyndham Street, thick with accountants and lawyers fattening themselves on sweeping away the wreckage, became known as 'Wind-'em-up Street'.[9]

The depression shook the thinking of people who had sailed to the ends of the earth to improve their lot. Now, like Banquo's ghost, painfully obvious signs of stagnation and unemployment haunted their streets. Used to seeing the jobless gather to seek assistance after seasonal work ran out each winter, Aucklanders were shocked to see the numbers who clogged lower Queen Street throughout 1885 and '86. Dunedin's unemployed sought help to emigrate. Many did. Husbands deserted families, often with the collusion of their wives, so that their children could get charitable aid. Soup kitchens appeared in the towns and cities and Methodist and Salvation Army church missions kept busy. Men tramped the roads fruitlessly. In 1892 Otago's Morven Hills station logged 400 jobseekers.[10] A few took up small patches of marginal land under the Village Settlement scheme. Thousands more fossicked — kauri gum was 'the great staple of the Waitakerei Riding of Waitemata County', gold elsewhere. Others shot rabbits for the pittance their skins and carcasses brought in.

People sought answers or culprits. The colony was a swirl of ideas, nostrums, declamations and predictions as newspapers, bookshops and public halls aired the issues of the day: land

North Otago Museum

CB Russell, Canterbury Museum

Because most people walked just about everywhere, poverty was very visible in colonial streets. Poorer citizens made a precarious living by doing odd jobs or by hawking. Ned Pickett, who sold fish on the streets of Oamaru, lived on the foreshore in a shack made of sheets of iron and rubble until it burned down in 1900, which probably added to his careworn looks. Ned stuck to the streets but swaggers, such as this man photographed about 1910, were familiar to country folk as well as townies.

nationalisation and tax reform; elected governors; tariff protection; legislative protection for workers' rights; no 'sweated' labour; restrictions on 'alien' immigration; trade unionism; early closing of shops and offices; dress reform; votes for women; banning alcohol, gambling and prostitution — a heady mix.

Unemployment and uncertainty opened eyes and ears to ideas that would have been thought too radical just a few years earlier, such as socialism. The fast-growing Knights of Labour (who also preached land nationalisation) championed Henry George's single tax on the 'unearned increment' within the value of land. Edward Bellamy's *Looking Backward* (1888), a utopian novel about a society that had abolished poverty, sold by the dray-load. William Pember Reeves, the Christchurch politician soon to enter government, read and popularised progressive thinkers. The air was thick with talk of a new social order based on co-operation and brotherhood; everyone noticed the explosive growth of friendly societies and trade unions.

Unseemly displays of privilege and exploitation also fuelled this debate. Employers had been responding to contracting markets and competition from cheap foreign goods by introducing machinery, cutting wages and replacing adult males with female and child labour. Between 1881 and 1886 the ratio of female to male labour soared from 1:17 to 1:5. It was not all bad —

female customers of Bendix Hallenstein's new DIC department stores expected to be served by women — but some employers in the clothing, rugmaking, bootmaking, printing and other trades were just ratbags. Dunedin printers Mills, Dick & Co employed 13 boys and just one adult. They paid the boys nothing for the first three months (after which they might be sent away) and let them use the toilet only between nine and ten each morning.[11] But it was the plight of women clothing workers, the future mothers of the nation, which tore at Victorian heartstrings. In 1888 Dunedin readers had been following the House of Lords inquiry into 'sweating' in London quietly until Rutherford Waddell, minister at St Andrew's Church on the edge of the 'Devil's Half-Acre', dropped a bombshell; his sermon 'The Sin of Cheapness' warned that this Old World evil existed here.

Sweating, strictly defined, was the system whereby middlemen contracted to supply manufacturers at fixed rates. They then hired the cheapest labour they could find. But the term soon covered any worker exploitation. George Fenwick, editor of the *Otago Daily Times* (and son of a Yorkshire Chartist), investigated and in early 1889 shocked colonists with a three-part report that revealed that 'starvation wages are paid to a large number of seamstresses in Dunedin'. One woman earned about two shillings a 12-hour day, finishing moleskin trousers

Many people worked in the clothing and footwear industries, usually in small workshops. In McDairmid's in Oamaru in 1918 there was a clear gender and age division of labour; women and a youth worked the machines while older males supervised. North Otago Museum

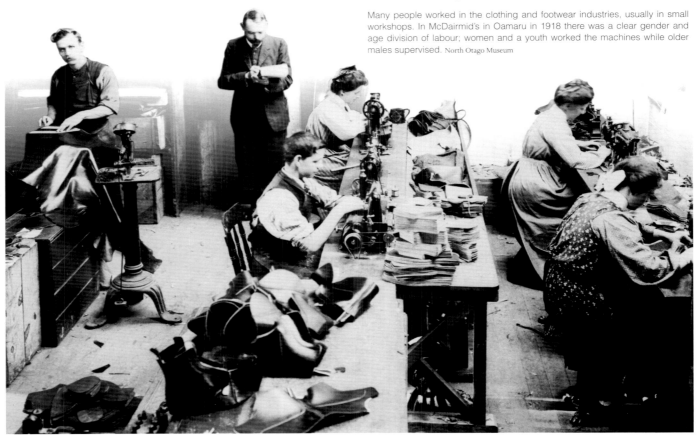

for 2d a pair. Girls worked to late hours for less than 14 shillings a week. 'Are these old world curses to be allowed to eat their way into the heart of this young community?' Fenwick demanded.[12] Premier Sir Harry Atkinson's royal commission toured the main centres gathering evidence, interviewing women such as 'Miss Y', who:

> worked in the ironing room, ironing shirts. It was heavy, hot work. The irons weighed nine or ten pounds each; Miss Y and the other ironers stood all day. The room was over-heated from the stoves which were kept burning all day to heat the irons. In summer the temperature was particularly unbearable. Working days started at 8 am and finished at 6 pm, six days a week, the only holidays being Sundays, Christmas Day, and sometimes New Year's Day. The only break in the day was a half-hour for dinner at midday.[13]

The commission's split report nit-picked — London-style full-fledged sweating did not exist here and Dunedin was a special case, worse than other centres — but the commissioners had unearthed enough evidence of overcrowded, dirty, insanitary premises, long and irregular hours, low wages and bad employers to prick colonial consciences opposed to Old World evils haunting New World dreams. Richard Seddon voiced their concerns during the 1890 election campaign: 'God's own country, but the devil's own mess.'

Trade unionism became a popular remedy. On 11 July 1889 at the Dunedin Choral Hall 300 people formed the Dunedin Tailoresses' Union and elected Rutherford Waddell president, John A Millar secretary and former premier Sir Robert Stout a trustee.[14] With the help of vice-president Harriet Morison and others, they signed up 600 women within a month.[15] Nationally, union membership surged from about 3500 in 1885 to 40–50,000 in the winter of 1890, driven by international factors (global interest in semi-skilled and unskilled unionism, the so-called 'new unionism') and local issues (sweating and the 1890 Maritime strike). The tailoresses were conciliatory and co-operative but later helped form the Otago Trades Council and levied their members to support the New Zealand Maritime Council. This council, founded in 1889, and led by Millar, a savvy Anglican socialist, had doused the Northern Steamship Company's fires by running a union-owned shipping line against it. Its strongest affiliates were the seamen, railway workers', watersiders' and miners' unions — muscular, nationally organised unions that shared Millar's belief that 'Labour is one, and an injustice to one is an injustice to all'. By 1890 the council claimed, over-optimistically, 20,000 members, its ranks swollen by several victories.

On 26 August 1890 the seamen and wharfies at Port Chalmers struck in support of their Australian colleagues. James Mills

Rutherford Waddell was a Christian socialist. As the Long Depression settled in he opened a mission hall, a savings bank and a free library; he also supported women's suffrage. His sermon on 'The Sin of Cheapness' was the most influential sermon ever preached in New Zealand. He died in 1932.

Presbyterian Church Archives of New Zealand

chose to throw the weight of the Union Steam Ship Company ('the Southern Octopus') behind the Australian shipowners, causing a reluctant Millar to proclaim a general seamen's strike, which quickly escalated to include most council affiliates. Eight thousand struck (about 13 per cent of the colony's unionists), making this New Zealand's first nationwide, multi-industry strike. Most stayed out for 10 weeks, but their timing was bad and Mills's tame shipmasters' union kept enough of his ships moving. The employers refused to compromise. After the strike collapsed the Union Company blacklisted many men. But the strikers gained a new sense of solidarity and retained considerable public respect, which bore fruit at the general election. In Dunedin a 'Labour Party' middle- and working-class coalition triumphed; Mills just edged out Millar for the Port Chalmers seat, but voters put bootmaker David Pinkerton and brass finisher William Earnshaw into Parliament.

THE DEVIL'S HALF-ACRE

All cities had slum areas, but Dunedin's 'Devil's Half-Acre' was more notorious than most; respectable tongues wagged that it was a 'celebrated nest of vice', a 'special locality of abominations'.[16] Satan's patch of God's own was bigger than a half-acre. Its black heart beat strongest near the lower end of Walker Street (modern Carroll Street) but the term covered an area bounded fuzzily by Maitland, Maclaggan and Princes streets, rising gently above the main business area. By modern standards its denizens lived remarkably close to the elite. Before electric trams and cars there was less residential segregation and Maitland Street itself was a fashionable address. The Dunedin Club wined and dined in Johnny Jones's old home, Fernhill, at the lower end, and James Mills lived comfortably near the top.

The Devil's Half-Acre became a tent town during the gold-rush; it was close to the old landing site and just a drunkard's stumble from Shadrack Jones's Provincial. Wood later replaced canvas, but the area stayed low rent, with businesses, accommodation houses and shacks all crammed

ABOVE: Walker Street runs through the centre of this view, an eclectic mix of solid masonry buildings, factories and wooden shacks.

This child sat in the narrow street in a feature entitled 'Assyrian [Lebanese] houses, off Walker Street', which the *Otago Witness* ran on the area's slum dwellings in 1904. Most of the houses had just one or two rooms, shared toilet facilities and an outside tap.

together along a warren of dark, narrow lanes. On one small section barely 21 m wide and 54 m deep, 14 dwellings and several shops crowded together. Here people like 'Opium Mag' — Margaret Williams, an alcoholic prostitute — plied their trade in the late 1870s.[17]

There were 'foreign devils' too: the Chinese, who had moved in during the gold-rushes, and the Lebanese or 'Syrians'. But from the late 1880s economic uncertainty and closer living had Dunedinites fretting over signs of urban squalor and racial decay. Even workers, keen to avoid any reminder of 'the gutter', viewed 'street Arabs', larrikins, drunkards, and fan-tan and pakapoo games coolly. The 1900 bubonic plague scare was the last straw. Church groups such as the Salvation Army and Waddell's Walker Street Mission had been trying to clean up the street's morals with modest success, but it took the council to clean up the worst buildings. Within a few years the brothels closed or became more discreet and the Chinese agreed to maintain their dwellings to European notions of order.

At least these children were off the street, where people increasingly preferred them to be. Infants from the Walker Street kindergarten (the country's first) in 1895.

Liberal New Zealand's battle against privilege

All these concerns about Old World evils, privilege and tears in the colonial social fabric coalesced at the 1890 election. The so-called 'Continuous Ministry', conservatives kept in power in the lean 1880s by Atkinson, had run out of what little steam it had left. But who would have predicted that when Wanganui printer John Ballance formed a government early in 1891 it would last a generation? The South Island and many northern towns and cities had voted overwhelmingly for change, Dunedin, Invercargill and Nelson voters going further by electing trade unionists. In a highly symbolic battle 'Plain Bill' Earnshaw from the Hillside Railway Workshops took the Otago Peninsula seat off the king of the castle, William Larnach. 'In the two-storeyed houses, in those with servants' quarters, in the city clubs, in the high country of the "sheep kings" and in Government House, men with money and men in debt felt cold.'[18] Shocked by the prospect of working-class parliamentarians, the Wellington Club no longer offered politicians automatic membership.

The Liberal Party, the first semi-modern party to run an election campaign with a programme that candidates pledged to support, was unlike anything the country had seen before and its unbroken term in office has never been matched. Why was it so enduring and so endearing? The words 'He loved the people' on Ballance's ghastly statue in Parliament grounds hint at the party's hold on those values that many colonists feared were threatened by unemployment, poverty, sweating and land monopoly. Liberal leader John Ballance may not have been a great orator, but his faith in 'the people' and in democracy and his choice of signs of privilege to target helped him unite factions. Intelligent, honest and modest, Ballance could talk to anyone. People applauded him for declining a knighthood, the usual colonial premier's bauble. His Cabinet was also striking. Only two ministers had any secondary schooling, and one of them, the Christchurch radical intellectual William Pember Reeves, was considered a traitor to his class. Uncouth was the general verdict on Ballance's deputy, Lancashire-born Richard Seddon, a rotund, pugnacious former West Coast publican. The others included John McKenzie, a fiery Otago farmer; Joseph Ward, a suave Southland businessman, soon to become Postmaster-General; former Thames sawmiller Alfred Jerome Cadman (Commissioner of Stamp Duties and Native Minister); and Patrick Buckley, a Wellington lawyer, who was Attorney-General.[19]

The Liberals got unintended help from the anti-democratic behaviour of the governor and the Legislative Council. Straight after their defeat Atkinson and his henchmen stacked the Legislative Council, the toffs who sat in the upper house on lifetime appointments. As Sir John Hall warned, 'it will . . . be a serious disaster if the Council is not strengthened before the Reds get into the saddle'.[20] By rubber-stamping the appointments (which now included Atkinson), Governor Lord Onslow gave Ballance the perfect rallying cry — democracy versus privilege! Then Onslow compounded the offence of acting on the advice of a defeated ministry by refusing Ballance's request to appoint councillors, alleging that it would 'swamp' an institution he and Atkinson had just shamelessly saturated. Onslow bolted in 1892, but his successor, Lord Glasgow, just as biased and even more obtuse, also refused to give the premier his constitutional dues. The conservative Legislative Council savaged bill after government bill.

The ministry mobilised popular support by buying the *New Zealand Times* and by establishing the National Liberal Association. When colonists showed that they hated privilege as much as sweating, the government's growing popularity tempered some of the nervous Council's excesses. In 1894 the

New Zealanders associated John Ballance's premiership with the return to prosperity and called him 'The Rainmaker'. Born in County Antrim, Ireland, in 1839, he emigrated to Wanganui in 1866 where he worked as a journalist and publisher. WP Reeves described him as 'absolutely the most unassuming and unpretentious' man he knew, adding that 'as a Premier — and I say it emphatically — he knew how to be master in his own house'. Ballance won his seat by a mere 27 votes in 1890 but led the innovative Liberal government.

PT Cole, Alexander Turnbull Library, G-606

'THE CLOVEN HOOF IN THE TANKARD'S FOAM'

Temperance societies pre-dated colonisation, but fuelled by a virulent strain of moral evangelism flowing from middle-class Protestant churchgoers, the anti-drink crusade took off in the 1880s. The Women's Christian Temperance Union (WCTU) was formed in 1885; a year later the New Zealand Alliance emerged as a modern political pressure group. Politicians and editors liked to lampoon the 'wowsers', but as historian Keith Sinclair observed, they were ably and energetically led and 'in speech the "wowsers" were, indeed, the least temperate people in the country'.[21] The 1880s saw riots between pro- and anti-temperance supporters.

LEFT: Moral evangelists crusaded against the 'demon drink'. The Protestant churches took the lead during the 1880s as the emphasis shifted from temperance to prohibition. The Independent Order of Rechabites had appeared in New Zealand as early as 1843, just eight years after being formed in Britain.

BELOW: Many men signed the pledge; but alcohol consumption had been falling, thanks more to male domesticity than to noisy moral crusading. As gender ratios balanced and the idea grew that a man's wage should be big enough to support an entire family, men spent more time at home and less in the pub. And even in the pub, beer ousted spirits.

North Otago Museum

James McAlister Collection, Alexander Turnbull Library, G-10209-½

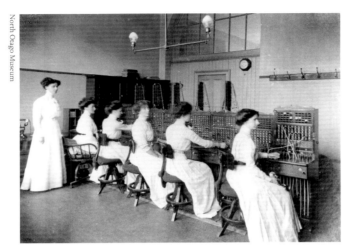

For young women the world changed more radically than it did for their brothers in the decades after they gained the vote. Although they were discouraged from entering many occupations and expected to leave paid employment on marriage, new fields opened up in places such as the post office, which recruited 'cadettes' from the early 1890s. By 1910 women dominated the Oamaru exchange (though not the rest of the post office). Girls also made better use of education. In 1910 these girls at the Stratford Technical School were learning milk acidity testing.

Colonial Office slapped Glasgow into line; no British monarch had rejected prime-ministerial advice since 1707! The governorship survived — although Grey's Elected Governors Bill came within a vote of passing its second reading stage — and later gained in stature as imperial fervour surged around Queen Victoria's jubilee; but the Legislative Council — its new members put on seven-year terms in 1891, and diluted by successive Liberal appointments — atrophied, becoming an increasingly irrelevant political retirement home.

Ballance died on 27 April 1893 of cancer, his doctors' desperate attempt to keep him alive by injecting champagne as a stimulant doing him no good. He had already anointed Sir Robert Stout, the intellectual leader of colonial Liberalism, his successor. Cabinet agreed, but there were two problems. Although he had helped build the middle- and working-class coalition in Dunedin, Stout had not stood in 1890. Deputy leader Richard Seddon, the rough, tough, ex-publican had, and did not intend to be passed over. 'There followed the most extraordinary cabinet crisis in New Zealand's history.'[22] Seddon remained 'acting premier', promising to put the issue to Cabinet when Parliament reconvened. In the meantime he appealed over the heads of ministers to the people and to cranky old Liberal icon Sir George Grey, who hated Stout and who had once said of Seddon, 'I have never met a manlier man.'[23] By the time Stout returned to the House in the Inangahua by-election in June 1893, Seddon had outmanoeuvred him; everyone knew it was choose Seddon or split the party. Campaigning skilfully, invoking the memory of Ballance and helped by an improving economy, Seddon triumphed.

That was the start of the remaking of the publican from Kumara as 'King Dick', but his grudge match with Stout had just begun. That feud (which extended to their wives) would colour colonial politics for years. Stout counterattacked on two popular issues he knew would discomfort the Premier: alcohol and women's suffrage. There was considerable crossover of people, institutions and ideas between them. Stout's prohibition bill was shelved in committee narrowly, forcing Seddon to do something. So, from the mid 1890s the country held local licensing polls to decide whether electorates remained 'wet' or went 'dry'. Most voters favoured prohibition at every election between 1902 and 1911, but by requiring a 60 per cent threshold for change, Seddon kept most of God's own grog's own.[24] The drink issue generated more heat than any other, but the movement lacked stable leadership in Parliament, where a leading 'dry', the impossibly principled and erratic Tommy 'Tea' Taylor, fell out with mainstream Liberals.

Suffragists did better than wowsers. The issue had been big throughout the 1880s when Seddon had done more than anyone to defeat women's suffrage. In 1887, the year he torpedoed the bill, the WCTU made Kate Sheppard, a Christchurch Christian socialist, national superintendent of its franchise and legislation department. Women had already made modest gains: the Married Women's Property Act (1884) made matrimonial property settlements fairer, women could go to university (even if not everyone welcomed them) and they could vote in charitable aid board elections. Sheppard, popular with suffragists, was a smart choice; she was an energetic, good-looking woman who knew how to lobby male politicians, use the press and network with groups such as the New Zealand Alliance, which hoped that women would vote out alcohol. Many in the social purity movement believed that women were more virtuous than men and would therefore reform the conduct of politics once enfranchised.

THE SUFFRAGISTS

The Women's Christian Temperance Union (WCTU) attracted many suffragists and was the largest women's group at the time. Suffragists who did not care much for the 'C' or the 'T' in the WCTU formed their own franchise leagues. These were women like Margaret Bullock — painter, novelist, journalist, travel-writer, parliamentary correspondent and widow with five sons — who founded a league in Wanganui and, once the franchise was won, visited every house in the town to tell women why they should vote.

And those more interested in the 'U' formed groups that welcomed men as members. The Canterbury Women's Institute, formed in September 1892, advocated a broad platform of women's rights and included in its membership feminist novelist Edith Searle Grossman, eccentric scientist Alexander Bickerton, and socialist Eveline Cunnington, along with leading temperance advocates like Sheppard.

Many suffragists were well-heeled, with husbands, fathers, or brothers in business, on the bench, in the church or in politics. There were the 'political wives' of the Liberals, like Maud Pember Reeves who confirmed that 'we are going to have the franchise after all . . . My husband is to be relied on. I have seen to that.'[25] Most had small families or were childless, like Jean Smalley, wife of a Wesleyan minister and active in the Waimate and Oamaru franchise leagues.

These women had time and energy to devote to the cause. But there were also women of more humble means who squeezed suffrage work into their hectic working days. Firebrand Rachel Grimmett, whose husband ran a building business, stalked the streets of Caversham and South Dunedin for women's suffrage and, as an ardent Salvation Army foot-soldier, to fight 'Satan's strongholds' in the pubs and clubs. Elizabeth Caradus, mother of 15 (eight of whom survived infancy), kept a shop in Auckland's Freeman's Bay to support her husband's carpentry business, and worked in the local mission and the Ladies' Christian Association before becoming active in the Women's Franchise League as its treasurer. The shop stayed in the family for a half-century. It fell to the wrecker's ball in 1969 when, as the Kiwi Grocery, and said to be Auckland's oldest shop, it made way for the Harbour Bridge–Southern Motorway link. *Bronwyn Dalley*

There is a quiet nod to suffrage whenever a $10 note circulates; the face of Kate Sheppard (above) graces its reverse side.

NEW ZEALAND INTRODUCES WOMEN'S SUFFRAGE : "Female suffrage has made much greater headway in New Zealand than at home. Not only did the women exercise their new right at the recent general elections, but a member of the fair sex has been elected Mayor of Onehunga. The women at the Borough Council Chambers exhibited unmistakable signs of triumph during the morning's Poll, for in working hours they were in possession of the whole field"

November 1893 was a busy month for New Zealand women politically. They voted for the first time at national elections on the 28th, and next day the electors in the Auckland suburb of Onehunga brought in Elizabeth Yates as the first woman mayor in the British Empire. Yates took no great interest in women's suffrage. And she had no truck with the temperance lobby either, seeing prohibition as an infringement of personal liberty.

'You should always keep something up your sleeve for next year,' Seddon advised Joe Ward. 'Keep the buggers on a string and they'll keep you in office.' Seddon strung the voters along for the 13 years he reigned as 'King Dick'.

Not all suffrage supporters had such grand hopes. Most were simply ordinary men and women. Many were men, especially if they were political radicals or religious nonconformists. In the industrial suburbs of Caversham and South Dunedin artisans and skilled men strongly supported suffrage; so did 65–70 per cent of women by 1893, confounding critics like Dunedin mayor Henry Fish, whose hysterical attacks on suffragists and dodgy petitions backfired. Nationwide, about 25 per cent of women signed the 1893 suffrage petition, the final of three such petitions in the early 1890s. By any standards it was a monster. When Sir John Hall theatrically rolled it out across the Chamber that year it reached almost 300 m in length.

But demographic changes were easy to lose sight of in the early to mid 1890s as Seddon struggled to take the sting out of Stout's electoral ambushes. Against the odds, he corked (but did not completely quiet) the prohibition issue. But he failed with suffrage, despite cynically letting the House pass Sir John Hall's Electoral Bill, confident that the Legislative Council would kill it and take the blame. At the last minute his shiftiness enraged two councillors who voted for it after learning that Seddon had telegraphed another councillor asking him to change his mind. On 8 September 1893, therefore, the bill was passed 20 to 18, the *New Zealand Herald* commenting that 'it is hardly too much to say that the enfranchisement of the woman has been accomplished by her enemies'.[26] By the narrowest of margins New Zealand women got the vote and Seddon hypocritically telegraphed Sheppard his congratulations 11 days later when Governor Glasgow signed it into law. He would later boast about the decline in licensed public houses.

The break-up of the Cheviot Hills property was the Liberals' greatest propaganda coup. In fact, the heirs of the hated 'Ready Money Robinson' happily pocketed the government's £260,200 for their isolated 34,300-ha station. Many of the new farm units were uneconomically small, and two farmers out of every three left within 15 years; the stayers survived mostly by bending the rules and amalgamating units. But there were 311 separate properties here in 1914.

'I played on them like a pianner': Seddon's one-man-one-party rule

That telegram to Sheppard was vintage Seddon. His sharp political antennae, cunning and tactical flexibility astonished friend and foe alike. He personified pork barrel politics in 'God's Own Country', as he loved to call it, a tubby, egotistical political dynamo who ran everything, meeting deputations, dishing out political favours and finding people jobs. As Sir John Hall spluttered, 'he canvasses & promises and appears at the Polling Booth in his shirt sleeves'.[27] No wonder he had no real hobbies or relaxations. He was larger than life, meddlesome, egotistical and vulgar in speech, the first New Zealand populist politician to outsmart people by appearing dimmer than he was. 'I hate having to let them think me a fool,' he once confessed, but that was all part of playing them 'like a pianner'.[28] In 1893 few expected him to last long, but he fought the election ably as 'first mate', as he put it, winning even more soundly than Ballance had. Seddon never lost an election.

Women's suffrage was just one of the reforms of the Liberal era. For them land reform was the most important way to create a just and prosperous society. Hulking great 'Red Jock' McKenzie, Ballance's capable, sometimes volatile Minister of Lands, still harboured bitter childhood memories of the Highland clearances. Land had an almost spiritual improving quality for him — 'getting men on the land' would solve poverty and unemployment. Despite attacks from the pastoralists, his Land and Income Assessment [Tax] Act 1891 created a modest graduated land tax. The Land Act 1892 brought the lease-in-perpetuity, McKenzie's famous 999-year lease.

The issue was both symbolic and real. Few pastoralists thought themselves colonial aristocrats and many had been subdividing recently,

hampered only by a shortage of credit for purchasers. But 'land monopoly' was the symbolic issue of the day, and many colonists angered by the arrogance of the sheep lords in the Legislative Council thought them the embodiment of privilege. Even though New Zealand was urbanising fast, thousands wanted to own their own farms, or at least thought they did, and in towns surrounded by large estates most people favoured 'bursting them up'. In 1893 the cry of 'lands for the people' went up at Robinson's Cheviot Hills estate of all places. 'Ready Money' Robinson, arrogant in life and a Legislative Councillor to boot, had died in 1889. After rejecting the government's valuation for death duties, his executors challenged it to put up or shut up. By purchasing, subdividing and helping over 400 settlers onto Cheviot, the Liberals caught the attention of rural New Zealand.

That set the pattern. Most owners of 'burst up' estates sold willingly to the government, the only buyer with sufficiently deep pockets. In fact, they offered four times more land than the government bought. Just as important as the Land for Settlements Act 1894 (which mandated state purchase) was Seddon and Ward's Advances to Settlers Act 1894, which put state resources into settling the North Island. These two Acts and some lesser instruments put 7000 farmers and their families onto the land, revitalising the countryside 'and accelerating New Zealand's move away from a "plantation" type of agriculture to family farming'.[29] The 100,000 southern settlers lured to the new North Island frontier districts accelerated the drift north, where many displaced the chief victims of the Liberals' land policy, Maori. Democracy and ethnocentrism went hand in hand, especially with an overwhelmingly South

Schooled in the democratic, argumentative Free Kirk, Liberal Lands Minister John McKenzie migrated to Otago in 1860, speaking better Gaelic than English but determined to push leasehold tenure and closer settlement. AV Hunt, Alexander Turnbull Library, A-122-004

197

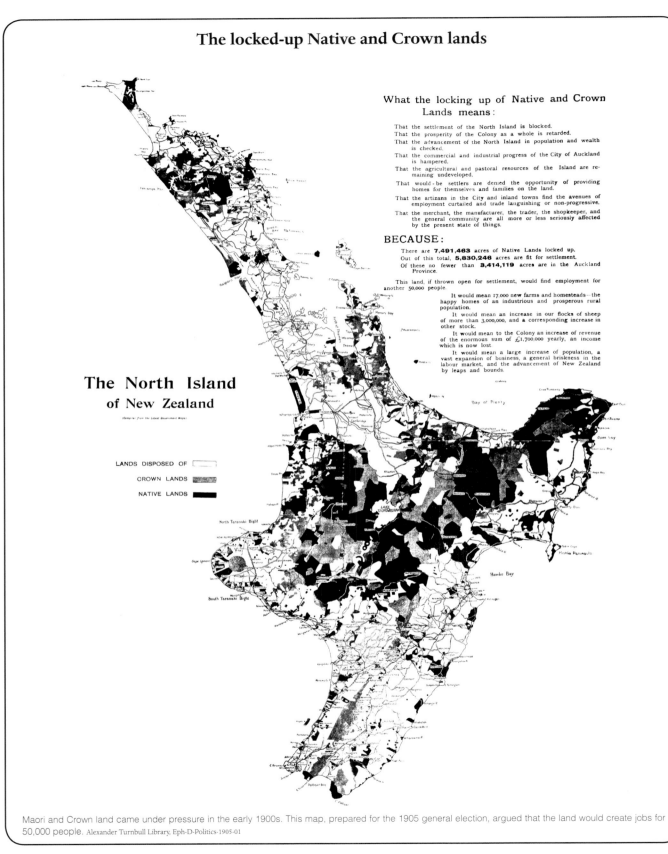

The locked-up Native and Crown lands

What the locking up of Native and Crown Lands means:

That the settlement of the North Island is blocked.

That the prosperity of the Colony as a whole is retarded.

That the advancement of the North Island in population and wealth is checked.

That the commercial and industrial progress of the City of Auckland is hampered.

That the agricultural and pastoral resources of the Island are remaining undeveloped.

That would-be settlers are denied the opportunity of providing homes for themselves and families on the land.

That the artizans in the City and inland towns find the avenues of employment curtailed and trade languishing or non-progressive.

That the merchant, the manufacturer, the trader, the shopkeeper, and the general community are all more or less seriously affected by the present state of things.

BECAUSE:

There are **7,491,463** acres of Native Lands locked up.

Out of this total, **5,830,246** acres are fit for settlement.

Of these no fewer than **3,414,119** acres are in the Auckland Province.

This land, if thrown open for settlement, would find employment for another 50,000 people.

It would mean 17,000 new farms and homesteads—the happy homes of an industrious and prosperous rural population.

It would mean an increase in our flocks of sheep of more than 3,000,000, and a corresponding increase in other stock.

It would mean to the Colony an increase of revenue of the enormous sum of £1,700,000 yearly, an income which is now lost.

It would mean a large increase of population, a vast expansion of business, a general briskness in the labour market, and the advancement of New Zealand by leaps and bounds.

The North Island
of New Zealand
(Compiled from the Latest Government Maps)

LANDS DISPOSED OF

CROWN LANDS

NATIVE LANDS

Maori and Crown land came under pressure in the early 1900s. This map, prepared for the 1905 general election, argued that the land would create jobs for 50,000 people. Alexander Turnbull Library, Eph-D-Politics-1905-01

198

North Otago Museum

In 1878 shop assistants worked very long hours. The Employment of Females Act did not apply to shops, so they worked as long as the shop was open, until 7 p.m. Monday to Friday and 10 or 11 p.m. on Saturdays — often 70 hours or more a week. By 1902, when 'Bulleid's shop girls' hammed it up at Cape Wanbrow, Oamaru, legislation placed some curbs on their employer.

Island party in charge. McKenzie expedited the transfer of 2.7 million acres (1.1 million ha) of Maori land to the government and another 400,000 acres (162,000 ha) to private purchasers. Modern observers might find it ironic that McKenzie, so angered by the clearances and who did more than anyone to promote the Queen's Chain, should have engineered this, but the Liberals wanted northern votes and, a Social Darwinist at heart, McKenzie thought communal ownership wasteful.

That rejection of communal ownership put him in step with Seddon's dilution of the labour influence in the 1890 'Lib-Lab' compact. Reeves, who led the 'Labour Party' in the House and fashioned the Liberals' labour policies and their place in New Zealand mythology, was the son of a wealthy partner in and manager of the *Lyttelton Times*. 'Willie' learned Latin at a prep school and went to Christ's College, where some classmates thought the future socialist too 'snobby'. After drifting aimlessly, Reeves caught the intoxicating whiff of printer's ink and from 1885 he edited his father's *Canterbury Times*. Two years later he won St Albans and threw in his lot with Ballance, his social ostracism by friends only confirming his radicalism. In 1891, Ballance made him Minister of Education and Justice. Next year he became the Empire's first Minister of Labour.

The colony was receptive to Reeves' ideas. Trade unionists and radicals, determined that Old World evils had no place in God's Own Country, were calling for a government department for labour, a labour bureau, factory laws, a worker's lien law, support for trade unionism and compulsory arbitration. In 1891 Ballance got a badly mauled Factory Act past the Legislative Council, but real progress had to wait until Reeves took charge of labour bills next year. The Shops and Offices Act established the state's right to regulate hours and conditions of work for shopworkers. The Contractors and Workmen's Lien Act made better provision for paying contractors and workmen. His Labour Department bill had to be dropped, and the council mauled his Industrial Conciliation and Arbitration (IC&A) bill so savagely that the government ditched it.

Reeves' greatest achievement was the Industrial Conciliation and Arbitration (IC&A) Act, which transformed New Zealand's industrial relations and trade unionism, and lasted 90 years. Reeves knew that compulsory arbitration was essential and tried to introduce it each year from 1891. His first bill died in the House and the Council killed the others; but in return for Reeves's support, Seddon backed the IC&A bill, which finally passed in 1894. The Act set up industrial districts, each

THE YOUNG MAORI PARTY

Young Maori Party leaders Peter Buck and Apirana Ngata with James Carroll at Wairoa before the war. Ebullient, a born raconteur who enjoyed most things in life, Carroll provided the whakaruruhau (mantle of care) in Parliament, sheltering the young saplings of the Young Maori Party. Tairawhiti Museum

Top-down history overgenerously credits those top-hatted cultural boundary-crossers, the Young Maori Party (YMP), for the Maori recovery that pre-dated them. The Young Maori Party tag dates from 1907 and was applied to graduates from the elite Te Aute College in Hawke's Bay. Te Aute headmaster John Thornton encouraged his pupils to go into higher education. Many did, making substantial contributions to New Zealand society — Ned Ellison in health and public administration, Reweti Kohere in writing, Paraire Tomoana in sports and composition — but the best remembered are the politician knights, Sir Apirana Ngata, Sir Peter Buck (Te Rangi Hiroa), and Sir Maui Pomare. It helped that these fluent Maori speakers also spoke polished garden-party English.

Christian, bilingual, more scholarly than most settlers, they were assimilationists, valuing teachers above tohunga. They also spoke for the 'flax roots', since Maori parents, while keeping te reo alive in their homes, knew the value of having their children taught in English. Their emphasis on hygiene and sanitation and on temperance on the marae also struck a chord.

Apirana Ngata, Ngati Porou, born 1874, was the lynchpin. Appointed travelling secretary for the Te Aute College Students' Association in 1899, this consummate networker spread the gospel of hygiene and temperance throughout the East Coast, the Ureweras, the Bay of Plenty, and Wanganui. He shared Maori criticism of the Native Land Court but thought a separate Maori

James Carroll (standing, right) became King Dick's right-hand man. This stiffly formal portrait was taken to record the Premier's visit to Huntly in 1898. The Maori King, Mahuta Tawhiao Potatau Te Wherowhero, sits beside Seddon; his advisors Tupu Taingakawa and Henare Kaihau stand beside Carroll.

parliament impractical. Inevitably he came to the attention of the first Maori minister for Native Affairs, James Carroll, who co-opted Ngata and Hone Heke Ngapua to help him draft the Maori Councils Act and the Maori Lands Administration Act, laws designed to outflank the Kotahitanga and Kingitanga by devolving power to elected Maori councils. The Te Aute College Students' Association also drafted the by-laws, which mandated the scientific approach. In a parallel to the work of European health reformers such as Truby King, medical administrators Pomare and Buck wielded this new broom vigorously, even if the Maori councils satisfied neither Maori nor those settlers who thought they detected the whiff of 'Home Rule' in them.

Ngata won Eastern Maori in 1905. He worked closely with Carroll while also fostering tribal incorporations, managing communal farms and his own model sheep station. In 1908 he was joined in Parliament by Buck (Pomare followed three years later), to form with Carroll a powerful bloc that seemed to prove that Maori could compete with Europeans. These men may have been exceptional and settlers may have claimed too much credit for their achievements, but that does not diminish the fact that the degree of equality that existed here was unusual by New World standards. Maori had had universal male franchise since 1879 (Maori women got the vote with other women in 1893), and in 1909 and 1911 Carroll was acting prime minister, an inconceivable idea in Australia, South Africa or Canada.

with its own conciliation board. Registered trade unions and employers chose an equal number of members, who selected an independent chair. If they could not settle a dispute, either party (or the board itself) could appeal to an arbitration court, comprising a judge plus assessors selected by the union and the employer. Unions did not have to take advantage of its provisions. They could still register under the 1878 Trade Union Act and, deeply suspicious of state involvement, they stayed aloof until 1896, when the Denniston Miners' Union dragged the Westport Coal Company into conciliation. When the parties failed to agree the union appealed to the court. It rejected most of the union's claims; but by forcing the WCC to recognise the union and to give 'preference' to hiring Denniston miners, it encouraged other unions to try the Act. Then the Seamen's Union took on the Union Company, winning several concessions from the court; this set the union on course for a full recovery and spelt the end for the company's mutual benefit society, the hated 'Deaf & Dumb Society'.

Because the court heard most cases, no matter how trivial, by 1900 it was in danger of becoming the victim of its own success. For trade unionists who had seen their unions crushed or expire just 10 to 15 years earlier, the gains were remarkable. By 1900 a new form of unionism had appeared 'which owed its very existence to the Arbitration Act and which depended on the coercive power of the state to achieve its ends'.[30] More striking to contemporaries, the new law seemed to have rendered strikes obsolete; there would be none between 1894 and 1906. Henry Demarest Lloyd, the great American progressive, called New Zealand 'a country without strikes'.[31] Not surprisingly, union membership soared, making it the third most unionised society in the world by 1913.

Seddon's pretensions to kingly status extended to its Maori equivalent, rangatira. Here he drew on the support of James Carroll. Born in Wairoa in 1857 to a Sydney-born Irishman and a Ngati Kahungunu mother, Carroll grew up bilingual. His mother was a woman of mana, but Carroll was not a traditional leader; instead he was one of the new type of men who were looking for new answers in politics, religion, newspapers, and even new forms of carving and figurative painting. He won Eastern Maori in 1887. Believing that all Maori could, like him, master the skills necessary to work in both cultures, he 'aimed at empowering Maori within modern economic life and securing their equality with Pakeha'.[32] His criticism of the Native Land Act 1888 inspired Ballance to appoint him to an inquiry into native land laws, then from March 1892 to the Executive Council to represent the 'native race'. Carroll considered customs such as competitive feasting wasteful and saw leasing — combined with compulsory investment of the rent on behalf of the owners — as a way of stimulating development. The paternalistic Native

Land Court Act 1894 restored Crown pre-emption to protect Maori from improvidence.

This put him offside with the other Maori members of the House of Representatives, who urged Maori to boycott the court and to stop selling or leasing land. Maori had been struggling to counter Wellington's parliament with one of their own, but had been held back by disunity. From time to time hui were held as Maori 'parliaments'; Te Tii, in the Bay of Islands held several. In April 1892, 96 chiefs met at Te Tiriti o Waitangi marae; by June

Photographer ES Pegler called this portrait 'pensioners at home'. These were model examples of the 'deserving' poor, for there was a strong streak of moral evangelism to the rules that New Zealand pensioners had to meet to get their pensions. They also had to be the right colour — Asian New Zealanders could not get the old-age pension. National Publicity Studios Collection, Alexander Turnbull Library, F-22951-½

nearly 21,000 had signed the covenant of Kotahitanga (the Maori Unity Movement). The Maori Parliament met for the first time at Waipatu marae in Heretaunga that month.[33] It would meet for another decade in several places and demand devolution of powers from Wellington; but settler politicians closed their ears, and with Te Whiti, Te Kooti and the Kingitanga hanging back, Carroll easily dismissed its demands.

But in 1895 the sale boycott drove the government to amend

the law to permit direct dealing. That and intertribal jealousies broke resistance; Ngati Maniapoto alone sold 700,000 acres (283,500 ha) between 1892 and 1899, finally opening up the King Country to Europeans. In 1893 Carroll had jumped waka: he had left Eastern Maori for the general seat of Waiapu, becoming the first Maori to hold a general seat. In the mid 1890s he twice accompanied Seddon on extensive treks through Tuhoe settlements in the rugged Ureweras. He piloted through the Urewera Native Reserve Act 1896, preserving the fragile land

from settlement and also pioneered the East Coast-style land incorporations, all part of his scheme to slow the settler inrush while helping Maori to acquire the skills and capital to compete with them. His Maori Councils Act 1900 offered an alternative to the Maori Parliament — tribal councils somewhat akin to local authorities. By 1910, however, most had fizzled out.

Meaningful opposition to 'King Dick' had also fizzled out. By 1900 Seddon had sidelined all opponents. He could ignore the Opposition — it formally disbanded in 1899. The urban radicals had been swamped by new Liberals elected from 1893, all of whom signed loyalty pledges to 'King Dick' before they could run; consequently the 'Lab' part of 'Lib-Lab' was heard less often now. In 1896 Reeves left for London as agent-general. Three years later Seddon muzzled Stout by making him chief justice. In 1897 and '98 Seddon capped off the Liberals' reform burst with a measure of his own — old-age pensions. Although modest, given only to the 'deserving' poor, withheld from Asian New Zealanders, and not taken up very readily — in 1901, 62.5 per cent of New Zealanders eligible by age to the pension did not collect it — state-funded pensions were a landmark measure.[34] They were also a mark of Seddonian paternalism, since they were partly inspired by the plight of ageing former miners. Seddon's other social reforms were also rooted in personal experience. The former railway fitter abolished the railway commissioners appointed by Atkinson in 1887 and improved working conditions and career paths. Although he made Labour Day a holiday from 1896 and gave administrator Edward Tregear a free hand at the Labour Department, little more was done apart from the Workers' Dwellings Act 1905 and a modest state-housing scheme.

King Dick's interests turned increasingly towards other countries. He tried to exclude unwanted foreigners from God's own country, notably Asians and Austrians (the Dalmatians who began settling in the Far North in 1898 and '99). Seddon, a hapuka in a rock pool, had kept New Zealand out of Australia in 1901, hoping instead to make it the heart of a mini Pacific empire. He dreamed of federating Hawai'i, Fiji, Tonga, Samoa and the Cooks with New Zealand and Niue but had to settle for the Cooks in 1901. During the South African War he whipped up patriotic fervour, meddled in officers' commissions and appeared more John Bullish than the British. In London for imperial conferences or coronations, he strutted the imperial stage in his magnificent privy councillor's uniform.

Seddon was a colossus, totally dominating Cabinet, caucus, Parliament and the electorate, which lapped it up. Once Jock McKenzie resigned in 1900, he was without an equal in Cabinet. Visitors came from far and wide to see the future and how it worked, for it was said that New Zealand was the birthplace of the 20th century. But Seddon pushed himself too hard and from the late 1890s his health worried insiders (the worst problems were kept from the public). Then on 10 June 1906, off the Australian coast, his heart failed not long after he telegrammed 'just leaving for God's own country'. His death shocked New Zealand. He was not just premier, he was the government, as even those who had mocked his diction or his pretensions acknowledged. 'It might be said of my late premier that his was of latter years benevolent despotism rather than pure constitutional government,' Governor Plunket said, 'but the Colony trusted him.'[35] It erected a statue in front of Parliament that 'has come to represent the authority of the state in New Zealand'.[36]

Between 1881 and 1896 the birth rate fell by 40 per cent, trimming family sizes, though the fall varied according to class, ethnicity and geographical location. For rural New Zealand children in a time when ready-made toys were rare, play required much improvisation, as these illustrations show. A box serves as a cart for Maori children, who are playing surrounded by heavily logged land; and an old bent tin is being used by boys playing cricket on the road in a West Coast mining town.

BELOW: In 1908 the North Island main trunk line was completed, 30 years after the mainland's. This photograph shows a Public Works Department train and construction workers on the main trunk line near Waiouru, with Mounts Ruapehu and Ngauruhoe in the background.

'The twentieth century begins here': prosperity and cultural vitality

The economy climbed out of the doldrums in the mid 1890s as wool prices picked up and the new pastoral industries, fathered by refrigeration, fat-lamb farming and dairying, flourished. Construction, gold mining using dredges and manufacturing also stoked the engines of growth, but the pastoral industries were the ones that would largely underwrite the country's standard of living for almost another century. Of course it helped that the British market was prospering and could afford these products, but New Zealand producers also proved remarkably successful at outperforming Southern Hemisphere rivals.

They started with sheep breeds such as James Little's Corriedale, a dual-purpose crossbred beast that fattened farmers' accounts by efficiently processing the south's exotic grasses into high-quality wool and meat. Traditional breeds remained important; but many breeders favoured dual-purpose breeds such as the New Zealand Romney, which emerged somewhat later in the North Island. Then the discovery in the early 1900s that rape grew well in Canterbury's early spring enabled farmers to fatten their lambs in time for them to hit British tables for Christmas. By 1905 the colony was exporting more lamb than mutton.

A sophisticated processing and transport system linked London to its town milk supply colony half a world away. Now the costly, publicly funded infrastructure of ports, railway lines and telegraph lines began to pay dividends. The Union Company's steamers were the tip of an efficient and often underrated coastal trade. The south's railways were already sophisticated, and during the first years of the new century the northern system was capped off by the hurried completion of the main trunk, with its heroic engineering feats of tunnels, spirals and viaducts. Parliamentarians adjourned proceedings to take the train up to welcome the visiting American Great White Fleet in 1908, but more importance should perhaps be attached to the train that raced Bluff oysters to the Queen City to honour the ships' officers at a banquet. Goods still had to be trans-shipped into steamers to cross Cook Strait, but at last New Zealand had a national railway system worthy of the name.

The massive freezing works, 31 of them by 1901, were the most obvious signs of the pastoral revolution. Most started out locally owned, but British companies such as Borthwicks and Vestey's bought into the trade. They were soon joined by British shipping companies. From the late 1880s steamships of 5000 to 7000 tons displaced 1000-ton sailing ships from the United Kingdom trade, dramatically cutting transport costs

Rails ringed city streets, too. In the early 1900s the major cities all built extensive electric tram systems, which sped the growth of suburbanisation. Here workmen are laying tramlines at the corner of Cuba and Manners streets in Wellington in 1903.

and voyage times for passengers. British interests bought the New Zealand Shipping Company in the late 1880s and in 1917 would go on to take over the Union Steam Ship Company. Meat companies, closely associated with shipping lines, were also linked to insurance companies and banks in forging an efficient, innovative, and profitable conveyor belt between New Zealand and Britain. Octopus? Oligopoly? Who cared? It worked.

Dairying benefited from the infrastructure of shipping, banking and insurance created for the frozen meat trade. Like fat-lamb production, dairying also owed a debt to William Saltau Davidson, who had pioneered the industry at Edendale in Southland. The Waireka Dairy Factory Company opened a cheese factory in North Otago in 1883. But dairying took off fastest in hitherto depressed Taranaki, a region that quickly became synonymous with dairying, exporting more butter than the rest of the country together. In the 1890s Taranaki exports

grew by 234 per cent and its population by 72 per cent. Taranaki farmers were tough and innovative. At first milk was collected from farms, separated at creameries and taken to a central factory to be made into butter or cheese. From the 1890s the co-operatives, a distinctively New Zealand phenomenon, expanded rapidly, with groups of individuals combining to build and run the factory while preserving their individuality as producers. They succeeded in enabling New Zealand farmers to produce butter and cheese, ship them to the other side of the world and still compete with the Danes and the Argentinians. In the 1900s home separating of cream from milk cheapened the cost of collection, eliminated the local creamery and encouraged the growth of larger, centralised factories. Cow-cockies were technology-mad magpies, picking up the American Babcock test (which measured the butterfat content of milk and cream) and then the first milking machines.

The government came to the party by enacting legislation to improve and safeguard quality, important to an industry that required technical advance and expert help. The Liberals' Department of Agriculture began looking after animal welfare in 1892, eight years before they sanctioned a health department to care for people. Their Dairy Industry Act 1908 was highly influential. In general the government provided capital, advice, help in achieving quality control, and selective subsidies. By registering, licensing and inspecting slaughterhouses, abattoirs, meat-export works and dairy factories it ensured that New Zealand primary produce was respected in Britain for its quality, purity and value. That clean, green image boosted the dominion's market share from less than five per cent of Britain's butter and three per cent of its cheese imports in 1900 to almost nine per cent and over 30 per cent respectively in 1914.

Like waste in a cowshed, prosperity trickled down haphazardly and unevenly. While the white-collar sector grew and women moved into some clerical fields, many New Zealanders still remained dependent on seasonal or broken work, especially in small towns and rural areas. Despite Seddon's pensions, survival could be precarious for the elderly, the sick or the single.

The early 20th century also brought evidence of a Maori revival. The 'dying race', all 45,000 of them (just over five per cent of New Zealanders in 1901) appears to have shrugged

off its winding sheet during the 1890s and walked away. The revival was aided in part by intermarriage, which helped diffuse immunities to Old World bacteria and viruses. Maori death rates remained high but birth rates were higher still in a population that was now overwhelmingly rural, 'isolated from, and marginal to, the urbanising Pakeha socio-economy'.[37] Many Maori communities survived on a mixture of subsistence agriculture, seasonal hunting, fishing and gathering, and casual or seasonal work on road gangs, farms and sawmills. It kept them going but without much to fall back on when times got tight or when illness struck.

The news that the race was not dying would please many who began this period convinced of that. From the 1880s and 1890s Auckland artists such as Charles Goldie and Gottfried Lindauer urgently painted what they called the 'Old Time' Maori, the ageing warriors and elders of the 1860s. Scholars, many of them amateur gentlemen or politicians, busied themselves with the literary equivalent of salvage archaeology. Journalist and historian James Cowan published *The Maoris of New Zealand* (1910) and *The Adventures of Kimble Bent* (1911). S Percy Smith, Hoani Turei Te Whatahoro, Elsdon Best, Augustus Hamilton, and TL Buick all wrote about Maori history and ethnography, Buick rekindling some non-Maori interest in the Treaty of Waitangi. 'Young Maori Party' members wrote

For many people in rural and small town New Zealand, work was often seasonal, short term and broken by periods of unemployment or under employment. For Maori it was especially so. In the north gum-digging provided a welcome source of income. Northwood Collection, Alexander Turnbull Library, G-6280-¹/₁

widely, with Peter Buck being particularly influential. Labour bureaucrat Edward Tregear published *The Maori Race* in 1904. Politician and runholder Robert McNab wrote widely on 'Old New Zealand'. These non-fiction writers had more influence than the poets, short story writers and novelists, and several still haunt general knowledge. Smith and Te Whatahoro 'smithed', as one historian put it, the still persistent myth that the Moriori of the Chathams were a separate and primitive race. From Britain Reeves influenced the political and historiographical agenda for decades to come — perhaps even still — with his classics *Land of the Long White Cloud* (1898) and *State Experiments in Australia and New Zealand* (1902).

Settler history, too, was patchily noted and celebrated as New Zealanders, like their Australian cousins, wrote their own 'colonial book of Genesis'.[38] In Wellington and Dunedin respectively, cultural magpies Alexander Turnbull and Thomas Morland Hocken amassed collections that formed the core of later national institutions. Dunedin's jubilee celebrations kick-started the Otago Early Settlers' Association, which went on to found the country's first social history museum. Away from such genteel havens, fire, saws, axes and ploughs, the progress industry's weapons, still ruled the land, but even here there was some stocktaking. In 1887, Te Heuheu Tukino IV, Horonuku, paramount chief of Ngati Tuwharetoa, preserved the sacred peaks of Ruapehu, Tongariro and Ngauruhoe by giving them to the nation, thereby creating the world's second national park. A few sites such as Ship Cove were also reserved before 1903, when the Scenery Preservation Act added many more to, it must be said, lure tourist pounds as much as preserve heritage.[39]

Of the higher arts, painting most closely explored the antipodean light and textures. The arrival in 1890 of two immigrants, Scot James Nairn and Dutchman Petrus van der Velden — the latter remembered by Otira Gorge locals as 'that queer old bird . . . sitting there on the verandah in the sun, with a pot of ale in one hand, and his pipe, waiting for a decent storm to brew up' — marked 'the beginning of a new era in New Zealand painting', having a major impact on local painters and on the public art schools established in Dunedin (1870), Christchurch (1882) and Auckland (1890).[40] Van der Velden's Otira Gorge studies brood darkly, while Nairn's sunlight dapples across southern seas. In an era when governors' ladies went sketching in the Antipodes Islands or Fiordland, leisured women took up paintbrushes in considerable numbers, although some of the younger ones, such as Frances Hodgkins, flitted overseas and challenged the old notions of the sedate 'lady painter'.

Fiction flourished. For women, 'writing love stories (or poetry) was an acceptable literary activity'.[41] Prominent writers included Edith Grossman, Jessie Mackay and Blanche Baughan. Literary critics have tended to underrate the period before

Puke Ariki

In 1885 Taranaki's first co-operative dairy factory, the Moa Farmers' Co-operative Dairy Company, opened at Inglewood. Taranaki and the Waikato were soon thick with them, since the time it took to transport milk cans over primitive roads set a practical limit from farm to factory of about 5 km. Until the factories set up tributary skimming stations in the 1890s with steam-driven centrifugal separators, they were places at which to swap news, as these fellows seem to be doing.

North Otago Museum

Taking time off. In the cities people took ferries or electric trams to the beaches or trains out into the countryside. In the countryside traction engines, such as this one belonging to 'Darkie Hill' from Herbert, helped transport district folk to their picnic just outside Oamaru.

North Otago Museum

By the early 1900s ball sports such as rugby, soccer and league were promoted as manly preparations for life, a point appreciated by cod-liver oil tonic manufacturer Lane's Emulsion, which sponsored some of the players in the Oamaru Auctioneers and Grain Merchants' team of 1911.

the 1920s and have built an industry around the famous expatriate writer, Katherine Mansfield, whose best work was written after 1913, while ignoring Edith Lyttelton because 'she was an expatriate New Zealander and . . . much of her writing was consciously aimed at a popular readership'.[42] Lyttelton, who wrote under the pen name GB Lancaster, had grown up on a Canterbury farm under the thumb of a harridan of a mother. In the first half of the 20th century, however, she produced 11 novels, a collection of stories, two serialised novels and over 250 stories, most published by reputable publishers, and wrote almost exclusively about 'the formation of colonial identity, and the legacy of imperialism in the lives of settlers and their descendants'.[43]

Male writers, a more diverse bunch, might with retrospect be divided into those who wrote for the campfire and those who waited for each Home boat to discharge its letters, papers and books. Some, most notably Alfred Grace with *Maoriland Stories* (1895) and *Tales of a Dying Race* (1901), did with their pens what Goldie and

'No one really knew who I was until I finally left N.Z. – that end of the world'. Like Reeves before her and Katherine Mansfield later, GB Lancaster — Edith Lyttelton — New Zealand's most widely read writer of the first half of the 20th century, wrote her greatest works overseas. Alexander Turnbull Library, S-L27-260

Lindauer did with paint, capturing the supposed last gasps of Maoriland. Others, rural romantics, were influenced by the Australian balladeers such as Henry Lawson (who spent time here in the late 1890s), with their homosocial imagery of mateship and rough antipodean democracy. In some ways antipodean literature was as trans-Tasman as shearing. Many New Zealanders cut their teeth writing for the Sydney *Bulletin* — Lyttelton called it her 'literary father' — and from 1905 the country had its own version of the crusading Australian newspaper *Truth*. In 1898, just as he was starting to outrage Oamaruvians by preaching against their urban vice, poet-cum-congregationalist minister David McKee Wright had published *Station Ballads and Other Verses*, which portrayed country life as full of manly virtue and womanly purity, and town life as full of strikes, criminals and effeminacy. He hated grasping station bosses and strikers equally.

Reeves loathed the former and helped the latter, but his famous poem 'A Colonist in His Garden' is a declaration of faith in the transplantability of

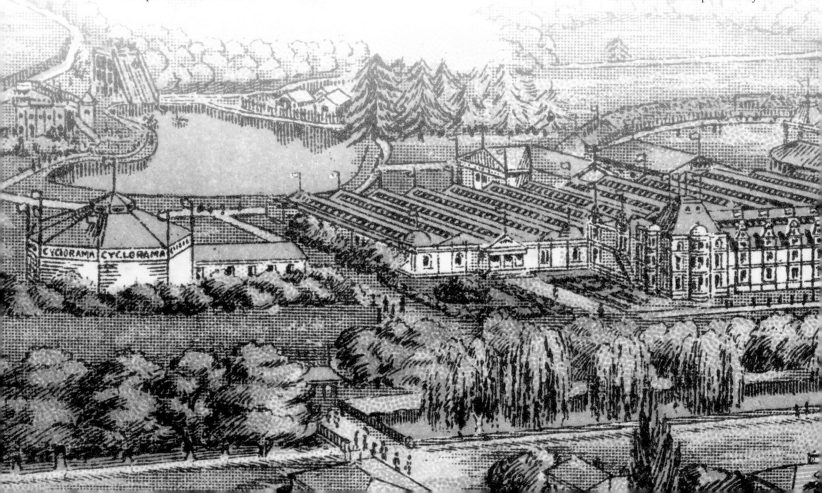

God's Own Country

British culture, written 'after he had already abandoned his antipodean garden for the "the old, green land"'.[44] Most women writers (though not Lyttelton) and many men preferred bone china tea services to billies and thought Englishness superior to antipodean nationalism and the cult of mateship. Charles Baeyertz, who founded *The Triad* in Dunedin in 1893, disliked colonial accents and saw egalitarianism as mediocrity. It will come as no surprise to learn that *The Triad* enjoyed its best circulation in the South Island. Or that it later moved to Sydney.

Musical scores contributed to the minuscule local publishing industry, churning out such delights as 'The Zealandia Polka Mazurka', 'On the Ball' (a 'football song'), the 'Colonial Mazurka' or 'The Huia Waltz'. In 1878, Thomas Bracken's 'God Defend New Zealand' was published as the national anthem. A decade and a half later, German immigrant Michael Balling, appalled at the prominence given to sport, ventured into the isolated Urewera with his viola, and built a music conservatorium at his new

Schools of art flourished in the large towns and cities. In 1876 prominent Dunedin citizens formed the Otago Art Society to promote 'the exaltation of sentiment and the refinement of mind'. James Kilgour's painting shows the first art school director, DC Hutton and his wife Nellie at work. J Kilgour, Hocken Library, University of Otago

home town, Nelson.[45] Balling spoke highly of Maori chants, but the musician who turned most famously to Maori themes was New Zealand's first composer of note, Alfred Hill, who knew Goldie and replicated his efforts. Hill's 'Waiata Poi' 'kept John McIndoe's Dunedin presses busy meeting the demand for New Zealand's first international best-seller'.[46] His most popular major works were the cantata *Hinemoa* (1896) and the opera *Tapu* (1902); in the latter, toured memorably by the Pollard Opera Co, the second scene opened with steam ascending from a replica Pink Terrace. Hill's music was said to be whistled in the streets of Sydney, but modern eyes and ears might wonder whether 'Tapu', with its plot about federation with Australia, emancipated women cyclists, and natives and cooking pots, was art or merely artful cultural shoplifting.[47]

Many of these cultural and intellectual strands came together at the International Exhibition in Christchurch, King Dick's statement 'proclaiming New Zealand's distinctiveness and imminent greatness'.[48] Seddon laid the foundation

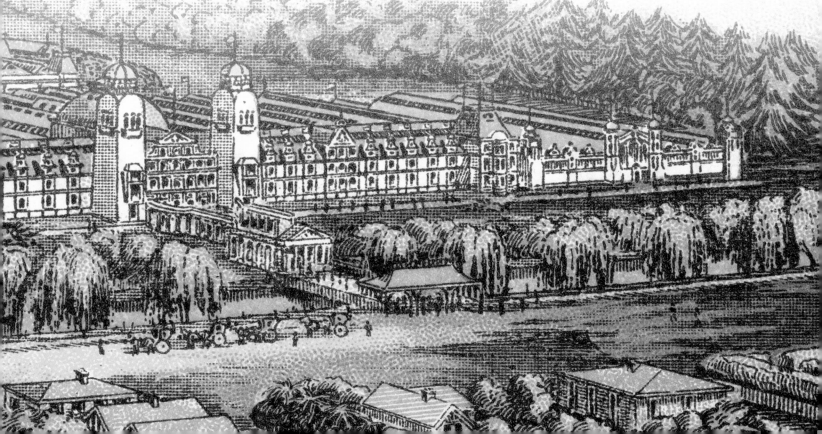

BELOW: New Zealand held several international exhibitions between 1865 and 1940, all but one in either Dunedin or Christchurch. For several months visitors would flock to the elaborate temporary palaces, exhibition halls and fun parks. The New Zealand International Exhibition at Hagley Park over the summer of 1906–07 was a colossal celebration of 'God's own country' and drew just under two million visitors, twice the country's population at that time. D Thompson Collection, Alexander Turnbull Library, PAColl-0892-1

stone, but had been laid low by the time it opened. As James Cowan noted in the official record, 'it came as a distinct impetus to virile nationhood and helped to a rather more exact realisation of our value as a civilised state than New Zealanders had hitherto grasped'. Running a postcolonial eye over events in Hagley Park, historian Jock Phillips saw seven tableaux — A Land of Abundance, Beautiful New Zealand, The Social Laboratory of the World, The Britain of the South, A Man's Country, Maoriland and A Respectable People. Pride there certainly was. After locals protested at the appointment of an English-born Australian as conductor for the exhibition orchestra, the government stepped in and appointed Hill.[49] Hill also wrote the music for Johannes Andersen's 'Exhibition Ode'. But we should not exaggerate the nationalistic flourishes. British and Australian art was popular, people took pride in the visiting Royal Navy squadron, they nicknamed the orchestra 'Hill's Brigands' because of the cost to the taxpayer, and the show-stealers were the members of the Lancashire working-class Besses o' th' Barn Band.

Science was also on display in Christchurch. New Zealand's greatest scientists, like the writers, became expatriates, men like physicist Ernest Rutherford, though the ones who stayed proved remarkable at adapting new inventions to money-making activities. In 1889, for example, Karangahake was the first mine in the world to test the new MacArthur-Forrest process for extracting gold from quartz deposits by cyanidation.[50] Fewer natural scientists flew the coop, because New Zealand, long isolated from the rest of the world and still being reworked by fire and earthquakes, was nature's equivalent of the social laboratory. Leonard Cockayne, the great botanist and a founder of modern science, published his seminal *New Zealand Plants and Their Story* in 1910. Small cores of scientists at the universities and the major museums worked alongside amateurs, recording species, unearthing moa skeletons, and studying Maori and Pacific Islanders — 'native' to them encompassing people as readily as forest or fiord. Here, too, the sense of specialness was accompanied by a feeling of loss as the countryside was drained, burned and fenced to form London's dairy farm. In the Hawke's Bay, farmer and autodidact William Herbert Guthrie-Smith was writing articles about the environment long before the publication of his classic *Tutira: The Story of a New Zealand Sheep Station*. On first Resolution Island in Fiordland and then Kapiti Island, Richard Henry pioneered the island sanctuary approach to species protection, something in which New Zealand would become the world leader.

For New Zealanders looking for entertainment, circuses or stage shows filled the bill. Amateur 'coon shows' or 'nigger minstrel shows', as they were called, were common and popular. North Otago Museum

'Hayseed Hussars and Wobblies': the 1890 consensus splinters and re-forms

Sir Joseph Ward, Seddon's successor, won the 1908 election even more convincingly than 'King Dick' ever had — with 58.7 per cent of the vote — but it was the last Liberal victory. It was as misleading as it was magnificent. The dandyish Ward, political to the very tips of his splendidly waxed moustache, lacked the strength and animal magnetism by which Seddon had held everything together. 'Listening to his sentences I always feel like the man who watched the slow procession of the dredge buckets, dreamily waiting for the last bucket to come up,' an observer wrote in 1909. 'Time disappears, the world fades away.'[51]

For some time the consensus of 1890 and its ageing architects had also been fading away. Sectional divisions were deepening, as a glance around Ward's own caucus would have shown. Some new Auckland and Christchurch urban radical Liberals were virtually independents and there were now no full-time farmers in the caucus.[52] And, with Ballance, Seddon and McKenzie dead and Reeves out of politics, the Cabinet of ageing mediocrities had lost touch with the newer forces in society. On the right had emerged the heirs of refrigeration and the Liberal land policies, the new family farmers suspicious of city interest groups, trade unions and the Farmers' Union's other nemesis, 'inefficient' manufacturers. On the left, many workers were growing discontented with their lot. Each time Ward tried to placate one group he offended the other. Any cow-cocky might have

told him that it was foolish to fence-sit on barbed wire, but the Liberals, who distrusted interest groups and appeals to sectional loyalties, stayed put.

Some of the pushiest challenges to the Liberals' gradualism were coming from the towns and cities where trade unions, nurtured by the Arbitration Court, were signing up large numbers of unskilled workers for the first time. Socialism had influenced Reeves and other leaders of the 1890s but it had not entered the popular vocabulary. From 1906 to 1908, however, socialists of every shade of red canvassed manual workers, making converts in the coal mines, the flax mills and on the wharves. John A Lee recalled that 'in those pre-1914 days, at every smoko, at every few minutes of idleness at the pit mouth . . . a grim dungareed orator mounted the soapbox to bless the coming socialist dawn'.[53] New Zealand was no different to the other Western nations just before the war; syndicalists (who believed in revolutionary industrial unionism), and anarchists and 'Wobblies' (members of the Industrial Workers of the World) 'preached class war, direct action, industrial unionism, and One Big Union as the means of achieving a socialist millennium'.[54] Revolutionaries as colourful as their nicknames — Australians Bob Semple, 'Bob the Ranter' or 'Fighting Bob', and Paddy Webb — savaged 'Labour's leg-iron' (their name for the Arbitration Court), which they thought had emasculated unionism by weaning unions away from direct action. A tough apprenticeship in some of the worst mines in the United States had taught Pat Hickey, 'Wild Bill Hickey', one of the few New Zealand-born revolutionaries, that 'class warfare was inevitable, class solidarity essential, and revolutionary industrial unionism

Brass bands were extremely popular. Towns, friendly societies, churches and even factories and trade unions formed them but Christchurch went one further when Fred Painter combined playing and pedalling. One day an unwary woman cyclist crossed the path of the Christchurch Bicycle Band while it was performing in the street. Band members took evasive action, she fell off, but the music continued uninterrupted!

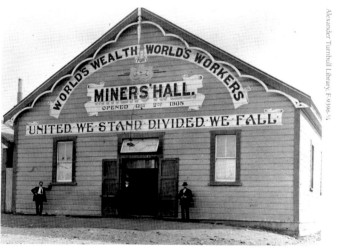

Labour's rallying cry adorns the miners' hall at Runanga. The West Coast mineworkers led the radicals' challenge to the old Lib-Lab system.

the only defence and hope for the "wage slave"'.[55] No wonder Edward Tregear, Secretary of the Department of Labour, wrote in 1908 about New Zealand feeling 'the heavy ground-swell presaging the coming storm and pulsing against her shores both from the Old and New Worlds'.[56]

That year a tsunami struck at Blackball, where Hickey led the country's first meaningful strike since 1891. The 'tucker-time strike' began quietly enough. On 27 February 1908 Webb and six mates were sacked for taking 30 minutes for 'crib' (lunch), twice the time allowed. In striking to support them, the Blackball Coal-Miners'

months later, a tactical victory for tucker-time, but a strategic one for the revolutionaries by discrediting the court, making striking attractive, and raising industrial unionism's stocks.

The miners' unions led the flight from arbitration. The court had its problems. It could take a year to make a decision and wages were falling behind living costs, to the frustration of people accustomed to prosperity but convinced that working people were missing out on their fair share of the national wealth. In contrast, some of the first unions to break from arbitration made quick gains for their members.[57]

Dominion status. 'Kiwi: "I think that I would look better without it."' In 1907, Sir Joseph Ward, who liked big gestures, got the Imperial Conference to give New Zealand dominion status, but cartoonist Trevor Lloyd captures public antipathy. Many New Zealanders distrusted the strutting Ward (it was once said his speeches were as stiff as his moustache) or anything that smacked of loosening the ties of Empire. T Lloyd, Alexander Turnbull Library, C-109-023

Union deliberately breached its arbitration award. But in refusing to pay the £75 fine imposed by the court, it blew a colossal raspberry at the arbitration system. Then it made officials look like bumbling pantomime villains. When bailiffs seized miners' assets to auction to pay the fine, the union rigged the bidding, ensuring that the auction raised an insulting pittance. Then a huge procession accompanied Hickey to the train when he was gaoled. Thwarted and ridiculed, the mine company caved in a few

In 1909, Hickey and Semple organised the New Zealand Federation of Miners, which a year later became the Federation of Labour, or 'Red Feds' as it became known, covering many miners', seamen's, wharfies', flax workers', labourers' and other unions. Conservative New Zealand trembled as wave after wave of 'foreign agitators' (mainly Australian), as the press called them, swept through the mining towns and the cities, preaching revolution and denouncing timid reformism of the type practised by the Lib-Labs. Their hopes that the absence of a strong Labour Party would help speed revolution were mistaken, though. Most unionists still clung to the system, even if the trades and labour councils had to move leftwards to pre-empt Red Fed challenges.

Faith in direct action and revolutionary contempt for tinkering political parties spread, especially around Auckland. It then grew rapidly as that city attracted the lion's share of the country's immigrants — in 1911, 39 per cent of inner-city Auckland residents were immigrants, 59 per cent of them men.[58] There the leaders of the wharfies, labourers, freezing workers and seamen, plus gold-miners at Waihi and coal-miners at Huntly, breathed revolutionary fire and talked openly of industrial warfare. In 1912

but like the one man killed by the police and scabs, Fred Evans, they achieved a glorious martyrdom in Harry Holland's best-selling polemic, *The Tragic Story of the Waihi Strike,* which aroused indignation throughout the country and helped reunite labour. Many unionists had sympathised more with the engine drivers than with the miners, but police brutality and the expulsion of miners from their homes reunified the labour movement. Waihi became a rallying cry.

By then working-class voters had deserted Ward's Liberals. Since 1906, Ward had wiggled uncomfortably, making noisy imperialist gestures that alienated the left. Dominion Day in 1907 put New Zealand on an equal footing with Australia and Canada,

Bush life was rougher than pastoralism. In these huts from the 1890s, canvas sheets covered the roof and rough slabs formed the walls. The fireplace and chimney, sheathed in corrugated iron, were stuck on the end to minimise the ever-present fire danger. Alexander Turnbull Library, G-17832-¹⁄₂

the strike at the Waihi gold-mine polarised the country. It started when the miners struck after the company, teetering on the verge of insolvency, recognised a separate union for engine drivers. The strike dragged on for six months, sustained by worker solidarity, money from Australia and the women pickets who fought 'The Battle of Rosettes' on the town's footpaths.[59] But it ended in violence when the police helped 'blacklegs' and 'scabs' to reopen the mine and drive the strikers out of town. They had lost,

and Premier Ward became Prime Minister Ward. In 1909 he brought in compulsory military training and gave the Royal Navy HMS *New Zealand.* But his 'very long, rambling and incoherent speech' at the 1911 imperial conference in favour of imperial federation stunned even federationists.[60] He created further troubles for himself in 1909 by accepting a baronetcy (Ballance and Seddon, far cannier, had rejected knighthoods), leading *The Maoriland Worker* to crack that:

Sirjo has got his title,
He scored it years ago,
When Seddon wouldn't take it
They passed it on to Joe.

Another self-inflicted wound was his Land Bill, which opened the door philosophically to Reform's symbolic rallying call for the freehold. The government that unleashed the police at Waihi had been a Reform one, not Liberal. The cowpats hurled from the right did Ward more damage than the revolutionary left's noisier thunderbolts. The Opposition had disbanded in 1899 and for some years the 'land without strikes' was also a land without a parliamentary Opposition, Seddon getting more gyp from his own backbiting backbenchers than from anyone else. But in 1909 bluff, gruff, bull-necked William Ferguson Massey, 'Farmer Bill', formed the Reform Party, the parliamentary focus for the earlier Reform Leagues. Massey was an unlikely successor to the throne of Seddon, and as 'foreign' (he was an Ulsterman) as the foreign-born radicals he denounced; but, as efficiently as a dairy farmer clearing bush, he whipped Reform into shape — a disciplined party with its roots strongest in cow-cocky country, in rich city seats and in the 'neglected North', as the *New Zealand Herald* carped.[61] This farmer from Mangere shared the *Herald's* resentment of 'our Southern Ministry' and articulated his fellow northerners' call for development, the old litany of roads, railways, bridges, ports and post offices.

Crucially, Massey now had numbers on his side. Between the 1891 and 1901 censuses the North Island overtook the South. With more ships now calling at Auckland and Wellington than Port Chalmers and Lyttelton, most immigrants landed there, supplementing the 100,000 southerners who had crossed Cook Strait to take up the new bush farms. By 1911 Reform spoke for the North Island and those southern urban enclaves where the new white-collar middle class and old money worried about strikes, Red Fed rhetoric and republican/unpatriotic gestures.

Prime Minister William Massey (1856–1925) liked to say that 'we've turned the corner'. For most of his long prime ministership (1912–25) he needed a sense of optimism. His Reform government seldom had a workable majority and had to weather industrial unrest, a world war, a difficult wartime coalition, a flu epidemic and post-war recession. Schmidt Collection, Alexander Turnbull Library, G-1539-½

Reform was not strong on articulating its philosophy, but its opposition to socialism and revolution, its promise to reform the Liberals' corrupt and costly bureaucracy, its call for freehold farm tenure rather than the Liberals' leasehold, and its encouragement of home-ownership appealed to many.

Massey lacked Joe Ward's panache and Seddon's boisterous bravura, but in 1911 his party took four more seats than the divided, befuddled Liberal Party. After stretching credibility with a Speech from the Throne that 'embraced every proposal that has ever been advocated, or even dreamt of, by the Labour Party and extreme Radical Wing', and that required Governor Lord Islington to 'summon to my aid all the training in Constitutional demeanour, which a Governor of New Zealand is so unstintingly furnished with, to make me deliver it with becoming gravity', Ward stepped down.[62] Now the Liberals, yesterday's men, huddled behind a ministry headed by Thomas Mackenzie. Propped up unsteadily by Labour and independent members of the House of Representatives, Mackenzie's ramshackle ministry lingered painfully until Massey proposed a second vote of no confidence in June 1912 and tetchy old John Andrew Millar, of Maritime Council fame, furious at being passed over for the leadership, dragged himself from his sickbed. Like an avenging Old Testament god, 'still clad in his pyjamas under his tweeds and overcoat', 'though stricken with illness and with one side of his features slightly twisted with paralysis', the old mariner whose dramatic interventions bookended the Liberal era, led his colleagues into the Noes lobby to bring down the Liberals by 41 votes to 33.[63]

It must have disconcerted young New Zealanders who had grown up knowing nothing but a Liberal government. And if, as Massey and other leading Reform politicians claimed, Reform was merely building on and legitimising the Liberals' legacy, the immediate, turbulent events of 1913 and '14 might have reinforced that sense of change. After Reform crushed the Waihi miners, the left began to change course. Two unity conferences produced general support for a

United Federation of Labour and a Social Democratic Party. In September and October 1913 major disputes broke out in the mines and on the wharves. With talk of 'class war' filling the air and large crowds demonstrating in the Wellington streets, Massey, Governor Liverpool and Commissioner of Police John Cullen (fresh from quashing Waihi), convinced themselves that even Parliament was threatened. Unsure of the loyalty of police rank and file (which he had just prevented from unionising), Massey called for volunteers to help keep order. Briefly (and to the embarrassment of the Admiralty and the Colonial Office) he and Liverpool convinced the commanders of the cruisers HMS *Psyche* (Wellington) and HMS *Pyramus* (Auckland) to put on displays of force.

By 30 October the first of 'Massey's Cossacks' (one paper dubbed them 'Cullen's Cossacks'), as the special constables were called, were riding into Wellington, blunt instruments swinging menacingly at their sides. This provocation brought more workers out on the streets, where several bloody battles were fought and shots discharged. The specials were a mixture of territorials (in Wellington especially), white-collar workers (the foot specials who made up a third of the volunteers) and farmers and farm workers. The cockies stuck together; one Tauranga contingent called themselves the 'Hayseed Hussars'. 'Cow spankers! Teet pullers!' angry citizens shouted as they rained rocks and insults down on the specials. The *Sydney Morning Herald* called it 'a sort of modified civil war between the town and the country'.[64]

Trouble spread whenever the specials rode into town. Westport, Greymouth, Lyttelton and Port Chalmers ground to a halt, perhaps not surprising for port town strongholds of militant miners, seamen and wharfies, but then Auckland staged a remarkable general strike. The coal workers and wharfies lit the fuse and the Farmers' Union added the gunpowder by sending hundreds of Waikato specials into the city, effectively shutting it down on 8 November. For almost a fortnight tram drivers, carpenters, bricklayers and others backed the miners, seamen, stokers and wharfies; even the paperboys refused to sell the *Herald*. But by mid November the farmers had the wharves working again. In December the seamen went back to work, followed by the wharfies. By January 1914 the last of the miners had also returned to work, defiant but defeated.

The 1913 strikes taught everyone important lessons. Workers learned the value of unity and of having friends in Parliament if they wanted to avoid another hammering from the coercive force of the state. That took the steam out of syndicalism and stilled criticism of 'Parliamentary Cretinism', as *The Maoriland Worker* had called parliamentary Labour. 'The Wobbly left and the Lib-Lab right had been discredited', although the middle had indeed moved leftwards by the standards of just a few years earlier.[65] Now, confronted by Reform's hard-faced men, Bob Semple, Peter Fraser, Harry Holland, Joe Savage and others headed down the path that led to forming the New Zealand Labour Party in 1916. Yet, if Reform had converted most Red Feds to politics, it, too, had changed its ideas about industrial relations, unions and arbitration. 'The very fact that the arbitration system had been so bitterly attacked by the Red Feds rendered it more appealing to those on the right.' In 1913, Massey, who had once called arbitration 'un-British', told Parliament that it 'has done a great deal of good and I am prepared to certify as to its usefulness'.[66] Although many Wobblies left the country and some union leaders suffered, the unions remained intact and the country was the third most unionised in the world after Britain and Australia. To a greater extent than once acknowledged, Seddon's 'God's own' lived on under 'Farmer Bill'.

Smith Collection, Alexander Turnbull Library, G-49061-½

Smith Collection, Alexander Turnbull Library, G-48932-½

The 1913 waterfront strike pitched town against country and labour against capital. In Wellington the two sides took to the streets. In the right-hand photo, trade unionists and supporters stretch along Riddiford Street, Newtown, behind the Federated Seamen's Union's banner. Guns rule Buckle Street in the left-hand picture.

Chapter 8

War clouds that had been gathering in Europe for years cast a shadow over New Zealanders. Their prosperity was bound up with Britain's, but few could have predicted the full price of Empire. WB Wollen's sombre depiction of *Fleurbaix, Christmas 1916*, captures the horrors that awaited so many of their young men.

WB Wollen, Archives New Zealand, NCWA 493

The Price of Empire
1897–1918

New Zealand had come into existence behind the shield of imperial naval power. The Pax Britannica, resting on the might of the Royal Navy, allowed small isolated communities far from the imperial centre to flourish with little concern for their security. But as the 19th century drew to a close, other powers challenged British naval supremacy. Maintaining the Empire's position now seemed to demand a united effort by all its constituent parts, and the lion's cubs must do their bit. New Zealanders, linked culturally, emotionally and economically to Britain, did not hesitate.

At first they barely noticed the price of Empire. New Zealand soldiers tested themselves on a foreign battlefield for the first time in South Africa, at little cost. But then the price grew steeper. When the hundred-year peace in Europe shattered in 1914, New Zealanders found themselves fighting in a war of unprecedented scale and violence. Standing shoulder to shoulder with imperial and dominion troops, they grew to appreciate their own distinctive national identity within the imperial fold. New Zealand's age of innocence ended on the stinking, blood-soaked battlefields of France and Flanders.

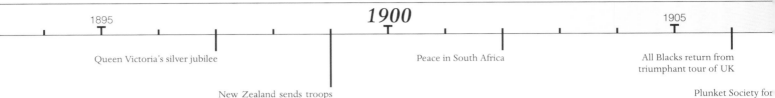

Willing imperialists and playing-field patriots

The 60th anniversary of Queen Victoria's accession to the throne in 1897 touched off an orgy of celebration throughout the Empire. In the imperial capital, colonial leaders met for the first time in solemn conclave with British ministers. In the streets, Londoners gazed in rapturous awe on the martial panoply of Empire. Among the many brilliantly bedecked contingents that paraded before them were 50 New Zealanders, 20 of them Maori, led by Colonel Albert Pitt. The first New Zealand troops sent overseas, they represented a colony that rejoiced in its ties to the greatest empire the world had ever seen.

Their Premier 'King Dick' Seddon had also made the six-week journey to London to take part in the celebrations. A true believer in the 'best of British' and a strident colonial-nationalist, he never forgot his British roots. 'God's own country' was but part of a mightier whole, he later reminded Parliament:

> We are a portion of the dominant family of the world — we are of the English-speaking race. Our kindred are scattered in different parts of the globe, and wherever they are, no matter how far distant apart, there is a feeling of affection — there is that crimson tie, that bond of unity, existing which time does not affect, and as years roll by it grows firmer, stronger and in the end will become indispensable.[1]

Few disagreed.

Conscious that families stick together in strife, Seddon did not hesitate to show his colours when Britain faced the possibility of war in southern Africa in September 1899. New Zealand would assist the mother country in the looming struggle with descendants of the original Dutch colonists, the Boers, in the South African Republic (Transvaal) and its ally, Orange Free State. Ever the populist, he had sensed the public mood perfectly. Parliament overwhelmingly endorsed his proposal to offer a contingent for service if war broke out.

On 21 October 1899, 40,000 people gathered at Wellington's Queen's Wharf to farewell the first troops sent by New Zealand to a foreign war. The 214-strong contingent was going, Seddon

proclaimed, to fight 'for one flag, one Queen, one tongue, and for one country — Britain'.[2] He had struck political pay dirt: within weeks his government's soaring popularity would be reflected in the ballot box. With war fever sweeping the country, men flocked to volunteer for the four further contingents that were rapidly dispatched. Two comprised 'rough riders' — men with no military experience but who were adept with horses and rifles.

Maori wanted to go, too, to 'Kiki te Poa' — 'Kick the Boer' — to use the words of a contemporary haka.[3] Seddon sympathised, but the British authorities did not — this, they insisted, would be a 'white man's war'. The only Maori men to go to South Africa did so as 'honorary whites', blending into contingents because of their European names and English language proficiency.

Expectations in 1899 of a quick victory soon proved misplaced. British forces overcame early setbacks to occupy the Boer capitals, but the outnumbered and outgunned Boers refused to submit. They turned to guerrilla tactics, which inevitably provoked ruthless countermeasures aimed at cutting the Boer commandos off from their support. As the war

Alexander Turnbull Library, F-29354-½

Richard Seddon and New Zealand soldiers bound for the South African War. The idea of assisting the Empire in war grew stronger in the late 19th century. Until then the nearest New Zealand came to making a contribution was in 1885. When war between Britain and Russia over Afghanistan seemed imminent, Premier Robert Stout moved to offer a 1000-man force. But the crisis subsided before any action could be taken.

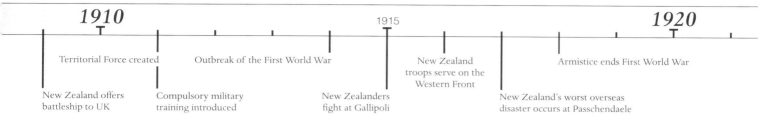

Territorial Force created

New Zealand offers
battleship to UK

Compulsory military
training introduced

Outbreak of the First World War

New Zealanders
fight at Gallipoli

New Zealand
troops serve on the
Western Front

New Zealand's worst overseas
disaster occurs at Passchendaele

Armistice ends First World War

dragged on, New Zealand soldiers took part in the despoliation of Boer farms and the herding of women and children into concentration camps.

The mobile, irregular fighting on the high veldt suited New Zealand's amateur soldiers. One of them was provincial rugby rep David Gallaher:

We have been all over S. Africa pretty well I believe, on the trek the whole time & it looks as if we will be trekking till the end . . . We have had a fair share of fighting all the time and I am still alive & kicking, although I have had a couple of pretty close calls.[4]

At home, a military ethos gripped the public. Praise of New Zealand troops' performance in South Africa by British generals boosted self-esteem. The dispatch of further contingents —

10 went in all — kept the jingoistic drums beating. Thousands flocked into the Volunteer Force, New Zealand's part-time military forces.

New Zealand played its part on the imperial stage with gusto — and without a high cost that might have awakened doubts about its role. Of the 6500 who served in South Africa, 230 died; most succumbed to disease and accidents, including a train crash.

The war not only strengthened imperialist sentiment but also heightened New Zealand's sense of identity. The idea of subsuming that identity within an Australasian state, never popular, lost further ground — as became apparent when New Zealand, in 1900, faced the choice of joining the six Australian colonies in a federation. In turning his back on the proposed

An artist's impression of the first New Zealand contingent's action at Slingersfontein on 15 January 1900. About 30 mounted riflemen under Captain Madocks saved the day when the Boers made a strong attack on a Yorkshire Regiment detachment on a hill. The New Zealanders drove the Boers back. The hill was thereafter known as New Zealand Hill. GD Giles, Auckland Museum

Lieutenant-Colonel Albert Robin, who commanded the first contingent sent to South Africa, enjoyed a high profile as his country's first prominent soldier on an overseas battlefield and was lauded as a hero on his return in 1901. The frontispiece of an illuminated address presented to him depicted Zealandia descending from her throne to welcome home the victorious soldier. Robin's subsequent career was equally distinguished, culminating with his command of the forces in New Zealand during the First World War.

The relaxed demeanour of some of the 35 nurses who served in military hospitals during the South African War belies the unpleasantness of the conditions many had to endure. 'The place was a hotbed of fever, and the dreaded enteric raged everywhere,' one complained in a letter home; 'and no wonder, with no sanitary arrangements whatever, animals lying dead everywhere, water bad, buildings covered black with flies, and patients covered with vermin.'

federation, Seddon had again correctly interpreted the country's preference. A royal commission set up to consider the pros and cons soon endorsed his approach. When the Commonwealth of Australia came into being on 1 January 1901, New Zealanders were present as spectators — another military contingent had been sent across the Tasman for the occasion — rather than as participants.

Far from looking westwards to Australia, Seddon had his sights set northwards on the wider Pacific. His efforts in the 1890s to interest London in annexing Hawai'i fell on deaf ears.[5] Anxious to keep foreign powers away from New Zealand's vicinity, he focused on Samoa. In 1899, as factional strife grew, he implored the British to let him send a force there, pointing to the availability of Maori and men 'accustomed to bush life and with experience in the backwoods' for the purpose. But British thumbs remained firmly down. With imperial diplomatic objectives outranking New Zealand wishes, Seddon could only gnash his teeth as Germany and the United States took over the group.[6]

A cult of manhood and a growing military ethos permeated society in the early 1900s. The former had been born in the struggle to tame the frontier, the masculine world of the bush. It had roots, too, in the public school virtues that underpinned education in the colony. Chasing Boers on the veldt had provided a new test of manliness. In peacetime the game of rugby football provided a less taxing substitute for war. Commonly believed to develop the spirit of manly courage and teamwork needed on the battlefield, rugby assumed new importance in the New Zealand psyche after New Zealanders had proved themselves on the playing fields of Britain.

Notions of racial superiority went hand in hand with an overwhelming sense of imperialist-nationalist pride. Viewing the world through imperial lenses, most New Zealanders looked down on Africans and Asians as inferior. Fear intensified such attitudes. For many the teeming millions of Asia constituted a 'Yellow Peril', threatening to submerge the small white colonies on the continent's periphery. Keeping out such people became a national imperative, one that seemed threatened by imperial actions when Britain entered an alliance with Japan in 1902. New Zealand remained determined that no diplomatic exigencies would be allowed to influence its discriminatory immigration policies.

Such attitudes made life uncomfortable for Chinese and Indians already in New Zealand. Seddon had no qualms about playing the race card. Populist racism underpinned measures that discriminated against these residents, including the £10 (later £100) poll tax imposed on all arriving Chinese — an imposition not formally removed until 1944. Sometimes the climate of hate took on a more menacing aspect, as, for example, when in 1905

RUGBY — A MAN'S GAME

Boer War veteran David Gallaher's 'All Blacks', as the New Zealand representative team was dubbed, made a triumphant progress through the British Isles, France and North America in 1905–06, winning all but one of their games (a century later rugby fans still argue about a disallowed try resulting in the only loss). They returned home to acclaim; New Zealanders took pride in colonial tweaking of British noses. More than 20,000 Aucklanders crowded the wharf as Seddon welcomed the team home. 'Like lambs they entered, but like lions they departed, from the Motherland,' the *New Zealand Herald* exulted.[7]

THE MOA AND THE LION.

Trevor Lloyd's cartoon glories in New Zealand's trouncing of the British teams.
T Lloyd, Alexander Turnbull Library, F-21875-½

David Gallaher, the successful captain of the 1905 All Black team, in his South African War uniform. Alexander Turnbull Library, F-25342-½

FIGHTING FIT

Beneath all the hype about New Zealand's victories on the veldt and the football fields in grey old Blighty lay a deep uncertainty over the nation's security, and not just from the covetous eyes believed to be trained on New Zealand from afar. The rapid social change of the period, seen in the growth of towns, fed the belief that New Zealand had not escaped the problems of the Old World. The place seemed to be crawling with social, moral and physical degenerates: unemployed, paupers, prostitutes, criminals, drunkards, and the mentally unsound — a 'swarm of parasitical organisms', in the words of Dr Duncan MacGregor, the Inspector-General of Hospitals and Asylums.[8] The 'better classes' did a woefully inadequate job of reproducing themselves, while the 'unfit' had, allegedly, an unbounded capacity to breed. Popular publications such as WA Chapple's *The Fertility of the Unfit* prophesied doom if things continued; never should the unfit mingle with the fit, for whom it was a civic duty to reproduce. It was enough to make the country's movers and shakers ponder the very future of the race; and it fuelled a cult of motherhood that extolled women's role as mothers of the race. Even that arch-imperialist Seddon argued that 'it is clearly undesirable that the colonies should be populated by the inferior surplus people of older and alien countries'.[9]

There certainly was a spectacular decline in Pakeha fertility, only a third of enlistees and conscripts to the armed forces between 1914 and 1918 were deemed completely fit, and there were social problems enough in towns and rural areas, but there was a lot of alarmist nonsense behind the claims of a population in peril. Belief won out, and New Zealand, along with the rest of the Western world from the later 19th century, proved a receptive climate to eugenics — the science of racial fitness through correct breeding and a proper environment. There were those who espoused the grim end of the eugenic agenda in compulsory sterilisation or lethal chambers for the unfit, and there were some harsh penal

a mentally disturbed Englishman murdered an elderly Chinese man in Wellington's Haining Street.

Asians were not the only ethnic minorities to bear the brunt of public hostility early last century. Caucasians of obviously non-British origin also suffered discrimination, Dalmatians who came to dig kauri gum in northern parts being a notable example.

Towards war

After the South African War, New Zealanders' concerns about security grew. The expansion of other navies, especially Germany's, had set alarm bells ringing in London and elsewhere in the Empire. The response to this challenge included Britain's alliance with Japan, increased warship building, and the concentration of the Royal Navy in the North Sea as the naval arms race between Britain and Germany intensified.

New Zealanders knew the economic health of their country was at stake. Superior naval power could ensure their access to the

People, money and ideas had crossed the Tasman freely, but in 1901 New Zealand politicians declined to board the new Commonwealth of Australia and paddled their waka off on a separate course. That ended a long but seldom impassioned debate; the heat had long gone out of the issue because intercolonial trade had been weakening as the British market increased in importance for every colony.

and 'corrective' policies enacted in the name of a better race; but for the most part, eugenics led to an increased emphasis on public, and particularly children's, health.

Most famously, the Plunket Society, founded by self-trained paediatrician Frederic Truby King in 1907, emerged from this. Believing that 'the destiny of the race is in the hands of its mothers', King, with his band of nurses and volunteers, set out to improve maternal and infant health in the national interest.[10] Infant mortality was already in decline, and dropped further with the Plunket system of hygiene, 'humanised milk', and regular, orderly child-rearing practices. Inevitably perhaps, in this time of rising militarism, the latter had a distinct disciplinary air. Babies needed to be in top physical condition: boys to grow up to defend the Empire, and girls to breed for it. *Bronwyn Dalley*

LEFT: Body culture was a more benign expression of interest in health and efficiency. Strongman Eugen Sandow toured New Zealand and Australia in 1902–03 extolling exercise as a way to heal the nation. David Chapman Collection

RIGHT: Founder of the Plunket Society Frederic Truby King (1858–1938) was, ironically, a sickly child, and he and his wife Isabella had no children of their own. SP Andrew Collection, Alexander Turnbull Library, F-018662-¹⁄₁

McNeur Collection, Alexander Turnbull Library, F-19148-¹⁄₂

Chinese gold miners with the Reverend Alexander Don outside a cob dwelling in Tuapeka, Otago about 1900. One pillar of New Zealand society early last century was a racial exclusivism that often descended to outright racism.

only market that mattered — Britain. Since 1887 New Zealand had paid a subsidy towards the Royal Navy. This helped keep up regional naval strength in the South Pacific while ensuring the stationing of two cruisers in New Zealand waters. But the arrangement fell victim to Australia's desire to create its own navy. New Zealand's Prime Minister, Sir Joseph Ward, firmly opposed any attempt to follow suit. A professional force would, he feared, drain government funds desperately needed to develop the country. Nor did he like the prospect of being a junior partner in a joint Australia–New Zealand navy. Not till the Reform Party took over the Treasury benches in 1912 did New Zealand shift tack. New Minister of Defence James Allen persuaded a reluctant Admiralty to provide the ageing cruiser HMS *Philomel* as a training ship.

Changes in naval defence were matched by a far-reaching reorganisation of New Zealand's citizen-soldier-based military forces. New Zealand's amateur soldiers had performed well in South Africa, but could they foot it with the troops of a major enemy? The government's military advisors thought not; the ramshackle Volunteer Force could never provide the necessary

HMS *NEW ZEALAND*

The importance of the Royal Navy maintaining its superiority over the growing German fleet impressed itself upon New Zealand leaders. In 1909 fears that the Germans were winning the naval arms race produced a public outcry in Britain. Prime Minister Sir Joseph Ward responded by dramatically offering to pay for a battleship (or two) to augment the Empire's main fleet. In the event a battle cruiser, HMS *New Zealand*, was built at Glasgow and launched in July 1911. An *Indefatigable*-class ship, she displaced 18,750 tons, mounted eight 12-inch guns as her main armament, and carried a crew of 800. When she visited New Zealand in 1913, tens of thousands went on board at the various ports.[11]

HMS *New Zealand's* commander, Captain Lionel Halsey, received numerous gifts, including a piupiu from a Maori

chief who urged him to wear it in action. Halsey did that at Heligoland Bight in 1914, also donning a tiki he had received in New Zealand. When *New Zealand* came through unscathed, her crew were convinced that the tiki and piupiu had had a talismanic effect. They insisted on him wearing them again in the next action, at Dogger Bank in 1915. At the Battle of Jutland Halsey's successor wore the tiki, but, being somewhat portly, merely hung the piupiu in the conning tower. Although hit, the ship suffered no casualties. *New Zealand* remained with the Grand Fleet until the end of the war, carried Lord Jellicoe on a naval mission that took it to New Zealand in 1919, and was broken up as a result of a naval disarmament agreement in the 1920s. The tiki is in Canterbury Museum; the piupiu is still in the hands of the Halsey family.

BELOW: A 1911 painting of HMS *New Zealand* in Portsmouth Harbour. WL Wylie, Archives New Zealand

ABOVE: HMS *New Zealand's* visit to the dominion in 1913 provided many festive occasions, as thousands flocked to visit the ship. The Press Collection, Alexander Turnbull Library, G-2284-¹/₁

training, they warned. In 1909 the government finally agreed. A new 30,000-strong Territorial Force would replace the Volunteer system. Not only would it provide a more effective home defence force but also, more importantly, it would make raising an expeditionary force for imperial service in emergency much easier. Standardisation with British and other imperial forces became the order of the day. To ensure units were fully manned, all men between 18 and 25 became subject to compulsory military training. Cadet training from the age of 12 would prepare them for this military duty.

Imperial military luminary Lord Kitchener endorsed these plans when he visited in February 1910. New Zealand, he suggested, should send cadets to the new Australian military college at Duntroon — an idea that the government quickly took up, beginning a long association. A group of imperial officers brought out for the purpose implemented the new Territorial Force scheme. Major-General Alexander Godley oversaw the process as General Officer Commanding.

Not everyone approved. Anti-war organisations encouraged men to default on their training obligations. Some went to prison. Such opposition irritated the authorities. But it did not hinder the introduction of the new scheme.

Few New Zealanders gave more than passing thought to news of the assassination, on 28 June 1914, of the Austro-Hungarian Archduke Ferdinand and his wife Sophie by a Serbian nationalist. This seemingly unimportant Balkan event touched off a cataclysm in Europe unmatched since Napoleonic times. The division of Europe into confronting alliances — the Central Powers (the German and Austro-Hungarian Empires) and the Triple Entente (the British, Russian and French Empires) — provided the powder. When Germany, seeking to defeat France before facing the Russians, invaded neutral Belgium, it triggered British intervention on 4 August. Britain went to war for more fundamental reasons — its own security, it feared, would be threatened by a tilting of the European balance of power Germany's way.

King George V's declaration of war (on the advice of his British ministers) encompassed all his territories and dependencies, including the self-governing parts of the British Empire. New Zealanders had no qualms about their automatic involvement. Indeed, many shared

'K of K looks in.' British war hero 'Kitchener of Khartoum' visited New Zealand in 1910.
JC Blomfield, Alexander Turnbull Library, MNZ-916-¼

HMS *Philomel* arriving at Wellington in 1917. New Zealand's contribution to the naval war, *Philomel* offered no great accretion to British naval strength because of her decrepit state. After initial escort duties in the South Pacific, she operated in the Red Sea area until 1917. She showed the flag and made occasional landings. About a quarter of her crew were New Zealanders. Following her return to New Zealand, she was decommissioned and became a depot ship.

BELOW: The New Zealand (Rifle) Brigade marching through Wellington streets on the way to their transports for embarkation overseas. New Zealand rapidly raised two expeditionary forces in 1914, thanks to the preparatory work of the preceding four years. Between 1914 and 1918, 42 per cent of men of military age (20–34 years of age) would go overseas for war service.
Kippenberger Military Archive, Army Museum

the enthusiasm that swept through Britain and the European empires at the onset of the war. Almost 15,000 were present at 1 p.m. on 5 August 1914 to hear Governor Lord Liverpool read on the steps of Parliament a terse telegram received from London: 'War has broken out with Germany.' That evening an even larger crowd marched through the streets of the capital 'in rows four, five and six deep, upon military lines' in a 'remarkable display of enthusiasm'.[12] The response elsewhere was no less excited.

Although at war, the dominion was under no formal obligation to assist Britain. But New Zealanders did not hesitate. Their own wellbeing, they believed, was bound up with the fate of the Empire. They feared the likely traumatic consequences of defeat, with annexation by the victor a real possibility. They also recognised the equally traumatic impact of their country being cut off from its market, the source of its prosperity. In Parliament six days before the outbreak, Prime Minister William Massey had reflected public sentiment in pledging to dispatch an expeditionary force if needed; now he quickly asserted New Zealand's willingness to do all in its power to support the imperial cause. Steps began immediately to raise two expeditionary forces. One would seize the wireless station in German Samoa — following a request from

London that reawakened long-held aspirations in Wellington. The other, much larger, would go to the European theatre to join the British Expeditionary Force in France.

Men flocked to the colours — 14,000 by the end of the first week of the war.[13] With an average age of 23, they were the vanguard of the 70,000 who would enlist in the next four years. Many families had more than one member at risk. Dannevirke farmers Herbert and Ellen Knight, for example, soon had three sons, Douglas, George and Herbert, serving. So too did lighthouse keepers Samuel and Caroline Hart — railways clerk Leonard, blacksmith Adrian and engineer Harry. Parents were torn between pride and foreboding as they watched their young respond to the call. 'Well Len,' Samuel Hart wrote to his son, 'I feel proud of being your Father. Good men like you are going to save the Empire.'[14] George Knight's mother wrote in similar vein:

My dear Georgie I tried to write last night to tell Dad, I could not face it alone. I had a good blub & feel better, of course I knew we could not hope to keep out of it, nor did I want to as I told the others if you were needed & you felt you ought to go; it will be very hard to part with any of you I dare say it will mean the three, but I am ready to do my duty always as you are to do yours.[15]

Readily identifying with the British Empire, recruits accepted the need to stand with their kith and kin against the common enemy. Reports of German atrocities in Belgium inflamed feeling against German militarism. For some the opportunity to escape from difficult or disliked conditions at home provided further incentive. Social pressure also played a part: 'When I was home and saw the soldiers going off,' George Knight wrote to his mother, 'I felt I was sort of mean and wanted to hide because I was not there and have dreaded anyone asking me if I am going or want to go.'[16] But for most, including the Knights and the Harts, the main incentive to enlist was adventure, an escape from the tedium of everyday life. Overseas travel was slow and expensive; so for working men wanting to see the world, this was an opportunity not to be missed.

Few opposed the war. Although churches had sponsored anti-militarist activities before the war, such sentiment was muted after its outbreak. Only Quakers stood firmly opposed as the main churches rapidly came in behind the war effort. Prominent Wellington Presbyterian minister James Gibb actively encouraged recruitment for the expeditionary forces.[17] A few non-church anti-war groups — the National Peace Council, the Canterbury Women's Institute and the New Zealand Freedom League — opposed the war. Yet the strength of 'war fever'

Archives New Zealand, C1370

Men of the light railway unit that formed part of the Samoa Expeditionary Force. They repaired the line between Apia and the wireless station.

induced even the Peace Council to suspend its public campaign.

War fever engendered extreme chauvinism. Enemy aliens — the 4000 Germans and 2000 Austro-Hungarians in the country in August 1914 — bore the brunt of public hostility as antagonism gave way to hysteria. Rumours abounded of German spies or plots to subvert the war effort, perhaps by poisoning water supplies. A female-dominated Anti-German League appeared, determined to root out this threat. Even naturalised Germans or Austro-Hungarians were not immune to abuse and hostility.

Sometimes the mob ran loose. Buildings were burned down, including a Lutheran church. In Wanganui in 1915 a 3000-strong crowd rampaged in response to rumours of disloyalty among the town's 'alien' population. They smashed the windows of Heinhold's butcher's shop, then did the same to the Hallenstein Brothers store and a German piano shop. As a soldier raised the Union Jack over the butcher's shop, the mob sang the National Anthem.

Official action against enemy aliens intensified. More than 400 were interned on Motuihe or Somes Island. Others found themselves on the wrong end of government efforts to combat the more insidious perceived threat they posed to young minds. The Alien Enemy Teachers Act 1915 gave powers that were used, most notably, to oust Professor GW von Zedlitz from his position at Victoria University College. Even men of German extraction who served in the New Zealand Expeditionary Force (NZEF) against Germany were not immune to discrimination and public hostility.

Maori response to the outbreak of war depended largely on tribal allegiances. Tribes that had suffered defeat and despoliation in the 19th century wars remained unenthusiastic about the conflict. But kupapa (tribes that had fought alongside imperial or colonial troops) took a very different stance; the war was an opportunity to bolster their mana by once again taking up arms. Some volunteered for the NZEF, and entered the ranks of its battalions to serve on the same basis as their Pakeha comrades.

But there was a desire also to form a specifically Maori unit. At first it seemed the South African War experience would be repeated, as the British once again indicated that the conflict in Europe would be a 'white man's war'. Such pretensions soon evaporated, however, as the British and French looked to use their huge reservoirs of colonial manpower. Objections to a Maori unit vanished with news that Indian troops would be deployed. The four Maori MPs and Sir James Carroll oversaw the recruitment of a 500-strong 'Native Contingent'. Fears about the future of the Maori race ensured a protective (some would say racist) attitude; it was understood that Maori troops would be used as non-combatant garrison troops. After training, the contingent left New Zealand for the Middle East in early 1915 and eventually took up station in Malta. They were the first of 2227 Maori to serve in the NZEF.[18]

228

The landing at Anzac Cove on the Gallipoli Peninsula, now in modern Turkey. From here the Allies hoped to go on to threaten the heart of the Ottoman Empire.

For a time it seemed the Maori soldiers might be sent to help garrison Samoa, where New Zealand, in the first month of the war, had had a signal success. On 15 August 1914, 1400 men had set out from Wellington in two hastily fitted out troopships. When the Union Jack was run up in Apia two weeks later, Samoa became the second German territory, after Togoland, to fall to the Allies. Although the Germans offered no opposition, the occupation set the stage for the first New Zealand–German armed confrontation of the war. On 16 September New Zealand field gunners deployed on the beach at Apia stared down the gun barrels of the German Asiatic Squadron's armoured cruisers *Scharnhorst* and *Gneisenau*. But the cruisers withdrew without firing any shots, leaving a New Zealand military administration to control the islands for the rest of the war.

Worries about the escort available for the NZEF's Main Body delayed its departure. When the 10 troop transports finally left Wellington on 16 October 1914, British and Japanese warships guarded them. The 8400 men and 3800 horses remain the largest bodies of men and horses to leave the country at one time. As they steamed towards the Suez Canal, the soldiers expected that within weeks they would be confronting the Hun on the Western Front. Developments soon ensured that their first encounter with the enemy would take place in a very different location.

Baptism of fire

While the Australasian convoy was crossing the Indian Ocean, the Ottoman Empire entered the war on the enemy side. With the Suez Canal, the vital imperial link, in jeopardy, the Australians and New Zealanders were landed in Egypt as a precautionary measure. Camped at Zeitoun, the men trained hard in the desert heat. Off duty, they toured the pyramids and other ancient monuments. For many, visiting the bars and brothels of Cairo provided another form of adventure — or misadventure, for the venereal disease rate climbed. Accepting that soldiers would always be soldiers, NZEF commander Sir Alexander Godley quietly ensured that they had access to treatment kits and advice.

For some of the troops the serious business began in early 1915. Deployed along the Suez Canal, they helped repel an Ottoman force that had crossed the barren Sinai. During the fighting, Private William Arthur Ham became the first NZEF soldier to fall in battle. Back in Cairo, some troops soon afterwards engaged in less glorious action. On 2 April 1915 they and Australian troops ran amok during a drunken riot in Cairo's brothel district of Wazza.

But the prospect of action overshadowed such indiscretions. Linked together as the Australian and New Zealand Army Corps — ANZAC — the New Zealanders and Australians took

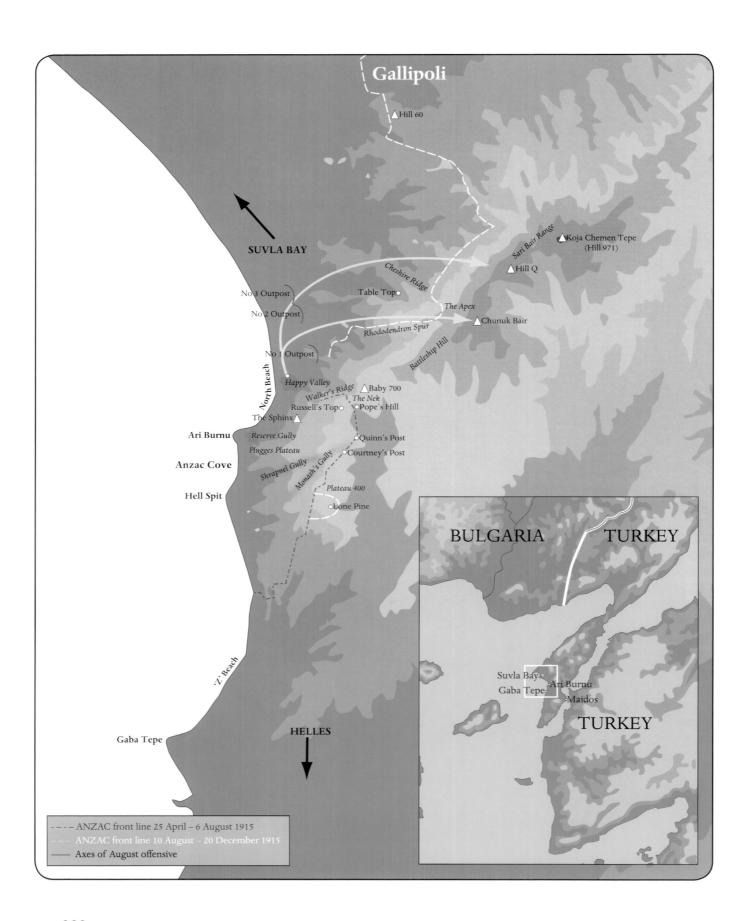

Gallipoli

△ Hill 60

SUVLA BAY

Sari Bair Range

△ Koja Chemen Tepe
(Hill 971)

Cheshire Ridge

△ Hill Q

No 3 Outpost

No 2 Outpost

Table Top ○

The Apex

△ Chunuk Bair

Rhododendron Spur

No 1 Outpost

Battleship Hill

North Beach

Happy Valley

Walker's Ridge

△ Baby 700

The Nek

Russell's Top ○ ○ Pope's Hill

The Sphinx △

Ari Burnu

Reserve Gully

Plugges Plateau

○ Quinn's Post

Anzac Cove

Shrapnel Gully

Monash's Gully

○ Courtney's Post

Hell Spit

Plateau 400

○ Lone Pine

BULGARIA   TURKEY

'Z' Beach

Suvla Bay
Gaba Tepe ·Ari Burnu
·Maidos

Gaba Tepe

HELLES

TURKEY

– · – · – ANZAC front line 25 April – 6 August 1915
– – – ANZAC front line 10 August – 20 December 1915
——— Axes of August offensive

part in the Allies' effort to knock the Ottoman Empire out of the war by seizing the Dardanelles, the gateway to Constantinople (now Istanbul). The plan called for them to make a flanking diversionary attack while British forces landed at the tip of the Gallipoli peninsula on 25 April. But because of a navigational error the ANZACs went ashore in rugged terrain north of their objective. The Turks soon threatened to drive them back into the sea. Only by frantically digging were the ANZACs able to cling to their tiny enclave. By the end of the first day, hundreds had been killed or wounded.

George and Herbert Knight were among those struggling to beat off the Turks, who overlooked the ANZAC positions. But on 13 May, a sorrowful George advised his mother of the 'greatest sorrow that has ever happened in our family'. Herbert had fallen victim to a sniper on the previous Sunday evening. 'He was shot thro the heart & so suffered no pain; death being instantaneous,' he assured his mother. 'It was as great a shock to me as it would be to you.'[19]

In August the New Zealanders, now including the Maori contingent, played a key part in an attempt to break the shackles by seizing the dominating Sari Bair range. The men of Lieutenant-Colonel William Malone's Wellington Battalion took the summit of Chunuk Bair and held off ferocious Turkish counter-attacks for a day. Their many casualties included Malone, killed by a shell burst. When the Turks soon afterwards forced relieving British troops off the summit, the slender chance of the Allies grabbing victory had gone. In the end the Allies acknowledged defeat. By the end of January 1916 all their forces had been evacuated from the peninsula.

The campaign cast a long shadow. Many New Zealanders believed that their country had come of age in the struggle, the first time it had fought in the big league. They took pride in the fortitude shown by the men in terrible circumstances. Commemorating the day of the landing in 1916, Anzac Day, they began a lasting tradition in New Zealand. Although bolstering New Zealanders' sense of national identity, the fighting at Gallipoli had shattered their illusions. The nature of modern warfare had been brutally revealed; of the 8500 New Zealanders who landed on the peninsula, 2721 were dead and many were maimed. But Gallipoli proved to be merely the prelude to an even greater trial.

For New Zealanders, the war at sea was just as important as the battle on land. British sea-power was the key. Grand Fleet commander (and future governor-general of New Zealand) Sir John Jellicoe would later be described as 'the only man on either side who could lose the war in an afternoon'.[20] When the rival fleets clashed at Jutland in 1916, his caution ensured that there would be no Trafalgar-like triumph. Even so, as the enemy fleet scurried back into its ports, the Allied naval clamp on Germany

Soldiers of the Wellington Regiment man a trench at The Apex on Gallipoli. In the foreground is Robert William Dyer.

remained unimpaired. HMS *New Zealand* had been in the thick of things; although struck by a shell, she suffered no serious damage or casualties.

Behind the shield provided by the Grand Fleet, other forces protected vital sea lanes against commerce-raiding cruisers and armed merchant vessels. But submarines soon emerged as the most potent threat to Allied sea movements. U-boats hit New Zealand hard, sinking numerous cargo ships off Britain.

They also greatly increased the danger of transporting troops over the sea. Nonetheless, none of the 90,000 men and women who followed the Main Body out of New Zealand in 42 reinforcement drafts between 1914 and 1918 fell victim to them.

The brunt of trade protection fell on the Royal Navy. Some 500 New Zealanders played a part in this effort. Aside from those serving on *Philomel*, the cruiser *Pyramus* had about 90 among her crew. Others were called up as naval reservists or joined the Royal Navy voluntarily. In 1916 the Royal Navy was also permitted to recruit several hundred men for service in motor-boats. New Zealand seamen fought in all phases of the naval war, including the vital struggle against the U-boat. Auckland-born William Edward Sanders won a VC for successful attacks on U-boats while commanding a disguised warship (Q-ship).

Not all New Zealanders in the navy served at sea. Those who fought on land included former New Zealand swimming champion and future 2NZEF commander Bernard Freyberg. He distinguished himself serving with the Royal Naval Division at Gallipoli. Later, on the Western Front, his bravery in an attack in which he was severely wounded earned him a VC. Wimbledon tennis champion Anthony Wilding died while serving with a Royal Naval Air Service armoured car squadron in France. A handful of New Zealand naval officers served in armoured cars in Russia.

New Zealand merchant seamen also contributed to the imperial war effort. Many lost their lives as U-boats took their toll. Only occasionally did opportunities arise to hit back. In March 1917 the New Zealand Shipping Company steamer *Otaki* fought an epic duel with the German armed merchant raider *Moewe*, inflicting severe damage on it before being sunk.

New Zealanders also fought in the air. About 700 served in British or Australian air units. Although most fought on the Western Front, New Zealand's only military aviator at the outset of the war, Lieutenant William Burn, was killed in action in Mesopotamia (today's Iraq) in 1915. Some men proceeded to the United Kingdom on their own initiative to join up; some transferred from the NZEF or British regiments; and others underwent initial training at flying schools in New Zealand before proceeding overseas. Some men rose to command British squadrons.

When most of the NZEF left for France in early 1916, its Mounted Rifles Brigade stayed on in Egypt. With Australian mounted horsemen, they formed a mounted division, the renowned ANZAC Mounted, commanded first by an Australian officer and later by New Zealand's 'Terrible Ted' Chaytor. During the next two and a half years the New Zealand mounted troopers campaigned against the Turks in the biblical lands of Sinai and Palestine. They did so with élan, not least at the Battle

The sinking of the Otaki *by the German raider* Moewe *1917. Otaki's* master, Captain Archibald Bisset Smith, who went down with his ship, was awarded a posthumous Victoria Cross for this action. His heroism is still commemorated by a shield donated by his family to his old school, Robert Gordon's College, awarded annually to the 'Otaki Scholar' for pre-eminence in 'character, athletics and leadership'.

of Rafa in January 1917. Two companies of New Zealanders also served in the Imperial Camel Corps. Water problems hampered operations, but by the end of 1917 the Allies were in Jerusalem. By the time the Turks submitted on 31 October 1918, nearly 1500 New Zealanders serving in the Middle East had become casualties, more than a third of them killed.

A handful of New Zealanders also served in Mesopotamia, some in British regiments or as pilots. A New Zealand unit was also present, a specially raised 63-strong wireless troop sent in 1916. Operating as part of an ANZAC Wireless Squadron, it suffered five fatalities before being transferred to France in 1918.

The Western Front

Meanwhile, in April 1916, the remainder of the NZEF had at last reached its original destination, the Western Front. A doubtful New Zealand government reluctantly agreed to British proposals for the establishment of a full New Zealand Division. Reinforcements already in Egypt and the New Zealand (Rifle) Brigade, which had been dispatched in 1915, made up the numbers. The New Zealanders arrived in France to find a New Zealand presence already established. A tunnelling company, specially recruited at British request, had reached the front in early 1916; it operated mainly in the Arras area.

The battlefield was very different from, and more dangerous than, that endured at Gallipoli. Forced below ground level by the power of defensive weaponry, the two sides faced each other in an elaborate trench system stretching 700 km from Switzerland to the English Channel. The big gun ruled over this battlefield, and men in the trenches faced the constant threat of a direct hit.

Although shelling caused steady attrition, the real slaughter occurred when the men went 'over the top' in major offensives. Exposed to the enemy's machine guns and artillery, they suffered horrendous casualties without ever breaking through the opposing line. An Anglo-French offensive launched on the Somme on 1 July 1916 left 20,000 British dead on the first day alone, with little ground gained.

A new phase in this offensive provided the setting for the New Zealanders' first major operation in France. On 15 September 1916 they took part, near the village of Longueval, in an attack that was notable for the debut of a new weapon, the tank. The New Zealanders took their objective, and later made a series of subsidiary pushes, all at fearful cost. In 23 days, more than 1500 men were killed and 6500 wounded. No breakthrough ensued.

The New Zealanders endured the misery of their first winter in the trenches. 'Mud, and slush are the most prominent things about our trenches at present,' Len Hart wrote home in November 1916, 'and the weather is steadily getting colder and wetter.'[21] Trench raids and shelling took a steady toll of lives.

When the summer returned, the New Zealanders prepared to help seize the Messines ridge in Belgium. On 7 June 1917, after huge mines had been exploded under the defenders, they crossed no-man's-land to capture the village of Messines. All objectives were quickly occupied and counter-attacks repulsed. But German shelling of the newly gained territory soon took a fearful toll among its captors. By the time the New Zealanders were pulled out, 700 had been killed. Four months later, on 4 October, the New Zealanders went over the top again, at Ypres. They seized their objective, the Graventafel Spur, without difficulty. But like all First World War attacks the cost was high. Among the many victims was Boer War veteran David Gallaher, who succumbed to his wounds — the 43-year-old former All Black captain was one of 13 All Blacks killed on the Western Front. Two of his brothers would also fall during the war, while serving with Australian forces.

Eight days later the New Zealanders returned to the fray. Their objective this time was the Bellevue Spur immediately before the battered remains of Passchendaele village. For the troops moving up to the start line, conditions were atrocious. Junior officer George Knight, the Dannevirke farmer's son, was among those waiting to advance during the early hours of 12 October. His company included the lighthouse keeper's son, Len Hart. 'We struggled on through this sea of mud for some hours, and everyone was feeling pretty well done,' Len later recounted. 'It was quite common for a man to get stuck in the mud and have to get three or four to drag him out.'[22]

Meanwhile the gunners had been engaged in a desperate struggle to drag their pieces into position in time. Not all had succeeded when the barrage opened. The mud also hindered operation of the available guns. Accuracy suffered, as Len Hart and other soldiers waiting on the start line found to their cost. Part of the initial bombardment fell in their lines. 'It was a truly awful time — our own men getting cut to pieces in dozens by our own guns.'[23] Worse was to follow.

The 'friendly fire' setback did not prevent the men from stoically setting off towards the dark ridge at 5.30 a.m. Only a ragged and inadequate barrage preceded them. When they reached the enemy wire they were horrified to find it remained uncut. Previous bombardment, designed to open the way, had failed to do the job. Only a few gaps existed, death traps covered by enemy machine guns.

Courage alone — and there was plenty on display — could not overcome this fatal deficiency. Enemy machine guns cut a swathe through the New Zealanders. George Knight was among their victims, shot in the chest. Len Hart described his death: 'He fell immediately without a word or sound and did not speak again. Two of us were endeavouring to bind up his wound when another bullet pierced his throat and he immediately breathed his last.'[24]

THE AGONY OF PASSCHENDAELE

The Battle of Passchendaele in October and November 1917 was the final phase of an offensive launched by the British Expeditionary Force on 31 July 1917. Its aim was to push the Germans off the high ground surrounding the vital Belgian town of Ypres (now called Ieper) and to open the way for a substantial advance that would have a significant strategic impact on the Western Front. After some early gains, the attack quickly faltered in August as bad weather left the troops bogged down.

A new phase of the battle opened in September. A way forward seemed to have been found in a 'bite and hold' approach — with effective artillery support the infantry could seize a portion of the enemy territory and hold it against the inevitable counter-attacks. Two attacks in September demonstrated the effectiveness of such tactics. The third, on 4 October, involving the New Zealanders and Australians of II ANZAC, was also successful. But even as the enemy appeared to the British commander to be tottering, heavy rain turned the battlefield into a morass. Two further hastily prepared attacks, on 9 and 12 October, failed disastrously, mainly because proper artillery preparation proved impossible. Hundreds of New Zealanders died in the second of these failed attacks.

By this time the capture of the ruined village of Passchendaele had lost all strategic significance. When Canadian troops pressed forward in a series of well-supported attacks to take it in early November, the cost in lives had been in no way commensurate with the advantages gained. Five months later the ruins were back in German hands.

Kippenberger Military Archive, Army Museum

ABOVE: Watercourses destroyed by shelling and constant rain rendered the Passchendaele battlefield a hideous bog, in which the troops struggled to carry out their duties. 'The mud is a worse enemy than the German,' divisional commander Sir Andrew Russell lamented on 4 October 1917. Its effect on the artillery support that could be provided when his division attacked eight days later would be fatal for many New Zealanders. Here gunners jack up a field gun as they attempt to move it forward in the morass.

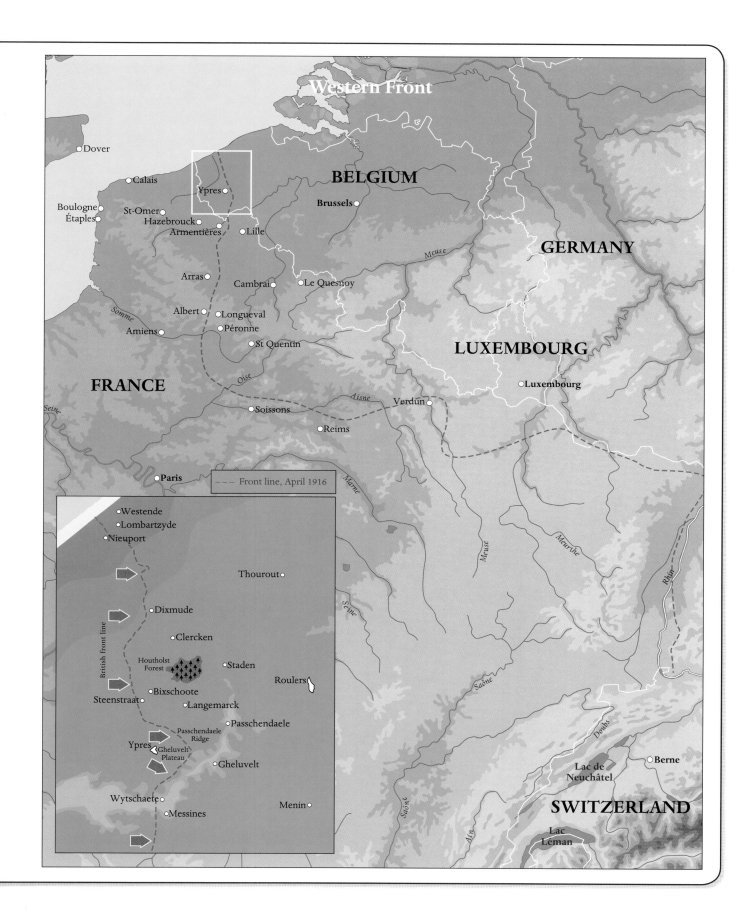

Western Front

Dover

Calais

Boulogne
Étaples

St-Omer
Hazebrouck
Armentières
Lille

BELGIUM

Brussels

GERMANY

Ypres

Arras

Cambrai
Le Quesnoy

LUXEMBOURG

Albert
Longueval
Péronne
St Quentin

Luxembourg

FRANCE

Amiens

Soissons

Verdun

Reims

Paris

--- Front line, April 1916

Westende
Lombartzyde
Nieuport

Thourout

Dixmude

British front line

Clercken

Houtholst
Forest
Staden

Bixschoote
Roulers

Steenstraat
Langemarck

Passchendaele

Passchendaele
Ridge

Ypres
Gheluvelt
Plateau
Gheluvelt

Berne

Lac de
Neuchâtel

Wytschaete
Menin

SWITZERLAND

Messines

Lac
Léman

Only by going to ground in the innumerable shell holes could men survive this maelstrom of fire. Plans for a renewal of the attack were mercifully cancelled. By nightfall the survivors had pulled back to near their start line. Scores of badly wounded men lay in the mud of no-man's-land. For these men the aftermath of the attack became a private hell as the numbing shock of being hit gave way to agonising pain; many died before they could be rescued.[25] The attack took the lives of 840 New Zealanders, the country's worst catastrophe in an overseas battle.[26] The grisly toll included at least six sets of brothers.

Those who survived the inferno included Bright Williams who recovered from his wounds and died in 2003, New Zealand's last First World War veteran. Len Hart came through unscathed. A week later he conveyed his bitterness in a letter home:

Some terrible blunder has been made. Someone is responsible for that barbed wire not having been broken up by our artillery. Someone is responsible for the opening of our barrage in the midst of us instead of 150 yards ahead of us. Someone else is responsible for those machine gun emplacements being left practically intact, but the papers will all report another glorious success, and no one except those who actually took part in it will know any different.[27]

Battle scene with soldiers crossing a road, painted by Arthur Lloyd.
Auckland Museum

But New Zealanders at home had no illusions about the scale of the disaster. The long casualty lists cast a pall over the community, the grief unleavened by any sense that the lives had not been sacrificed in vain. Countless families received the dreaded telegrams reporting the death, disappearance or wounding of a husband, son or brother.

For Mary Ann Newlove of Takaka, the pain can only have been acute. Over a period of three weeks, she received word successively of the deaths at Passchendaele of all three of her sons serving in the NZEF.

Historians still argue about who was responsible for this Passchendaele fiasco. Quite apart from the controversial question of whether the offensive should have been continued at all, the New Zealanders had, in the circumstances existing on 12 October, been given an impossible task. The conditions reduced almost to zero the chances of success in anything but a carefully organised and well-supported attack. For New Zealanders at home, Passchendaele became a symbol of extreme military futility and epitomised the tragedy of the First World War — a seemingly endless stalemate in which incompetent generals expended the lives of their troops in tens of thousands to make gains that were measured in yards. The disaster added greatly to war-weariness among the population at large as the war dragged into its fourth year.

The home front

The outbreak of war in 1914 unified the community. With unions promising not to strike, and labour leaders proclaiming their loyalty, resentments over the tribulations of the previous year faded. A new mood of conciliation and consensus prevailed. The government released men imprisoned for activities during the 1913 industrial unrest, and the rhetoric of class conflict was muted.

New Zealand enjoyed a doubly fortunate situation. Far distant from the main battlefields, its citizens feared little more than raids against them — unless the Empire lost the war. They could, moreover, contribute to the war in a way that increased their own prosperity. Unable to feed its population by its own efforts, Britain depended on New Zealand's food products. From March 1915, farmers received a huge boost from the introduction of bulk-purchase arrangements; all the frozen beef, mutton and lamb they could produce would henceforth be taken by Britain and at a price that left them smiling. Cheese and butter later came within the bulk-purchase orbit as well.[28] So, too, did wool.

The war effort at home was not, however, all plain sailing. Maintaining production and exports at the required levels depended on overcoming three significant problems: labour shortages caused by enlistment, shortages of materials or shipping, and industrial dissension. Freezing workers, wharfies and coal-miners occupied strategic positions in the chain of supply to the United Kingdom.

Farmers did not face major labour shortage problems at first, even when their labourers enlisted. They just worked harder. Family members helped out, and neighbours co-operated on a give-and-take basis to overcome labour shortfalls. The output from farms remained high. The problems arose off-farm. Labour shortages impacted heavily on processing and transporting of produce, and also on business and other support services. Expanding manufacturing exacerbated the problem. The production of military uniforms, boots and other accoutrements greatly expanded.

Retired men and school-leavers helped make up the shortfall in towns and cities. Women did too. Many entered the paid workforce for the first time, especially in teaching and office jobs. Workers, men and women, were on the job longer as overtime increased. Efficiency became a byword. The authorities frowned on absenteeism and anything else that seemed to hinder production, including the demon drink.

Inflation posed another major danger for the war effort on the home front. Rising prices, the government recognised,

would inevitably cause dissension and strikes as workers strove to maintain their position. The answer seemed to lie in the imposition of price controls. But the system did not prevent food prices from rising 16.5 per cent in the first year of the war. By November 1918 they were 25 per cent higher than at the outbreak of war, while wages had risen less than 16 per cent.

As the war progressed, workers in some sectors became increasingly restive. They were goaded to action by the apparent unfairness of farmers enjoying high prices for their exports as a result of the imperial commandeer. A series of strikes threatened the flow of produce to the United Kingdom. Manufacturing for the war effort also suffered a decline in productivity.

In early 1917 miners and waterside workers began go-slows in support of pay demands. When leaders of the mine workers were arrested in April, a full-scale strike ensued. Although a settlement was reached in this particular dispute, other miners struck soon after. The government used the threat of conscription to coerce the strikers, normally exempted as essential industry workers, back to work. Powers provided under the War Regulations were used to suppress any incitement to strike.

External influences also affected New Zealand's export effort. In particular, shipping services were disrupted. Any delay in the arrival of cargo ships presented problems as perishable produce piled up in cool stores. The creation of further storage capacity helped overcome this difficulty.

Efforts to sustain the NZEF began to divide the community as the war dragged on. Finding men to replace those who were killed or wounded or to fill new units offered for the imperial cause initially presented few problems. A surge of volunteering followed news of New Zealanders in action at Gallipoli. Men wanted to support 'the boys at the front' and to be part of a great national effort. Their path to the front led them through a camp system that had been hastily expanded to meet war needs. During 1915 the main training centre was at Trentham, with smaller camps at Avondale and Narrow Neck in Auckland, Awapuni near Palmerston North, and Papawai, near Masterton. In early 1916 a major camp capable of holding 7500 men was built near the southern Wairarapa town of Featherston.[29] From that time most reinforcements for the NZEF spent time there before embarking for Europe or the Middle East.

By 1916 the number of volunteers had fallen, even as New Zealand expanded its commitment with the formation of the New Zealand Division. The dream of adventure or travel had long since lost its seductive gloss. The patently inglorious nature

Archives New Zealand, C1370

A mine laid by the German raider *Wolf* washed ashore on Awana Beach, Great Barrier Island, on 4 March 1918. *Wolf* laid mines off both North Cape and Cape Farewell in 1917. These immediately claimed a cargo ship and later the intercolonial liner *Wimmera*. The 26 who drowned from the latter were the only New Zealanders killed by enemy action within territorial limits during the war. Although no other raider entered New Zealand waters, a prisoner of war, Felix von Luckner (the raider *Seeadler*'s captain), escaped in 1918 from Motuihe Island, seized a scow, and made off with 10 others. Within a week he had been run down in the Kermadec Islands; he spent the rest of the war in Fort Jervois in Lyttelton Harbour.

of the fighting — and the long casualty lists — had seen to that. Nor did soldiers have to leave New Zealand to find themselves at risk. Epidemics of various diseases swept the military camps. Trentham was completely evacuated in July 1915. A poll indicating that many men had no intention of volunteering worried the authorities. Recruiting for the Maori contingent had also all but dried up, partly owing to resentment at the way it had been treated by the higher command in 1915 (when four officers were returned home as unsuitable).[30] Against this trend, the community increasingly favoured equality of sacrifice, at least of lives. 'Shirkers' — men of eligible age for military service still in the community apparently without good cause — faced increased hostility.

To keep NZEF units up to strength, the government introduced conscription. Many men continued to volunteer, but from November 1916 successive ballots determined the fates of those who did not. More than 30,000 conscripts went to the front in the next two years. Conscription ensured the mobilisation of almost one in five male New Zealanders, compared with one in seven Australians and Canadians and one in four Britons.[31]

Not everyone accepted the coming of compulsion. Left-wing politicians opposed it, as did the labour movement generally.

Robert Semple condemned the introduction of 'the octopus of conscription, Prussianism'; Peter Fraser spoke of the war wending 'its weary, corpse-strewn way'.[32] Conscript wealth as well as men, they demanded. In December 1916 the authorities responded; Semple, Fraser and three others found themselves behind bars, convicted of sedition. They were the most visible of a small army of resisters; in the next two years more than 200 others would be convicted for sedition or disloyalty, and 71 of these would be gaoled.[33]

Others resisted less overtly, though just as firmly. Taking part in war was an anathema for some; it was morally wrong. The authorities took a very narrow view, allowing only members of churches with long-established anti-war credentials to stand aside. A few score of Quakers, Christadelphians and Seventh-Day Adventists benefited. Political or humanitarian arguments against involvement in war cut no ice with those responsible for hearing appeals against conscription.

Several hundred appellants took the option of serving as non-combatants. Those who refused to serve after having their cases dismissed were dragged in front of courts martial. Imprisonment with hard labour was their lot. Fourteen of the most 'troublesome' defaulters, including Archibald Baxter and

Children of Wellington's Te Aro School show their support for the war effort.

Archives New Zealand, ABHO W3771

two of his brothers, faced a harsher punishment, intended to set an example to others in the same predicament. Dragged to France, they endured repeated field punishment — including being positioned periodically in no-man's-land — as the authorities tried to break their resistance. Several became stretcher-bearers, but Baxter, with one other (Mark Briggs), would not budge. Eventually Baxter was hospitalised, diagnosed as 'melancholic' and returned to New Zealand in August 1918.[34]

About 5000 men avoided the appeal process altogether. By failing to register, they never entered the system and became liable to being balloted. Police scoured the country for these evaders and caught several hundred. They joined defaulters in gaol, where some would remain until late 1920. For years after their release they would be irritated by civil penalties.

Defaulters and evaders revealed cracks in the consensus that sustained New Zealand's war effort. But they represented no more than seven per cent of the men who volunteered or were called up for service with the NZEF.[35] They presented a nuisance to the authorities rather than a serious threat to New Zealand's ability to meet the commitments it had undertaken.

Some Maori also resisted involvement in the war. Still angry at their treatment in the New Zealand Wars, some tribes, especially the Waikato under the leadership of Te Puea Herangi, resisted the recruitment of their younger men for the Maori contingent. Others considered the commitment of the contingent to combat operations a breach of the understanding of non-combatant service on which the force had been recruited; they feared the implications for Maoridom of the loss of young men in battle. Numbers told the story — the rate of recruitment for Maori was less than half that of Pakeha.[36]

Apparent Maori 'resistance' and pacifism riled the government, which was conscious of the difficulties in sustaining the contingent. Action seemed necessary against messianic prophet Rua Kenana and his separatist community at Maungapohatu, deep in the Urewera. A police party trekked into the area in April 1916. The affair ended in tragedy. Shots were exchanged, and two Maori died. Rua, arrested with five others, faced sedition charges.[37]

In June 1917 all North Island Maori became liable to conscription. Only the resistant Waikato were targeted, but the effort proved a dismal failure for the authorities. Individual and collective resistance made it well-nigh impossible to register men in the tribal area. Even so, four ballots were held, the upshot being a further hundred men under arrest for refusing to serve and more in hiding. A few changed their minds when treated leniently at the Maori training camp at Narrow Neck, and 11 drew sentences of hard labour from courts martial. But by the time the war ended no Maori conscript had left the country.[38]

If the NZEF depended on the home front for a steady supply of reinforcements, it also benefited greatly from the women's support. Women's attitudes to the war were ambivalent. At the outset, many were caught up in the enthusiasm that swept the country. They supported the government's decision to provide an expeditionary force. Some pressured seemingly enlistment-shy young men by handing them white feathers, a symbol of cowardice. Anti-German measures found strong support among women. But recognition of the war's possible consequences for their loved ones soon tempered such feelings.

With half the men of military age involved during the course of the war, there were few women who did not have a close relative overseas with the forces. They lived with constant fear that their loved one's adventure might end in tragedy, that he might be killed or badly maimed (a feeling shared, of course, by men as well). The lengthy casualty lists in the newspapers from 1915 soon exacerbated such fears. The telegram boy, the harbinger of ill tidings in the form of a telegram from the Minister of Defence advising of a soldier's fate, became dreaded.

The evident futility and waste of lives in a seemingly inescapable quagmire left women frustrated, bitter and grief-stricken. Some gained relief from their sense of helplessness by throwing themselves into voluntary work, doing something practical for the boys. Patriotic organisations such as Lady Liverpool's Women's War Fund provided an outlet. Women helped organise fundraising carnivals, they knitted garments and made jam, and they packed parcels for the soldiers. Otago and Southland women alone sent overseas more than 47,000 articles in 1915, including balaclavas, socks, and hussifs (flannel or silk cummerbunds).[39] For the men at the front, these goods provided much-appreciated variety in their daily fare and much-needed practical items; and it was a welcome reminder of home. Maori soldiers were not forgotten. Each month the Maori Soldiers' Fund set up by Miria Woodbine Pomare (wife of Sir Maui Pomare) sent off 2000 parcels for Maori and Cook Island soldiers.[40]

The war also affected the employment of women in the paid workforce. Unlike their Second World War counterparts, women did not face the discomfiture and inconvenience of being directed to work by the state. But gaps in the labour force left by men departing for the NZEF provided opportunities for employment for many women who might not otherwise have sought a paid job. Unofficial initiative led to the appearance of a Women's National Reserve, which prepared lists of women willing to do certain jobs. Most women who took up wartime jobs were just 'keeping seats warm' for men overseas. Even so, the war opened up new employment areas to women, especially in the public service and retailing. From mid 1916 they could sit the public service exams. The dominance of women in teaching increased.

THE SIAMESE TWINS

Although the main political parties had called a political truce on the outbreak of war, they had resumed hostilities in the December 1914 general election. So close was the outcome that it was not until June 1915 that William Massey finally secured a tenuous majority. Almost immediately Reform entered into a 'National' coalition with the Liberals. The two parties shared the portfolios in the new ministry, which was announced on 4 August 1915.

Massey remained Prime Minister with Sir Joseph Ward as Minister of Finance. Both men would spend prolonged periods out of the country, attending imperial meetings in London. They would be dubbed the Siamese twins because they appeared everywhere together. In their absence James Allen had charge of the day-to-day administration of New Zealand's war effort as acting prime minister.

The National coalition remained in place for the rest of the war. With its formation, the six Labour MPs became the official opposition in Parliament. This change of status was soon bolstered by organisational change — in 1916 the United Labour Party and the Social Democratic Party came together to form the New Zealand Labour Party.

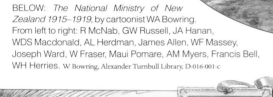

BELOW: *The National Ministry of New Zealand 1915–1919*, by cartoonist WA Bowring. From left to right: R McNab, GW Russell, JA Hanan, WDS Macdonald, AL Herdman, James Allen, WF Massey, Joseph Ward, W Fraser, Maui Pomare, AM Myers, Francis Bell, WH Herries. W Bowring, Alexander Turnbull Library, D-016-001-c

ABOVE: Massey (centre) and Ward salute troops as they march past during a visit to the Western Front. Between them is the commander of the New Zealand Division, Major-General Sir Andrew Russell. Archives New Zealand, IA76/13

For women on the margins of society, the war proved less satisfying. Repression increased, driven by fears in the community that prostitution would lead to the rapid spread of sexually transmitted diseases among soldiers. The authorities' apparent 'moral laxity' came under increased scrutiny. Police, as a result, received new powers to suppress brothels. Even the hitherto largely untouchable 'one-woman' establishments became fair game.

Conscription prompted many women to become political activists. Some, horrified by the waste of life, promoted pacifist thinking. They formed a section of the Women's International League for Peace and Freedom (WILPF) in Auckland in 1916. The new organisation — there were also short-lived sections in the other main centres — aimed to end the war by negotiation and to resolve future conflicts by arbitration and conciliation. Before long, however, the WILPF amalgamated with the Auckland Women's Political League to form the Women's International and Political League. The war also encouraged the resurrection of the National Council of Women, which had fallen into abeyance in 1906.

Women also fought their own war in New Zealand, against the liquor menace. The Women's Christian Temperance Union succeeded in having barmaids registered and in securing early closing of bars. Its campaign complemented official efforts to curb the effects of liquor not only on young soldiers in camp but also on the workforce. Sly-grog selling, especially near camps, was banned. With 'treating' or 'shouting' outlawed, buying a mate a drink meant breaching the law. Partly in an effort to curb prostitution, women were excluded from bars after 6 p.m. At the end of 1917, 6 p.m. became the closing time, an 'emergency' measure that would become a feature of New Zealand life for the next five decades.

Women also served overseas, especially in Britain. To support the New Zealand effort in France, a rear base had been established there in 1916. Training camps at Sling on the Salisbury Plain (marked by New Zealand badges carved in the chalk of a nearby hill that can still be seen today) and at Brocton, Boscombe, Grantham and Ewshot provided way stations for reinforcements on their journey to the front. Wounded or sick men came back from France for treatment at hospitals at Walton-on-Thames, Brockenhurst, and Codford. There was also a convalescent hospital at Hornchurch.

Among the nurses who staffed the hospitals were many New Zealanders. A dedicated New Zealand nursing service had been formed in 1915, the brainchild of Australian-born nursing administrator Hester Maclean. Nurses had served in the Mediterranean, and 10 had drowned when the troopship *Marquette* was torpedoed en route for Salonika in October 1915 — the worst loss of life of New Zealand service women in any war. They also helped staff the New Zealand hospital at Hazebrouck, in France. They learned, Maclean wrote, to 'sleep to the sound of the guns and the bombs falling nearby', to endure trench foot sometimes so bad that shoes could not be worn, and to deal with the sudden influxes of patients during offensives.[41]

Nurse Elsie Grey was at Hazebrouck in June 1917 when the casualties of Messines poured in:

. . . it is terrible to see these men wounded in the head — numbers of them became paralysed and quite a number were minus arms and legs and eyes. For the first few days they were quite silly — lost their reason and some speechless. Oh it was ghastly and desperately busy — we just went on and on doing dressings no hope of finishing.[42]

More than 600 New Zealand women served overseas with the NZEF during the war, either in stationary hospitals or on the New Zealand hospital ships *Maheno* and *Marama*. Other New Zealand women toiled independently of the NZEF, such as doctors Agnes Bennett and Jessie Scott in

Among those who excelled in the fighting to halt the Germans was Opotiki-born former horse-breaker Sergeant Richard Travis, who earned a reputation for his audacious conduct in no-man's-land leading a section of snipers and observers known as Travis's Gang. A stray shell would kill him in July 1918, one day after he had attacked a series of German machine-gun posts with such bravery that he was awarded a posthumous Victoria Cross. Alexander Turnbull Library, F-103803-½

Cairo and Salonika. About a hundred provided nursing or Voluntary Aid Detachment (VAD) services in British or French military facilities. Most did so in France, Belgium or the United Kingdom; a few were to be found in hospitals in Mesopotamia, Serbia or Russia.

A constant stream of men coming across from France on leave supplemented the New Zealand presence in England. There were usually more New Zealanders in England than in France, and unofficial facilities had sprung up to cater for their needs. Many made a beeline for the New Zealand Soldiers' Club in London's Russell Square. Run by Ethel Burnett with the help of 200 female volunteers, this home away from home for the troops sold them more than a quarter of a million meals, and countless guidebooks and packets of tobacco. The main attraction was the New Zealand women who served them, symbols of home and 'Mum' for homesick men, who could eat buttered scones with tea and sympathy.

New Zealand soldiers on leave in Britain took the opportunity to visit relatives and see the sights — though always with the knowledge of what awaited them when their all-too-short respite ended. Len Hart, observing the dejection of the soldiers in a carriage as their leave ended, commented on this: 'the comparison between sitting in the stalls of the Criterion theatre, and a day or two after to be trudging through the cursed mud of Flanders is too ludicrous.'[43] Young New Zealanders also tasted the delights of Paris and had their eyes opened. Len Hart wrote home of the joys of being brought breakfast in bed by French maids and of the surprising attentions that would be bestowed on a generous tipper: 'Some of them were rather embarrassing for a start, but I soon discovered that it is not customary to get embarrassed at anything in Paris.'[44]

Whether in London or Paris, the troops sought the company of women. Like soldiers since the beginning of time, they also suffered the consequences in the form of venereal disease. In 1917 the rate soared to 134 per 1000 troops. Official stupidity hindered the military authorities' attempts to deal with the problem. Sensible measures introduced by NZEF commander Sir Alexander Godley had to be curtailed. It was left to private efforts to fill the gap and provide ways to protect the men from this scourge.

In the vanguard was Ettie Rout, a Tasmanian-born office worker and labour activist. In 1915, she had formed the New Zealand Volunteer Sisterhood, which began its work with 12 volunteers in the YMCA canteen in Cairo. By 1917 Rout was in London. She provided prophylactic knowledge and equipment to the soldiers until the NZEF at last adopted her kit and made it freely available, the only official recognition she ever received.

New Zealand and British troops move forward with Mark V tanks near Grévillers on 26 August 1918. Imperial War Museum

Victory — at a price

Even during the dark days of 1916–17 most New Zealanders still believed that the sacrifice was worth it. To expend so much blood without securing victory was unthinkable. To stop short of this objective would be an unforgivable betrayal of the tens of thousands who had fallen. The war to end all wars had to be won. But in early 1918 defeat, not victory, seemed the more likely outcome, despite the United States entry to the war on the Allied side.

For the New Zealanders who had endured a bitter winter in the line near Ypres, the immediate prospect was rest and recuperation. Shortly before the division was relieved Len Hart was left nearly blind after being caught in a gas attack. 'Our division was to have been relieved . . . three nights after I was sent away,' he wrote home from his hospital bed in England. 'Whether this has been done or not I do not know, but none of us would be sorry to have to say goodbye to that hideous graveyard of Ypres for ever.'[45]

The storm broke just weeks later. German forces, reinforced from the now defunct Eastern Front, launched a massive offensive on 21 March. The yawning gap torn in the Allied line seemed to portend catastrophe. Among the reserves thrown into the path of the oncoming German infantry was the New Zealand Division, now one of the strongest in the British Expeditionary Forces thanks to conscription. Hastening back to the Somme in forced marches, it joined the struggle to stem the German flood and, after losing many men, eventually stabilised the line in its sector. Adrian Hart expressed the thoughts of many: 'I think it is Germany's last throw and if we can hold them here the end is not very far off for they must already have lost an immense number of men.'[46] He was right. By April the offensive had run out of steam.

In August the Allies attacked. In the 'Hundred Days Offensive' from August to November 1918, New Zealand troops were to the fore. Revelling in the opportunity to fight in open country, they advanced from Bapaume to Le Quesnoy. But tragedy struck the Knight family once again, when on 1 September Douglas was killed. A comrade wrote to Douglas's mother: 'a better chum & friend it was not possible to have. What talks we would have in our bivvy, needless to say about NZ. He of the work among the sheep, his college days & of the work in connection with the sawmilling & the farms, about the home & the happy days, of the sisters & the brother about

18 & in the talking he revealed himself for the wonderful character that he was.'[47]

Individual initiative counted for much in this new phase of the fighting, as was demonstrated when the New Zealanders swept past the ancient fortified town of Le Quesnoy on 4 November in their longest one-day advance of the whole war. Some troops set out to capture the bypassed town. Subaltern Leslie Averill was first up a ladder used to scale the walls. Once the New Zealanders were in the town, the demoralised German garrison quickly gave up. This dashing incident caught the imagination of the townsfolk, forming a bond with New Zealand that still remains strong.

This exploit was the division's swan song. A week later Germany gave in. An armistice ended the fighting at 11 a.m. on 11 November 1918. The tired troops greeted it with little emotion. In the weeks that followed they marched to Cologne as part of the occupation force. This German sojourn did not last long; by March 1919 men were heading for home in a steady stream.

At home relieved New Zealanders also adjusted to the peace. For a small community of just over a million, the price of Empire had been huge. More than 18,000 — one in six of those who went overseas — had not returned. Two-thirds fell on the Western Front, a toll that surpassed New Zealand's total dead in the Second World War. The dice of death had rolled capriciously: whereas all three Knight brothers had been killed, the Hart brothers all survived.

The dead lie buried or are memorialised in war cemeteries near where they fell. Many have no known grave. David Gallaher is buried in Nine Elms Cemetery, near Poperinge, Belgium, while the Knights lie in three countries: Herbert at Gallipoli; George in the vast Tyne Cot Cemetery, near Passchendaele, Belgium; and Douglas in Bancourt Cemetery, France. Battlefield memorials at Gallipoli, Longueval, Messines, Graventafel and Le Quesnoy commemorate the efforts of the men 'From the Uttermost Ends of the Earth', the phrase that appears on each of them. In New Zealand, war memorials throughout the land and the solemn proceedings of Anzac Day every 25 April continue to remind New Zealanders of their country's bloodiest overseas conflict.

A roadside cemetery near Neuve Eglise. A greater percentage of New Zealand's males of military age lost their lives in the First World War than did those of any other dominion or colony. Contrary to a myth that later developed, New Zealand was not one of the hardest hit by the war. Britain, France, Italy, Serbia, Rumania, Germany, Austria-Hungary, Turkey and Bulgaria all lost much higher proportions of their military-aged men than did New Zealand.
G Butler, Archives New Zealand, NCWA 471

Chapter 9

Unemployed men on relief work replace tramway tracks in High Street, Christchurch, in 1932. After the electric trams, motor power and 'labour-saving' innovations that epitomised the material progress and optimism of the 1920s, the pick and shovel of the relief gang symbolised the great leap backwards of the Depression years.

J Fitzgerald, Canterbury Museum, 16298

The Rise and Fall of Happy Homes

1918–1935

The years from the end of the Great War until the advent of New Zealand's first Labour government in 1935 have always had a bad press. The shattering economic slump of the early 1930s overshadows the period. New Zealand also endured its deadliest disease outbreak (the 1918 influenza pandemic) and its worst natural disaster (the Hawke's Bay earthquake of 1931). But the period was not without achievement and innovation — particularly between 1922 and 1929, when New Zealand crackled with energy and ideas. Electricity and fuel oils challenged coal as the driving force of the economy, while down on the farm mechanisation and science boosted productivity to new levels. Public trams, private automobiles and the Californian bungalow with its 'mod cons' forged a new suburban frontier of 'happy homes' and gave New Zealand probably the highest home-ownership rate in the world. Innovations in fashion, recreation and the media — especially radio, cinema and gramophone records — helped create a new popular culture, which, to the alarm of many, often had an American accent. In many ways, these trends foreshadowed the prosperity, stability and consumerism of the 1950s and 1960s. Before then, however, the hopes of thousands of New Zealanders would be dashed in a great Depression and another great war.

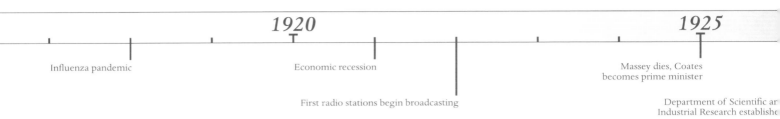

A land unfit for heroes

The immediate aftermath of the Great War was a worrying time for New Zealanders. Although the dominion was spared the devastation and upheavals that stalked Europe, the human cost of the war was massive and ongoing. More than 100,000 men and women had served overseas; 18,000 had died. There were few New Zealanders who had not lost a relative, friend or neighbour. Many who did return were physically or psychologically scarred, and would endure discomfort, pain or nightmares for the rest of their lives. Most suffered in silence, unable or unwilling to talk about the horrors of war. Others were embittered by the apparent comforts enjoyed by civilians back home and by what they perceived as society's failure to acknowledge their sacrifices. Although the government spent over £25 million to help returned servicemen train for new careers, buy houses or get on the land, post-war New Zealand seemed anything but a 'land fit for heroes'; the state's farm settlement scheme in particular has been harshly criticised. Many disgruntled diggers found refuge in the camaraderie of the Returned Soldiers' (later Returned Services') Association, which soon emerged as one of the country's most influential pressure groups.

But the slaughter of the Great War did little to dampen New Zealanders' enthusiasm for imperial escapades. When the Chanak crisis briefly threatened to reignite war between Britain and Turkey in 1922, 13,000 men and nearly 400 nurses dashed to enlist within two weeks.[1]

Canterbury Museum, 583/1

Contagious crowds throng Christchurch's Cathedral Square on Armistice Day 1918. Instead of joyous celebrations, the immediate aftermath of the war delivered more misery and fear, as a lethal influenza pandemic claimed over 8600 victims in two months — almost half as many as the country lost in four years of war. Despite, or perhaps partly because of, the scale of the tragedy, the flu pandemic was largely swept under the carpet of New Zealand history.

The Rise and Fall of Happy Homes

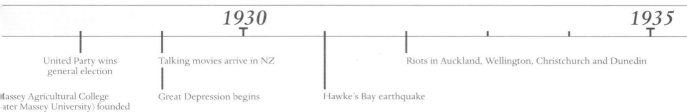

1930   1935

United Party wins general election

Talking movies arrive in NZ

Riots in Auckland, Wellington, Christchurch and Dunedin

Massey Agricultural College (later Massey University) founded

Great Depression begins

Hawke's Bay earthquake

The end of the 'war to end all wars' contained a terrible sting in its tail: a deadly influenza pandemic that swept the world, killing between 20 and 40 million — two or three times as many as the war itself. The 'Spanish flu' or 'Spanish Lady', as it was often called, arrived in New Zealand in October 1918, probably with returning troops; by the time it abated in December the death toll had topped 8600, including at least 2160 Maori.[2] As the death rate was highest among people in their 20s and 30s, it compounded the terrible toll of the war. At the height of the crisis, in November, the whole country held its breath; schools, factories, shops, hotels, theatres and hairdressing salons were closed, and Auckland's Armistice Day celebrations were postponed until the following year. The virus struck with little warning, and apparently healthy people often collapsed within hours of the first symptoms appearing. Some died within a day. After death many of the corpses turned purple or black, adding to the grief of survivors and evoking images of the Black Death of the 14th century. Schools and halls across the country became makeshift hospitals, and much of the burden of caring for the sick fell on volunteer caregivers, especially women. Among the victims were at least 14 doctors, including Margaret Cruickshank, who in 1897 had become New Zealand's first registered female doctor.

The virus had an especially deadly impact on Maori, whose death rate, 4.2 per cent, was about seven times that of Pakeha. Much of the blame was laid at the door of substandard housing — many Maori dwellings had earthen floors and were damp and overcrowded. But the small size and isolation of Maori rural settlements also compounded the misery. Such was the speed of the flu's spread that the remotest communities had little or no warning of its arrival. In the absence of outside help, there were often not enough locals left standing to care for the sick. Adding to the shock was the failure of traditional remedies; many Maori believed that the disease had magical causes and looked to tohunga to save them. Whole communities were decimated. At Mangatawhiri in Waikato, Te Puea Herangi's future husband, Rawiri Katipa, was one of only three adults unaffected in a community of 200; at least 50 died. At Panguru on the Hokianga Harbour most of the 40 residents were stricken, as Whina Cooper recalled:

The Press Collection, Alexander Turnbull Library, G-8545-½

In what looks more like a cowshed than a medical facility, Christchurch citizens line up in an 'inhalation chamber' for a dose of zinc sulphate; like many supposed cures for the flu, it probably did more harm than good.

Archives New Zealand, H11, W2615

The appalling standard of housing in many isolated communities was one of the factors that made the Maori death rate from flu seven times higher than that of Pakeha. Photographed in 1925, this rudimentary whare was at Te Kaha in the Eastern Bay of Plenty.

REMEMBERING THE FALLEN

The most striking expression of the nation's sorrow and pride in its wartime sacrifices were the more than 500 war memorials that sprouted across the country in the years after the Armistice. Monuments were erected in even the smallest of hamlets, the long lists of the fallen reading like a street directory of local families. In Taranaki over 30 settlements built memorials; Stratford alone has seven. Most were funded by donations from local communities. With almost all the dead buried overseas, they served as a surrogate grave for grieving families and friends, especially on Anzac Day when they became the focus of wreath-laying and speech-making.

Monuments came in all shapes and sizes: statues of soldiers or symbolic figures, arches, gates and obelisks and (less commonly) utilitarian amenities such as halls, bridges, clocks and libraries. The grandest are Auckland's imposing War Memorial Museum (1929), William Trethewey's elegant sculpture outside Christchurch Cathedral (1937), and Wellington's 50-m-high carillon (1932) — a monstrous musical instrument. Despite the war's supposed role as the midwife of New Zealand nationalism, few memorials feature home-grown symbolism; their iconography and inscriptions instead reflect an eclectic mix of loyalties to God, king and country.[3]

RIGHT: A stone sentry stands guard in the tiny Southland settlement of Riversdale. This memorial, unveiled in 1924, reveals a story of loss that was repeated across the country: the 23 names listed represented around 10 per cent of the local male population. Ministry for Culture and Heritage

BELOW: The construction of a National War Memorial in Wellington was delayed for years by quarrels over funding, location and design, but finally, on Anzac Day 1932, the towering carillon was dedicated before a gigantic crowd. Another part of the original design, a Hall of Memories beneath the carillon, was not completed until 1964, by which time there was another generation of war dead to remember. Grand plans for a tree-lined boulevard sweeping down to the harbour came to nothing. SC Smith Collection, Alexander Turnbull Library, G-20293-1⁄1

Everyone was sick, no one to help, they were dying one after the other. My father was very very sick then. He was the first to die. I couldn't do anything for him. I remember we put him in a coffin, like a box. There were many others, you could see them on the roads, on the sledges, the ones that were able to drag them away, dragged them away to the cemetery. No time for tangis.[4]

The carnage in Maori communities, however, paled in comparison to Western Samoa, then under New Zealand military rule. There, over 7500 — a staggering 20 per cent of the population — succumbed to the virus, at least partly because of the negligence of the New Zealand authorities in enforcing a quarantine.[5]

As the Spanish flu graphically demonstrated, Maori and Pakeha remained worlds apart. In 1921 over 90 per cent of Maori lived in rural areas, compared to only 40 per cent of Pakeha. Although Maori had readily adopted European clothing, foods, tools and other aspects of material culture, their physical isolation — and the failure of the state to implement its long-standing policy of 'race amalgamation' — enabled them to preserve much of their traditional way of life. Attachments to hapu, iwi and whakapapa, and customs such as tangi and hui, remained extremely strong. Most Maori still consulted tohunga and relied on traditional cures, and in 1930 many Maori children spoke only Maori at home.[6] Maori had lost most of their land. Only a tiny minority retained enough to farm commercially or lease to others; the majority were either landless or possessed small plots suitable only for subsistence agriculture. Maori in the interwar years remained a rural people without the economic and political resources to sustain their way of life.

The flu pandemic eased in mid December, but its terrible toll contributed to the simmering sense of trauma that stalked New Zealanders into the early 1920s. In this time of turmoil Pakeha society faced challenges on several fronts: ongoing class conflict, an alarming upsurge in sectarian tensions, deep divisions over the prohibition question, and a severe economic recession in 1921–22.

The threat of a radical labour movement was sharpened by the strains of war, the 1917 Bolshevik revolution in Russia and post-war upheavals across Europe. The failure of militant unionism in 1912–13 encouraged many Red Fed leaders to seek more effective strategies to realise their socialist utopia on earth. A new, united New Zealand Labour Party, formed in 1916, sought to achieve radical socialist objectives — the nationalisation of the means of production, distribution and exchange — not through revolutionary or industrial action but via the ballot box. By skilfully exploiting war-weariness and resentment at inflation and profiteering, Labour snatched three by-election victories in 1918, then captured 24 per cent of the vote at the 1919 general election, more than doubling the support various Labour candidates had received in the 1914 election.[7]

The centrepiece of Labour's 1919 manifesto was a programme of land nationalisation far more radical than anything proposed by contemporary British and Australian Labour parties. This committed the party to prohibit land sales other than to the state, so that over time the government would accumulate a vast landed asset leased out for productive use. Although Labour was dedicated to achieving nationalisation through constitutional means, its policy was anathema to New Zealand's extensive propertied classes. A sudden upsurge in strikes — a railway strike in 1920 briefly stranded the Prince of Wales in Rotorua — and the formation of the Alliance of Labour, an umbrella union organisation with militant aims, added to fears that the tide of revolution was rising.

An unexpected spasm of sectarian strife, which culminated in the trial for sedition of Catholic Bishop James Liston in 1922, added to the climate of unease.[8] Simmering resentment towards New Zealand's largely Irish Catholic minority (around 14 per cent of the population), stirred by Protestant disgust at Ireland's Easter Uprising of 1916, led to the formation of a Protestant Political Association (PPA) in 1917. The PPA whipped up anti-Catholic fears by accusing Papists of undermining the Allied war effort and the New Zealand Catholic Church of conspiring with 'disloyalists' to foment revolt in Ireland. Its leader, Baptist minister Howard Elliott, was a demagogue with a knack for manipulating crowds and attracting media attention with lurid allegations, including tales of drowned nuns and dead children buried in convent grounds.

By the end of 1917, sensing the propertied classes' anxiety at the revival of socialism, the PPA tweaked its message to mobilise their support. Elliott alleged that the Catholic Church was in bed with the Labour Party (whose leadership certainly contained several Irish Catholics), that Labour stood for Bolshevism, and that Bolsheviks were sabotaging the war effort. By the end of 1919 the PPA boasted 225 branches and 200,000 members. Its campaign against Catholic and Labour candidates at that year's general election helped sweep Reform to victory and probably helped defeat many Liberal candidates, including the party's Catholic leader, Sir Joseph Ward.

Another deep division in Pakeha society immediately after the war was the decades-old struggle between 'wets' and 'drys' over the prohibition of alcohol. Since the 1880s the prohibition campaign led by the New Zealand Alliance had developed into a powerful mass movement. By 1908, 12 electorates had voted to go dry under the local liquor polls introduced in 1893. In 1910 a triennial national referendum was added to the local option, and the following year almost 56 per cent of voters

THE RISE OF RATANA

In November 1918, as influenza cut a swathe through Maori communities, Tahupotiki Wiremu Ratana of Ngati Apa and Nga Rauru experienced visions that were later interpreted as omens. A mysterious whirlwind cloud appeared before him, striking him dumb; when he spoke, it was with the voices of the Holy Spirit or the archangels Gabriel or Michael. They told him to turn his people away from belief in spirits towards Jehovah, and to preach the Gospel to Maori all over New Zealand. At first his family thought he was mad, but his aunt Mere Rikiriki, a well-known faith healer who had predicted the coming of a prophet in 1912, recognised Ratana as the Mangai (the Mouthpiece) of the Holy Spirit. He cleared out his house and urged others to do the same; those who failed to follow his advice succumbed to the deadly flu. When he showed an ability to heal the sick through prayer, a stream of visitors began to arrive at his farm near Wanganui, which became known as Ratana pa. The Pakeha press seized on the story and the 'Maori Miracle Man' became a national celebrity; in 1919 and 1920 the train to Ratana station was disgorging up to 100 visitors a day.

Ratana's spiritualist revival initially avoided politics and land issues, but the movement expanded rapidly in the early 1920s; soon there were Ratana bands and choirs, rugby teams, a newspaper, even a bank. In 1923 he publicly committed himself to a political programme; during a 1924–25 visit to Europe he attempted — without success — to present a petition on the Treaty of Waitangi and land confiscations to King George V and the League of Nations in Paris. Ratana's early attacks on 'tohungaism' had won warm support from other Christian clergymen, but the formal establishment of his own church in 1925 (and his subsequent rejection of monogamy) triggered an enduring breach with mainstream Christianity.

To his many Maori followers, Ratana's faith and leadership were a source of great consolation in uncertain times. The movement's increasing devotion to politics promised landless and destitute Maori rewards and justice on earth as well as in heaven. Ratana's mission to capture the Maori electoral seats — the four quarters of his body, as he called them — was eventually achieved in 1943, by which time his 'party' had sealed a long-standing alliance with Labour. Six decades after the Mangai's death, both church and party endure as powerful forces in Maori society.[9]

ABOVE: In 1921 and 1922 Ratana led a sweeping religious revival among Maori, travelling widely through both islands; his motorcade from Napier to Tauranga is said to have cost £1300. Whole communities converted to his teachings, and by 1928 the Ratana faith claimed more than 20,000 followers or morehu (survivors), about a third of the total Maori population.
RR Woodcock Collection, Alexander Turnbull Library, F-89569-½

LEFT: A growing pile of discarded walking sticks, crutches and spectacles — seen here in a museum at Ratana pa — seemed to confirm the success of Ratana's faith healing, but many dismissed him as a charlatan.

backed prohibition, falling just short of the 60 per cent majority required. Prohibitionists redoubled their efforts during the war years, when sobriety was promoted as patriotic duty, and in 1918 Parliament introduced a new system of national referenda. A special poll was to be held in April 1919, with a choice between prohibition, continuance, and state control of the industry — and a simple 50 per cent threshold. If prohibition were rejected, essentially the same question would be put to voters at each succeeding general election.

Both sides campaigned feverishly in the lead-up to the poll, churning out reams of newspaper advertising, posters and leaflets. Prohibitionists staged mass rallies and concerts, their halls and podiums ringed with blue and white ribbons, while gig-loads of children belted out hymns and temperance jingles. One of the most popular tunes, based on the hymn 'Throw Out

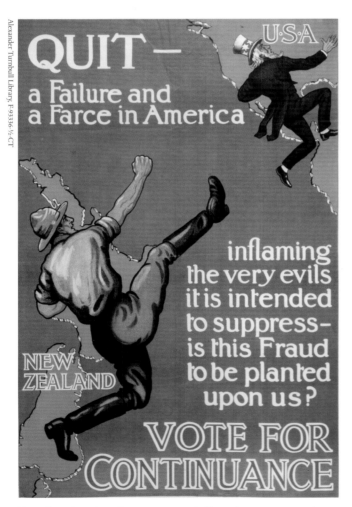

Alexander Turnbull Library, F-93336½-CT

Liquor licensing referenda were accompanied by an intense propaganda war. While prohibitionist posters typically highlighted the threat of the 'demon drink' to family life and public order, in the 1920s the 'continuance' camp, funded by powerful brewing interests, often pointed to America's failed experiment with prohibition.

the Life-line', beseeched electors to 'strike out the first line' on the ballot paper. On 10 April the drys appeared to have won a stunning victory by 246,000 votes to 232,000. But the votes of the nearly 40,000 servicemen who were overseas, on board troopships, or in camps or hospitals, were still to be counted. Fighting for the Empire was thirsty work, and the soldiers' overwhelming rejection of prohibition — by 32,000 to 7700 — ensured that their beloved beer kept flowing. On election day in December 1919, prohibitionists again scented victory, but fell 3260 votes short of their target. While the prohibition movement was to remain a formidable political force throughout the 1920s (and national referenda would continue to be held at each general election until 1987), the two 1919 polls were as close as it ever got to banning the bottle.[10]

The short, sharp economic recession of 1921–22 added to the country's woes. The downturn was sparked by a slump in the prices for primary produce in the glutted British market, and was felt all the more keenly as it followed hard on the heels of an immediate post-war boom. Struggling to balance its budget, the Reform government retrenched state spending and slashed public servants' wages by up to 10 per cent. Unemployment soared. The Arbitration Court resisted employer demands to axe post-war cost-of-living bonuses until May 1922, when it began to order some reductions. Union resentment boiled over, but with a large pool of replacement labour and state backing, employers picked off the big Alliance of Labour unions one by one; strikes by seamen, freezing workers and coal-miners in 1922 and '23 all ended in defeat, and government railwaymen met the same fate in April 1924.

Farmers were also hard hit by recession, none more so than the returned servicemen assisted onto the land under the Discharged Soldiers Settlement Act 1915. Under this scheme a million hectares of Crown and private land was sold or leased to 10,500 ex-servicemen. But the injection of £13.5 million into the property market during the brief post-war boom sparked a frenzy of land speculation. Prices peaked in 1921, when 1.8 million hectares was sold for £82 million in 56,000 transactions. When produce prices tumbled in 1921 and '22, many soldier settlers faced the impossible task of servicing huge debts on overcapitalised properties with sharply reduced incomes. For some, failure was aggravated by inexperience and the hopelessly marginal nature of the land, as symbolised by the doomed settlement at Mangapurua, inland from Wanganui, with its ghostly 'bridge to nowhere'. Though the popular image of thousands 'walking off the land' is exaggerated — most soldier settlers were still farming in 1934, even if many were struggling at subsistence level — the scheme still ranks as one of the less successful experiments undertaken by the New Zealand state.[11]

Calmer waters

So far, so bad. But what was remarkable about New Zealand after 1922 was that post-war turmoil gave way to a period of considerable stability, consensus and material progress. How did this reversal of fortunes come about? Certainly, some of the earlier flashpoints receded more through good luck than good management. Prohibitionist agitation declined after the peak of 1919, partly because the temperance movement's success in shackling the demon drink in a web of restrictive laws had diminished the public evils of drunkenness. Sectarian tensions also waned after 1922, as Reform's supremacy eased Protestant fears of Catholic domination and the settlement of the Irish question helped defuse one of the most explosive issues of domestic religious debate.

The economy remained highly unstable throughout the 1920s, with another recession in 1926–27, but the overall trend was one of modest economic expansion. New Zealand's performance was at least superior to Australia's, where the economy stagnated during this period. The main driver of economic growth in New Zealand was an increase in the volume of meat, wool and dairy exports, in turn stimulated by technical advances: electricity and motor power, the application of artificial fertiliser (superphosphate) to the lowlands, improvements to pasture and stock, and a cure for the 'bush sickness' that had hampered livestock farming in the North Island's volcanic centre. Government scientists, notably those employed by the Department of Scientific and Industrial Research (established in 1926), were heavily involved in these innovations. Farmers took to new technology with gusto — between 1919 and 1931 the number of electrified milking sheds leapt from 7000 to 22,000 and tractors from around 100 to 5000.[12]

Overt class conflict also appeared to ease in the mid 1920s. The incidence and severity of strikes fell sharply. Between 1921 and 1925, 581,000 working days were lost to industrial stoppages; between 1926 and 1930, only 130,000.[13] At the same time, electoral support for the Labour Party, which was gunning for power after the gains of 1919, stagnated at around 25 per cent throughout the 1920s. Recurring electoral disappointments prompted the party to review its fundamental objectives, and it concluded that its radical land policy was a liability. John A Lee argued, 'My God, that land programme is a hell of a grill to toast

New Zealand's economy in the 1920s was dominated by British trade and British ships, with over 80 per cent of our exports 'Home'-ward bound. In 1922 the British-owned shipping companies that controlled New Zealand's export trade — the New Zealand Shipping Company and the Federal Steam Navigation Company; Shaw, Savill and Albion; and the Commonwealth and Dominion (or Port) Line — formed a cartel. Joined in 1933 by Blue Star, this cartel was to retain a stranglehold over the UK–NZ sea lanes until the advent of container shipping in the 1970s. SL Thompson, Christchurch Art Gallery

a candidate on when the audience is hostile.' In 1927 Labour discarded nationalisation in favour of more moderate policies barely distinguishable from those of the Liberals and Reform.[14] While Labour's shift towards the political centre did not reap immediate rewards at the 1928 and 1931 elections, it did much to soothe class conflict and lower the emotional temperature of New Zealand politics.

There were other reasons for Labour's electoral failure in the 1920s, including the unsympathetic public image of Harry Holland, who led the party from 1919 to his death in 1933. A man of unquestionable conviction and sincerity, Holland was clever and remarkably well read. He even, somewhat incongruously, penned highly sentimental poetry, one collection being entitled *Red Roses along the Highway*. But he lacked warmth, and his sermons on scientific socialism, delivered in a harsh, metallic voice, evoked the stormy spectre of the Red Feds rather than the kindly ghost of King Dick.

Perhaps most important of all was the success of the Reform governments led by William Massey and Gordon Coates in isolating and defeating their political opponents. Reform had first come to power in 1912 and ruled continuously (apart from an uneasy wartime coalition with the Liberals) until 1928. Contrary to his free-market rhetoric, between 1912 and 1924 Massey oversaw a 40 per cent increase in the state's share of gross domestic product, making his administration 'the most interventionist in New Zealand's history' so far.[15] The establishment of a Meat Producers' Board (1922) and Dairy Produce Control Board (1923) to co-ordinate the production, transport and marketing of farm produce was condemned as 'agrarian socialism' by some conservatives. Reform governments not only maintained their predecessors' lavish spending on railways and other public works, but sharply increased expenditure on education, health and welfare; they raised old-age and widows' pensions, brought in pensions for the blind, and in 1926 introduced the world's first system of fully state-funded family allowances.[16]

Reform's greatest achievement in the 1920s was to devise and entrench new means for political consensus, chiefly by expanding opportunities for social advancement in secondary education, which offered working-class children admission to the white-collar workforce, and home-ownership, which promised workers economic independence — 'a stake in society'.[17] Government spending on education trebled between 1912 and 1926. The number of children attending secondary schools soared from 11,500 in 1915 to 31,000 in 1930; the proportion of primary-school leavers going on to secondary school jumped from 37 per cent in 1917 to 55 per cent by 1932.[18] With more free places in secondary schools, many more children were able to pass the civil service or matriculation examinations that were essential for those aspiring to professional and white-collar jobs.

Of perhaps even greater significance was Massey's success in creating property-owning opportunities for urban workers. The key institution was the government's State Advances Department, which lent mortgage money on easy terms to settlers, workers and local authorities. Its Advances to Workers Branch, first established in 1906, expanded greatly under Reform, especially after 1923 when the maximum loan was raised to 95 per cent of a property's value. Between 1923 and 1929, £10.7 million was advanced to almost 16,000 workers, making the state the largest mortgagee in the country. The proportion of employees owning their own homes climbed from 35 per cent in 1916 to 50 per cent in 1926. By then New Zealand enjoyed possibly the highest home-ownership rate in the world, with 60 per cent of all household heads kings of their own little castles — even though this 'property-owning democracy' was in reality more a 'mortgagors' democracy'.[19]

The acquisition of property, referred to colloquially as 'getting on', had been a fundamental ambition of working people since the early colonial era. It was also a recurrent theme of immigrant propaganda, which often hawked New Zealand as a 'workingman's paradise'. Massey understood these desires and sought to exploit them, rightly recognising that home-owners make reluctant revolutionaries. 'If you want to knock Bolshevistic notions and revolutionary socialistic notions out of men, you give them a stake in the country — something to lose, something to take a pride in.'[20] Reform's policy was also, of course, calculated to woo working-class votes at election time, and the lure of the picket fence must have cornered at least some of the sizeable anti-Labour working-class vote during the 1920s.[21]

Although it restrained working-class radicalism, Massey's home-ownership programme came with a steep price tag. Financed largely through overseas borrowing, it contributed greatly to the debt-servicing burden that would plague the government during the slump of the 1930s. Its success also contributed to the degeneration of electoral politics. Vote-buying had always been a feature of the hustings, but in the interwar years it was accentuated by the popularity of Massey's housing programme. The rival parties' desperation to out-promise each other descended into farce during the 1928 campaign, when Reform was challenged by the new United Party, a hodgepodge of disaffected Reformists and the dispirited rump of the Liberals. In his opening address United's ageing leader, Sir Joseph Ward, misread his notes and pledged to borrow the staggering sum of £70 million in one year (instead of over 10 years as he intended to say). The electorate lapped up this bold Vogelite vision of progress, and United rode 'the musical chink of the seventy million' into power against all the odds.[22]

REFORM'S 'KING BILLY'?

New Zealand's longest-serving Prime Minister after Seddon, William Ferguson Massey dominated the political scene from 1912 until his death in 1925. While he shared some of Seddon's looming bulk and political nous, he has received nowhere near the same popular or scholarly acclaim. Even his nickname, 'Farmer Bill', pales beside 'King Dick'. The savagery with which Massey's government crushed the Waihi and general strikes of 1912–13 would earn him the eternal hatred of the New Zealand left. His heavy-handed suppression of the Maori prophet Rua Kenana in 1916, attacks on civil liberties during and after the war and support for a 'White New Zealand' immigration policy in the 1920s have likewise done little to endear him to liberal historians. Looking back, Massey seems the very embodiment of the much-maligned Reform era: he lauded the farmer as the backbone of the country, insisted that a woman's place was in the home, and was more pro-British than the British. But while he was certainly no visionary, 'Farmer Bill' was far more capable and forward-thinking than opponents and historians have generally given him credit for.

The Press Collection, Alexander Turnbull Library, G-8607-⅟₂

ABOVE: Belying his backwoods image, Bill Massey flicks the switch to open the new state-owned hydroelectric power station at Mangahao, Horowhenua, in November 1924. The Reform government initiated a massive programme of electricity generation and reticulation in the 1920s.

BELOW: Massey's grandiloquent tomb on Point Halswell, overlooking Wellington Harbour, squats on the site of an old gun emplacement dating from the Russian scare of the 1880s. It was completed in 1930 at a cost of £15,000, a third of which was raised by public donations, the rest by the state. A more appropriate monument to a prime minister who strongly promoted agricultural science and education was the establishment of Massey Agricultural College at Palmerston North in 1927. John Cao

A MEMORIAL OF LOYAL AND FAITHFUL SERVICE TO KING AND COUNTRY

In 1925 Gordon Coates led Reform to its greatest election victory on the back of a slick presidential-style campaign that heralded a new era in New Zealand electioneering. Rather than presenting the detailed policy statements of earlier years, Reform's newspaper advertisements, posters and leaflets urged electors to vote for 'Coates and Confidence' and get their 'Coats off with Coates', 'The Man who gets things done'. Alexander Turnbull Library, Eph-C-POLITICS-1925-01

The creativity of the Reform government in the 1920s was also evident in its relationship with Maori. The calamity of the 1918 pandemic sparked a flurry of interest in Maori health, hygiene and housing reform, long-standing concerns of Dr Maui Pomare, Minister of Health from 1923 to 1926. Reform also took the first, tentative steps towards settling long-standing Maori grievances. Agreements with Te Arawa in 1922 and Ngati Tuwharetoa in 1926 led to the establishment of trust boards with some government funding, and recognition of their respective rights over the Rotorua lakes and Lake Taupo. The government set up royal commissions in 1920 to study Ngai Tahu grievances and in 1926 to investigate the Waikato and Taranaki confiscations, each of which recommended that compensation be paid. Although the eventual monetary settlements were modest, these were significant developments in the context of the time.[23] Apart from Pomare, these efforts were largely driven by a partnership between two far-sighted politicians — one Pakeha, one Maori; one Reform, the other Liberal. These two men were Gordon Coates and Apirana Ngata.[24]

Coates was far more sympathetic to Maori aspirations and needs than any of his Pakeha colleagues. A farmer from Kaipara, north of Auckland, he had mixed with local Maori, had an early relationship with a Maori woman who bore two children to him, and had learnt some Maori language. Tall, manly and energetic, Coates was a snappy dresser with a casual, charming manner. He had entered Parliament in 1911 and, after a distinguished war career, became Massey's Native Minister in 1921; he was also a dynamic Minister of Railways and of Public Works, and following Massey's death, Prime Minister from 1925 to 1928.

Even though they belonged to opposing parties, Coates worked closely with the Ngati Porou leader Apirana Ngata throughout the 1920s. New Zealand's first Maori university graduate, Ngata had entered Parliament in 1905 as the Liberal member for Eastern Maori. He was to hold his seat for 38 years but enjoyed real political power for only six — from 1928, when he became Native Minister in the new United government, until 1934, when he was forced to resign over revelations of departmental mismanagement. Unlike Ratana, Ngata worked within the system. Rather than spiritual zeal, his success was based on his skill, persistence, understanding of tribal politics and ability to operate in the Pakeha world. Drawing on Ngati Porou's promising involvement in commercial farming, Ngata launched a highly ambitious programme to promote the economic development of all rural Maori by consolidating small, unproductive landholdings and developing them into economic farms.

Auckland Star Collection, Alexander Turnbull Library, F-153604-½

The ground-breaking Maori land development schemes promoted by Apirana Ngata in the 1920s and 1930s sought to group fragmented, unproductive Maori landholdings into viable economic units through co-operative local effort. As it was almost impossible for Maori to borrow money from European lending institutions, most of the capital for the schemes was lent through Maori land boards.

As well as persuading Coates to investigate long-standing grievances, Ngata fostered Maori scholarship and education, and encouraged his people to preserve and nurture their traditional arts and culture. He convinced the government to establish and support a Board of Maori Ethnological Research (1923), a Maori Purposes Fund Board (1924), which subsidised cultural and educational activities, and a School of Maori Arts and Crafts in Rotorua (1926), which played a crucial role in the revival of woodcarving. Ngata also had Maori accepted as a university subject in 1923 and himself published an important collection of traditional Maori songs and sayings.

Given the lack of resources, economic uncertainty and Pakeha indifference, Ngata's achievements were remarkable. In the impoverished Hokianga district, for example, over 8000 ha were developed by 1938, carrying almost 6000 dairy cattle and supporting 3200 local Maori. 'The children got milk regularly for the first time,' recalled Whina Cooper. 'The owners were soon able to bring in beef cattle, pigs and sheep for meat. All this was good for health and good for family life.' Moreover, as people got healthier and happier, 'they were more interested again in their Maoritanga, in making more use of their marae and learning their language and traditions. They had more food and more money to run huis and tangis.'[25] But many Maori had no land to develop, and Ngata's schemes were only a stopgap. The long-term future of this largely landless and undereducated rural people remained far from certain.

A culture of consumption

In the 1920s and 1930s New Zealand hummed with the sound of new technologies: electricity, motor vehicles, radio, 'talking' movies, aeroplanes. Motor power and electrification helped spark a boom in farm productivity in the 1920s, and by the early 1930s electric power had supplanted steam as the driving force of industry. While coal was still king on the tracks and around coastal ports, the country's refrigerated exports were increasingly shipped 'Home' on big, modern motor ships. Electric lighting brightened city streets and homes, and the better-off households brimmed with the latest labour-saving appliances. New Zealanders took to these innovations like ducks to water — if they could afford them. Many also rushed to embrace the new fashions and recreations of the time, including, for young women, the 'flapper' look with its short hairstyles and looser, more comfortable clothing. Shorter working hours and the greater mobility afforded by expanding rail, tram and road networks provided new leisure opportunities, including team sports and family holidays at the beach or in the mountains.

New Zealand's urban landscape was re-shaped in the 1920s. Suburbs of detached homes with large sections grew so rapidly that they became the dominant features of cities and towns. In Auckland, the suburban push was mainly to the south and west of the city, into Mount Albert, Balmoral, Sandringham, Mount

The Rise and Fall of Happy Homes

Roskill, Westmere, Point Chevalier and Avondale. In Wellington, subdivisions initially sprouted to the south and east, in Island Bay, Hataitai, Kilbirnie, Lyall Bay and out on the Miramar peninsula; by the end of the 1920s they were edging out into the Hutt Valley. In Christchurch the main direction of growth was westwards towards Fendalton and Riccarton and south-west to Spreydon. Secondary centres, notably Hamilton and Palmerston North, also had their share of suburban sprawl.

With the new suburbs came a new architectural style, the Californian bungalow, which quickly supplanted the colonial villa as the prime symbol of urban New Zealand. The bungalow was imported from California around 1909, not by architects but via pattern-books of plans and specifications that cost only £2–3 each. As bungalows required less timber than the standard villa and made greater use of factory-made materials such as plywood and fibrous cement sheets for internal lining, they were comparatively cheap and quick to build. Another attraction was that bungalows were designed to incorporate the latest labour-saving household conveniences: electric ceiling lights, built-in kitchen cupboards and benches, a gas or electric water heater, a purpose-built bathroom with hot and cold running water, and often a flushing water closet. As water and sewerage systems became available, the old outhouse or lean-to laundry and lavatory were brought inside, usually as part of the back porch — although most housewives still faced the drudgery of hand-washing clothes in a wood- or gas-fired copper. Electric 'hotpoints' allowed better-off bungalow dwellers to enjoy an ever-expanding array of shiny gadgets, the height of urban refinement in the 1920s: toasters, irons, sewing machines, radios, gramophones, vacuum cleaners, and even sophisticated 'laun-dry-ette' washing machines.[26]

The popularity of these mod cons was a reflection not only of the long-term decline of domestic service, but also the rapid development of electric power. In the early 1920s Minister of Public Works Coates established a regulative framework for electricity generation and reticulation, and initiated the construction of hydroelectric schemes. Dams at Mangahao in Horowhenua, Arapuni on the Waikato River and Waikaremoana were completed by 1929, and in 1931 total electricity generation was over 40 times greater than in 1911. Supply fostered demand, and slick advertising helped convince householders and farmers of the advantages of this cheap, clean power source for lighting, heating, cooking and powering farm equipment like milking sheds. Electricity consumption surged by 22 per cent per annum during the 1920s, and by the end of the decade most urban dwellers and farmers were switched on.[27]

Overseas fashion trends quickly made their mark in post-war New Zealand, as this photograph of Wellington dental school students in the mid 1920s illustrates. Younger women readily adopted the short bob or shingle cut as part of the boyish, 'flapper' look; hemlines, edging upwards since about 1910, now reached the uncharted territory of the knee. These easier-to-wear styles reflected the new employment and leisure opportunities for young women in the 1920s. Archives New Zealand, ABKI 667/1

Another vital ingredient in the growth of the suburbs was the expansion of the transport system, which enabled workers to live beyond walking distances from their place of employment. Motor cars rolled out in increasing numbers, but the primary people-mover was the electric tramway. Electric trams supplanted horse-drawn or steam-powered ones in the main centres in the 1900s, and new lines snaked outwards through the 1910s and 1920s. In Auckland, the last major extensions pushed the network out into the burgeoning bungalow suburbs of Westmere, Avondale, Mount Roskill and Point Chevalier in the early 1930s. Boosted by council-subsidised fares, annual passenger numbers peaked at 168 million in 1925, before competition from motor buses and private cars began to bite.[28] The ubiquitous rattling tram and the daily commute became a shared ritual for suburban men of all classes:

There's a plumber and a printer,
A natty office toff,
A porter and a policeman —
Who pops in on and off —
And a little pale bookkeeper
With a nasty kinda cough,
On the tram that takes us home
At 5 o'clock.[29]

Along with cheap mortgage money, the bungalow, electricity, trams and cars, the suburban push of the 1920s was fostered by new attitudes to the home. The traditional rural family economy, in which men, women and children laboured together on the land, was being displaced by the urban household of male breadwinners, housewives and schoolchildren. Less important as a productive unit, the family home was increasingly championed as a centre of domestic bliss. The concept was epitomised in the expression 'the happy home', widely used at the time in advertising, journalism, political rhetoric and literature. Political organisations and parties from the right-wing Welfare League to the Labour Party promoted the creation of 'happy and comfortable homes' as a definition of their ideal society. Women's pages in newspapers and magazines such as *New Zealand Home Magazine* and the *New Zealand Woman's Weekly* (established in 1932) combined practical domestic tips with sentimental articles about home life.

The home was also a preoccupation of much New Zealand fictional literature, including the work of Katherine Mansfield, Jane Mander and Robin Hyde. In Hyde's autobiographical novel *The Godwits Fly* (1938), the mother yearns to escape Wellington's Newtown, with its 'rows of grimy little streets and terraces', loafing drunks and drippy-nosed slum kids, for a better life 'amongst the respectable' in the outer suburbs — a dream eventually realised with the helping hand of State Advances.[30]

Viewed from the summit of Mount Albert, Auckland's suburban frontier sprawls into Sandringham and Three Kings in 1926. The popularity of low-density suburban housing was enhanced by the widespread belief that the crowded inner city was a breeding ground for vice, disease and crime. Politicians and town planners alike promoted spacious 'garden suburbs' as an essential environmental reform that would produce healthy, vigorous and patriotic citizens. Auckland City Libraries

The Rise and Fall of Happy Homes

Billed as a 'gorgeous ultra-modern love-drama', Cecil B De Mille's *Feet of Clay* (1924) was one of the hundreds of Hollywood movies that dominated New Zealand's screens in the interwar years.

The rapid development of the telephone network was another symbol of progress in the 1920s. Although telephones had been in New Zealand since the 1880s, in 1905 there were only 1.4 subscribers per 100 people; by 1930, this had leapt to over 10 per 100, the third highest rate in the world behind the United States and Canada (and almost twice that of Britain). This 1937 Post Office advertisement extols the advantages of the phone in isolated rural areas.

Ownership of private motor cars rocketed from 71,000 in 1925 to 155,000 in 1930; by 1939, despite the impact of the Depression, there were 215,000. But car ownership was not yet widespread among working people, who typically travelled to work on trams, bicycles or on foot. And many of those who did own cars used them mainly for special trips: the Sunday drive, family holidays or the weekly trip into town for farming families.

This cult of domesticity had an especially powerful impact on women, reinforcing Victorian beliefs that their rightful role was as homemaker, nurturer of children and dutiful companion to their husbands. These ideals were promoted by representatives of all classes and by most women's organisations. After the influx of women into paid work during the war years, in the 1920s the employment of married women in particular was actively discouraged. The state lent a helping hand, introducing compulsory domestic education for schoolgirls and banning the permanent employment of women in the public service. Factory legislation, Arbitration Court awards and unions kept women out of many occupations or ensured that they were paid less than men. While new opportunities were opening up for unmarried women in shops and offices, the overall participation of New Zealand women in paid employment between the wars was among the lowest in the Western world.

At the same time, both sexes joined voluntary organisations, which sprang up all over the country in the 1920s, especially sports clubs. Before the war, few women and children were involved in voluntary groups other than churches, and male membership was largely confined to the middle class. In the 1920s, participation was democratised. Working-class men flocked to join friendly societies and suburban or work-based sports teams and clubs, especially rugby and cricket. Children joined age-group sports teams and youth movements such as scouts and guides. Young women became involved in hockey, basketball (netball) and other sports, as well as community groups for mothers. Increased participation in sport was matched by a surge in spectator numbers. International rugby matches and Ranfurly Shield challenges drew enormous crowds in the 1920s and 1930s.

Evening Post Collection, Alexander Turnbull Library, G-529-½-EP

The increasing popularity of the automobile produced a mounting road toll, and car crashes soon topped that old colonial curse — drowning — as New Zealand's leading accidental killer. In 1929 there were 178 deaths in motor vehicle accidents, an increase of 158 per cent since 1921. This smash occurred on Wellington's Salamanca Road.

Gordon Burt Collection, Alexander Turnbull Library, F-117814-½

Jobs in big department stores like James Smith's in Wellington, Farmers in Auckland, and DIC and Ballantyne's in Christchurch were keenly sought after by young women in the 1920s. In 1905 James Smith's had almost no female workers; by 1925 it employed about 100 single and a handful of married women, on wages not much less than those paid to its 50 male workers. Customers were also largely women, mainly the better-off — as the herd of fur coats in this photograph suggests.

The real revolution in interwar leisure, however, flowed from the impact of new media, especially radio, cinema and the gramophone. Radio stations were established in the main centres and larger provincial towns in the early 1920s, and listening to the wireless, especially popular serial shows, became a favourite family activity. The impact of the medium was initially limited to the middle class — in 1925 there were only 4702 radio licences in the country, or one for every 64 dwellings. But radio ownership doubled in the next five years, and then rocketed in the 1930s, with 152,808 sets in 1935 and 345,682 in 1940 — by which time four out of every five households were tuning in.[31]

More popular than radio in the 1920s were the movies. First established around 1910, purpose-built cinemas sprouted everywhere between the wars. By the early 1930s there were almost 500, and the average New Zealander was going to the flicks once a fortnight. Some cinemas in the main centres, such as Dunedin's Empire De Luxe (later St James) and Auckland's Civic, were veritable 'Picture Palaces', as famous for their spectacular decor as their features. In the 1920s cinemagoers mainly saw Hollywood imports — 350 out of 400 features screened in 1927 were American-made — but official and voluntary efforts to promote British films were partially successful in the 1930s.[32] Most popular were comedies like Charlie Chaplin's *The Gold Rush* and Buster Keaton's *The General*, swashbuckling adventures like *The Mark of Zorro* and *Robin Hood*, biblical epics like *The Ten Commandments* and *Ben Hur* and, following the arrival of 'talkies' in New Zealand in

Rather than threatening the cosy family home, listening to the wireless became a favourite activity for Mum, Dad and the kids. Even the family dog assumes the 'His Master's Voice' pose in this 1930s advertisement for Atwater Kent radios.

1929, musicals like Al Jolson's *The Singing Fool* and the lavish *Gold Diggers of Broadway*. But this was also a fertile period for local film-making, with 22 features shot in New Zealand between 1914 and 1936 — including Rudall Hayward's *Rewi's Last Stand* (1925) and *The Bush Cinderella* (1928) — a remarkable output given that only another six would follow in the next 35 years.[33]

New technologies made new heroes. Many came from the fantasy world of Hollywood: comedians like Chaplin and Keaton, and heart-throbs like Rudolph Valentino, Greta Garbo, Gloria Swanson, Douglas Fairbanks and Mary Pickford. Traditional figures like the British royal family retained enormous respect and popularity, and tours by the Prince of Wales in 1920 and Duke and Duchess of York in 1927 drew vast crowds. A handful of heroes were New Zealanders, mostly sportspeople, their feats increasingly publicised by radio coverage and newsreel footage in theatres. Among them were the young Maori fullback George Nepia and other members of the All Blacks 'Invincibles' of 1924; boxer Tom Heeney, who challenged for the world heavyweight title in New York in 1928; wrestler Lofty Blomfield, with his famous 'octopus clamp'; and the aviatrix Jean Batten, whose long-distance solo flights and movie-star looks transfixed the nation in the mid 1930s. Perhaps most famous of all was a big red racehorse from Timaru called Phar Lap, who lived fast, died young and left a beautiful corpse, which was lovingly dismembered after his death in California in 1932; his heart went to Canberra, his hide to Melbourne and his skeleton to New Zealand's Dominion Museum.

But despite the new rhythms and recreations, New Zealand remained a powerfully conformist and conservative society.

Happy home ideals reflected a persistent strain of Victorian puritanism and emphasised the virtues of thrift, sobriety and self-discipline. Although churchgoing was in decline, religion remained an influential force in society, and the whole country closed down on Sundays. In 1930, Thames clergymen complained about children using swings on the Sabbath; two years later a Chinese market gardener was fined £5 for picking peas on a Sunday.[34] Even radio stations fell silent on Sunday mornings for a moment of hushed prayer. When novelist Jane Mander returned in 1932 after two decades overseas, she was dismayed by New Zealand's conformity and puritanism, its 'barren wastes of Victorian Philistinism'.[35] Indeed, the 1920s and 1930s are commonly seen as the 'most artistically barren' decades in New Zealand's history,[36] a cultural wasteland that forced its leading literary and artistic lights — notably Mansfield and the painter Frances Hodgkins — to play the expatriate game.

In the 1920s moralists and public officials warned of a new serpent slithering into this puritan paradise — a cultural invasion of American comics, 'pulp fiction' novels, dance music, radio serials and gangster movies. Even American cars were suspect. In the short term at least, happy homes ideology and a combination of voluntary and formal censorship helped safeguard British cultural dominance and moral harmony. Radio regulations in the 1920s prohibited any content of 'a controversial nature', and 1930s government policy drove popular American serials off air in favour of more morally sound British and Australian ones. The state also happily wielded the censor's knife, banning or snipping 262 films in 1932. The same year, a department store manager was fined £5 for selling the comic *Gangster Stories*, an 'indecent publication'

A crowd welcomes Charles Kingsford Smith's *Southern Cross* at Wigram after his flight across the Tasman, 11 September 1928. The interwar years were a golden age of aviation, when the daredevil ocean crossings of Charles Lindbergh, Amy Johnson, the New Zealander Jean Batten and others captured the public's imagination.

PICTURE PALACE

The great cathedral of New Zealand cinema was Auckland's Civic Theatre, a building of unparalleled splendour with seating for 3500. The Civic was the brainchild of entrepreneur Thomas O'Brien, who built a movie empire in Auckland's inner suburbs in the 1920s and brought the 'atmospheric' cinema — in which coloured lights played across the ceiling to recreate the night sky — to New Zealand when he opened Dunedin's Moorish-styled Empire De Luxe in 1928. He then persuaded a group of wealthy Auckland businessmen to build a massive atmospheric cinema in Queen Street and sweet-talked a cool £180,000 out of the Bank of New Zealand. But like many Queen City speculations, all was not what it seemed. The BNZ loan and soaring construction costs raised eyebrows in Parliament, and the final price tag ballooned to over £200,000. The Civic opened amid great fanfare in December 1929, but the onset of the Depression contributed to disappointing attendances — as did O'Brien's stubborn insistence on showing British rather than the more popular American films. When his company went belly-up in 1932 O'Brien skipped town, later turning up in Australia, where he died in straitened circumstances in 1948. Despite the decline in cinema attendance in the television age, and the threat of the wrecker's ball in the 1980s, the Civic survives as one of Auckland's best-loved buildings.[37]

The Civic's sumptuous interior wowed moviegoers with a riot of Indian, Moorish and Persian imagery, including elephants and panthers, swaying palm trees, a twinkling starscape and female ushers in billowing pantaloons. Robin Morrison

judged likely 'to deprave and corrupt' impressionable young minds. But American invaders were not the only victims of the moral guardians. Ettie Rout's book *Safe Marriage*, which promoted contraception as a safeguard against venereal disease, was banned in 1923; so was Jean Devanny's 1926 novel *The Butcher Shop*, a tale of domestic confinement and extramarital love that the Censorship Appeal Board denounced as 'sordid, unwholesome and unclean'.[38]

The emphasis on family, motherhood and Empire was also dubiously expressed through the eugenics movement. Although subsequently tainted beyond repair by its association with Nazi racial ideology, in the 1920s eugenics was the height of respectability, a modern science blending the latest research in genetics, biology and demography. Eugenicists exploited anxiety over falling birth rates — the average number of live births per married Pakeha woman plummeted from 6.5 in 1880 to 2.4 in 1923 — and age-old fears of the 'yellow peril' to argue that the white race had to 'populate or perish'. Contraception and abortion were condemned as instruments of race suicide, except of course in the case of those deemed 'unfit' — criminals, 'imbeciles', alcoholics, epileptics, prostitutes and other undesirables — who must be prevented from breeding to avoid racial degeneration. Under the Child Welfare Act 1925 increasing numbers of orphans and juvenile 'delinquents' were committed to public institutions. The same year, a Committee of Inquiry into Mental Defectives and Sexual Offenders, which included Plunket guru Sir Truby King, concluded that the 'unchecked multiplication of the feeble-minded and epileptic' was causing 'the serious deterioration of the race'. Among its (unsuccessful) recommendations were the compulsory segregation and sterilisation of 'incurable' mental defectives.[39]

Nevertheless, the order, stability and optimism of 1920s New Zealand were significant achievements, especially given the troubles that had plagued society in the decade before 1922. Much of the credit for this belongs to the consensus-building policies of the Massey and Coates governments. But how pervasive and robust was this consensus? Certainly, only a minority of workers, especially among the unskilled, had escaped inner-city slums for the new garden suburbs. Many who did soon discovered that heavy mortgages and low-paid white-collar jobs offered the illusion rather than the reality of promotion to the middle class. Maori had been excluded from the suburban push altogether, while new employment and leisure opportunities for women threatened the long-term stability of the happy home ideal. A more immediate menace loomed, however. The Depression of the 1930s would not only shatter the consensus but completely overshadow the interwar period, obscuring the fact that the 1920s was a generally positive decade that paved the way for the stable years following the Second World War.

Alexander Turnbull Library, PAColl-5936-10

George Nepia, the incomparable fullback in the 'Invincible' 1924 All Blacks, in action for New Zealand Maori against Wellington at Athletic Park in 1935. During the 1920s rugby union became firmly established as the dominant sport among both Pakeha and Maori males.

Alexander Turnbull Library, Eph-E-TOURISM-ca 1932-01

Château Tongariro

NATIONAL PARK
BEST REACHED BY RAIL
NORTH ISLAND MAIN TRUNK TRAINS TO NATIONAL PARK STATION, THENCE 11 MILES BY CONNECTING MOTORS

NEW ZEALAND

Modelled on North American and European alpine resorts, the majestic Chateau Hotel in Tongariro National Park was the jewel in the crown of New Zealand's promising tourism industry. But like Auckland's Civic Theatre, it had the misfortune to open just as the slump loomed in late 1929, and within 15 months it was threatened with closure. A reluctant Tourist Department eventually assumed ownership from entrepreneur Rodolph Wigley, but only cost-cutting and clever marketing would keep the Chateau afloat through the Depression years.

Let them eat grass: politicians and the slump

As in other Western societies the Great Depression of the early 1930s had a profound impact on New Zealanders. The unprecedented suffering and insecurity it unleashed swept away the new consensus of the 1920s, and fractured the popular image of New Zealand as 'God's own country', a prosperous, progressive 'land of plenty'. Although the Depression's impact was uneven, the shock and sombreness of these years were inescapable; despair stalked the land like an 'unwanted stranger, a grey and ghostly visitor to the house'.[40] Its psychological imprint would remain long after the economy had recovered, instilling in New Zealanders a sense of anxiety and obsession with security that would last for half a century.

Despite what most people believed at the time, the main causes of the slump were outside anyone's control, including the government. New Zealand's heavy dependence on overseas trade made it especially vulnerable to a sharp fall in prices for its meat, wool and dairy exports. In 1929–30 the dominion's income from exports fell by about 20 per cent compared to the previous year. That was bad enough, but no one could have imagined that it would plunge by another 20 per cent next year — virtually halving overseas earnings in two years.[41] As farmers stopped spending, a shockwave rippled through the economy. The severity of the slump was deepened by a credit squeeze as banks restricted funds, and by a collapse of domestic consumer and investment confidence, which was in turn exacerbated by the government's deflationary policies.

When the dying Joseph Ward resigned as prime minister in May 1930, the task of dealing with the slump fell to his successor, 'Honest George' Forbes. His response was highly orthodox; the government would retrench its way out of trouble by taking a razor blade to state expenditure. It shaved public servants' wages and salaries by 10 per cent, axed the 1931

A familiar scene outside Parliament in the early 1930s, as Prime Minister George Forbes struggles to pacify an angry demonstration. A small farmer from North Canterbury, Forbes had no answers to the overwhelming problems of the slump. Keith Sinclair described him, perhaps a little unfairly, as our 'most improbable Premier'.

census, and even trimmed expenditure on meat for cats living in government offices.[42] The Arbitration Court followed suit, imposing a 10 per cent across-the-board reduction in award wages. But things only got worse. As the crisis deepened, business interests demanded still deeper cuts and a government of national unity based on wartime precedent. United and Reform formed a coalition in September 1931, ending two decades of three-party politics and leaving Labour as the only serious opposition. Despite its easy victory in the general election in December that year, the Coalition was doomed to be the most unpopular government in New Zealand history.

Although the floundering Forbes remained Prime Minister, Coates (Minister of Public Works, Transport and Unemployment) became the driving force of the Coalition. He added the finance portfolio in 1933 when William Downie Stewart, a wheelchair-bound Dunedin lawyer and intellectual, resigned in protest at Cabinet's decision to devalue the New Zealand pound. Unlike the deeply conservative Downie

Stewart, Coates was prepared to prescribe increasingly unconventional medicine to cure the country's economic ills, including devaluation and the establishment of a Reserve Bank in 1934. To counteract the narrowness of Treasury advice, he recruited a group of university-educated economists — RM Campbell, WB Sutch and Horace Belshaw — who became known as the 'brains trust'. But the Coalition was deeply divided, and Coates's high profile made him the butt of poisonous rumours, including stories that he had hit the bottle and, most famously, that he had advised the unemployed to eat grass.

Following the recommendations of a National Expenditure Commission (made up mostly of businessmen), in 1932 the Coalition sharpened its knife for a fresh round of cuts. Programmes that only a few years before had been trumpeted as symbols of enlightened humanitarianism were now under threat. The government reduced old-age, widows' and war veterans' pensions and family allowances, raised the school

Evening Post Collection, Alexander Turnbull Library, G-8646-½-EP

Demeaning make-work schemes, bleak relief camps and hungry, solemn queues became potent symbols of the failure of the Coalition government's unemployment relief policies, and what many saw as its cruel indifference to human suffering.

SHAKE, RATTLE AND ROLL

As if the country's economic woes were not enough, on the morning of 3 February 1931 Hawke's Bay was smacked by an earthquake measuring 7.8 on the Richter scale. Within two and a half minutes much of central Napier and Hastings had been flattened. Fires swept through the wreckage destroying much of what was left. Dozens of buildings collapsed, including Napier's cathedral, public library and nurses' home, where eight nurses died. Huge slips crashed down from Bluff Hill. The sea rushed out of Ahuriri Lagoon, uplifting 3600 ha of dry land. The shock brought down buildings in Wairoa and Gisborne, and toppled chimneys from Taupo to Wellington. Sailors from HMS *Veronica* were on hand to provide immediate help, but 30,000 homeless huddled in tents for weeks while hundreds of aftershocks frayed their nerves. With an official death toll of 256, the Hawke's Bay quake remains the worst disaster on New Zealand soil, topped only by the 1979 air crash in Antarctica.[43]

PTW Ashcroft Collection, Alexander Turnbull Library, F-139885-½

Napier rose stylishly from the ashes of 1931, celebrating its resurrection with a carnival in 1933.

R Hipkins, Hawke's Bay Museum

Not everyone was obsessed with unemployment and protest during the Depression. 'Humour amongst hard-pressed unemployed' ranks low down the news in this 1933 press billboard, behind the wedding of an actress, the spiteful 'bodyline' cricket series between Australia and England, and the spectacle of female surfers. Movies, sport, horse racing and other pastimes provided a welcome distraction from everyday troubles.

entry age from five to six, shut two teachers' training colleges, deferred the intake of new dental nurse trainees, and virtually stopped advancing mortgages to home buyers and farmers. It canned compulsory military training and slashed the defence budget by a third. Public servants' pay packets were lightened by another 10 per cent, the 1934 election was postponed for a year and the Department of Immigration was abolished. So many employees of the Railways and Public Works departments were laid off that the latter all but disappeared. The Coalition also acceded to business demands to abolish the requirement for compulsory arbitration, effectively creating a system of free wage-bargaining — a green light for employers to exploit high unemployment and cut wages.[44] At the same time, the government legislated for a compulsory 20 per cent reduction in interest rates and rents, a remarkably radical intervention for the time.

To those in the firing line, the state's assault on their jobs, wages and pensions was inexplicable and malicious. But there was some method to the Coalition's madness. The bottom line was the need to service New Zealand's mountain of overseas debt, the legacy of decades of voracious borrowing by successive administrations. Fearing that hard-pressed British creditors would call in their loans, the Coalition resolved to pay back all loans reaching maturity, which could only be achieved through massive savings in more vulnerable areas of state spending. The only alternative was defaulting on the loans, a drastic step that would have destroyed the creditworthiness of the New Zealand government and made future borrowing impossible except at exorbitant interest rates. Measured on its own terms, the Coalition's policy was successful — the government was able to stop overseas borrowing in 1932 and begin repaying debt in 1935. But the brakes were kept on far too long. As the recovery gathered pace after 1933 Coates could, and should, have spent more to ease the misery.

The Coalition also directly relieved farmers. Plunging incomes and heavy debt burdens reduced farmers' net incomes to zero and even negative levels in three successive years from 1930. Coates feared that if droves of farmers quit the land or if farms were sold up by creditors the farming sector would collapse, taking the whole economy down with it. As well as lowering farmers' costs by deflating the prices they paid for goods and services, in early 1933 the Coalition devalued the New Zealand pound against the pound sterling in an attempt to increase the value of farmers' overseas earnings in New Zealand currency. Coates went to extraordinary lengths to keep farmers on the land. The government established mortgage adjustment commissions with sweeping powers to defer farmers' interest payments, reduce interest rates and write off a portion of the debt owed — without the consent

of the mortgagee or the payment of compensation. Although the contribution of the Coalition's policies is hard to measure, the farming sector survived the slump in reasonably good shape. The volume of farm production rose by 24 per cent between 1928–29 and 1933–34 and, contrary to legend, there were on average under 100 farm bankruptcies a year during the Depression — fewer than during the 1920s.[45]

Coates and the Coalition were far less successful, however, in their efforts to relieve unemployed workers. In the depths of the Depression an estimated 12–15 per cent of the workforce was registered as unemployed — although if non-registered, women and Maori jobless are taken into account the true figure may have been twice as high.[46] The government's response was constrained by budget pressures and the prevailing belief in the principle of no pay without work. Responsibility for relief lay with an Unemployment Board, established in 1930 by the previous United government, which was partly funded by a special annual levy on all wage-earners over 20. Initially at least, entitlement to relief work was highly discriminatory; women, males under 20, adult males who failed to pay the levy, and men who could not work because of old age, illness or disability received nothing. Moreover, relief pay rates were a passport to poverty, providing about half the wage of a labourer lucky enough to keep his job.

The Unemployment Board relied on local government to soak up most of the unemployed through a programme called Scheme 5. But as the ranks of unemployed swelled, Scheme 5 relief had to be rationed — men worked for three weeks at a time and were then 'stood down' for a week without pay. When local bodies ran short of useful construction projects like roads, parks and playing fields, they resorted to demoralising make-work tasks: 'You had men shifting this heap of clay and rubbish from one spot to another and back again,' recalled one man. 'You can't conceive of a worse form of degradation.'[47]

In late 1931, with Scheme 5 bursting at the seams, the government introduced its most notorious solution, Scheme 6A: rural labour camps where unmarried men were put to work cutting roads, draining swamps and clearing scrub. The camps were managed by the Public Works Department, itself reeling from cutbacks, and conditions were often appalling, especially in winter. At one camp, a newspaper reported that 'the floors of the tents are earthen, uncovered by boarding . . . The men bathe in drains, wash in a horse trough.'[48] Although relatively few relief workers — less than 10 per cent — were sent to these 'slave camps', their muddy desolation came to symbolise Coalition failure and indifference. To be fair, after the riots in April and May 1932 the government tried to alleviate some of the worst aspects of its relief regime, abolishing the Scheme 5 stand-down in some parts of the country, introducing a dole for those unfit for relief work, and gradually improving conditions in Public Works camps. But it was too little, too late.

Adding to despair was the collapse of the state's long-standing vehicle of poor relief, charitable aid. Mostly funded by central government, local Charitable Aid boards assisted the 'deserving' poor largely through 'outdoor relief' — grocery and rent vouchers, fuel and clothing — after rigorous case-by-case assessment, backed up by intrusive inspections. Prior to the slump the number of recipients ranged from 4000 to 6000 a year; in 1932, it soared to almost 94,000. Long, sullen queues snaked along the streets outside board offices. Private charity provided some assistance. Mayor's or mayoress's relief funds sprouted in many towns, while churches and other charitable institutions doled out soup, warm beds, and hand-me-down clothes and boots. But demand outstripped supply. In just six months in 1932, the Auckland City Mission supplied 37,000 free beds and 102,080 meals.[49]

Home-ownership dreams fell by the wayside as the government retrenched, the flood of State Advances mortgage money dried to a trickle. Although the Coalition's mortgage relief measures helped protect farmers, they offered little to urban mortgagors unable to service their loans because of wage cuts or unemployment. Thousands of homes were sold up by their creditors, and the proportion of household heads who owned their own homes slid from 60 per cent in 1926 to 50 per cent in 1936. Massey's land of happy homes threatened to unravel before his successors' eyes.

The Depression's impact was severe, but also highly uneven. Overall retail prices fell by 21 per cent between 1929 and 1933, so that despite wage cuts the real incomes of most of those who kept their jobs probably remained stable or even increased.[50] Consumption of some luxury items like ice-cream, brandy and cigars plunged, but sales of electricity and household appliances continued to rise. In general, the cities were harder hit than the country, with Auckland worse off than Dunedin. Although 8000 Maori registered as unemployed and undertook relief work — mirimiri rori, or 'stroking the road', as they called it — most were left to fend for themselves in their predominantly rural communities.[51] Unemployed women also suffered from official indifference: 975 were registered in 1933, but their true numbers may have reached 7000; the government was loath to provide meaningful relief, while local unemployment committees persisted in training young women for domestic service jobs that simply did not exist.[52] Hardest hit of all were those who had been most at risk of unemployment and poverty before the slump: older men and unskilled workers. How did ordinary New Zealanders, especially the unskilled who bore the brunt of the Depression, respond to the crisis, and to the Coalition government's assault on their living standards?

Making do

New Zealanders responded in many different ways, from rhetoric to riots, petty capitalism to petty crime. Some turned their despair inwards, reflected in a leap in the suicide rate, but drinking declined and interpersonal violence was surprisingly rare. Some responded with acts of generosity and self-sacrifice, others with greed and selfishness. Most tightened their belts, scrimped and saved, and hoped that better times were just around the corner. These were not victims, but resourceful, resilient people making do as best they could. Families shacked up to save money, farmers sent surplus food to urban relatives, and benevolent butchers and grocers gave away scraps of meat, stale bread and broken biscuits. Young couples put off marrying, raising the average age of marriage to its highest-ever level, and there was probably an upsurge in abortions. Many urban New Zealanders, still close to their frontier and rural roots, eked out uncertain incomes through 'do-it-yourself' activities — growing their own food in a backyard vegie patch, keeping poultry, hunting and fishing, and making their own clothes — or through 'penny capitalism': taking in boarders, collecting and selling bottles, sacks and firewood, or making jams, cordials and furniture polish and hawking them door to door.

The most startling response was a brief spasm of rioting that swept through the four main centres in 1932. Trouble first flickered in Dunedin in January, when a crowd of unemployed besieged a grocery store, and again in April, when protesters stoned the mayor's relief depot and tried to storm the hospital board's offices before being scattered by police batons.[53] By far the most violent disturbance was Auckland's famous Queen Street riot of 14 April. Post and Telegraph Association members marching to a Town Hall meeting were joined by a large crowd of relief workers, swelling numbers to perhaps 15,000. Angry at being turned away from the overflowing hall, some demonstrators scuffled with the police barring the entrance. When a leader of the unemployed, Jim Edwards, rose to speak — apparently to urge calm — he was struck down by a policeman. The crowd erupted and surged down Queen Street. Armed with fence palings and stones from a mini golf-course in Civic Square, they smashed hundreds of shop windows and looted jewellery, liquor, clothing and tobacco. One chemist shop was cleaned out of contraceptives; a man was seen staggering off with a grandfather clock on his back, and the department store Milne and Choyce 'grieved over the spoliation of their very costly wax "dummies"'.[54]

Reinforced by armed sailors and volunteers, the police wrested back control of the central city several hours later. Hundreds were injured, including several policemen, and 35 looters arrested. The forces of order were bolstered the next day by 98

Waikato Territorials and 1000 'special' constables, but violence flared again that night. As crowds massed in Karangahape Road, scuffles broke out and more windows were smashed; the night ended with another 35 arrests and 50 injuries.

The next riots were associated with a strike by Christchurch tramwaymen against pay cuts. On 6 May, union pickets, backed by relief workers, engaged in a 'running battle' with 400 specials enrolled to protect strikebreaking ('scab') tram-drivers. The next day a 'howling crowd' of 2000 besieged the Christchurch Rugby Club team, whose players included specials, outside Lancaster Park, until police batons cleared an escape route. Wellington got in on the act a few days later, on 10 May, when up to 7000 relief workers converged on Parliament demanding to see Coates. When a delegation returned empty-handed, 30 to 40 men careened up Lambton Quay smashing 200 shop windows. The next morning, 2000 unemployed unable to get into a meeting at Trades Hall spilled into an empty section in nearby Cuba Street. When police hauled down a speaker, the crowd hurled bricks and stones; foot and mounted constables waded in with batons, leaving dozens battered and bleeding.[55]

A state of siege settled on the main centres, with specials guarding the streets, all outdoor meetings banned and shop windows boarded up for weeks, but there was no more major trouble. The government reacted decisively for once by rushing through Parliament a Public Safety Conservation Act that gave the authorities draconian powers to maintain order, and undoubtedly helped deter further disturbances. In all, 185 offenders were prosecuted for their part in the riots; several — including Jim Edwards, who had eluded police for six weeks before giving himself up — received prison sentences of up to two years with hard labour. Many other agitators were arrested in the following years for 'inciting disorder', breaching by-laws against public speaking and distributing 'seditious' literature.

As the Christchurch tramway dispute showed, the trade union movement also attempted to resist Depression cutbacks through direct action. An open trade union conference in

The worst outbreak of rioting during the 'angry Autumn' of 1932 was Auckland's Queen Street riot of 14 April 1932, which produced a level of violence not seen on New Zealand streets since the 1913 strike. Here, onlookers survey the wreckage on the corner of Swanson and Queen Streets.

March and April 1932 promised a campaign of petitions, demonstrations and meetings, but it too fell victim to the government's post-riot clampdown. In late 1932 and early 1933 the major industrial unions — freezing workers, waterside workers, coal-miners and seamen — each struck in protest at wage cuts, but with a huge pool of jobless to draw on, employers easily prevailed. Thereafter, union militancy fell away rapidly. Union membership tumbled from 104,000 in 1928 to 72,000 in 1933, and the number of working days lost to strikes fell from 108,000 in 1932 to a record low of 10,000 in 1934.[56] Relief workers, organised by the communist-influenced Unemployed Workers' Movement (UWM) and other competing groups, also protested noisily and even went on strike, with predictable results. In Auckland the UWM's Anti-Eviction Committee barricaded tenants' houses against bailiffs, and a hunger march from Gisborne to Wellington in early 1934 attracted widespread attention but few concessions from the government.

The Depression also spurred the growth of political movements of right, left and centre. The tiny Communist Party attracted new recruits and police harassment in equal measure;

its members worked to alleviate distress and co-ordinated UWM resistance, but it never threatened the authority of the state or the Labour Party's popularity. New forces on the right included the New Zealand Legion, a movement for moral and civic regeneration established in early 1933 and led by the Wellington surgeon Dr Robert Campbell Begg, and the Democrat Party, founded by businessman William Goodfellow in 1934. These appealed to professional and middle-class New Zealanders alienated by Coates's 'socialistic' legislation. Each grew quickly — by the end of 1933 the Legion boasted 20,000 members, while the Democrats won eight per cent of the vote (but no seats) in the 1935 election. But they both faded away almost as fast.

A more influential middle-class protest movement was the Social Credit Political League, established in 1934. The League was not a political party but a crusading pressure group devoted to the monetary theories of its Canadian sage, Major CH Douglas. It blamed the slump on a lack of purchasing power and offered a painless panacea — the creation of cheap credit by the state. The credit credo spread rapidly, especially among dairy farmers and small-town businessmen in the North Island,

Evening Post Collection, Alexander Turnbull Library, G-84197-½

A land of plenty? Unemployed men in Newtown, Wellington, display a cornucopia of vegetables grown as part of a local-body scheme that provided allotments to those who lacked their own patch of soil. Gardening was strongly promoted as a self-help solution for those struggling on relief; there were even competitions to find the unemployed 'gardener of the year'.

and was enormously influential within the Labour Party, many of whose leading figures — including Frank Langstone, John A Lee and Rex Mason — were convinced 'credit men'.

Personal responses to the slump were just as varied. One reaction, hopeless despair, was graphically expressed in the suicide rate, which leapt from 1.2 per 10,000 people in the mid 1920s to 1.65 in 1932, before declining again until the 1960s. 'Plenty of fellows went over Grafton Bridge, and plenty of girls, too.'[57] In contrast to modern trends, those most prone to suicide were middle-aged and elderly men. On the other hand, people did not rush to drown their sorrows in drink — no doubt partly because they could not afford it. Per capita consumption of alcohol actually fell to one of its lowest recorded levels (although homebrew and moonshine undoubtedly helped fill the gap), and the conviction rate for drunkenness halved between 1929 and 1934.[58]

Nor did New Zealanders lash out at one another. Whereas convictions for crimes against property (including theft, fraud and wilful damage) jumped by 40 per cent between 1929 and 1932, 'offences against the person' dropped by a quarter.[59] The homicide rate, which had been falling since the 1850s, continued to decline through the slump years, reaching one of its lowest points in New Zealand's history. Despite intense personal pressures, most kept their emotions in check; where frustration boiled over, it was often turned inwards, as the rise in suicide suggests. Although New Zealand's powerful culture of puritanism and self-repression has been much criticised, and justly so, it did at least help restrain violence in desperate times.

Although New Zealand women led the world in gaining the right to vote in 1893, they were barred from sitting in Parliament until 1919. Three women contested seats at that year's election, but it was another 14 years before the first woman MP, Labour's Elizabeth McCombs, was elected. In 1933 McCombs won a by-election in Lyttelton following the death of the sitting MP, her husband James. Her parliamentary career was cut short by her own death two years later.
Advisory Committee of Women's Affairs Collection, Alexander Turnbull Library, F-150372-½

What is remarkable about New Zealand during the Great Depression is not that it produced so much disorder and violence, but so little. The authority of the state was never threatened. There were none of the mass street battles between extremists of right and left that afflicted many other democracies. The weakness of the trade unions and Communist Party, and the Coalition government's crackdown, helps explain the modest level of working-class unrest. Equally, in contrast to most other states — even Australia with its New Guard — no fascist movement emerged. Unlike other countries, where fascism fed off the collapse of the property-owning classes and race hatred, New Zealand's middle classes were bent but not broken; home-ownership rates fell, but the vast majority survived. And racial minorities could hardly be blamed for the slump: Maori were a rural people with no economic power; Chinese, Indians and Jews were too few.

Perhaps most important of all, popular discontent and anger were channelled into conventional forms by the rise of the Labour Party. Led since Holland's death in 1933 by Michael Joseph Savage — a benign figure who 'smelt of the church bazaar and not at all of the barricades'[60] — and riding the popular wave of credit reform, Labour seemed to offer a practical and painless way of rebuilding the land of happy homes. On election night in 1935, huge crowds roared as the results boards turned crimson with Labour triumphs:

They had been without fires, many of them, for months; without the warmth of security for years. They had been shuffled and cut like a pack of greasy cards . . . one for the relief camps, one for hoeing weeds, one for the small farm with the mortgage that looked so large. Their lit faces were all glowing, the roughish pink putting the floodlights to shame.

Labour leaders who tried to speak were drowned out by the din, 'but it didn't matter. Nothing mattered, except that the crowd-body, a long time cold and scared in its softest spots, courage, pride and respectability, should suddenly be awake and singing again.'[61]

Chapter 10

The Centennial Exhibition, held in Wellington in 1939–40, was a triumphant blast of modern — and modernist — New Zealand. The buildings, designed by Edmund Anscombe and depicted here on the cover of a souvenir booklet, were expansive, soaring structures that embodied New Zealand's sense of national progress.

SPECIAL SOUVEN

NEW ZEALAND CENTENNIA

Hope and Heroes
1935–1949

A golden dawn seemed to break over the country in 1935 when Labour came to power. Gone was the gloom of the Depression, and once more the world watched as New Zealand charged ahead with economic and social reform. The entire place hummed as Labour poured money into everything it could find — welfare, health, education, the arts, broadcasting, Maori affairs, and farming. Government took centre stage in this new welfare state.

All good things had to end. The Second World War shattered the lives and dreams of many New Zealanders. After the war, Labour could not work its magic again, as the hard times of war lingered long after the last blasts of the conflict. Its reforming fire flickered, then died in 1949. But by then, Labour had changed New Zealand irrevocably, and in ways that would be felt for another half-century and more.

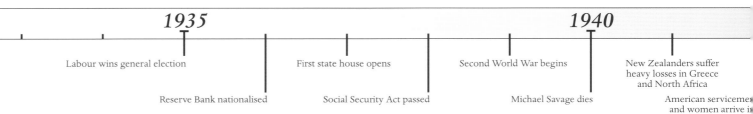

1935   1940

Labour wins general election   First state house opens   Second World War begins   New Zealanders suffer heavy losses in Greece and North Africa

Reserve Bank nationalised   Social Security Act passed   Michael Savage dies   American servicemen and women arrive in New Zealand

Building Jerusalem down under

The impact of the 1935 election was bigger than *Ben Hur*. This 'civil war of a democracy' trounced an old order and ushered in a new era that would influence New Zealand life and politics for decades to come.[1] Over 90 per cent of the electorate voted, with Labour taking 46 per cent of the vote, and 53 of the 76 European seats in Parliament. A swathe of rural and country-town electorates flipped to Labour. The defeated opposition skulked away to re-form itself in 1936 as the National Party.

New Zealanders wanted a new, more humane way of responding to need and crisis. Labour would deliver, immediately and over time. Wellington Central Labour MP Peter Fraser declared, 'Let us go forward with fitting humility . . . to our great task of building "Jerusalem in our most green and pleasant land".'[2] The biblical analogy was apt. Many in the Labour government, including leader Michael Joseph Savage, saw themselves as erecting the kingdom of God on earth.

Labour's first Cabinet was unlike any other that had sat in Parliament. These were men sharply moulded by their experiences and long wait to gain power — most were in their 50s. Four had been imprisoned for opposing conscription in the First World War; several were former union organisers and members of the Red Feds; five were Australian migrants; some had grown up in poverty.

Labour had campaigned on a ticket of a greater role for government. In social policy, it would pick up where the Liberals had left off and expand from there. Labour promised a security blanket to the sick, the aged, the needy and the unemployed. No longer would New Zealanders have to suffer the chill of charity when misfortune came their way. Labour hoped to elude misfortune altogether, but if it did come, then there would be a generous safety net to catch everyone.

This was 'sentimental socialism': 'the Red Flag had been furled, replaced by . . . [a] cornucopia of pink candy floss.'[3] 'Decent' and 'decency' were favoured adjectives of these

A baker's dozen: the first Labour Cabinet. Standing (left to right): William Lee Martin, Paddy Webb, Frank Langstone, Rex Mason, Frederick Jones, Dan Sullivan, Tim Armstrong. Seated: Bill Parry, Peter Fraser, Michael Joseph Savage, Walter Nash, Mark Fagan, Bob Semple.

1945

1950

Canberra Pact

'Native' dropped from official usage

Referendum restores peacetime
compulsory military training

Peace; universal family
benefit introduced

Labour men, particularly Finance Minister Walter Nash. The nationalisation Labour had advocated through the previous decade, and which seemed to frighten voters, was gone. Some of its socialist objectives remained, notably the redistribution of wealth. This would be done through measures that improved the lot of all: guaranteed prices for farm products that would raise farmers' standards of living; and a statutory minimum wage to lift the hopes of workers.

Once the election was over, the sense of relief and anticipation was almost palpable. Broadcaster Colin Scrimgeour recalls: 'What a load lifted from hundreds of thousands of hearts the night Labour was elected. It was as if the sun was to shine for the first time in years.'[4] Crowds cheered Savage on his arrival in Wellington from Auckland on 2 December. They lined the streets, perched on the tops of cars and trucks, and clambered on awnings and roofs to catch a glimpse of the diminutive new leader with the big heart and shy smile. Savage had become New Zealand's 'secular saint'.[5]

Within hours of the swearing-in of Cabinet, a Christmas bonus for the unemployed and those on charitable aid was announced. No matter that the previous administration had promised this. Labour went further, topping up the Coalition's pledge with another £100,000 to be spread among all receiving sustenance or on the lower scales of relief pay. Maori relief levels were boosted to match Pakeha, and all relief workers received seven days of paid holidays. The tidy nest-egg that the Coalition had tended since 1932 — including £38 million in overseas funds — came in handy here. The declining number of unemployed and rising export prices allowed the new regime to be generous; the ground had been prepared for these white knights of Labour who charged to the rescue.

Labour started as it meant to continue. It reversed Depression cuts and closures: pension rates were restored, teacher training colleges were reopened, five-year-olds returned to school, and relief rates of pay were raised. In Wellington, Parliament's public gallery was the place to go. Whoever would have thought that debates on the Finance Bill, the Reserve Bank Amendment Bill, the Primary Products Marketing Bill, and more besides, would have been crowd pullers?

By the end of 1936, Labour had implemented many of its promises. The Pensions Amendment Act increased the rate of pensions for the nation's elderly, and gave assistance to deserted wives. One woman wrote to Savage: 'There are many like myself, refined, sensitive, and too proud to accept charity of any kind, so you can understand why tears of joy came to my eyes when I realised what this pension would mean to me.'[6]

A state-owned broadcasting system came into effect. Morning listeners could tune in to the half-hour of handy hints, recipes and general chat hosted by Maud Ruby Basham, known as 'Aunt Daisy'; in the afternoons, they could hear Parliament broadcast. The Finance Act restored all award rates and eliminated the cuts to public service and other salaries. Labour restored power to the Arbitration Court, required it to introduce a 40-hour week for workers wherever possible, and instituted a basic wage sufficient for a man, his wife and three children. Legislation governing factories, and shops and offices, also laid down maximum hours of 40 or 44 a week, along with minimum levels of pay. True to its collectivist origins, Labour saw power in the unions. Membership became compulsory for workers covered by an Arbitration Court award or industrial agreement. Union members soared from 81,000 in 1935 to 249,000 in 1938.[7]

Santa Claus arrived early in 1935, dispensing bonuses and higher rates of pay to those at the bottom of the social heap. Labour's measures were synonymous with Christmas goodies for more years yet. Its mid-year budgets — such as this one in 1941— were dubbed 'Christmas in July'.

HIGH AND SPRY

The Labour government was not the only thing to blitz New Zealand's record books in 1936. In the midst of the Nazi theatre of the Berlin Olympics, Oxford-based medical student Jack Lovelock sprinted to victory in the 1500 metres, breaking the world record. It was New Zealand's first Olympic gold medal in athletics. Later in the year, Jean Batten continued her series of solo flights from one side of the world to the other. She flew her Percival Gull 6 from England to New Zealand, arriving at the Mangere aerodrome 11 days and 45 minutes after take-off. Six thousand fellow New Zealanders turned out to greet her. She zipped down to Wellington a few days later, where one of her admirers — who knows why — presented her with a tiny black kitten that certainly added the finishing touch to her chic fur-lined fly-girl image.

Lovelock Collection, Alexander Turnbull Library, MSX-2261-062

Most significantly for more long-term financial planning, the government bought out the Reserve Bank's private shareholding to enable it to control currency, credit and the funds earned by exports. Why 'so delicate a set of machinery' should be run by private bankers and not the men elected to govern the country was a mystery to the Labour government.[8]

Implementing guaranteed prices for farm products was more difficult. It took five months of negotiations within Cabinet, with economists, and with industry before things were settled. The Primary Products Marketing Act regulated prices only for dairy products, but it was a significant step, and one that materially improved the lot of dairy farmers; their first payout was much higher than expected.

Archives New Zealand, AALF 6112

Great views, shame about the access; state housing designed by a man without a pram. Orakei, 1950s.

Social policies lay at the core of Labour's platform. Its aim was to meet the needs — articulated now as rights — of every New Zealander to a decent home, an adequate income, sufficient respite in times of want, and security in old age. The state would provide for everyone's needs, from the cradle to the grave. There would be no stigma of charity. 'I want to see humanity secure against poverty, secure in illness or old age . . . We are here to serve, not merely to talk,' Savage said.[9]

The government moved early to provide public housing for rent, not necessarily because of the state of accommodation — 55,000 houses in need of urgent repair, 27,000 better off demolished — but because housing had a central role to play in Labour's notions of decency.[10] Good housing was the basis for strong families, in turn the foundation of a stable society. After urging from John A Lee, parliamentary under-secretary with special responsibility for housing, the Reserve Bank released £5 million in credit for the construction of state houses, to be paid back at rates of interest that were low by anyone's standards — 1.25 per cent.

By the end of 1936 Labour had established a Housing Construction Branch in the State Advances Corporation, led by Arthur Tyndall, with Gordon Wilson as the chief architect. The branch commissioned designs for the houses that the government demanded be built to a high standard and with the best of materials. Each house was to embody modern, comfortable New Zealand: power points in all the rooms, concrete paths to house and clothesline, copper piping, meat safe, tiled roof wherever possible.

Alexander Turnbull Library, C-10529-½

Labour had initially wanted the state to build the houses, but there was neither the expertise nor the capacity for this in the public sector. Instead, the government tendered out to the private sector the contracts for the construction of houses. The first contract was let in December 1936 for the Wellington suburb of Miramar. With much fanfare, Savage opened the first state house there the following year.

This house — still standing at 12 Fife Lane — was built by Fletcher Construction. James Fletcher had talked to Labour soon after the 1935 election to discuss ways of building high-quality houses quickly and cheaply enough that their rental would remain in reach of the average New Zealander. When the first contracts were let, Fletchers won them. The company was the only one capable of building the number of houses that Labour wanted — 400 in Miramar and the Hutt Valley — but Fletcher's special relationship with the government brought criticism from smaller players in the building trade. Future tenders were modified so that smaller companies could compete, but Fletchers still gained about half up until late 1938, almost bankrupting itself in the process.

Communities of state houses were also part of Labour's vision. Graced with open spaces and the full range of recreational, educational and other facilities, these suburbs would embody the sense of community. The Hutt Valley suburb of Naenae, with its town centre designed by (but not built to the plans of) Austrian modernist architect Ernst Plischke from the early 1940s, was the most complete example of such 'designer communities'.

Lee was a man with a mission. He aimed to have 5000 houses built a year. It was an impossible goal, and a combination of rising costs, an overextended building industry and insufficient local supplies of materials stymied it. Still, two and a half years after the first contracts were let, there were 3500 new state houses; it was, even the National Party was rumoured to have noted, one of the 'outstanding successes of the Labour Party's programme'.[11]

Social security was Labour's big achievement. It came into force on 1 April 1939, hardly an auspicious date for legislation that led the world. Funded through a tax levy on all earners, it gave an old-age pension to everyone — male and female, Maori and Pakeha — at age 60, and universal, free health care for maternity services and visits to the doctor. It seemed beautifully simple: a single piece of legislation, and no messy or complex funding system. It took some getting, and the government lost a few battles in the process.

Labour became government with barely an inkling of the cost of comprehensiveness. Once the sums were done, the annual bill for universalism came to £30 million. There was barely this in the kitty. Between 1936 and mid 1938, politicians and public servants threw around ideas and figures. They did what so many others would later do, and went on a retreat, in this instance to Lake Waikaremoana, for a period of thinking in the summer of 1937–38. Economists were in their element; would there be a special tax, higher income tax, means-testing, targeting, or an interest-bearing accumulated fund? Would it cost £10 million, £18 million, or £30 million? Could the country afford it now, and in the future?

283

THE SHOT-GUN WEDDING

The introduction of free medical care had Labour fighting with the medical profession, whose members almost seemed to favour Mammon over Hippocrates. The doctor–patient relationship — always useful to trot out — could not weather the GP receiving a payment from the government; there was nothing so personal, some medics argued, 'as the personal relationship between the patient and the doctor, and in that relationship the patient is the doctor's first consideration before everything, and it was the patient's payment to the doctor that ensured that'. [12] Money was probably not the key issue though, for doctors were more worried about the loss to their status through being 'socialised' by the government.

The British Medical Association, the medical 'union', led the doctor lobby. Its spokesperson was the uncompromising James Jamieson, who hated Savage and all that Labour stood for. The association balked at a system where their fees would be set and paid by government. It formulated an alternative that divided the population into four income groups, with only the poorest receiving free health care.

Labour rejected that, and negotiations with the medical profession broke down. The Social Security legislation enshrined free health care for all, but it was introduced piecemeal, with the medical profession screaming and kicking all the way. Doctors were slow to take up the contracts for maternity benefits; by mid 1939, only 30 out of 900 had accepted. Savage finally laid down the law. He told a seething Jamieson: 'Let us be quite frank. We are not going to do any more waiting. We have done too much waiting already . . . If the medical profession show some desire to meet us that makes all the difference. To be quite frank I do not see much evidence of that.' He gave doctors 48 hours to fall into line. Characteristically, they took two weeks, but agreed to accept a fixed payment for maternity services with only obstetric specialists charging higher fees. A similar process dogged the general practitioner benefit, but it was eventually implemented in 1941. [13]

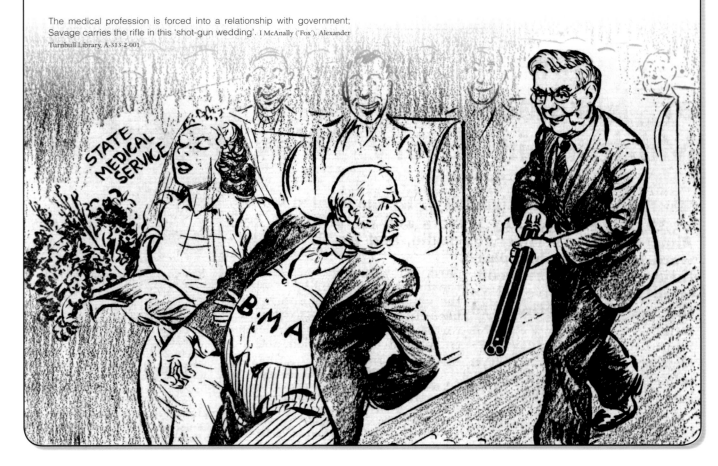

The medical profession is forced into a relationship with government; Savage carries the rifle in this 'shot-gun wedding'. I McAnally ('Fox'), Alexander Turnbull Library, A-313-2-001

We all know the answer to that last question; but for Labour, the principle of universalism was paramount. Its final solution for the elderly was a compromise. The weekly pension of 30 shillings would go to those earning less than £1 a week; there would also be a universal superannuation of £10 a year at age 65, regardless of income.[14]

Social security helped Labour to a resounding victory over the National Party, led by Adam Hamilton, in 1938. This time, Labour was elected on its achievements. People heeded Labour's call not to 'put the clock back', and with its allies it got more than 55 per cent of the vote. Labour publicity played up the rising standard of living. Wages were higher than before, there were jobs aplenty, savings were healthy, and there were more consumer items to purchase.

New Zealand's international credit was at rock bottom though. The £38 million of overseas funds in 1935 declined as the government went on a spending spree. It became £28.6 million in April 1938, then £8 million in November. To sustain any type of growth, as well as to meet the cost of its social security scheme, Labour quickly needed to secure money and markets.

John Pascoe Collection, Alexander Turnbull Library, F-32-¼

Schoolkids gulping down free milk is one of the abiding images of Labour's measures aimed at boosting the health and welfare of young New Zealanders. Department of Health officers had been suggesting such a scheme for nearly a decade. Backed by Education and Health Minister Peter Fraser, the scheme began in 1937 and was available to over 80 per cent of schoolchildren by 1940.

Cover art by WW Stewart

With more money in their pockets, people started travelling again, for work and pleasure. Now they had a choice: the main trunk rail, or its air equivalent that began operation between Auckland and Dunedin in 1936, with stops in Palmerston North, Blenheim and Christchurch. For those wanting to go further afield, PanAm began long-haul flights between Auckland and San Francisco in 1937, with stops at Honolulu and Pago Pago.

Alexander Turnbull Library, Eph-E-AVIATION-1930s-01

NEW ZEALAND ON PARADE

Five years in the planning, the centennial celebrations were a testament to material progress, a benevolent state and the glories of God's own — and they went ahead despite the clouds of war. The 1940 centennial displayed New Zealand to itself, and to whomever else watched.

The key message was pride in the nation and its peoples. The government commissioned booklets and projects to chart the national story. 'Pioneers' received special note in official publications and events. History tended to be Pakeha; Maori appeared as largely incidental, in roles of helpers, forerunners and hazards to Europeans.[15] Not surprisingly, some Maori disapproved of the entire enterprise. But most people joined in the celebrations. Communities staged shows and pageants that depicted the past and extolled the present.

The centrepiece was a six-month-long fair in Wellington, touted as the greatest exhibition ever held in the Southern Hemisphere. Over 2.5 million people visited. The 22-ha site bulged with attractions. All manner of companies advertised their wares. The 'Government Court' promoted the varied achievements of the state. There were technological wonders galore — the Health Department's walking–talking robot Dr Well-and-strong was a huge hit.

'Playland' was the drawcard, and New Zealanders lapped it up. This was Disneyworld down under, 1940s style. The Ghost Train thrilled, the Crazy House amused, and the Scoota Boats and Dodgem Track upped the adrenalin. The Cyclone Roller-coaster gave its shrieking passengers the ride of their lives. Less tasteful, but as popular, was the Odditorium with its selection of 'freaks'.[16]

M Matthews, Archives New Zealand, TO1, 28/27/4

In April 1939 Nash scurried off to London, that seemingly inexhaustible source of credit. Normally the money men welcomed petitioners from across the sea. This time, the Brits were barely civil. Labour had already instituted import controls, although they were hardly effective; in the first half of 1939, imports were greater than for the same period in 1938. Those controls, and the cost of the social security scheme, were stumbling blocks. It was an unhappy time, and Nash found himself being lectured on the excesses of Labour social policy and central control of the Reserve Bank.

The British finally drove a tough bargain. New Zealand would get £16 million, to be repaid over five years at annual instalments of £3.2 million paid into a special account made up directly from export receipts. Labour believed the terms to be almost intolerable; but although Savage huffed and puffed, there was little he or Nash could do but sign on the dotted line in mid July. At least the terms had been amended from annual repayments of £4 million made monthly. New Zealand's dire economic situation was only saved by the war.

Meanwhile, Labour squabbled with itself, and personal clashes took over from political differences. The worst were between Savage and Lee. Despite his image, Savage was not always of a kindly disposition. He could hurl his toys from the sandpit if things did not swing his way; his biographer describes him as 'undeniably sensitive, possibly over-sensitive, to criticism'.[17] Lee was stubborn, and had an enormous sense of his own importance and an unmatched turn of invective. He had no time for Nash, whom he referred to as 'never more than a travelling salesman who became a travelling political salesman', and he loathed Savage, 'the god with clay feet'.[18]

Things worsened after the 1938 election. Lee's *Psychopathology in Politics* (1939) was a thinly veiled attack that called into question Savage's mental state; at the time, Savage was dying of cancer and was frequently in pain. The Labour Party's 1940 Easter conference was the final showdown. Savage's report — read out by Fraser because Savage was too ill to attend — recorded how his life had been made a living hell by 'venom and lying innuendo'. Lee was expelled from the party and went on to form the Democratic Labour Party. Two days later Savage was dead, and Peter Fraser took over the reins; the country went into mourning for Savage.[19]

Fighting fascism

By then New Zealand was at war again. For the second time in 25 years it took up arms against Germany, now in the grip of Adolf Hitler's brutal and aggressive dictatorship. Successive crises had beset Europe in the late 1930s, culminating in Hitler's invasion of Poland. In doing so he had crossed a line drawn in the sand by the belatedly resolved British and French governments. Their declarations of war confronted New Zealand with its most momentous decision — for Britain no longer spoke for the dominions. Savage and his Cabinet had hesitated not at all. New Zealand backdated its declaration of war to the exact moment of Britain's — 3 September 1939.[20]

Savage's words were stirring stuff: 'Where she goes, we go; where she stands, we stand.'[21] New Zealanders would fight alongside their kith and kin, but self-interest buttressed emotion. As in 1914, trade and defence realities made standing aside unthinkable. New Zealand still relied on the imperial link for both prosperity and security. The increasingly uncertain shield of British seapower was all that lay between New Zealand and the menace of militaristic Japan. Only a few pacifists and communists demurred from the decision to fight.

New Zealand mobilised thousands of men and women. More than 200,000 New Zealanders served in the Second World War. First in action were 500 New Zealanders already serving in the Royal Air Force, most on short-service commissions, plus some who had made their careers in the force after the previous war. From 1941 many more of their countrymen would join them. Because the RAF's needs went far beyond the ability of Britain alone to provide, Commonwealth leaders at a meeting in Ottawa in late 1939 hammered out a scheme to make up the shortfall. A steady stream of airmen from the dominions was soon passing through training schools in Canada to enter the RAF. More than 7000 of them were New Zealanders.[22]

The navy was quick to take the fight to the enemy. Even before the declaration of war the cruiser *Achilles* joined a British squadron off South America. On 13 December 1939 she and two other cruisers defeated the German pocket battleship *Admiral Graf Spee*, later scuttled, a startling victory that boosted morale throughout the Commonwealth. For *Achilles'* sister ship, *Leander*, no such opportunities for glory existed; she endured the monotony and frustration of patrolling in New Zealand waters. Like the air force, the navy sent men to serve with the Royal Navy, and they were spread around the fleet. More than 700 flew with the Fleet Air Arm.

An infantry division was New Zealand's main contribution to the war effort. Commanded by British Army officer Bernard Freyberg, the First World War VC winner who had spent his youth in New Zealand, it went overseas in three echelons in 1940. Unlike the situation in 1914, Second New Zealand Expeditionary Force (2NZEF) was not handed over lock, stock and barrel to the British for use as an integral part of the imperial forces. But asserting the national interest within a British military hierarchy was problematical. For this reason Freyberg took with him a 'charter' carefully delineating his role and duties as commander of a small national force.

The first and third echelons landed in a familiar stamping ground, Egypt, which was under threat from large Italian forces in Libya. The second echelon joined them in 1941 via the United Kingdom, where it had formed part of the forces that prepared to repel invasion during the Battle of Britain. Among the troops in Britain in 1940 were hundreds of Maori. With the exception of those from Taranaki and the Waikato, where a sense of injustice remained strong, Maori had responded enthusiastically to Apirana Ngata's call to form a Maori unit in 2NZEF. This would not be a non-combatant unit, as in 1914. This time Maori would fight shoulder to shoulder with Pakeha in 28 (Maori) Battalion. After training, the Maori soldiers had embarked with the second echelon in May 1940.[23]

Once all its units had reached Egypt in early 1941, 2 NZ Division stood ready to enter the fray. But it would do so not, as expected, against the 'Eyties' in Egypt's Western Desert — the Italian invader had been driven far to the west by a tiny British force — but against the 'Jerries' in Greece; New Zealanders had to cross the Mediterranean for their baptism of fire. Deployed with an Australian division to bolster the beleaguered Greeks, they quickly found themselves beating a hasty retreat when German forces invaded.

Successfully evacuated from mainland Greece by the navy, most of the New Zealand division ended up in Crete. But the

Air Force Museum

Keith Park, who was one of New Zealand's greatest and most decorated military commanders, served in the RAF. He took a lead role in the Battle of Britian and later commanded the British air forces in the Middle East.

Evening Post Collection, Alexander Turnbull Library, G-123832-½

More than 10,000 Kiwis served with the RAF, on the ground and in the air; here five strike a pose before a Supermarine Spitfire fighter plane in England. The RAF had seven 'New Zealand' squadrons, but New Zealanders were part of other squadrons, too. Their jobs were very high risk. Casualties were heavy, especially in the bombers.

troops' respite proved brief. On 20 May 1941 German airborne troops landed. The Luftwaffe bombed and strafed the defenders mercilessly. Even so, the invaders faced disaster. They had incurred huge casualties in the assault without seizing any of the vital airfields needed for their reinforcement. But for a series of mistakes by New Zealand commanders at the key point, Maleme aerodrome, they might have suffered a humiliating defeat. Once the Germans had control of Maleme and began flying in troops and equipment, defeat for the Allied forces on Crete was inevitable. Yet another evacuation followed. Back in Egypt the troops licked their wounds. A thousand of their number had fallen and several thousand more were heading for prisoner-of-war camps in Germany. The fact that they had given the German paratroopers a bloody nose provided little consolation.[24]

The division re-entered the fray in Libya in November 1941 against an Italian foe stiffened by German forces under Erwin Rommel, who effectively controlled the Axis effort. Fighting with great purpose, the New Zealanders helped relieve Tobruk. But Rommel's forces overran a brigade HQ and several battalions. Another 2000 men went into the bag as POWs. Operation Crusader would prove to be 2NZEF's costliest battle of the war.

After recuperating in Syria in early 1942, the division rushed back to the Western Desert to help halt a new enemy thrust — and narrowly escaped disaster at Minqar Qa'im. Only a dramatic breakout saved the division when Rommel's forces surrounded it. Rommel's onrush towards Cairo was halted at El Alamein, but an attempt to push him back in early July led to new disasters for Freyberg's men. Several thousand more POWs began the long, and dangerous, journey to camps in northern Italy.[25]

In October 1942, the tide finally turned. Under a new commander, Sir Bernard Montgomery, the Commonwealth forces of the 8th Army launched an offensive at El Alamein that soon forced Rommel into retreat. In both the battle and the pursuit, the New Zealanders were in the vanguard. They had by then become a highly experienced and proficient unit. They advanced right across North Africa, trying in a series of left hooks to encircle the enemy forces. By the time the Axis forces in North Africa surrendered on 13 May 1943, they had reached Enfidaville in Tunisia.

Meanwhile, war had come to the Pacific. On 7 December 1941 Japan struck. While carrier-borne air forces savaged the US battlefleet at Pearl Harbor and attacked targets elsewhere in the western Pacific, Japanese forces landed in Malaya. Pushing down the peninsula, they threatened the vital British base at Singapore. The destruction of the British fleet off the Malayan coast by bombers based in Indo-China came as a shock to New Zealanders. So too, in February 1942, did the fall of Singapore, which had long been presented as impregnable.[26] They watched in horror as Japanese forces flooded into the Dutch East Indies (now Indonesia) and reached as far south as the Solomons. Japanese planes bombed Darwin.

Although New Zealanders feared imminent invasion, Japan never seriously contemplated this. Its attempt to cut off Australia and New Zealand failed when US forces won the Battle of the Coral Sea in May 1942. But more important was the showdown that occurred at Midway a month later. The decisive American victory there left Japan on the back foot. It effectively ended the possibility of an invasion of New Zealand — unless the Japanese could turn the tables in a future naval battle. The scale of American naval building made this unlikely.

Captain Charles Upham (centre) is congratulated by his platoon sergeant on the award of the first of his two Victoria Crosses.

Expatriate New Zealand cartoonist David Low was famed for his biting commentary on the pre-war failure of the Western democracies to respond to the challenge posed by fascism. This December 1941 cartoon was prompted by Japan's surprise attack on the US fleet at Pearl Harbor while negotiations were still under way.

Shortly after the Midway battle a friendly invasion of New Zealand began. American troops landed in mid June 1942, and their presence in New Zealand and the islands to the north provided further reassurance to the public. It was soon obvious that New Zealand, far from facing an enemy invader, would instead become a support base for an American counter-offensive in the Solomon Islands. United States Marines sailed from New Zealand to land on Guadalcanal in August 1942.

Uniquely in the Second World War, the Solomons campaign involved all three New Zealand services. New Zealand's two cruisers operated in the dangerous Solomon seas. Both suffered serious damage that forced their withdrawal. In January 1943 a recently arrived minesweeping flotilla made its mark when two of its minesweepers destroyed a Japanese submarine. Two motor launch flotillas took part in the latter stages of the campaign. But RNZAF fighter and bomber squadrons provided the main New Zealand effort in the islands. They helped sweep the Japanese from the skies and later bombed enemy positions in New Britain and Bougainville. By early 1945, 8000 RNZAF personnel were deployed.

New Zealand also took a limited part in ground operations. Some served in Fijian units that joined the fray. New Zealand also sent an under-strength infantry division commanded by Harold Barrowclough, which moved forward to the battle zone by way of New Caledonia. Three times the troops took on the Japanese in island jungles and performed with credit. On Mono Island in October 1943, they made the first opposed amphibious landing by New Zealand troops since Gallipoli.

But in 1944, 3 NZ Division fell victim to manpower shortages at home. Sending food to Britain was an important part of New Zealand's war effort, and commitments to maintaining economic production left New Zealand unable to sustain two divisions in the field. In line with the overall Allied strategy of beating Hitler first, the government ordered the withdrawal and ultimately the disbandment of 3 NZ Division.[27]

This left 2 NZ Division to fight on against the Germans. Landing in Italy late in 1943, it spent the next 18 months taking part in the slow Allied slog up the peninsula, battling against

The New Zealanders experienced one of their most dramatic moments in North Africa at Minqar Qa'im in 1942. Surrounded by Axis forces, the division was forced to make a desperate breakout attempt. A violent night attack opened a gap for a large segment of the division; most of the rest used the distraction to find another way out. The division was saved, but the price was staggering: nearly 1000 casualties. P McIntyre, Archives New Zealand, NCWA 20, AAAC898

HERE OR THERE?

Should New Zealand have brought home 2 NZ Division from the Mediterranean to bolster home defences after Japan entered the war? Among historians, this Pacific versus Mediterranean focus is the most hotly debated issue surrounding New Zealand's war effort. Pointing to the return of two of the three Australian divisions in the Mediterranean in early 1942, some scholars have condemned the New Zealand government's failure to recall 2 NZ Division, citing this as evidence of a lack of independence — a willingness to put British interests ahead of New Zealand's. They contrast Prime Minister Peter Fraser's approach with that of his Australian counterpart, John Curtin, who, they claim, had to fight to assert Australian interests.

But their argument rests on a myth. Australia's redeployment was made as a result of a British request, not an Australian demand (even if recriminations between London and Canberra would subsequently occur during the redeployment itself). Later, after the victory at El Alamein,

Curtin did insist on the return of the third division. To his intense anger New Zealand failed to follow suit and pull back 2 NZ Division. But by then the home defence danger had passed.

The issue of 2 NZ Division's continued involvement in the Mediterranean theatre was revisited a number of times, but the division did not return home until after the end of the war against Germany. New Zealand's decision to leave 2 NZ Division in the Mediterranean theatre stemmed partly from recognition that it could be used more effectively there than in the South Pacific. It was fully in accord with Allied strategic priorities — the war against Germany, considered more important to the overall Allied cause, took precedence over that with Japan — and it was also in line with American wishes. It reflected, too, New Zealand's own war strategy of using its resources where they could best achieve its objective — a victorious Commonwealth would ensure New Zealand's physical and economic security.[28]

For Australians and New Zealanders, the threat from Japan only assumed menacing proportions early in 1942. Encouraging Kiwis to keep up the war effort at home in case of a Japanese attack relied on old stereotypes of the 'yellow peril'. The focus of the New Zealand fighting remained in the Mediterranean.

German forces that had taken over when Italy surrendered in early September 1943. Rugged terrain and harsh weather conditions made campaigning a miserable experience in winter, and this was compounded by the strength of enemy resistance. The New Zealanders crossed the Sangro River on the east coast only to find the German strongpoint of Orsogna an insuperable barrier to their advance. Morale sagged as mud and cold added to the troops' miseries. But they would soon face an even worse ordeal.

Pulled out of the line in January 1944 and deployed across the mountainous spine to the west coast, 2 NZ Division took part in attacks on Cassino in February and March. Despite the controversial destruction of the monastery overlooking the shattered town, the New Zealanders could make no progress against their old adversaries, the paratroopers. They experienced the horrors of close quarters fighting among the rubble.

More than a thousand were killed or wounded in this mini-Stalingrad, but Cassino remained firmly in German hands when they pulled out in March.

After recovering, the division was committed to the advance north to the Senio River. The New Zealanders helped capture Florence. But German resistance remained strong, and the New Zealanders on the Senio grimly confronted the prospect of another Italian winter. Not until April 1945 did the enemy begin to falter. A massive Allied offensive, helped by growing partisan operations, finally broke the line. The New Zealanders raced north to reach Trieste on 2 May, the day German forces in Italy capitulated. There followed an uneasy but eventually resolved confrontation with Tito's partisans, who had also entered the town.[29]

By this time, Italy had long since become a sideshow. In June 1944 the Western Allies had opened the Second Front in Normandy. Many New Zealanders serving in British navy and air units took part in this, the

greatest amphibious operation to that date. They harried enemy forces pulling back across France, while the men of Bomber and Coastal Commands continued their long campaign against enemy industry and shipping. All these efforts contributed to the wearing down of German strength as the Russian juggernaut bore down on Berlin from the east. On 8 May 1945, shortly after Hitler had killed himself in his bunker, Germany gave in.

One enemy remained — in the Pacific. New Zealand warships joined the British Pacific Fleet that, with massive American naval forces, carried the fight to Japanese waters. Japan teetered as US forces seized islands from which devastating air attacks could be mounted on it. Savage fighting on Iwo Jima and Okinawa aroused fears that an invasion of the home islands would be a bloody affair.

New Zealand, with some trepidation, was preparing to provide a force to take part in these operations when an unexpected development brought a quick and brutal end to the war. On 6 August 1945 the Americans dropped an atomic bomb on Hiroshima. Three days later, Nagasaki suffered the same fate. Japan capitulated. New Zealand troops would later become part of the occupation forces, and would remain in Japan until 1948.

Practice Landing, New Caledonia by Russell Clark, official war artist with the New Zealanders in the Pacific. Like that of other official war artists such as Peter McIntyre, Clark's task was to capture something of the heroic aspects of Kiwi soldiers. R Clark, Archives New Zealand, AAAC-898

The home front

While New Zealand men and women took the fight to the enemy on distant battlefields, those at home adjusted to wartime realities. The home front demanded a national effort on an unprecedented scale. For the first time, New Zealanders faced the prospect of their own country becoming a battleground. Liberties were severely curtailed.[30]

War had unified the community. Maintaining the consensus in favour of full participation in the Commonwealth war effort became a major concern of the government. New Zealand's distance from immediate danger seemed to demand firm action to ensure that dissent remained limited and did not lead to a fall-off in support. Freedom of speech became an early victim.

Few contested the state's need to control the dissemination of information that could be helpful to the enemy. 'Loose lips sink ships', the posters proclaimed. But control of the media extended to embrace opinion as well. Anything likely to undermine public support for the war effort was fair game for the censor, JT Paul. A fine line existed, however, between opposing the war effort and criticising the government. And censorship at times crossed that line and entered the political realm.

The government clamped down on any who persisted in publicly expressing their opposition to New Zealand involvement in the war. Outspoken pacifists were first to bear the brunt. The most conspicuous, First World War veteran

War savings schemes were pushed hard. They not only helped finance New Zealand's war effort, but soaked up excess cash in the economy and helped keep a lid on inflation.

Being 'manpowered' into a food dehydration plant in Pukekohe for the duration was probably not every woman's dream. It is no wonder that these women were smiling, though. Some of the alternatives — munition factories or freezing works — were hardly ideal jobs.

Ormond Burton, found himself behind bars when he persisted in publicly denouncing involvement in the war. Others joined him. Communists, too, came under fire. The only political grouping to oppose involvement, they took their lead from Stalin's collusion with the Nazis in the rape of Poland. When Soviet troops invaded Finland, their stocks fell even further. Few regretted the government's suppression of the communist organ *People's Voice*. Not until Hitler turned on Russia in June 1941 did the communists finally change course to fully support the war effort.

Once conscription began in 1940 another group faced the discomfort of public disapproval — men who refused, on grounds of conscience, to accept the dismissal of their appeals against being called up. Conscientious objection presented a ticklish issue for a Cabinet that comprised several men, including Fraser, who had gone to prison for opposing conscription in the previous war. Although widening the scope for men to stand aside, they did not hesitate to come down heavily on the 800 who refused even to undertake non-combatant duties. The public, hostile towards 'shirkers', fully approved the imprisonment of these men in work camps for the duration. Their POW-like existence would continue even into peacetime.

The 'Conchies' were not the only prisoners of the war in New Zealand. Fears of a 'Fifth Column' had led to early action against German citizens when the war began. Internment on Somes Island in Wellington Harbour awaited those deemed a threat. A number of Italians and Japanese would later join them.

Supplying food to Britain was again an important facet of New Zealand's war effort. No time had been wasted in reinstituting arrangements for the bulk-purchase of New Zealand's exports. Once more the dominion found itself in the fortunate position of being able to make a major contribution to the war effort merely by doing what it already did well, and this was to its advantage economically. But maintaining production demanded labour. The problem of balancing the needs of farming with those of the military services would plague the government throughout the war.

The importance of production increased with the onset of war in the Pacific in 1941. With the influx of American troops to the South Pacific, a new demand developed. Supplying them with food put a strain on an economy already stretched in meeting commitments to Britain. One answer was to further mechanise New Zealand's farming operations. Seven thousand tractors, obtained from the United States under Lend Lease, boosted production.

The need for greater self-sufficiency also increased as imports dried up and wartime needs emerged. Local production expanded, notably shipbuilding. Yards were soon turning out a range of small craft for British and later American as well as local use. Factories were built or converted to produce munitions and other war-related items.

Controlling the economy was imperative. The government acted to stem inflationary pressures, which were bound to cause disruptive strikes, by imposing a wage and price clamp in late 1942. By this time it had already ensured that labour needs were met. From the outset certain industries had been deemed essential and men were prevented from leaving them to join the forces. With the mobilisation of the home defence forces in early 1942, more drastic action kept farms and factories running as men headed off to camp. 'Manpowering', as the direction of labour became known — a word derived from the title of the regulations — began in early 1942. All men of military age, and an increasing cohort of women, were henceforth employed at the whim of the state.

The war's impact on women was immense. As in the previous conflict, they watched their loved ones set off overseas and awaited the outcome with trepidation. Once again they feared the arrival of the telegram boy with a message of disaster that dashed their hopes of a reunion. Many sought relief from their sense of helplessness by throwing themselves into efforts 'to help the boys'. Like their mothers before them, they knitted, baked and packed parcels. Others moved into the workforce to fill positions vacated by men entering the services.[31]

Under the umbrella of the Maori War Effort Organisation (MWEO), the Maori contribution to New Zealand's war effort was both military and civilian. They sustained a volunteer infantry battalion overseas, manned another in the Territorial Force at home, and entered the workforce in large numbers. Here Maori members of the Women's Auxiliary Army Corps wave to departing soldiers on Wellington wharf.
John Pascoe Collection, Alexander Turnbull Library, F-1636-¼

Other women yearned for more direct involvement in the war effort. The lure of a uniform proved strong. Many hastened to join the Women's War Service Auxiliary when it was formed in 1940. The creation of women's services in the following year opened new opportunities. Thousands of women became Waacs, Waafs or Wrens, as the women's services became known from their acronyms. They did clerical work, drove vehicles, operated searchlights or worked in intelligence organisations.

For those at home, life became increasingly constricted. Shortages tested homemakers, who struggled to keep food on the table as rationing kicked in with a vengeance in 1942. With sugar and butter in short supply, they had to use ingenuity in their baking. Clothing shortages demanded much revamping of existing garments. Luxury items like silk stockings disappeared. Everywhere people just had to make do.

Women in the workforce, especially those who were married, could struggle. Child care was difficult, and many endured awkward situations living with in-laws. Conditions at work could be trying. Although at first only 20- and 21-year-olds were 'manpowered', the regulations were steadily extended to encompass all those between the ages of 18 and 40, single or married (unless with children under 16).

Despite women's greater involvement in the economy, their participation was still regarded as temporary. Once the troops came home, married women in particular were expected to vacate their positions and resume their roles as homemakers. But their war effort gave women new confidence. The war ensured that some 50,000 who would not normally have entered the paid workforce did so.

Maori also gained new confidence from their contribution to the war effort. To sustain their battalion overseas they created a Maori War Effort Organisation (MWEO) based on tribal committees. A Maori initiative to meet a Maori problem, the organisation ensured a flow of volunteers to keep the battalion's ranks filled.

Although they could not be forced to serve in the forces, Maori could be 'manpowered'. The needs of employment encouraged a major demographic shift into the towns and cities. Often for the first time, Pakeha and Maori were in close contact, at work or in hostels. This development had long-term significance — at war's end Maori did not return to their tribal areas, as many expected. The urban Maori was here to stay.

Many faced discrimination, especially over accommodation, which the MWEO sought to alleviate. Prejudices were sometimes enhanced by the sub-standard lodgings many Maori endured.

THE AMERICAN INVASION

Between June 1942 and late 1944 more than 80,000 American troops were deployed to New Zealand, along with several times that number who transited through it in ships or aircraft. Americans — women and men — flavoured wartime life in Auckland and Wellington, the cities nearest their main camps.

As they came to train or recuperate, the 'Yanks' had a big impact on social life here. They brought new habits — coffee-drinking, for example — and attitudes that provided a tonic to the staid wartime New Zealand. The different demeanour and manners of the American soldiers appealed to women. Society frowned on women entering into relationships with the Americans, but many did. For the men of 2NZEF, located far from home, much heartache followed as word percolated through of infidelities, real or imagined. The American presence would leave a legacy — more than a thousand war brides and more than a few children with American fathers.

Relations between Americans and New Zealanders were generally amicable, but there were occasional flare-ups. Men clashed, as during the infamous 'Battle of Manners Street' in April 1942, a series of brawls in the capital that apparently began with a confrontation between Americans and some New Zealand merchant seamen. Another battle royal in Auckland soon afterwards left some men in hospital.

As the Pacific fighting shifted north, the American presence wound down. Most US personnel had gone by the end of 1944.[32]

In March 1943, 500 Americans joined local Maori to watch the annual regatta at Ngaruawahia. Some American servicemen used to the hard traditions of the American South found the comparatively friendly relations between Maori and Pakeha a surprise. Te Puea Herangi worked hard to build bridges between the two groups, and organised a series of visits to Turangawaewae from the end of 1942. John Pascoe Collection, Alexander Turnbull Library, F-352-¼

But on the whole the war experience had a positive effect on race relations. Shared danger and effort helped break down previous barriers. Pakeha widely admired the courage and commitment of 28 (Maori) Battalion, for whom the war was, as Ngata noted, the 'price of citizenship'.

For most on the home front the war's defining moment came in early 1942, when invasion seemed to loom. Men of the home defence forces poured into camp to prepare to meet the enemy. Behind them stood the 100,000-strong Home Guard, poorly armed older men and boys ready to do their bit. Others toiled over concrete mixers to throw up defences at likely landing beaches that bristled with pillboxes and gun emplacements. Roadblocks were constructed. In the cities, air-raid shelters reminded civilians that they too could be in the firing line.

New Zealanders faced the prospect of the horrors of modern warfare in their own backyard, and for women there was the additional fear of violation by rampaging enemy soldiers. But the enemy never came — and had never planned to do so. American

naval victories at Coral Sea and Midway soon allayed fears, as did the subsequent arrival of American troops in New Zealand.

By July 1942 the sense of crisis had faded. Men of the home defence forces were stood down and returned to their civilian jobs. People got on with their lives amid continuing restrictions and shortages. Rationing was extended. War-weariness grew as the conflict dragged on through 1943 and 1944, a feeling alleviated only by the sense that victory was now only a matter of time.

Everyone was relieved when German resistance faltered in early 1945. New Zealand received the news of war's end in Europe on 8 May, and people let their hair down immediately, despite the government trying to curb excitement until the official celebrations could begin. The war against Hitler had been their war — the one in which their country's forces were most directly engaged and the one that held the key to ultimate victory. Three months later it was all over. New Zealanders hit the streets again on 15 August to celebrate the defeat of Japan. Bad weather put a damper on the crowds' spirits in many centres, but most were buoyed by expectations of what peace would bring and by anticipation of the return of those serving overseas and the 8000 prisoners of war.

War's shadow

It ended with bangs and whimpers: 'six long, anxious, worrying, dangerous, tragic years' were over, Prime Minister Peter Fraser announced in August 1945.[33] It was time for the rebuilding to begin, but things were never going to be easy. Emotions ran high, but the great expectations of reunion were not always realised. Physical and emotional scars were raw. How could they be otherwise when 17,000 New Zealanders had returned injured in body and spirit, and over 11,500 did not return at all?

Scars on the heart and in the mind would never heal quickly. Many returned soldiers and their families fought the war for the rest of their lives. Maurice Costello, in 1994, said:

I think, God, I wish I could go to sleep and forget all this, that's what I feel. The trouble is you go to sleep and then suddenly wake up and you're dreaming the whole damn thing all over again . . . You can't really forget it. As soon as I start to think about that I start to tense up. Like I feel tensed up now. It's there. You're sort of living it all over again.[34]

The government wanted to avoid the same mistakes that had dogged the rehabilitation of soldiers after the First World War. A rehabilitation department had been established in 1943 to manage the process, and guidelines were developed — returned men were to move back into the positions they would

New Zealand Journal of Agriculture, 1944

The homecoming was romanticism idealised, and this was fully exploited in advertising everything from vitamin supplements to blankets. The reality could be very different. Families went through the often painful process of renewing relationships. Bedrooms were places of love and joy, but also disappointment and misery; more New Zealanders divorced in 1946 than in any previous year.

have obtained had they not gone to the war. The manufacturing sector had expanded during the conflict, providing work for many men on their return. Special training schemes came on line towards the end of the war. The building industry needed skilled workers, so carpentry centres trained up returned men. There were seven such centres in 1944, and 28 four years later.[35]

The aim was to match manpower and training with national needs. Houses were in woefully short supply, so in addition to training carpenters, centres provided men with skills in other aspects of the building trade: joinery, plumbing, bricklaying. Loans were available for men to purchase tools, or for buying and setting up a business. Money was there for purchasing farms as well, with priority given to men with farming experience. In all, the rehabilitation scheme was 'a major success story'.[36]

Most people just wanted things to get back to normal — and in a hurry. Normality generally meant Mum at home with the kids, and Dad out at paid work. Women's departure from the paid workforce, and especially that of married women, mirrored the winding-down of the conflict. At war's end, 'women voted with their feet', freeing up jobs for men to resume. In the end, the war did little to shift fundamental attitudes towards the gender order; it had been a 'waiting time' for women, a brief interruption of the transition from girlhood to womanhood.[37]

The government and employers nudged women back to the home, and not always gently. Just days after Japan's surrender, all married women were released from work direction on the condition that they assume home duties. In banks, women tellers found themselves demoted to ledger duties as a first step towards departure. Single women tended to remain in the paid workforce, but married women clocked out for good — or for some years at least, until a surfeit of jobs drew them back.

Settling down, starting a family, and re-establishing relationships were high priorities for the great majority of women and men. 'I was one of those persons who thought that I was lucky and blessed to get an ex-Maori Battalion husband, and just wanted to spoil him, do everything I could,' Harata Solomon said of her marriage to her soldier cousin, Matuwai, whom she wed in 1947.[38] Marriage and motherhood were careers, not alternatives to them, and most women were happy with this. Some felt the pressures to wed the man who had gone away a boy and whom they now scarcely knew. The expectations to help returned soldiers get back to a normal life were too much for others. Forty years after the war some women still remembered the pressure to marry ex-servicemen: 'It's all very well for them to say, "You have to rehabilitate them." Nobody has to do that at all. You don't have to.'[39]

A trip to a shop, like this one in Te Kaha, could be fraught for Maori families, for some shopkeepers controlled their benefit payments. Overzealous officials also regulated how Maori mothers could spend their family benefit. Out of bounds in Ruatoria were tobacco and cigarettes, soft drinks and biscuits, pickles and sauces, hardware, taxi fares, and food for hangi.

THE NEW LOOK

High glam hit dowdy old New Zealand in 1948 with the New Look, the sartorial brainchild of French designer Christian Dior. When he launched this chic style in war-weary Europe the year before, the fashionista pounced upon it. It was a pointed rejection of the drab, militaristic clothing that had dominated women's dress during the war era. The New Look was lush, and provocatively wasteful. Yards of material swathed the body; skirts swirled seductively around the calf; waists were cinched in, shoulders padded and hips puffed out.

New Zealand women were cautious about adopting the style initially. It seemed to demand a disciplining of the body in tight undergarments, or the need to diet and exercise obsessively. Even worse, it seemed old-fashioned. One young woman commented, 'My mother wore clothes like that 35 years ago.'[40]

But New Zealand women eventually embraced the new style and there were none of the street protests that greeted its introduction in Australia or Britain.[41] Eager for a little bit of luxury after the hardships of the war, and no doubt wanting to appear sexier, more alluring and more feminine, New Zealand women bought and stitched their own versions of the New Look in the late 1940s.

The New Look lent a swankiness to activities like beer drinking. But this advertisement was far from the realities of most pubs, where crowds of men jostled each other to get to the bar.

FOR HAPPY MEMORIES . . .

D B LAGER

with its

Refreshing and Fragrant Flavour

A PRODUCT OF DOMINION BREWERIES LTD., AUCKLAND

For men, a stay-at-home wife confirmed their capacity to be a good husband, father and provider. Six years' absence at war no doubt accentuated men's need to have their role as breadwinner and family man reconfirmed. A working wife seemed to call manhood into question, and women could be acutely aware of this.

It was not just a desire for normality and ideas about 'natural' roles for married women and men that encouraged nesting after the war. Labour's social security scheme continued its pre-war emphasis on family-building. The family benefit became 'universal', and was payable direct to the mother of every child from birth to 16 years from April 1946. Initially, 'all' really meant 'just some'. At first, the payments did not apply to the children of war widows or war pensioners who were already in receipt of a benefit. Children born out of wedlock and brought up by their single mothers were also excluded from the state's largesse, although their mothers could be entitled to discretionary payments administered through the government's child welfare organisation.[42] Political and public opinion brought all these families into the fold, and within a week of the first payments being made, true universality was implemented.

The benefit demonstrated Labour's egalitarian philosophy that all New Zealanders were entitled to social security, regardless of their wealth or social status. In marked contrast to what would happen to perceptions about welfare in the 1980s, support like the family benefit reinforced the idea that state assistance was the birthright of all.

The level of the family benefit was generous; for a time it was about one-sixth of the female minimum wage. In a family of three children, the family benefit brought in the equivalent of half the female minimum wage. It was like manna from heaven for some women; as one wrote, 'For my cousin, it was her saviour:

CULTURAL SECURITY

The arts received their own social security with a huge boost under Labour, for whom providing New Zealanders with access to their culture was the mark of a civilised government. The 1940 Centennial was one opportunity for local writers and artists to speak, write, compose and paint New Zealand. Under the energetic direction of Joe Heenan of the Department of Internal Affairs, and with the full support of Peter Fraser, a host of other cultural supports came on line, all with government assistance.

The National Film Unit began work in 1941 and the New Zealand National Orchestra was playing by 1947. The Literary Fund subsidised publishing from 1946, with the literary journal *Landfall* one of its first beneficiaries in 1947. State patronage buoyed the vibrant arts scene, and enabled major figures to emerge: Denis Glover, Charles Brasch, Rita Angus, Doris Lusk, Douglas Lilburn. And the receptive climate for the arts also flowed into more popular forms, including jazz and swing.

The New Zealand label TANZA — To Assist New Zealand Artists — had its first hit in 1948 with 'Blue Smoke'. Written by Ruru Karaitiana and crooned by Pixie Williams, the tune was redolent of New Zealand and the Pacific, in a sort of country-and-western way. People loved it, and snapped up 50,000 copies.

they had five children and things weren't easy at all; she had money of her own she could spend on herself and the children.'[43]

Struggling Maori families found their circumstances notably improved through the regular assistance. Teachers in rural communities reported children arriving at school better clothed and fed than previously. But Pakeha minds could be suspicious. There were claims of Maori squandering their payments on booze and fags, gambling and taxis. Maori communities were said to be dependent on social security; benefits were the 'chief industry' in some areas, and government was apparently 'debauching Maori with easy money'.[44]

Overcoming such attitudes would be a long haul, but Maori welfare officers, first employed as part of MWEO, played a key role here. They advised Maori women how to manage the family benefit, and other payments to which they were entitled. In the cities, they helped bridge the gap between rural and urban life.

The MWEO was a beacon of Maori autonomy in the 1940s, but it was not to last. Many Maori leaders — Ngata excepted — wanted to keep it going in some form. Its by-Maori, for-Maori aspects appealed; but, importantly, it was not the Department of Native Affairs, an agency almost universally disliked because of its unhelpful, Pakeha way of operating. In its turn, the department looked sideways at the MWEO's 'encroachment' on its activities, especially as it had enhanced its own welfare and housing functions through the early 1940s. Minister of Native Affairs Rex Mason, 'a man with few Maori contacts and no real grasp of the organization's significance', was hostile to the organisation continuing at all.[45]

Maori demanded a Department of Maori Welfare, and through the work of MP Eruera Tirikatene, this almost eventuated. Tirikatene organised national conferences and urged a thorough investigation of the administration of all

TEN-POUND POMS

Bringing in labour from overseas was one solution to the post-war labour shortage, and it would also boost New Zealand's population, which some thought was dangerously low. If you were aged between 20 and 35, had no dependent children, and were prepared to work in a specified job for two years, then ten quid would get you from the 'grey UK' to 'the greatest little country on earth'.

The assisted immigration scheme fell on receptive ears in Britain, where discontent with rationing was high. The scheme began in 1947 with a batch of 158 migrants, and New Zealand officials in London could receive 170 written and 75 personal inquiries about it in a day. The scheme had its ups and downs in terms of the number and type of applicants, and the New Zealand government steadily amended its parameters. By 1950 it was open to married couples with two children, the list of targeted jobs — such as nursing or construction initially — was expanded, and the £10 charge was removed. Nearly 3000 assisted migrants had arrived in the country by then, with around 20,000 more making their way under their own steam.

The new migrants had mixed views on the greatest little country; 'frankly I found NZ boring' was one assessment. Of the 26 psychiatric nurses brought out in a trial run in October 1946, three had left within the month, and another seven had departure plans in hand. For the migrants who stayed — and they were the great majority — the opportunities, the absence of a rigid class system, and the light and the open spaces were novel attractions. Not so appealing was the relative quiet. 'I tried to keep an open mind, but it was all rather strange,' Grace Flynn confessed in 1949. 'I was born and bred in the centre of London, I felt lost here — so few people, such small houses, so many wide open spaces, so little organized entertainment.'[46]

To single men and women

GOOD JOBS

GOOD PAY

GOOD LIVING

Emigrate to NEW ZEALAND

..for a *NEW* way of life

New Zealand has a place for YOU in her future development. There are many jobs awaiting the new settler.
For **MEN**—Building, Engineering, National Development and Farming.
For **WOMEN**—Nursing, Factory, Domestic and Office.
If you are under 36 **enquire** about the Free and Assisted Passages being offered to **single** British men and women by calling on or writing to the **Chief Migration Officer, New Zealand Government Offices, 415 Strand, London, W.C.2**

Archives New Zealand, L1, 22/2/14

Maori affairs. His Maori Social and Economic Reconstruction Bill sought to retain Maori autonomy in Maori affairs, but in the end Mason's Maori Social and Economic Advancement Bill became law in 1945. The MWEO's structure of tribal and executive committees fell into the government's net and much of its independence was lost.

'We didn't get very far in our efforts to run our own affairs because at that stage there was a lot of opposition from the establishment, from senior officers in the department itself, and in the organisations above it,' recollected Charles Bennett who joined the new department after service with the Maori Battalion.[47] Many Maori remained uncertain of the revamped Department of Maori Affairs, as Native Affairs had been renamed in 1947 when government symbolically divested itself of the term 'native'. MWEO members, as well as soldiers from the Maori Battalion, assumed prominence within the new department, but they sometimes had a rough road in convincing their constituents that they were not lackeys of the state intent on sacrificing Maori culture on the altar of Pakeha progress.[48]

Post-war inflation eroded everyone's benefit levels, which had never really managed to keep pace with the rising cost of living. People on fixed incomes, old-age pensioners especially, felt disadvantaged. Families — the very group at which much of the welfare state was targeted — could be in the worst position.

The scant supply of housing lay at the heart of much of the trouble. House construction had slowed in the war years. As early as 1941, welfare and housing officials declared there was a 'national problem' in housing larger families. A special scheme came on line in the following year to subsidise the rents of, or find accommodation for, such families, and 300 were assisted in this way within 18 months.[49] But it was rearranging deck chairs on the *Titanic*.

'House hungry' New Zealand was ravenous by 1944, when construction recommenced, with 26,000 families waiting for state houses. The growing population and the move to the cities was not helping. Labour built over 32,000 houses between 1937 and 1949, but supply dragged behind demand. Maori families especially were in dire need of accommodation. Rangi Royal of the Native Department estimated at least 1200 houses — 500 of them urgently — were needed for Maori in Auckland in 1944. At war's end, there were 15,000 applicants for state houses in Auckland alone; this included more than 2000 returned servicemen, who were meant to receive priority housing.[50]

Workers were also in short supply. The restriction on imports during the war had boosted the local manufacturing sector, and industries of all sorts cried out for workers. Labour's post-war strategy of ensuring full employment was realised. In 1945 an estimated 50,000 workers were needed, especially in the main centres and in the new public works schemes such as hydro developments.

Shortage was one thing that New Zealand was not short of. Making do and going without were expected in wartime, but not in the peace that followed. The import controls introduced in 1938 meant that various consumer goods were scarce. Rationing was still in effect in many areas. Tea-drinkers squeezed out every precious leaf, butter and cream were in short supply, and sugar was rationed. Meat-lovers had to be satisfied with what they could get, as exports to Britain took meat from their dinner tables. People wanted to enjoy the peace and the comforts for which they had fought. Labour had delivered much since 1935, but there was rising discontent by the late 1940s and the lingering rationing was behind much of it.

Labour had remained in government during the war (though co-operating with the National Party in a War Cabinet that oversaw the war effort from 1940 to 1945), but the first post-war election, in 1946, was a close-run affair. Labour promised tax concessions and 'turned on the spending tap': subsidies for the construction of war memorials, logging in state forests to supply timber, a new pay scale for teachers, and a free dental care scheme for children. It was enough — just. Labour won 51 per cent of the vote with 30,000 more votes than National, but gained victory only through retaining the four Maori seats.[51] It was hardly a mandate for radical reform.

There was little enough initiative for change in the Labour ranks in any case. Fraser was focusing on international politics, as he had been for some time. Early in 1944 he had signed the Australia–New Zealand Agreement, commonly known as the Canberra Pact, which allowed for co-ordination of the two country's policies in civil and military matters. Later, New Zealand's focus was the new United Nations. New Zealand had enthusiastically played a part in its creation at the 1945 San Francisco Conference in the hope of forging a peaceful post-war world.

Rationing dwindled during the final years of the decade, although it would not finally vanish until 1950. The restrictions on tea, meat and sugar were history by the end of 1948, but the reintroduction of petrol rationing in 1947 was unpopular. People had to improvise. Eve Ebbett recalls:

When I married in 1949, my husband-to-be had been promised the loan of a car for our honeymoon. It was marvellous to have wheels, but not owning a car of our own meant that we had no access to petrol coupons. Only a little bartering and the kind hearts of friends who offered us some of their coupons made the honeymoon possible. This was more than four years after the end of the war and ten years after the introduction of petrol rationing.[52]

Hocken Library, University of Otago

Rationing of material and women's clothing still operated in 1949, prompting claims from overseas fashion experts that New Zealand women looked dowdy and drab. Finance Minister Walter Nash rushed to the defence of local sartorial standards, perhaps unwisely. He was dubbed the 'dress dictator' and National Party leaflets made the most of his controls over female clothing.

Labour became its own worst enemy in the lead-up to the 1949 election. A strike by Auckland carpenters in early 1949 exposed the cracks in the labour movement, and the government's handling of the dispute, which involved deregistration of the Auckland branch of the carpenters' union, was universally unpopular among unionists. Fraser's push for compulsory military training upset the Labour applecart even further. He was convinced of the need for it in the new Cold War climate, but his colleagues, traditionally opposed to peacetime military training, took some persuading. Caucus supported him narrowly, but the wider Labour Party and unionists were opposed.

Sid Holland's National Party had a field day. The coupling of rationing and the shortage of consumer goods boosted their arguments that Labour strangled the economy and freedom of choice. National had pushed this pro-consumption, anti-control button for several years. 'When we become the Government, every opportunity will be given for people to own things,' Holland had declared in 1943.[53] This time, it would get results.

Labour's achievements had been enormous; now it could only hark back to what it had done. 'Don't Gamble With Prosperity' one 1949 election leaflet proclaimed; 'An Era of Plenty' reminded another. But voters wanted more than the status quo; 'the Government stood there, waving back at its record, and the crowd moved on.'[54] National took 52 per cent of the votes, and 46 of the 80 seats in the House. Conceding defeat in Wellington, outgoing Prime Minister Peter Fraser was greeted with boos. Fourteen years on from the landmark victory in 1935, the tide had finally turned.

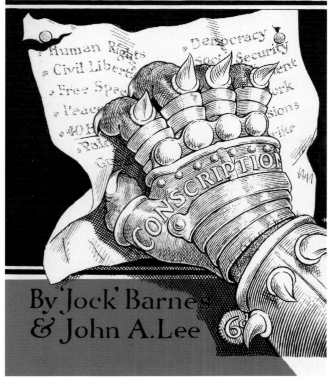

Labour took the issue of reviving peacetime compulsory military training to the people in a national referendum in 1949. Over 500,000 New Zealanders wanted it, more than three times the number that voted against. Many of the 'No' votes were in Labour electorates; the general election was not looking good for the government.

Chapter 11

Friday night in the city meant bright lights, shopping, the flicks. Hollywood met New Zealand in films like *Runaway*, with its heady blend of sex, flesh and mystery. The cities were the places to be, and people flocked there in the post-war decades.

WW Stewart, courtesy Grantham House Publishing

The Golden Weather
1949–1965

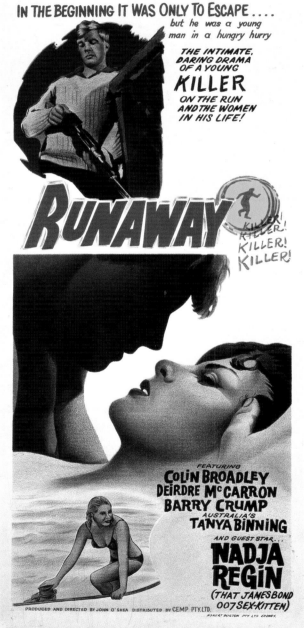

IN THE BEGINNING IT WAS ONLY TO ESCAPE....
but he was a young
man in a hungry hurry

THE INTIMATE, DARING DRAMA OF A YOUNG
KILLER
ON THE RUN AND THE WOMEN IN HIS LIFE!

RUNAWAY

KILLER!
KILLER!
KILLER!
KILLER!

FEATURING
COLIN BROADLEY
DEIRDRE McCARRON
BARRY CRUMP
AUSTRALIA'S
TANYA BINNING
AND GUEST STAR...
NADJA REGIN
(THAT JAMES BOND 007 SEX-KITTEN)
PRODUCED AND DIRECTED BY JOHN O'SHEA DISTRIBUTED BY CEMP PTY.LTD.
ROBERT BURTON PTY LTD SYDNEY.

Pacific Film Collection, New Zealand Film Archive

As the 456th freshly-shorn ewe bolted from the shearing shed on Akers Station, Opiki, Godfrey Bowen ended his nine-hour marathon of blood, sweat and shears. His 1953 world shearing record was appropriate in a country where sheep outnumbered people by 33 million. Between 1949 and 1965 the golden fleece propelled New Zealand to one of the highest standards of living in the world. These were glory years. We climbed higher, ran faster, and jumped further than anyone else. Creative arts blossomed. Teenagers embraced movies, fashions, rock 'n' roll and all things American with breathless enthusiasm. We were a passionate people — our prodigious procreative energy produced nearly a million babies. The population we could not generate ourselves was imported in the biggest immigration scheme since Vogel's. Suburbs burgeoned. Cities sprawled. Maori, predominantly rural before the war, recognised the promise of the city, and were urban within a generation. There was conservatism and stability, but in these decades New Zealand was more than just a pavlova paradise; it was expansionist, energetic and exciting.

A passionate people

Comfort, security and a return to normality were all that most people wanted in the 1950s and 1960s. Romance, marriage and family were in the air; social pressures and government policy directed towards helping young families supported Kiwis' nesting aspirations and their desire to turn 'in on themselves'.[1]

Family was at the heart of it, and New Zealanders wed and bred with a gusto not equalled before or since. Over 20,000 couples swarmed up the aisle in 1946, more than in any other year until 1964; the number of petitions for divorce in 1946 also reached a level that was unmatched for another 20 years. The just-married became younger than ever. A quarter of all brides were under 21 between 1950 and 1954, and a decade later nearly 40 per cent were under 21. Men waited till they were a little older before making the commitment. But by the mid 1960s, over half of all grooms and almost three-quarters of all brides were under 25.[2]

Newly-weds got right down to business: around three-quarters of first babies made their appearance within two years of marriage. More than 47,000 babies came in 1946 and the number kept climbing: 56,351 in 1956, and an unsurpassed high of 65,390 in 1961. The average number of births to each woman went from 2.3 in the 1930s to peak at 4.3 in 1961.[3] It was even higher for Maori — around 6 in 1962. The boom had to end, and while the number of Maori babies grew as a proportion of all born, the total number of births and the fertility rate declined relatively steadily thereafter.[4]

The pill, available from 1961, had some effect: 'Within just five years women were swallowing some 100,000 packets of the pill each month,' Dr Margaret Sparrow, an early pill user, recalled. 'The representatives of the drug companies leave sample packets [of the pill] with the doctors before they're introduced to the country generally, and [my husband] brought home a couple of packets of these new fangled pills and threw

OUT OF WEDLOCK

Archives New Zealand, AALF 6112

There was a lot of idealising of romantic love, but marriage was not always on the cards. More babies were born on the 'wrong' side of the blankets from the 1950s, many to women under 21, evidence of the teenage sexual 'semi-revolution' and earlier marriage in action. In 1954 about four per cent of babies were 'illegitimate' (the less condemnatory label 'ex-nuptial' came into use in 1969) and a decade later the figure had risen to about 10 per cent. Maori figures, included in the statistics from 1962, boosted the percentage, but it was clear that ex-nuptial births were on the rise. And they kept surging ahead, to reach 14 per cent by 1971.[8]

Single motherhood was an enormous financial and emotional strain. 'The unfortunate woman was branded as immoral, humiliated, and treated like dirt,' one 1950s single mum recalled. Some women moved town to give birth; Taihape was said to be the place to go in the 1950s, though where Taihape women went was anyone's guess. Community disapproval could be strong.

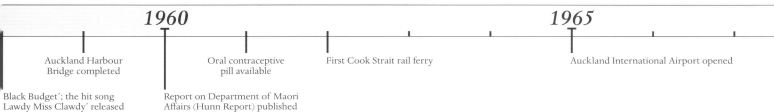

Auckland Harbour
Bridge completed

Oral contraceptive
pill available

First Cook Strait rail ferry

Auckland International Airport opened

Black Budget'; the hit song
Lawdy Miss Clawdy' released

Report on Department of Maori
Affairs (Hunn Report) published

them on the table and said, "Chomp away at these".'[5] The pill could change a woman's life, but its particular role in the baby bust is harder to pinpoint. The boom was a brief, if spectacular, reversal of a longer-term decline in fertility levels. Shifting attitudes towards career motherhood, and a growing tightness in the economy that made large families seem less viable, are just as likely to lie behind the changes from the mid 1960s, but we can only speculate.[6]

Those without their own babies were keen to adopt. The emphasis on home and family upped the ante on family formation. Adoptions peaked at nearly 4000 in 1971 and the 1955 Adoption Act ensured neither birth parents, adoptive parents nor children had access to adoption records; almost everyone in this secret process was, and would remain, a stranger to each other. It was mainly a Pakeha system, although the 1955 legislation restored the right, which had been taken away in 1909, for Maori to adopt Pakeha children; Maori 'adoptions' or

whangai still occurred, reflecting a more complex and whanau-based system of child-raising.[7]

Babies were healthier than ever. In the early 1960s Pakeha infant mortality was the third lowest in the world. Maori infant mortality figures were still twice the Pakeha level, but they also fell once serious child health problems were overcome. A polio vaccine was available from 1956, effectively wiping out the disease that had crippled so many young children. Tuberculosis also faded out; Maori children had suffered the most from this illness, as it was generally related to poor living conditions.

Put all these things together and you get a population blow-out of under-16s. In 1961, the boom year for births, children comprised a third of the population. Maori children were more numerous still — for most of this period they were over 40 per cent of the Maori population, and reached half of it in 1966. The flow-on effects of the kiddie blip were vast (and are still being felt today as these same kids grey). The welfare

The welfare state aided young families, but there was scant financial help for the single mother, and this could place her under relentless pressure to 'give up' her child. Yet most women struggled against the odds and kept their babies.[9]

Of course everyone had an opinion on the state of affairs. Much was heard of the permissive society, the disappearance of the chaperone, declining standards of morality, loose parental control, the lure of free maternity care, trashy literature, peer pressure. Inevitably, women were blamed.

LEFT: Babyville: the waiting room at the Waterloo Plunket Clinic, Lower Hutt, 1950s. Plunket was one of the few organisations to assist single mums.

RIGHT: *Out of Wedlock*, a two-part radio documentary, aired in 1964, and was featured in the *Listener* where the message was blunt: 'The ultimate decision is made, in most cases, by the girl, however unwilling she may be later to accept the responsibility and blame. It is fitting, therefore, that nemesis — pregnancy and the birth of an illegitimate child — is hers.' Young women clearly had to accept the consequences if they snuggled up to a bloke in a darkened car.

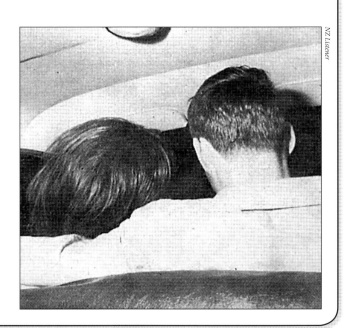

NZ Listener

state focused on families and family-building across many areas: health, education, housing and income support. Over 300 new primary and secondary schools shot up between 1950 and 1965 for the thousands of extra students needing desks. With each school costing about £250,000 to build, the financial outlay was enormous.[10]

New families needed somewhere to live, some urgently as houses were in short supply following the war. Post-war governments continued with state houses but the philosophy changed. Labour had built houses to rent; the National government elected in 1949 had no interest in being landlord or builder. Instead, it sold off state houses to tenants, and made available loans for constructing houses. By the mid 1950s it was financing about a third of all houses built. In a move away from the Labour vision of state housing for ordinary Kiwis, it was mainly those on low incomes who would be eligible for a state house. State house communities now started to be the domain of poorer families.

The level of home-ownership climbed steadily and this was aided by cheap state loans, down to a low of three per cent from 1958. Seventeen thousand new house building permits were issued in 1950, 20,000 in 1955, and 21,000 a decade later. 'Nappy Valleys' — new communities financed in some way or another by the state — spread through towns and cities, in areas such as Mangere, Hillcrest, Titahi Bay, Aranui and Corstorphine.[11]

Maori were more likely to be tenants than owners. In keeping with the official line of integration and assimilation, Maori and Pacific Island families were 'pepper-potted' among Pakeha. An 'allowance' of one Maori family per block of Pakeha families seemed to be the maximum before white flight set in and property prices tumbled. Or Maori left, alienated, isolated and discriminated against. Nowhere near as well off as Pakeha, Maori families clustered in areas with cheaper housing. Residents of a stretch of South Auckland suburbs were, in culture, lifestyle, opportunities and expectations, light years away from those living in Remuera and other suburbs nestling in Auckland's more picture-perfect spots.

Most Maori could not afford to own homes in the cities. Low incomes obviously contributed to this. The complicated Maori housing programme also played a part. The government's key lending agency, the State Advances Corporation, preferred to lend money to Maori who would live in the 'Pakeha way', as a nuclear rather than an extended family. Maori could also access loans and housing through the Department of Maori Affairs, but this was often a more expensive option. Despite these problems, and the outright racism some encountered trying to obtain rental accommodation or financial assistance, Maori still benefited from the increased housing available through the 1950s and 1960s.

The weekend gained new meaning. The mandatory 40-hour (or 44 in some workplaces) week (for paid work) from 1936 had demarcated 'work' from 'leisure', and this became even more pronounced after the war. Late-night shopping on Friday was the end of the Monday to Friday grind — except for those working

Porirua was born in the 1950s. Bulldozers and graders worked furiously for a decade shaping the landscape to accommodate the largest town planned and created by the government. More than £10 million was spent and nearly 3000 houses built. Over three years, the city centre was laid out, with shops, small businesses, transport networks and car-parking facilities. *AJHR*, 1962, H-38

SEPARATE SPHERES

Traditional gender roles were to the fore. All Blacks were heroes for the sporting man and boy. Tough opponents such as the Springboks, touring in 1956, were worthy foes in the manly and often bloody showdowns. Women's magazines suggested how to craft desirable homes. Anne Else says: 'I picked up the message very early, mainly from the pages of my mother's fat weekly bundle of magazines, showing fascinating floor plans of the right and wrong way to arrange furniture, or ten bright ideas for trimming lamp shades.'[12] 'Hospitality culture' was prized, and visitors expected home-made goodies with their cup of tea.

RIGHT: No smoky bars and leering labourers here. Wearing dressy clothes, smoking cigarettes and drinking cocktails, 1960s chic poses at the Chateau Tongariro. Clothes maketh the man, and woman. Women's dresses curved around the feminine and maternal bust and hips, while the men's slick, short-back-and-sides haircuts and swanky suits suggested successful men of business.

BELOW: The pub was a man's world until the end of six o'clock closing in 1967. G Tapper, Auckland Art Gallery, Toi o Tamaki

in the shops and cinemas. Then there was 'Saturday's business': 'A couple got engaged, bought a section, in their spare time built the house, and contributed their bit to the baby boom.'[13] This was family time for Mum and Dad at least — doing the lawns, pottering in the shed, digging the vegie patch, pouring the concrete, watching the kids play sport, sewing a new dress. Staying at home or spending Saturday night at the movies were always options, but once television beamed into homes from 1960, the big screen lost out to the box. City channels transmitted daily from mid 1962, and by the middle of 1965, nearly half of New Zealand homes had a TV set. Programmes screened every evening till 11 p.m. during the week (and midnight on Friday), and then from 2 p.m. in the weekend. During this period, attendances at the flicks fell substantially.[14]

In the home, the 'electric servant' — the only type of servant now available — reigned supreme. Ovens, ranges, freezers, cake mixers, toasters, vacuum cleaners and jugs were all meant to make women's domestic lives easier, but they probably just freed them up for other tasks. Half of households had the big-ticket items like washing machines and refrigerators by the mid 1950s and they were virtually universal a decade later, although Maori and rural people were slower to obtain them.[15]

Appliances and gadgets cost. Borrowing through hire purchase surged massively. Over £8 million was owed in 1956, double the amount of 20 years earlier; this increased to £20 million by 1963 and £30 million by 1965. For families whose aspirations outran their means, a government-funded community budgeting service operated, first in Kaikohe in 1960 and then in major towns by the end of the decade.[16]

Domestic ideology was important, but a revolution was under way. The ready availability of jobs encouraged married women into the workforce from the early 1950s, and about 45 per cent of these workers were in their child-bearing years. Married women made up 25 per cent of the female workforce in 1951, 41 per cent by 1966. The percentage increase matched that between 1966 and 1980, a period normally seen as the boom time of married women's employment.[17] Some women worked to meet family finances; others sought outlets beyond home, especially once the kids started school. Domestic routines and culture changed for good. The baking binges and the passion for preserving petered out from the 1960s as women had no time to slice, boil and knead away their days. Visitors still expected a biscuit with their cuppa, but from the early 1960s, that biscuit was more likely to have come from Mrs Griffin.[18]

Electric machines removed some of the elbow grease from washing clothes, but things still had to be bright white.

Patrolling the borders

The ideals of security, comfort and progress that drove home-life also oiled the political wheels and foreign policy. The National government elected in 1949 promised security and freedom, opportunity and prosperity for all. Rationing lingered until the end of 1950, but as if drawing a line under those dark years, wartime Prime Minister Peter Fraser died in December 1950.

Freedom, opportunity and security at home depended on a 'free world'. That phrase spoke volumes in the chill of Cold War tensions between the Soviet Union and communist states on the one hand, and the 'free world' on the other. The new alliances and new enemies that emerged from the rubble of the Second World War carried through for many years to come.

Communism was one of the big enemies. From this distance, the attitude seems straight out of a James Bond movie. But there was real fear in the early 1950s that a third world war loomed, that the communists — Russians and Chinese — would be behind it, and that an atomic bomb would be used. Perhaps it is not surprising that between 10 and 15 per cent of New Zealand's budget went on defence in the 1950s and 1960s, two or three times the level of the mid 1980s.[19]

Reds could lurk anywhere. Even sheep-shearing hero Godfrey Bowen found himself in a potentially difficult situation. After a demonstration of his prowess in the Soviet Union he was made a Hero of Socialist Labour in 1963. It was a grand title, but questionable back in red-scared New Zealand. *Truth* screeched about suspected communists arriving as new migrants; shopkeepers complained of commies speaking on street corners. Cecil Holmes, member of the Communist Party and apprentice film-maker at the National Film Unit, became a fall-guy in 1948 and '49. His satchel, containing his party membership and details of industrial action the film unit was considering through the Public Service Association, was taken from his vehicle during a meeting of left-wing intellectuals in Parliament Buildings. Within weeks, Holmes' political affiliations were splashed across newspapers.[20]

Prime Minister Sid Holland's claims about treacherous communists helped National win the snap election that was called as the 1951 waterfront dispute hobbled to an end. Militant unionism, its alleged links with communism and the disruption the dispute had caused would have no place in New Zealand. The public mood was belligerent but buoyant, even if the dispute had cost upwards of £40 million. The exhausted Waterside Workers' Union was broken up into more than 20 port-based organisations,

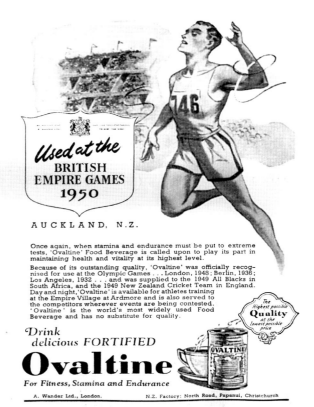

ROWING
AND
SCULLING

**PROGRAMME
OF EVENTS**
for
**Monday, 6th February
1950**

to be held on
**LAKE KARAPIRO
CAMBRIDGE, N.Z.**

Imperial allegiances were strong. Everyone came out to see the young Queen Elizabeth tour the country in the summer of 1953–54. New Zealand had already flown its imperial colours earlier when Auckland hosted the British Empire Games in 1950 — and supplied the athletes with good old imperial Ovaltine.

THE ENEMY WITHIN

Links between communism and unions seemed especially sinister. Relations between the watersiders on the one hand, and their employers and government on the other, had festered for years. Watersiders went out on strike 28 times in 1949 alone. National aimed to get tough.

The 1951 waterfront dispute became the big showdown. Each side was led by men who enjoyed a good scrap: Jock 'The Bull' Barnes (head of the watersiders), 'almost pathologically bold, aggressive and stubborn'; versus the former communist and thug Fintan Patrick Walsh who was Vice-President of the Federation of Labour that supported the government; and Prime Minister Sid Holland, 'who may have never read a book in his life but was a skilled if overexcitable professional politician and amateur magician'. Some believe that these three could have avoided confrontation had hearts and minds been willing. But they were not, and strongmen Barnes and Walsh were looking for a stoush.[21]

Things came to a head in early 1951 following a general wage order. What watersiders wanted and what employers offered was just threepence an hour. When things stalled, the watersiders banned overtime. Employers locked them out. The dispute was on — whether you called it a 'lockout' or a 'strike' showed your leanings. It lasted for 151 days — a numerical harmony from 15 February 1951 through to 15 July 1951 — and involved upwards of 20,000 workers downing tools. Traditionally stroppy unions of miners, seamen and freezing workers supported their friends on the wharf; over 200,000 unionists kept on working.

BELOW: Police swung their batons on a unionist march in Wellington's Cuba St in May, and again two weeks later in Auckland. 'Bloody Friday', on 1 June, left police, unionists and their families injured following police curtailment of a march led by unionist wives. Harry Rose, Roth Collection, Alexander Turnbull Library

National's reaction was tough: unionists would never win this battle. Normal civil liberties such as free speech were curtailed in a State of Emergency. Watersiders and supporters clashed with police in ugly incidents.[22] The government banned assistance, including food supplies, to families of watersiders and supporters. Times were tough, but help came via a well-organised relief network arranged by supporting unions, and especially the wives, girlfriends and daughters of those involved in the industrial action. 'Somebody produced a slaughtered sheep to share. I got the impression it was stolen but now I know that there were friendly farmers who donated sheep, and market gardeners who gave vegetables, and tradespeople who provided other goods and services for nothing, or next to nothing.'[23]

ABOVE: The majority of watersiders stuck it out for the entire 151 days, and their union issued a certificate to all who 'Stood Loyal Right Through'.
Alexander Turnbull Library, Eph-A-Labour-1951-01

effectively halting concerted action. Few New Zealanders appeared to notice the irony that National, elected in 1949 on a ticket of freedom and liberty, had within two years restricted the civil liberties of those who dared to disagree. The borders of freedom and security would be patrolled at home, and if that meant limiting the freedoms of some to safeguard the freedom of the many, then it seemed that most New Zealanders agreed.

Patrolling international borders mattered too in the effort to hold the line against the encroachment of the communist world. New Zealand's global position depended on whom it chose as friends; for once friendships were made, enmities became clear. There was little choice, of course. Ancestral links died hard. Mother Britain had always been a fulcrum of New Zealand's foreign policy; so a secure United Kingdom was the basis for a secure New Zealand.

Increasingly, New Zealand became more aware of its geography and also realised that Britain was no longer the global power it had been. The United States played a key role in the Asia-Pacific region in the 1940s, and post-war New Zealand wanted this continued guarantee of regional security.

It came first in the shape of the 1951 Pacific Security Treaty, the ANZUS alliance. All for one and one for all, Australia, New Zealand and the United States agreed to regard a threat to the peace and security of one of them as a threat to all. They also pledged to maintain and develop, separately and jointly, individual and collective capacity to resist armed attack. Britain was miffed. New Zealand tried to develop some type of 'BRITANZUS' to appease political opinion in Britain and also public opinion at home, which wanted to keep hold of the apron strings. Superpower United States set its own rules; it would be ANZUS for as long as it suited.

Frank Corner, First Secretary at the New Zealand embassy in Washington in 1951, summed up the position with regard

Sid Holland sits flanked by Vice-President Richard Nixon, left, and American Consul Robert Scotten, at the State Luncheon held at Parliament Buildings in 1953. This was the first American vice-presidential visit to New Zealand and it reaffirmed the links between the two countries.

POST-WARS

Holding the line against further 'communist aggression' would involve the 'free world', including New Zealand, in armed conflicts in Asia for over two decades. With the British, New Zealand forces fought communist guerrillas in the jungles of Malaya in the Malayan Emergency — if a conflict stretching from 1948 to 1960 can be called an 'emergency'.

By 1950, New Zealanders were battling on the Korean peninsula. Trouble had been brewing there for some time after the United States and the Soviet Union carved up the spoils at the end of the Second World War. Conflict broke out between South and North Korea when the northern communist regime — armed by the Soviet Union — crossed the 38th Parallel dividing the region to invade its southern neighbour. New Zealand sent two frigates in 1950 to take part in the United Nations operations to assist South Korea. The conflict escalated into a full-scale, three-year struggle between the US- and UN-assisted South on the one hand, and the North, backed by the communist People's Republic of China and the Soviet Union, on the other.

'Kayforce' was New Zealand's main contribution, sent over in December 1950 and forming part of the Commonwealth Division under the control of the British. About 4700 eventually served in Korea, with another 1300 on board the frigates. Forty-five New Zealanders lost their lives on the peninsula; one Kayforce member was a prisoner of war for 18 months. Fighting halted in mid 1953 with the signing of an armistice, but members of Kayforce stayed for a further four years; Korea remained divided. Back home, the public was scarcely bothered by the war, and Kayforce came to be considered the 'Forgotten Force'.

to ANZUS: 'Basically . . . the American unwillingness to include Britain . . . springs from a refusal to share real power in the Pacific with any other country. They will talk to Australia and NZ, and will be most forthcoming with us, because we are so unequal and represent no real challenge to their right of decision. But the British are a different proposition.'[24]

Foreign policy boffins were on a roll. New Zealand signed the South-East Asia Collective Defence Treaty, commonly known as the Manila Pact, in 1954. The Treaty partners — the ANZUS triumvirate, Britain and France (the local colonial powers), and Thailand, Pakistan and the Philippines — agreed to separate and joint development of individual and joint capacities to counter-attack, and allowed for economic and technical assistance to the region. Next year the South-East Asia Treaty Organisation (SEATO) came into being. For New Zealand, it was an opportunity to engage in complex military planning for the defence of the region. New Zealand and its friends were not the only ones interested. The world watched as South-East Asia began a messy divorce from the colonial European powers, and then a flirtation — marriage even — with the Soviet Union and China.

Vietnam was shedding its French colonial legacy and embracing communism. With the French out and the country split into two in 1954, the scene was set for a civil war between the communist North and the US-backed South. New Zealand watched with alarm but was reluctant to send troops, as the United States requested from the early 1960s. The National government thought external intervention would do little good, and fears of an unwanted conflict with China loomed large. But America was nothing if not persuasive. A small civilian surgical team was sent in 1962, and in 1964, 25 army engineers. This would never be enough, especially as the Australians had toed the line. Sending combat troops to Vietnam, as New Zealand would do from 1965, confirmed the shift in external relations; for the first time, New Zealand waged war without Britain. Regional security and upholding the ANZUS alliance — with emphasis on the 'US' — now motivated New Zealand's view of its geopolitical place.

The golden fleece

A natural population increase of over 37 per cent in 15 years is impressive. During the Great New Zealand Lamb Boom of 1949–65 our sheep flock grew from 33 million to 54 million. Their produce, and that of their bovine paddock-mates, formed about 90 per cent of the country's exports in the early 1950s. The expanding economy ran on sheep and cows.

War History Collection, Alexander Turnbull Library, M-3092

Maori soldiers played a key role in the post-wars. Here members of the New Zealand Battalion enjoy a hangi and beer before moving further into the Malayan jungle in 1958. The army also provided a career path for young Maori men not necessarily open to them in the civilian world.

Ships stacked high with meat, butter, cheese and wool left New Zealand ports, mostly for British markets. In 1955, 70 per cent of the sheep meat on the plates of British diners came from New Zealand. Until 1954, Britain bulk-purchased New Zealand meat, guaranteeing two-thirds of this country's export earnings.

Apprehension about a secure market for fleece vanished with a wool boom caused by the Korean War. Some thought that the United States bought up bales to make uniforms for its troops — a little bit of New Zealand on the backs of Americans fighting in Korea. The truth was less romantic; the United States was stockpiling in case of long-term conflict.[25] But a wool rush was on, and it mattered little who was buying, or why.

Almost overnight, wool prices trebled. Money poured in. A previous record high of £46 million in 1949 soared to over £74 million worth of wool exports in 1950, a whopping £128 million in 1951 and £82 million in 1952. In 1951 wool alone accounted for over half the total value of exports. The stuff was like gold, and every scrap counted. There were stories of farming families bundling up and selling the stray tufts plucked from gorse bushes, thistles and barbed wire. Shearing gangs could make decent money.

The heady days of the wool-rush soon vanished, but its effects endured. The fleece lured some farmers from their meat

P McIntyre, courtesy S McIntyre

Shearing could be relatively lucrative work for Maori, some of whom formed whanau-based gangs.

MANNA FROM HEAVEN

Aerial top-dressing of fertiliser and seeds was a boon to many farmers. Properties on the cobalt-deficient volcanic plateau and in hilly regions, always liable to revert to scrub, could now be developed. The 1067-ha hill-country Ngahere Station in Hawke's Bay increased its stock numbers, and the number of stock per hectare, once it began aerial top-dressing in the mid 1950s.

Early flights — such as that of Alan Prichard, who aerial-sowed seeds along Ninety Mile Beach in 1941 — convinced the government to conduct trials. In 1948 a tankload of superphosphate spewed from the modified reserve petrol tank of an Air Force Grumman Avenger over the tarmac at Ohakea. The aerial top-dressing industry had taken off.

Old war-birds came in handy. Surplus de Havilland Tiger Moths were converted to top-dressers by removing the spare front seat; by 1954, there were 160 top-dressing planes in the skies, 146 of them Tiger Moths. They could be bought for as little as £100 and fitted out for another £150; £250 all up and a bored ex-RNZAF pilot had a lucrative business. Eager farmers obliged them with airstrips, sometimes just a cleared bit of flat paddock that allowed pilots to land and take off. They could land anywhere, though. Pilots soon gained reputations for adventurous drops. The first fatal crash occurred near Hunterville in 1950.

National Publicity Studios Collection, Alexander Turnbull Library, F-60913-½

or dairy herds, even when the government paid guaranteed or fixed prices for dairy produce. This was a boom time for farming. Farm output doubled between the mid 1940s and the mid 1960s: dairy production increased by 50 per cent, wool and sheep-meat production was up by 200 per cent, and beef by 300 per cent.[26]

Chemicals, technology, and better farming methods contributed. Farmers reaped the benefits of 30 years of scientific research into improving crops and grasses. A good deal of the advice was about greater use of fertiliser, especially superphosphate. From the 1950s, a significant boost for farm productivity fell from the sky, in the form of top-dressing.

With cash to spare, farmers rapidly mechanised. Tractors were a must-have. Nineteen thousand rumbled around farms in 1946, and almost 90,000 in 1965.[27] The trusty steed and various hand-operated machines disappeared. Dairy farmers took advantage of the spread of electricity, packed away their milking stools and installed milking machines. Separators vanished as tankers arrived at the farm gate to pick up the day's supply of whole milk for the local dairy factory.

Good times on the farm flowed to local communities. Farmers drove into town to shop, visit the bank, maybe have a drink at the pub. Rural towns that serviced farming areas — Marton, for instance — enjoyed a mini-population boom.

The volume of meat exported put pressure on small freezing works, and from the early 1960s, large new freezing works were opened.

For a time, the farming community expanded: from 86,000 farm holdings in 1946 to 92,000 in 1955. But overall, this period brought a decline, and after the 1950s the farming community shrank absolutely as well as relatively. Farming was profitable; though it was still the hard graft it had always been, even with new gadgets in the shed and paddocks. Profitability pushed up prices of land and farm holdings, putting farm ownership beyond the aspirations of many. Dairying, which had given way in some areas to the golden fleece, fell most dramatically — from 40,000 dairy farmers in 1950 to around 17,000 two decades later.[28]

Things had been fine while there were arrangements for British bulk-purchasing of New Zealand meat. There was less certainty from the mid 1950s. Britain had its own farmers to satisfy, and there were countries enough in Europe that could put butter and cheese on British tables. New Zealand had to exploit the old ancestral link to get an assured, if fairly open, market for its agricultural produce.

Hard bargaining finally gained a guaranteed, unrestricted and duty-free entry to the United Kingdom until 1967 for New Zealand dairy products and pork. But by the early 1960s, Britain's new European focus was a potential threat to New Zealand.

Archives New Zealand, AANR 6329

The backbone of the country. Farmers yarn at an East Coast stock sale of cattle in the 1950s.

From 1961 Britain flirted more seriously with the European Economic Community (EEC), hoping to gain entry. But that community had little sympathy with preferential agricultural agreements with some piddling nation across the world at the expense of its own produce.

British dalliances caused much heart fluttering in New Zealand. There was 'filial disbelief, then horror. The Mother Country was flirting with moustachioed, amoral foreigners and casting the child loose upon the world.'[29] That New Zealand managed to keep cosy agreements with Britain for so long owed much to many, and to the skills of one man in particular — John Ormond, chair of the Meat Board from 1951 until 1972, who negotiated the bulk-purchasing and unrestricted right of entry agreements during the 1950s.

Ormond also saw the writing on the wall and tried to develop new markets. Suspicious of British motives — Ormond believed that Commonwealth ties could be weak as water if it suited Britain — he urged the exploitation of alternative markets. Of increasing importance was the United States. Beef meat had never been a huge export, but from the late 1950s the Americans took most of what we had to offer. Alert farmers converted their herds to meat producers.

By 1965, Britain still remained the single biggest market for New Zealand export produce. Diversification aside, most of that produce was the big three: wool, dairy products and meat. The umbilical cord remained for now, and government protections insulated farmers from some of the vicissitudes of the international marketplace.

The promise of prosperity had brought National to power in 1949. The wool boom seemed a tailor-made fulfilment of that pledge. The sudden jump in earnings created a false sense of security, and by the early 1950s problems loomed. Doing its bit for a recovering Europe led New Zealand to relax import controls. Goods flooded in. High exports supported this, and it was fine while the 'sterling area', the group of Commonwealth countries that settled their overseas debts through London, maintained a balance of payments with that global economic powerhouse, the United States. American dollars were in short supply as collectively the sterling area bought more from the United States than it sold there. The order to cut imports went out from London. New Zealand fell into line. Import licences were cancelled. This eased things, and reduced New Zealand's balance of payments deficit created by the import rush. But the bad old days returned; shortages and controls came in 1952 and lasted until 1954.

Great expectations made it hard to understand why everything could not be had when agricultural produce attracted high prices overseas and there was virtually full employment at home. The government's tactic to close the gap between realities and expectations was to alternate between curbing and indulging desires. Election year 1954 saw import controls lifted, then the predictable ordering and buying frenzy. Just as inevitably, there followed cutbacks and financial controls. A similar thing happened in the next election year, 1957, but this time National was punished.

Sid Holland, Prime Minister since 1949, stepped down, ill and tired, just 10 weeks before the election. Unassuming Keith Holyoake took over. Many thought him a bit of a bore but that did not stop them voting for him. Opposite him was the comfortable figure of Walter Nash, stalwart of the 1935 Labour government. Labour promised expansion — cheap housing loans, the proper selection and handling of imports, and a rebate of up to £100 on the tax payable on the new PAYE system to be introduced in 1958.

Voters warmed to Labour's simple message. Their parliamentary majority of two gave scant margin for things to go wrong. The first day in office obliterated any complacency

Nash Papers, Archives New Zealand

Walter and Lotty Nash in 1960, still going strong. Walter was getting on — 75 years old and in Parliament since 1929 — but was still energetic enough to lead Labour to victory in the 1957 election. It had been a long while between drinks for Labour; it had been thrown out in 1949, and would be out again in 1960 and not back until 1972.

they might have had. The opening of the books revealed a dire financial predicament needing immediate action. Export prices had dropped more than anyone had realised, while bills for imports had bounded ahead of the ability to pay. The trade deficit was plain ugly and getting worse by the day; £4 million in September, it reached £30 million by December.

Tried and loathed solutions returned from the beginning of 1958 — increased control, and reduced and judiciously selected imports. Prices for dairy products and wool fell through 1958 and looked set to drop by £50 million towards the end of the year. This Labour government would be long remembered for its budget announcement in the winter of 1958. 'Increase' was the word, and this was applied to pensions and benefits, to personal income tax and petrol tax (effectively raising its price). Nash and Minister of Finance Arnold Nordmeyer, both non-smokers and non-drinkers, priced up booze and fags, never a popular move among Labour's traditional voters. Contemporary economists praised the budget, but to most people it was the 'Black Budget', and it cost Labour the next election.[30]

New Prime Minister Holyoake preached a philosophy of 'Steady Does It'. He quietly steered the country through the mini-crises of the 1960s when agricultural prices fell, just managing to mask financial and economic woes that escalated during the rest of the decade.

Gains as well as losses marked the period. On the whole, there was economic growth and rising prosperity, satisfyingly attractive prices for agricultural produce on the international market and expansion across society. Maybe it was a long, slow boom, but a boom is a boom, and it lay behind much of the comfort in this period.[31]

Bulldozer blitz

Industrial development was the other prong to growth. Its effects were obvious, immediate and long-lasting. Bulldozers cut the landscape, rivers were diverted, bush and wildlife were disrupted, rock-art sites were destroyed, and huge steel and concrete edifices were erected in town and country. Maori and community groups murmured their protest at some schemes, but New Zealanders generally welcomed the developments. The expansion rivalled that of the Vogel era 80 years before, and once again, the state was behind much of the activity.

After the war, demand for electricity far exceeded supply. Most of the country was electrified by the 1940s, but people and business wanted more. There was simply not enough power to go around and restrictions were imposed periodically through to the mid 1950s. Domestic users were most affected, but if the country's manufacturing, farming and industrial base was to expand further, more power was needed, and quickly.[32]

National continued Labour's efforts to harness the geothermal resources of the central North Island. The result was the Wairakei geothermal power station where drilling began in 1950. The station, completed in 1963, was the second-largest of its kind in the world. Hydroelectric schemes were the main focus. The Waikato River, with stations on it since the 1920s, continued as the North Island hub. More stations were added from the late 1940s. The river became a series of adjoining lakes, separated by towering concrete dams and enormous stations: Karapiro, Mangakino, Maraetai, Whakamaru, Atiamuri, Waipapa and so into the gorges and rapids of Aratiatia. When that last station was completed in 1964, 20 years of construction on the Waikato closed.

Down South, the Waitaki and Clutha rivers were dammed. The Roxburgh station, constructed between 1949 and 1956, was the country's largest hydro project at the time, with digging and tunnelling machines operating round the clock for six days

ECNZ/Transpower, Energyinfo

Serious planning for the Cook Strait cable had been under way since 1950. The three cables — the largest, heaviest submarine cables at the time — were laid over a period of a month. The crew of the *Photinia* began work at Oteranga Bay on Wellington's rugged coast at noon on 12 November 1964, reeling out cable for six hours, after which the vessel turned, made a six-hour voyage to Fighting Bay in the outer Marlborough Sounds and laid the other end of the cable. On land, over 1600 steel towers carrying transmission lines formed a giant's pathway through Canterbury and Marlborough.

READY-MADE TOWNS:
MANGAKINO

Localised mini-booms could last only as long as the construction of power stations. Temporary villages appeared almost overnight, with clusters of huts, cookhouses, maybe a small shop, and a recreation hall that doubled as a bar. These were frontier settlements of mainly young single men, many of them Maori, who worked hard and probably partied even harder.

The Waikato schemes needed a more permanent base. Planning for the town of Mangakino began in 1946 and within two years there were 500 houses. The idea was to have a cross-section of the population, workers and their families as well as single men. All a family would expect to find in a small town would be there: civic centre, shops and schools, a bus station and a post office.

For a time, settlement was too quick. Houses had no inside water or lighting, the roads were unsealed, shops not yet open and for some months there was no resident doctor. But by the end of 1948 things were on the up. A maternity hospital and district high school were established in that year, and a couple of years later most of the usual urban facilities were available.

Almost 6500 people lived at Mangakino at its height in 1959. But there was always a feeling of uncertainty — would the government give the go-ahead on the next hydro development and guarantee work? The cancellation of a scheme in 1961 wrought havoc. Within two years the population had plummeted to 2000 as people moved elsewhere in search of work. Mangakino now services the surrounding dairy farms.[33]

New Zealand modern: Mangakino was designed by Ernst Plischke, one of this country's most prominent architects. Archives New Zealand

a week. Its completion ended power restrictions in the South Island, but northerners still languished in the dark. Getting more power from South to North was high on the government's agenda. The development of Benmore on the Waitaki River was crucial. Here was the southern end of the Cook Strait cable that siphoned power from the South Island to the North. Holyoake flicked the 'on' switch at Benmore in May 1965, firing up the cable that provided the North Island with around 13 per cent of its power in the next year.

Jobs went begging on many of the developments. Filling the vacancies was one reason for a new immigration scheme. Between 1947 and 1975 the New Zealand government assisted 77,000 Britons and over 6000 Dutch to migrate. Free or cheap passage was provided in return for work, including work on the hydro projects. Over half the workers at Roxburgh were migrants from Britain, the Netherlands and Germany.[34]

Forestry also needed workers. The exotic pine forests in the central North Island were ready for milling by the early 1950s. In

LEFT: Air travel took off in the 1950s and 1960s. National Airways Corporation (NAC) connected main and provincial centres for the traveller and producer who needed quick, long-distance transport. Best of all were the big jets that sped here from the other side of the world, touching down in Auckland first in 1963. Two years later Air New Zealand headed off to Los Angeles in its own DC8s. The world would never look the same again. Museum of New Zealand, Te Papa, Tongarewa

BELOW: John Johns photographed for the New Zealand Forest Service during the 1950s and 1960s. His images provided a stunning visual record of the flora and fauna of indigenous and exotic forests, such as this Canterbury pine forest, photographed in 1955. Auckland Art Gallery, Toi o Tamaki

1955 Tasman Pulp and Paper Company's huge mill at Kawerau became operational, and with it the new towns of Murupara and Kawerau. Mill and forest were the lifeblood of these places. Maori plugged many of the gaps in the forestry gangs, which provided steady work for communities in surrounding districts.

Big growth also came in the manufacturing sector. Relaxed import controls helped, as imported parts boosted the number of vehicles and machinery assembled locally. High standards of living created intense consumer demand for appliances, especially once electricity flowed: 56,500 radios and 38,500 refrigerators were made in 1952; 140,000 and 44,000 a decade later.[35]

Parts of Auckland became industrial parks. The region's manufacturing production all but equalled that of the entire South Island and it continued to swell. Greater consumer demand and population, and proximity to the public works and forestry schemes attracted investors and entrepreneurs. Mt Wellington, Penrose and South Auckland morphed into factory zones producing motor vehicles, clothing and consumer products.

Development demanded good transportation networks. The rail line reached its peak length and coverage in 1952. Government policy here went beyond building tracks and running the system. Railways were protected, to some extent, from competition from road transport. With the exception of goods such as livestock, or where there were no rail services, road haulage firms were only permitted to transport goods up to a distance of 48 km. The establishment of the Cook Strait rail–road ferry in 1962 provided a vital link by allowing easier movement of goods,

and passengers, between the islands. For the first time, there was a true national railway system. Despite protections, road steadily became more important for getting goods around the country, and the government revised upwards the distance that trucks could carry goods — 64 km from 1961, 150 km from 1976. Tarsealing the last portion of State Highway One between Auckland and Wellington in 1954 must have helped here.[36]

Bright lights, big city

In the cities there were shops, supermarkets, malls, new houses, ample work, a varied nightlife, bars, dance venues and, even from the early 1960s, a few high-class restaurants. Parts of the cities may have shut down in the weekend, but the lights were bright and they were where people wanted to be. They were hardly New York or London, but New Zealand's cities were bigger and better than they had ever been before.

Maori led the charge. Maori and Pakeha worlds had existed largely separately before the Second World War, with most Maori in country areas, working on their own farms, in local industries or as seasonal labourers. War work attracted Maori to towns and cities, and during the 1950s and 1960s this became a full-blown migration, adding another travel saga to Maori history. Before the war, about 75 per cent of Maori lived in the country; two decades later, around 60 per cent lived in urban areas. Such a massive relocation of people over a generation is startling, and is central in shaping recent events.[37]

Push and pull factors came into it. Land pushed. The development schemes launched by Apirana Ngata in the 1920s were never going to be sufficient to make viable much of the four million acres of land still held by Maori. Good-sized chunks of that land were poor quality and would neither sustain development nor provide its owners with a decent livelihood. Only 54 of the 500 residents of the Te Rarawa community of Ahipara in the Far North made a living working for the nine full-time farmers there in the 1950s. It was not enough.[38]

Demography pushed as well. The Maori population nearly doubled between 1951 and 1966. This can be explained by more babies and children, as well as better health and longer life expectancy — the 'Maori death bust'.[39] No amount of development on marginal lands was likely to support the population.

Employment pulled. First step for some was the industries of the central North Island, hydro and timber especially, which attracted workers from nearby areas. Tuhoe from Ruatahuna went to timber towns reasonably close to home, such as Kaingaroa, in preference to centres further afield. The pay was better too, and Maori there in the early 1960s could earn above the Maori national median wage — though still less than the Pakeha median.[40] Bay of Plenty timber created new Maori communities: Murupara, Tokoroa, Kawerau and Putaruru.

Policy pulled, too. The Department of Maori Affairs ran an urban 'relocation' programme from 1960. Families trying to eke out a subsistence living on their kainga, supplemented by seasonal work, could get assistance to move to town. Within five years, 400 families had been relocated, and nearly 500 more had found jobs or houses.[41]

Work, money and pleasure — 'the big three' — were to be had in the cities, and the majority of Maori moved there without government assistance, taking their chances on getting a house and job.[42] The metropolitan sprawls of Auckland and Wellington offered plenty of jobs, normally unskilled and blue-collar work, in manufacturing or on construction sites. This was safe enough in the booms of the 1950s and 1960s, but it carried the seeds of future Maori unemployment in the economic crises that came from the mid 1960s.

The urban lifestyle posed particular challenges. 'Taking permanent employment, coping with a total cash economy . . . that had little scope for subsistence activities, and meeting . . . rent, time-payment, hire purchase, rates and mortgages' occupied them.[43] Financially, Maori were better off than they had ever been, but making it in the city required a thick skin, and not just because of the considerable racism and hostility many encountered. Department of Maori Affairs welfare officers visited stressed families wrestling with the demands of

Urbanisation meant depopulation of the rural hinterlands, or at least a shift in their demographic structure as younger people moved away. Culture and language remained strong in many of the rural communities — such as this one in 1963 — giving the lie to official ideas about integration.

the new environment. A Whangarei Home Counselling Service saw 70 families in 1963, a third of whom had migrated within the previous five years, with 'a pile of debts and judgement summonses'.[44]

It wasn't just the daily practicalities of the Pakeha system, either. Urbanisation meant, to some extent, 'redefining aspects of Maoriness'. People now had to think about the things they had taken for granted back home: how to run a hui, how to keep the language going, what to do for tangihanga.[45] The risk of dislocation from cultural roots was high and this occurred frequently, but voluntary associations, sports clubs and religious networks tried to keep cultural links vibrant.

Te Ropu Wahine Maori Toko i te Ora (the Maori Women's Welfare League) was one group that supported Maori through the difficult urban transition, both in terms of coping with 'Pakeha-ness' and retaining 'Maori-ness'. The league offered advice and material assistance on health, education, child care, and a host of other matters. Under Whina Cooper's leadership from 1951, the league walked the difficult line of presenting a Maori view and being pragmatic.

The Maori Council assumed some of that role from 1962. This pan-tribal organisation was established by Holyoake's government to form a cadre of National-leaning Maori leaders who would help parry the Maori MPs who had been solidly Labour

Ans Westra

The Community Centre in Auckland, opened in 1948, was one of the important facilities Maori established for the urbanising population. It rocked all weekend with dances and live bands. The big names in entertainment played there, including the Howard Morrison Quartet, the Maori Volcanics, the Hi Fives, and Kiri Te Kanawa. It provided the comforts of home, too, with boil-ups, rewena paraoa and kaimoana on the menu.

Archives New Zealand

'You'll have better prospects if you korero Pakeha.' The relatively healthy state of te reo (language) had crumbled through education policies and the urban rush. Hoani (Johnny to his friends) Waititi was one who worked above and beyond to remedy this. He was behind the Maori Education Foundation, his *Te Rangatahi* textbooks became classics, and he taught te reo at schools such as the Queen Victoria School for Maori Girls in the 1950s.

for two decades. It was one of the outcomes of the Report on the Department of Maori Affairs (the Hunn Report), commissioned by Nash's government but not released officially until 1961. The report was both a snapshot and a reasonably comprehensive study of urbanisation and its effects on Maori and the country as a whole. It was not without controversy, and its recommendations about 'racial policy' troubled many Maori greatly. 'Evolution is clearly integrating Maori and Pakeha' — 'Pakeha' here meaning modern — and such integration was behind policies such as the 'pepper-potting' of Maori families into Pakeha state-housing areas. The report also noted the need for 'some continuation' of Maori culture, although Maori themselves had to decide what features 'of their ancient life are . . . to be kept alive'.[46]

Working beyond one iwi was essential in the mix of the urban environment. Culture clubs, community centres and urban marae picked up the challenge of providing space for all iwi, as

Urban Motorways . . .

More vehicles travel safely when people invest in Modern Roads; Journeys are shorter & cost less.

Motorways seemed the solution to Auckland's traffic woes in the 1950s.

Auckland was a city built for cars. Its love affair with them caused problems that have stretched into the 21st century. In 1955, the Farmers Trading Company erected New Zealand's first multi-storey car-parking building. It could accommodate 500 cars over six levels in the heart of Auckland.

well as 'detribalised' people, to gather. Several leaders, including Whina Cooper and Maori Battalion leader Arapeta Awatere, who founded a cultural club and also taught marae protocols through the adult education programme at the University of Auckland, dreamed of a marae where all could gather. It was easier dreamed than done, but in 1965 the marae Te Puea opened at Mangere under the Tainui confederation of tribes and was made available to all migrants regardless of iwi. Pan-tribal marae would follow.[47]

Maori migration showcased the shifting distribution of population. Main centres became larger, both through natural increase and as a result of the greater employment opportunities. Once-provincial centres such as Hamilton emerged as major cities. Southern centres such as Christchurch and Invercargill spread some more, but people continued to favour the North. The gap between the islands became more pronounced in these years.

The Big Two — Wellington and Auckland — burgeoned through rampant suburbanisation. The combined population of Wellington and the Hutt Valley jumped from around 200,000 in 1951 to almost 290,000 in 1966, with much of the growth occurring in the state-housing suburbs in the Hutt Valley and new suburbs up the coast.[48]

More and more, however, it was just the Big One. Auckland grew massively, both in numbers and space. The 330,000 people who lived there in 1951 were joined by another 220,000 by 1966; within another decade, a third of New Zealand was there. 'Auckland' was a misnomer. In the mid 1960s it was made up of a clutch of cities: Manukau, Takapuna, Papatoetoe and Auckland. Together with a host of boroughs and suburbs they fanned out across the bays, plains, isthmus and remains of volcanoes that distinguished the landscape. The conglomeration was mammoth by international standards: 40 km from north to south, 25 from east to west, and it just kept spreading.[49]

Auckland was, and still is, a suburban sprawl. Not all was fairly gained, even in the 20th century. Orakei was built over the traditional and ancestral lands of Ngati Whatua who had been dealing with the government about their land since the 1930s. They were finally evicted in 1952 to allow in the developers. Protesting and weeping, the people were relocated to new state houses. Kuia and kaumatua passed away within a year of the forced shift, and the houses they had left were razed to the ground. Te Puea Herangi sent a message to the Minister of Maori Affairs — she could still smell the smoke of the burning buildings: 'The suburb of Orakei inherited a fine playground. Ngati Whatua inherited a legacy of bitterness, division and defeat.'[50] It was a legacy that would erupt in years to come.

Auckland's suburbs contained all the mod cons, and it was probably no accident that they appeared first in Auckland's vastness. In 1957 the first supermarket opened there; the next — in Otahuhu 1958 — had parking for 150 cars. Pakuranga,

developed from the early 1960s, had a shopping mall by 1965, one of the country's first, with space for 150 cars. A new experience in one-stop shopping had begun, and supermarkets eventually took over from small dairies and specialist stores. But importantly, they symbolised a mobile population that loaded up the boot or back seat in weekly or fortnightly buying sprees.[51]

All New Zealand was mobile, lagging only behind the United States, Canada and Australia as the most motorised countries. But where Wellingtonians used an extensive public transport system, Aucklanders relied on cars; traffic lights were introduced there in 1947 to control the flow of traffic. Out in the suburbs, people could live in one area, and work and shop in another. An estimated 40 per cent of commuters surged into central Auckland by car every weekday in 1954.[52]

Gridlock highlighted just how much the infrastructure struggled to match its growth. Public transport systems were running down, and trams disappeared from streets in the 1950s. Motorways would be the answer to traffic problems that were already only too apparent for people trying to go about their daily business. A key link was the Harbour Bridge, opened in 1959. Planners expected that it would take 19 years for the volume of bridge traffic to reach eight million vehicles a year. Five years was too many, and the bridge was enlarged with clip-on lanes within the decade.

The expanding city displayed other problems associated with sudden growth. Social services lagged. Child welfare officers in Otahuhu in the early 1960s recalled the overwork from rising caseloads: 'four nights a week, probably through to nine or ten at night . . . just doing office work . . . just doing catch-up work . . . and you'd also spend one day in the weekend working full-time in the office.'[53] Extremes of rich and poor were visible, as they had always been, but the rush to the cities threw differences into sharp relief. Migration, especially of Maori in the 1950s and Pacific Islanders in the 1960s, lifted the lid on simmering social and racial problems.

The golden weather

Just mention the term 'post-war', and a mantra is likely to begin among many who grew up then. Dull, boring, grey — any dowdy epithet will do to describe an oh-so-tedious time brought to life by a few rowdy teenagers. As many remember it as exciting Friday nights cruising the streets, great music, lots of cash, fantastic clothes, good sex. These more energised baby-boomers seem to have fallen quiet as they have aged; their ennui-ridden youthful counterparts, burst forth from repressive suburbia, have shaped our views of the period. Their story of the pavlova paradise is only a partial one, and cries for revision.[54] This was not a time of mass protest and challenges to the status quo, for that would

A LITTLE NIGHT MUSIC

For those who knew where to go, Auckland and Wellington offered more in the way of entertainment than the picture theatre or dance hall found in the majority of towns. The much-criticised six o'clock closing of pubs at least allowed a bit of nightlife to bloom. There were cabarets and nightclubs, jazz and dance clubs, and coffee bars where intellectuals and 'bohemians' gathered before heading off to parties where alcohol and marijuana were on offer. Auckland's 'Angels', beautiful young things clustering around Rainton Hastie, later a striptease entrepreneur, bragged of a lifestyle of loud music, bars and cafes, booze and casual sex.[55] Wellington had Harry Seresin's coffee bar, established in 1958, and the Sorrento Coffee Bar. Auckland had the Montmartre, the Polynesian Club,

the Peter Pan Cabaret and the Picasso Jazz Basement where patrons could be assured of music until all hours. The Maori Community Centre, opened in 1948, buzzed for two decades.

The sex industry ticked along. Lifestyles could be full-on — all-night drinking parties, a few drugs, sex and more sex. In Ponsonby, Flora McKenzie's exclusive brothel employed 'sophisticated' women for the city's leading men. Randy sailors looked for action; 'shipgirls' and 'shipqueens' worked the boats, although in this respect provincial New Plymouth rivalled the big centres. Massage clubs and strip bars did business along Vivian Street and K Road, scarcely bothered by the police. Same-sex networks existed largely underground in the big cities; those who needed to, knew.

The Sorrento Coffee Bar — one of Wellington's reefer clubs. It was home to the coolest of the cool: jazz musicians, beat poets à la Ginsberg, men with slim pants and women with big hair.

The Top Twenty Club was at the top of Auckland's Vulcan Lane. Max Merritt and the Meteors was its resident band for a time in the 1960s.

come later, and even then only from a few; the status quo was just a lot more interesting than is often assumed. Nowhere was this more evident than in culture both popular and high.

The young reaped the benefits of the prosperous economy. For many, aspirations were not constrained by the traumatic events of depression and war that had disrupted their parents' lives. There was plenty of work; they could afford to go to the movies or dances, buy cars or motorbikes. Teenagers feasted on the popular culture streaming out of North America and replayed here on the radio, in the movies, in books, comics, language and speech. Clothing styles showed it all. Young Maori in Ruatoria sported oversize cowboy hats in imitation of Gene Autry, 'the Singing Cowboy'; young women wore the matador pants or straight, tight skirts seen on Hollywood stars; young men poured themselves into tight pants and leather jackets in the style of James Dean. English styles were not abandoned. Suave young men adopted the narrow tie, Edwardian dress-coat and duck-arse haircuts so beloved among London's 'teddy boys'.[56] Bob Jones recollected:

> I can remember the first pair of stovepipe trousers in Lower Hutt. In a group of perhaps 50 or 100 kids we followed this fellow . . . down the street gazing in awe at the stovepipe trousers, pointing and laughing and mocking . . . We were all wearing them, of course, a few years later, and another ten years passed and the public servants were wearing them.[57]

Distinctive groups emerged. 'Milkbar cowboys' frequented the ever-popular milk-bar and rode round on motorcycles. Some raced up and down Auckland's Queen Street; Christchurch milk-bar cowboys — 'self-styled charmers and their "pillion pets"' — made a swift invasion of Timaru one weekend, much to the consternation of startled locals. Bodgies and widgies, dressing in American styles, listened to the latest music releases. In the 1960s, mods appeared, more influenced by the British scene.[58]

A good number of teenagers also spent their adolescence wearing twin-sets and pearls or freshly laundered shirts and corduroy slacks. Pimples, homework, getting the latest single and finding a partner at the dance were the big challenges. But the teenage world was under intense adult scrutiny, especially during the 1950s. It was not that this world was any better or worse than that of earlier generations, but the clothes, entertainment opportunities, money and lifestyles created a culture that adults found mysterious and rebellious.

'Juvenile delinquency' is synonymous with 1950s teenagers. The famous episode was in the Hutt Valley in 1954, one of four separate inquiries into teenage behaviour in the area in the 1950s. After a young woman admitted that she was leading a 'depraved sexual life' among a group of adolescents, police inquiries revealed there were 50 of them who frequented milk-bars and met in private homes or parks to have sex. The report of a special committee to inquire into youth moral delinquency, released in 1955 and sent to every home receiving a benefit, told a story of juvenile immorality. Working mums, insufficient healthy leisure pursuits in new housing suburbs like the Hutt Valley, the forwardness of young women, and the pernicious effects of American culture were all considered to be causes. Government reaction was predictably knee-jerk, legislating against various types of publication and adolescents who performed 'indecent' acts.

A storm of interest in juvenile delinquency was unleashed. It was looked for, and found, everywhere. Parents were advised on how to check for bodgie signs in their children — watch the 'odd clothing cults'. Hordes of milk-bar cowboys, bodgies and widgies were said to be running riot. And they were in a couple of places. In 1958 teenagers trashed trains in Hutt Valley's Manor Park; and in 1960 some of the 5000 who travelled up to the Hastings Blossom Festival ran amok. Academics and other specialists got in on the act. Psychological reports were published, radio documentaries aired, pages of print filled.[59]

But the extent of juvenile delinquency has been overrated. The big fuss occurred as appearances before the children's court were declining. There was an upsurge in cases from the mid 1950s, but by then, people were looking for signs of trouble. Young people had acted up in the 1940s — 1944 was the high point for appearances before the children's court — to little public comment. Police and other inquiries into teenage behaviour in the later 1950s and 1960s passed with nary a murmur. In 1964, police interviewed 400 teenagers and their parents in Grey Lynn and Panmure concerning 'sexual misbehaviour'. *Truth* squawked about these 'Pyjama parties without pyjamas'; but no one noticed. Public interest in the affairs of youth had come and gone.[60]

New Zealand enjoyed the world revolution in music and dance. Big bands, swing, jazz, and country-and-western ballads had dominated the music and dance scene for some time. These are not the sounds that are remembered, or that were essential to teenage dance and music culture. Rock 'n' roll, an overnight sensation, hit in the mid 1950s. Jukeboxes became a fixture of milk-bars, and by the end of 1956 there were rock 'n' roll venues for teenagers to jive and twist away in. Dance endurance contests became popular. The first took place in Wellington's Roseland Cabaret in April 1957. Twenty-three hours into the contest the still-gyrating couples were trucked to the Town Hall where they went on for another three hours.

Local stars strutted their stuff. Johnny Cooper, 'The Maori Cowboy', recorded a couple of Bill Haley covers in the mid 1950s; they were not hugely successful, but his 'Pie Cart Rock 'n' roll' was arguably the first Kiwi rock classic. Its story was uniquely New Zealand anyway — a song written in exchange for the promise of free meals at the Wanganui pie cart.

AE Manning's work was published in 1958 and traced the background of 30 bodgies and widgies from both sides of the Tasman. The illustrations were by Dennis Turner. Interviewed in *The Rising Generation*, broadcast in 1958, one bodgie stated, 'We're just ordinary sensible jokers.'

Distinctive new buildings showcased experimentation and adventure among local architects. John Scott's Futuna Chapel (1961) in the Wellington suburb of Karori was a radical departure in church design.

GANGS OF AUCKLAND

Talk of gangs and subcultures led to an inquiry into teenage gang activity in 1958. Auckland, with its burgeoning social problems, was the target. Alan Levett, formerly director of Dunedin's Kensington Youth Centre, had a roving commission to mix and mingle with gangs in the newer parts of town — 'a "follow your nose" procedure, indirect questioning and informal chat mixed with hamburgers and cheap coffee'.

Levett collected information on 41 gangs with about 700 members all up, ranging in age from 12 to 24. Gang names came straight from Hollywood, comics or the latest hit: Red Ram Rockers, Rebels, Holy Rockers, Earth Angels. Others advertised their patch: Avondale Virgins, Epsom Boys, Kingsland Roughs, and more prosaically, Balmoral Dairy Company (whose attitude, if not their name, was 'insolent'). Jeans, leather jackets, long hair and colourful clothes were the usual dress, with few — the Arcade Boys among them — noted as 'slick'. 'Hanging around' seemed the favoured activity, along with fighting, drag-racing, a bit of stealing, parties, sex — and 'police baiting'.[61]

More serious and out-to-shock than the gangs Levett chatted with were the Auckland motorcycle gang Hell's Angels. They ruffled the feathers of the good citizens of New Plymouth in 1966 with their clothing and Nazi memorabilia, seen to be in particularly bad taste just two decades on from the war.

THE SATIN SATAN

Wanganui played a key part in New Zealand's rock 'n' roll history. Johnny Devlin, 'The Wanganui Elvis', 'New Zealand's Elvis Presley', and more impressively, 'the Satin Satan', made his stage debut yodelling in a talent quest at its Opera House in 1951. Johnny Cooper spotted him in a talent quest in Marton in early 1957 and gave him some hints on presentation and voice control (the yodelling routine was history by now). Devlin won the next talent quest he entered, in Dannevirke, and from there it was up to the throbbing music scene of Auckland. His first performance at the Jive Centre was startling; the audience screamed hysterically as he sang and moved across the stage. 'I guess I shook my leg or something and they screamed. Then I shook it again, and they screamed again.'

Hits like 'Lawdy Miss Clawdy' came in 1958. Devlin toured to ecstatic audiences. He sped off from one show in a pink Cadillac, accompanied by a fur-wearing Mabel Howard, Minister in Charge of Child Welfare. Shrieking women queued for a look at their idol, but most wanted something more. Devlin took to throwing bits of his clothes into the audience, and his agents sewed his shirts so that fans could rip them from his back. In Invercargill, riotous fans tore off his trousers, broke into backstage, and Devlin had to escape out a toilet window; in Greymouth, minders turned the fire hose onto fans intent on groping their hero.[62]

A year or so after its introduction in New Zealand, Johnny Devlin became Coke's poster boy. Coca-Cola sponsored Devlin's national tour of 1958.

New Zealand Magazines Archive

Ray Columbus and the Invaders released 'She's a Mod' in mid 1964; it stayed at the top of the Australian charts for eight weeks. In 1965 the band opened for the Rolling Stones. Invercargill became news; Ray Columbus and the Invaders got a rapturous welcome there, but the Stones were pelted with rotten tomatoes and eggs. Television helped bands get valuable exposure. *Time Out for Talent*, run by the Christchurch studios of the NZBC in 1961, was followed by *In the Groove* and *Let's Go*.

Maori musicians, and especially show bands, were to the fore. The Hi Fives and others performed to audiences who thrived on the verve and excitement generated up on stage. Energy was high. The Howard Morrison Quartet burst from Rotorua with a string of irreverent and peculiarly Kiwi hits like 'My Old Man's an All Black' and 'The Battle of the Waikato'. By 1964 the Quartet was one of the country's most popular family entertainers. Maori musicians and artists received a huge boost when the New Zealand Opera Company toured *Porgy and Bess* with a strong Maori cast headed by Inia Te Wiata; the show played to packed houses in every town in 1965.

The entire cultural and artistic sector experienced a surge of energy and creativity. Ground-breaking work altered cultural and artistic boundaries — Colin McCahon's 'Northland' panels in 1958; the haunting poetry of James K Baxter and Allen Curnow. Major writers of the later 20th century made their entry: Janet Frame, Maurice Gee, Maurice Shadbolt, Alistair Campbell and Hone Tuwhare. Professional theatre companies

toured, and when Wellington's Downstage Theatre opened its doors in 1964, it became the country's first professional theatre. Some years earlier, Bruce Mason's play *The End of the Golden Weather* had marked the 'arrival' of local drama.

Important infrastructures for the arts were established. In 1961 the Arts Advisory Council put subsidies to artists on a regular footing and more funding was made available. New groups such as the Historic Places Trust emerged, putting the protection of New Zealand's built heritage on the national agenda after 1954. The government continued to sponsor the arts. The New Zealand Ballet Company was formed in 1953, and the Opera Company the following year. At the Auckland City Art Gallery, the country's first full-time professional director provided a national focus for artists. There were festivals, and the gallery took a lead in bringing major works to New Zealand — in the later 1950s, 50,000 people turned up to view the Henry Moore sculpture exhibition.

The New Zealand of 1965 was light years away from that of 1949. People looked different, their expectations were higher, they lived in different places, and they had freedoms and opportunities that earlier generations lacked. When evangelist Billy Graham toured in 1959, 40,000 people packed Wellington's Athletic Park to hear his message of love and faith. One was Johnny Devlin; Walter Nash was another. Devlin, Nash and Graham — rocker, politician and evangelist — were photographed together; the frameworks of family, law and order were still reasonably secure.

Met At Park

ence."

spiritual things. Devlin described himself as "vitally interested" after his discussion with Mr. Piatt.

Late Shipping

Wellington. — Sunday; Arrived, Tanea (4.55 p.m.), Dunedin; Kokiri (11.5 p.m.), Westport.

FIGHT OR LOSE

NEW YORK, April 5.—The New York State Athletic Commission has ordered Sugar Ray Robinson to sign up to defend his world middleweight title against Carmen Basilio by April 15 or face the loss of his crown.

DR. BILLY GRAHAM, Mr. Nash, and Johnny Devlin, photographed at Dr. Graham's opening crusade meeting in Athletic Park, Wellington, yesterday.

Who would have expected the lurex-wearing, guitar-toting Kiwi rocker Johnny Devlin (right) to turn up at the open-air ministry of Billy Graham (left) in Wellington in 1959 wearing a suit and looking for all the world like a teenaged choirboy? This photograph of Devlin and Graham with Prime Minister Walter Nash captured some of the underlying social stability in the 1950s. *Dominion,* 6 April 1959

Chapter 12

Identity politics, whether on an individual, social or national level, helped shape the ethos of New Zealand life between 1965 and 1984. Jacqueline Fahey's painting captured some of the feminist elements of the changing moods that swept the country.

J Fahey, Auckland Art Gallery, Toi o Tamaki

Generations
1965–1984

It could have been Rob's finest moment. It was the National Party conference in 1974. Robert Muldoon, counter-puncher and economic wizard, had just been elected leader of the party. The press were captivated by him; the party faithful, loving his energy and belligerent wisecracks, were eating out of his hand. At one point he bellowed from the platform that no one in the hall could possibly advocate the legalisation of marijuana. Back came a lone voice, 'I would.' The speaker was Gavin Muldoon, Rob's son, sitting among the Young Nats.[1]

The confrontation of father and son, or rather parent and child, was in one sense the motif of these years. Between 1965 and 1984 the value system that had been largely accepted by most New Zealanders for over half a century came under challenge. Whether it was beer or drugs, 'horis' or 'tangata whenua', war or peace, 'Mrs' or 'Ms', these were the years when slogans flourished and arguments flew. People marched in the streets and shouted on talkback shows. The period ended with a country seemingly more divided than it had been for a hundred years; and the new values that would emerge reshaped the way New Zealanders saw themselves.

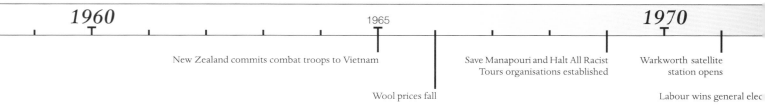

1960   1965   *1970*

New Zealand commits combat troops to Vietnam   Save Manapouri and Halt All Racist   Warkworth satellite
Tours organisations established   station opens

Wool prices fall   Labour wins general elec

Roots of revolution

'Don't trust anyone over 30,' proclaimed Tim Shadbolt, leader of the Auckland University Society for the Active Prevention of Cruelty to Politically Apathetic Humans, on *Gallery*, a much-watched television programme of the late 1960s.[2] One way of seeing the conflict of values is to explore the distinctive life experiences of two generations. Many people who ruled New Zealand in these years had been born in the 1920s: they were 35–45 in 1965, 55–65 in 1984. They had grown up into economic depression and then war. Hard work, the need to save, the value of the welfare state was the legacy of the slump; a belief in the Empire/Commonwealth and international security was the legacy of the war. The baby-boomers, born after 1945 and aged 20 or under in 1965, 40 or under in 1984, grew up in affluence and full employment. They were freer to challenge the quest for security in lifestyle and politics and to imagine a new culture. Tim Shadbolt explained, 'Our generation isn't just kicking its heels against the establishment, we are preparing a whole new lifestyle; we are almost a sub-culture with a whole new set of ideas.'[3]

In retrospect, 1965 was the end of the 'golden wether'. The following year, as the country was encouraged by a young politician, Robert Muldoon, and a catchy jingle to look forward to a decimal currency economy on 'July the 10th of next year', wool prices collapsed. By the end of the season the Wool Commission had bought over a third of the clip. Although there were brief respites, the country was to face a continuing struggle for the next 18 years. Prices for agricultural products remained low; prices for imports rose. Between 1972 and 1975 the terms of trade fell by 40 per cent, meaning that nearly three lambs or bales of wool had to be exported for every two previously. The 'oil shocks' of 1973 and 1979 accentuated the problem and annoyed a community in which cars had become an expected convenience.

Britain's entry into the European Common Market in 1973 was of greater long-term significance. In 1965 New Zealand sent over half its exports by value to the United Kingdom, but the days of the British housewife paying New Zealanders' bills

Eymard Bradley

During the 1960s and 1970s migrants from Tonga, Samoa, the Cook Islands and other Pacific Islands moved to New Zealand's main cities, especially Auckland, where work seemed abundant. These women found jobs in a canning factory. But like many Maori, migrants from the Pacific clustered in the low-paying jobs that were the first to go when times got tough.

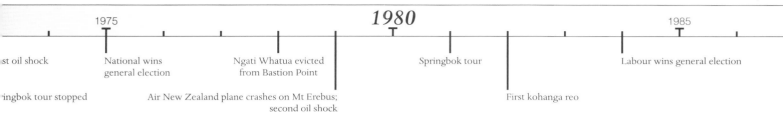

1975   *1980*   1985

st oil shock

National wins
general election

Ngati Whatua evicted
from Bastion Point

Springbok tour

Labour wins general election

ringbok tour stopped

Air New Zealand plane crashes on Mt Erebus;
second oil shock

First kohanga reo

were over. Ten years later just over a fifth of our exports went to Britain; in 1984 only a tenth.[4] From 1970 New Zealand began to suffer from rising prices, growing unemployment and a stubborn lack of growth. Unemployment, which was under 10,000 in the census of 1966, was over 100,000 twenty years later. New Zealand fell precipitously from the sixth most wealthy country per person in 1965 to 19th in 1980.[5]

Economic problems contributed to the noisiness and bitterness of these years — housewives CARPing (Campaign against Rising Prices), unionists calling for better pay, farmers whingeing. The pressures were especially severe down on the farm. This was farm and small town versus big city. The traditional troika of wool, meat and dairy products, which had sustained farming incomes for 50 years, fell by 1984 to just over half our export receipts.[6] As the payouts fell in value, costs for fuel rose. Young farmers struggling to meet mortgages as interest payments escalated vented their frustrations on bankers or freezing workers who were also trying to 'keep pace'. In the small towns shops closed, paint began to peel. There were pockets of rural growth: kiwifruit in the Bay of Plenty, the beginnings of a wine expansion. But these were relatively small in value and were likely to be investments of the urban wealthy. So the rural sector looked with jealousy and suspicion towards the concrete towers and unsettling ideas of the city.

In the city slow growth also brought pain and anger. Many rural Maori and immigrants had moved there for a better life and they were often the first to get the redundancy letter. Yet the city saw areas of growth — manufactured goods rose from 16 per cent of exports in 1974 to 28 per cent 10 years later —

As New Zealand became more confidently urban, the farmer became a fond figure of the past. The best examples were John Clarke's television caricature of the gumbooted black-singleted Fred Dagg pictured here, and Murray Ball's cartoon and later film, *Footrot Flats*. Peter Bush

and it was here that new values were born.[7] There was a major expansion in the size of New Zealand cities during the 1950s and early 1960s, but the style of life had remained essentially suburban. At 5.30 p.m. every weekday, Aucklanders sped along new motorways and Wellingtonians boarded commuter trains to seek peace and harmony in the suburbs. At the weekend, one British immigrant noted, 'you could have shot a rifle in the street and you wouldn't have hit anybody'.[8]

By the late 1960s the scene was changing fast. There was an increase in nightlife, which included theatre, trendy restaurants and more than the traditional Hollywood fare at the movies. Auckland held its first film festival in 1968; three years later Wellington followed. The young middle class left the suburbs for the inner city. In Ponsonby and Herne Bay in Auckland, in Mt Victoria and Thorndon in Wellington, they restored old houses. The recent migrants, especially Pacific Islanders, moved out. As the city grew in size (by 1984 a quarter of New Zealanders lived in Auckland) and confidence, it became aware of how foreign the old rural mythology was. Aucklander Robin Morrison's photographs of rural South Island were published in what became a prize-winning book. Urbanites laughing at farmers and small-town New Zealanders looking enviously at the trendies of the city were part of the flavour of the period.

Behind the rise of urban culture lay another crucial revolution. Jobs in the city were increasingly dependent upon education. Lawyers, bankers, computer specialists, social workers, civil servants, teachers, actors — all needed a formal education. In the 1950s universal secondary education had led

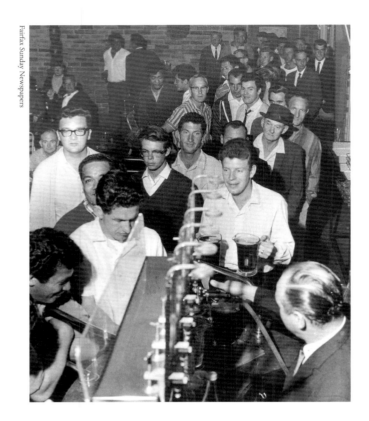

to a dramatic increase in high schools. Now it was the turn of universities and polytechnics. In 1965, when the first baby-boomers arrived on campus, there were some 20,000 students. Twenty years later the figure was almost 50,000. These young people were encouraged to think for themselves and to question. They were exposed to ideas from the international community of learning. They had the time and opportunity to take part in protest marches. They were articulate. Higher education provided a seedbed for new values and an audience for new urban entertainments.

New forms of communication were another catalyst for change. Jet travel took New Zealanders to the world, where they developed a taste for urban sophistication, and brought travellers here who already had it. The overseas tourists did not want New Zealand 'closed'; they wanted good food, slick entertainment and long shopping hours.

A growing nationalism gave urgency to debate. Throughout these years the number of foreign-born people in the society

In September 1967 New Zealanders voted overwhelmingly to end the 'six o'clock swill' — the 6 p.m. closing of pubs. On this first night of 10 p.m. closing (left), not much seems to have changed. It is still blokes drinking from jugs. But within a few years the pubs would have become more inviting to women, with the provision of comfortable chairs, more wines available behind the bar and live band entertainment.

The official opening day at Mangere International Airport, two months after the first jet had landed there in November 1965. Jets made overseas travel fast and relatively cheap. 'OE' (Overseas Experience), the expression coined by cartoonist Tom Scott, became an obligatory experience for young New Zealanders. When they returned they brought new tastes — cappuccino, pasta, wine. Jets brought incomers too. In 1965, 122,000 visitors arrived in New Zealand; 20 years later there were 596,995.[9]

SQUARE EYES

Only five years old in 1965 and broadcasting 50 hours a week, television still had the allure of a novelty. When colour arrived in 1973, the allure was tinted. Many popular programmes confirmed old attitudes. The majority of them were from Britain, and whether *Coronation Street* or Sunday night historical dramas, they reinforced the British heritage. American programmes — middle-class soap operas like *Peyton Place* or *Dallas* or popular westerns like *Gunsmoke* — idealised material success. Yet television provided an entranceway for new ideas. Stylish programmes like *The Avengers* brought an image of Carnaby Street sophistication. Documentaries and news clips brought the debates and incidents of overseas politics straight into the living room. For the first time New Zealanders watched a war, the Vietnam War, played out before their eyes. They saw the Chicago convention, Woodstock and the moon landing. Overseas ideas and fashions became available for imitation, especially after 1971 when the Warkworth satellite station allowed direct international feeds. Television also provided a forum for debate. Until 1975 there was only one channel, and thereafter only two. News and current affairs programmes like *Gallery* were watched closely and debated at workplaces and in newspapers. National Party television advertisements, prepared by Hanna Barbera in 1975 were given some credit for the subsequent National landslide. Talkback radio swept the nation in the 1970s, symbolising the desire to talk through the conflicts that had come to vex society.

Alexander Turnbull Library, EPH-C-CABOT-Music-1968-01

ABOVE: Among the local programmes that attracted a following was the Saturday night music programme, *C'mon*, hosted by Pete Sinclair and first screened in 1966. With slick dancing and bouncy vocalists like Dinah Lee, *C'mon* evoked the spirit of the 'swinging '60s'; it was also a popular stage show.

BELOW: During the 1969 general election the studio at WNTV 1 announced results on a national link. Fairfax Sunday Newspapers

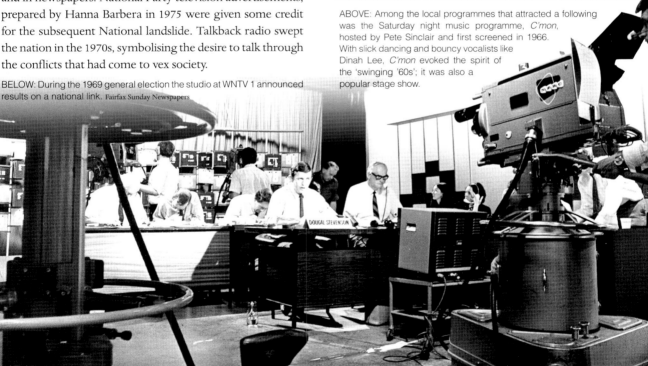

was always less than 15 per cent. Not surprisingly the native-born yearned for a stronger sense of nationhood. The decline of Britain's political and economic power and its entry into the Common Market in 1973 forced New Zealanders into a nationalist phase. This was expressed in several symbolic actions: the selection of the governor-general from among local-born dignitaries, rather than British aristocrats (Sir Arthur Porritt in 1967 was the first New Zealand-born, Sir Denis Blundell, who succeeded him in 1972, the first local inhabitant); and the acceptance in 1977 of 'God Defend New Zealand' as an official National Anthem now that 'God Save the Queen' was no longer played in cinemas.

New Zealand's cultural life began to mature. Local publishing expanded and the tables once devoted to New Zealand books in shops became too small. Writers like Maurice Gee graduated from short stories to novels. Painters like Colin McCahon and Toss Woollaston sold their paintings for decent prices. On the stage, New Zealand plays were more common and some, such as Roger Hall's *Glide Time* and Greg McGee's *Foreskin's Lament*, went to the centre of contemporary debate. Critics and defenders of the old order, people like Trevor Richards and Robert Muldoon, shared this desire for a stronger national identity. The effect was to heighten the urgency attached to particular issues.

Generation gaps, small town versus city, new media, a backdrop of economic distress and an aroused nationalism were some of the factors that made for loud voices and conflicting principles. Of course, although the arguments raged, there were many things that did not change. Kiwis still yearned for

In the 1960s there had been only two New Zealand feature films. But in the late 1970s local films took off. From 1980 to 1984 there were no less than 35. The most successful at the box office was *Goodbye Pork Pie* (1981), featuring Kelly Johnson (pictured here with the Groucho Marx glasses) and a yellow Mini. The film was as popular as Hollywood hits like *Star Wars*.

summers at the beach, followed sport, discussed weather, were shocked at accidents and fascinated by crime. Yet few of these pursuits were entirely free of debate. Families on the beach complained of the layabout habits of the surfies with their loud transistor music. Sport, which had once united New Zealanders, eventually divided them. Natural disasters continued to occur — the *Wahine* storm in 1968 when 51 people were drowned in Wellington Harbour, the Inangahua earthquake the same year, and the Abbotsford landslide in 1979. Yet even here there were larger ideological debates. For example, the question arose as to whether the Abbotsford slip was caused by suburban sprawl on unstable soil and the effect of the neighbouring motorway. As for crime, the Arthur Allan Thomas case provided the big headlines. Thomas was accused and convicted of murdering two neighbours. Initially the case confirmed in urban-dwellers' minds an image of strange goings-on down on the farm; but as the trial, retrial, and eventual pardon proceeded it appeared that the police had in fact planted evidence. The upshot was a wider questioning of an established institution. During these years it was simply impossible to escape the fact that New Zealanders were involved in major debates about values.

'Yankee go home!'

'Something is happening to New Zealanders. They are behaving in ways quite uncharacteristic of the species as recognised by their ancestors,' wrote the *New Zealand Monthly Review* in May 1965.[10] The magazine was referring to demonstrations greeting the American Secretary for State, Henry Cabot Lodge, when he arrived in Wellington on behalf of President Lyndon B Johnson (often referred to in slogans by his initials LBJ) to press for New Zealand's military involvement in the Vietnam War. New Zealanders were not often seen waving placards in the streets in 1965; most were more interested in the birth of the Lawson quintuplets or Kiri Te Kanawa winning the Mobil Song Quest. But by the end of the decade thousands were marching about the war in Vietnam. The first challenge to the values that had ruled New Zealand for half a century came in foreign policy.

Lodge's visit to brief the New Zealand Cabinet was calculated. Unlike the Australian government, which accepted a military engagement in Vietnam with few apparent doubts, New Zealand's National government and in particular Prime Minister Keith Holyoake were more cautious. The Vietnamese leader and communist Ho Chi Minh had been campaigning since 1945 for independence for his country — first against the French, and then after defeating them in 1954 and expecting nationwide elections that never came, against the regime propped up by the Americans in South Vietnam. By 1965 this propping-up required thousands of American troops, and the Americans were turning to their allies in Asia and the Pacific to give a hand.

Holyoake never questioned the morality of New Zealand involvement. Like most New Zealanders he accepted that the world was divided into a communist and a 'free' world and that New Zealand's security depended on a policy of forward defence — stop the reds on the Mekong or we will be fighting them on the Waitemata. He accepted the 'Munich analogy' (that you should not appease dangerous dictators as Hitler had been appeased at Munich), and he accepted the 'domino theory' (that if Vietnam fell to the communists the other countries of South-East Asia would fall like 'dominoes').

New Zealand's defence depended on the system of collective security: if we supported our allies, they would defend us. By the 1960s our significant ally was not Britain with whom we had always fought, but the United States and Australia with whom we had signed the ANZUS treaty in 1951. So Holyoake accepted that we should be involved. His caution came from doubts as to whether the war could be won, and even more from his instincts about politics at home. 'Kiwi Keith' feared that the war's expense and a large number of casualties might rock the boat. He refused to consider conscripting men. New Zealand's contribution was 'psychological or symbolic', as Lodge said, a matter of waving another flag. The first combat commitment, announced by Holyoake in May 1965, was a four-gun artillery battery of 120 men. Even at the height of New Zealand's involvement in 1968 the force was only 540 men (Australia's, by contrast, was over 6000 by 1966).[11]

Holyoake went only part of the way with LBJ, yet over the next five years New Zealand involvement in the Vietnam War triggered a re-examination of the nation's foreign policy and identity by growing numbers of younger New Zealanders. At first the numbers were not great. As Jack Marshall recalled later, in May 1965 the government was not worried by the domestic opposition, for 'quite frankly the New Zealand public was quite docile at that stage'.[12]

Early demonstrators were largely drawn from the 'Old Left', traditional opponents of the American alliance such as members of the Communist Party or Christian Pacifists. But in June 1966 a new organisation emerged, the Auckland Committee on South-East Asia, which first met in the tutorial room of the Auckland University history department. The executive included six university staff, seven students and two journalists. Seven weeks later Victoria University hosted the first 'teach-in', an American campus idea. Over 1000 people came to listen to 14 hours of speeches on both sides of the Vietnam debate. Within three months another 10 teach-ins had been held.[13] Elsewhere, intellectuals like the poet James K Baxter spoke out; Baxter's poem 'A Bucket of Blood for a Dollar' summed up a growing unease.

'Kiwi Keith' Holyoake was close to the people. He left school at 12 to help on the family farm, played rugby for Golden Bay and was active in the Farmers' Union. He first entered Parliament in 1932, and in 1965 was into his second term as prime minister — a reign that would not end until he handed over to Jack Marshall in 1972. Despite an image as slightly pompous, Holyoake had an instinct for popular attitudes and always kept his telephone number listed.

In September 1966 Lyndon B Johnson became the first American president to visit New Zealand. During his hectic 24-hour stopover there were large crowds in the streets. The American Ambassador reported that it was 'the greatest welcome ever accorded any public figure in the history of New Zealand'. But if LBJ had turned to his left from his position here in front of the national war memorial he would have seen about 1500 placard-waving demonstrators against the Vietnam War.

Fairfax Sunday Newspapers

ABOVE: Visits by American and Vietnamese politicians and generals provided regular opportunities for protest against the war. There was little love lost between police and demonstrators on such occasions. This photograph was taken outside Air Vice-Marshal Ky's hotel in Auckland in 1967; according to one newspaper, in this period before non-sexist language became de rigueur, 'It would be enough to make anyone drop his placard.'

BELOW: The Campaign for Nuclear Disarmament Easter March in 1964 at Kaiwharawhara, Wellington.

WR (Bill) Sykes, Private Collection

Out of this academic environment emerged a new sense of New Zealand's place in the world. Imitating the American anti-war movement, New Zealanders questioned the ideas of a monolithic communist force and the domino theory on the grounds that nationalism was stronger than ideology. The Vietnam War was said to be primarily a civil war, and South Vietnam hardly a 'free' society. Where New Zealand anti-war groups were distinct was their nationalist view that New Zealand should find its own independent place in the world, and not kowtow to big brother across the Tasman or the bigger one across the Pacific. Critics pointed out that New Zealand was further than London from Vietnam and because of its isolation the country could forge its own viewpoint, become at worst a neutral power, at best a force for peace and anti-militarism. As the leading historian of the anti-war movement concludes, 'Ultimately, the debate opened by the antiwar movement was neither about Vietnam nor the United States but about New Zealand and its place in the world.'[14]

A new vision called for methods of protest new to this country. At first they reflected the values of the academy — teach-ins, publications, a 'Peace, Power and Politics' conference. Then there was a progression to new methods, which, to quote protester Tim Shadbolt, were 'loud, extravagant and colourful, an insult to the quiet, rational, intellectual crap that's supposed to flow around university precincts'.[15] Song-sheets were handed out and chants chanted ('1, 2, 3, 4, we don't want your bloody war!'). There was street theatre, and rock concerts before

marches. There were amusing placards, such as 'Get smart, Maxwell' (in reference to the popular TV series *Get Smart,* which starred the fictional agent Maxwell Smart) when US General Maxwell Taylor and presidential advisor Clark Clifford visited in 1967. When Secretary of State William Rogers visited, flour bombs, eggs and paint were thrown. An effigy of President Nixon was burnt. There were increasing clashes between protesters and police, which reached a peak when Vice-President Spiro Agnew visited in January 1970 bearing some moon rock from the successful landing six months before; just before midnight, 500 demonstrators and 200 police clashed outside his hotel.[16]

Popular protest against the war increased. Between 1970 and 1972 there was a series of mobilisations and mass marches; one in April 1971 attracted 35,000 people. By now a majority of New Zealanders were against the war.[17] Criticism widened to unease about the whole American alliance. There were protests about plans to build an Omega navigation system in the Southern Alps that would allegedly assist America's Polaris submarines, US warships were picketed, and there was violence amid the grandeur of the southern lakes when 300 young people barricaded the road to Mt John observatory near Tekapo because of its alleged involvement in a nuclear tracking system.

Concern about the Vietnam War had spawned a larger vision about New Zealand foreign policy and a questioning of established values. Individuals who had learnt protest methods in anti-war protest graduated to other causes. By 1971 Barry Mitcalfe and Roger Boshier, two colleagues from Wellington's Committee on Vietnam, were active with the Peace Media Research Project organising to send a flotilla of boats into France's South Pacific nuclear test area. Tim Shadbolt wrote *Bullshit & Jellybeans,* in which there was a blueprint for the practical protester. By the turn of the decade other movements had appeared. New Zealand was in protest mode.

'Make love not war'

The greatest public support went into the battle to prevent the raising of Lake Manapouri. This campaign represented another major value shift for many New Zealanders. Like most 'colonial' societies, Pakeha New Zealand had regarded the frontier as something to be tamed for material progress — the bush should be cut down and made 'productive'. Wilderness became English pastures, rivers were dammed for cheap power. As early as 1960 the Forest and Bird Society had organised a petition against the Manapouri scheme that attracted about 25,000 signatures. But this was a small and not very noisy minority. Ten years later another petition included almost 265,000 signatures, the largest in New Zealand history up till that time. Everyone knew about Manapouri.

The Save Manapouri Campaign issued 30,000 share certificates. Campaigners pointed out that the shores of the lake would be littered with rotting tree stumps, its beaches would slump, and 17 islands, mostly predator-free, would be inundated. Precious flora, such as a unique orchid, would be drowned. Bird life would suffer. The battle was won in 1973 when the Labour government changed the dam design and appointed six of the campaigners as Guardians of the Lake.

The issue was simple. Should Lake Manapouri be raised by 8.4 metres to provide additional electricity for the Comalco aluminium smelter at Bluff; or should one of New Zealand's 'loveliest lakes' be saved from desecration? The initial leaders in the campaign were older people — an Invercargill city councillor and later MP, Norman Jones; a 55-year-old farmer and former bomber pilot, Ron McLean; and a university botanist, Alan Mark. But the long-term effect was to energise a new generation and give birth to a new vision about the environment.[18]

Many argued that the country's resources were not abundant, and its environment was unique and fragile. Living in harmony with the natural world was a higher value than material progress. A new generation set up new groups for new campaigns: in 1971 the Environmental Defence Society and Ecology Action, and two years later the Beech Forest Action Committee to oppose the selective logging of the South Island's beech and podocarp (mainly rimu) forests. This committee evolved into the Native Forests Action Council (NFAC), and at 9 p.m. on 4 July 1975, 40 members gathered around a fire on the snow-covered banks of the Maruia River to sign the Maruia declaration. It was a characteristic ceremony of the new politics. The declaration, among other principles, called for an end to the logging and burning of indigenous forests and their protection in law. It eventually carried 341,160 signatures when presented to Parliament in 1977.

The greenies faced opposition. The sawmilling community of Minginui, for example, blocked the road to prevent Guy Salmon, the NFAC research director, from entering. But the environmentalists' arguments increasingly won wide support. In 1978 the massive logging of the South Island beech forests

STONED AT SWEETWATERS

In 1967, following Bob Dylan's 'Mr Tambourine Man' ('Take me for a trip upon your magic swirling ship') and the Beatles 'Sergeant Pepper', marijuana use, previously confined to an underground of beat musicians and poets, became more widespread. A Wellington detective reported that 'pot smokers were young people not prepared to accept the standards of the older generation'.[19] Over the next three years the scene took off. In Wellington the Duke of Edinburgh pub became a centre for poets, artists, musicians and pot-smokers, student newspapers were open in their discussion of 'dope', and 'head' shops openly sold flavoured rolling papers, roach clips, Indian chillums, incense and oriental trinkets. Artists like Philip Clairmont and Tony Fomison composed canvases 'under the influence'. The international trade in drugs continued and in 1976 New Zealand was rocked by the stories of 'Mr Asia's' huge drug-importing business.

Drugs abounded at music festivals, the first of which occurred at Ngaruawahia in January 1973, modelled very much upon Woodstock four years earlier. In the early 1980s came gatherings at Nambassa and Sweetwaters. Here the playing of rock music and the smoking of pot sat alongside stalls providing vegetarian food, palm readings, incense and information about tenants' rights. The festivals were instant communities, the physical expression of a new world dawning. At the first Ngaruawahia gathering, Split Ends bombed; as Split Enz they went on to better things. Split Enz played games with their audience's minds. With their bright clothes and weird hairdos, they appealed to the psychedelic impulse. They played at every Sweetwaters festival.

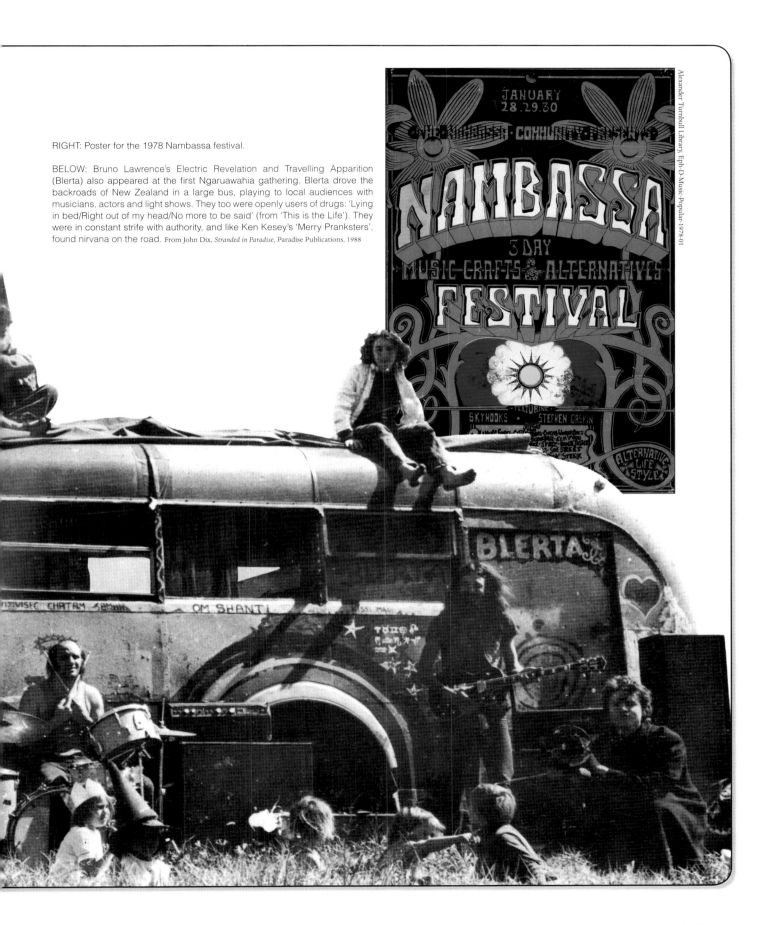

RIGHT: Poster for the 1978 Nambassa festival.

BELOW: Bruno Lawrence's Electric Revelation and Travelling Apparition (Blerta) also appeared at the first Ngaruawahia gathering. Blerta drove the backroads of New Zealand in a large bus, playing to local audiences with musicians, actors and light shows. They too were openly users of drugs: 'Lying in bed/Right out of my head/No more to be said' (from 'This is the Life'). They were in constant strife with authority, and like Ken Kesey's 'Merry Pranksters', found nirvana on the road. From John Dix, *Stranded in Paradise*, Paradise Publications, 1988

was abandoned. Up north, logging ceased in Pureora, one of the few remaining locations of the blue-wattled kokako, after a bare-footed botanist, Stephen King, and 13 other members of NFAC camped in a treetop vigil in a 1000-year-old totara.[20]

Some environmental successes engaged the nation's imagination, and none more so than the Wildlife Service's campaign to save the black robin. This tiny bird, said to be one of the world's rarest, was brought back from the brink of extinction. One of the robins, 'Old Blue', became a household name.

Saving lakes, forests and birds was the emotional heart of the 'Green' movement, but environmentalism drew people in other directions. There were groups to protect rivers and whales and to oppose mining. Later in the 1970s, Jeanette Fitzsimons convinced Devonport on Auckland's North Shore to begin weekly collections of glass, paper, plastic and tin cans, the first place this practice was adopted. Others put their energies into issues of efficient power use, and Campaign Half Million petitioned against nuclear power.

From 1972 New Zealanders became concerned about nuclear issues outside the country. Here the new environmental consciousness and the vision of an independent foreign policy came together. The French had been testing nuclear bombs and there was an anxiety that the Pacific was being polluted with radioactive 'fallout'. Strontium 90 had been detected in New Zealand milk. Activists sent a series of small boats into the testing zone.

At this point the Labour government, elected in 1972, despatched the frigate *Otago* and then *Canterbury* as a protest and joined Australia and Fiji in taking France to the International Court of Justice in The Hague. This was an interesting move. The Labour Party had a distinctly ambivalent relationship with the protest movement. The party had not wholeheartedly opposed the Vietnam War, but had emphasised a medical, rather than military, contribution in Vietnam. Prime Minister Norman Kirk, by background a working-class trade unionist, was uncomfortable with urban intellectuals and street protesters. The most explicit political expression of the new value system came in May 1972 when a public meeting at Victoria University formed the Values Party. A *Gallery* programme featuring the young leader, Tony Brunt, created huge interest, and at the election that year the party took two per cent of the vote, despite standing in only half the electorates. It was an impressive result.

But 'Big Norm' Kirk owed his election victory to more than the 'youth revolt'. Inflation had been running at high levels, and the government's delay over Lake Manapouri was expressive of its failure to listen. Holyoake had been eased out in early 1972, and his long-time deputy Jack Marshall seemed lacking in energy. It was 'time for a change', as the Labour Party proclaimed. Kirk took note of what was happening in the streets. He let his hair grow a shade longer; he became unequivocal against the Vietnam War. Upon its election his government withdrew the remaining troops and recognised communist China. Raising of the Manapouri dam was stopped. Kirk committed his government to opposing French nuclear tests, and refused to allow United States nuclear-powered ships to visit New Zealand ports. There were other symbolic concessions to the new environmentalism. A scheme of national walkways provided for access to the great and beautiful outdoors; and ohus (communes on largely unspoilt and inaccessible land for people wanting an alternative lifestyle) were promoted.

When Kirk died, a mere 20 months into the government, long-haired protesters joined thousands of others in genuine mourning. The Values Party did not immediately disappear. Despite internal divisions and a decision immediately after the 1972 election to work at a community level without a national leader, the party won over five per cent of the national vote in the election of 1975.

Outside politics the greening of New Zealand sprouted other movements ranging from hippies who dropped out of the system to moderate changes in suburban lifestyles. There were certain paradoxes here. The ideas were anti-materialistic, but they were in part a product of consumer fashion. Music, a highly

R. Angus, Museum of New Zealand, Te Papa Tongarewa

The late 1960s saw the emergence of movements to save some of the historic areas of New Zealand's cities. There was a bitter fight in Wellington when it was announced in 1968 that the motorway would carve through historic Thorndon and the old Bolton Street cemetery. Rita Angus expressed her concern in 1969 with images of cemetery stones in this work, *Flight*, one of her last paintings before her death.

commercial medium, was often the vehicle for communicating new values. The long-haired styles of The Beatles and the psychedelic messages of their album *Sergeant Pepper's Lonely Hearts Club Band* clearly had an impact. When Radio Hauraki's ship, *Tiri*, sailed off into international waters in 1966 to play a continuous programme of rock music, it marked one of the first signs of the new culture.

New values began with a vision of changing society, but they often ended up with a cultivation of the self. People who had revolted over the Vietnam War began to explore personal growth. Chris Wheeler, who in 1968 had established a radical magazine, *Cock*, published the *Cannabis Cultivators' Guide*. Those who took up the 'weed' were likely to drop out and go back to the land. Here they expressed their alienation from the 'system' by growing their own vegetables and building alternative houses like geodesic domes or reusing railway carriages. The hippie community expected the new world to be born from the grass roots, not from reform of existing institutions. The 1975 edition of the *New Zealand Whole Earth Catalogue*, the hippie bible, described the back-to-the-landers:

They tend to be in their 20s, well educated, idealists, pacifists, individualists, often creative, usually long haired and resistant to pressures of social conformity. They tend to be concentrated in Northland, Westland, the Nelson area, Coromandel, the Gisborne area, and for some strange reason, Christchurch. They are the anti-war and civil rights protestors of the 1960s, who have by now realised that their protests will eventually result in success, but that the social system will continually create new problems.[21]

Hippies were the extreme of the new value system, but many others were also affected. Not everyone had hair down to their waist, but by the mid 1970s even the All Blacks had longer locks. Tee shirts and jeans had replaced corduroy trousers and ties. Rock music achieved an extraordinary popular following. Few institutions were left unchanged by the new consciousness. In the schools there was an emphasis on freeing the inner child, on learning by doing, in reaction against the more repressive disciplines of the past. Where the dropouts and the environmental protesters led, many followed.

James K Baxter's funeral at Jerusalem. By 1972 Baxter had moved from being an anti-war poet, and later a friend of urban dropouts and addicts, to becoming 'Hemi', the long-haired figure living in his community at Jerusalem. He had become the Jesus Christ of a new faith in which Pakeha learnt from Maori and lived in harmony with the environment. Baxter's tangi in October 1972 was a gathering of the new order.

The home front

In 1970, the year the counter-culture became visible in New Zealand, the first women's liberation groups were founded. Characteristically, the founders were generally young, tertiary-educated, urban people who had been active in other social movements and often took their models from overseas.[22] They represented the first explicit challenge for a generation to assumptions about the family and social order in New Zealand. Feminists would picket and march for the next 15 years on the politics of gender. Yet long before the public banners, a silent revolution had begun as thousands of individual women challenged older assumptions.

The suburban nuclear family was at the heart of the trad-itional value system. Social order, it was believed, required people to live in detached houses with gardens in the suburbs, where they were safe from the dangers of the city and where Mum could stay at home and look after the kids while Dad earned the living. The generous provision of the family benefit, the assumption in pay negotiations of a family wage (a wage sufficiently large to support a wife and two kids), the state's encouragement of new subdivisions and own-your-own housing, the restrictions on obtaining a divorce, and the institution of six o'clock closing, which kicked the blokes out the pub door to go back home — all expressed this family ideal.

With jobs available and aspirations rising, married women entered the workforce from the late 1950s; by 1961 about one in six were in full-time employment. The figure was up to one in four by 1971, and 10 years on, despite rising levels of unemployment, well over a third of married women were working full-time with another 20 per cent in part-time employment. Equally striking, women were no longer only in traditional occupations. Most nurses, typists, and primary teachers were still women, but by 1981 so were about a fifth of doctors and lawyers (up from three per cent in 1966), a quarter of dentists, and one in 10 government officials.[23] Feminist campaigns brought some victories, which aided the cause. The fight for child-care centres won success, especially in public sector organisations. In 1980

D Black, Alexander Turnbull Library, Eph-D-Women-1980-01

EQUAL PAY IS YOUR RIGHT

WOMEN SHOULD RECEIVE THE SAME WAGES AS MEN FOR SUBSTANTIALLY THE SAME JOB DISCUSS THE MATTER WITH YOUR EMPLOYER- YOUR UNION WILL BACK YOU UP

Feminists worked hard to get women a decent deal in the workplace. The fight for equal pay bore fruit in the 1972 Equal Pay Act, and five years later discrimination on the basis of sex, race or religion was outlawed.

Marti Friedlander, Pentecostal March (II) 1972, Auckland Art Gallery, Toi o Tamaki

Not everyone welcomed a more open display of sexuality. Patricia Bartlett, secretary of the Society for the Promotion of Community Standards, toured the country in 1970 in a campaign to ban pornography and 'girlie' magazines. Some religious groups, such as these Pentecostal adherents in 1972, took up the tools of the protest generation and marched with banners.

a working women's charter was accepted by the Federation of Labour and the Labour Party.[24] By 1984 there were more women in public life, and there were 10 Labour women MPs.

As women attained more power in the world, they became more reluctant to be swallowed up in child-centred domesticity. Family life became less popular. Men and women no longer rushed to the marriage altar — the average age for both spinsters and bachelors marrying rose by two years, to 24 and 26 respectively, from the early 1970s to the mid 1980s. Others ignored marriage completely and lived as de facto couples. The marriage rate fell by a third. Divorces increased dramatically — from under five per thousand marriages in 1970 to well over 15 in the early 1980s, partly as a result of the introduction of no-fault divorce.[25]

Naturally households became smaller. By 1981 in almost one in five households one person lived alone, and in half there were no more than two people. Even more remarkably, only just over a third consisted of the traditional norm — Mum, Dad and at least one kid.[26] Households were now a varied assortment of solo parents, single people, childless couples and multi-family groups.

There were fewer kids. The post-war baby boom had reached its peak in 1961 and the fall continued apace. By the early 1980s a woman might expect to bear fewer children than the replacement level of two. In 1961 the figure had been over four.[27] Whether this came about from the woman's desire to find her place in the world, from economic pressures such as the growing costs of housing and child-rearing or the reduced value of the family benefit, or from improved contraception, is unclear.

New patterns of sexuality were undoubtedly part of the story. Changes had begun in the early 1960s with the arrival of the pill. By the early 1970s discussion about the repression of sexuality had become explicit, with controversies about the availability of contraceptive-vending machines and mixed flatting, and growing pressures to unbutton strict censorship laws. Women's fashions in the late 1960s were openly provocative with the mini-skirt reaching a 'highpoint' in 1969.

Changes were not necessarily to women's advantage. The contraceptive pill raised male expectations that women would deliver sexual favours. It was not until the early 1970s that women in public, as well as in private, claimed the right to control their own bodies and their own sexuality. There were campaigns against pornography offensive to women, and against sexist language and events considered exploitative, such as beauty contests. There was action against domestic violence. In 1974 the first women's refuge opened and a decade later there were 34 refuges helping over 20,000 women and children each year. In marches to 'reclaim the night', Rape Crisis campaigned on women's right to occupy public space without danger of attack from men. There was also an active women's health movement,

Germaine Greer, celebrated author of *The Female Eunuch*, visited in March 1972 and was promptly arrested and fined for using the word 'bullshit'. In Wellington the 'Society for the Protection of Society from the Society for Protection of Community Standards' led a demonstration of women chanting the offending words down to the central police station.

IDENTITY POLITICS

Women found many ways of asserting identity in these years. Some kept their family names or adopted the prefix 'Ms'. Others uncovered women's history. From 1971, 19 September became commemorated as Suffrage Day. Women's groups and *Broadsheet* magazine, edited by Sandra Coney from 1972, promoted the idea of a proud women's culture.[28] Women also met in national conventions. Four United Women's Conventions, held every two years from 1973 to 1979, took the feminist message to a wider audience. A unanimous motion, at the first convention in Auckland, that the prime minister have a women's advisor was rejected by Norman Kirk on the grounds that there were four women Labour MPs and he had 'his wife'. In Wellington in 1975, the International Year of Women, 2200 people attended the second convention.

The final United Women's Convention in Hamilton in 1979 was highly divisive. Despite Robin White's poster, which set out to attract Maori women, at the convention itself Maori women demanded greater representation, as did lesbian women.

which blacklisted offensive male doctors and encouraged clinics in which women would conduct pelvic self-examinations.[29]

A woman's right to choose to have a child, or to have an abortion, aroused fierce arguments. Under the Crimes Act provision for 'killing an unborn child', abortion was a serious crime unless carried out to preserve the life of the mother. Commonly women resorted to back-street abortionists, and in the 1960s up to 300 women were admitted to hospital each year following illegal attempts. Women's liberation argued for the right to abortion on request.

No sooner had women made this demand than the Society for the Protection of the Unborn Child (SPUC) was established in 1970. Henceforth the battle was intense. On the one side were younger women who set up groups such as the Abortion Law Reform Association and Women's National Abortion Campaign (WONAC). In 1974 the Remuera Abortion Clinic opened to provide a service within the law. On the other side was the Catholic Church and more conservative older sections of the community. They looked to Parliament for a tightening of the law; and in 1975 Gerard Wall's Hospitals Amendment Bill became law. The Remuera clinic was raided and closed. For the rest of the decade the battle raged. Eventually, in 1977, the Contraception, Sterilisation, and Abortion Act maintained restrictive conditions against abortion, but established an administrative system of 'certifying consultants', which, in practice, from 1979 allowed abortion services under the public health system.

Lesbian women and gay men began to 'come out'. In 1972 the Gay Liberation movement was formed, and the following year there appeared Sisters for Homophile Equality and the first lesbian magazine, *Circle*. By the end of the decade the 'lesbian nation' had its own social clubs, sports teams, newsletters and a 'Lesbian Line' at the end of the phone. Gay men followed where their sisters had led. In 1974 came the first effort promoted by Venn Young to decriminalise homosexuality. The bill did not pass, but it brought into the open both prejudices and the case for an end to discrimination.

Although the family was changing, old attitudes died hard. The career woman was also likely to be the Mum at home vacuuming the floors and picking up the kids from school. Men still on average earned considerably more than women. Yet there was now a greater range of personal options and family types — the extended family of Pacific Islanders, the occasional family with a house-husband, and gay men living in the inner city.

Changes in the family had wider effects. With both partners working full-time, shopping had to change. Supermarkets with parking became universal. From 1980 restrictions on Saturday shopping were relaxed, and shopping became a weekend leisure activity for both men and women. As women took up jobs they had more spare cash and less interest in or time for cooking, so they would go out to eat or give the kids money for takeaways. If they stayed at home, the prepared meal from the supermarket freezer could replace the home-grown vegies and preserves on the table.[30] Alcohol tastes also changed. In 1961 the first New Zealand restaurants had been licensed to serve alcohol, and New Zealand vineyards began to produce more table wines instead of fortified liquor. Between 1975 and 1982 the area planted in wine grapes increased from 2351 ha to 5901; and wine consumption rose from 8.6 litres per head in 1975 to 14.5 six years later.[31]

Islanders in Auckland City moved out to South Auckland. As the suburban dream faded for some privileged New Zealanders, it became compulsory for others.

'The Treaty is a fraud'

For half a century until the mid 1960s the widespread view among Pakeha, and among many Maori, was that New Zealand had the best race relations in the world. As Maori moved to the

Fish and chips remained the most popular takeaway, but from the 1970s the busy family had more fast-food options. Kentucky Fried Chicken opened its doors in 1970, Pizza Hut in 1975, and the first McDonald's opened in Porirua in June 1976. R White, Auckland Art Gallery, Toi o Tamaki

As the baby boom bust, housing pressures eased. This was accentuated from 1975 when assisted immigration from Britain ended. With the economy turning down, flight across the Tasman began. From 1976 to 1983, 150,000 more people left New Zealand permanently than arrived. Governments began a long retreat from assisting the construction of new houses. Instead, with house prices rising and interest rates rising even more, governments focused assistance on those in financial need.[32] There was also an interesting shuffling of houses as Maori and recent immigrants were squeezed out of the inner city by yuppies keen to restore the older houses and be close to city entertainment. Maori and Pacific

city in large numbers in the post-war years, they were expected to assimilate, and many did so while there were plenty of jobs. There was general self-satisfaction at the apparent lack of social prejudice within New Zealand — not that New Zealanders spent much time looking at race issues overseas. In 1965 a whites-only Springbok rugby team toured the country and the protests were all but invisible.

Over the next 20 years some people put forward a different view about race here. Maori questioned the assimilation model, while reasserting identity and eventually a vision of Maori sovereignty. From the Pakeha side came a vision of a more ethnically diverse society with a role to fight racism both at home and abroad, especially in apartheid South Africa.

The first movement originated in the social changes following Maori migration to the city. Despite the official policy of 'pepper-potting', Maori did congregate, at first in the inner city and then in new suburbs such as Otara or Porirua. As the economy turned sour, city streets were no longer paved with gold. In 1970, a Young Maori Leaders' Conference on urbanisation at Auckland University brought together kaumatua and young people, graduates and gang members from groups like the Storm-troopers and Black Power. There emerged a commitment to strengthening Maori language and culture, and stronger political action. A new organisation emerged, Nga Tamatoa — the young warriors. In Wellington the Maori Organisation on Human Rights attacked discrimination in housing, employment, sport and politics.

Both groups fought consistently for Maori language and culture, especially within the schools. Over the next 15 years there was a considerable response. Maori language day — which eventually became a week — was introduced. Radio and television announcers practised Maori pronunciation. In 1982

the first kohanga reo or 'language nest' for the teaching of te reo to pre-schoolers began. There was an upswelling of creativity as Maori adapted traditional culture to the modern urban world. Artists such as Ralph Hotere brought Maori aesthetics into new media. There was a reinvigoration of carving styles with marae in the city and in educational institutions. Kapa haka was revived.[33]

Maori political action took new forms. This focused particularly on Waitangi Day, which had become an official day of commemoration in 1960. In 1971 Nga Tamatoa disrupted the ceremony and the next year they staged a walkout. The Labour government determined to give more credence to the Treaty by changing the name to New Zealand Day and making it a public holiday. When he announced this on 6 February 1973, Kirk expressed his vision for the nation by taking the hand of a young Maori boy. In 1975 the Waitangi Tribunal was established to hear contemporary breaches of the Treaty. But such acts did not stop a growing level of protest. The Waitangi Action Committee, which had won attention when they raided a Pakeha haka party at Auckland engineering school in 1979, led the annual protest. By 1983, 4000 demonstrators turned out at Waitangi, the

Reed Publishing Ltd

Penguin Books Ltd

Witi Ihimaera's *Tangi* (Heinemann) was the first published novel by a Maori writer when it appeared in 1973. Others followed; especially from Patricia Grace, who also combined with the Maori artist Robyn Kahukiwa to prepare children's books telling Maori stories (above: *The Kuia and the Spider*, first published by Longman Paul, 1981).

BASTION POINT

In 1977 new urban-based Maori radicalism and older concerns about land loss came together at Bastion Point on Auckland's waterfront. Originally the home of Ngati Whatua, Auckland's local iwi, the land had been acquired by the Crown through a series of compulsory and negotiated purchases. Some had been used for state housing, some for reserves including the memorial to Michael Joseph Savage. For over 100 years Ngati Whatua had fought for land rights here, their last land-holding in Auckland. When in 1976 the Cabinet decided to dispose of the last uncommitted 60 acres (24 ha) for housing, Joe Hawke, who had witnessed the eviction of his people and the burning of their houses at Okahu Bay in the early 1950s, led Maori onto the site in January 1977 and occupied it. Despite a settlement that Robert Muldoon believed generous, Hawke refused to accept it. On 25 May 1978, 600 police backed by the army forcibly removed the occupiers and arrested 230 of them. The television and newspaper images of this action, far more than the details of the land case, came to symbolise the confrontation of Muldoon's government and land rights protesters.

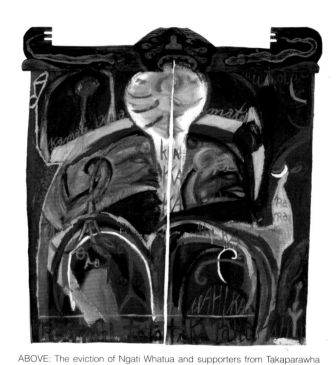

ABOVE: The eviction of Ngati Whatua and supporters from Takaparawha — Bastion Point — embedded itself in late twentieth-century Maori politics. Artist Emily Karaka explored the themes of protest and dislocation a decade after the eviction. The volcano Rangitoto is the maunga tapu (sacred mountain) of Ngati Whatua. E Karaka, Victoria University of Wellington Art Collection
BELOW: Archives New Zealand

grounds were cordoned off, and the police donned riot helmets and brandished long batons.

There was also growing attention to the question of land. Old grievances were triggered in 1967 when the Maori Affairs Amendment Act allowed the bundling together of small shares of Maori land for onselling. The issue reached wider groups with the Maori Land March led by Whina Cooper in 1975. The march brought together people of many iwi, and after setting off from Te Hapua in the Far North it attracted thousands as it crossed over Auckland Harbour Bridge and arrived in Wellington on 13 October 1975. The organisation, Te Roopu o te Matakite, which had been formed for the Land March, soon collapsed, but the fight for Maori land now had wide Maori support.

Issues of race also energised young Pakeha. In July 1969 a new organisation HART (Halt All Racist Tours) was founded to campaign against sporting contact with South Africa. This was a major challenge to New Zealand values. Victory over the Springboks in 1956 began over a decade of great success for the All Blacks, who remained central to the country's self-image.

The Springboks were defeated again in 1965. Throughout these years there had been some protest over rugby contact with South Africa. In 1960 some had campaigned over the exclusion of Maori from the All Blacks team to tour South Africa. By 1966 the National government had accepted, in Holyoake's words, that 'in this country we are one people', and 'No Maoris, No Tour' was imposed on the Rugby Union. A proposed tour in 1967 was cancelled. HART went a stage further and said that even if Maori were included, tours to the republic should be opposed as a statement against apartheid. HART became committed to a policy of 'non-violent disruption'.[34]

As the anti-apartheid movement took off, passions were aroused on the other side. Organisations like WARD (War Against Recreational Disruption) emerged. The Rugby Union, largely an organisation of older short-back-and-sides males, held to the dictum 'Keep Politics out of Sport (or 'KEEPOOS', as Tim Shadbolt noted),[35] while Jack Marshall on becoming Prime Minister argued for 'building bridges' as he defended plans for a Springbok tour here in 1973. Kirk, too, had promised before the

Gil Hanly

A hikoi from Turangawaewae passes through South Auckland on its way to Waitangi in February 1984. In 1981 Muldoon had described the protesters at Waitangi as a minority of 'outcasts'. But this hikoi signalled the full involvement of the Kingitanga in the protest movement. It was led by Eva Rickard who had won her spurs fighting for the recovery of the Raglan golf course. Maori protesters could no longer be described as 'outcasts'.

1972 election not to interfere. Things changed when he took office; on the grounds that any tour would bring massive civil disruption and the withdrawal of many nations from the 1974 Christchurch Commonwealth Games, Kirk stopped the tour.

The Labour government began to see itself as an opponent of racism, and followed through in other ways. In 1975 assisted immigration from the United Kingdom was stopped, and for the first time immigrants were chosen on the basis of qualifications rather than national or ethnic background. In effect, the de facto 'white New Zealand' policy had gone. The office of Race Relations Conciliator had been established earlier, in 1971.

Robert Muldoon, elected leader of the National Party in 1974, was an older New Zealander who fully accepted the racial attitudes of many of his generation. During the campaign of 1975 the National Party ran advertisements with brown faces overrunning New Zealand cities. This was a clear reference to the migration of Samoans, Tongans and Cook Islanders, which had quickened during the good times of the 1960s as employers sought out cheap labour to staff Auckland's factories. In the decade from 1966 to 1976 the numbers of Pacific Islanders in New Zealand more than doubled, to about 50,000. Following the election there were dawn raids on alleged Pacific Island overstayers.

Muldoon had also campaigned in 1975 on the principle of no interference in sport, and indicated that the Springboks would be welcome. He determined to keep to that stand. His government made clear its support for the All Black tour of the republic in 1976 — a government minister attended the farewell, and Muldoon attacked HART for 'spreading lies about New Zealand' overseas. In the very month when South Africa, and the world, was rocked by the Soweto riots, Muldoon refused to meet with Abraham Ordia, President of the Supreme Council for Sport in Africa. Black Africa responded and made New Zealand an international pariah with a partial boycott of the 1976 Montreal Olympic Games. Not even John Walker's victory in the 1500 metres could save New Zealand from embarrassment.[36]

Pressures intensified when the Commonwealth Heads of Government Meeting in London in June 1977 forced Muldoon to sign the Gleneagles Agreement, which committed governments to withhold support for, and take 'every practical step' to discourage, sporting contact with South Africa. Muldoon chose to implement this by sending the agreement to sporting bodies with a preface that 'under a National Government there will be no political interference in sport in any form'. Then in September 1980 the Rugby Union issued an invitation to a Springbok team. When he heard the news, Muldoon reportedly said, 'I can see nothing but trouble coming from this.'[37] But speaking on television 11 days before the Springboks arrived, Muldoon described the South Africans as 'our kith and kin' and promised not to order cancellation. The tour went ahead.

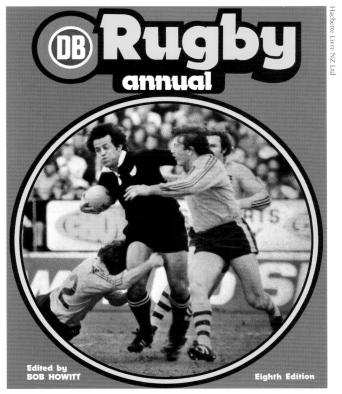

Hachette Livre NZ Ltd

In the 1970s many people still considered the All Blacks the personification of the Kiwi male. The *DB Rugby Annual* paid tribute to two parts of the old rugby, racing and beer cliché, but Auckland-born Samoan winger Bryan 'BG' Williams represented the beginnings of the 'browning' of the national team late last century as Pacific Islanders and Maori formed an ever-larger part of the ABs.

Fairfax Sunday Newspapers

Dick Tayler wins the 10,000 metres on the opening day of the 1974 Commonwealth Games in Christchurch. The games had come under threat from the proposed Springbok rugby tour of New Zealand, but when the tour was stopped they went ahead and opened sensationally with this victory by the local boy. The games also ended dramatically with a wonderful race in the 1500 metres in which the New Zealander, John Walker, was just pipped by Tanzanian Filbert Bayi in world-record time.

Over the next 59 days, New Zealanders were divided against each other in the largest civil disturbance in the country since 1951. On one side lay 'Rob's Mob', older or provincial New Zealanders, people who believed in the centrality of rugby to the national way of life. On the other side, marching every time a game was played, were many of the generation who had come to political consciousness in the years of the Vietnam War. They were largely urban people, many of them tertiary educated and working in the caring professions as teachers or social workers.[38] There was strong support from the union movement and from Maori active in defence of Maori rights. It was a battle about New Zealand values — between the traditional sense of national identity and the dreams born in the late 1960s.

The tour had its epic moments. There was the game in Hamilton when the protestors broke onto the ground and stayed there huddling and chanting 'The Whole World is Watching', while Waikato rugby supporters bayed for blood; and the batoning in Wellington's Molesworth Street in the falling dusk on the day of Charles' and Diana's wedding. There were the incredible street confrontations during the tests at Christchurch and Wellington, with police donning riot gear, and the protesters wearing padding and cycle helmets. And there was the final test in Auckland, when a full-scale riot occurred outside while inside fans watched behind rows of barbed wire as the two teams struggled in an epic match that was periodically interrupted by flour bombs dropped from a plane above. Few New Zealanders did not take sides. On the streets, the jeering abuse of the rugby supporters was balanced by the chants of 'Amandla' and 'Remember Steve Biko' from the protesters.[39]

Tyrant or economic wizard?

Throughout these years the New Zealand economy struggled. Yet it was not until the early 1980s that a new vision emerged about the state and the economy. This was partly because the man who managed the economy for all but three years from 1967 to 1984 was Robert Muldoon. The story of the New Zealand economy and how the state should manage it cannot be separated from his story.

Muldoon had been passed over for a Cabinet post immediately after the 1966 election, but in 1967 after Harry Lake died, 'Bob' Muldoon ('Rob' came later with the 'Mob') became the youngest Minister of Finance in the 20th century to that date. Brought up in poor circumstances in the Depression before prospering as an accountant in the 1950s, Muldoon believed intensely in the welfare state and the central role of government in the economy. It took him a long time, even during

his second period as Minister of Finance after 1975, before he believed that New Zealand's problems were other than short-term, and he never gave up the view that government should intervene to ease short-term pain and pick winners. Despite his noisy blustering against uppity unions and selfish financial institutions, Muldoon was a conservative man and a pragmatic tinkerer.

In the late 1960s the main institution for Muldoon's tinkering was the mini-budget. He would appear on the nation's television screens, his gruff manner projecting a man in control. With a slight adjustment of interest rates or government charges, things would be back on track. There were occasional crises in the labour relations area, such as the nil wage order of 1968. But usually 'man-to-man' talks with Federation of Labour boss Tom Skinner got things back on an even keel.

In 1972 the Labour Party was elected. At first the economy boomed and Kirk won plaudits as an international statesman.

Rugby fans and anti-Springbok tour protesters slug it out in the streets of Auckland on the occasion of the final test there in September 1981. Despite the obvious intensity of the fighting, no lives were lost during the tour. And some New Zealand traditions remained intact. Close by this scene, police used rubbish bins to provide protection and block off streets. While the battle raged, some people seized the opportunity to fill the bins with household rubbish. Dominion Post Collection, Alexander Turnbull Library, EP-1981-3106-17A

Dad in suit, daughter and son-in-law in hippie smock — the generation gap in clothing, 1972: Muldoon, on the occasion of the marriage of his daughter, Barbara, to Kevin Williams.

Then in July 1974 Muldoon ousted Marshall as leader of the Opposition, and a month later Kirk died. Bill Rowling, Kirk's successor, suffered from a high-pitched voice and a lack of charisma. He could not compete with Muldoon's brilliant use of the new media — both television and talkback radio. In November 1975 Muldoon won a spectacular victory with a majority of 23 seats.

There were many reasons for the result; but two are important. Muldoon presented himself as the spokesman of the ordinary bloke, the decent New Zealander, the representative of traditional Kiwi values. In a famous interview before the election he said that he wanted to leave New Zealand 'at least as good as when I took over'; there were no millennial dreams for our Rob.[40] He had always opposed the protest generation. He raved against trendy lefties, Maori radicals, pommie trade unionists, Pacific Island overstayers. His slogan in 1975 was 'New Zealand — the Way You Want It'. He promised a universal national superannuation scheme available at the age of 60, which was, in the words of his mate Bert Walker, recognition of those who had 'gone through two world wars and the Great Depression'.[41] Muldoon's first Cabinet was dominated by men like himself — it included no fewer than seven war veterans. Later he invited

American ships back into New Zealand ports, unleashing periodic flotillas of protest, and in accord with imperial tradition despatched a frigate to help Britain in the 1982 Falklands War.

Muldoon also presented himself as the economic wizard. When the first oil shock hit in 1974 and there was an eight per cent decline in the standard of living, Rowling and his Minister of Finance, Bob Tizard, responded in traditional ways and borrowed, rather than deflated. They feared that a repeat of the 1958 'Black Budget' would be electoral death. But Muldoon raised fears about the levels of international debt. He promised to restore 'New Zealand's shattered economy'.

When Muldoon became both Prime Minister and Minister of Finance, restoring the economy turned out to mean 'no fundamental restructuring', but, in his favourite phrase, 'tidying up our economic problems'. There were increases in government charges and a freeze in the public service, but no slashing at the welfare state. Muldoon, like the predecessors he had criticised, assumed that the fall in the terms of trade was temporary and could be tided over by borrowing. His fine-tuning meant giving assistance to traditional producers. He refused to remove protection on local manufacturing and instead gave them export incentives, showing faith in his ability to pick winners and support them. Farmers received incentives to increase livestock numbers, low-interest loans, tax rebates for fencing, fertiliser subsidies and the Supplementary Minimum Prices scheme to guarantee minimum prices. Farmers and manufacturers became like the old, welfare beneficiaries.

Nor did the unions escape Rob's heavy hand. Labour relations had become increasingly strained over the previous decade. As economic conditions tightened and price inflation increased, there were pressures for wage increases. Working days lost annually from industrial stoppages rose from under 100,000 every year before 1967 to over 350,000 after 1975. Standing aside and allowing free wage-bargaining was not Muldoon's style. He imposed a year-long wage and rents freeze and then brought back the Arbitration Court, which had been abolished in 1971. He intervened in some disputes and solved problems over a couple of gins with Tom Skinner. Believing in negotiation and control, he resisted the abolition of compulsory unionism.[42]

Fine-tuning did not work. By 1978 unemployment, just over 10,000 when Muldoon took office, had reached over 45,000; and although he could point to a reduction in inflation to 12 per cent, the voters had doubts. At the 1978 election National won fewer votes than Labour, despite gaining a majority of 10 seats. Things did not improve the following year, when there was another huge increase in the price of oil. A programme emerged that came to be called 'Think Big', although it was not quite the clear-sighted strategy the name implied.

National passed the National Development Act in December 1979 to speed up the programme. It drew opposition predictably from greenies and, more surprisingly, from within National's ranks. Three MPs — Michael Minogue, Ian Shearer and Marilyn Waring — crossed the floor on one clause. Their act reflected a widening concern within the party that executive authority was becoming too strong. National had long stood as the party of free enterprise, and during Muldoon's early years some had pushed a liberal agenda. They had some successes, such as a freeing-up of the financial sector and the signing of Closer Economic Relations with Australia in 1982, but not enough for many in the party. New voices appeared within the major right-wing interest groups, such as Federated Farmers and the Manufacturers' Federation. While some were loath to lose the import controls or the agricultural subsidies that sustained their incomes, others argued that such intervention brought high costs, inflationary pressures and an inefficient use of resources. The voices for more 'market economics' became louder as Margaret Thatcher took office in the United Kingdom in 1979 and Ronald Reagan became President in 1981.

Unrest boiled over with the attempted 'colonels' coup against Muldoon in 1980, led by Derek Quigley, Jim McLay and Jim Bolger, and finding eager support from economic liberals. Muldoon returned from overseas to stave off defeat. It was a temporary respite. In 1981 two young apostles of liberal economics, Ruth Richardson and Simon Upton, entered Parliament. Both spoke, but did not vote, against 1982 legislation

to allow the Clyde high dam to progress. The legislation was only passed because Social Credit gave support, counterbalancing the opposition of the 'Waikato liberals', Minogue and Waring. In the same year Quigley spoke out against 'Think Big' and resigned from Cabinet.

Two acts further inflamed the liberals. The first was the Income Tax Amendment (No 2) Bill, designed to prevent tax rip-offs in the kiwifruit industry. The second was the wage and price freeze. After prolonged and damaging strikes of the drivers in 1979 and at the Kinleith mill the next year, both employers and unions pressed for free wage-bargaining. The director of advocacy, Max Bradford, spoke for the Employers' Federation; the fiery Jim Knox, who had replaced Tom Skinner, and the FOL secretary, Ken Douglas, spoke for the unions. In 1982, although inflation was running at over 15 per cent, Muldoon offered a five per cent wage increase and tax concessions. When the FOL turned this down, Muldoon imposed a 12-month freeze on wages and prices using the 1948 Economic Stabilisation Act. The Act did not give him power to control interest rates, and as his suspicions rose that the bankers and finance houses were as 'evil as money-lenders in the temple' he introduced the Finance Bill of 1983.[43] This time Ruth Richardson, Quigley and Dail Jones crossed the floor, and the finance sector was up in arms.

In January 1983, Bob Jones — property magnate, talkback king and former mate of Muldoon — announced he was standing

Muldoon campaigned brilliantly in 1975, using charts and graphs to raise fears about the level of overseas debt.

THINK BIG

'Think Big' referred to a bundle of projects intended to exploit New Zealand's energy resources and remove our dependence on a small number of agricultural products. Several projects involved the use of Maui gas, which came on stream in May 1979 and which the government was committed to buy whether the gas was used or not. The gas would be used for methanol and ammonia-urea plants at Waitara, for synthetic petrol at Motunui, and for compressed CNG and LPG. Dependence on imported oil was also to be reduced by expansion of the Marsden Point oil refinery. And New Zealand's apparently abundant electricity and gas were to be used in high-energy projects such as a third aluminium pot-line at Tiwai Point, a second smelter at Aramoana on Otago Harbour, the expansion of New Zealand Steel and the electrification of the North Island main trunk rail line.

The term 'Think Big' itself had initially been coined by Duncan MacIntyre in connection with the fishing industry (following the expansion to a 200-mile maritime zone in 1977), and most of the schemes had begun as disparate ad hoc projects. But Muldoon grabbed hold of the term and ran with it. It was a programme of government-led investment in the tradition of Julius Vogel or the power stations of the 1950s. Its implementation was in the hands of Bill Birch, Minister of Energy and of National Development.

The programme was always controversial. It required an enormous investment of capital, which diverted funds away from growing areas such as tourism, fishing, kiwifruit and wine. Some of the projects, especially the synthetic petrol plant, were a wasteful use of energy with a poor rate of return and were dependent upon shaky economic assumptions. It was assumed, for instance, that oil prices would reach about US$60 a barrel, when in fact through most of the 1980s they were about US$15.

Environmentalists opposed the proposed smelter at Aramoana, which was sited on one of the few salt marshes in the South Island and directly opposite Taiaroa Head — the only mainland albatross colony in the world. A Save Aramoana campaign eventually declared Aramoana an independent state with border posts, postage stamps and 'passports'.

'Think Big' also came up against Maori opposition. The Motunui synthetic petrol plant was designed with an outfall that would discharge untreated waste onto traditional fishing reefs. Aila Taylor, of Te Atiawa, lodged a claim with the Waitangi Tribunal concerning traditional rights to collect kai moana. The tribunal was unequivocal in its support, and although Muldoon's government initially refused to concede the water right, eventually the level of public concern was such that an existing Waitara outfall was used instead.

David Wall Photography

This image of Te Atiawa women gathering shellfish from the reefs at Motunui was used by the iwi to fight the proposed outfall of the Motunui synthetic petrol plant.

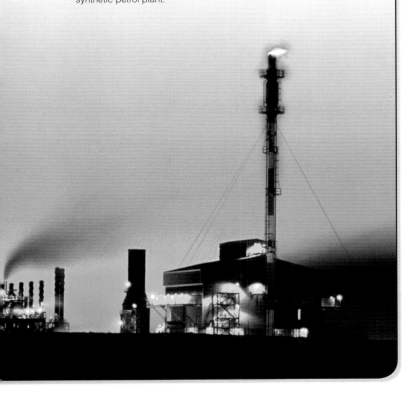

as an independent in the seat of Ohariu. Before long, former National supporters flocked to Jones's New Zealand Party (or as Muldoon called it, the 'Jones party' or 'the Greedies'). Muldoon was now opposed by the very people expected to support the National Party, especially younger people working in business, finance or farming. They argued against economic regulation and a lavish welfare state, and for entrepreneurial freedom.

New Right ideas were also bubbling up from Treasury. There a 'think tank' of men, who were all under 40 in 1980 and had imbibed neo-liberal economics at university, came to believe in the superiority of the market to government in determining economic choices. Muldoon would scrawl across their papers 'waste of time putting in a paper like this'.[44]

Others were more receptive to such ideas. In 1983 Rowling was replaced as leader of the Labour Party by David Lange. Lange surrounded himself with people who had come to political prominence in the late 1960s and 1970s — people like Mike Moore, still only 34 in 1983, Michael Bassett who had cut his teeth in the anti-war movement, and Roger Douglas, dismissed from the front bench by Rowling in 1980 for writing an alternative budget. These men became convinced of the need for a deregulated economy, especially after Treasury seconded Doug Andrew to the Opposition in 1983.[45]

By 1984 the forces of a new generation were mounting against Muldoon. One segment of the baby-boomers, those who tended to be in the 'sharing and caring' professions, were antagonised by his stands on Springbok tours, the environment and visits by nuclear ships, and also by his macho aggressive style. They became active on behalf of the Labour Party. Another group, young lawyers, business people and even some farmers, were frustrated by his antagonism to economic liberalism. Some remained critics within the National Party, others supported the New Zealand Party, a few even gave support to Labour. The unions felt angry at Muldoon's overregulated state which prevented free wage-bargaining. The values of these groups had once been minority interests; by 1984 they were widely shared perspectives that would eventually determine the direction New Zealand took for the remaining years of the century. In the short term Muldoon was the defender of the old order. But his days were numbered. As the pressure rose, he became more isolated; he indulged in night-time drinking of whisky. The final crisis came on 14 June 1984, when Marilyn Waring, lesbian, feminist, economic liberal and opponent of the Springbok tour, expressed opposition to the nuclear ships policy. Despite her promise not to bring down the government, Muldoon saw red and, allegedly 'pissed as a fiddler's cat' he went to Government House and called an election.[46] It was the last throes of the Depression generation.

*Chapter*13

Queer guys for straight eyes. From 1986 same-sex relationships between consenting adults were legal. Later human rights legislation banned discrimination on the grounds of sexual orientation, although some rights that other couples enjoyed remained closed to same-sex couples and in 2004 Anglican leader Whakahuihui Vercoe could dream of 'a world without gays'.

Phil Walter, Fotopress

Breaking Free
1984–2005

Forget street protests. After 1984 the baby-boomers who really shook up the pavlova paradise did so from the Beehive. Labour's libertarian young things broke traditional defence ties, restructured the economy and offered new freedoms to gays and Maori. A more insidious revolutionary, technology, hit the delete button on thousands of jobs. At first, while Aucklanders built mirror-glass towers and messed about in boats, the increasingly mythic 'heartland' did most of the bleeding. Then the share-market crash spread the pain to the cities. In the mid 1990s we ended our latest flirtation with being the 'laboratory of the world', although we still retained the market economy and our 'Man Alone' foreign policy. Prosperity returned for many, powered by the servicing and niche technology industries. The technological changes were less important — cellphones and satellites merely continued the globalisation begun by Polynesian canoes, British submarine cables and American Boeings. Political changes were also of less importance. The big revolution was social. Early 21st century New Zealand — less blokey and egalitarian, more racially divided, ethnically diverse, pluralistic, urban and better educated — was more culturally self-confident, and culture leads politics. The stage has been set for the dreams of the under 30s who now shop at Asian foodmarkets, listen to Polynesian or Maori radio as often as ZMFM, and whose career and lifestyle choices may be between Amsterdam and Auckland, Dunhuang or Dunedin.

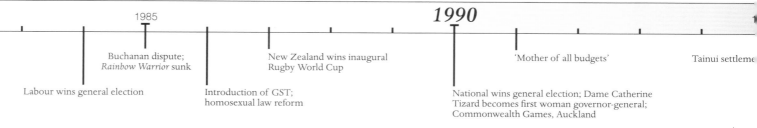

1985   *1990*

Buchanan dispute;   New Zealand wins inaugural   'Mother of all budgets'   Tainui settleme
Rainbow Warrior sunk   Rugby World Cup

Labour wins general election   Introduction of GST;   National wins general election; Dame Catherine
                               homosexual law reform   Tizard becomes first woman governor-general;
                                                                    Commonwealth Games, Auckland

New Zealand's silent war of independence

Governor-general Sir David Beattie must have been getting sick of Sir Robert Muldoon. Just a few months earlier his prime minister had, with comically inept mistiming, gate-crashed the annual Government House media dinner to ask for the 'schnapps election'. Now, a day after being hung out to dry by voters, Muldoon was again disrupting things, this time the bankers' bash at the fashionable eatery Le Normandie. Constitutional convention required defeated ministries to play it straight between an election and the swearing-in of their successors. But Muldoon, who cared little for constitutional niceties, seemed out to 'booby-trap . . . the command bunker before vacating it'.[1] By publicly refusing to follow prime minister-elect David Lange's request to devalue the dollar — which Reserve Bank and Treasury officials had also been trying to get Muldoon to do — he fed an already damaging speculative frenzy.[2] New Zealand's foreign reserves were draining faster than the whisky in his glass. Then a currency crisis threatened to turn into a constitutional crisis as Lange accused Muldoon on television

of 'committing economic sabotage'.[3] 'Throughout the latter part of the evening the Government's chief economic advisers held a number of meetings in the bar and toilets of the restaurant, out of sight of others at the dinner.'[4] At midnight Beattie told the head of the Prime Minister's Department that if caucus overruled Muldoon next morning he would appoint a temporary prime minister to devalue while there were still dollars left to play with. At the last moment, however, Muldoon backed down, grumbling churlishly.

New Zealand's overseas reserves settled down but little else did. That currency crisis set the tone for a turbulent decade, which many like to call revolutionary. Certainly it seemed like that to many who lived through it, with all the privatisation and corporatisation, the railway station and post office closures, the share-market boom and bust, the removal of subsidies and the tearing down of tariff barriers.

The first fireworks came in foreign policy and they gave an international stage to David Lange. There must be something in the air of Mangere, which was home politically to two of last century's more memorable prime ministers, Massey and Lange. But this slice of South Auckland was multicultural, suburban and industrial, not small-farmer-Protestant, when Christian socialist doctor Roy Lange's son moved into the ninth floor of the Beehive.

David Lange's rise had been rapid since 1977 when, in a plot twist straight out of a Greek myth, Muldoon's muckraking over the MP Colin Moyle's lifestyle opened the parliamentary door to Lange, his ultimate nemesis. Now, seven years and one stomach-stapling operation later, the 41-year-old lawyer led a new Cabinet that was probably the youngest since the formation of political parties.[5] 'The government passed overnight from the RSA generation to the baby-boomers.'[6] Energetic, untrammelled by previous experience in Cabinet, but aware of the country's desire for change, many ministers had little regard for existing conventions. Unlike Muldoon's Cabinet, where 'there were only two shades of opinion . . . "yes" and "yes, sir"',[7] Lange's Cabinet heaved and bubbled like a Rotorua mud pool with new ideas, some equally volcanic.

The first eruption splashed Uncle Sam, though it came from the party, not Cabinet. On Monday 16 July, with Muldoon still in his bunker and the currency crisis mesmerising the media,

Muldoon's behaviour soured the taste of victory for Lange and set the tone for a tetchy decade. Six years later it would be National's turn to complain about finding a post-election turd in the celebratory punchbowl — the Bank of New Zealand crisis.

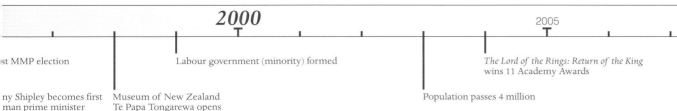

American Secretary of State George Schultz flew into Wellington for an ANZUS Council meeting. Lange smelt a big fat rat in the timing. It was, he said, 'a calculated attempt to embarrass the new Labour Government'. The council communiqué was 'intellectual dishonesty which allowed the representatives of a defeated government to put their country's name to a document that all who signed it knew did not represent the views of the country's future government'.[8] Angry as he was, Lange promised to talk to his party. Twenty years later the Secretary of Foreign Affairs felt that Schultz 'convinced himself' that this amounted to an assurance that he would overturn Labour's policy, and subsequently felt betrayed.[9]

Officials and politicians searched for a way out. Parliamentary Labour was in a difficult position. Party activists were in no mood to draw distinctions between nuclear propulsion and nuclear weapons. The times were against that. The papers were full of the military posturing between Reagan's America and the Soviet Union, the war in Afghanistan, the nuclear winter theory and post-Armageddon TV chillers such as *Threads* and *The Day After*. By late 1984 nearly 40 towns and boroughs had declared themselves nuclear-free.[10]

Between 1978 and 1984 opposition to nuclear-armed ship visits had risen from 31.5 per cent to 72.4 per cent.[11] Dissent became orthodoxy. Even Social Credit and the New Zealand Party went anti-nuclear; Bob Jones knew that mushroom clouds were bad for business. Few New Zealanders felt threatened by the Soviet Union, Britain and America's great bogey, but they feared The Bomb and agreed with Lange that 'there's only one thing worse than being incinerated by your enemies, and that's being incinerated by your friends'.[12]

In 1984 Labour had campaigned against nuclear power and nuclear weapons but not against ANZUS, the country's main defence alliance. Since becoming leader Lange had tried to keep the Americans on side, but he hit a brick wall when they refused to confirm or deny that their ships were nuclear-powered (easy to work out) or nuclear-armed (impossible, when missile systems such as ASROC could fire either nuclear or conventional warheads). Washington refused to follow the rules of its host, fearing that if it did, other countries might catch 'New Zealanditis'.

Late in 1984 the Americans tested the political waters by requesting a visit by the guided missile destroyer USS *Buchanan*. The *Buchanan* was not exactly toothless — she had ASROC — but the Americans hoped that this 23-year-old veteran (which had visited Auckland as recently as 1979) might slip under the political radar. No such luck. 'Near-uncertainty was not now enough for us,' Lange recalled. 'Whatever the truth of its armaments, its arrival in New Zealand would be seen as a surrender by the government.'[13] Lange still hoped that the Americans might offer to send something less ambiguous, but a leak to the press scotched that. It was the *Buchanan* or nothing.[14]

On 4 February 1985 the government said no. Just days later Washington severed intelligence and military ties, and downgraded political and diplomatic exchanges.[15] Schultz confirmed that the United States was no longer willing to maintain its security guarantee to New Zealand, although the treaty structure remained in place. Lange could live with his rear-admirals missing out on American cocktail parties. By then, in the shadow of the uneasy stand-off between Reagan and the Soviets, he had become the poster boy for nuclear disarmament. At a widely televised Oxford Union debate with right-wing evangelist Jerry Falwell, Lange drew thunderous applause by telling a young conservative, 'I can smell the uranium on your breath.'[16]

David Lange said he came to power 'at a time of calculated crisis, with a former prime minister having a licence to ringbark us, and scattering termites all around our wooden legs'. Lange had a gift for one-liners that made his press conferences the best show in town between 1984 and 1989. This 1987 polling day photo captures the quieter side of the man.

Ventures Two Ltd

Traditional trade links weakened along with traditional defence alliances. By the 1980s New Zealand was no longer London's antipodean dairy farm. In trade, as in defence, Australia was New Zealand's largest partner. Thanks to Muldoon's Closer Economic Relations trade agreement, container ships such as the *Canterbury Express* were kept busy. By 1999 Australia, which took just one per cent of our exports in 1950, was buying over 21 per cent of them.

In 1987 Labour passed the New Zealand Nuclear Free Zone, Disarmament and Arms Control Act and the United States Congress passed the Broomfield Act, confirming that New Zealand's status had been formally downgraded from ally to friend.[17] By then each knew the other's position. As Lange said, there cannot be any 'security alliance with a nuclear power on any terms other than those set by a nuclear power', and if the security alliance was the price New Zealand must pay to remain nuclear free, 'it is the price we are prepared to pay'.[18] By 1989, when he wrote that, public opinion (which in the period 1984–85 had included a big middle ground who wanted to reconcile the anti-nuclear policy with continued membership of ANZUS) had translated into political will.[19] Take the 'Z' out of the acronym, and that is where the Yanks could stick their alliance, many said. Even National signed up to anti-nuclearism. In 1989, 52 per cent of New Zealanders preferred to break defence ties rather than admit nuclear-armed ships. And with that

nationalism came anti-militarism — another 1989 poll showed that only 38 per cent would fight to defend their country, compared to 60 per cent of Australians and 77 per cent of Americans.[20] A national psychological shift had occurred; this reworking of relations with traditional allies was a long way from subsidising the imperial fleet, going where Britain went, or going even half the way with LBJ.

Economic policy: from wets to dries and then back to damp

Twenty years later, Sir Roger Douglas said that 'whether the nuclear ships issue distracted potential critics and made my job easier I will leave for others to make a judgement'. Many believed so, also naming the exchange crisis, which Douglas admitted opened a window for fast, furious action. 'We didn't create crises but we weren't above taking advantage of them,' a Treasury official remembered.[21]

There were plenty of distractions in the years 1984–85 as Labour unpicked Muldoon's 'economic vision of the Mad Hatter's Tea Party'. On Wednesday 18 July Lange, still prime minister-designate, announced a 20 per cent devaluation and a three-month freeze on wages and prices. Then, in old Labour fashion, it was time to consult, beginning with a widely publicised Economic Summit Conference. In 1986 it appointed Sir Ivor Richardson to head the Royal Commission on Social Policy, which produced *The April Report*. The Royal Commission's consultative approach 'alarmed Douglas and the planners who were mapping out a more austere path'. *The April Report* was a last-ditch attempt to return to the gentler world of the 1970s and to hold onto the 'principle of "belonging and participating"'.[22] Bulky, and unloved by Douglas or Treasury, the *Report* made itself useful at the Royal Commission's farewell party as a doorstop.

In fact the summits and commissions had already been sidelined by the new minister, who, as Lange once quipped, like rust never slept. Douglas had made his name in 1972–75 for restructuring broadcasting. Since then he had been demoted to the shadow cabinet for upstaging his leader. In 1980 he published his secular tract — all capital letters, exclamation marks and sound bites — *There's Got to Be a Better Way!* Transitional it may have been (it still argued for selected intervention and regulation), but entries such as 'KILLING THINGS (The case for departmental euthanasia)' pointed the way ahead — freeing up the economy, culling dying industries and cutting red tape.

Douglas was surfing a wave, generated earlier by the Chicago and Austrian schools of economics and popularised by economist Milton Friedman. There were many cross-currents, and the jargon was ugly, confusing and little read by most politicians, but everything flowed in the direction of less state intervention in the market, a smaller state and the elimination, reduction or at least targeting of social spending. Even Muldoon had stuck his toes in the waters of liberalisation with CER and some other measures. 'Rogernomics', the nickname given to Douglas's policies, followed those given to Margaret Thatcher's Thatcherism and Ronald Reagan's Reaganomics. Political scientists quibble over calling it 'libertarian', 'neo-liberal' or 'New Right'. Derivative, perhaps, Rogernomics could be described as Reaganomics with a little Rogering thrown in. Unlike Thatcher's Tories or Reagan's Republicans, most Labour dries were not social conservatives or Cold War warriors. They were also prepared to liberalise social policy in areas such as homosexual law reform and Treaty issues. This, at least, kept them in step with more traditional party activists and backbenchers, for whom the increasingly disgruntled new MP and former party president, Jim Anderton, provided a rallying point.

Douglas's thinking matched Treasury's. Traditionally, Labour and Treasury had been suspicious of each other, but events had drawn them closer. Treasury's run-ins with Muldoon had raised

From blue seas to blue helmets, defence continued to divide politicians. How much should a small independent nation spend? In the late 1980s, against the wishes of party activists who saw frigates as Cold War toys, Labour joined the Australasian 'Anzac Frigate programme'. Just two joined the fleet — HMNZS *Te Kaha* (pictured) and HMNZS *Te Mana* — and after 1999 a new Labour-led government scrapped the air force combat wing. The 2004 'Project Protector' fleet programme emphasised patrol vessels and logistical support for peacekeeping.

its stocks with the Opposition, and a younger generation of neo-liberal Treasury economists had worked more closely with Douglas in the early 1980s. The aims of Treasury's radical 1984 post-election briefing document, *Economic Management* — microeconomic reform, efficiency in government and fiscal discipline, and an anti-inflationary, independently administered monetary policy — matched Douglas's evolving thinking. *Economic Management* aimed to 'insulate the activity of economic management from problematic currents within Cabinet, Parliament and the community'.[23]

Douglas and Treasury moved quickly, giving rise to urban legends of a Treasury line, TINA — 'There Is No Alternative' — and of bumper stickers saying 'Vote for Treasury and cut out the middlemen'. Early in 1985 Douglas floated the dollar, traditionally controlled by politicians. The Kiwi soared in value — 'it stopped a growing economy in its tracks' one economist

Visits from warships like the USS *Texas* had been controversial long before Labour demanded confirmation or denial that they carried nuclear weapons. When the British refused to declare the Royal Yacht *Britannia*, the Royal Navy's wimpiest 'warship', nuclear-free for the Queen's 1990 visit Lange remarked, 'I was once laid low by a prawn I ate on board, but I thought that was about the limit of its lethal powers.' British ships later returned but not American ones. Fairfax Sunday Newspapers

FRENCH TERRORISM
IN AUCKLAND

Just after midnight on 10 July 1985 the *Rainbow Warrior*, Greenpeace's protest ship, sank alongside Marsden Wharf, drowning a crewman. The weeks that followed produced a trail of stories of camper vans and Zodiac inflatables left behind by the bumbling killers, Major Alain Mafart and Captain Dominique Prieur, spooks from a supposedly friendly country, France. Their president first denied France's involvement, then admitted guilt and finally paid compensation. Later even Lange, who had once defended Auckland crooks for a living, was taken aback by French duplicity

when they repatriated their agents on bogus medical grounds.

Even so, Gallic gall probably did more for Lange and Greenpeace than the *Warrior* could have achieved off Moruroa Atoll. This incident in our silent war of independence also 'interacted decisively with an upsurge in New Zealand nationalism'. New Zealanders were disenchanted with Washington and London, who though quick to condemn terrorism elsewhere, sat on their hands while France blackmailed New Zealand over its exports.[24] With allies like these, who needed enemies?

In 1985, in peacetime, France did what Germany and Japan had failed to do in war 40 years earlier — sink a merchant ship in a New Zealand harbour. The failure of traditional allies, Britain and the United States, to condemn this state-sponsored terrorism only hardened support for a more independent foreign policy line. Fairfax Sunday Newspapers

considered — and the funds inflow from overseas investors encouraged a new gold-rush. The Barclays share-market index surged from 1900 points to 3790 in 1986 alone. In 1989 the Reserve Bank of New Zealand Act effectively 'Muldoon-proofed' monetary policy by taking it out of the hands of elected politicians and giving it to the governor of the Reserve Bank.[25] A universal goods and services tax (GST) of 10 per cent (later raised to 12.5 per cent) took effect from 1 October 1986, while top tax rates came down from 66 cents in the dollar to 48 cents.

of managers who were expected to run their corporations along private sector lines. The sprawling Post Office was broken into three: New Zealand Post, Post Office Bank and Telecom. On April Fool's Day 1987 a raft of new state-owned enterprises (SOEs) came into being. They cut staff drastically — 50 per cent at Coal Corp and 25 per cent at the Electricity Corporation immediately, 30 per cent in Telecom's first two years and 72 per cent in Railways Corporation between 1983 and 1990.[26]

Dominion Post Collection, Alexander Turnbull Library, EP/1994-0914-18A

'Downsizing', 'restructuring', 'rationalising', 'rightsizing', it all amounted to laying people off. Thousands upon thousands of them. Like many Maori, Steve and Robert Reriti went through the disruption of the times. By 1994 they felt fortunate to be working as Taskforce Green (subsidised) employees on this sports pavilion in Lower Hutt.

For decades governments had used the state sector to minimise unemployment. But this was not the way of the Lange–Douglas government. Douglas was willing to accept higher levels of unemployment as part of the price of getting the 'economic fundamentals' right. Labour took the scalpel to the core public sector, starting with its commercial activities. There were already state-owned corporations (such as the Shipping Corporation, Railways, Broadcasting and Air New Zealand) but many ministries and departments combined regulatory roles with trading activities. The State-owned Enterprises Act 1986 placed these trading activities in the hands

More corporations and job losses followed. But for Douglas even the best-run SOE was too far removed from the disciplines and incentives of the market and still left the government exposed to risk. In December 1987 he announced a big privatisation programme — selling the family silver, critics called it. It was far from popular, especially when news of the fees paid to consultants leaked out. Sales ranged from Communicate New Zealand ($64,000) to Telecom ($4.25 billion).

In the remaining core public sector, the State Sector Act 1988 replaced departmental permanent heads with fixed-term chief executives, who now employed their departments' staff. Almost everyone underwent at least one major carve-up or recon-figuration. The big Ministry of Transport was broken up into many smaller units, as was the Department of Scientific and Industrial Research. A new Department of Conservation was assembled from elements of Lands and Survey, the Wildlife Service and the Forest Service. In many (but not all) areas, policy advice was also separated from service delivery, making New Zealand, a former defence secretary complained, 'the only country in the world with two Defence departments – one to reflect and one to fight'![27] The Public Finance Act 1989 introduced accrual accounting. Now ministers would purchase specific outputs from their departments.

Local government reform followed a similar trajectory. The year 1989 produced the biggest shake-up in local government since the abolition of the provinces in 1876. Thirteen new regional councils, 14 city councils and 57 district councils replaced approximately 620 territorial and ad hoc bodies.[28] The harbour boards' commercial operations were transferred to publicly owned port companies. There were efficiency gains — between October 1989 and February 1990 the cost of moving a container across the Auckland wharves fell from $350–$400 a box to $220 — but thousands of waterfront jobs went, almost half of the workforce in 1989, and more later as the port companies further streamlined their operations.[29]

The restructuring costs fell heaviest on the unskilled and the semi-skilled, traditionally the first to be laid off when the going got tough. Maori unemployed — 14.1 per cent in 1981 compared to 3.7 per cent for non-Maori — approached 20 per cent in 1989.[30] It was even worse for Pacific Islanders, whose unemployment levels were always higher than the rest of the population and stayed that way for longer: 6.1 per cent in 1987 compared with four per cent in the rest of the population, and a whopping 28.8 per cent in 1992, compared with 10.6 per cent. Even when the economy had picked up a decade later, Pacific Islanders still struggled to catch up. In 2001, their unemployment rate was 11.2 per cent, double that of the wider population, and those in work earned proportionately less of the national median income than they had in 1986.[31]

Rural and small-town New Zealand suffered. Whole industries shut down in some places, effectively closing towns. The killing chains at the Whakatu freezing works in Hawke's Bay stopped in 1986, putting 1500 locals, mainly Maori, out of work in an instant.[32] It was a pattern repeated elsewhere as forestry and mining shed workers, and private companies — Bendon and Crown Lynn, for example — found it cheaper to run their businesses offshore.

People drifted away from rural areas and small towns in search of work and opportunity. Oamaru's population, 13,550 in 1978, had dropped 1000 people by 1987.[33] Places like that never seemed to recover, despite investment in sunrise industries or heritage, and the chance to nab a historic house at a bargain price. A decade later, Oamaru was still going down, and between 1996 and 2001 its population declined by over five per cent.[34]

New Zealand's smokestack industries went down for the count late last century. In 2004 Patea resembled an open-air industrial heritage park. The harbour (rear) closed in the early 1960s. The freezing works (foreground) closed in the 1980s. Thousands of manual jobs vanished from the cities and the countryside. Marty Melville, Fotopress

CITY OF SALES, CITY OF SAILS

Mirror glass hides what goes on behind its walls while borrowing its finery from the neighbours. That makes it a fitting symbol for the 1980s, when spec builders filled city centres with nondescript concrete-and-glass boxes. Chase Corporation's Mid-City cinema and shopping complex buildings were the vilest. All tacky neon, glass and drag-queen quality glitter, they sprouted in Queen Street, Auckland and in Manners Street, Wellington before the crash stopped the spread of the contagion.

In the 1980s conspicuous consumption rode high in those parts of the City of Sails unaffected by plant closures and factory lay-offs. Every month *Metro*, a slick city glossy, advised the chattering classes which new watering hole was hot, which was not and — in a thinly disguised gossip column — who was up whom. Its advertising spreads would have been unthinkable in Muldoon's 'Fortress New Zealand'. Able to buy overseas funds freely, retailers could now offer consumers whatever they fancied, from bidets to BMWs. For Aucklanders in a hurry, there was even a helicopter shuttle service between the airport and the city.

Others messed about in boats. In the 1980s Michael Fay and David Richwhite, gung-ho merchant-banker symbols of the times, decided to go after the America's Cup. New Zealand had a fine yachting tradition, but its sportspeople had never thrown money at a yacht race the way Fay, Richwhite and their supporters did. For the 1986 Fremantle challenge Bruce Farr designed a revolutionary 'plastic fantastic', a fibreglass yacht. Two years later the bankers created the lowpoint in the long history of the Cup, a challenge with *KZ1*, 'the big boat'. The Americans creamed it with a catamaran, and the farce degenerated into acrimonious litigation. Without this crew of money men, Team New Zealand went on to win the Cup in 1995, defend it successfully in 2000 and lose it in 2003. BELOW: Fairfax Sunday Newspapers

Listener cartoonist Trace Hodgson was one of the harshest critics of the transformation of the economy, portraying Lange as economically illiterate and Douglas as cynical and exploitative. That oversimplification masked Lange's role in the changes, or at least during Labour's first term. By 1988, however, the pigs' paper towers had collapsed and the bananas were being inserted in painful places. T Hodgson, NZ Cartoon Archive, Alexander Turnbull Library

Meanwhile, large towns serving the rural hinterland swallowed up people. Hamilton, centre of dairying and the racing industry, and conveniently close to the Auckland metropolis, just kept on expanding, outstripping the growth in the wider population.[35]

At the August 1987 election Labour increased its share of the vote, something few governments had done that century. It had helped that the earliest reforms had bitten two sectors of less interest to traditional Labour loyalists, agriculture and the financial markets. But a near-win in Remuera coupled with defections in traditional city seats suggested that the party's electoral support was becoming more true-blue than blue collar. Money had flowed freely after Douglas loosened things up, high interest rates and high inflation encouraging a spending boom. From being overregulated, New Zealand went to cowboy country. These were the years when Roger Hall moved on from *Gliding On* to *The Share Club* and television celebrated the minority lifestyle in *Gloss* — all shoulder pads, big hair, bitchiness and boardroom beastliness.

Lange–Douglas Labour now depended on an uneasy coalition of traditional but increasingly disaffected Labour voters, issues-driven environmental peaceniks and the economic liberals who favoured Rogernomics. It took just two things — an economic collapse, and a falling-out between Lange and Douglas — to derail everything.

The economy nose-dived just months after the election. The October 1987 share-market crash popped the speculative bubble that had dazzled the middle class. In just one day $10 billion was wiped from the value of the New Zealand share-market. And it just kept falling. Worth $50 billion before 'Black Tuesday', New Zealand's share-market finally bottomed out at $14.5 billion in January 1991. No other developed country's market fell as far or stayed down longer.[36] Down came the corporate high-fliers — Ariadne, Chase Corp, Charter Corp, Judgecorp, Equiticorp — and soon the corps were corpses. 'For lease' signs went up, the mirror-glass spec jobs ground to a halt, and builders went bust, leaving jagged gaps in city streets. Tales of insider trading, and of incompetent and illegal behaviour, would fill the news for years to come. Many small investors lost their savings, a few their houses.

The political fallout was damaging, for the crash spread the pain from *Truth* readers to the *Metro* mob, who fled on their Gucci-shod feet back to National. Until now, the booming financial, professional consultancy and construction sectors had

World share-markets collapsed on 'Black Tuesday', 21 October 1987. Corporate high-fliers and Hooray Henrys lost their Versace shirts, but because New Zealanders had taken to shares like Lotto tickets, 40 per cent of adults also suffered when this bubble burst. That week at share-brokers Francis, Alison, Symes & Co, Grant Taylor (left) and Stuart Beadle sweated while New Zealand took a bath.

insulated middle-class Auckland and Wellington from much of the pain. Not any more. By the late 1980s urban, white-collar workers also found themselves on the scrapheap as government agencies restructured and as businesses closed, consolidated, retrenched or exported their top jobs to Sydney and Melbourne. Teachers, doctors and nurses became economic migrants. Registered unemployment would go from 100,000 in early 1988 to 216,000 in early 1992 (or 265,000 if the more broadly defined 'jobless' figure was used).[37] Long before then, Labour's caucus hit what Deputy Prime Minister Geoffrey Palmer called 'speed wobbles'. Lange lost confidence in Douglas and wanted to suspend the restructuring — 'pausing for a cuppa', he called it — but the Rogernomes, who were more espresso folk anyway, cried 'crash through or crash!' As Douglas, remembering that the 1972–75 Labour government had lost office before being able to reform health or local government, later put it:

Implement reform in quantum leaps, using larger packages . . . speed is essential. It is almost impossible to go too fast . . . once you build the momentum, don't let it stop rolling . . . don't blink. Public confidence rests on your composure.[38]

By now Lange was 'a lonely figure, tossed by forces far greater than he could ride, let alone tame'. He may, as Colin James suggests, have been 'more a salesman . . . for those who drove the policy change[s]' but early in 1988 Lange struck out at Douglas's favoured low flat-tax rate. Later he sacked Douglas's acolyte, Richard Prebble, from Cabinet. Douglas was next on the list. But caucus was not ready to recant and when it invited Douglas and Prebble back in 1989, 'Lange was stranded in the hard glare of market economics and efficiency and his titular leadership died there'.[39] He resigned in August 1989.

Lange's replacement was Geoffrey Palmer, sharp-minded, but too academic for some, and not a natural on television, making him fair game for the cartoonists.[40] Plunging poll figures panicked his colleagues into handing the poisoned chalice to Mike Moore just weeks from the 1990 election. To no avail. The party polled 35 per cent of the vote, its poorest result since 1931.[41] Jim Anderton, who had left Labour in 1989 to found New Labour, added to the damage.

When Jim Bolger's National government took power the mood was gloomy, made worse by another unexpected financial crisis, this time over the Bank of New Zealand. Bolger had his doubts about Treasury, but these were not shared by his Minister of Finance, Ruth Richardson, the self-styled 'peppery little conviction politician', who planted her foot on Ruthanasia — Rogernomics turbo-charged. She made the most of the BNZ crisis. 'As Roger Douglas knew only too well, a crisis inherited from your predecessor can give you a flying start in terms of impetus and goodwill.'[42]

Doctor Ruth went straight for the fiscal enema. In December 1990 National announced $1.275 billion worth of social welfare cuts. Among other things, her controversial 1991 'mother of all budgets' put cash registers and credit card machines into hospitals, or CHEs (Crown Health Enterprises) as they became known. State housing was put into an SOE which charged tenants market-based rents. 'National was moving decisively away from the social-citizenship model of the welfare state towards the residual or minimalist model.'[43] The Employment Contracts Act and the sale of the railways also carried the restructuring into areas considered off-limits by Labour. For the next two years Richardson and Jenny Shipley — 'the two hair shirts' — held the line against big-spending colleagues. A rare sacred cow that managed to slip by was the controversial new Museum of New Zealand.[44]

National's welfare cuts jolted the population, and perhaps none more than the elderly. Contrary to its election pledges, national superannuation fell under Richardson's knife. Labour's deeply unpopular surcharge on superannuation, introduced in 1985, would be abolished — or so National promised — but leaked plans from the Department of Social Welfare showed that the government meant to replace the tax with a tough income-tested abatement regime. In the end, the surcharge remained, and at a higher rate than before; it was finally dropped in 1998.

The elderly had been galvanised into action at National's 'most provocative and unpopular move'. Activist groups such as

New Zealanders showed little enthusiasm for republicanism, but late 20th-century governments welded new figureheads to the ship of state by appointing different sorts of people to Government House. Dame Catherine Tizard, a television panellist and mayor of Auckland, was the first woman governor-general. She brought a new look to Government House, or 'State House Number One' as she called it. Dominion Post Collection, Alexander Turnbull Library, EP-1992-4512-34

Grey Power gained new members who were prepared to march on Parliament, picket electorate offices, and jam radio talkback lines.[45] Yet those who shouted the loudest were not necessarily hardest hit. Between 1987 and the mid 1990s, the equivalent disposable income of households whose main income was national superannuation remained relatively stable; that of other beneficiaries — sole parents, the unemployed and sickness beneficiaries — fell by an average of 20 per cent.[46]

Labour's final honours list, which included knighthoods for Palmer and Douglas, only added to public disillusionment, which grew as the recession deepened. National had a huge majority but barely six months after winning office it was so unpopular that Governor-General Dame Catherine Tizard told the Queen that she was studying constitutional issues.[47]

By late 1991 recession had become depression (in contrast to the rest of the world, which was prospering) and unemployment — despite years of migration outflows — had reached a frightening 11 per cent. The government talked about 'a hand up' replacing 'a hand out', but the electorate responded with a two-finger salute. For a while Richardson and Shipley travelled with police escorts.

At the 1993 election voters remained wary of Labour and weary of change but, furious with National for breaking a promise to remove pension surcharges, they left it clinging to power by one seat. 'Roger Douglas had had a David Lange to charm New Zealanders. I had not,' Richardson mused amidst the wreckage.[48] Bolger, 'The Great Helmsman', dropped the pilot and steered into the centre of the channel. There would be some further reforms, such as to shipping in 1994, but the high-water mark had been passed and there had been some hasty backtracking on superannuation and health.

The 'revolution' remains controversial, over-hyped by as many of its instigators as of its detractors. While some called it counter-revolutionary, Colin James maintained that the

'1984–87 Parliament smashed the icons of the 1950s consensus', not just in overthrowing Keynesian economics, but also because Labour 'ploughed up every policy field, in some cases very innovatively'. He saw the leaders of the Vietnam generation — the 'gimme generation' — as being less concerned with security than their parents; their 'temperament was in tune with the psychology of individual freedom from constraint implied by libertarian theories'.[49] They fought a cultural war of independence, 'indigenising' ethnic Europeans and 're-indigenising' Maori. 'New Zealand policymakers behaved rather like adolescents in the 1980s, recklessness mixed with experimentation', accelerating, broadening and deepening the change beyond what occurred in similar societies. They were helped by New Zealand's 'village-like polity', which enabled a few well-connected people to drive through change quickly. Muldoon's discrediting — National did not recover properly before the 1987 election and essentially adopted Douglas's course — meant that 'we had, from 1984–87, effectively a one-party state, controlled from the top and incorporating top officials in the key ministries'.

It may be that the attitudinal changes of 1984–93 are more significant than the much-debated economic restructuring. Seeing Britain's entry into the EEC as more important, historian James Belich calls 1984 a 'blue herring'. 'Its architects freed up the fiddle market while Rome burned, restructured the stable door after the horse had bolted.'[50] Economist Brian Easton believes that the New Right policies actually added to the problem. The crude relative rankings of Gross Domestic Product per capita — disputed by some economists — show that the real action had happened earlier. In 1950 New Zealand was ranked fifth of the OECD 24 nations, in 1966 sixth, then 11th in 1971, reflecting the wool price collapse. The oil shocks of the 1970s took that to 19th by 1980, where it rested through Muldoon's last term, Rogernomics and Ruthanasia until 1997, when it slipped slightly to 20, its current standing.[51]

The 'revolution' had even less effect on social policy, and more particularly its delivery. Between 1984 and 1990 divisions within Labour's own constituency and within caucus prevented the Rogernomes from drastically reforming social services (though their broader emphasis on individual choice and consumption helped to ringbark the idea of universal rights to welfare). Richardson had no such inhibitions. The 1991 budget amounted to 'a radical plan to reduce welfare to a marginal safety net and to eliminate all forms of universal provision in the long term'.[52] Some Social Welfare offices had to hire bouncers to protect staff as community frustration boiled over.[53] But ACC, the DPB and universal superannuation survived, as did large government agencies administering growing education, health and social welfare budgets.

Many New Zealanders failed to see how cutting benefits, supposedly to give beneficiaries greater incentive to move into the workforce, would work when unemployment just kept on climbing. There were 245 food banks dispensing charity by 1994 when 17-year-old Lower Hutt resident Daniel Middleton took his case to passing motorists.

Dumped from finance by Jim Bolger after the 1993 election, Ruth Richardson took pride in the Fiscal Responsibility Act, which reinforced 'the concepts of prudence, stability and certainty in fiscal management'. By the time Tom Scott drew her as a Starfleet officer, an electorate sick of radical reform had decided that 'the engines cannae take any more, Captain'. MMP, confirmed in the 1993 referendum, put a tractor beam on the ideologues.

Richardson did not survive. Why? The New Right's panzer charge faltered in close-quarters fighting in the blackboard jungles and the emergency wards. Treasury's mandarins were less sure-footed with social policy than they were with economic policy. Inevitably, when the spending ministers' advisors regrouped, politicians like Bolger, sensing the voters' 'predilection for exercising choice collectively rather than individually', 'kept pulling the wings off the reforms', as Richardson later said.[54] 'The reforms of 1991 were perhaps inevitably doomed because they failed to appreciate the impossibility of completely replacing earlier notions of social policy', social historian Michael Belgrave concluded. 'New Zealand's welfare state is still a product of its historical development . . . despite the pressures of globalisation and an open economy.'[55]

Voters took revenge. In the 1993 election Labour's vote slipped marginally, but National's plunged over 12 per cent to 35.1 per cent. The Big Two's combined share of the vote was the lowest in 65 years. But disenchantment ran deeper. Heylen polling showed that trust in Parliament and politicians had slumped from 33 per cent in 1975 to an embarrassing 11 per cent in 1985; seven years later it barely registered at four per cent. Bolger (like Bill Birch, Lange, Helen Clark and others) disliked proportional representation; so voters took out some insurance against fast, radical change when he kept a promise he might not have been expected to, and held a referendum on changing the electoral system.[56] In 1992, 85 per cent voted for a referendum on the first-past-the-post system. In a second referendum, in 1993, the voters took 'revenge on politicians they had come to distrust', and made the biggest change to the electoral system since 1893 by selecting Mixed Member Proportional (MMP).[57] It was the political equivalent of sending a troublesome tomcat to the vet. Since 1996 governments have been coalitions or minority governments.

In late 1997 a coup deposed Bolger and made Jenny Shipley New Zealand's first woman prime minister. Shipley was tough-minded. 'This isn't a damn beauty contest,' she once said, 'if you

Dominion Post Collection, Alexander Turnbull Library, EP 1993-2927-28

'Want a good reason for MMP?' asked the *Footrot Flats* character Wal, the creation of Murray Ball and the embodiment of a traditional Kiwi lifestyle that was dying. 'Look at the people who are telling you not to.' Journalist Jo Walker took to Wellington streets in 1993 to counter Business Roundtable criticism of MMP.

come into politics to be popular, then you've picked the wrong sport.' She veered right, ignoring the nation's mood, and paid the price in 1999 when a Labour–Alliance coalition swept aside her wobbly government.[58] National almost disappeared as a major party in the 2002 election, winning just over 20 per cent of the vote.

In 1999 Labour's Helen Clark became prime minister, leading a Labour-dominated government in coalitions, formal or otherwise, with the Alliance Party (which self-destructed in 2002), and then after the 2002 election, with the Progressive Coalition and supported by United Future New Zealand. Labour was determined to distance itself from the previous regime and especially the Labour government of 1984–90. The 1999 Speech from the Throne sought to lay the 1980s ghosts to rest: 'New Zealanders . . . are weary of radical restructuring . . . The next three years will be marked by responsible, pragmatic change in the interests of the many.'[59] Voters were convinced enough to give Labour another chance in 2002.

Various policies highlighted this brave new world under an older-style Labour. It rolled back many of the unpopular changes to the health sector, and reversed National's decision to hold superannuation levels constant in real terms for several years; by 2000, this benefit had emerged from the melee of reforms 'virtually unscathed'.[60] There was a royal commission into genetic modification, although not everyone liked its findings and the whole GE issue would eventually drive a wedge between Labour and the Greens. There was more funding for science and research, industry development and social services. The policy of SOE — 'sell off everything' — stopped, and even famously reversed when the government bailed out the privatised Air New Zealand (and almost had to do the same for the rail network). A healthy economy with decent growth — sometimes higher than the OECD average — generated budget surpluses and allowed cash to be injected into education, health and social services, for example. Unemployment fell to the more manageable levels of 5.7 per cent by 2001 and 3.6 per cent by early 2005.[61]

In 2000 the Employment Contracts Act vanished, and many workers and unionists merrily danced a jig on its grave. The new Employment Relations Act began an era of collective bargaining to reduce inequalities. Employment agreements replaced contracts, and unions won the right of access to the workplace to recruit for members, something they could do previously only with permission.

The business sector prophesied doom and gloom. Unions' hopes of growth and some employers' worries about payback did not eventuate. When the Act came into effect in 2000, union membership was at a record low of 17 per cent of the employed labour force; in March 2003, it was 17.6 per cent. Members were

The economy recovered from the mid 1990s, but the new jobs were different. The big multinationals had either crashed or they went back to 'core business'; even Fletcher Challenge split apart. Many factory jobs had been exported to the Far East or the Pacific, so new businesses tended to be small and either service sector or high-tech. Dunedin, once the centre of Victorian manufacturing and 'sweating', became a centre for biotechnology, home to new companies such as cancer researchers Pacific Edge Biotechnology Ltd.

more likely to be the professional white-collar woman than the traditional blue-collar man. Rather than pursuing industrial action — although some key groups did this after 2000 — unions focused on developing relationships with employers and being associations for workers. 'Unions are now about any issues that workers face,' commented one organiser.[62]

A survey of businesses found that the new legislation had, in the main, made no impact on them.[63] Some employers blamed the Act for their problems in a growing economy. Late in 2002 Carter Holt Harvey announced it would issue redundancy notices to over 250 maintenance workers at the Kinleith pulp and paper mill. 'Delays, stopwork meetings and extensive consultation under the Employment Relations Act have slowed down the changes at Kinleith,' the chief executive was quoted as saying.[64]

Employers could be equally as suspicious about the effects of paid parental leave, one of the major Labour–Alliance policy planks, introduced in 2002. Most of the gripes were about paying the 12 weeks leave (extended to 14 from December 2004) to new parents, male or female; it was estimated to cost $51 million annually, rising to almost $60 million in 2005. There were some grumbles about the level of payment (a maximum of $325 a week before tax), that the self-employed missed out, and that there were anomalies in the timing — it was available for babies due on or after 1 July 2002, so those born prematurely in May or June were in while those due in those months were not. By early 2004, over 19,000 women (and a few men) had received the leave.[65]

'AOTEAROA, RUGGED INDIVIDUAL'

Cultural nationalism boomed from the mid 1980s. A Maori cultural renaissance was to the fore. *Te Maori*, the exhibition, returned in 1986 from a triumphant tour of the United States. Nearly 200,000 people visited the exhibition in Wellington, some probably looking again at taonga 'to which, as schoolchildren, they had been dragged to museums to view'.[66] Maori painters and writers explored Maori themes, or produced work in te reo — a version of *The Merchant of Venice* played in 2002. Popular musicians took Maori-inflected sounds or te reo mainstream.

The small screen showed more of New Zealand — in *Shortland Street* (from 1992) or on Maori TV, for example. But many local shows, such as *Shark in the Park* and *Gloss*, had a short shelf-life, and some mercifully so. The big screen carried films like *Footrot Flats* (1986), *The Piano* (1993) and *Once Were Warriors* (1994). There were distinctly local stories, such as *Whale Rider* (2003), and others that we tried hard to make local, most

notably Peter Jackson's *The Lord of the Rings* (2001–03), which showcased New Zealand directing talent, technical wizardry and landscape. Jackson's blockbusters hit the stratosphere, with the third film cleaning up at the 2004 Academy Awards; if there had been an award for best supporting country, New Zealand would have won that too.

One of the boldest depictions of local culture was the bicultural national museum, Museum of New Zealand Te Papa Tongarewa, which opened in 1998 as a 'forum for the nation'. The branding said it all: Te Papa, Our Place. All New Zealanders could see their culture and heritage on display, and the meanings of those terms were deliberately broad.

BELOW: Te Papa opened on Wellington's waterfront in 1998. The arts establishment bristled at the placing of a Colin McCahon painting next to a refrigerator, and the traditionalists rolled their eyes at theme park rides and hordes of screaming kids charging around the exhibits, but the punters loved the place. Over a million visitors clocked in during the first year alone, and numbers remained high. Museum of New Zealand, Te Papa Tongarewa

ABOVE: Homage to the roots: Maori and Pacific beats and stories defined New Zealand hip hop and rap from the mid 1990s. Artists like Che Fu (left) and Nesian Mystic, performing here at the New Zealand Music Awards in 2003, took local sounds to a new generation of New Zealanders.

BELOW: No dusty artefacts and papier mâché sets here; Te Maori showcased taonga to the world.

Te Maori
A recovered *The return home*

AUCKLAND CITY ART GALLERY
JUNE 28-SEPTEMBER 10, 1987

Yet Clark's Labour did not seriously challenge Douglas and Richardson's politics-proofing of the economy. The extremism was abandoned, but the principles of a more open economy endured. This was partly because the economy flourished after 1999, partly because of the fiscal policies of Clark and her finance minister Michael Cullen, and partly because, in the view of commentators such as Brian Easton, the government had no mind to reverse some of the changes of Rogernomics.[67] Buoyed by a throbbing economy, Labour turned to fostering knowledge-based growth and, more controversially, implementing race relations initiatives.

It also set about strengthening national identity through arts and culture. The state supported growth in the cultural sector, just as it had in the 1930s and 1940s, that other great period of soaring cultural nationalism. And just as a key minister in the first Labour government (Peter Fraser) translated an interest in the arts into concrete support, so too did Clark from 1999. A 'cultural recovery' package injected over $80 million across the arts and culture spectrum in 2000, and additional government support thereafter enabled more of New Zealand to be seen, heard and experienced.

Dialling in the changes

The jury is divided on whether 1973 or 1984 was the greater turning point in recent history. Already, there are whispers that 1999 may have been another of New Zealand's quiet revolutions, or even the 2004 budget.[68] Our recent history rivals 20th-century Russia's in revolutions in quick succession, but everyone seems in agreement about the cultural and social shifts since the mid 1980s. Some of the shifts continued the existing trends — for example, Auckland's spread and the trek north. Some came about as a consequence of economic or political reforms, while others occurred more or less independently, such as the drop-off in fertility.

A theme of growing diversity captures the flavour of New Zealand from 1984. In lifestyles, opportunities, ethnicity and the differences between rural and urban, North Island and South, or rich and poor, more variation flowed into New Zealand life. Things that were unheard of in 1984 had become commonplace by the end of the period.

Take communication technology. The Internet arrived here in 1986, but only a few scientists and computer nerds seemed aware of it. Around 1200 host computers were hooked into the Internet by 1991, with connection speeds we would find numbingly slow now, and there were fewer than 150 websites in the world to surf. The technology took off in the 1990s: 180,000 computers had Internet access by 1999, and by 2001 New Zealand was among the top 10 webbed countries. Websites were numbered in the hundreds of millions. We seized on mobile phones and text messaging even more eagerly. An estimated 58 per cent of households had at least one mobile phone in 2001, more than double the number four years earlier, and school teachers bemoaned the 21st-century 'teen-speak' that came in the wake of texting.

But as with all gadgets and new technology, access fell unevenly. Predictably, the better-off, big-city folk, Pakeha and Asians were the main beneficiaries. Growing use did not mean universal use either: around 60 per cent of households were without Internet access in 2001.[69] Technology made the rest, the best and the worst of the world just a finger click away. Internet chat rooms seem light years removed from toll calls, but the bigger changes may actually have occurred a century earlier, when cables allowed communication with the other side of the world in a day, rather than weeks or months.

The politics of MMP even brought diversity into Parliament, which started to look more like the wider society it represented. Parliament contained more women, and more Maori and

Nigel Longstaff

Despite the changes over the late 20th century, the 'Super-Mum' phenomena still seemed entrenched for some women, who were holding down a career and raising a couple of kids, all the while looking good.

people from Pacific Island and Asian communities; in the 2002 election 34 women, 19 Maori, three Pacific Island and two Asian MPs were elected. New Zealand got its first openly gay politician, its first dreadlocked Rastafarian MP and, world famously, a transgendered MP. The first MMP Parliament had some complete greenies, and not just in the ecological sense; previously unemployed grandmothers and 20-somethings with little political experience.

Since the early 1990s the number of women in Parliament — as well as the range of women on top in politics, representing the Queen, in the judiciary, steering major companies and heading an Anglican diocese — seem to have fulfilled some of the feminist ambitions raised in the 1970s. A Ministry of Women's Affairs opened in 1986 to give the government policy advice on gender issues, although political support for this small office was never universal. A dedicated Equal Employment Opportunities Commissioner joined the Human Rights Commission in 2002. The policies of some of the shoulder-padded 'polifemmes' through the 1980s and early 1990s made the women's movement shudder. 'Girls Can Do Anything' slogans seemed to have come horribly true when the gals in the Beehive acted a lot like the blokes.

There were reminders, too, that not all attitudes towards women had shifted. Everyone shuddered when details came to light in 1987 about the 'unfortunate experiment' with sufferers of cervical cancer at Auckland's National Women's Hospital. The subsequent inquiry into treatment at the hospital was a landmark in women's public health issues. Marches by women to 'reclaim the night' dwindled from the mid 1980s, but sexual assault and domestic violence remained realities for some women. Child abuse and sexual abuse became major issues of public concern.

To young women growing into adulthood in the last 15 years of the 20th century, the organised feminist movement of the 1970s seemed like ancient history. Many things they took for granted were won hard by the generation that had gone before: equal pay, access to abortion and contraception, wider educational and job opportunities, greater equality. More of this generation's women attend university; they are marrying later, if they marry at all, and are having children later, if they have them at all; and they tend to be earning more than their grandmothers ever dreamed of. Yet by the early 21st century, women still earned less than men — about 80 per cent of the weekly male wage in 2002, and less for Maori and Pacific Island women. They were clustered in a comparatively narrow range of occupations that tended to be lower paying, and found it harder to save for their retirement. Within the home, unpaid work fell unevenly, and women still did most of the child care and household tasks.[70]

Sheer demographics loom large in this period and they changed the basis of New Zealand society. Nearly 15 per cent of New Zealanders, or one in seven, were Maori in 2001, up by 21 per cent in 10 years. Significant gaps remained between Pakeha and Maori. There was a depressing list of 'disproportionates' and 'lower thans': median annual income, education, life expectancy, standard of housing. Government policy focused on closing these gaps or reducing inequalities in the 21st century. Seen in the longer term, many measurable gaps between Pakeha and Maori have lessened, though whether that reduces inequalities is another matter; but this lessening is probably cold comfort to Maori who were hit harder by, and took longer to recover from, the changes from the mid 1980s.

But there were counter-currents. Maori population growth matched a resurgence of Maori culture. The Maori Language Act 1987 recognised Maori as an official language of New Zealand and established a Maori Language Commission. Along with kura kaupapa Maori (Maori language schools), the first of which opened in 1984, such moves helped to push te reo. In 2001, around 25 per cent of people of Maori ethnicity spoke some te reo; significantly, half of them were aged under 25 years.[71] Maori tertiary education institutions — whare wananga teaching traditional Maori subjects — gobbled up students eager to connect with Maori culture. In 1999 there were fewer than 1500 students at whare wananga; by 2003, there were over 13,500.[72]

One of the big news stories for New Zealand, and for Maori in particular, from the late 20th century was the heightened place of the Treaty of Waitangi in public consciousness. The Treaty settlement process was perhaps the most powerful, and controversial, manifestation of this. Treaty settlements, made possible by Labour's 1985 backdating of the Waitangi Tribunal's purview to 1840, opened up new avenues for the settlement of historic grievances. In 1988, the Tribunal's powers were enhanced

further when it gained the power to order — not just recommend — that land held by SOEs that had been acquired in breach of the Treaty be reacquired by the government and returned to Maori owners. For some, such measures were a 'bold and necessary enterprise' that would assist in rectifying past injustices; for others, there was concern over how far the claims would go, how much they would cost, and how many there would be.[73]

Maori did not delay in lodging claims with the Tribunal. By early 1991, there were 200 claims on the Tribunal's books, and the number kept growing; there had been over 1000 claims lodged by 2004. Progress on inquiring into the claims, some of which were grouped together, and reaching a settlement

Fotopress

Some people looked sideways at the number of claims Maori filed with the Waitangi Tribunal from the mid 1980s, seeing only the media reports of protests rather than the issues behind them. Hawke's Bay Maori (below) in 2003 draw attention to a wahi tapu (sacred place), subject to a Tribunal claim, that the local council was trying to sell. Meanwhile, the thousands of people — Maori and Pakeha — turning up to kapa haka festivals (above) went largely unnoticed by the media. Fotopress

New Zealand's growing Asian population brought diverse cultural events into the local scene. Here Chinese New Year dragon dancers participate in a Christmas parade in Auckland in 2002.

acceptable to both Maori and the Crown was slower. Under the National government of the 1990s, and particularly its Minister in Charge of Treaty Negotiations, Doug Graham, considerable progress was made in reaching agreement with some iwi.

Substantial problems meant substantial settlements — $170 million each in the case of Tainui (1995) and Ngai Tahu (1998), and $170 million for the settlement of commercial fisheries claims (1992) — and these took some negotiating. Ngai Tahu's multi-volume Tribunal report appeared in 1991, with the settlement offer, all 1800 pages of it, taking a couple of years to work out. When invested wisely (not all settlements were), they brought the promise of new jobs, training and other benefits for iwi members; the 1993 Sealord deal was a major investment in one of the growing export industries, deep-sea fishing. Other settlements were smaller: nearly $44,000 for Rotoma (1996), nearly $130,000 for Te Maunga (1996). For some iwi, the official apology that came with settlements was worth more.

In the early 1990s the National government thought that a 'fiscal envelope' of $1 billion would do for Treaty settlements, it claimed. Maori firmly rejected it. There were Pakeha who bridled at the settlements and demanded that the Tribunal be abolished. Some bristled at the contents of Tribunal findings such as the 1996 Taranaki report which likened 19th-century events there to the Holocaust. They had little time for what they saw as the 'antics' of Maori 'activists' — Mike Smith taking an axe to the tree on One Tree Hill in 1994; the 79-day occupation in 1995 of Wanganui's Moutoa Gardens, known to Maori as Pakaitore; the increasing tension at Waitangi Day events; and the 15,000 marchers in the 2004 hikoi protesting over the government's plans for the foreshore. Playing the race card was as popular a political party trick as it had been 40 years before, as National Party leader Don Brash discovered in 2004.

Despite the protest, the Tribunal continued to inquire into and report on claims, and the government continued to reach settlements with iwi, at the rate of about one every six months by 2004.[74]

The big change in New Zealand's mix was the growth of the Asian population — nearly seven per cent of New Zealanders by 2001, double the proportion a decade earlier. Changes in immigration policy were important here, as New Zealand saw advantages in seeing itself as an Asia–Pacific nation. New criteria introduced from 1987 broke down our traditional favouritism towards British (and European and South Pacific) migrants. Wealthy Asian migrants, particularly Hong Kong Chinese beginning to eye uncertainly the pending handover to China of the colony, were particularly welcome.[75]

Or at least that was the rhetoric. Asian migration brought out the ugly side of some Kiwis, who were jealous of Asian wealth and success or just plain racist. There were shrill cries for keeping the number of Asian migrants 'manageable' to retain the New Zealand 'way of life'. Politicians saw gains in plugging an anti-Asian prejudice that had been relatively muted for some years. At the same time, in 2002 the government made a formal apology to Chinese for the 19th-century poll tax and the legacy of discrimination that Chinese had experienced. Chinese New Zealanders, some with roots in the country stretching back three or more generations, suddenly felt themselves treated as 'gate-crashers' in their own homes as other New Zealanders lumped all Asians together and failed to distinguish between them and the new arrivals. One second-generation Chinese New Zealander noted that 'people often asked me, as if I represented all my race, certain questions like, "What would Chinese do in this sort of [situation]". I felt like saying, "what the f*** are you asking *me* for?!"'[76]

Light of the Pacific. Saturday's Otara Flea Market started out as a place for Auckland's Pacific Island population to stock up on Pacific foods and other products. It has become a multicultural market for the city's diverse ethnic groups.

If changes in migration policy favoured Asian migrants and others with the desired levels of wealth and skills, they disadvantaged those from the Pacific Islands. From the mid 1980s, most Pacific peoples migrating to New Zealand did so on the grounds of reuniting families. By 2001, Pacific Islanders made up around 6.5 per cent of the population — less than the Asian percentage — and most lived in Auckland, the world's largest Polynesian city.

In 2003 New Zealand's population passed the four million mark, an important milestone for a country this small. It had taken some doing. There were two million of us in 1952 and three million 21 years later, but the next million took 30 years. A drop in the number of migrants partly explains this, and a 'brain drain' out of the country accounted for some external flow. Human biology was the big factor. New Zealanders stopped breeding — the average number of births to each woman in 2002 was 1.9 children (2.47 for Maori women), a drop of nearly two-thirds on the 1960s highs. For all but two years since the mid 1980s, fertility has run below the population replacement level.[77] This fertility drop is part of a long slow decline — the mid century baby-boom was a freakish reversal — and it has major flow-on effects.

Prams and pushchairs go out, walking frames and mobility scooters come in. The number of people aged 65 and over more than doubled between the 1950s and the early 2000s, and the elderly make up a growing proportion of the population, reaching 11.9 per cent in 2003.[78] Whether Maori, Pakeha, Pasifika or Asian, women and men also live longer, although important differences remain between these groups. Not only did life expectancy rise over the period, but the older generation was fitter, healthier and stayed in work for longer than before.

Ageing has become big business. Strings of retirement complexes and rest homes appeared from the 1990s. The odd

This may look like a job centre for the unemployed of the 1980s and early 1990s, but it is Student Job Search at the University of Auckland in 1999. Increasingly, students took on part-time work to put themselves through tertiary education.

Growing old, 21st-century style. Residents from 30 Auckland rest homes took part in the 'Rest Home Games' in 2001.

'Masonic Village' opened its gates, but many of these homes and villages sported more stylish monikers that hinted at a sedate or upmarket lifestyle: Malvina Major Retirement Village (Wellington), Ngaio Marsh Retirement Village (Christchurch). Few places were named after men, perhaps reflecting the higher levels of female clientele. Knightsbridge Village (Auckland) advertised 'facilities and privileges that are more akin to those of a resort', and its promotional material, along with that of four related villages, sounded like the advertising for swanky inner-city apartments: restaurants, bars, indoor heated swimming pools, gymnasiums, hairdressing salons, billiard tables, indoor and outdoor bowling rinks, petanque courts, newsletters, villas with attached garages and internal access, camper van and boat parking. Only the more prosaic respite rooms, nurses' stations, and 24-hour emergency call service distinguished the complex, but that was the idea. A 2003 survey found that almost half the respondents in retirement villages stated they had moved there to 'have fun', and if the catalogue of facilities was anything to go by, there was fun — and active fun at that — to be had.[79]

Gloomy forecasts about Generation X-ers — those born after about 1961 — and their Generation Y children having to support hordes of greying baby-boomers while receiving less state support themselves made private superannuation schemes more essential, in theory at least. In 1995 the government established a Retirement Commission to help New Zealanders see the need to save for their retirement. It soon became clear that the need was to encourage people just to save, and in 2001 the commission launched the 'Sorted' website that provided financial plans and hints on saving. But Kiwis could barely pay off their credit cards let alone save for retirement. High levels of debt and low rates of savings characterised New Zealand households, and these levels were notably more extreme than those in other developed

SPORTS, 1990s-STYLE

Consumption, leisure and entertainment came together in the new era of professional sports from the mid 1990s. Rugby union was the big winner, recovering some of the hammering it took following the 1981 Springbok tour of New Zealand, and the rebel 'Cavaliers' tour of South Africa in 1986. Winning the inaugural William Webb Ellis Trophy (the Rugby World Cup) in 1987 helped. Professionalism took off in the mid 1990s, with the All Blacks winning the first professional tri-series against Australia and South Africa in 1996. The contracts and endorsements earned by some players became the stuff of legend.

The development of the Super 12 series in 1996 showcased the new rugby spectacle — at the expense of the provincial games, which never quite matched the hoopla from the blend of internationalism and parochialism surrounding the Super 12. These were games to be enjoyed by the whole family. Mum, Dad and the kids could readily kit themselves out in team colours and paint their faces. On the field, action was complemented by a pre-match entertainment extravaganza. Instead of pies and warm beer at half-time, spectators could expect some type of show to keep them occupied for the 10-minute hole in the middle of the game. Traditionalists could huff away at the behaviour of the crowds and their level of rugby knowledge, or the reinvention of Lancaster Park, home of Canterbury rugby for many a year, as Jade Stadium in 1998 but the consumption of the rugby spectacle had come to stay.

Other national teams and sporting codes, and the less exalted levels of rugby, fared more modestly in the professional age. Members of the national netball team, the Silver Ferns, held down day jobs while doing their bit for the sponsorship dollar. Here they play a game in the sponsor's Christchurch car park; the following year the firm became the team's premier sponsor.

countries. Household indebtedness climbed from the late 1980s, partly because New Zealanders got more access to credit. The level of money owed on credit cards increased by 10 per cent a year between 1993 and 2003, reaching $3.3 billion; households owed a whopping $80 billion all up by the end of 2002. The only thing that seemed to decrease from the mid 1990s — just before New Zealanders almost unanimously rejected a compulsory superannuation scheme in a nationwide referendum — was the number of people saving for retirement.[80]

New Zealanders headed into their golden years with most of their money locked up in their houses. From the 1990s fewer people were interested in signing up to a mortgage, reversing a long-standing Kiwi ethos of home-ownership. Demographics partly explained this — with fewer people having children, some of the traditional attractions of home-ownership lessened. Changes in social behaviour, with people delaying nesting till

they were older, also meant that house-buying was put off. Economics came into it as well; mortgage interest rates rose in the late 1980s — up to 25 per cent and more at some points — then house prices in areas like Auckland shot up through the 1990s and early 2000s. It cost $264,000 (as a median price) to buy in Orakei in 1992; 10 years later, people had to fork out $473,000.[81] Prices like that made it extra tough for Pacific Island people and Maori — less well-off, on average, than their Pakeha or Asian counterparts — to buy their own place, and their home-ownership rate fell more markedly.

The 20- and early 30-somethings were the group that most turned away from house and mortgage. The student loans scheme is identified as one of the main hurdles for this 'Generation Debt'. Loans to finance the cost of a tertiary education were introduced in 1992, hard on the heels of the rise in tuition fees in 1990 and the tightening-up of access to

OFF PONSONBY ROAD

The latte set was hardly middle New Zealand. For most Kiwis, coffee came in powdered form and sliced white proved a lot easier — and cheaper — for school lunches than olive ciabatta infused with truffle oil. The extent to which changes in more upmarket cuisine and eating and drinking habits affected the wider population is difficult to assess. The traditional Sunday roast was already history by the early 1980s, replaced with a greater variety of meals, but this was part of a longer change dating from the 1960s.[82] In 2001 around 25 per cent of the home food bill went on ready-to-eat meals or food eaten away from home. Lest we think that some of that was spent on fine dining, the top-selling supermarket food items should hint at New Zealanders' food tastes. Heading the list in 2002 was toast-sliced white bread, followed by blue-top milk, then 1.5-litre bottles of Coca-Cola; 2.25-litre bottles were in fourth place.[83]

Down at the shop, everyone wanted a bargain. Daily national sales at The Warehouse averaged $4.7 million from the 80 stores and 39 stationery outlets in 2003; back in 1982 the first shop had turned over $4900 on its opening day. The Warehouse had become the third-largest company on the stock exchange by 2003. Inner-city apartment types may not be seen dead in the Red Shed, but the rest of New Zealand was happy enough to snaffle up the goods — an estimated 82 per cent of New Zealanders shopped there in one survey month in 2003. Some small towns went out of their way to

get a store. These places, hit hard by the 1980s recession, saw the shop as a way to keep local customers local. Dannevirke, population 5500, was a case in point, receiving its Warehouse in mid 2001 following intense lobbying.[84]

The 'Cash-register Carol' is played at full volume in Hamilton's Warehouse, Christmas 2000.

allowances. By early 2004, 379,000 students and ex-students owed $7 billion, despite some freezes on fees or even no fees offered by institutions such as the Southland Polytechnic. The average student graduated with a debt of $12,643 in 2004, and the top debtor owed almost $180,000.[85] New Zealanders galloped into tertiary education, fees or no fees: 50,000 students in 1975, 210,000 in 1995, and over 300,000 in 2003.[86]

'Generation Debt? More like Generation Spend,' some commentators declared. The rising emphasis on lifestyle that came in the wake of mid 1980s glitz created, some believe, a new culture of consumption. New Zealand's young generations spend a whole lot more money than their parents ever did. According to 'Sarah' — not her real name — discussing her lifestyle choices in early 2003, 'It's much more important to go out for lunch, get a new pair of shoes . . . I've been working for three years and what do I have to show for it?' 'It's no small

coincidence,' the interviewer sniffed, 'that many of the interviews conducted for this story took place in cafés. This is a lifestyle-focused generation.'[87]

Leisure opportunities certainly expanded from the 1980s. There had always been entertainment in towns and cities, although it was not always easy to find. Inner-city growth fuelled nightlife. Pubs, bars and clubs, open all hours, concentrated in entertainment districts such as Wellington's Courtenay Place or in the streets around Dunedin's Octagon. Changing attitudes towards gambling made way for the opening of casinos, most notably in Auckland's Sky City in 1996. Despite these entertainment industries, the average New Zealander was a lounge lizard. Watching the box, either TV or video, came out the top leisure activity in 2001, followed by 'socialising and conversation'; more physically active pursuits took up a fraction of people's time.[88]

The heady days (and nights) of 1980s business deals struck over bottles of Bolly in fashionable eateries at least boosted the cuisine scene. The chattering classes took up café culture, and the streetscapes of many large centres sported outdoor tables where suits and others liked to be seen and to linger over espresso. Foodie culture emerged, and magazines like *Cuisine*, launched in 1986, took off; its readership 17 years on was nearly 80,000.[89]

For some, shopping developed into a distinct leisure activity. The liberalisation of shop trading hours in 1980 meant that Saturday and later Sunday shopping boomed. 'Late night Friday' became a thing of the past, as did weekends for those behind the counters. Although there were some, particularly unions, who held out for shops to be shut for at least part of the day on certain days of the year — in particular Anzac and Christmas Day, and Good Friday — more and more shops opened their doors. Garden centres made a point of opening over the Easter break from the later 1990s, regardless of fines dished out. Changes in the importation of goods at the end of the 20th century brought a whole new range of goodies into the local market, and at cheap prices. Shopkeepers and local industry balked at this, but shoppers were in retail heaven.

Heartland New Zealand reinvented itself, particularly in the 1990s. Diversifying helped. The expansion of the wine industry through the 1980s, buoyed by the international successes of sauvignon blanc, saw farmland in areas such as Marlborough given over to the grape, while 'new land' in other areas, notably Otago, was brought under cultivation. The amount of land planted in vines more than quadrupled between the mid 1980s and the early 2000s.[90] Wine put once quiet townships on the foodies' map. The small Wairarapa town of Martinborough gentrified steadily through the 1990s, with every second house seeming to advertise itself as a 'cottage B & B', ideal for that weekend away.

Bruce Jenkins, courtesy Art Deco Trust, Napier

Sixty-odd years after the 1931 earthquake devastated the town, Napier capitalised on the new architecture erected in its wake. This self-styled 'Art Deco Capital of the World' promoted its look (not to mention its climate, and the local wine and food scene) through art deco weekends and festivals. Predictably, 1990s 'art deco' buildings also sprang up.

BELOW: Whakapapa Productions Ltd

Tourism, especially of the eco variety, boosted some places. In Kaikoura, which had been gutted by the decline of the railways, Maori entrepreneurs — not without some rancour — turned whale-watching into a cash cow, reinvigorating the town. Adventure tourism spiced up a visit to Queenstown, which had become a mecca for international tourists with as many shop signs in Japanese as in English. By 2004, tourism was the country's biggest money-earner, displacing the dairy industry.[91]

Diversity within the country was matched by a growing sense of New Zealand's difference from the rest of the world. Geography played a role here. By the end of the 20th century, New Zealand may have had cultural roots in Britain and the Pacific, but locale had won out. Being a wee dot at the bottom of the map, with links to Asia and the Pacific, was something to boast about. Connections were not always made with the much larger blob off to the west; but that was probably because New Zealand liked to distinguish itself from Australia in the long tradition of trans-Tasman rivalry — a rivalry that has probably been felt more acutely on this side of the ditch.

Being different counted as the world got closer. Whether or not the marketplace was actually any more global in 2005 than in 1984 or 1934, the last 20 years have also been about 'New Zealandness', recognising and celebrating place, history, culture and peoples within this country.[92] Events like the 1990 sesquicentennial of the signing of the Treaty of Waitangi were part of a mounting emphasis on distinctiveness, and awareness of race relations. It was often the indigenous peoples or their culture or the landscape that set New Zealand apart or that were believed to mark off the country. Marketing New Zealand as a green Elysium — '100 per cent pure' — touted the environmental treasures we believed the rest of the world had lost.

According to population projections produced by Statistics New Zealand, the age profile of the population will continue to shift.[93] Half the country will be over 45, and one in four over 65 in 2051. Some population groups will have a higher proportion of aged people than others. There will be more Maori and Pacific peoples of working age, but fewer Asian and European. The birth rate, estimated to fall slightly to 1.85 births per woman by 2051, will sit below the replacement level; a migration gain of 5000 people a year would produce only a slow population growth. Couples without children will take over from two-parent families as the most common family type. How to finance the aged hordes will be one of the big questions in this future scenario.

Another puzzle is how New Zealand will support itself with over half its people squeezed into roughly a seventh of the land-mass and well over a third of them jostling for space in the Auckland region's two per cent of the countryside. Thirty-seven per cent of the population will live in the Auckland region by 2021, and less than a quarter in the South Island; Manukau, rather than Christchurch, will be the second-largest city behind Auckland. Even now the mega-city of the North grows by one person every 29 minutes.

New Zealand from the mid 1980s always seemed to be in search of the Holy Grail of national identity. Dick Seddon may have felt right at home with that sense of nationhood, but white imperialist, booster and promoter of children and population growth that he was, he may not have liked the way the place was heading. The latest population projections predict greater ethnic and cultural diversity in the future. People of Maori, Pacific and Asian ethnicity are set to comprise more of the total population, partly because of higher fertility levels, and partly because of migration. By 2021, 17 per cent of the population will identify as Maori, 9 per cent as Pacific Islanders, 13 per cent Asian, and 60 per cent European. This should pose interesting questions about what it means to be a New Zealander, and what New Zealand may be.

Notes

ATL   Alexander Turnbull Library
AJHR   *Appendix to the Journals of the House of Representatives*
ANZ   Archives New Zealand
AUP   Auckland University Press
BNZW   Charlotte Macdonald, Merimeri Penfold & Bridget Williams (eds.), *The Book of New Zealand Women*, Bridget Williams Books, Wellington, 1991
BWB   Bridget Williams Books
CUP   Canterbury University Press
DNZB   *Dictionary of New Zealand Biography* (vols 1–5)
JPS   *Journal of the Polynesian Society*
NZHA   Malcolm McKinnon (ed.) *New Zealand Historical Atlas*, David Bateman, Auckland, 1997
NZJH   *New Zealand Journal of History*
NZOYB   *New Zealand Official Yearbook*
NZH   *New Zealand Herald*
NZPD   *New Zealand Parliamentary Debates*
OCNZMH   Ian McGibbon (ed.), *The Oxford Companion to New Zealand Military History*, OUP, Auckland, 2000
OHNZ   Geoffrey Rice (ed.), *The Oxford History of New Zealand*, 2nd edn., OUP, Auckland, 1993
OHNZL   Terry Sturm (ed.), *The Oxford History of New Zealand Literature in English*, 2nd edn., OUP, Auckland, 1998
OUP   Oxford University Press
Paradise   James Belich, *Paradise Reforged: A History of the New Zealanders from the 1880s to the Year 2000*, Allen Lane Penguin Press, Auckland, 2001
Peoples   James Belich, *Making Peoples: A History of the New Zealanders from Polynesian Settlement to the End of the Nineteenth Century*, Allen Lane Penguin Press, Auckland, 1996
PHNZ   Michael King, *The Penguin History of New Zealand*, Penguin, Auckland, 2003
UOP   University of Otago Press
VUP   Victoria University Press

Introduction

1. Belich, *Peoples*, p. 8.
2. www.penguin.co.nz/Book
3. For recent discussions of the popularity of history on television elsewhere, see David Cannadine (ed.), *History and the Media*, Palgrave Macmillan, Basingstoke, 2004; articles in 'Screen Histories', *History Workshop Journal*, 56, 2003, pp. 153–216.
4. Belich, *Peoples*, p. 7.

Chapter 1: The Last Place on Earth, Prehistory–c. 1300

1. David Bellamy, Brian Springett & Peter Hayden, *Moa's Ark: The Voyage of New Zealand*, Viking, Auckland, 1990, p. 97.
2. Trevor Worthy & Richard Holdaway, *The Lost World of the Moa: Prehistoric Life of New Zealand*, CUP, Christchurch, 2002, pp. xvi–xvii.
3. Worthy & Holdaway, pp. xviii.
4. David Young & Bruce Foster, *Faces of the River*, TVNZ Enterprises, Wellington, 1986, pp. 129–30.
5. Jefley J. Aitken, *Rocked and Ruptured: Geophysical Faults in New Zealand*, Reed Books, in association with the Institute of Geological and Nuclear Sciences Limited, 1999, Lower Hutt, p. 22; Worthy & Holdaway, p. xvi; Geoff Hicks & Hamish Campbell (eds.), *Awesome Forces: The Natural Hazards that Threaten New Zealand*, Te Papa Press in association with EQC & IGNS, 1998, Wellington, pp. 5–7.
6. Brian Parkinson, *Reed Field Guide to New Zealand Alpine Fauna and Flora*, Reed Books, Auckland, 2001, p. 7.
7. Gordon Stephenson, *Wetlands: Discovering New Zealand's Shy Places*, Government Printer, Wellington, 1986, pp. 64–67.
8. David Young, *Our Islands, Ourselves: A History of Conservation in New Zealand*, UOP, Dunedin, 2004, ch. 1.
9. Penelope Jane Forsyth, *Rocks and Minerals: A Beginner's Guide to New Zealand*, Government Printer, Wellington, 1985, pp. 8–9, 23–26.
10. Nic Bishop, *From the Mountains to the Sea: The Secret Life of New Zealand's Rivers and Wetlands*, Reed, Auckland, 1994, pp. 13–14.
11. www.tvone.co.nz/programmes/dinosaurs
12. Geoff Park, *Nga Uruora: Ecology and History in a New Zealand Landscape*, VUP, Wellington, 1986, p. 36.
13. Stephenson, pp. 22–23, 64, 76.
14. Pam Crisp, Lindsay Daniel & Philip Tortell, *Mangroves in New Zealand: Trees in the Tide*, GP Books for Nature Conservation Council, Wellington, 1990, p. 18.
15. Worthy & Holdaway, p. 548.
16. Worthy & Holdaway, p. 139.
17. Quoted in John Cawte Beaglehole, *The Life of Captain James Cook*, Hakluyt Society, London, 1974, p. 109.
18. Patrick Vinton Kirch, *The Lapita Peoples: Ancestors of the Oceanic World*, Blackwell, Maldon, 1997, pp. 65–66.
19. Geoffrey Blainey, *A Short History of the World*, Viking, Ringwood, 2000, p. 234.
20. Kirch, pp. ixx–xx.
21. Kirch, pp. 14, 53, 62–63, 199–203.
22. Simon Best, *Lapita: A View from the East*, New Zealand Archaeological Association Monograph 24, Auckland, 2002, pp. 11, 17, 48; Kirch, p. 68.
23. Accidental drift was popularised by Andrew Sharp, *Ancient Voyagers in the Pacific*, Polynesian Society, Wellington, 1956.
24. Thor Heyerdahl, *The Kon-Tiki Expedition: By Raft Across the South Seas*, Allen & Unwin, London, 1953.
25. Quoted in David Lewis, *Shapes on the Wind*, 2nd edn., HarperCollins, Sydney, 2000, p. 11.
26. European scholars remain oblivious, however. *The Earliest Ships*, vol. 1 in the prestigious 12-volume Robert Gardiner (ed.) *Conway's History of the Ship*, Conway Maritime Press, Greenwich, 1996, completely ignores Pacific craft.
27. Belich, *Peoples*, p. 31.
28. John Cawte Beaglehole (ed.), *The Voyage of the Endeavour 1768–1771*, Cambridge University Press, Cambridge, 1955, pp. 164–67.
29. David Lewis, *We, The Navigators: The Ancient Art of Landfinding in the Pacific*, 2nd edn., University of Hawai'i, Honolulu, 1994, pp. 53–71.
30. Ben Finney, *Voyage of Discovery: A Cultural Odyssey Through Polynesia*, University of California Press, Berkeley, 1994, pp. 127–29.
31. John Cawte Beaglehole (ed.), *Joseph Banks, The Endeavour Journals*, vols. I & II, 1768–1771, Angus & Robertson, Sydney, 1962, p. 366.
32. Lewis, *We, the Navigators*, pp. 82–83.
33. Lewis, *We, the Navigators*, p. 145.
34. Lewis, *Shapes on the Wind*, p. 74.
35. Geoffrey Irwin, 'Exploring the Pacific, Strategies and Motives' in *Bearings*, vol. 5, no. 2, 1993, p. 44.
36. Irwin, p. 44.
37. Lewis, *We, the Navigators*, p. 352.
38. *NZHA*, plate 10b.
39. Irwin, p. 45.

Chapter 2: Treasure Islands, c. 1300–1769

1. Herbert Guthrie-Smith, *Bird Life on Island and Shore*, Blackwood and Sons, Edinburgh, 1925, pp. 1, 128–29.
2. Bradford Joseph Teapatuoterangi Maaka Haami, 'The Kiore Rat in Aotearoa; A Maori Perspective', *Science of Pacific Island Peoples*, vol. III, Institute of Pacific Studies, 1994, pp. 65–76.
3. Richard N Holdaway, 'A Spatio-Temporal Model for the Invasion of the New Zealand Archipelago By the Pacific Rat Rattus Exulans', *Journal of the Royal Society of New Zealand*, 29 Jun 1999; Janet Wilmshurst, pers. comm., 2 Apr 2004.
4. Finlay Lloyd Phillips, *Nga Tohu a Tainui Landmarks of Tainui: A Geographical Record of Tainui Traditional History*, Tohu Publishers, Otorohanga, 1989, pp. 5–12.
5. Helen Leach, *A Thousand Years of Gardening in New Zealand*, AH & AW Reed, Auckland, 1984, p. 54.
6. Patrick Vinton Kirch & Roger Green, *Hawaiiki, Ancestral Polynesia: An Essay in Historical Anthropology*, Cambridge University Press, New York, 2001, pp. 126–28.
7. Helen Leach & Phillip Houghton, 'Palliser Woman', *BNZW*, pp. 484–85.
8. Bruce McFadgen, pers. comm., 7 Mar 2004.
9. Trevor Worthy & Richard Holdaway, *The Lost World of the Moa: Prehistoric Life of New Zealand*, CUP, Christchurch, 2002, p. 546.

10. Phillips, p. 6; Chris Winitana, *Legends of Aotearoa*, HarperCollins, Auckland, 2001, p. 90.
11. Belich, *Peoples*, pp. 44–45, 53–54.
12. Atholl Anderson & Richard McGovern-Wilson, 'Maori settlement on Lee Island' in Atholl Anderson & Richard McGovern-Wilson, *Beech Forest Hunters: The Archaeology of Maori Rockshelter Sites on Lee Island, Lake Te Anau, in Southern New Zealand*, New Zealand Archaeological Association Monograph, 18, Auckland, 1991, pp. 76–82 (quote).
13. Philip Simpson, *Dancing Leaves: The Story of New Zealand's Cabbage Tree, Ti Kauka*, CUP, Christchurch, 2000, p. 155.
14. Leach, p. 49.
15. Alexander H McLintock (ed.), *An Encyclopaedia of New Zealand*, vol. 1, Government Printer, Wellington, 1966, p. 55.
16. Elizabeth Pischief, *Assessment of Heritage Significance: Otatara Pa Historic Reserve*, Department of Conservation, Napier, 1997; Mark Horrocks, Martin Jones, Ross Beever & Doug Sutton, 'Gourds, truffles and coprolites', *New Zealand Geographic*, 51, May–Jun 2001, pp. 8–9; Roger Green & Doug Sutton, 'Field School Uncovers Pouerua's Past,' *Historic Places*, Sep 1986, p. 14.
17. Matthew McGlone, 'Polynesian Deforestation of New Zealand: A Preliminary Synthesis', *Archaeology Oceania*, vol. 18, 1983, p. 16.
18. McGlone, p. 22.
19. Belich, *Peoples*, p. 68.
20. Bruce McFadgen, 'Impact on the Landscape: Environmental Change', in John Wilson, Tipene O'Regan & Atholl Anderson (eds.), *From the Beginning: The Archaeology of the Maori*, Penguin Books with New Zealand Historic Places Trust, Auckland, 1987, pp. 49–51, 55; Atholl Anderson, *When All the Moa Ovens Grew Cold*, Otago Heritage Books, Dunedin, 1985, p. 24.
21. Tim F Flannery, *Future Eaters: An Ecological History of the Australasian Lands and People*, Reed Books, Sydney, 1994, pp. 54–55; Matthew McGlone, Atholl Anderson, Richard Holdaway, 'An Ecological Approach to the Polynesian Settlement of New Zealand' in Douglas G Sutton (ed.), *The Origins of the First New Zealanders*, AUP, Auckland, 1994.
22. Geoffrey Irwin (ed.), *Kohika: The Archaeology of a Late Maori Lake Village in the Ngati Awa Rohe, Bay of Plenty New Zealand*, AUP, Auckland, 2004, pp. 239–48.
23. Jared Diamond, *Guns, Germs and Steel: A Short History of Everybody for the Last 13,000 Years*, Vintage, London, 1998, p. 54; Michael King suggests 'on the balance of probabilities' that they made landfall prior to the 14th century, but archaeological sites appear on current evidence no older than the 15th century; *Moriori: A People Rediscovered*, Viking, Auckland, 1989, p. 22, 28.
24. Richard Holdaway, Trevor H Worthy & Alan JD Tennyson, 'A Working List of Breeding Bird Species of the New Zealand Region at First Human Contact', *New Zealand Journal of Zoology*, vol. 28, 2001, p. 119; Trevor Worthy, 'What Was on the Menu: Avian Extinction in New Zealand', *New Zealand Journal of Archaeology*, vol. 19, 1997, pp. 140–41.
25. Leach, p. 43.
26. Leach, pp. 64–65.
27. Atholl Anderson, *The Welcome of Strangers: An Ethnohistory of Southern Maori AD 1650–1850*, UOP, Dunedin, 1998.
28. Quoted in Kirch & Green, p. 254; Agnes Sullivan, 'Nga Paiaka o te Maoritanga: The Roots of Maori Culture' in Sidney M Mead (ed.), *Te Maori: Maori Art from New Zealand Collections*, Heinemann, Auckland, 1984, p. 60 (quotes 2, 3).
29. Waitangi Tribunal, *Muriwhenua Fishing Report*, Wellington, 1988, pp. 13, 14, 73.
30. William Colenso, 'On the Maori Races of New Zealand', *Transactions of the New Zealand Institute*, vol. 1, 1868, p. 368.
31. Belich, *Peoples*, pp. 102–3.
32. William Colenso, 'On the Vegetable Food of the Ancient New Zealanders', *Transactions of the New Zealand Institute*, vol. 13, 1880, p. 5.
33. Belich, *Peoples*, p. 178.
34. Sidney Moko Mead, 'Ka Tupu te Toi Whakairo ki Aotearoa: Becoming Maori Art' in Mead (ed.), pp. 64–66; Gilbert Archey, *Whaowhia: Maori Art and Its Artists*, Collins, Auckland, 1977, pp. 20–21, 28–29, 51–53, 62–63, 70–74.
35. Raymond Firth, *Economics of the New Zealand Maori*, Government Printer, Wellington, 1972, pp. 84–85; Peter Buck/Te Rangi Hiroa, *The Coming of the Maori*, Maori Purposes Fund Board, Whitcombe & Tombs, Christchurch, 1949, pp. 168–70.
36. David Young, *Woven By Water: Histories from the Whanganui River*, Huia, Wellington, 1998, ch. 9.
37. Barry Brailsford, *Greenstone Trails: The Maori and Pounamu*, AH & AW Reed, Wellington, 1984, pp. 61–62.
38. Winitana, p. 12.
39. Mead in Mead (ed.), p. 64.
40. Charles Royal, unpublished ms, in possession of author.
41. Buck/Hiroa, pp. 346–47.
42. Kirch & Green, p. 239.
43. Buck/Hiroa, pp. 346–47.
44. Buck/Hiroa, p. 401.
45. Firth, pp. 254–55.

Chapter 3: When Worlds Collide, 1642–1839

1. Philip Bosscher (ed.), *The Heyday of Sail: the Merchant Sailing Ship 1650–1830*, Conway Maritime Press, London, 1995, pp. 47–51.
2. There is a rich tradition of amateur claims for pre-European 'discoverers' of New Zealand. For the latest, see Gavin Menzies, *1421: The Year that China Discovered the World*, Bantam, London, 2002.
3. Anne Salmond, *Two Worlds: First Meetings Between Maori and Europeans 1642–1772*, Viking, Auckland, 1991, p. 78.
4. King, *PHNZ*, p. 96.
5. Salmond, *Two Worlds*, pp. 63–84.
6. King, *PHNZ*, pp. 39–42. King notes that the word could more properly be rendered 'Land of the Long Clear Day' or the 'Long White World'.
7. David Mackay, 'James Cook' in *DNZB*, vol. 1, p. 92.
8. In 1769 'bark' meant a ship-rigged vessel with a plain bluff bow but a full stem with windows. It should not be confused with the American spelling bark (barque), which is a vessel of three or more masts carrying fore-and-aft rig on the mizzen.
9. Quoted in Anne Salmond, *The Trial of the Cannibal Dog: Captain Cook in the South Seas*, Allen Lane, London, 2003, p. 95.
10. Quoted in Salmond, *Two Worlds*, p. 122.
11. Salmond, *Two Worlds*, p. 138.
12. Anne Salmond, *Between Worlds: Early Exchanges Between Maori and Europeans 1773–1815*, Viking, Auckland, 1997, p. 194.
13. Michael Roche, *History of Forestry*, New Zealand Forestry Corporation Ltd/GP Books, Wellington, 1990, p. 17.
14. Judith Binney, 'Two Communities 1820–1839' in Judith Binney, Judith Bassett & Erik Olssen, *The People and the Land, Te Tangata me Te Whenua: An Illustrated History of New Zealand 1820–1920*, Allen & Unwin, Wellington, 1990, p. 19.
15. Alan Grey, *Aotearoa and New Zealand: A Historical Geography*, CUP, Christchurch, 1994, p. 126.
16. For more on whaling see: Harry Morton, *The Whale's Wake*, UOP, Dunedin, 1982; A Charles Begg & Neil C Begg, *The World of John Boultbee*, Whitcoulls Publishing, Christchurch, 1979; Don Grady, *Sealers and Whalers in New Zealand Waters*, Reed Methuen, Auckland, 1986.
17. Morton, p. 50.
18. Quoted in Grady, p. 131.
19. Quoted in Rhys Richards & Jocelyn Chisholm, *Bay of Islands Shipping Arrivals and Departures 1803–1840*, Paremata Press, 1992 (np).
20. Belich, *Peoples*, p. 153.
21. *NZ Gazette and Wellington Spectator*, Apr 1844.
22. Morton, p. 169.
23. Linda Colley, *Captives: Britain, Empire and the World 1600–1850*, Pimlico, London, 2003, p. 134.
24. Grady, 'Elizabeth Guard' in *DNZB*, vol. 1, pp. 164–65.
25. Morton, p. 247.
26. For more on the *Boyd* see: Wade Doak, *The Burning of the Boyd: a Saga of Culture Clash*, Hodder & Stoughton, Auckland, 1984; Tony Simpson, *Art and Massacre: Documentary Racism in the Burning of the Boyd*, The Cultural Construction Company, Wellington, 1993; Louise Callan, *Shipwreck: Tales of Survival, Courage and Calamity at Sea*, Hodder Moa Beckett, Auckland, 2000 and the accompanying Greenstone TV series, *Shipwreck*.
27. Salmond, *Between Worlds*, p. 388.
28. Angela Ballara, *Taua: Musket Wars, Land Wars or Tikanga? Warfare in the Early 19th Century*, Penguin, Auckland, 2003, pp. 312–13.
29. Quoted in Frances Porter & Charlotte Macdonald (eds.), *'My Hand Will Write What My Heart Dictates': The Unsettled Lives of Women in 19th-Century New Zealand As Revealed to Sisters, Family and Friends*, AUP/BWB, Auckland, 1996, p. 36.
30. Ballara, p. 99. For more specific detail, see Atholl Anderson, *Te Puoho's Last Raid: The Battle for Tuturau 1836–37*, Otago Heritage Books, Dunedin, 1986; Alfred Crosby, *The Musket Wars: A History of Inter-iwi Conflict 1806–45*, Reed Books, Auckland, 1999; *NZHA*, plate 29.
31. Paul D'Arcy, 'Maori and Muskets From a Pan-Polynesian Perspective', *NZJH*, vol. 34, no. 1, Apr 2000, pp. 117–134.
32. Frederick Edward Maning, *Old New Zealand: A Tale of the Good Old Times by a Pakeha Maori*, Golden Press, Auckland, 1973, p. 216.
33. Lawrence M Rogers, *The Early Journals of Henry Williams*, Pegasus Press, Christchurch, 1961, p. 42.
34. Belich, *Peoples*, p. 13.

35. Harry Evison, *Te Wai Pounamu The Greenstone Land: A History of the Southern Maori During the European Colonisation of New Zealand*, Aoraki Press, Christchurch, 1993, p. 61.

36. Anderson, *The Welcome of Strangers*, p. 84.

37. King, *PHNZ*, p. 139.

38. Belich, *Peoples*, p. 164.

39. Fergus Clunie, *Historic Bay of Islands: A Driving Tour*, Reed Books, Auckland, 1998, p. 6.

40. Belich, *Peoples*, p. 135.

41. Judith Binney, 'Two Communities 1820–1839', p. 14.

42. Judith Binney, 'Kendall, Thomas 1778?–1832', *DNZB*, updated 31 Jul 2003, www.dnzb.govt.nz

43. Clunie, p. 12.

44. Clunie, p. 16.

45. King, *PHNZ*, p. 143.

46. Penny Griffith, Ross Harvey & Keith Maslen, *Book and Print in New Zealand: A Guide to Print Culture in Aotearoa*, VUP, Wellington, 1997, p. 29.

47. Belich, *Peoples*, p. 167.

48. King, *PHNZ*, p. 144.

49. Bledisloe to Prebendary W Cash, Church Missionary Society Papers, MS Papers 4485, ATL.

50. Quoted in Duncan Mackay, *Frontier New Zealand: The Search For Eldorado 1800–1920*, HarperCollins, Auckland, 1992, p. 21.

51. Edward Markham, *New Zealand or Recollections of It*, Government Printer, Wellington, 1963, p. 40.

52. Eva Wilson, 'Howell, John 1810?–1874', *DNZB*, updated 31 Jul 2003, www.dnzb.govt.nz

53. Trevor Bentley, *Pakeha Maori: The Extraordinary Story of the Europeans Who Lived as Maori in Early New Zealand*, Penguin, Auckland, 1999, p. 133.

54. Bentley, p. 103.

55. Roger Wigglesworth, 'Marmon, John 1798–1800?', *DNZB*, updated 31 Jul 2003, www.dnzb.govt.nz

56. Warren E Limbrick, 'Selwyn, George Augustus 1809–1878', *DNZB*, updated 31 Jul 2003, www.dnzb.govt.nz

57. Gavin McLean, *Captain's Log: New Zealand's Maritime History*, Hodder Moa Beckett, Auckland, 2001, p. 39.

58. Peter Entwistle, *Behold the Moon: The European Occupation of the Dunedin District 1770–1848*, Port Daniel Press, Dunedin, 1996, p. 63.

59. Ian Wards, *The Shadow of the Land: A Study of British Policy and Racial Conflict in New Zealand 1832–1852*, Government Printer, Wellington, 1968, p. 7.

60. Quoted in Andrew Porter (ed.), *The Oxford History of the British Empire: Vol. III, The 19th Century*, OUP, Oxford, 1999, p. 578.

61. Wards, p. 8.

62. Baron Karl von Hugel, 'Sydney, New Zealand and Norfolk Island From 10 February to 16 April 1834', MS 90-389-6/18, ATL.

63. He was not the only one. See also William Marshall, *A Personal Narrative of Two Visits to New Zealand, in His Majesty's Ship* Alligator, *AD 1834*, London, 1836, pp. 108–9.

64. von Hugel.

65. Stuart Park, 8 Nov 1996, www.crwflags.com/fotw/flags. See also Ministry for Culture and Heritage, www.mch.govt.nz/nzflag/history/united.html

66. Manuka Henare, 'Tangata Whenua: For Frontier of Dreams' notes, 15 Mar 2002, Ministry for Culture and Heritage.

67. Binney, 'Two Communities', p. 29.

68. David Savill, *Sail to New Zealand: The Story of Shaw Savill & Co. 1858–82*, Robert Hale, London, 1986, pp. 39–40.

69. King, *PHNZ*, p. 154.

70. Quoted in John O'C Ross, 'Busby and the Declaration of Independence', *NZJH*, vol. 14, no. 1, Apr 1980, p. 89.

71. Quoted in Wards, p. 14.

72. Claudia Orange, *The Treaty of Waitangi*, Allen & Unwin/Port Nicholson Press, Wellington, 1987, p. 21.

73. David Landes, *The Wealth and Poverty of Nations*, Norton, New York, 1998, p. 89.

74. Ross, p. 84.

75. Claudia Orange, 'The Maori and the Crown' in Keith Sinclair (ed.), *The Oxford Illustrated History of New Zealand*, OUP, Auckland, 1990, p. 42. See also Pat Moloney, 'Savagery and Civilisation: Early Victorian Notions', *NZJH*, vol. 35, no. 2, Oct 2001, p. 168.

76. Paul Moon, *Te Ara Ki Te Tiriti: The Path to the Treaty of Waitangi*, David Ling, Auckland, 2002, p. 66.

Chapter 4: Flags and Nations, 1839–1852

1. Philip Temple, *A Sort of Conscience: The Wakefields*, AUP, Auckland, 2002 is the most recent treatment of the Wakefields. For the scheme, see Patricia Burns, *Fatal Success: A History of the New Zealand Company*, Heinemann Reed, Auckland, 1989; and for a critique, Michael Turnbull, *The New Zealand Bubble: The Wakefield Theory in Practice*, Price Milburn & Co, Wellington, 1959.

2. For the development of British policy and its context see Alexander H McLintock, *Crown Colony Government in New Zealand*, Government Printer, Wellington, 1958, ch. 2; a more detailed treatment that deals with both the frontier and British policy is Peter Adams, *Fatal Necessity: British Intervention in New Zealand 1830–1847*, AUP/OUP, Auckland, 1977, pt. I.

3. Claudia Orange, 'The Treaty of Waitangi: A Study of its Making, Interpretation and Role in New Zealand History', PhD thesis, University of Auckland, 1984, ch. 2 gives a full discussion of these details.

4. Normanby to Hobson, 14 & 15 Aug 1839, Colonial Office (CO) 209/4, pp. 251–82, and 157–63. These can be found in an abridged form in W David McIntyre & WJ Gardner (eds.), *Speeches and Documents on New Zealand History*, OUP, Oxford, 1971, pp. 10–18.

5. Adams, p. 245.

6. Claudia Orange, *The Treaty of Waitangi*, Allen & Unwin/Port Nicholson Press, Wellington, 1987, ch. 3 for a detailed discussion; for another view see King, *PHNZ*, pp. 151–67.

7. William Colenso, *The Authentic and Genuine History of the Signing of the Treaty of Waitangi*, Government Printer, Wellington, 1890, pp. 16–17 gives this account, which is taken almost verbatim from notes Colenso took during the meeting. For the notes of Hobson's speech see Notebook in Colenso Papers, X, Hawke's Bay Museum.

8. Orange, *The Treaty*, pp. 45–46, describes the care with which Williams claimed he explained the Treaty.

9. The speeches are fully recorded in Colenso.

10. Quoted in Orange, *The Treaty*, p. 51.

11. Colenso Journal, 6 Feb 1840, Hawke's Bay Museum.

12. Quoted in Orange, *The Treaty*, p. 54.

13. The names and moko or signatures that appear on the Treaty copy signed at Waitangi are a muddle, many having been added after 6 February. For a listing and attempt to identify names and dates of signing see www.nzhistory.net.nz/Gallery/treaty-sigs/index.htm

14. Quoted in Orange, *The Treaty*, p. 55.

15. Archives New Zealand in Wellington holds these Treaty copies in its Constitution Room for public viewing.

16. McLintock, p. 43.

17. Quoted in John Miller, *Early Victorian New Zealand: A Study of Racial Tension and Social Attitudes 1839–1852*, OUP, Wellington, 1958, p. 42. The account of Wellington's early days is drawn from Miller; also from David Hamer & Roberta Nicholls (eds.), *The Making of Wellington 1800–1914*, VUP, Wellington, 1990.

18. Quoted in Miller, p. 45.

19. For Nelson, see Miller, ch. 5 and 6, and Ruth M Allen, *Nelson: A History of Early Settlement*, AH & AW Reed, Wellington, 1965, on which this section is based; also Pamela Hall, 'The Nelson Settlement' in *New Zealand's Heritage*, vol. 1, pt. 15, Paul Hamlyn Ltd, Wellington, 1971.

20. Miller, pp. 70–80 covers the Wairau and FitzRoy's response; also Angela Ballara, 'Te Rangihaeata' in *DNZB*, vol. 1, pp. 488–91.

21. This section is based on RCJ Stone, *From Tamaki-makau-rau to Auckland*, AUP, Auckland, 2001, pp. 180–315 which gives the best coverage of the background to and founding of Auckland; RCJ Stone 'The founding of Auckland' in *New Zealand's Heritage*, vol. 1, pt. 14, Paul Hamlyn Ltd, Wellington, 1971; John Horsman, *The Coming of the Pakeha to Auckland Province*, Hicks Smith & Sons Ltd, Wellington, 1971; Lady Martin, *Our Maoris*, London, 1884; William Swainson, *Auckland, the Capital of New Zealand, and the Country Adjacent*, London, 1853.

22. The term is used by Stone, *From Tamaki-makau-rau*, p. 308.

23. RCJ Stone, *Young Logan Campbell*, AUP, Auckland, 1982.

24. Horsman, p. 77.

25. Steven Oliver, 'Wiremu Kingi Maketu' in *DNZB*, vol. 1 p. 262.

26. Belich, *Peoples*, p. 215.

27. Stone, 'The Founding of Auckland', p. 382.

29. Freda Rankin Kawharu, 'Hone Wiremu Heke Pokai', in *DNZB*, vol. 1.

30. This section is based on James Belich, *The New Zealand Wars and the Victorian Interpretation of Racial Conflict*, AUP, Auckland, 1986, pp. 43–44.

31. Miller, pp. 80ff.

32. Belich, *The New Zealand Wars*, pt. I.

33. Quoted in Orange, *The Treaty*, pp. 118–19.

34. Orange, *The Treaty*, pp. 125ff.

35. McLintock, ch. 13.

36. Orange, *The Treaty*, pp. 137–39.

37. Orange, *The Treaty*, pp. 118–26 discusses the Northern War and the re-erection of the flag.

Chapter 5: The Explosive Frontier, 1852–1884

1. Raymond P Hargreaves, 'Maori Flour Mills of the Auckland Province 1846–1860', *JPS*, Jun 1961, pp. 228–29; 'Maori Flour Mills South of the Auckland Province (1847–1860)', *JPS*, Mar 1962, p. 102.
2. Paul Monin, *This Is My Place: Hauraki Contested, 1769–1875*, BWB, Wellington, 2001, p. 124.
3. Raymond P Hargreaves, 'The Maori Agriculture of the Auckland Province in the Mid-Nineteenth Century', *JPS*, vol. 68, 1959, p. 61.
4. Keith Sinclair, 'Maori Nationalism and the European Economy, 1850–60', *Historical Studies Australia and New Zealand*, May 1952, p. 124.
5. Frances Porter, *Born to New Zealand: A Biography of Jane Maria Atkinson*, Allen & Unwin/Port Nicholson Press, Wellington, 1990 reprint, p. 58.
6. Quoted in Porter, pp. 55–56.
7. Quoted in Porter, pp. 63–64.
8. Quoted in Sinclair, p. 121.
9. Quoted in Porter, pp. 129–30.
10. Quoted in James Belich, *The New Zealand Wars and the Victorian Interpretation of Racial Conflict*, AUP, Auckland, 1986, p. 92.
11. Quoted in Belich, *New Zealand Wars*, p. 95.
12. R McNicoll, 'Pratt, Sir Thomas Simson (1797–1879)', *Australian Dictionary of Biography (ADB)*, vol. 5, Melbourne University Press, Melbourne, 1974, pp. 455–56.
13. Quoted in Porter, pp. 152–53.
14. Quoted in Belich, *New Zealand Wars*, p. 113.
15. Sinclair, p. 125.
16. James Cowan, *The New Zealand Wars: A History of the Maori Campaigns and the Pioneering Period*, vol. 1, Government Printer, Wellington, 1983 reprint, p. 232.
17. Sinclair, p. 119.
18. Claudia Orange, *The Treaty of Waitangi*, Allen & Unwin/Port Nicholson Press, Wellington, 1987, p. 148.
19. Orange, p. 157.
20. Cowan, p. 231.
21. James Belich, 'Cameron, Duncan Alexander. 1808–1888', *DNZB*, vol. 1, pp. 65–66.
22. John Eldon Gorst (Keith Sinclair, ed.), *The Maori King*, Paul's Book Arcade/OUP, Hamilton & Auckland/London, 1959, p. 180.
23. Belich, *New Zealand Wars*, p. 147.
24. Quoted in Belich, *New Zealand Wars*, p. 152.
25. M Orbell, *Maori Poetry: An Introductory Anthology*, Heinemann Educational Books, Auckland, 1978, pp. 52–53.
26. Quoted in Belich, *New Zealand Wars*, p. 158.
27. Quoted in Belich, *New Zealand Wars*, p. 160.
28. Quoted in C Pugsley, 'Walking the Waikato Wars: Farce and Tragedy at Rangiaohia: 21–22 Feb 1864', *New Zealand Defence Quarterly*, no. 17, 1997, p. 32.
29. Elsdon Best, *Tuhoe: The Children of the Mist*, vol. 1, 2nd edn., AH & AW Reed, Wellington, 1972, pp. 570–71; Cowan, pp. 368–69.
30. Quoted in Best, *Tuhoe*, vol. 1, p. 572.
31. Quoted in Belich, *New Zealand Wars*, p. 180.
32. Quoted in Belich, *New Zealand Wars*, p. 207.
33. Chris McConville, 'Chute, Sir Trevor (1816–1886)', *ADB*, vol. 3, 1969, p. 397.
34. James Belich, 'Whitmore, George Stoddart, 1829–1903', *DNZB*, vol. 1, p. 592.
35. James Belich, *'I Shall Not Die': Titokowaru's War, New Zealand, 1868–9*, Allen & Unwin/Port Nicholson Press, Wellington, 1989, pp. 151–52.
36. Rival chief Wi Pere, in J Binney, 'Te Kooti Arikirangi Te Turuki, ?–1893', *DNZB*, vol. 1, p. 463.
37. Translated by Margaret Orbell, in I Wedde & H McQueen (eds.), *The Penguin Book of New Zealand Verse*, Penguin, Auckland, 1985, pp. 91–92.
38. Judith Binney, *Redemption Songs: A Life of Te Kooti Arikirangi Te Turuki*, AUP/BWB, Auckland, 1995, p. 2.
39. Jeremiah 31:17, in Binney, *Redemption Songs*, p. 66.
40. Belich, *'I Shall Not Die'*, p. 213.
41. Belich, 'Titokowaru, Riwha, ?–1888', *DNZB*, vol. 1, p. 545.
42. Belich, 'Titokowaru', p. 544.
43. Belich, *New Zealand Wars*, p. 256.
44. David V Williams, *'Te Kooti Tango Whenua': The Native Land Court, 1864–1909*, Huia, Wellington, 1999, p. 1.
45. Quoted in G Young, 'Nga Kooti Whenua: The Dynamics of a Colonial Encounter', PhD thesis, Massey University, Albany, 2003, p. 16.
46. Alan Ward, *A Show of Justice: Racial 'Amalgamation' in Nineteenth Century New Zealand*, AUP, Auckland, 1973.
47. Ann Parsonson, 'He Whenua Te Utu', PhD thesis, University of Canterbury, 1978; Young.
48. Monin, p. 246.
49. Hargreaves, p. 231.
50. 'Notes of the Journey of Sir George F. Bowen . . .', enclosure in GF Bowen to Earl of Kimberley, 15 May 1872, *AJHR*, 1872, A-1, no. 66, p. 86.
51. *NZPD*, vol. 1, part 2, 10 Sep 1867, p. 863.
52. James H Kerry-Nicholls, *The King Country; or, Explorations in New Zealand*, first pub. 1884, Capper reprint, Christchurch, 1974, p. 8.
53. Quoted in Keith Sinclair, *Kinds of Peace: Maori People After the Wars, 1870–85*, AUP, Auckland, 1991, p. 56.
54. Quoted in Sinclair, *Kinds of Peace*, p. 73.
55. Quoted in Sinclair, *Kinds of Peace*, p. 124.
56. Alan Ward, *An Unsettled History: Treaty Claims in New Zealand Today*, BWB, Wellington, 1999, pp. 62–63.
57. Second Report of the 'West Coast Commission', *AJHR*, 1880, G-2, pp. xlii–xliii.
58. Quoted in Sinclair, *Kinds of Peace*, p. 60.
59. Quoted in H Riseborough, *Days of Darkness: Taranaki, 1878–1884*, Allen & Unwin, Wellington, 1989, pp. 178–79.
60. Calculated from figures in *NZOYB*, 1893, pp. 60–61.
61. David Ian Pool, *Te Iwi Maori: A New Zealand Population Past, Present & Projected*, AUP, Auckland, 1991, pp. 77–78.

Chapter 6: The Rush To Be Rich, 1848–1882

1. Alexander Bathgate, *Colonial Experiences*, James Maclehose, Glasgow, 1874, p. 26.
2. *Statistics of New Zealand 1879*, p. 18.
3. www.waitangi-tribunal.govt.nz/doclibrary/researchwhanui
4. Atholl Anderson, *The Welcome of Strangers: An Ethnohistory of Southern Maori AD 1650–1850*, UOP, Dunedin, 1998, p. 194.
5. *Otago Witness*, 2 Nov 1861.
6. Stevan Eldred-Grigg, *Pleasures of the Flesh: Sex & Drugs in Colonial New Zealand 1840–1915*, AH & AW Reed, Wellington, 1984, p. 39.
7. Ray Hargreaves, *Barmaids, Billiards, Nobblers & Rat-pits: Pub Life in Goldrush Dunedin*, Otago Heritage Books, Dunedin, 1992, pp. 23–24.
8. James McNeish, *Tavern in the Town*, AH & AW Reed, Wellington, rev. edn., 1984, p. 308.
9. Robert Hoskins, *Goldfield Balladeer: The Life and Times of the Celebrated Charles R. Thatcher*, Collins, Auckland, 1977, p. 151.
10. Tom Field & Erik Olssen, *Relics of the Goldfields, Central Otago*, John McIndoe, Dunedin, 1976, p. 12.
11. Joanne MacCormack, 'Chaos and Calm: The Tuapeka Goldrush and Beyond', BA (Hons) long essay, University of Otago, 1996, p. 5.
12. Field & Olssen, p. 23.
13. Quoted in MacCormack, p. 37.
14. Philip Ross May, *Hokitika: Goldfields Capital*, Pegasus Press, Christchurch, 1964, p. 11.
15. Alan Grey, *Aotearoa and New Zealand: A Historical Geography*, CUP, Christchurch, 1994, p. 267.
16. Quoted in May, p. 29.
17. See for example, MacCormack, May, or Sandra Jane Quick, 'The Colonial Helpmeet Takes a Dram: Women Participants in the Central Otago Goldfields Liquor Industry 1861–1901', MA thesis, University of Otago, 1997.
18. Christine Dann, 'Isabella Graham' in *BNZW*, p. 249.
19. Anne Hutchison, 'Weldon, Barbara 1829–37? –1882', *DNZB*, updated 11 Feb 2002, www.dnzb.govt.nz
20. *Hokitika Star*, 18 Mar 1869.
21. James Ng, *Windows on a Chinese Past*, vol. 1, Otago Heritage Books, Dunedin, 1993, p. 123.
22. Ng, p. 124.
23. *NZOYB*, Wellington, 1893, p. 240.
24. Quoted in WHS Roberts, *North Otago From the Earliest Days*, Oamaru Mail, Oamaru, 1906, p. 286.
25. WJ Gardner, 'A Colonial Economy', in *OHNZ*, p. 62.
26. Belich, *Peoples*, p. 189.
27. Gary R Hawke, *The Making of New Zealand*, Cambridge University Press, Cambridge, 1985, p. 33.
28. Atholl Anderson, *Race Against Time: the Early Maori-Pakeha Families and the Development of the Mixed-Race Population in Southern New Zealand*, Hocken Library, Dunedin, 1991, p. 31.
29. Syd Cormack, as told to Joanna Irwin, *Four Generations From Maoridom: the Memoirs of a South Island Kaumatua and Fisherman*, UOP, Dunedin, 1997, p. 24.
30. John Wilson, *Waikakahi: the Promise Fulfilled*, Waikakahi Centennial 1999 Incorporated Society, Waimate, 1999, p. 20.

31. Belich, *Peoples*, p. 257.
32. Buddy Mikaere, *Te Maiharoa and the Promised Land*, Heinemann, Auckland, 1988, p. 125.
33. Grey, p. 208.
34. Belich, *Peoples*, p. 303.
35. Graeme Wyn & Garth Cant, 'The Bonanza Wheat Boom' in Garth Cant & Russell Kirkpatrick (eds.), *Rural Canterbury: Celebrating its History*, Daphne Brasell Associates Ltd with Lincoln University Press, Wellington, 2001, p. 64.
36. Jim McAloon, 'The Colonial Wealthy in Canterbury and Otago: No Idle Rich', *NZJH*, 30/1, 1996, p. 59.
37. WJ Gardner, 'Robinson, William 1813/1814? – 1889', *DNZB*, updated 11 Feb 2002, www.dnzb.govt.nz
38. DC McDonald, 'Campbell, Robert 1843–1889', *DNZB*, updated 11 Feb 2002, www.dnzb.govt.nz
39. John E Martin, *The Forgotten Worker*, Allen & Unwin/Port Nicholson Press, Wellington, 1990, p. 175.
40. John E Martin, 'The Struggle for £1: The Emergence of the Shearers' Union in the 1870s', *NZJH*, vol. 24, no. 1, Apr 1990, p. 66.
41. Martin, 'The Struggle for £1', p. 70.
42. Bruce Collins, *Rocks, Reefs and Sandbars*, Otago Heritage Books, Dunedin, 1995, p. 53.
43. Quoted in WHS Roberts, *History of Oamaru and North Otago*, Andrew Fraser, Oamaru, 1890, p. 303.
44. Quoted in *Otago Daily Times*, 2 Apr 1892.
45. *Statistics of New Zealand, 1879*, p. 244.
46. Belich, *Peoples*, p. 370.
47. Lionel Frost, *The New Urban Frontier: Urbanisation and City Building in Australasia and the American West*, New South Wales University Press, Kensington, 1991, p. 49.
48. Les Dew, *The Tidal Travellers: The Small Ships of Canterbury*, A&M Publishers, Christchurch, 1991.
49. Trevor Burnard, 'An Artisnal Town — The Economic Sinews of Christchurch' in John Cookson & Graeme Dunstall (eds.), *Southern Capital: Christchurch, Towards a City Biography 1850–2000*, CUP, Christchurch, 2000, p. 117.
50. David Leitch & Bob Stott, *New Zealand Railways: The First 125 Years*, Heinemann Reed, Auckland, 1988, p. 17.
51. For a virtual tour of the *Euterpe*, see www.sdmaritime.com/360india
52. Henry Brett, *White Wings*, vol. 1, Brett Publishing Co, Auckland, 1924, pp. 127–28.
53. Judith Bassett, 'A Paradise for Working Men' in Judith Binney, Judith Bassett & Erik Olssen, *The People and the Land, Te Tangata me Te Whenua: An Illustrated History of New Zealand 1820–1920*, Allen & Unwin/Port Nicholson Press, Wellington, 1990, p. 165.
54. Grey, p. 227.
55. *AJHR*, 1870, B.2, p. 19.
56. www.nzhistory.net.nz/gallery/brit-nz/irish.htm
57. E.g., the Oamaru–Moeraki line, see Kenneth C McDonald, *White Stone Country: The Story of North Otago*, North Otago Centennial Committee, Oamaru, 1962, p. 123.
58. Raewyn M Dalziel, *The Origins of New Zealand Diplomacy: The Agent-General in London 1870–1905*, Price Milburn for VUP, Wellington, 1975, p. 36.
59. See Jo-Anne Smith, 'Harriet Simpson', *BNZW*, pp. 610–11.
60. Followed later by Taranaki, although before too long all three provincial agencies were working for central government.
61. Joshua Charlesworth, 13 Dec 1879, Diary and letters, 1879/80, MS Papers 4564, ATL.
62. George James Lister, diary 1879, MS Papers 1820, folder 1, ATL.
63. Charlotte Macdonald, *A Woman of Good Character: Single Women as Immigrant Settlers in Nineteenth-century New Zealand*, Allen & Unwin, Wellington, 1990, p. 75.
64. Tony Simpson, *The Immigrants*, Godwit Press, Auckland, 1997, p. 137.
65. Lister, diary.
66. Charlesworth, 13 Dec 1879, diary.
67. Simpson, p. 191.
68. Lister, diary, p. 7.
69. Belich, *Peoples*, p. 287.
70. Charlesworth, 14 Sep 1879, diary.
71. Charlesworth, 31 Aug 1879, diary.
72. Brett, p. 62.
73. Lister, p. 85, diary.
74. Charlesworth, letter, 10 Jan 1880.
75. Burnard, p. 115.
76. The 2500 figure was set by the US Bureau of Statistics.
77. Frost, p. 38
78. John Cookson, 'Pilgrims' Progress — Image, Identity and Myth in Christchurch' in Cookson & Dunstall (eds.), p. 14.
79. Hargreaves, p. 14.

80. Geoffrey W Rice, 'Public Health in Christchurch 1875–1910' in Linda Bryder (ed.), *A Healthy Country: Essays on the History of Medicine in New Zealand*, BWB, Wellington, 1991, p. 94.
81. Rice, p. 90.
82. Geoffrey Rice, *Christchurch Changing*, CUP, Christchurch, 1999, p. 42.
83. Margaret Tennant, *Paupers and Providers: Charitable Aid in New Zealand*, Allen & Unwin/Port Nicholson Press, Wellington, 1989, p. 19.
84. Alma Rutherford, *The Edge of the Town: Historic Caversham as Seen Through its Streets and Buildings*, John McIndoe, Dunedin, 1978.
85. John S Parker, *Timaru Centenary 1868–1968*, Timaru City Council, Timaru, 1968, p. 2.
86. Burnard, p. 119.
87. Sharyn Cavanagh, *The Junction: A Brief History of the Thornbury District 1883–1983*, Thornbury School Centennial Committee, Thornbury, 1983.
88. Jim McAloon, *Nelson: A Regional History*, Cape Catley, Whatamango Bay, 1997, p. 57.
89. Judith Bassett, 'Hannah Ward Barron', *BNZW*, p. 52.
90. Brett, p. 149.

Chapter 7: God's Own Country, 1878–1913

1. David Hamer, *The New Zealand Liberals: The Years of Power, 1891–1912*, AUP, Auckland, 1988, p. 197.
2. Gary R Hawke, *The Making of New Zealand: An Economic History*, Cambridge University Press, Cambridge, 1985, p. 83.
3. Peter Holland, Kevin O'Connor & Alexander Wearing, 'Remaking the Grasslands of the Open Country' in Eric Pawson & Tom Brooking (eds.), *Environmental Histories of New Zealand*, OUP, Melbourne, 2002, p. 80.
4. Russell Stone, *Makers of Fortune: A Colonial Business Community and Its Fall*, Auckland/OUP, Auckland, 1973, p. 49.
5. Stone, p. 59.
6. Stone, p. 63.
7. Stone, p. 65.
8. *NZHA*, plate 57b.
9. Belich, *Paradise*, p. 36.
10. Erik Olssen, *A History of Otago*, John McIndoe, Dunedin, 1984, p. 91.
11. RT Robertson, '"Sweating" in Dunedin 1888–90', PGDA thesis, University of Otago, 1974, p. 12.
12. Olssen, p. 100.
13. Charlotte Macdonald, 'Miss Y and Miss Z', *BNZW*, p. 749.
14. Maryan Street, 'Working Women and Trade Unions in New Zealand 1889–1906' in Pat Walsh (ed.), *Trade Unions, Work and Society: The Centenary of the Arbitration System*, Dunmore Press, Palmerston North, p. 47.
15. Penelope AE Harper, 'The Dunedin Tailoresses' Union 1889–1914', PGDA thesis, University of Otago, 1988, p. 26.
16. JMA Tuck, 'The Devil's Half-Acre: 1900–1910, The Work of the Dunedin City Council and St Andrew's Presbyterian Church in the Slum Area Known as the Devil's Half-Acre', BA (Hons) long essay, University of Otago, 1983, p. 6.
17. Bronwyn Dalley, 'Margaret Williams alias Opium Mag' in *BNZW*, p. 736.
18. Keith Sinclair, *William Pember Reeves: The New Zealand Fabian*, Clarendon Press, Oxford, 1965, p. 126.
19. Timothy McIvor, *The Rainmaker: A Biography of John Ballance*, Heinemann Reed, Auckland, 1989, p. 181.
20. McIvor, p. 179.
21. Keith Sinclair, *A History of New Zealand*, Harmondsworth, rev. edn., 1988, p. 185.
22. Sinclair, *Reeves*, p. 167.
23. RM Burdon, *The New Dominion: A Social and Political History of New Zealand Between the Wars*, AH & AW Reed, Wellington, 1965, p. 106.
24. Only 12 electorates went dry.
25. Quoted in Sandra Coney, *Standing in the Sunshine: A History of New Zealand Women Since They Won the Vote*, Viking Penguin Books, Auckland, 1993, p. 23.
26. Dorothy Page 'Introduction' in *The Suffragists: Women Who Worked for the Vote, Essays From DNZB*, BWB/DNZB, Wellington, 1993, p. 13.
27. Jean Garner, *By His Own Merits: Sir John Hall — Pioneer, Pastoralist and Premier*, Dryden Press, Hororata, 1995, p. 238.
28. Burdon, p. 283.
29. Tom Brooking, 'John McKenzie' in *DNZB*, vol. 2, p. 296.
30. James Holt, *Compulsory Arbitration in New Zealand: The First Forty Years*, AUP, Auckland, 1986, p. 53.
31. Henry Demarest Lloyd, *A Country Without Strikes: A Visit to the Compulsory Arbitration Court of New Zealand*, Doubleday, Page & Co, New York, 1902.
32. Alan Ward, 'James Carroll', *DNZB*, vol 2, p. 79.
33. Ranginui Walker, *Ka Whawhai Tonu Matou: Struggle Without End*, Penguin Books, Auckland, 1990, p. 165.

Notes

34. Gaynor White, *'Beyond the Statute: Administration of Old-age Pensions — the first forty years'* in Bronwyn Dalley & Margaret Tennant (eds.), *History and Social Policy: The New Zealand Experience*, UOP, Dunedin, 2004, pp. 125–40.
35. Plunket to SSCols, 9 Jul 1906, CO 209/268–209, Micro-Z-1799, ANZ.
36. David Hamer, 'Richard John Seddon', *DNZB*, vol. 2, p. 451.
37. Belich, *Paradise*, p. 191.
38. Graeme Davison, 'The Parochial Past: Changing Uses of Australian Local History' in Paul Ashton (ed.), *The Future of the Past? Australian History After the Bicentenary*, Royal Australian Historical Society, Nowra, 1990, p. 8.
39. Gavin McLean, 'Where Sheep May Not Safely Graze: A Brief History of New Zealand's Heritage Movement' in Alexander Trapeznik (ed.), *Common Ground? Heritage and Public Places in New Zealand*, UOP, Dunedin, 2000, p. 27.
40. TL Rodney Wilson, 'Notes Toward a van der Velden Mythology', www.art-newzealand.com/Issues1to40; Gordon H Brown & Hamish Keith, *An Introduction to New Zealand Painting 1839–1980*, enlarged edn., David Bateman & Collins, Auckland, 1982, pp. 49–50.
41. Lydia Wevers, 'The Short Story' in *OHNZL*, p. 253.
42. Terry Sturm, *An Unsettled Spirit: The Life and Frontier Fiction of Edith Lyttelton (GB Lancaster)*, AUP, Auckland, 2003, p. 5.
43. Sturm, p. 5.
44. MacD P Jackson, 'Poetry' in *OHNZL*, p. 417.
45. John Mansfield Thompson, *The Oxford History of New Zealand Music*, OUP, Auckland, 1991, pp. 129–30.
46. Thompson, p. 213.
47. John Mansfield Thompson, *A Distant Music: The Life and Times of Alfred Hill 1870–1960*, OUP, Auckland, 1980, p. 79.
48. Jock Phillips, 'Exhibiting Ourselves: The Exhibition and National Identity' in John Mansfield Thompson (ed.), *Farewell Colonialism: The New Zealand International Exhibition Christchurch 1906–7*, Dunmore Press, Palmerston North, 1998, p. 17.
49. John Mansfield Thompson (ed.), '"A Triumph for Instrumental Music of the Highest Type": From the Exhibition Orchestra to the Besses O' Th' Barn Band' in Thompson (ed.), *Farewell Colonialism*, p. 80.
50. David V Fenby, 'Going for Gold With Cyanidation' in Denis Hogan & Bryce Williamson (eds.), *New Zealand is Different: Chemical Milestones in New Zealand History*, Clerestory Press, Christchurch, 1999, p. 199.
51. Desmond Hurley, *A Dictionary of New Zealand Political Quotations*, OUP, Auckland, 2000.
52. Erik Olssen, 'Strife in the Laboratory 1906–1914' in Judith Binney, Judith Bassett & Erik Olssen, *The People and the Land, Te Tangata me Te Whenua: An Illustrated History of New Zealand 1820–1920*, Allen & Unwin, Wellington, 1990, p. 285.
53. John A Lee, *Rhetoric at the Red Dawn*, Collins, Auckland, 1965, p. 21.
54. Erik Olssen, *The Red Feds: Revolutionary Industrial Unionism and the New Zealand Federation of Labour 1908–1913*, OUP, Auckland, 1988, p. xiv.
55. Erik Olssen, 'Patrick Hodgens Hickey', *DNZB*, vol. 3, pp. 215–16.
56. Fran Shor, 'Bringing the Storm: Syndicalist Counterpublics and the Industrial Workers of the World in New Zealand, 1908–14' in Pat Moloney & Kerry Taylor (eds.), *On the Left: Essays on Socialism in New Zealand*, UOP, Dunedin, 2002, p. 59.
57. Tom Brooking & Paul Enright, *Milestones: Turning Points in New Zealand History*, Mills Publications, Lower Hutt, 1988, p. 115.
58. Olssen, *Red Feds*, p. 108.
59. Olssen, *Red Feds*, p. 155.
60. Keith Sinclair, *A Destiny Apart*, Allen & Unwin, Port Nicholson Press, Wellington, 1986, p. 100. For Ward's speech and the questions and comments of his fellow prime ministers, see AB Keith, *British Colonial Policy*, vol. II, London, 1918, pp. 247–97.
61. Michael Bassett, *Coates of Kaipara*, AUP, Auckland, 1995, p. 30.
62. Lord Islington, quarterly report, 10 Jan 1912, CO209/275–276, Micro-Z-1804, ANZ.
63. Michael Bassett, *Three-party Politics in New Zealand 1911–1931*, Historical Publications, Auckland, 1982, p. 14.
64. Olssen, *Red Feds*, p. 188.
65. Olssen, *Red Feds*, p. 210.
66. Holt, p. 113.

Chapter 8: The Price of Empire, 1897–1918
1. *NZPD*, vol. 110, 28 Sep 1899, p. 76.
2. Ian McGibbon, *The Path to Gallipoli: Defending New Zealand 1840–1915*, GP Books, Wellington, 1991, p. 49.
3. McGibbon, p. 116.
4. Gallaher to 'old Sis', 18 Oct 1901, MS Papers 3576, ATL.
5. McGibbon, pp. 164–65.
6. McGibbon, p. 140.
7. *NZH*, 7 Mar 1906.

8. Quoted in Margaret Tennant, *Children's Health, the Nation's Wealth: A History of Children's Health Camps*, BWB, Wellington, 1994, p. 20.
9. Quoted in Linda Bryder, *A Voice for Mothers: The Plunket Society and Infant Welfare 1907–2000*, AUP, Auckland, 2003, p. 1.
10. Quoted in Bryder, p. 12.
11. McGibbon, p. 222.
12. Paul Baker, *King and Country Call: New Zealanders, Conscription and the Great War*, AUP, Auckland, 1988, p. 15.
13. Hart to Hart, 19 Feb 1915, MS Papers 2157, folder 1, ATL.
14. Baker, p. 15.
15. Nancy Croad (ed.), 'My dear Home, The letters of three Knight brothers who gave their lives during WWI', unpublished typescript, Auckland, 1995, p. 196.
16. George Knight to his mother, 13 Nov 1914?, MS Papers 5548-02, ATL.
17. Peter Lineham, 'Religion and war' in *OCNZMH*, pp. 443–44.
18. Baker, p. 221.
19. Croad, p. 47.
20. Winston S. Churchill, *The World Crisis, 1911–1918*, Thornton Butterworth Ltd, London, 1931, p. 589.
21. Hart to 'Mother, Father & Connie', 3 Nov 1916, MS Papers 2157, folder 4, ATL.
22. Hart to 'Mother, Father & Connie', 19 Oct 1917, MS Papers 2157, folder 5, ATL.
23. Hart to 'Mother, Father & Connie', 19 Oct 1917.
24. Hart to Sybil M Lee, 3 Feb 1918, in Croad, p. 213.
25. For a moving description of the plight of such men, see OE Burton, *The Silent Division: New Zealanders at the Front 1914–1919*, Angus & Robertson, Sydney, 1935, pp. 248–50.
26. These figures are derived from a printout of New Zealand deaths on 12 Oct 1917 provided by the Commonwealth War Graves Commission.
27. Hart to 'Mother, Father & Connie', 19 Oct 1917.
28. John Martin, 'War economy' in *OCNZMH*, p. 582.
29. Lt-Col. JT Sleeman, 'The Supply of Reinforcements during the War' in HTB Drew (ed.), *The War Effort of New Zealand*, Whitcombe & Tombs Ltd, Wellington, 1923, pp. 4–5.
30. Ashley Gould, 'Maori and the First World War' in *OCNZMH*, p. 297.
31. Baker, p. 138.
32. Michael Bassett with Michael King, *Tomorrow Comes the Song: A Life of Peter Fraser*, Penguin Books, Auckland, 2000, p. 73.
33. Baker, p. 167.
34. David Grant, 'Conscientious objectors' in *OCNZMH*, p. 116.
35. Baker, p. 208.
36. Baker, p. 221.
37. Baker, pp. 214–17.
38. Baker, pp. 217–20.
39. Jane Tolerton, 'Women and the First World War' in *OCNZMH*, p. 613.
40. Tolerton, p. 613.
41. Miss H. Maclean, 'New Zealand Army Nurses' in Drew, p. 99.
42. Quoted in Anna Rogers, *While You're Away: New Zealand Nurses At War 1899–1948*, AUP, Auckland, 2003, p. 122.
43. Hart to 'Mother, Father & Connie', 16 Aug 1917, MS Papers 2157, folder 5, ATL.
44. Hart to 'Mother, Father & Connie', 4 Feb 1918, MS Papers 2157, folder 6, ATL.
45. Hart to 'Mother, Father & Connie', 1 Mar 1918, MS Papers 2157, folder 6, ATL.
46. Adrian to 'Mother & Father', 5 Apr 1918, MS Papers 2157, folder 2, ATL.
47. Colin W Matheson to Mrs Knight, 27 Oct 1918, in Croad, p. 227.

Chapter 9: The Rise and Fall of Happy Homes, 1918–1935
1. Ian McGibbon, 'Chanuk Crisis' in *OCNZMH*, p. 82.
2. Geoffrey Rice, *Black November: The 1918 Influenza Epidemic in New Zealand*, Allen & Unwin, Wellington, 1988, pp. 142–43.
3. Jock Phillips & Chris MacLean, *The Sorrow and the Pride: New Zealand War Memorials*, GP Books, Wellington, 1990; 'Lest We Forget: War Memorials of the First World War', www.nzhistory.net.nz/Gallery/Anzac/memorial
4. Quoted in Rice, p. 110.
5. Rice, pp. 139–40.
6. Belich, *Paradise*, p. 204.
7. For the origins and early years of the Labour Party see Barry Gustafson, *Labour's Path to Political Independence*, AUP, Auckland, 1980.
8. On Liston, see Rory Sweetman, *Bishop in the Dock: The Sedition Trial of James Liston*, AUP, Auckland, 1997.
9. Angela Ballara, 'Ratana, Tahupotiki Wiremu 1873–1939', *DNZB*, updated 16 Dec 2003, www.dnzb.govt.nz
10. John Prince, 'Look Back in Amber: The General Licensing Poll in New Zealand, 1919–87', *Political Science*, vol. 48, no. 1, Jul 1996; Neill Atkinson, *Adventures in Democracy: A History of the Vote in New Zealand*, UOP, Dunedin, 2003, pp. 125–29.

11. Ashley Gould, 'Soldier Settlement in New Zealand After World War I: A Reappraisal' in Judith Smart & Tony Wood (eds.), *An Anzac Muster: War and Society in Australia and New Zealand 1914–18 and 1939–45*, Monash Publications, Melbourne, 1992, pp. 114–29; Alexander H McLintock (ed.), *An Encyclopaedia of New Zealand*, Government Printer, Wellington, 1966, vol. 2, p. 265.

12. GT Bloomfield, *New Zealand: A Handbook of Historical Statistics*, GK Hall & Co, Boston, 1984, p. 189. See also Ross Galbreath, *DSIR: Making Science Work for New Zealand*, VUP, Wellington, 1998.

13. Bloomfield, p. 148.

14. Quoted in Erik Olssen, *John A Lee*, UOP, Dunedin, 1977, p. 33.

15. Michael Bassett, *The State in New Zealand, 1840–1984: Socialism Without Doctrines?*, AUP, Auckland, 1998, p. 147.

16. Margaret McClure, *A Civilised Community: A History of Social Security in New Zealand 1898–1998*, AUP, Auckland, 1998, pp. 38–42.

17. The best account of Reform's achievements during these years is Miles Fairburn, 'The Farmers Take Over' in Keith Sinclair (ed.), *The Oxford Illustrated History of New Zealand*, 2nd edn., OUP, Auckland, 1996. On housing, see also Anthony Ward, 'Aspects of New Zealand Housing, 1920–1930', MA Thesis, Victoria University of Wellington, 1977.

18. Bloomfield, p. 113.

19. *NZOYB*, 1930, pp. 663–65; Fairburn, p. 206.

20. *NZPD*, 1919, vol. 185, p. 375.

21. For a discussion of 'working-class Toryism' and its impact on Labour's electoral fortunes in the 1920s see Fairburn, pp. 204–05.

22. Olssen, p. 46.

23. In 1931 Taranaki tribes accepted an annual payment of £5000; Waikato negotiated until 1947 before accepting the same amount.

24. Each has been the subject of a major recent biography: Michael Bassett, *Coates of Kaipara*, AUP, Auckland, 1995; and Ranginui Walker, *He Tipua: The Life and Times of Sir Apirana Ngata*, Viking, Auckland, 2001.

25. Michael King, *Whina*, Hodder & Stoughton, Auckland, 1983, p. 125.

26. Jeremy Ashford, *The Bungalow in New Zealand*, Viking, Auckland, 1994, pp. 68–70.

27. John E Martin (ed.), *People, Politics and Power Stations: Electric Power Generation in New Zealand 1880–1998*, 2nd edn., Electricity Corporation of New Zealand, Wellington, 1998, especially ch. 4 and app. 3; Bloomfield, p. 206.

28. This total was only surpassed during the Second World War when petrol rationing sparked a revival in tram usage. See Graham Stewart, *The End of the Penny Section*, rev. edn., Grantham House, Wellington, 1993, p. 172.

29. Stewart, p. 86.

30. Robin Hyde, *The Godwits Fly*, AUP, Auckland, 1970, pp. 17–18, 77–78.

31. Patrick Day, *The Radio Years: A History of Broadcasting in New Zealand*, vol. 1, AUP, Auckland, 1994, p. 321.

32. NJ Elliot, 'Anzac, Hollywood and Home: Cinema and Film-Going in Auckland, 1909–1939', MA Thesis, University of Auckland, 1989; Belich, *Paradise*, pp. 251–52.

33. *NZOYB*, 2000, p. 288.

34. Gil Dymock (ed.), *Good Morning New Zealand: News Stories of the Day from the 1930s*, Moa Publications, Auckland, 1990, pp. 11, 44.

35. Quoted in Lawrence Jones, 'The Novel' in *OHNZL*, p. 136.

36. JM Thompson, *The Oxford History of New Zealand Music*, OUP, Auckland, 1991, p. 94.

37. Nerida Campbell, 'O'Brien, Thomas Alexander 1888–1948', *DNZB*, updated 16 Dec 2003, www.dnzb.govt.nz; Gavin McLean, *100 Historic Places in New Zealand*, Hodder Moa Beckett, Auckland, 2002, p. 159.

38. Elliot, pp. 126–30; Dymock, p. 45; Sandra Coney, *Standing in the Sunshine: A History of New Zealand Women Since They Won the Vote*, Viking/Penguin Books, Auckland, 1993, p. 268.

39. *AJHR*, 1925, H-31A, p. 23; Coney, pp. 70–71.

40. John Mulgan, *Report on Experience*, Blackwood & Janet Paul, Auckland, 1967, p. 10.

41. Malcolm McKinnon, *Treasury: The New Zealand Treasury 1840–2000*, AUP, Auckland, 2003, pp. 114–15.

42. Herbert Roth, *Trade Unions in New Zealand: Past and Present*, Reed, Wellington, 1973, p. 51.

43. Matthew Wright, *Quake: Hawke's Bay 1931*, Reed Books, Auckland, 2001.

44. For an assessment of the impact of this decision, see John E Martin, 'The Removal of Compulsory Arbitration and the Depression of the 1930s', *NZJH*, vol. 28, no. 2, Oct 1994, pp. 124–44.

45. Barrie MacDonald & David Thompson, 'Mortgage Relief, Farm Finance and Rural Depression in New Zealand in the 1930s', *NZJH*, vol. 21, no. 2, Oct 1987, pp. 228–50.

46. Belich, *Paradise*, p. 255; *NZHA*, plate 79; Keith Rankin, *Unemployment in New Zealand at the Peak of the Great Depression*, AUP, Auckland, 1995, p. 28.

47. Tony Simpson, *The Sugarbag Years*, Alistair Taylor, Martinborough, 1974, p. 93.

48. Quoted in Simpson, p. 7.

49. Simpson, p. 7.

50. Martin, 'The Removal of Compulsory Arbitration', p. 135.

51. Erik Olssen, 'Depression and War' in Sinclair (ed.), *The Oxford Illustrated History of New Zealand*, p. 212.

52. Melanie Nolan, *Breadwinning: New Zealand Women and the State*, CUP, Christchurch, 2000, pp. 170–73; Coney, pp. 230–31.

53. Graeme Dunstall, *A Policeman's Paradise?: Policing a Stable Society, 1918–1945*, Dunmore Press, Palmerston North, 1999, pp. 87–88.

54. Gillian Boddy & Jacqueline Matthews (eds.), *Disputed Ground: Robin Hyde, Journalist*, VUP, Wellington, 1991, p. 269.

55. Dunstall, pp. 93–96.

56. Roth, pp. 51–53, 169, 172.

57. Robin Hyde, *Nor the Years Condemn*, New Women's Press, Auckland, 1986, p. 315. See also *NZOYB*, 1928, pp. 163–64; *NZOYB*, 1934, pp. 116–17.

58. Bloomfield, p. 121.

59. *NZOYB, 1935*, p. 163.

60. Keith Sinclair, *A History of New Zealand*, 3rd edn., Penguin Books, Harmondsworth, 1980, p. 266.

61. Hyde, *Nor the Years Condemn*, p. 347.

Chapter 10: Hope and Heroes, 1935–1949

1. Keith Sinclair, *Walter Nash*, OUP, Auckland, 1976, p. 111.

2. Robert Chapman, 'From Labour to National' in *OHNZ*, p. 354; Bassett & King, p. 136.

3. Sinclair, pp. 112–13.

4. Colin Scrimgeour, in CG Scrimgeour, John A Lee & Tony Simpson, *The Scrim-Lee Papers: C.G. Scrimgeour and John A. Lee Remember the Crisis Years 1930–40*, AH & AW Reed, Wellington, 1976, p. 55.

5. Margaret McClure, *A Civilised Community: A History of Social Security in New Zealand 1898–1998*, AUP, Auckland, 1998, p. 93.

6. Quoted in McClure, p. 66.

7. Chapman, p. 356.

8. Quoted in Sinclair, p. 125.

9. Quoted in Barry Gustafson, *From the Cradle to the Grave: A Biography of Michael Joseph Savage*, Penguin, Auckland, 1988, p. 224.

10. Erik Olssen, *John A. Lee*, UOP, Dunedin, 1977, p. 93.

11. Quoted in Olssen, p. 109; Gael Ferguson, *Building the New Zealand Dream*, Dunmore Press, Palmerston North, 1994, pp. 127–37.

12. McClure, pp. 76–77.

13. Quoted in Sinclair, p. 162.

14. Quoted in Gustafson, p. 24; Elizabeth Hanson, *The Politics of Social Security*, AUP/OUP, Auckland, 1980, pp. 117–21.

15. Chris Hilliard, 'A Prehistory of Public History: Monuments, Explanations and Promotions, 1900–1970' in Bronwyn Dalley & Jock Phillips (eds.), *Going Public: The Changing Face of New Zealand History*, AUP, Auckland, 2001, pp. 35–36.

16. www.nzhistory.net.nz/gallery/centennial/intro

17. Gustafson, p. 231.

18. Lee, in Scrimgeour, Lee & Simpson, pp. 60, 104.

19. Gustafson, pp. 255–68.

20. FLW Wood, *Political and External Affairs*, War History Branch, Wellington, 1958, pp. 7–12.

21. Wood, p. 11.

22. For a more extended discussion of New Zealand's war effort generally see Ian McGibbon, *New Zealand and the Second World War: The People, the Battles and the Legacy*, Hodder Moa Beckett, Auckland, 2004.

23. JF Cody, *28 (Maori) Battalion*, War History Branch, Wellington, 1956; Wira Gardiner, *Te Muru o te Ahi: The Story of the Maori Battalion*, Reed, Auckland, 1992.

24. On this campaign see Dan Davin, *Crete*, War History Branch, Wellington, 1953; Megan Hutching, *'A Unique Sort of Battle': New Zealanders Remember Crete*, HarperCollins, Auckland, 2001; Ian McGibbon, 'Freyberg, ULTRA and the Battle of Crete' in Christian Leitz & Joseph Zizek (eds.), *Writing Europe's Pasts*, Australian Humanities Press, Unley, 2003, pp. 336–47.

25. For more on POWs see Megan Hutching (ed.), *Inside Stories: New Zealand POWs Remember*, HarperCollins, Auckland, 2002.

26. On the place of the Singapore naval base in New Zealand's defence strategy see W David McIntyre, *New Zealand Prepares for War, Defence Policy 1919–39*, CUP, Christchurch, 1988; Ian McGibbon, *Blue-water Rationale: The Naval Defence of New Zealand 1914–1942*, Government Printer, Wellington, 1981.

27. McGibbon, *New Zealand and the Second World War*, pp. 129–43, 198–200.

28. McGibbon, *New Zealand and the Second World War*, pp. 104–05. For another view see Belich, *Paradise*, pp. 270–87.

29. Megan Hutching (ed.), *A Fair Sort of Battering: New Zealanders Remember the Italian Campaign*, HarperCollins, Auckland, 2004.

30. For an exhaustive treatment of the home front see Nan Taylor, *The Home Front*, 2 vols, Historical Publications Branch, Wellington, 1986.

31. Deborah Montgomerie, *The Women's War: New Zealand Women 1939–45*, AUP, Auckland, 2001.

32. On the US presence in New Zealand see Harry Bioletti, *The Yanks are Coming: The American Invasion of New Zealand 1942–44*, Century Hutchinson, Auckland, 1989; Denys Bevan, *United States Forces in New Zealand 1942–1945*, Macpherson Publishing, Alexandra, 1992; Jock Phillips with Ellen Ellis, *Brief Encounter: American Forces and the New Zealand People, 1942–1945*, Department of Internal Affairs, Wellington, 1992.

33. Quoted in Taylor, *The Home Front*, vol. 2, p. 1265.

34. Quoted in Alison Parr, *Silent Casualties: New Zealand's Unspoken Legacy of the Second World War*, Tandem Press, Birkenhead, 1995, p. 130.

35. Taylor, vol. 2, p. 1277; McGibbon, *New Zealand and the Second World War*, pp. 212–13.

36. McGibbon, *New Zealand and the Second World War*, p. 212.

37. Montgomerie, pp. 171, 183.

38. Quoted in Montgomerie, p. 173.

39. Quoted in Montgomerie, p. 179.

40. Quoted in Chris Brickell, 'Exploring the Contours of Resistance: The example of Dior's "New Look" in New Zealand' in Catherine Brennan (ed.), *Social Diversity and the Politics of Exclusion: Sociological Association of Aotearoa (New Zealand) Proceedings of Conference 2001*, Massey University, Palmerston North, 2002, pp. 72–73.

41. Fiona McKergow, 'Opening the Wardrobe of History: Dress, Artefacts and Material Life of the 1940s and 1950s' in Bronwyn Dalley & Bronwyn Labrum (eds.), *Fragments: New Zealand Social and Cultural History*, AUP, Auckland, 2000, pp. 176–78.

42. Quoted in McClure, pp. 106–07; Bronwyn Dalley, *Family Matters: Child Welfare in Twentieth Century New Zealand*, AUP, Auckland, 1998, p. 217.

43. McClure, pp. 105–09.

44. McClure, pp. 117, 122.

45. Claudia Orange, 'An Exercise in Maori Autonomy: The Rise and Demise of the Maori War Effort Organisation', *NZJH*, vol. 21, no. 1, 1987, p. 164.

46. Megan Hutching, *Long Journey for Sevenpence: Assisted Immigration to New Zealand from the United Kingdom 1947–1975*, VUP, Wellington, 1999, pp. 60, 141, 145, 177–79.

47. Quoted in Anna Rogers & Miria Simpson (eds.), *Te Timatanga Tatou Tatou: Early Stories from the Founding Members of the Maori Women's Welfare League*, Maori Women's Welfare League & BWB, Wellington, 1993, p. 318.

48. Aroha Harris, 'Maori and "the Maori Affairs"' in Bronwyn Dalley & Margaret Tennant (eds.), *Past Judgement: History and Social Policy in New Zealand*, UOP, Dunedin, 2004, pp. 191–205; Bronwyn Labrum, '"Bringing Families Up to Scratch": The Distinctive Workings of Maori State Welfare, 1944–1970', *NZJH*, vol. 36, no. 2, 2002, pp. 163–66.

49. Dalley, *Family Matters*, pp. 154–57.

50. Ben Schrader, 'Labour at Home: The First Labour Government and the Familial Suburban Ideal' in Barbara Brookes (ed.), *At Home in New Zealand: History, Houses, People*, BWB, Wellington, 2000, pp. 126–27; Ferguson, pp. 167–68, 172–74.

51. Bassett & King, pp. 311–12; Neill Atkinson, *Adventures in Democracy: A History of the Vote in New Zealand*, UOP, Dunedin, 2003, p. 160.

52. Eve Ebbett, *When the Boys Were Away: New Zealand Women in World War II*, Reed, Auckland, 1984, p. 113.

53. Chris Brickell, 'Labour, National and the Postwar Consumer', *History Now*, 7, 4, 2001, p. 18.

54. Chapman, p. 372.

Chapter 11: The Golden Weather, 1949–1965

1. King, *PHNZ*, p. 411.

2. Figures from *NZOYB*, 1957, pp. 79–81, 1972, pp. 112–17.

3. This is the average number of births per woman in child-bearing years, or the total fertility rate.

4. Figures from *NZOYB*, 1972, pp. 112–17, 2000, p. 98.

5. Helen Smyth, *Rocking the Cradle: Contraception, Sex and Politics in New Zealand*, Steele Roberts Ltd, Wellington, 2000, pp. 94–97.

6. Belich, *Paradise*, pp. 493–96.

7. Bronwyn Dalley, *Family Matters: Child Welfare in Twentieth-century New Zealand*, AUP, Auckland, 1998, pp. 224–26.

8. Belich, *Paradise*, p. 506. *NZOYB*, 1972, pp. 90–91.

9. Quoted in Anne Else, *A Question of Adoption: Closed Stranger Adoption in New Zealand, 1944–1974*, BWB, Wellington, 1991, p. 7. See figures in Dalley, *Family Matters*, p. 222.

10. *NZOYB*, 2000, pp. 106–07, 224; *NZHA*, plate 70.

11. Figures from Gael Ferguson, *Building the New Zealand Dream*, Dunmore Press, Palmerston North, 1994, pp. 177–96.

12. Quoted in Bronwyn Labrum, 'Persistent Needs and Expanding Desires: Pakeha Families and State Welfare in the Years of Prosperity' in Bronwyn Dalley & Bronwyn Labrum (eds.), *Fragments: New Zealand Social and Cultural History*, AUP, Auckland, 2000, p. 201.

13. Lloyd Jones & Bruce Foster, *Last Saturday*, VUP for National Library, Wellington, 1994, pp. 137–38.

14. *NZOYB*, 1966, pp. 361, 370.

15. Graeme Dunstall, 'The Social Pattern' in *OHNZ*, p. 459. Jean-Marie O'Donnell, '"Electric Servants" and the Science of Housework: Changing Patterns of Domestic Work, 1935–1956' in Barbara Brookes, Charlotte Macdonald & Margaret Tennant (eds.), *Women in History 2*, BWB, Wellington, 1992, pp. 168–83.

16. Labrum, 'Persistent Needs', pp. 201, 203; *NZOYB*, 1966, p. 608.

17. *NZOYB*, 1966, pp. 960–61, 1970, pp. 930–31, 1975, p. 866, 1980, p. 793, 1985, p. 870. Melanie Nolan, *Breadwinning: New Zealand Women and the State*, CUP, Christchurch, 2000, pp. 192–229.

18. Ray Bailey with Mary Earle, *Home Cooking to Takeaways: A History of New Zealand Food Eating 1880–1990*, 2nd edn., Massey University, Palmerston North, 1999, pp. 90–97.

19. Figures from Belich, *Paradise*, p. 437.

20. Ron Palenski, 'Bowen, Walter Godfrey 1922–1994', *DNZB*, updated 16 Dec 2003, www.dnzb.govt.nz; Redmer Yska, *All Shook Up: The Flash Bodgie and the Rise of the New Zealand Teenager in the Fifties*, Penguin Books, Auckland, 1993, pp. 16–18.

21. Belich, *Paradise*, pp. 300–01, Dick Scott's *151 Days*, New Zealand Waterside Workers' Union (Deregistered), Auckland, 1952, provides a good idea of the tone at the time.

22. Scott, pp. 111–17, 183–92.

23. Maureen Birchfield, *She Dared to Speak: Connie Birchfield's Story*, UOP, Dunedin, 1998, p. 148.

24. Ian McGibbon (ed.), *Unofficial Channels: Letters between Alister McIntosh and Foss Shanahan, George Laking and Frank Corner, 1946–1966*, VUP, Wellington, 1999, p. 112.

25. 'Korean War' in *OCNZMH*, p. 270.

26. Figures in this, and preceding paragraph, from *NZOYB*, 1957, p. 308; *NZHA*, plate 89.

27. *NZOYB*, 1966, p. 405.

28. Figures from Dunstall, p. 461.

29. Gordon McLauchlan, *The Farming of New Zealand*, Australia & New Zealand Book Company, Auckland, 1981, p. 15.

30. Figures in previous two paragraphs from Robert Chapman, 'From Labour to National' in *OHNZ*, pp. 379–81.

31. Belich, *Paradise*, p. 313.

32. See John Martin (ed.), *People, Politics and Power Stations: Electric Power Generation in New Zealand 1880–1998*, 2nd edn., Electricity Corporation of New Zealand, Wellington, 1998.

33. Martin (ed.), pp. 151–54.

34. More than twice that number arrived without assistance. See Megan Hutching, *Long Journey for Sevenpence: Assisted Immigration to New Zealand from the United Kingdom 1947–1975*, VUP, Wellington, 1999, p. 179; *NZHA*, plate 88.

35. *NZOYB*, 1957, p. 644, 1966, p. 509.

36. Gary R Hawke, 'Economic Trends and Economic Policy, 1938–1992' in *OHNZ*, pp. 428–29.

37. Good studies of Maori migration in this period include Ranginui Walker, 'Maori People since 1950' in *OHNZ*, pp. 498–509; King, *PHNZ*, pp. 466–84.

38. *NZHA*, plate 91.

39. Belich, *Paradise*, p. 470.

40. DR Chapple, 'A Timber Town' in IH Kawharu (ed.), *Conflict and Compromise: Essays on the Maori Since Colonisation*, Reed, Wellington, 1975, pp. 191, 210.

41. Figures in Walker, p. 501.

42. Ranginui Walker, *Ka Whawhai Tonu Matou: Struggle Without End*, Penguin Books, Auckland, 1990, p. 199.

43. Walker, *Ka Whawhai Tonu Motou*, p. 198.

44. Quoted in Bronwyn Labrum, '"Bringing Families up to Scratch": The Distinctive Workings of Maori State Welfare, 1944–1970', *NZJH*, vol. 36, no. 2, 2002, p. 169.

45. King, *PHNZ*, pp. 472–73.

46. 'Report on Department of Maori Affairs, with Statistical Supplement', *AJHR*, G-10, 1961.

47. Walker, 'Maori People', pp. 504–5, *Ka Whawhai Tonu Matou*, pp. 200–01.

48. *NZOYB*, 2000, p. 95.

49. *NZOYB*, 2000, p. 95.

50. *Report of the Waitangi Tribunal on the Orakei Claim* (Wai-9), Waitangi Tribunal, 1987, pp. 124–26.

51. *Home and Building*, Aug 1958, pp. 52, 63–65.
52. *NZHA*, plate 75.
53. Quoted in Dalley, *Family Matters*, p. 174.
54. Recent revisions include Frazer Andrews, 'The Man in the Grey Flannel Suit: White-collar Masculinity in Post-war New Zealand' in Caroline Daley & Deborah Montgomerie (eds.), *The Gendered Kiwi*, AUP, Auckland, 1999, pp. 191–212; Belich, *Paradise*, pp. 297ff; Caroline Daley, *Leisure and Pleasure: Reshaping and Revealing the New Zealand Body, 1900–1960*, AUP, Auckland, 2003; Bronwyn Dalley, *Living in the Twentieth Century: New Zealand History in Photographs*, BWB/Craig Potton, Wellington, 2000; Labrum, 'Persistent Needs'; Fiona McKergow, 'Opening the Wardrobe of History: Dress, Artefacts and Material Life of the 1940s and 1950s' in Dalley & Labrum (eds.), pp. 163–87.
55. Redmer Yska, *New Zealand Green: The Story of Marijuana in New Zealand*, David Bateman, Auckland, 1990, pp. 59–76, *All Shook Up*, pp. 182–83.
56. Material regarding juvenile delinquency drawn from Dalley, *Family Matters*, pp. 177–99. See also Yska, *All Shook Up*.
57. Bob Jones, Radio New Zealand *Spectrum* documentary, no. 731.
58. Dalley, *Family Matters*, p. 197.
59. Dalley, *Family Matters*, pp. 196–97.
60. Dalley, *Family Matters*, pp. 177–201.
61. AE Levett, 'Gangs in Auckland', Feb 1959, SS, 8/10/11, pt 1, ANZ.
62. John Dix, *Stranded in Paradise: New Zealand Rock 'n' Roll, 1955–1988*, Paradise Publications, 1988, pp. 19–29; Yska, *All Shook Up*, pp. 195–212.

Chapter 12: Generations, 1965–1984

1. Barry Gustafson, *His Way: A Biography of Robert Muldoon*, AUP, Auckland, 2000, p. 146.
2. Tim Shadbolt, *Bullshit & Jellybeans*, Alister Taylor Ltd, Wellington, 1971, p. 166.
3. Shadbolt, p. 168.
4. *NZOYB*, 1977, p. 545; 1985, p. 609.
5. *NZOYB*, 1987–88, p. 338; Brian Easton, 'New Zealand's Post-war GDP performance', www.eastonbh.ac.nz
6. *NZOYB*, 1985, p. 609.
7. *NZOYB*, 1985, p. 609.
8. Megan Hutching, *Long Journey for Sevenpence: Assisted Immigration to New Zealand from the United Kingdom 1947–1975*, VUP, Wellington, 1999, p. 145.
9. *NZOYB*, 1967, p. 1000; 1987–88, p. 321.
10. *New Zealand Monthly Review*, May 1965.
11. David McCraw, 'Reluctant Ally: New Zealand's Entry into the Vietnam War', *NZJH*, vol. 15, no. 1, 1981, pp. 50–53.
12. Quoted in Roberto G Rabel, 'The Vietnam Antiwar Movement in New Zealand', *Peace & Change*, 17, 1992, p. 21.
13. Rabel, pp. 5–11.
14. Rabel, p. 27.
15. Elsie Locke, *Peace People: A History of Peace Activities in New Zealand*, Hazard Press, Christchurch, 1992, p. 215.
16. Locke, pp. 207–11.
17. Rabel, p. 22.
18. Neville Peat, *Manapouri Saved! New Zealand's First Great Conservation Success Story*, Longacre Press, Dunedin, 1994.
19. Redmer Yska, *New Zealand Green: The Story of Marijuana in New Zealand*, David Bateman, Auckland, 1990, p. 86.
20. Roger Wilson, *From Manapouri to Aramoana: The Battle for New Zealand's Environment*, Earthworks Press, Waiwera, 1982.
21. Quoted in Yska, p. 119.
22. Charlotte Macdonald (ed.), *The Vote, the Pill and the Demon Drink: A History of Feminist Writing in New Zealand, 1869–1993*, BWB, Wellington, 1993, p. 161; Christine Dann, *Up from Under: Women and Liberation in New Zealand, 1970–1985*, Allen & Unwin/Port Nicholson Press, Wellington, 1985, p. 5.
23. Anne Horsfield, *Women in the Economy*, Ministry of Women's Affairs, Wellington, 1988, pp. 257, 259, 281, 283.
24. Dann, p. 75.
25. *NZOYB*, 2000, p. 123.
26. *NZOYB*, 1984, p. 84.
27. *NZOYB*, 2000, p. 98.
28. Sandra Coney, *Standing in the Sunshine: A History of New Zealand Women since they Won the Vote*, Viking, Auckland, 1993, pp. 140ff.
29. Dann, passim.
30. Ray Bailey with Mary Earle, *Home Cooking to Takeaways: A History of New Zealand Food Eating 1880–1990*, 2nd edn., Massey University, Palmerston North, 1999, pp. 263–66.
31. —
32. Gael Ferguson, *Building the New Zealand Dream*, Dunmore Press, Palmerston North, 1994, p. 235.

33. Ranginui Walker, *Ka Whawhai Tonu Matou: Struggle Without End*, Penguin Books, Auckland, 1990, pp. 197–212.
34. Trevor Richards, *Dancing on Our Bones: New Zealand, South Africa, Rugby and Racism*, BWB, Wellington, 1999, pp. 15–50.
35. Richards, p. 47.
36. Richards, pp. 134–85.
37. Gustafson, p. 311.
38. Jock Phillips & Peter King, 'Who Were the Springbok Tour Protestors?' in David Mackay et al (ed.), *Counting the Cost: The 1981 Springbok Tour in Wellington*, Victoria University, 1982.
39. Geoff Chapple, *1981: The Tour*, Reed, Wellington, 1984.
40. *Seven Days*, BCNZ, 27 Jul 1975.
41. Gustafson, p. 238.
42. Jonathan Boston, *Incomes Policy in New Zealand: 1968–1984*, VUP, Wellington, 1984.
43. Gustafson, p. 351.
44. Malcolm McKinnon, *Treasury: The New Zealand Treasury, 1840–2000*, AUP, Auckland, 2003, p. 304.
45. William H Oliver, 'The Labour Caucus and Economic Policy Formation, 1981–1984' in Brian Easton (ed.), *The Making of Rogernomics*, AUP, Auckland, 1989, pp. 11–52.
46. An anonymous witness who spoke at the Stout Centre conference on Muldoon, Apr 2003.

Chapter 13: Breaking Free, 1984–2005

1. Belich, *Paradise*, p. 407.
2. Roger Douglas, *There's Got to be a Better Way*, Fourth Estate Books, Wellington, 1980, p. 22.
3. Roger Douglas & Louise Callan, *Toward Prosperity*, David Bateman, Auckland, 1997, p. 57.
4. Barry Gustafson, *His Way: A Biography of Robert Muldoon*, AUP, Auckland, 2000, p. 393.
5. Michael Cullen, 'Reflecting on the Fourth Labour Government', Stout conference, 30 Apr 2004, reported in *NZH* 1 May 2004, www.nzherald.co.nz
6. Gerald Hensley, 'Reflecting on the Fourth Labour Government', Stout conference, 30 Apr 2004, reported in *NZH* 1 May 2004, www.nzherald.co.nz
7. Paul East, *Evening Post*, 24 Dec 1992.
8. David Lange, *Nuclear Free — The New Zealand Way*, Penguin, Auckland, 1990, p. 97.
9. Colin James, 'A Mistaken US Impression that Left an Indelible Mark', www.synapsis.co.nz/herald
10. Malcolm McKinnon, 'Realignment: New Zealand and its ANZUS Allies' in Bruce Brown (ed.), *New Zealand in World Affairs III 1972–1990*, VUP/NZIA, Wellington, 1999, p. 153.
11. McKinnon, p. 154.
12. Lange, p. 97.
13. Lange, p. 87.
14. Stuart McMillan, *Neither Confirm Nor Deny: The Nuclear Ships Dispute Between New Zealand and the United States*, Allen & Unwin/Port Nicholson Press, Wellington, 1987, p. 80.
15. Malcolm McKinnon, *Independence and Foreign Policy: New Zealand in the World Since 1935*, AUP, Auckland, 1993, p. 233.
16. Lange, p. 114.
17. Richard Kennaway, 'The ANZUS Dispute' in Richard Kennaway & John Henderson (eds.), *Beyond New Zealand II: Foreign Policy into the 1990s*, Longman Paul, Auckland, 1991, pp. 70–71.
18. David Lange, 'Calling a Dead Letter a Dead Letter', *New Zealand International Relations XIV/4*, Jul/Aug 1989, p. 25.
19. Malcolm McKinnon, 'The End of the Alliance?', *NZIR XIII/3*, May/Jun 1988, p. 17.
20. McKinnon, 'Realignment', p. 167.
21. McKinnon, *Independence and Foreign Policy*, pp. 319–20.
22. Margaret McClure, *A Civilised Community: A History of Social Security in New Zealand 1898–1998*, AUP, Auckland, 1998, pp. 226–27.
23. McKinnon, *Independence and Foreign Policy*, p. 314.
24. The 'war of independence' suggestion is from McKinnon, *Independence and Foreign Policy*, p. 298; Belich offers a Boston Tea Party comparison in Belich, *Paradise*, p. 439.
25. McKinnon, *Independence and Foreign Policy*, p. 357.
26. Colin James, *New Territory: The Transformation of New Zealand 1984–92*, BWB, Wellington, 1992, p. 179.
27. Hensley.
28. Bryan Gilling & Alan Henderson, *Town and Country: The National Associations and Insurance Companies of Local Government in New Zealand*, Dunmore Press, Palmerston North, 2000, p. 120.
29. Tasman Express Line minutes, 15/16 Feb 1990, McKay Shipping Ltd, Auckland.
30. Belich, *Paradise*, p. 474.
31. *Pacific Progress: A Report on the Economic Status of Pacific Peoples in New Zealand*, Statistics New Zealand, Wellington, 2002, pp. 47–50, 90.
32. Bronwyn Dalley, *Living in the Twentieth Century: New Zealand History in Photographs 1900–1980*, BWB/Craig Potton, Wellington, 2000, p. 32.

33. *NZOYB*, 1979, p. 59 and 1988–89, p. 153.

34. Statistics New Zealand, 'Oamaru Urban Area Community Profile', Statistics New Zealand, Wellington, 2002.

35. Statistics New Zealand, 'Hamilton Zone Urban Area Community Profile', Statistics New Zealand, Wellington, 2002.

36. Belich, *Paradise*, p. 406.

37. James, *New Territory*, p. 180.

38. Roger Douglas, *Unfinished Business*, Random House, Auckland, 1993, pp. 220–33.

39. James, 'Reflecting'.

40. Ian F Grant, *Public Lives: New Zealand's Premiers and Prime Ministers 1856–2003*, New Zealand Cartoon Archive, Wellington, 2003, p. 170.

41. Neill Atkinson, *Adventures in Democracy: A History of the Vote in New Zealand*, UOP, Dunedin, 2003, p. 250.

42. Ruth Richardson, *Making a Difference*, Shoal Bay Press, Christchurch, 1995, p. 76.

43. Geoffrey W Rice, 'A Revolution in Social Policy' in *OHNZ*, p. 493.

44. Richardson, p. 105.

45. McClure, p. 239.

46. Peter Travers, 'Living Standards of Older People and Policy Implications for their Grandchildren', *Family Matters*, 61, 2002, pp. 68–69.

47. *Evening Post*, 1 Jun 1991.

48. Richardson, p. 177.

49. James, *New Territory*, p. 92.

50. Belich, *Paradise*, p. 424.

51. Easton, www.eastonbh.ac.nz

52. Michael Belgrave, 'Needs and the State: Evolving Social Policy in New Zealand History' in Bronwyn Dalley & Margaret Tennant (eds.), *Past Judgement: Social Policy in New Zealand History*, UOP, Dunedin, 2004, p. 37.

53. McClure, pp. 235, 245.

54. Malcolm McKinnon, *Treasury: The New Zealand Treasury 1840–2000*, AUP, Auckland, 2003, pp. 398–99.

55. Belgrave, p. 38.

56. Jack Vowles, Peter Aimer, Helena Catt, Jim Lamare & Raymond Miller, *Towards Consensus: The 1993 General Election in New Zealand and the Transition to Proportional Representation*, AUP, Auckland, 1995, especially chapter 7 and Alan McRobie (ed.), *Taking it to the People? The New Zealand Electoral Reform Debate*, Hazard Press, Christchurch, 1993.

57. Belich, *Paradise*, p. 408.

58. Wendyl Nissen, 'Jenny Shipley', quoted in Grant, p. 184.

59. Helen Clark, 'Speech From The Throne', 21 Dec 1999, www.beehive.govt.nz

60. Travers, p. 68.

61. Brian Easton, 'Economic Directions: What does the Government think it's doing?', *NZ Listener*, 12 Jan 2002, and 'Manure and the Modern Economy: Has Economic Policy Hardly Changed?', *NZ Listener*, 7 Sep 2002.

62. Karen Skinner quoted in Mark Stor, 'The New Face of Unionism', *New Zealand Management*, 49, 4, 2002.

63. Paul Tremewan, 'Pain of New Law was Not Worth the Effort', *NZH*, 13 Oct 2003; Robyn May, 'Unions Reviving, but Not as Intended', *NZH*, 22 Oct 2002.

64. 'Kinleith mill workers to receive redundancy notices', *NZH*, 19 Dec 2002.

65. *NZH*: 'A tale of two babies — and $325 a week', 25 Jun 2002; 'The wages of motherhood', 25 Jun 2002; 'Paid parental leave increased to 14 weeks', 9 Mar 2004.

66. Tom Brooking, *Milestones: Turning Points in New Zealand History*, Mills Publications Ltd, Lower Hutt, 1988, p. 189.

67. Easton, 'Manure and the Macro Economy' and '1999 and all that', *NZ Listener*, 21 Jan 2004.

68. Easton, '1999 and all that'.

69. Statistics of New Zealand, 'Key statistics: April 2004. Household access to the Internet', and 'Information Technology', 'Hot Off the Press Household Economic Survey', www.statistics.govt.nz; Jock Phillips, 'History and the New Media' in Bronwyn Dalley & Jock Phillips (eds.), *Going Public: The Changing Face of New Zealand History*, AUP, Auckland, 2001, p. 150.

70. Anne Else & Barbara Bishop, 'Occupational Patterns for Employed New Zealand Women: An analysis of the 2001 Census Data', report prepared for Ministry of Women's Affairs, 2003 and CEDAW, *The Status of Women in New Zealand 2002*, Ministry of Women's Affairs, Wellington, 2002.

71. Statistics New Zealand, '2001 Census: Snapshot 4. Maori'.

72. Ministry of Education, 'Student Enrolments at Tertiary Institutions at 31 July 2003', www.minedu.govt.nz

73. Alan Ward, *An Unsettled History: Treaty Claims in New Zealand Today*, BWB, Wellington, 1999, p. 1.

74. 'Progress of claims', www.ots.govt.nz, 2004.

75. Statistics New Zealand, *Asian People*, 2002, pp. 11–12.

76. Manying Ip, 'Preface' in Manying Ip (ed.), *Unfolding History, Evolving Identity: The Chinese in New Zealand*, AUP, Auckland, 2003, p. xii; quoted in Beven Yee, 'Coping with Insecurity: Everyday Experiences of Chinese New Zealanders' in Ip (ed.), p. 231.

77. Statistics New Zealand, 'Demographic Trends 2003. Part 2: Fertility', www.statistics.govt.nz

78. Statistics New Zealand, 'Older People in New Zealand', 'Demographic Trends 2003, Part 1: Population change and structure', www.statistics.govt.nz

79. www.primecare.co.nz; 'Village People', www.consumer.org.nz, 1 Aug 2003.

80. Lesley Hull, 'Financial deregulation and household indebtedness', Reserve Bank of New Zealand discussion paper series, Jan 2003, pp. 5–7; AC Nielsen, 'Summary of Actions Taken in Response to Education Programme', prepared for Retirement Commission, Aug 2003; Mark Fryer, 'New Zealand's household debt at $80 billion and rising', *NZH*, 14 Dec 2002.

81. Simon Farrell-Green, 'Dial M for Mortgage', *Metro*, 261, Mar 2003.

82. Ray Bailey with Mary Earle, *Home Cooking to Takeaways: A History of New Zealand Food Eating 1880–1990*, 2nd edn., Massey University, Palmerston North, 1999, pp. 195–206; Ian Carter, 'Eternal Recurrence of the Trivially New: Food and Popular Culture' in Claudia Bell & Steve Matthewman (eds.), *Cultural Studies in Aotearoa/New Zealand: Identity, Space and Place*, OUP, Melbourne, 2004, pp. 96–98.

83. AC Nielsen, 'Grocery Report', www.acnielsen.co.nz

84. Margo White, 'The Shop that Ate New Zealand', *Metro*, 272, Feb 2004.

85. 'Protest as student debt hits $7 billion', *NZH*, 28 Apr 2004.

86. Ministry of Education, 'Student Enrolments at Tertiary Institutions at 31 July 2003', www.minedu.govt.nz

87. Farrell-Green.

88. *Around the Clock: Findings from the New Zealand Time Use Survey 1998–99*, Statistics New Zealand, Wellington, 2001.

89. Julie Dalzell, 'We've Come a Long Way, Baby', *Cuisine*, 100, 2003, pp. 148–49.

90. *Wine and Grape Industry Statistical Annual*, 2000–03.

91. Margaret McClure, *The Wonder Country: Making Tourism in New Zealand*, AUP, Auckland, 2004.

92. James, 'Reflecting'.

93. Figures in following two paragraphs are from 'National Population Projections 2001(base) – 2051', and National Population Projections 2001 (base) – 2021 for Maori, Pacific, Asian, Family and Households, Subnational, Projections Overview, www.statistics.govt.nz, 2002–03.

List of Artworks

Further Reading

General Works

Electronic

Dictionary of New Zealand Biography, www.dnzb.govt.nz/dnzb/ (also available in printed form, various years 1990–2000)
www.nzhistory.net.nz
Statistics New Zealand, www.statistics.govt.nz
Te Ara: The Encyclopedia of New Zealand, www.TeAra.govt.nz

Print

Belich, James, *Making Peoples: A History of the New Zealanders from Polynesian settlement to the End of the Nineteenth Century*, Allen Lane/Penguin Press, Auckland, 1996
———, *Paradise Reforged: A History of the New Zealanders from the 1880s to the Year 2000*, Allen Lane/Penguin Press, Auckland, 2001
Binney, Judith, Judith Bassett and Erik Olssen, *The People and the Land/Te Tangata me Te Whenua: An Illustrated History of New Zealand, 1880–1920*, Allen & Unwin/Port Nicholson Press, Wellington, 1990
Coney, Sandra, *Standing in the Sunshine: A History of Women Since they Won the Vote*, Viking, Auckland, 1993
Cumberland, Kenneth B, *Landmarks*, Readers Digest, Auckland, 1981
Dalley, Bronwyn, *Living in the Twentieth Century: New Zealand History in Photographs*, Bridget Williams Books/Craig Potton Publishing, Wellington, 2000
Grey, Alan, *Aotearoa and New Zealand: A Historical Geography*, Canterbury University Press, Christchurch, 1994
King, Michael, *Maori: A Photographic and Social History*, Reed, Auckland, 1983
———, *The Penguin History of New Zealand*, Penguin, Auckland, 2003
Macdonald, Charlotte, Merimeri Penfold and Bridget Williams (eds.), *The Book of New Zealand Women: Ko Kui Ma Te Kaupapa*, Bridget Williams Books, Wellington, 1991
McKinnon, Malcolm (ed.), *New Zealand Historical Atlas*, David Bateman/Internal Affairs, Auckland, 1997
Mein Smith, Phillippa, *A Concise History of New Zealand*, Cambridge University Press, Cambridge, 2005
Pawson, Eric and Tom Brooking (eds.), *Environmental Histories of New Zealand*, Oxford University Press, Melbourne, 2002
Phillips, Jock, *A Man's Country? The Image of the Pakeha Male: A History*, Penguin, Auckland, 1987
Rice, Geoffrey (ed.), *The Oxford History of New Zealand*, 2nd edn., Oxford University Press, Auckland, 1993
Sinclair, Keith, *A Destiny Apart: New Zealand's Search for National Identity*, Allen & Unwin/Port Nicholson Press, Wellington, 1986
———, *A History of New Zealand*, Pelican Books, Harmondsworth, 1959
——— (ed.), *The Oxford Illustrated History of New Zealand*, Oxford University Press, Auckland, 1990
Walker, Ranginui, *Ka Whawhai Tonu Matou: Struggle Without End*, 2nd edn., Penguin Books, Auckland, 2004
Wright, Matthew, *Reed Illustrated History of New Zealand*, Reed Books, Auckland, 2004

Chapter 1

Bellamy, David and Brian Springett with Peter Hayden, *Moa's Ark: The Voyage of New Zealand*, Viking, Auckland 1990
Evans, Jeff, *The Discovery of the Pacific*, Reed Books, Auckland, 1998
Finney, Ben, *Voyage of Rediscovery: A Cultural Odyssey Through Oceania*, University of California Press, Berkeley, 1994
Hutching, Gerard, *The Natural World of New Zealand: An Illustrated Encyclopaedia of New Zealand's Natural Heritage*, Viking, Auckland, 1998
Irwin, Geoffrey, *The Prehistoric Exploration and Colonisation of the Pacific*, Cambridge University Press, Cambridge, 1992
Lewis, David, *We, the Navigators: The Ancient Art of Landfinding in the Pacific*, 2nd edn., University of Hawai'i Press, Honolulu, 1994

Chapter 2

Archey, Gilbert, *Whaowhia: Maori Art and Its Artists*, Collins, Auckland, 1977
Brailsford, Barry, *Greenstone Trails: The Maori and Pounamu*, AH & AW Reed, Wellington, 1984
Buck, Peter/Te Rangi Hiroa, *The Coming of the Maori*, Historical Branch, Department of Internal Affairs, Whitcombe & Tombs, Wellington, 1962
Firth, Raymond, *Economics of the New Zealand Maori*, Government Printer, Wellington, 1972
Flannery, Tim, *Future Eaters: An Ecological History of the Australasian Lands and People*, Reed Books, Sydney, 1994

Leach, Helen, *A Thousand Years of Gardening in New Zealand*, AH & AW Reed, Auckland, 1984
Mead, Sidney Moko (ed.), *Te Maori: Maori Art from New Zealand Collections*, Heinemann, Auckland, 1984Simpson, Philip, *Dancing Leaves: The Story of New Zealand's Cabbage Tree, Ti Kauka*, Canterbury University Press, Christchurch, 2000
Sutton, Douglas G (ed.), *The Origins of the First New Zealanders*, Auckland University Press, Auckland, 1994
Wilson, John, Tipene O'Regan & Atholl Anderson (eds.), *From the Beginning: The Archaeology of the Maori*, Penguin Books with New Zealand Historic Places Trust, Auckland, 1987
Worthy, Trevor and Richard Holdaway, *The Lost World of the Moa: Prehistoric life of New Zealand*, Canterbury University Press, Christchurch, 2002
Young, David, *Our Islands, Ourselves: A History of Conservation in New Zealand*, University of Otago Press, Dunedin, 2004

Chapter 3

Ballara, Angela, *Taua: Musket Wars, Land Wars or Tikanga? Warfare in the Early Nineteenth Century*, Penguin, Auckland, 2003
Crosby, RD, *The Musket Wars: A History of Inter-iwi Conflict 1806–45*, Reed Books, Auckland, 1999
Manning, FE, *Old New Zealand: A Tale of the Good Old Times by a Pakeha Maori*, Golden Press, Auckland, 1973
Morton, Harry, *The Whale's Wake*, University of Otago Press, Dunedin, 1982
Salmond, Anne, *Between Worlds: Early Exchanges Between Maori and Europeans 1773–1815*, Viking, Auckland, 1997
———, *The Trial of the Cannibal Dog: Captain Cook in the South Seas*, Allen Lane, London, 2003
———, *Two Worlds: First Meetings Between Maori and Europeans 1642–1772*, Viking, Auckland, 1991

Chapter 4

Adams, Peter, *Fatal Necessity: British Intervention in New Zealand 1830–47*, Auckland University Press/Oxford University Press, Auckland, 1977
Belich, James, *The New Zealand Wars and the Victorian Interpretation of Racial Conflict*, Auckland University Press, Auckland, 1986
Friends of the Turnbull Library, *Edward Gibbon Wakefield and the Colonial Dream: A Reconsideration*, GP Publications/Friends of the Turnbull Library, Wellington, 1997
Hamer, David and Roberta Nicholls, *The Making of Wellington 1800–1914*, Victoria University Press, Wellington, 1990
McLean, Gavin, *Wellington: The First Years of European Settlement 1840–1850*, Penguin Books, Auckland, 2000
McLintock, AH, *Crown Colony Government in New Zealand*, Government Printer, Wellington, 1958
Monin, Paul, *This Is My Place: Hauraki Contested 1769–1875*, Bridget Williams Books, Wellington, 2001
Moon, Paul, *FitzRoy, Governor in Crisis 1843–1845*, David Ling, Auckland, 2000
Orange, Claudia, *An Illustrated History of the Treaty of Waitangi*, Bridget Williams Books, Wellington, 2004
———, *The Treaty of Waitangi*, Allen & Unwin/Port Nicholson Press, Wellington, 1987
Stone, RCJ, *From Tamaki-makau-rau to Auckland*, Auckland University Press, Auckland, 2001
Temple, Philip, *A Sort of Conscience: The Wakefields*, Auckland University Press, Auckland, 2002
Wards, I, *The Shadow of the Land: A Study of British Policy and Racial Conflict in New Zealand, 1832–1852*, Government Printer, Wellington, 1968

Chapter 5

Belich, James, *'I Shall Not Die': Titokowaru's War, New Zealand, 1868–9*, Allen & Unwin/Port Nicholson Press, Wellington, 1989
Binney, Judith, *Redemption Songs: A Life of Te Kooti Arikirangi Te Turuki*, Auckland University Press/Bridget Williams Books, Auckland, 1995
Dalton, BJ, *War and Politics in New Zealand 1855–1970*, Sydney University Press, Sydney, 1967
Porter, Frances, *Born to New Zealand: A Biography of Jane Maria Atkinson*, Allen & Unwin/Port Nicholson Press, Wellington, 1990
Prickett, Nigel, *Landscapes of Conflict: A Field Guide to the New Zealand Wars*, Random House, Auckland, 2002
Riseborough, Hazel, *Days of Darkness: Taranaki 1878–1884*, rev. edn., Penguin, Auckland, 2002
Ward, Alan, *A Show of Justice: Racial 'Amalgamation' in Nineteenth Century New Zealand*, Auckland University Press, Auckland, 1973
Williams, DV, *'Te Kooti Tango Whenua': The Native Land Court, 1864–1909*, Huia, Wellington, 1999

Chapter 6

Anderson, Atholl, *The Welcome of Strangers: An Ethnohistory of Southern Maori AD 1650–1850*, University of Otago Press, Dunedin, 1998

Arnold, Rollo, *The Farthest Promised Land: English Villagers, New Zealand Migrants of the 1870s*, Victoria University Press/Price Milburn, Wellington, 1981

Brett, Henry, *White Wings*, 2 vols, Brett Publishing Company, Auckland, 1924, 1928

Fairburn, Miles, *The Ideal Society and its Enemies: The Foundations of Modern New Zealand Society 1850–1999*, Auckland University Press, Auckland, 1989

Macdonald, Charlotte, *A Woman of Good Character: Single Women as Immigrant Settlers in Nineteenth Century New Zealand*, Allen & Unwin/Department of Internal Affairs Wellington, 1990

Simpson, Tony, *The Immigrants: The Great Migration from Britain to New Zealand, 1830–1890*, Godwit, Auckland, 1997

Chapter 7

Bassett, Michael, *Sir Joseph Ward: A Political Biography*, Auckland University Press, Auckland, 1993

Brookes, Barbara, Annabel Cooper and Robin Law (eds.), *Sites of Gender: Women, Men and Modernity in Southern Dunedin 1890–1939*, Auckland University Press, Auckland, 2003

Brooking, Tom, *Lands for the People? The Highland Clearances and the Colonisation of New Zealand: A Biography of John McKenzie*, University of Otago Press, Dunedin, 1996

Burdon, RM, *King Dick: A Biography of Richard John Seddon*, Whitcombe and Tombs, Wellington, 1955

Dow, Derek, *Maori Health and Government Policy, 1840–1940*, Victoria University Press, Wellington, 1999

Gustafson, Barry, *Labour's Path to Political Independence*, Auckland University Press/Oxford University Press, Auckland, 1980

Hamer, David, *The New Zealand Liberals: The Years of Power 1891–1912*, Auckland University Press, Auckland, 1988

Howe, KR, *Singer in a Songless Land: A Life of Edward Tregear 1846–1931*, Auckland University Press, Auckland, 1991

McIvor, Timothy, *The Rainmaker: A Biography of John Ballance*, Heinemann Reed, Auckland, 1989

Olssen, Erik, *Building the New World: Work, Politics and Society in Caversham 1880s–1920s*, Auckland University Press, Auckland, 1995

——, *The Red Feds: Revolutionary Industrial Unionism and the New Zealand Federation of Labour 1908–1913*, Oxford University Press, Auckland, 1988

Sinclair, Keith, *William Pember Reeves: The New Zealand Fabian*, Clarendon Press, Oxford, 1965

Stone, Russell, *Makers of Fortune: A Colonial Business Community and Its Fall*, Auckland University Press/Oxford University Press, Auckland, 1973

Thomson, David, *A World Without Welfare: New Zealand's Colonial Experiment*, Auckland University Press, Auckland, 1998

Walker, Ranginui, *He Tipua: The Life and Times of Sir Apirana Ngata*, Viking, Auckland, 2001

Chapter 8

Baker, Paul, *King and Country Call: New Zealanders, Conscription and the Great War*, Auckland University Press, Auckland, 1988

Bryder, Linda, *A Voice for Mothers: The Plunket Society and Infant Welfare 1907–2000*, Auckland University Press, Auckland, 2003

Crawford, John and Ian McGibbon (eds.), *One Flag, One Queen, One Tongue, New Zealand, the British Empire and the South African War 1899–1902*, Auckland University Press, Auckland, 2003

Harper, Glyn, *Spring Offensive: New Zealand and the Second Battle of the Somme*, HarperCollins, Auckland, 2003

McGibbon, Ian, (ed.), *The Oxford Companion to New Zealand Military History*, Oxford University Press, Auckland, 2000

——, *The Path to Gallipoli: Defending New Zealand 1840–1915*, GP Books, Wellington, 1991

Phillips, Jock, Nicholas Boyack and EP Malone (eds.), *The Great Adventure: New Zealand Soldiers Describe the First World War*, Allen & Unwin/Port Nicholson Press, Wellington, 1988

Pugsley, Christopher, *Gallipoli: The New Zealand Story*, Hodder & Stoughton, Auckland, 1984

——, *On the Fringe of Hell: New Zealanders and Military Discipline in the First World War*, Hodder & Stoughton, Auckland, 1991

——, *The Anzac Experience: New Zealand, Australia and Empire in the First World War*, Reed, Auckland, 2004

Rogers, Anna, *While You're Away: New Zealand Nurses at War 1899–1948*, Auckland University Press, Auckland, 2003

Tolerton, Jane, *Ettie: A Life of Ettie Rout*, Penguin, Auckland, 1992

Chapter 9

Bassett, Michael, *Coates of Kaipara*, Auckland University Press, Auckland, 1995

——, *Three-party Politics in New Zealand 1911–1931*, Historical Publications, Auckland, 1982

Burdon, RM, *The New Dominion: A Social and Political History of New Zealand Between the Wars*, AH & AW Reed, Wellington, 1965

Daley, Caroline, *Girls and Women, Boys and Men: Gender in Taradale 1886–1930*, Auckland University Press, Auckland, 1999

——, *Leisure and Pleasure: Reshaping and Revealing the New Zealand Body, 1900–1960*, Auckland University Press, Auckland, 2003

Day, Patrick, *The Radio Years: A History of Broadcasting in New Zealand*, vol. 1, Auckland University Press, Auckland, 1994

King, Michael, *Whina*, Hodder & Stoughton, Auckland, 1983

Rice, Geoffrey, *Black November: The 1918 Influenza Epidemic in New Zealand*, Allen & Unwin, Wellington, 1988

Simpson, Tony, *The Sugarbag Years*, Alister Taylor, Martinborough, 1974

Wright, Matthew, *Quake: Hawke's Bay 1931*, Reed Books, Auckland, 2001

Chapter 10

Bassett, Michael and Michael King, *Tomorrow Comes the Song: A Life of Peter Fraser*, Penguin Books, Auckland, 2000

Dalley, Bronwyn, *Family Matters: Child Welfare in Twentieth Century New Zealand*, Auckland University Press, Auckland, 1998

Ebbett, Eve, *When the Boys Were Away: New Zealand Women in World War II*, Reed, Auckland, 1984

Gustafson, Barry, *From the Cradle to the Grave: A Biography of Michael Joseph Savage*, Penguin, Auckland, 1988

McClure, Margaret, *A Civilised Community: A History of Social Security in New Zealand, 1898–1998*, Auckland University Press, Auckland, 1998

McGibbon, Ian, *New Zealand and the Second World War: The People, the Battles and the Legacy*, Hodder Moa Beckett, Auckland, 2004

Montgomery, Deborah, *The Women's War: New Zealand Women 1939–45*, Auckland University Press, Auckland, 2001

Olssen, Erik, *John A. Lee*, University of Otago Press, Dunedin, 1977

Sinclair, Keith, *Walter Nash*, Oxford University Press, Auckland, 1976

Taylor, Nan, *The Home Front*, 2 vols, Historical Publications Branch, Wellington, 1986

Chapter 11

Daley, Caroline and Deborah Montgomerie (eds.), *The Gendered Kiwi*, Auckland University Press, Auckland, 1999

Dalley, Bronwyn and Bronwyn Labrum (eds.), *Fragments: New Zealand Social and Cultural History*, Auckland University Press, Auckland, 2000

Dix, John, *Stranded in Paradise: New Zealand Rock 'n' Roll, 1955–1988*, Paradise Publications, 1988

Hutching, Megan, *Long Journey for Sevenpence: Assisted Immigration to New Zealand from the United Kingdom 1947–1975*, Victoria University Press, Wellington, 1999

King, Michael, *After the War: New Zealand since 1945*, Hodder & Stoughton, Auckland, 1988

McGibbon, Ian, *New Zealand and the Korean War*, 2 vols, Oxford University Press, Melbourne, 1992, 1996

Yska, Redmer, *All Shook Up: The Flash Bodgie and the Rise of the New Zealand Teenager in the Fifties*, Penguin, Auckland, 1993

——, *New Zealand Green: The Story of Marijuana in New Zealand*, David Bateman, Auckland, 1990

Chapter 12

Chapple, Geoff, *1981: The Tour*, Reed, Wellington, 1984

Dann, Christine, *Up from Under: Women and Liberation in New Zealand, 1970–1985*, Allen & Unwin/Port Nicholson Press, Wellington, 1985

Easton, Brian, *In Stormy Seas: The Post-War New Zealand Economy*, University of Otago Press, Dunedin, 1997

Gustafson, Barry, *His Way: A Biography of Robert Muldoon*, Auckland University Press, Auckland, 2000

Harris, Aroha, *Hikoi: Forty Years of Maori Protest*, Huia, Wellington, 2004

Peat, Neville, *Manapouri Saved! New Zealand's First Great Conservation Success Story*, Longacre Press, Dunedin, 1994

Richards, Trevor, *Dancing on Our Bones: New Zealand, South Africa, Rugby and Racism*, Bridget Williams Books, Wellington, 1999

Smyth, Helen, *Rocking the Cradle: Contraception, Sex and Politics in New Zealand*, Roger Steele, Wellington, 2000

Shadbolt, Tim, *Bullshit & Jellybeans*, Alister Taylor Ltd, Wellington, 1971

Ward, Alan, *An Unsettled History: Treaty Claims in New Zealand Today*, Bridget Williams Books, Wellington, 1999

Chapter 13

Belgrave, Michael, Merata Kawharu and David Williams (eds.), *Waitangi Revisited: Perspectives on the Treaty of Waitangi*, Oxford University Press, Melbourne, 2005

Douglas, Roger, *Unfinished Business*, Random House, Auckland, 1993

Easton, Brian (ed.), *The Making of Rogernomics*, Auckland University Press, Auckland, 1989

Guy, Laurie, *World in Collision: The Gay Debate in New Zealand 1960–1986*, Victoria University Press, Wellington, 2002

Lange, David *Nuclear Free—The New Zealand Way*, Penguin, Auckland, 1990

McKinnon, Malcolm, *Treasury: The New Zealand Treasury 1840–2000*, Auckland University Press, Auckland, 2003

Richardson, Ruth, *Making a Difference*, Shoal Bay Press, Christchurch, 1995

Index

Index

Index

Tuapeka goldfield, 156, 159, **223**
Tuckett, Frederick, 156
Tuhawaiki, 83, 156
Tuhoe, 59, 140, 143, 203, 326
Tuhua (Mayor Island), 41, 51
Tuki Tahua, 72
Tupaia, 66–7
Turangawaewae, 298
Turangunui River, **67**
Turnbull, Alexander, 207
Turner, Ellen, 96
Tuturau, 83
Tuwhare, Hone, 335
Tyndall, Arthur, 282

Uenuku, 144
Uereta, 60
umu ti, 46–7, **46**
Unemployed Workers' Movement, 276
unemployment: 1921–22, 254; 1978, 360; 1980s, 339, 371, 372, 375, 376, 377; 'Great Depression, 246, 281, 'Long Depression', 187, 188; Maori, 206, 326.
Unemployment Board, 273
unemployment relief schemes, 179–80, **269**, 273–4, 281
Union Airways, **285**
Union Steam-Saw Moulding Sash and Door Company, 187
Union Steam Ship Company, 182, 186, 189, 202, 204, 205
unions: action in protest at Depression cutbacks, 275–6, 277; and Industrial Conciliation and Arbitration Act 1894, 202; formed in 1800s, 189; growth in 1900s, 211–2; Labour policies, 379; membership, 189, 202, 281; National policies, 360; shearers', 168; support for Springbok tour protests, 358. *See also* strikes
United Future New Zealand, 379
United government, 259, 273
United-Reform coalition government, 269, 273–7
United Kingdom, *see* Britain
United Nations, 304
United Party, 256
United States: and NZ anti-nuclear policies, 348, 360, 363, 366–8; annexation of Samoa, 220; consul appointed to NZ, 100; exports to, 320; influence of culture in NZ, 265, 267, 298, 331; security, NZ role, 315–6, 343, 367–8; television programmes from, 341; Vietnam War, NZ protests, 342–5; whaling fleets in NZ, 99; World War II, 290–1, 298
United Women's Conventions, 352
universities, 340
University of Otago, 181
Upham, Charles, 290, **290**
Upton, Simon, 361
urban society: 1848–1882, 178–81; 1918–1935, 260–7; 1950s–1960s, 306, 325, 339; 'Great Depression', 274; impact of 'Rogernomics' and share-market crash, 374–5; inner-city living, 339, 352, 353; Maori, 297, 304, 310, 325–9; nightlife, 1950s–1960s, 327, **327**, 330, **330**, 339; 'pepper-potting' of Maori and Pacific families, 310, 320, 354; rural-urban tensions, 339, 342; suburbs, 180–1, 187, 260–1, 267, 283, 310, 329, 339, 350. *See also* names of specific cities and towns
Urewera (iwi), 143, 147
Urewera (region), 203, 209, 240
Urewera Native Reserve Act 1896, 203
utu, 60–1, 77, 78, 80, 112, 117, 143

Values Party, 348
Vancouver, George, 69
Velden, Petrus van der, 207
Venus, 88
Vercoe, Whakahuihui, 364
Victoria, 118, 129, 145, 158, 161, 164, 186
Victoria Cross, 232, 242, 290
Vietnam War, 316, 342–5; 348, 349, 358
Village Settlement Scheme, 187

violence, 277, 351, 382
Vogel, Julius, 173, 174, **174**
volcanism, 21, 23–4, 25, 27. *See also* names of specific volcanoes
Volkner, Carl, 142
voluntary organisations, 264
Volunteer Force, 223, 225
Von Tempsky, Gustavus, 139, 144–5, **145**

Waddell, Rutherford, 188, 189, **189**, 191
Waerenga-a-hika, 142
wages: cuts during Great Depression, 268, 269, 273, 274, 275–6, 281; equal pay, 350; freeze, 1980s, 360, 361; freeze, World War II, 297; Maori, 326, 382; minimum, 281; nil wage order 1968, 359; relief scheme pay rates, 273, 281; 'sweating', 188–9; women, 264, 382
Wahine storm, 342
Waiapu River, 142
Waihao, 167
Waiheke Island, 147
Waihi gold miners' strike, 213, 214, 257
Waikanae, 74, 130
Waikaremoana, 261
Waikato (chief), 86–7, **87**
Waikato (iwi), 81, 114, 116, 119, 129, 134, 136–7, 144, 240, 289
Waikato (region), 128, 144–5, 208, 259
Waikato Cavalry, 149
Waikato River, 135, 137, 261, 321
Waikato War, 135–40, **136**
Waikouaiti, 75, **172–3**
Waimate North mission station, 86, 103, 120
Waimate plains (Taranaki), 150–1
Waimea plains, 52
Waipa River, 137, 153
Waipori goldfield, 156
Waipoua Forest, 26
Wairakei geothermal power station, 321
Wairarapa, 113, 123, 129, 166
Wairau disaster, 109, 120
Wairau Bar, 46, 48, **48**
Wairau Purchase, 156
Waireka Dairy Factory Company, 205
Waitahuna, 161, **161**
Waitaki Boys' High, 181
Waitaki River, 48, 321, 324
Waitangi, 90, 91, **94–5**, 100, 101
Waitangi Action Committee, 354
Waitangi Day, 354, 384
Waitangi Tribunal, 156–7, 354, 362, 383–4
Waitara purchase, 130, 133, 135, 151
Waitara, 149, 362
Waitemata Harbour, 43, 54, 115. *See also* specific place names
Waititi, Hoani, 327
Waituna Wetlands Scientific Reserve, **26**
waka, *see* canoes
Waka Nene, Tamati, *see* Nene, Tamati Waka
Wakatipu goldfields, 161
Wakefield, Arthur, 109, **109**, 110–1
Wakefield, Edward Gibbon, 96, **96**, 99, 108, 110, 112–3, **125**, 156
Wakefield model of settlement, 96–7, 113–4, 157, 158
Wakefield, William, 91, 108–9, 110
Walker, Bert, 360
Walker, Jo, **378**
Walker, John, 357
Walker Street kindergarten, **191**
walkways, 348
Wall, Gerald, 352
Walsh, Fintan Patrick, 314
Wanganui: franchise league in, 195; New Zealand Company settlement, 110; occupation of Moutua Gardens, 384; ransacking of 'alien' property, World War I, 228; Te Ua attacks, 141, 148; Titokowaru

attacks, 144; 'wives, mothers and daughters' petition Queen Victoria, 144
war, *see* Falklands War; Korean War; Malayan Emergency; Maori warfare; New Zealand Wars; South African War; Vietnam War; World War II; World War II
War Cabinet, 295–7, 304
war memorials, 245, 250, **250**
WARD (War Against Recreational Disruption), 353
Ward, Sir Joseph, 196, 197, 211, **212**, 213–4, 223, 241, **241**, 251, 256, 268
Warehouse, 387, **387**
Waring, Marilyn, 361, 363
waterfront strikes: 1913, 215, **215**, 257; 1951, 313–5, **315–5**
Waterside Workers' Union, 313
weaving, Maori, 58
Webb, Paddy, 211, 212, **280**
Weld, Frederick, 113, 166
Weldon, Barbara, 164
welfare, *see* social welfare
Welfare League, 262
Weller, George and Edward, 75
Wellington: capital moved to, 142, 156; constitutional association activities, 124; entertainment district, 387; growth, 1950s–1960s, 329; Maori move to, 326, 354; motorway through, 348; National War Memorial, 250, **250**; New Zealand Company settlement, 99, 106, 107–10, 113–4; nightlife, 1950s–1960s, 330, **330**; painting by Heaphy, **106–7**; population, 156; public transport system, 329; riots during Great Depression, 275; road and telegraph communication between Auckland and, 147; shipping, 214; spec buildings, 1980s, 373; Springbok tour protests, 358; state housing, 283; suburbs, 261, 339; tensions between Auckland and, 109–10, 117–8; timber industry, 70; waterfront strike 1913, 215, **215**. *See also* Hutt Valley; Kapiti Coast; Kapiti Island; Porirua; Port Nicholson
Wellington Club, 192
Wellington Harbour, **110–1**
Wellington Regiment, 231
Wellman, Harold, **22**, 23
Wesleyan missions, 87, 97, 102
West Coast, 24, 59, 164–5
West Polynesia, 28
Western Samoa, 251. *See also* Samoa
Westport, 215
Westport Coal Company, 165, 202
weta, 21, **21**
wetlands, 25–6, 51
Whai, 105
whakapapa, 43, 53, 58
Whakatane, 143
whale-watching, 389
Whangarei Home Counselling Service, 327
whaling: pelagic (ocean), 70, 72, **73**, 97, 99; shore, 70, 74–5, 88, 157; stations and grounds, **71**
Whanganui River, 58
Whangaparaoa, 40, 43, 45
Whangaroa, 70, **76–7**, 77
whare wananga, 383
Wharepoaka, 88
Whatiwhatihoe, 149
wheat, 86, 128, 129, 147, 167
Wheeler, Chris, 349
Whitaker, Frederick, 116, 129, 144
White Island, 24
Whitmore, George, 142, 144
Wiffen, Joan, 25
Wigley, Rodolph, 267
Wilding, Anthony, 232
Wildlife Service, 348, 372
Williams, Bright, 236
Williams, Edward, 101